Of Odysseys and Oddities

Sheffield Studies in Aegean Archaeology, 10

SHEFFIELD STUDIES IN
AEGEAN ARCHAEOLOGY

Of Odysseys
and Oddities

Scales and modes of interaction between prehistoric
Aegean societies and their neighbours

Edited by
Barry P.C. Molloy

 **OXBOW** | books
Oxford & Philadelphia

Published in the United Kingdom in 2016 by
OXBOW BOOKS
10 Hythe Bridge Street, Oxford OX1 2EW

and in the United States by
OXBOW BOOKS
1950 Lawrence Road, Havertown, PA 19083

Paperback Edition: ISBN 978-1-78570-231-0
Digital Edition: ISBN 978-1-78570-232-7 (epub)

A CIP record for this book is available from the British Library

Library of Congress Cataloging-in-Publication Data

Names: Molloy, Barry.
Title: Of odysseys and oddities : scales and modes of interaction between
   prehistoric Aegean societies and their neighbours / edited by B.P.C. Molloy.
Description: Oxford ; Philadelphia : Oxbow Books, 2016. | Series: Sheffield
   studies in Aegean archaeology | Papers from the 2013 Sheffield Aegean
   Round Table. | Includes bibliographical references.
Identifiers: LCCN 2016007208 (print) | LCCN 2016008303 (ebook) | ISBN
   9781785702310 (paperback) | ISBN 9781785702327 (digital) | ISBN
   9781785702327 (epub) | ISBN 9781785702334 (mobi) | ISBN 9781785702341 (pdf)
Subjects: LCSH: Aegean Sea Region–Antiquities–Congresses. | Prehistoric
   peoples–Aegean Sea Region–Congresses. | Social interaction–Aegean Sea
   Region–History–To 1500–Congresses. | Intercultural
   communication–Aegean Sea Region–History–To 1500–Congresses. | Spatial
   behavior–Social aspects–Aegean Sea Region–History–To 1500–Congresses.
   | Material culture–Aegean Sea Region–History–To 1500–Congresses. |
   Aegean Sea Region–Relations–Congresses. | Neolithic period–Aegean Sea
   Region–Congresses. | Excavations (Archaeology)–Aegean Sea
   Region–Congresses. | Social archaeology–Aegean Sea Region–Congresses.
Classification: LCC GN776.22.A35 O34 2016 (print) | LCC GN776.22.A35 (ebook)
   | DDC 551.46/1388–dc23
LC record available at http://lccn.loc.gov/2016007208

Printed in the United Kingdom by Hobbs the Printers Ltd, Totton, Hampshire.

For a complete list of Oxbow titles, please contact:

UNITED KINGDOM
Oxbow Books
Telephone (01865) 241249, Fax (01865) 794449
Email: oxbow@oxbowbooks.com
www.oxbowbooks.com

UNITED STATES OF AMERICA
Oxbow Books
Telephone (800) 791-9354, Fax (610) 853-9146
Email: queries@casemateacademic.com
www.casemateacademic.com/oxbow

Oxbow Books is part of the Casemate Group

Front cover: The postern gate at the Mycenaean Citadel of Midea, Greece (Photograph Barry Molloy)

Contents

Acknowledgements

The 2013 Sheffield Aegean Round Table took place during a rather frigid January with snowfalls threatening to cut our plans short. Thankfully, we had a very fruitful meeting and a lively discussion over the course of three days. Most of those who engaged in the Round Table have been able to publish their papers in the volume, though the event was much enhanced by the oral contributions of John Bennet, Sue Sherratt, Sara Strack and Roger Doonan. We were also fortunate to have Kristian Kristiansen deliver a thought (and discussion) provoking keynote address and our meeting concluded with an eloquent final discussion by John Barrett.

The event took place during a Marie Curie Fellowship that the editor held at the University of Sheffield 2011–2013. I was very fortunate to work with and learn from Roger Doonan during this period. Along with acting as mentor for the fellowship, he co-organised the Round Table event with me and played a key role in designing the research agenda for the event and this publication. Thank you also to all of the student helpers who made the event run so smoothly. The Round Table is generously supported by the Institute for Aegean Prehistory, to whom we are most grateful.

The Sheffield Aegean Round Table is a type of event that is relatively rare these days, as it takes place in a relaxed atmosphere where people freely speak their minds. This is really made possible through the welcoming environment that is created by Debi Harlan, Valasia Isaakidou and John Bennet. The home baked fare that they so kindly made on the opening night (thanks also to Vuka Milić) set the guests up for a very comfortable and enjoyable event. Debi and John also hosted all of the guests at their home the next evening, making a very memorable climax to the convivial environment that makes the Round Tables such unique events.

The panel of reviewers, including many of the contributors, provided invaluable advice that was vital in bringing this volume to publication, for which we are grateful. I would finally wish to express my gratitude to the participants at the event and contributors to this volume who made the entire process so stimulating. It was indeed testimony to our aspiration to work across political and traditional boundaries that have influenced Aegean archaeology that we had participants representing eleven nationalities from institutions on three continents. A final note on behalf of the authors is that papers in this volume were submitted in 2013 and 2014, and as a consequence many will be missing citations to some important more recent publications.

Chapter 1

Introduction: Thinking of Scales and Modes of Interaction in Prehistory

Barry P.C. Molloy

Introduction[1]

Anton Adner died in 1822 when he was 112 years old. He had become something of a legend in his time in Bavaria because of his unique way to circumvent local taxation laws. A carpenter by trade, strict regulations meant that he could produce one specific product for local markets, and should he transport his goods across borders, a tax must be paid. That is unless the items were carried on him personally. Adner chose to manufacture wooden boxes. In his spare time he produced other craft items – from toys to woollen socks. He then placed his items in the wooden boxes, attached these to himself, and proceeded to walk not only across local borders, but throughout Bavaria, Austria and as far afield as Switzerland (Kastner 2015).

This volume is about scales and modes of interaction in prehistory, specifically between societies on both sides of the Aegean and with their nearest neighbours overland to the north and east. The story of Adner may be far removed in time and space, but it speaks of the quirks of a person's place in the world – how their knowledge is moulded by society yet how their choices can shape that society in return. To excavate his home, we may expect to find the sparse belongings of a Bavarian peasant craftsman, but his knowledge of the world was far broader than we might ascribe to his humble dwelling. We may invoke the individual agency of such a person who acted at his own behest to explain his particular case, yet it was the social and economic structures within which he operated and did business that drove his decision making. This reflects tensions at the very core of how we consider interaction in archaeology, particularly the motivations and mechanisms leading to social and material encounters or displacements. Linked to this are the ways we conceptualise spatial and social entities in past societies (scales) and how we learn about who was actively engaged in interaction and how and why they were (modes).

The Aegean has long been considered a powerful testing ground for evaluating the nature of connectivity in prehistory. This is to no small degree due to the wealth of material culture and high-standards of publication in this area. It provides an ideal environment for researching how we think about scales and modes of interaction there and in archaeology more generally. The ability to maintain connections with other, often distant, groups can be seen as a defining characteristic of the social dynamics of the peoples living around the Aegean. We find cultural practices and objects that have currency throughout areas that are distinguished by diverse land- and sea-scapes that range from enabling to dramatically restricting mobility. Our objective in this book has therefore been to evaluate practical approaches for recognising material correlates for connectivity within their local and regional contexts. Contributors take account of variable scales of both past interactions and contemporary analyses, along with a parallel consideration of functional and social elements influencing modes of interaction.

When we speak of scale, this is typically related to the component parts of ancient societies, from the intimate scale of the ground beneath the individual through to the land they inhabited and on to the world they lived in (Parkinson and Galaty 2010: 11–18; Knappett 2011: 28–36; 2012: 393–396). As we move through these scales, we progress from the local environment that was familiar to most individuals up to a wider world that becomes incrementally less familiar the farther they moved from home (Helms 1988; Barrett 1998). For the archaeologist, this question of boundaries and familiarity relates at once to the geographical scope of a case-study but also to the pragmatic issue of the volume and character of materials to be utilised in research (Roberts and Vander Linden 2011). We are also concerned with temporalities, and so scale further relates to the chronological parameters we select as appropriate for a given study. For these reasons, contributors were invited that covered a wide range of materials, places and prehistoric periods.

In relation to modes of interaction, we may simply define these as the ways in which people engage with each other and with their material and cosmological worlds (Kristiansen 2004; Knappett 2011: 3–36; Earle 2013; Fontijn 2013; Hahn and Weiss 2013a). The movement of people beyond their communities is commonly explored through the lens of trade and exchange, though interaction between people can include travel for religious reasons, political purposes, family reasons, exploration, violence, health and many more (Renfrew 1993; Kristiansen and Larsson 2005: 40). By taking a diachronic set of case-studies, the book is concerned with the longevity, resilience of character, and intensities of networks of connectivity and the ways these can be visible in the material record. With regard to exploring such pathways, contributors incorporated analyses of restricted circulation/elite objects alongside those representing practices intrinsic to the daily rhythms of life. This promoted a critical approach to various forms of interaction to account for stability and changes alike. The range of case studies is intended to better understand how global traditions shape local practices, while building from these heterogeneous arrays of local practices to contribute to

	8000	7000	6000	5000	4000	3000	2000	1800	1600	1400	1200	1000	800	600	400	200
Greece	Mesolithic		EN	MN	LN FN		EB	MB	LB I-II		LBIII		EIA		Archaic Class Hell	
Anatolia	Neolithic			Early Chalc		Late Chalc	EB	MB			LB		IA		Persian/ Class Hell	
Balkans	Mesolithic		EN	MN		LN	Chalc	EB		MB		LB		EIA	LIA	R
		Stone Age		Early Metal Ages					Minoan Mycenaean				Iron Age			

Figure 1.1: *General timeline for the subject matter of this book (there is considerable diversity in the naming of periods throughout the region, and in the date ranges allocated by different scholars within regions, and so these are for general orientation).*

less model-driven and therefore at times 'messy' bigger-scale narratives. This brings us to the 'Odysseys and Oddities' of the title, which is intended to reflect at once the diversity of purpose of ancient journeys alongside those often select array of objects we archaeologists invoke to characterise connectivity. For this reason we were as much interested in interaction within and between groups in their geographic and social environment as with the influences of interaction of an intercultural nature.

We begin in the Neolithic, a time when the place and permanency of settlements took on increased importance and visibility, as the growth of agriculture went hand-in-hand with evidence for greater mobility and transfers of cultural ideas and know-how. Beginning *c.* 8000 BC (in Anatolia, 7000 BC in Crete, and 6500 BC in the rest of Greece and the Balkans) and lasting broadly until *c.* 3500 BC (in Greece, *c.* 4500 BC the Balkans but until *c.* 5500 BC in Anatolia), there is considerable diversity in the dating and nomenclature of the phases of the Neolithic in the wider region. Following this, there are variable Final Neolithic, Chalcolithic and Eneolithic phases (Figure 1.1). While terminology and dating differ, the beginning of the Early Bronze Age leads us to a time with greater agreement in terms of its broad chronological boundaries amongst scholars, with an early Bronze Age lasting from around 3500/3000 BC through to *c.* 2000 BC, followed by a notably short Middle Bronze Age until around 1600–1500 BC and a Late Bronze Age lasting until around 1000 BC in many parts, or as late as 800 BC in more northern areas (Figure 1.1). The major urban centres of Crete emerged during the Middle Bronze Age, and the Mycenaean centres of the Greek mainland emerged at the beginning of the Late Bronze Age in southern Greece, while more modest villages dominate elsewhere. The romantically titled 'Dark Age' or Early Iron Age lasted into the second quarter of the first millennium to be followed by a series of more tightly bounded and regionally significant/employed phases from the seventh century BC onwards (Archaic, Classical, Hellenistic). It is in the Early Iron Age that connectivity is believed to have increased exponentially, with migrations of colonists and the adoption of closely linked forms of material culture and related practices throughout the Aegean.

For the periods in question, when looking at the larger spatial and temporal scales, we commonly consider how Neolithisation impacts upon Neolithic societies (Hadjikoumis *et al.*, 2011), the 'spread' of metalworking in the Early Bronze Age (Doonan and Day 2007), the development of complex trade systems of the Middle-Late Bronze Age (Broodbank 2013: 345–444; Sherratt 203; 2010), mobility and reform at the end of the Bronze Age and Early Iron Age (Drews 1993; Dickinson 2006; Kristiansen and Larsson 2007; Jung 2009; Molloy, in press), and colonisation in the developed Iron Age (Tsetskhladze 2006; Mac Sweeney 2013). While somewhat simplified, these themes are nonetheless preeminent in larger scale studies and are here intended to reflect varying prioritisations dependent on the period in question. We might even see a difference in our willingness to accept certain ideas (*e.g.* migration) in research for each period. How these varying priorities affect our approaches to the material record was a reason behind the wide chronological scale of this volume with the intention to stimulate dialogue between different material, geographic and temporal specialisms in discussion at the Round Table event in Sheffield in 2013 and in this volume.

Scales of interaction

Early in the history of archaeology, there was a marked concern with how big the ancient world was. This was seen as a function of defining what things were 'diffusing' and there was a significant interest in tracing such mobility between areas with defined cultural characteristics. The paragon of this perspective was V. Gordon Childe (*e.g.* Childe 1930), the great synthesiser who sought to explain where and when cultural traits spread across Europe and Asia (Halstead). The issue of *how* was of some concern, but that of *why* was perhaps not on centre stage at that point. In our globalising world today, we may reasonably invert the above question, with a similar objective, and ask how small was the ancient world? In this sense, connectivity is not seen as a euphemism for generalised links between cultural blocks or zones. It reflects our more general concern with what may be seen as overlapping configurations of connectedness defined by practices and identities (including their material correlates) at various social scales.

If the opening story of Adner tells us anything, it is that mobility can happen at all levels of society, its scale need not be technologically confined, and that motivations and mechanisms are subject to the vagaries of historical circumstances. As archaeologists, our bird's-eye perspective reveals the disposition of societies on spatial scales of our choosing (Barrett 1998: 22–23). The linkages we seek in material culture (in its broadest sense) can in turn reveal scales of social interaction that we can reasonably believe range from the familiar to the wholly unfamiliar in relation to the minds of past people. This is not to say that past peoples were ignorant of distant things, but that these were understood "through combined experience and myth" (Kristiansen 1993: 143; see also Kristiansen and Larsson 2005: 39–50).

Knowledge of individual experiences may have been relayed to 'home' communities with the objective of making experiences relevant to their particular forms of cultural understanding – that is tailored to suit the audience (and speaker). It is this local context of receptivity and (re-)interpretation that is of particular interest to many contributions in this volume, alongside considering the capacity of materials to reveal participation in transcultural practices and networks.

When we think of connectivity between entities, a point of reference is of necessity boundaries, or perhaps more aptly boundedness (Shanks and Tilley 1987: 170–172). What were the sizes, not only of social units, but of social worlds and cultural phenomena? For example, the home itself was no doubt intimately known by a person, as was their village/town and local hinterlands. Beyond this, the land of the social unit was part of both a spatial and conceptual entity (*e.g.* territory or ethnicity) known to occupants in different ways (*e.g.* a farmer versus a king). From this known environment, we proceed in asymmetrically increasing degrees of unfamiliarity in relation to the ways that different people made sense of distant people and places.

The scale of our 'question', the material (and contexts) selected and the methodology to define datasets (*e.g.* typology and/or chemistry) can be seen to link up any person or group in more than one way. That is less a philosophical platitude and more a recurrent issue in practical research infrastructures which are predicated upon finding material correlates for interacting entities. Parkinson and Galaty (2010: 11–18; see also Knappett 2011: 61–148, 2012: 394–396) have recently highlighted the complex interweaving of scales of past organisation and scales intrinsic to archaeological analyses, ranging from the micro-, through meso- and up to the macro-scale. With a clear debt to Braudel's (1973) temporal framework, this multi-scalar perspective also plays a pragmatic role for defining suitable datasets for particular issues (Molloy 2012: 94; Molloy *et al.* 2014a: 2–3). Any such discussion of scale we may define has to be flexible because it is relative to specific research environments (*e.g.* studying the context of a household in a settlement or the settlement in the context of a cultural entity). A broad set of definitions for heuristic purposes, following the above cited scholars, may therefore be:

1. Macro-scale – Typically associated with the supra-regional scale and long-term, though it may be construed as the level at which cultural differences between entities are pronounced. The time-frame of studies operating at this scale is typically extensive.
2. Meso-scale – This lies at the level of interaction between distinct entities within a cultural sphere, such as neighbouring settlements or towns. It may also work locally as relationships between households at a site.
3. Micro-scale – This may vary from the scale of a single archaeological context through to a household and is concerned with "the conjuncture of daily events" (Hodder 1999: 137). Typically, it relates to a specific unit within the system of analysis, and may be characterised (if not defined) by the relationships between people and/or things within a household.

Far from being conflicting approaches to the past, these are the overlapping layers that have enabled us to think in terms of social worlds more holistically. Theoretical trends often gravitate more towards one scale than another, for example the macro level was fundamental to the New Archaeology movement (Burström and Fahlander 2012: 1–2) as it was also to World Systems Analysis more recently (Sherratt 2010; Harding 2013; Knappett 2013). The macro-scale has often been approached using categories of artefacts whereby meaningful groups are constituted by formal similarities with other artefacts over and above the specifics of find context and related assemblages. At the other end of the scalar spectrum, with the development of post-processualism, focus came to be placed on the small-scale or local conditions of life and social reproduction. This often employed contextual analyses, thereby engaging with assemblages more closely linked to the life of those agents that were embedded in and enacting processes (Barrett and Damilati 2004). The attraction of being able to use meaningfully related datasets from fewer locations, at a time when the number of archaeological practitioners was also growing exponentially, meant that archaeologies of local circumstances came to numerically dominate research in the 1990s and into the 2000s. Roberts and Vander Linden (2011: 4) caution against this micro-scale route into a "cul-de-sac that means involuntarily learning more and more about less and less." This more intensive study of smaller datasets and local seriations, sequences and developments was accompanied by an increase in the promotion of theoretical positions.

In recent years, there has been a sharp turn to bottom up/data-rich analyses that seek to analyse an increasing range of social and spatial scales. We can see in this a self-conscious movement pursuing a perceived reversal trend (from a dominance of top-down modelling) in recent literature addressing connectivity and the scales at which we operate (Parkinson and Galaty 2010; Knappett 2011; Alberti and Sabatini 2012; Burström and Fahlander 2012; Maran and Stockhammer 2012a; Kristiansen 2014; Molloy 2014b). In not following theoretical pendulums, different contributors in this volume have sought to instrumentally use top-down approaches (if not specific methodological positions) alongside detailed treatment of primary datasets.

Modes of interaction

Modes of interaction primarily relate to the ways in which people encountered one another, which could range from the intimate but unfamiliar experiences of combat to formal and socially distant meetings between community representatives known well to each other. The high visibility of social or cultural markers such as ceramic or metal objects perhaps creates an imbalance in the forms of interaction we prioritise as archaeologists, with economic (*e.g.* trade/exchange) relations often emphasised. At the same time, modes of interaction can relate to actions involving people, people and things, or even people and concepts (*e.g.* deities). Indeed, even social encounters between people can convey the distinct ways individuals do things or think of material culture (materialities) which can vary in intensity from marital to martial experiences.

A fundamental factor underwriting any mode of interaction is mobility. Even within the household, the placement and movement of people and objects relates to the activities being undertaken, and interaction is integral to the preparation and undertaking of such acts. Moving outside the household, the diversity of mobility opens up exponentially. In the early days of archaeology, mobility was usually conceived in terms of people and objects moving together. In recent years, the transformative capacities of the movement of objects in their own rights and the ideas which they embody have been emphasised (Kristiansen and Larsson 2005; Alberti and Sabatini 2012; Maran and Stockhammer 2012b; Hahn and Weiss 2013b). The fundamental issue is not the possession of things, but the exchange of knowledge as people, things or ideas move through various fields of social discourse in their mobility.

Knappett (2010: 81–83) has usefully broken the second of these manifestations into things and objects. For him, objects are those pieces of material culture which we identify with and intentionally use to generate meaning in our lives (for example the visualisation of identity). Things on the other hand are the far more numerous background elements of life, perhaps no less important in structuring our lives, but they are facilitating materials without 'personality' that enable mundane actions. While the lines between may not be hard and fast, the former are the ones more likely to move over distances as they possessed a form of value, yet the latter are the ones that reflect better perhaps the typical material conditions of life. Such 'things', in reality, may better reflect diversity on the local scale and therefore be a better barometer of the impact of extra-group interactions than exceptional objects we often think of as exotica. Change (or stability) in the two need not be symmetric, and so provides a means for considering specific objects, practices or occurrences against the backdrop of the more general rhythm of life.

Leading from this, when assessing modes or scales of connectivity we must take stock of the heterogeneity of any social unit, because the mechanisms and motivations of interaction should vary significantly even within a community. Legarra Herrero emphasises that undue emphasis in Aegean archaeology has often been placed on elite interaction, whereby connectivity is considered in terms of negotiating power relationships, social differentiation, and ultimately change. He argues that the accessible scale of a small number of higher value objects has problematically been used as the primary or sometimes exclusive dataset to measure interaction in our studies. This risks isolating a specific stratum of interaction that may have had less impact on the lives of communities than the lower-level exchanges visible through things, in Knappett's terminology.

Encounters and engagements

Interaction takes place in many forms, though perhaps primarily through the transmission of things, actions, know-how or ideas between distinct parties. These may be occasional or part of a continuum of cultural flows. Apart from the trade or exchange of objects as items of value, other forms of mobility lead to ideas colliding in a variety of ways that are mediated by both material cultural and people's understanding of this. Recent research has highlighted the relevance of Post-Colonial Theory (PCT) for characterising the material outcomes of interactions that emerge from establishing new relationships or intensification of existing ones. In essence, when parties from different cultural backgrounds interact, the exchange of materials can be direct but sharing ideas can be asymmetric and built upon or into existing social and practical know-how. In most cases, it is this leading principle of PCT rather than a coherent body of theory that has become influential in the practical archaeology of objects (Fahlander 2007; Jung 2009: 81; van Dommelen and Rowlands 2012; Galaty 2014). Characteristically, the introduction of the material culture of one group to the social ambit of the other is not seen as the juxtaposition of a wholesale package of objects and associated practices, but an interpretation of these and other influences (*e.g.* social encounters) based on the prior knowledge and traditions of the receiving parties also (Alberti, Çilingiroğlu, Dawson, Legarra-Herrero, Molloy). Essentially (and non-exclusively) what we may expect to see archaeologically is an object with some local features created to perform elements of otherwise exogenous practices, or a local object being modified or otherwise used for a local interpretation of such practices. In this way artefacts and associated practices emerge from more than one tradition, but essentially constitute something new in themselves, often termed entangled, hybridised or creolised (Bhabha 1990: 210; *cf.* Fahlander 2007: 22; Stockhammer 2012).

What is fundamentally important for understanding interaction is that the encounters that give rise to entanglement (or whatever alternate term is acceptable) produce acts of interpretation that can be materially constituted at various stages of the *chaîne opératoire* (Stockhammer 2012; Hodder 2012; Molloy and Doonan forthcoming). This makes these acts open to archaeological investigation and potentially quantification. This could be revealed in the adoption of certain clay recipes or forming techniques, pyro-technological techniques, tool types for flint knapping, cooking pot functions or fabrics, weight or volume systems *etc*. This takes our view of interaction beyond the narrow confines of our typological groupings (*e.g.* Jones *et al.* 2002; 2007; Jung *et al.* 2008). As Kristiansen and Larson (2005: 13) have argued:

> When studying interaction, typological evidence may lead us on the way, but it may also betray us. Diffusion is the archaeological term for this phenomenon, but it does not tell us anything about the significance of the observed changes. Certain items and styles may be superficially or randomly applied, if contacts are superficial. But if they involve a recurring interaction over longer periods of time, this may lead to mutual and selective borrowing of more complex value systems and institutions.

We must also think of diffusion not as a directional transmission of objects and practices (or people) from one area into another, but a mediated phenomenon between people who recognise and choose to share certain practices to serve particular social purposes. There is an expectation in this to find material correlates for this state of affairs. For example, some aspects of the idea of communities of practice or recognised institutions, such as concepts of warriorhood (Kristiansen and Larsson 2007), may have created forums whereby shared understandings of materialities transcended culturally specific practices. In such contexts we may find the active promotion or acceptance of the exchange of specific objects, object forms and/or ways of making and using them. For Barrett (1998: 23), in Bronze Age Europe there were "practices which suppressed the strangeness of travel and displacement and which enabled at least a certain level of relocation and comprehension among a recognisable if distant community... Such systems of reference cut across the local social units upon which so much emphasis has been placed by archaeology." While the movement of objects beyond cultural boundaries remains a paramount indicator of mobility, following Knappett's (2010) differentiation between objects and things, this position is less conducive to explaining the transformation of day-to-day things or lifeways.

The movement of objects may nonetheless be considered to be something of a flag to pursue a critical approach to interaction that draws on a variety of methods. Our emerging challenge is to perhaps better appreciate reflexivity in the transformative outcomes of the local reception of objects within giving and receiving communities. As newly introduced objects and their derivatives become incorporated into local traditions, they at once become incrementally less foreign (Panagiotopoulos 2012; Maran 2013), while at the same time (on various scales) they have the capacity to transform what is typically local. People themselves can be considered in a similar light when we think of their migration, whether at the scale of the individual or a group. After a few short generations what were once ancestral homelands could evolve into unfamiliar or dimly/creatively remembered places where new social relations could be forged. What is familiar and what is foreign can be as much social as material, a state of affairs that could encourage non-linear histories as individuals and groups came to make the landscapes they inhabited their homes. Whatever our interest in geographic origins or how we demonstrate this through science, this can only be a part of the story of a person's perceived place in a social world.

Mobility and migration

It is difficult to speak about interaction in the ancient world without incorporating migration, though we have been particularly deft at doing this for over two decades now (Mac Sweeney; Halstead; Chapman and Hamerow 1997; Bergerbrandt 2013; van Dommelen 2014; Kristiansen, forthcoming). The phraseology sits more comfortably in Cultural Historical frameworks which are not popular in current theoretical discourses. In European archaeology debate is still very much active at conferences and in publications for certain periods (Dzięgielewski *et al.* 2010: 9–11). In the Aegean, the word migration hardly features in analyses of mobility, particularly in the Bronze and Iron Age, and it is increasingly typical to find discussion of mobility of people, things and ideas that need not commit to any single manifestation of mobility through those terms.

Of course, older views of waves of migration leading to culture change have largely fallen out of vogue, though we now face the challenge of accounting for coeval developments across wide areas and identifying actual instances of people moving. This must be viewed in relation to increasing evidence for real mobility (probably migration) of at least some people, as stable isotope and a DNA evidence is strongly suggesting (Manco 2013; Kristiansen 2014; Haak *et al.* 2015; Jones 2016). It is worth recalling in relation to this evidence for personal mobility the debates that raged over lead-isotope methods for provenancing copper-alloys. These were in part framed around scientific rigour of methods, but a fundamental strand was also in the reduction of biographies and lifecycles of objects to afterthoughts (Doonan and Day 2007: 6). The benefits of these new methods of creating linkages using genetic and isotopic evidence are well proven by now, though it remains fundamental to ground these in ongoing developments of methods for explaining as well as describing mobility (Halstead).

For this reason, we have to be clear – migrations did happen in prehistory, and so our priority should be to understand their form, intensity and extent (Anthony 1997; van Dommelen 2014). This is not the exclusive forum for socially transformative encounters, but equally it could impact significantly on social infrastructures and traditions in unpredictable ways and so cannot be subsumed in all cases into instances of mobility. Accepting the problems of using historic migrations in later societies as analogies, we can add to the circular migration typical to the Homeric cycles or the 'Celtic' incursions into Rome (*c.* 390 BC), Turkey (*c.* 287 BC) and Greece (*c.* 280 BC). Examples such as these make it clear that major events of movement can leave ephemeral archaeological traces, though they can be seen as elements of a long-term phenomenon in Europe (James 2005; Halsall 2008). We of course do not need to imply all migrations were of forms or scales that we find in historical times. For any period migrations are not, and cannot be, a catch-all explanation for culture change, one of the main objections to their role in archaeological explanation (Chapman 1997). Breaking this link between migration and culture change is therefore fundamental if we are to better understand the scales, modes and actual social impact of the movement of particular groups of people.

It is instructive that colonisation models have long been accepted as relatively wholesale movements of people during the Iron Age. Yet when the empirical foundations of this are challenged (Mac Sweeney) we find that such mass-movements are unlikely in many cases and that personal mobility and local receptivity were highly varied within each distinct social landscape. Even if only for this reason, a major challenge we face is to define material correlates for the mechanisms, temporality and purpose of the movements of people within the timeframe of individual lives. Anthony (1997) demonstrates that even with migration, many forms result in the majority of 'movers' returning to their place of origin, and not leaving unequivocal archaeological signatures of new material culture springing up en masse in supposedly settled areas. Both colonisation and migration appear best understood as dialectical relations between home and away, as well as between new and emergent communities of neighbours (Molloy). What is paramount is to shed the baggage of migration being a unilateral movement of a coherent ethnic or genetic group from one location to another, particularly as we move later in prehistory. In this volume, explicit analyses of migration are pursued in some of the papers, though it is clear that the tension surrounding the phrase increases incrementally as we move from the Neolithic towards the Iron Age as the range of sources available to analyse mobility increases.

Networks of connectivity

The resurgent interest in network approaches requires a brief comment, because it represents an (re-)emerging framework for analysing mobility and its advocates promote it as a bottom up method that has particular relevance for diachronic and multi-scalar analyses (Harding 2013; Knappett 2013), which are core concerns of this present book. It would be inaccurate to speak of network approaches as a unified whole or a theory as they are a suite of practical methods and theoretical perspectives that often have little more than the basic concept of 'networks' of connectivity in common. Brughmans (2013) provides a useful history of the use of these methods, and Knappett (in particular) has been involved in the development of practical applications of some network approaches in our study region (Knappett 2011; Rivers *et al.* 2013). Networks have been seen as a useful way of observing linkages across diverse scales of analysis, as they build from the micro- through the macro-scale using a consistent framework. It would be fair to say that there are few papers in recent decades that speak of connectivity in any period that omit the word network. We might see networks therefore as a fundamental aspect of how we generally consider ancient interaction to have been structured – that is there were inter-linked route-ways (physical and conceptual) through which people, things and ideas were transmitted.

In recent years, a critical approach has been applied to the term 'network' that seeks to formalise how we employ the concept and the terminology (Knappett 2011; Brughmans 2013). Social approaches to networks such as Social Network Analysis or Actor Network Theory have been adapted to serve as tools in archaeology to explain how social relationships are interlinked to form networks of relationships and/ or interaction between people. The latter has also been particularly influential in understanding person-object interactions. These are somewhat distinct from formal network analyses, typically using computer models, which require a more functional approach whereby we define relations between objects or places, often by abstracting data to form numeric values. This abstraction is an act of interpretation in itself that generally leads to a conclusion prior to conducting network modelling. Such networks when used in archaeology are therefore typically, if not exclusively, visualisations of connectivity defined through other means. Papers in this present volume draw on the former aspects of network thinking as a theoretical infrastructure when dealing with enchained relations and variable gravities in social interaction rather than the latter visualisations of networks (Alberti; Boyd; Dawson; Legarra Herrero; Mac Sweeney; Molloy).

Papers

The papers in this volume are arranged broadly in chronological order with similar themes located together where practical. Rather than discuss the papers in the order of their appearance, I choose here to contextualise each through issues that are common to more than one.

It may be fair to say that the use of select artefacts as exemplars of connections and networks of interaction has long been a problem for the entirety of the Balkan peninsula, including Greece (Tomas, 2010; Milić). In the case of obsidian, Milić demonstrates that the character of the material suggests irregularly appropriated objects that do not represent systemic or regular resource exchanges. She argues that procurement strategies reflect particular forms of engagements with distant places and groups. Milić sees connections as existing on the periphery of both Melian and Carpathian circulation ranges, which is somewhat in contrast to the wider distribution of spondylus shells from the Aegean in lands to the north. In turn, the distribution of this latter material may be seen to contrast with the partial transmission of ceramic manufacturing know-how (Urem-Kotsou). Together, these indicate that each proxy for 'connectivity' reflects different mechanisms, motivations and scales of mobility rather than individual facets of an otherwise linked-up social network. This is also reflected in Halstead's discussion of the bigger picture of Childe in which a common focus on origins and directionality set on this grander stage has for a long time restricted our ability to account for the structuring environment of local lifeways set within particular landscapes.

Çilingiroğlu argues that the geographies and maps that we use to visualise the ancient world may have carried little, if any meaning in the mind-sets and cosmologies of prehistoric peoples. She discusses how people may well have thought in more relational terms about the processes and observable phenomena that linked places, a point also raised by Dawson. Our concern with connectivity respecting logical pathways and emanating from point to point may be inherently problematic. In this way certain areas that we may think should have been better connected on the basis of least-cost routeways may have been bypassed or made liminal. The relative or absolute avoidance of places may arise for topographical, navigational, climatic or purely social reasons. The links between southern Anatolia and Greece, in Çilingiroğlu's example, share similarities that are not found in the eastern Aegean littoral, yet that latter region shares further features with the western Aegean region not found farther to the south east. The links between regions may thus be seen not only as islands in the stream, with the implied inevitability of encountering each, but also as social 'targets' that fulfilled purposes beyond our economic appreciation of time, distance and intentionalities (see also Milić).

Halstead uses the case of Greece in the Neolithic, and builds his position by demonstrating the ways in which the field has been transformed since the work of Gordon Childe with his grand scale discussions of diffusion. Horejs takes a more specific case using a multi-period site and its surroundings in the Izmir region of Anatolia. For both authors, local social conditions could create dislocations as well as links that can isolate places locally in certain ways even when they are still integrated globally. That this conflict could be in the form of open and violent hostilities in the form of warfare is suggested by the evidence Horejs presents, which emphasises the potential for this form of social interaction to have been highly formative at the local scale. For Halstead this potentiality of hardship, be it natural or anthropogenic, is a catalyst for maintaining distant or at least non-adjacent relationships in settlement traditions. As Çilingiroğlu and Milić discuss, however, we must also account for the material outcomes of longer distance relations that could be sporadic and historically contingent, as well as those that may be more regular or expected. The motivations for maintaining these relationships are unlikely to be evident within the gross temporal frameworks that we can bring to bear, but at the same time this highlights that we cannot take interaction as being *a priori* a mutually beneficial and reciprocity-focussed affair.

The actual movement of people as a force driving change is particularly emphasised in several contributions. This ranges from colonisation to the outcomes of social encounters that take their lead from PCT (Alberti; Dawson; Heyd *et al.*; Molloy). In other cases, the entire issue of the mobility of people is critiqued (Halstead; Mac Sweeney) on the basis that the impact of innovations that occurred across wider areas were variously articulated, and our first priority should be to define the regional disparity of this articulation at the local level. Halstead in particular considers that the local practical conditions of leading a Neolithic lifestyle need to be more accurately understood if we are to understand social reproduction, irrespective of points of origin of groups. Explaining who colonists were and where they came from is seen as subordinate to understanding the development of Neolithic societies as social phenomena within the landscapes of Greece. This emphasis on the structuring character of local landscapes and resources is raised also by Horejs and Mac Sweeney, when they emphasise the importance of continual flows of external interactions.

The issue of colonies and settlement of 'foreign' elements within existing groups is specifically raised by Heyd *et al.*, Mac Sweeney and Papadopoulos. The contrasting historical situations of each of their case-studies make them particularly salient in the context of this volume. Heyd *et al.* identify what they consider the embryonic form of the colonial idea in Early Bronze Age Thrace, while Mac Sweeney seeks to deconstruct the Classical concept of colony using the case of the eastern Aegean littoral. In both cases, it emerges that the active role of local groups operates alongside a less unidirectional and perhaps less organised concept of the colony by the 'colonisers' who occupy particular roles within societies. The transformation of existing cultural configurations, even in the Classical case, could be related to a process of ethnogenesis or at the very least the establishment of a distinctive group identity associated with one or more physical places (linked to myths of origin). This involved both migrants and local groups, often in areas particularly conducive to intercultural interaction. The colonisation process for both Heyd *et al.* and Mac Sweeney is a particularly intense form of interaction that is fuelled both by a receptive environment and personal mobility as much as an intentional policy of enculturation. For Papadopoulos, in Epirus in north-western Greece and southern Albania, the relationship between highly visible colonies and less visible 'local' forms of social organisation is seen as a mutually developing phenomenon of importance for understanding the emerging Hellenistic world of the Aegean more generally. The tribal entities of that region constituted a form of group identity quite different in their makeup to that of the Classical polis. As the latter concept became increasingly unstable, the relationship between urban spaces and the communities they were a component of changed. His parallel treatment of the Bronze Age and Classical world serves to emphasise the potential impact of non-palatial groups from areas of Greece far beyond the Mycenaean palace walls as playing a role in shaping their worldview and political regimes. Those who use urban places and diverse material culture as a device for performing power of necessity create a larger archaeological footprint than those who build the foundation of their power in the people they lead. The rapid and comprehensive rise of the military force of Phillip II is taken as an illustrative case in point by Papadopoulos.

Perhaps the most striking case where we "stress similarities over differences" (Parkinson and Galaty 2010: 9) is the concept of the Mycenaean world, or more precisely a perceived Mycenaean heartland. Our problem may arise from the traditional view of palaces as the top of a power pyramid, because the modes of being or performing 'Mycenaeaness' are both temporally and spatially far more heterogeneous than the above socio-spatial phrasing implies as argued by Boyd. In the lands neighbouring the palaces, there were different systems of social organisation apparent within this wider region using a closely linked suite of material culture. At the same time, the lands surrounding these clusters of urban centres such as the Ionian and Cycladic islands or places north and west of Boeotia are well known to subscribe to a variety of cultural practices that include Mycenaean ideas and material culture, but not exclusively. Boyd uses the case of burial practices and architecture, which are particularly visible modes of performing and presenting cultural identities, as a mechanism to explore some of the meanings underlying this diversity from the local to regional scales. This is particularly salient for understanding the character of internal connectivity within Bronze Age Greece, a theme also engaged with by Molloy for the Late Bronze Age. His exploration explores the interaction between Balkan and Italian groups with Mycenaean groups. This further reveals some consequences of the differential subscription to 'Mycenaeaness' within Greece and how this could be variably affected when outside influences become more visible around the time the people of the palaces were losing their place in the overall power structures of the region.

Kouka presents a case for the Early Bronze Age as a venue for the increased visibility of social differentiation in the north-eastern Aegean, drawing on detailed analysis of case study sites and their cultural interconnections. This extends across most fields of social discourse, with a primary focus on architecture but utilising other forms of material culture more broadly. She considers the built environment as a powerful vehicle for the development of authority structures, but also as a valuable resource for understanding how this was performed practically across a relatively large area and many different communities. An issue arises about at whose behest inter-settlement interaction was taking place, whether at the specific level of elites (Kouka) or at different levels through diverse mechanisms (Legarra Herrero). This is a crucial issue that we seek to address in the volume, because the relationship between agencies of interaction and the structures within which these operate have often been considered in terms where intentionality is restricted either by class or causality, and the daily rhythms that paralleled these are less overtly taken into account. This is significant for Legarra Herrrero and Papadopoulos and is discussed further by Dawson, who speaks about the importance of long-established routes that operated across multiple social strata. While these routes continue across significant social changes, the particular historical processes of any given period give greater or lesser weight to certain routes. Legarra Herrero is also particularly concerned with the prominence in Aegean archaeology of elites when discussing interaction. His paper considers how cultural interaction was not of necessity mediated by elites and that social encounters could occur at many social levels, which he argues moves us towards a better understanding of the social depth of connectivity that characterised the Mediterranean world.

Dawson's work on island resources in the Central Mediterranean provides a comparative example of the balance between desirable resources and the sense of place in the environments in which they would be used. This may materially remove them from many of the resources we might consider important or even essential to ways of life, but such concerns are one component in the ways that people chose to structure their lives and livelihoods. In this sense, access to external resources was due to the needs and perhaps actions of communities in the remote and/or resource poor areas, such that the patterns of connectivity are driven by what we may otherwise consider minor players or passive recipients. Dawson focuses on the islands surrounding Sicily as a context in which to explore islands as lived spaces, and the case is particularly salient for addressing the role of larger-scale and longer-term interaction within maritime societies of the Aegean.

Rahmstorf and Alberti highlight how ideologies of commodification spread from the Early Bronze Age onwards. This occurred as value became less relative and more absolute with reference to standards, such as silver (Alberti), and exchange or trade came to be based upon an understanding of materials as being possessed of value that could be both utilised and manipulated. Though weights and seals may often be poorly represented archaeologically, their very existence is testimony to this ideology that spread throughout much of the Aegean world by the Middle Bronze Age. Their use also provided a unifying sort of belief system that was widely understood and practised. Indeed, seals and weights may have constituted a form of communication network through which ideas of values were transmitted. Rahmstorf's contribution argues that these widely held understandings of measuring value emerged at a time that seafaring was linking an increasing number of sites in Early Bronze Age II. The much changed, that is more highly connected, world of the Middle and Late Bronze Age that Alberti discusses nonetheless retained a remarkable diversity in the systems of weighing used. She also highlights the importance of considering how different material categories may offer non-complementary, or even conflicting, patterns in relation to the scales and modes of interaction.

Changes in the actual technology, mechanisms and social ordering of maritime mobility in the Late Bronze Age are emphasised by Molloy and Alberti as fundamental aspects underwriting the changing patterns that we see materialised. Alberti stresses the potential role of 'delocalisation', in which the intentions of local communities are the driving force in adopting cultural features that derive from spheres of production and practice not traditionally associated with these same societies. Similarly, Molloy addresses the potential for intentional blending of traditions which can be mechanisms for intentional 'forgetting' or transformation of past norms within the context of changing political and social orders. The possibilities opened up by interaction are thus seen not as a flow of influence from extraneous forces, but in terms of variable utilisation of non-local ideas within each specific milieu.

The papers in this volume provide a broad chronological, spatial and material range, though taken together, they critically address many of the ways that scales and modes of interaction are considered in archaeological research. Ultimately, our intention has been to foreground material culture analysis in the development of the arguments presented herein, informed, but not driven, by theoretical positions.

Note

1.   All citations without a year given refer to papers in this volume.

References

Alberti, M.E. and S. Sabatini
2012 Introduction: Transcultural interaction and local transformations in Europe and the Mediterranean from the Bronze Ag to the Iron Age. In M.E. Alberti and S. Sabatini (eds.), *Exchange Networks and Local Transformations*: 1–5. Oxford: Oxbow Books.

Anthony, D.
1997 Prehistoric migration as social process. In J. Chapman and H. Hamerow (eds.), *Migrations and Invasions in Archaeological Explanation*: 21–32. Oxford: British Archaeological Reports.

Barrett, J.
1998 The politics of scale and the experience of distance: The Bronze Age World System. In L. Larsson and B. Stjernquist (eds.), *The World-View of Prehistoric Man* (KVHAA Konferenser): 13–25. Stockholm: Natur Och Kultur.

Barrett, J. and K. Damilati
2004 "Some light on the Early Origins of Them All": Generalization and the Explanation of Civilisation Revisited. In J.C. Barrett and P. Halstead (eds.), *The Emergence of Civilisation Revisited* (Sheffield Studies in Aegean Archaeology 6): 145–169. Oxford: Oxbow Books.

Bergerbrandt, S.
2013 Migration, innovation and meaning: Sword depositions on Lolland 1600–1100 BC. In M.E. Alberti and S. Sabatini (eds.), *Exchange Networks and Local Transformations*: 146–155. Oxford: Oxbow Books.

Braudel, F.
1973 *The Mediterranean and the Mediterranean World in the age of Phillip II.* London: Collins.

Broodbank, C.
2013 *The making of the Middle Sea: a history of the Mediterranean from the beginning to the emergence of the classical world.* London: Thames and Hudson.

Brugmans, T.
2013 Thinking Through Networks: A Review of Formal Network Methods in Archaeology. *Journal of Archaeological Method and Theory* 20: 623–662.

Burström, N. and F. Fahlander
2012 Introduction: To go with the flow or against the grain? In N.M. Burström and F. Fahlander (eds.), *Matters of Scale. Processes and Courses of Events in the Past and the* Present (Stockholm Studies in Archaeology): 1–10. Stockholm: USAB.

Burström, N.M. and F. Fahlander (eds.)
2012 *Matters of Scale. Processes and courses of events in the past and the present* (Stockholm Studies in Archaeology). Stockholm: USAB.

Chapman, J. and H. Hamerow
1997 On the move again Migrations and invasions in archaeological explanation. In J. Chapman and H. Hamerow (eds.), *Migrations and Invasions in Archaeological Explanation*: 1–10. Oxford: British Archaeological Reports.

Childe, V.G.
1930 *The Bronze Age.* Cambridge: Cambridge University Press.

Conolly, J. and M. Lake
2006 *Geographical information systems in archaeology.* Cambridge: Cambridge University Press.

Dickinson, O.
2006 *The Aegean from Bronze Age to Iron Age: Continuity and Change Between the Twelfth and Eighth Centuries BC.* London: Routledge.

Donan, R. and P. Day
2007 Mixed origins and the origins of mixing: Alloys and Provenance in the Early Bronze Age Aegean. In P.M. Day and R.C.P. Doonan (eds.), *Metallurgy in the Early Bronze Age Aegean* (Sheffield Studies in Aegean Archaeology 7): 1–18. Oxford: Oxbow Books.

Drews, R.
1993 *The End of the Bronze Age*. Princeton: Princeton University Press.

Dzięgielewski, K., M.S. Przybyła and A Gawlik
2010 Reconsidering Migration in Bronze and Early Iron Age Europe: Bridging a Gap in European Mobility? In K. Dzięgielewski, M.S. Przybyła and A Gawlik (eds.), *Migration in Bronze and Early Iron Age Europe* (Prace Archeologiczne No. 63 Studies): 9–36. Krakow: Księgarnia Akademicka.

Earle, T.
2013 The 3M: Materiality, Materialism and Materialization. In S. Sabatini and S. Bergerbrant (eds.), *Counterpoint: Essays in Archaeology and Heritage Studies in Honour of Professor Kristian Kristiansen*: 53–360. Oxford: British Archaeological Reports.

Earle, T. and K. Kristiansen (eds.)
2010 *Organising Bronze Age Societies*. Cambridge: Cambridge University Press.

Fahlander, F.
2007 Third space encounters: Hybridity, mimicry and interstitial practice. In P. Cornell and F. Fahlander (eds.) *Encounters|Materialities|Confrontations. Archaeologies of Social Space and Interaction*: 15–41. Newcastle: Cambridge Scholars Press.

Feuer, B.
2011 Being Mycenaean: A View from the Periphery. *American Journal of Archaeology* 115: 507–536.

Fontijn, D.
2013 Epilogue: cultural biographies and itineraries of things: second thoughts. In H.P. Hahn and H. Weiss (eds.), *Mobility, Meaning and the Transformations of Things: Shifting Contexts of Material Culture through Time and Space*: 183–195. Oxford: Oxbow Books.

Galaty, M.L.
2014 Review of Joseph Maran and Philipp W. Stockhammer (eds.), Materiality and Social Practice: Transformative Capacities and Intercultural Encounters. Oxford: Oxbow Books. *European Journal of Archaeology* 17: 162–167.

Haak, W. et al.
2015 Massive migration from the steppe was a source for Indo-European languages in Europe. *Nature*. 522.7555: 207-211.

Hadjikoumis, A., E. Robinson, and S. Viner-Daniels (eds.)
2011 *The dynamics of neolithisation in Europe: studies in honour of Andrew Sherratt*. Oxford: Oxbow Books.

Hahn, H. and H. Weiss
2013a Introduction: biographies, travels and itineraries of things. In H.P. Hahn and H. Weiss (eds.), *Mobility, Meaning and the Transformations of Things: Shifting Contexts of Material Culture through Time and Space*: 1–14. Oxford: Oxbow Books.

Hahn, H.P. and H. Weiss (eds.)
2013 *Mobility, Meaning and the Transformations of Things: Shifting Contexts of Material Culture through Time and Space*. Oxford: Oxbow Books.

Halsall, G.
2008 *Barbarian migrations and the Roman West, 376-568*. Cambridge: Cambridge University Press.

Harding, A.
2013 World systems, Cores and Peripheries in Prehistoric Europe. European Journal of Archaeology 16: 378–400.

Helms, M.W.
1988 *Ulysses' sail: an ethnographic odyssey of power, knowledge, and geographical distance*. Princeton: Princeton University Press.

Hodder, I.
1999 *The archaeological process: an introduction*. Oxford: Blackwell.
2012 *Entangled: an archaeology of the relationships between humans and things*. Malden: Wiley-Blackwell.

James, S.
2005 *The world of the Celts*. London: Thames and Hudson.

Jones, M.
2016 *Unlocking the Past: How Archaeologists Are Rewriting Human History with Ancient DNA*. New York: Arcade Publishing.

Jones, R., S. Levy and M. Bettelli
2007 Mycenaean pottery in the Central Mediterranean: Imports, imitations and derivatives. In I. Galanaki, H. Tomas, Y. Galanakis and R. Laffineur (eds.), *Between the Aegean and Baltic Seas: Prehistory Across Borders* (Aegaeum 27): 539–545. Liège: Université de Liège.

Jones, R., L. Vagnetti, S. Levi, J. Williams, D. Jenkins, and A. De Guio
2002 Mycenaean Pottery from Northern Italy. Archaeological and Archaeometric Studies. In *Studi Micenei Ed Egeo-Anatolici* XLIV: 539–546.

Jung, R.
2009 Pirates of the Aegean: Italy - the East Aegean - Cyprus at the end of the Second Millennium BC. In V. Karagheorgis and O. Kouka (eds.), *Cyprus and the East Aegean Intercultural Contacts from 3000 to 500 BC: An International Archaeological Symposium Held at Pythagoreion, Samos, October 17th-18th 2008*: 72–93. Nicosia: A.G. Leventis Foundation.

Jung, R., I. Moschos, and M. Mehoefer
2008 Fonevontas me ton idio tropo: Oi eirinekes epafes yia ton polemo metaxi dutikis Elladas kai Italias kata ti diapkeia ton opsimon Mukinaikon xronon. In S.A. Paipetis and Ch. Giannopoulou (eds.), *Politismiki Allilogonimopoisi Notias Italia Kai Dutikis Elladas Mesa Apo Tin Istoria*: 85–107. Patras: Periphereia Ditikis Ellados.

Kalafatić, H.
2011 *A Contribution to an Understanding of the Relationship between the Barice-Gređani Group, the "Bebrina-Type Hatvan Culture", the "Brod Culture" and "Posavina Culture"*. In Oposcula Archaeologica 35: 41–64.

Kastner, S.

2015 Anton Adner – Der älteste Berchtesgadener. In http://www.berchtesgadeninfo.de/de/
kultur-brauchtum-alpen/beruehmte-personen-zeitgeschichte/anton-adner.html (accessed
04/03/2015).

Knappett, C.

2010 Communities of Things and Objects: A Spatial Perspective. In L. Malafouris, and C. Renfrew
(eds.), *The Cognitive Life of Things: Recasting the Boundaries of the Mind*: 81–90. Cambridge: MacDonald
Institute Monographs.

2011 *An Archaeology of Interaction: Network Perspectives on Material Culture and Society*. Oxford: Oxford
University Press.

2012 A Regional Network Approach to Protopalatial Complexity. In I. Schoep, P. Tomkins and
J. Driessen (eds.), *Back to the Beginning: Reassessing Social and Political Complexity on Crete during
the Early and Middle Bronze Age*. Oxford: Oxbow Books.

2013 Introduction: Why Networks. In C. Knappett (ed.), *Network Analysis in Archaeology: New
Approaches to Regional Interaction*: 3–16. Oxford: Oxford University Press.

Kristiansen, K.

Forthcoming Interpreting Bronze Age trade and migration. In E. Kiriatzi, and C. Knappett (eds.)
Mobile Technologies across Dynamic Landscapes: Perspectives from Mediterranean Prehistory. London:
British School at Athens.

1993 From Villanova to Seddin. The reconstruction of an elite exchange network during the eighth
century BC. In C. Scarre and F. Healy (eds.), *Trade and Exchange in Prehistoric Europe*: 143–151.
Oxford. Oxbow Books.

1998 *Europe before history*. Cambridge: Cambridge University Press.

2004 Institutions and Material Culture in Bronze Age Europe: Towards and Intercontextual
Archaeology. In E. DeMarrais, C. Gosden and C. Renfrew (eds.), *Rethinking Materiality: The
Engagement of Mind with the Material World*: 167–178. Cambridge: McDonald Institute Monographs.

2014 Towards a New Paradigm? The Third Science Revolution and its Possible Consequences in
Archaeology. In *Current Swedish Archaeology* 22: 11–34.

Kristiansen, K. and T.B. Larsson

2005 *The Rise of Bronze Age Society: Travels, Transmissions and Transformations*. Cambridge: Cambridge
University Press.

2007 Contacts and Travels during the 2nd Millennium BC: Warriors on the move In I. Galanaki,
H. Tomas, Y. Galanakis and R. Laffineur (eds.), *Between the Aegean and Baltic Seas: Prehistory Across
Borders* (Aegaeum 27): 25–32. Liège: Univeritè de Liège.

Mac Sweeney, N.

2013 *Foundation myths and politics in ancient Ionia*. Cambridge: Cambridge University Press.

Manco, J.

2013 *Ancestral Journeys: The Peopling of Europe from the First Venturers to the Vikings*. London: Thames
and Hudson.

Maran, J.

2013 Bright as the sun: The appropriation of amber objects in Mycenaean Greece. In H.P. Hahn
and H. Weiss (eds.), *Mobility, Meaning and the Transformations of Things: Shifting Contexts of Material
Culture through Time and Space*: 147–169. Oxford: Oxbow Books.

Maran, J. and P.W. Stockhammer
2012a Introduction. In J. Maran and P.W. Stockhammer (eds.), *Materiality and Social Practice: The Transformative Capacities of Intercultural Encounters*: 1–3. Oxford: Oxbow Books.

Maran, J. and P.W. Stockhammer (eds.)
2012b *Materiality and Social Practice: Transformative Capacities of Intercultural Encounters*. Oxford: Oxbow Books.

Milić, M.
2014 PXRF characterisation of obsidian from central Anatolia, the Aegean and central Europe. In *Journal of Archaeological Science* 41: 285–296.

Molloy, B.P.C.
in press A picture of Dorian Gray (areas): Using bronze weaponry as a key to understanding cultural mobility in Late Bronze Age Southeast Europe. In C. Horn (ed.) *Warfare and Society in the Bronze Age: Proceedings of the Conference Held in University of Gothenburg 6-7th December 2012*. Cambridge: Cambridge University Press.
2012 Martial Minoans? War as Social Process, Practice and Event in Bronze Age Crete. *Annual of the British School at Athens* 107: 87–142.

Molloy, B.P.C. and R. Doonan
2015 A moving story: Some observations on the circulation of metal, metalworking and metal users in the thirteenth to eleventh century BC Balkan and Apennine peninsulas. In P. Suchowska-Ducke and H. Vandkilde (eds.), *Mobility of Culture in Bronze Age Europe. Proceedings of an International Conference and the Marie Curie ITN "Forging Identities" at Aarhus University June 2012*: 235–244 Oxford: British Archaeological Reports.

Molloy, B.P.C., J. Day, V. Klontza-Jaklova and C. Duckworth
2014a Of what is past, or passing, or to come: 5000 years of social, technological and environmental transformations at Priniatikos Pyrgos. In B.P.C Molloy and C. Duckworth, (eds.) *A Cretan landscape through time: Priniatikos Pyrgos and environs*: 1–7. Oxford: British Archaeological Reports.

Molloy, B., J. Day, S. Bridgford, V. Isaakidou, E. Nodarou, G. Kotzamani, M. Milić, T. Carter, P. Westlake, V. Klontza-Jaklova, E. Larsson and B.J. Hayden
2014b Life and Death of a Bronze Age House: Excavation of Early Minoan I Levels at Priniatikos Pyrgos. In *American Journal of Archaeology* 118: 307–358.

Panagiotopoulos, D.
2012 Encountering the foreign. (De-)constructing alterity in the archaeologies of the Bronze Age Mediterranean. In J. Maran and P.W. Stockhammer (eds.), *Materiality and Social Practice: The Transformative Capacities of Intercultural Encounters*: 51–61. Oxford: Oxbow Books.

Parker Pearson, M.
2005 Warfare, violence and slavery in later prehistory: An introduction. In M. Parker Pearson and I.J.N. Thorpe (eds.), *Warfare, Violence and Slavery in Prehistory*: 19–33. Oxford: British Archaeological Reports.

Parkinson, W.A. and M.L. Galaty
2010 Introduction: Interaction and Ancient Societies. In W.A. Parkinson and M.L. Galaty (eds.), *Archaic State Interaction: The Eastern Mediterranean in the Bronze Age*: 3–29. Santa Fe: SAR Press.

Renfrew, C.
1993 Trade beyond the material. In C. Scarre and F. Healy (eds.), *Trade and Exchange in Prehistoric Europe*: 5–16. Oxford: Oxbow Books.

Rivers, R., C. Knappett, and T. Evans
2013 What makes a site important: Centrality, Gateways and Gravity. In C. Knappett (ed.), *Network Analysis in Archaeology: New Approaches to Regional Interaction*: 125–150. Oxford: Oxford University Press.

Roberts, B.W. and M. Vander Linden
2011 Investigating Archaeological Cultures: Material Culture, Variability, and Transmission In B.W. Roberts and M. Vander Linden (eds.), *Investigating Archaeological Cultures Material Culture, Variability, and Transmission*: 1–22. New York: Springer.

Roberts, B. and M. Vander Linden (eds.)
2011 *Investigating Archaeological Cultures - Material Culture, Variability, and Transmission*. New York: Springer.

Rowlands, M.
2010 Concluding thoughts. In P. van Dommelen and B. Knapp (eds.), *Material Connections in the Ancient Mediterranean. Mobility, Materiality and Identity*: 233–247. London: Routledge.

Shanks, M. and C. Tilley
1987 *Re-constructing archaeology: theory and practice*. Cambridge: Cambridge University Press.

Sherratt, A.
1993 What would a Bronze Age world system look like? Relations between temperate Europe and the Mediterranean in later prehistory. In *Journal of European Archaeology* 1: 1–57.

Sherratt, S.
2003 The Mediterranean economy: "Globalisation" at the end of the second millennium BC. In W. Dever and S. Gitin (eds.), *Symbiosis, symbolism and the power of the past: Canaan, Ancient Israel and their neighbours from the Late Bronze Age through Roman Palaestina*: 37–62. Winona Lake: Eisenbrauns.
2010 The Aegean and the wider world: some thoughts on a world systems perspective. In W.A. Parkinson and M.L. Galaty (eds.), *Archaic State Interaction: The Eastern Mediterranean in the Bronze Age*: 81–197. Santa Fe: SAR Press.

Stockhammer, P.W.
2012 Entangled pottery: Phenomena of appropriation in the Late Bronze Age Eastern Mediterranean. In J. Maran and P.W. Stockhammer (eds.), *Materiality and Social Practice: The Transformative Capacities of Intercultural Encounters*: 89–103. Oxford: Oxbow Books.

Thornton, C., and B. Roberts
2014 Introduction. In B. Roberts and C. Thornton (eds.), *Archaeometallurgy in Global Perspective - Methods and Syntheses*: 1–10. New York: Springer.

Tomas, H.
2010 The World Beyond the Northern MargIn The Bronze Age Aegean and the East Adriatic Coast. In W.A. Parkinson and M.L. Galaty (eds.), *Archaic State Interaction: The Eastern Mediterranean in the Bronze Age*: 181–212. Santa Fe: SAR Press.

Tsetskhladze, G.R. (ed.)
2006 *Greek colonisation an account of Greek colonies and other settlements overseas.* Boston: Brill.

Van Dommelen, P.
2014. Moving On: Archaeological Perspectives on Mobility and Migration. *World Archaeology* 46(6): 477–483.

Van Dommelen, P. and M. Rowlands
2012 Material concerns and colonial encounters. In J. Maran and P.W. Stockhammer (eds.), *Materiality and Social Practice: The Transformative Capacities of Intercultural Encounters*: 20–31. Oxford: Oxbow Books.

Wallerstein, I.
1974 *The Modern World System I: Capitalist Agriculture and the Origins of the European World-Economy in the Sixteenth Century.* New York: Academic Press.

Chapter 2

An Elite-Infested Sea: Interaction and Change in Mediterranean Paradigms

Borja Legarra Herrero

A distinct Mediterranean

For archaeologists and historians, the Mediterranean world has been always inherently linked with ideas of human interaction (Braudel 1949; Horden and Purcell 2000; Abulafia, 2011; Broodbank 2013). The region presents a unique configuration in which the relatively calm waters of a closed sea connect the diverse histories of three continents. The stark differences of the lands around this sea, taken together with a very special kind of maritime 'glue' that allows for relatively easier connections than are possible by land travel alone, present a rare laboratory in human history to analyse how people, material and ideas move, meet and mix.

While ideas of *ex Oriente lux* among early 20th century scholars have already indicated the importance of the Mediterranean as a corridor for ideas and people to move, it was of course Braudel who presented a compelling case for approaching the Mediterranean as a context defined by its high connectivity (Braudel 1949). Braudel conveys the idea that interaction is a primary characteristic of the Mediterranean, as it transcends every single level of human experience in the region. The Mediterranean is not just about long journeys by the Phoenicians, or the Roman grain trade, but about the every-day experience of connectivity on every scale: the peddlers that move around using cabotage techniques, the products that reach local markets, the ideas that travel along with such mechanisms. The Mediterranean is a meshwork of movement at every social and geographical scale, and with an intensity difficult to match anywhere else.

Horden and Purcell's *The Corrupting Sea* (Horden and Purcell 2000) has inspired a new generation of archaeologists and ancient historians to re-examine the Braudelian paradigm. For example, the mosaic of Mediterranean landscapes, the uncertainties of the climate and the relatively easy connectivity made possible by the sea has taken a central place in the study of the Mediterranean (Blake and Knapp 2005;

Knapp and van Dommelen 2010; Demand 2011; Stockhammer 2012) and these approaches have led to new explicit attempts to develop an archaeology of the Mediterranean (Broodbank 2010, 2013).

This burst of academic interest cannot be explained solely by the inspirational academic work of Braudel, and Horden and Purcell. The interactivity that so starkly features in approaches to Mediterranean history seems to have come into focus as issues such as intercultural contact, fusion and mobility have become major concerns in our globalised modern world. We have started to look back to the ancient and prehistoric Mediterranean as a scenario that perhaps mimics both the potential and the problems unleashed by the mixture of cultures and ideas that define our modern-day reality (Rowlands 2010), as an interestingly distorted mirror in which to look at ourselves. A clear example of this phenomenon is the application of terms and approaches coined to explain the modern world, such as globalisation, to the past (Sherratt 2003; Hodos 2010; Maran 2011).

As interest in the connected Mediterranean grows, the models being developed to explain the way in which interaction moulded Mediterranean history are becoming increasingly complex. In particular, post-colonial theory has brought much more attention to ideas of local agency (Dietler 1998), and concepts such as hybridity (van Dommelen 1997), resistance (Dougherty 2003) and entanglement (Trochetti and van Dommelen 2005; Stockhammer 2013) are creating richer understandings of cultural contact and interaction in the Mediterranean. The spread of the Roman Empire is no longer a one-way process but a complex mosaic of cultural interactions (Mattingly 2011), Greek colonisation also opened up Greek populations to other culture influences (Antonaccio 2003), the east Mediterranean in the Late Bronze Age has been understood as an elaborated system of economic and cultural contacts under the approach of World System Theory (Sherratt and Sherratt 1998; Kohl 2011; Galaty *et al.* 2010), and there is much emphasis lately in approaching the flexible interaction of the Mediterranean using Network analyses (Knappett 2011).

So far, so good, it would seem. New perspectives introduced more complex ways of understanding the past and we have uncovered the rich ways in which people interacted. But, have we achieved this really? I would argue that the enriching approaches have not been able to identify and challenge some of the problems that are skewing our views of the Mediterranean past. Modern social and cultural paradigms concerning progress, trade, entrepreneurship, consumption and emulation have become deeply embedded in our visions of the Mediterranean, eroding the powerful social history that is at the core of the Mediterranean paradigm (Braudel 1949; Horden and Purcell 2000: 44). Too much of a characterisation of the Mediterranean based on modern values and conceptions of interaction presents problems in the ways mobility is understood. In particular, following recent archaeological literature (Kienlin 2012; Carballo *et al.* 2014) it seems opportune to revise the concept of 'elite', not only because it is a notion that is charged with modern meanings, but also because it plays a central role in explaining the major socio-political and economic changes that drive the history of the Mediterranean during the Bronze and Early Iron Ages.

Elite, social change and the Mediterranean: a flawed paradigm

Scholars who have cast their gaze over various areas of the Mediterranean would be only too familiar with the term 'elite' (Malkin 2002; Barceló 2005; Chapman 2005; Tronchetti and van Dommelen 2005; Russell 2010; Schoep 2010; Slootjes 2011). It would be inaccurate to characterise the rich and diverse literature as being solely elite driven, but it is also difficult to ignore the continual appeal of the notion in Mediterranean studies. While the term tends not to be defined (see discussion in next section), it is normally used to refer to the powerful in any society, the 'controlling few' (Marcus 1983: 7). In the particular case of the Mediterranean, elites repeatedly appear as crucial social agents in a wide range of studies: from the Neolithic (Tomkins 2011) to the Greek Colonisation (Riva 2010), from the Levantine coast (Ahrens 2011) to the waters of the west Mediterranean (López Padilla 2009). This constant referencing in such a variety of contexts, periods and approaches tends to be a good indicator of a term being overstretched. The significance of kings and Pharaohs in Mediterranean history cannot be denied and therefore elite is still a valuable term to approach the study of social organisation and change but studies have shown that there are many more social agents in the Mediterranean (Sherratt 1998; 2003; Jung 2012; Iacono 2013) that have been barely acknowledged.

There are several ways in which elites have been included in the explanation of the dynamic Mediterranean. For those authors who highlight the insecurities and dangers of living in such an arid landscape with an unreliable climate (Halstead 2004; Risch 2002), elites appear as figures who have exploited their managerial positions in the distribution of resources to acquire a privileged position. Hoarding and sharing are key strategies used to buffer against the inconstancies of Mediterranean weather conditions and to make the most of the different landscapes accessible to a given social group (Horden and Purcell 2000). These systems possibilitate the appearance of certain people at the centres of socio-economic networks to supervise the running of the organisation. These central figures, or elites, are normally understood to have naturally striven to entrench their position and it is this natural tendency for strengthening the system that brings social-change (Halstead 1989, 2004).

This vision has become less popular as the focus on Mediterranean studies has shifted over the last 20 years from the challenges of food production and survival towards connectivity. Still, the elites have kept their role as catalysts of change, now as key figures who channelled and fuelled interaction across the Mediterranean.

As mentioned above there are several reasons for this interest in interaction and cultural contact that have led to a wide variety of approaches. Our current view of the past Mediterranean is a rich combination of large scale economic movements with local responses that are defined in the archaeological record by a wide range of practices. This has encouraged many more types of studies. Interaction does not focus mainly on exchange anymore, and new studies have highlighted technological transfer (Brysbaert 2008), ethnogenesis processes (Blake 2013) and even large scale population movements (Voskos and Knapp 2008). It is rare, however, to find studies that examine the basic social mechanisms that make such processes possible. The application of network approaches illustrates well the problem. Network analyses are perhaps one of the methodologies that have shown more potential for the analysis of diverse types of interactions in the Mediterranean (Broodbank 2000; Knappett 2012; Isaksen 2013). It brings flexibility to our understanding of connectivity and allows us to approach broader patterns without losing the focus on local scales. However, when networks analyses are brought down to the realities of regional studies and there is a more pressing necessity to characterise the agents that represent the nodes in the network, the tendency to rely on notions of 'elite' to fuel the networks becomes apparent (*e.g.* Van Bremen 2007; Feldman 2008; Alberti 2013).

The role of elites becoming the kernels of change is based on an understanding that local privileged groups are the agents recognising the potential of new types of interaction for strengthening their social positions (Malkin 2002; Schoep 2006; Tronchetti and van Dommelen 2005; Slootjes 2011). This is understandable, as early documents such as the Amarna Letters or the archives from Ugarit point towards the significant role of oligarchies the east Mediterranean in establishing interactions across the Mediterranean (Bell 2012). At the other end of such interactions normally we encounter local elites creating a positive feedback loop between tighter control over resources that new colonist/traders may be interested in (both raw materials and the worforce needed to gather these materials; Dietler and Herbich 2001), and more exclusive control over the exchange links. Local elites seem easily capable of turning these new opportunities to their socio-economic advantage by a series of different mechanisms. They may use exotic materials and finished items to demonstrate their special status by means of the conspicuous consumption of such objects within meaningful social arenas (Cherry 2010). Such objects provide new material means to promote an ideology of distinction. Even the mere opportunity to travel to other places or connect with distant and mysterious peoples may add to their new ideological mystique (Helms 1994); they may claim links with other high-status groups as members of a similar koiné by adopting new customs (Dietler 1990), items (González Wagner 2013) or by claiming shared mythical links (Riva 2010: 58). In other cases, elites may lead the adoption of technical innovation (Brysbaert 2008) providing them with particular items to mark their differential status and giving them the opportunity to re-organise labour production. These mechanisms, isolated or in conjunction, provide the main explanations for how Mediterranean connectivity promoted socio-political change (*e.g.* Chapman 2005; Vianello 2011).

There are several cases in which specific versions of this approach, backed by detailed material analyses, have produced models of strong explanatory power. For example, in Iron Age Etruria, the case for local elites consolidating their position through economic and ideological links with Phoenician and Greek cultures is well documented (Malkin 2002; Izzet 2007). The clear case for elite emulation as evidenced by the Veii and Tarquinia tombs, has been backed by nuanced models that include a variety of responses to external influence that match the richness of the archaeological record (Riva 2010).

While such a model then is useful in particular cases, the repetition of such a picture in so many Mediterranean studies independently of the geographical area or the period studied indicates two major problems. First, as next section tries to show, that mechanisms of changes are not universal and the general idea of how elites work do not seem to fit current visions of power relationships in the anthropological cases that our models are based on. Specifically, they ignore the significance of taking into consideration the role of broader populations in processes of change. Secondly, as scholars are producing more nuanced theoretical points of view that build a much richer picture of the past, a comparable careful interpretation of the archaeological record is sometimes lacking. The relationship between items and social ideas of value is far from straight-forward. For example, while foreign materials and objects are relatively easy to identify in the archaeological record, detailed case-studies focused on deposition contexts have shown that they were not always significant to explain socio-political change (Legarra Herrero 2011a) and they did not always represent value-laden exotica (Tykot 2011).

How do elites work?

Despite its wide-spread use, the term 'elite' is ill-defined and escapes easy characterisation (Marcus 1983; Shore 2002). It is generally used to refer to a loose group of people with the power to make or influence decisions. It could be argued that the term is merely a word used to avoid unfashionable and meaning-laden labels such as 'chief' or 'big-man' (Kienlin 2012), and to keep our frame of reference consciously open. But such an assumption is dangerous as 'elite' carries with it a series of conventions and meanings of its own (Marcus 1983) that in most cases remain unchallenged under a guise of innocuousness.

At the heart of the term lies the concept of active agency (Marcus 1983; Shore 2002). The elite are the actual people who held and exercised power as opposed to more abstract and passive terms such as class. Elites do not simply exist, they act. So a working-definition of elite would be: a reduced group that wields much of the power to influence people and make decisions. While such definition includes highly formalised positions such as 'pharaoh', the focus here is in the use of the term in relation to formative periods of socio-political change that define much of Mediterranean history during the Bronze Age and Early Iron Age.

This very broad definition of the term elite may include several different groups in any given society (Scott 2008). Depending on their type of power, elites take on several personalities (military elite, political elite, religious elite, economic elite, and so on) that are differingly combined depending on the particular cultural environment. Therefore, elites may consist of several sub-groups sometimes of a very different nature, and that on many occasions oppose each other, although the case of certain individuals consolidating different kinds of power and deploying them accordingly in different circumstances is also well attested (Roscoe 2000). Such an articulated group of powerful people is in constant rebalancing depending on the shifting relationships between the different types of elite and the elites with the broader populations (Shore 2002). While the complex constitution of such elites has been acknowledged in several archaeological works (Bell 2012; Kienlin 2012; Schoep 2006) it is still rare to find definitions of elite within a specific cultural context.

More importantly, a workable definition of the notion must be aware that the changeable nature of the elite does not play out in a context isolated from the rest of the population, and much of its fluidity comes from the porous relationship between elites and the broader group, with a constant transfer of people amongst social positions. The fact is that our elites tend to be theorised as static and long-lived social groups in spite of the fact that the best studied cases, such as the strongly regulated Roman Empire (Hopkins 1983), have made clear that the nature of the ruling elite to be in constant flux due to their own internal battles, their permeable nature, and their changeable relationships with the rest of the population.

A possible reason for this simplification of the elite concept may have to do with the implicit assumption that past elites were governed by similar motivations as modern elites. In contrast to ideas of a 'Chief' or 'Big-man' the notion of elites is widely used in the modern world by the general population and by several academic disciplines (Savage and Williams 2008; Scott 2008; Daloz 2010). This makes it very easy for meanings and values related to its modern use to affect the study of elites in the past. Under modern socio-economic paradigms, elites are considered agents of change by deploying mechanisms such as conspicuous consumption, emulation and trickle-down effects. This agency tends to be seen as a positive force that brings social and economic benefits to the rest of the society (see for example the critique in Hamilakis 2002b and Legarra Herrero 2013). Elites are seen as the drivers of change and innovation, two notions charged with positive meanings in the modern world. Elites bring new prospects, opportunities, and technical developments to their societies as a by-product of the pursuit of their own interests (Savage and Williams 2008; Daloz 2010). Such a view seems to underpin the use of the concept of elites in the past. The connected Mediterranean is seen as a positive human context that encourages what in the modern world would be seen as beneficial dynamics of cultural contact and fusion, trade and exchange, economic development and technical innovation. Elites have become in many cases the personification of such processes in the Bronze and Iron Ages by being the main agents pushing the boundaries of trade, bringing innovations to local communities, and taking advantage of the cultural exchange that the connected Mediterranean made possible. Following such a paradigm and beyond studies on violence and warfare (Eckstein 2009; Jung 2009), it is difficult to encounter in Mediterranean studies an acknowledgement of the possible negative implications of cultural contact (disease, economic disparity, widening socio-political differentiation, xenophobia).

A final key trait of the concept of an elite is its relational nature (Marcus 1983). Elites can only exist in relation to the broader group they are trying to control. This relation again brings cultural particularities to the forefront, as the interaction between elites and the associated group is entirely dependent on shared social and ideological structures and on specific cultural mechanisms of social negotiation (Roscoe 2000). To add complexity, the interaction of elites with the related group relies on their multifaceted nature; the head of a kinship group would activate different aims, goals and means of interaction than a military leader would such variability is not played out in separate arenas by clearly differentiated groups but more often involves the same people reacting to a complex contextual awareness of the cultural relationships activated at each particular moment.

The complex nature of the relationship between elites and other parts of society has recently been subjected to the scrutiny of a range of anthropological and archaeological works (Roscoe 2000; Wiessner 2002; Roscoe 2009; Wiessner 2009; Blanton 2010; Hayden and Villeneuve 2010; Blanton and Fargher 2011; Carballo, Roscoe, and Feinman 2012; Kienlin 2012; Roscoe 2012). These works have shown that elites are not omnipotent individuals that can manipulate social relationships at will, but rather groups that need to engage in social conversation with the broader population in order to achieve their goals (Marcus 1983; Kienlin 2012). Such communication is limited by ideological and material restrictions imposed by cultural worldviews.

Anthropologists such as Polly Wiessner (Wiessner 2002, 2009) and Paul Roscoe (Roscoe 2000, 2009; Roscoe 2012) have revisited classic cases of Big-man societies in Papua New Guinea to offer a more modern understanding of power negotiations and socio-political change. It is beyond the scope of this article to dwell on the Big-man concept, and Papua New Guinea may seem a world away from the ancient Mediterranean, but the well documented ethnographic work in this part of the world has informed much of our models of formative periods of social stratification in the Mediterranean (Patton 1996; Broodbank 2000) so new research in this area makes a pertinent critique of Mediterranean studies.

Big-man figures (but also 'chiefs' or individuals with ascribed power) appear as restricted agents, people who must negotiate their power rather than simply impose it. In the cases presented, leaders form part of a complex web of social groups and relationships that contextualise their position, and in many cases limit it. For example, Polly Wiessner argues that long-established social arenas are particularly limited by tradition and that Big-men must create new areas of social activity in order to be able to negotiate new social relationships (Wiessner 2002). Even so, such new social arenas require the tacit approval of the rest of the population to be successful, approval which is dependent on whether they are perceived as beneficial. This particular point is especially interesting for our studies of the Mediterranean, as new connections would provide just such novel social arenas and social relationships in the form of new materials and customs for local cultures to contend with. The fact that elites are in many instances 'subjugated' to the group they command has two important implications for the Mediterranean: one refers to the aims and goals of the elite, the other to mechanisms of social interaction.

Elites are the visible heads of larger groups, such as extended families (Kienlin 2012; Roscoe 2012) or political organisations, and they act for their own benefit as much as for the benefit of the groups they represent (Scott 2008; Hayden and Villeneuve 2010). For most elites, securing a more powerful personal position in society is intrinsically related to the strengthening of the position of the specific group they lead. Decisions made by elites are driven by a combination of different types of reasons, ranging from seeking the benefit of the group they represent and widening their social appeal to more mundane motives, such as personal revenge or immediate physical satisfaction of the individual making the decision (Roscoe 2000). In addition, the goals of elites in the past do not necessarily follow modern paradigms of economic wealth and power. Much of their behaviour focuses on gaining social capital, symbolic capital and knowledge (Roscoe 2009; Hayden and Villeneuve 2010). Power depends not on material gains but on the ability to influence as many people as possible. Mechanisms such as conspicuous consumption, emulation, feasting and hoarding are part of wider social strategies for enlarging social influence (Roscoe 2009). Such mechanisms take different forms, with a shifting emphasis on ritual, economic and coercive activities dependent on the particular nature of each culture (Kienlin 2012). Most importantly, such mechanisms cannot be considered simple top-down strategies, as supporters represent active agents who will accept or reject these mechanisms based on the perceived benefits they provide them. The broader population is empowered by the cultural norms that frame their social relationships; in other words, the elite find themselves constrained by tradition and other social rules. At the same time ideological and material tools can help to manipulate messages that strengthen the position of an elite which is particularly patent in large socio-political systems (Smith 2003). However, this is never an automatic process, nor a perfect one and elites may always be involved in the constant maintenance of their social position (Roscoe 2000) against other elite groups, the groups they represent or even other socio-political entitites. Elites never can control social negotiation mechanisms at will.

This also brings us to the crucial point of how the interaction between elites, between elites and associated groups, and between these larger groups is managed. The nature of these relationships is entirely contingent upon its actual implementation, upon its practice (Shore 2002). The power relationships within a society may be shaped by ideological and social structures, but it is played out and constantly re-defined through repetitive practices ('habitus' in accordance to Bourdieu's terms; Bourdieu 1977). Such practices do not need to be heavily ritualised performances or highly visible events, but they are formed mainly through constant every-day customs and behaviours, and through a wide range of mundane material culture and activities that are open to the whole population, not only elites. It also depends on many more interactions than those related to social vertical differentiation, and the concept of 'heterarchy' has demonstrated (Crumley 2003) that many other social relationships are crucial to the structure of a culture.

In this light, some of the traditional models of elite behaviour seem to be crude caricatures. Let us focus, for example, on the concept of conspicuous consumption. This has been supported on many occasions by the idea that dangling an exotic object in front of people would attract attention and provoke admiration, thereby marking social differences. Modern views on conspicuous consumption have demonstrated that this is a complex mode of communication that allows for many responses (Patsiaouras and Fitchett 2012). Recent ethnographic studies have demonstrated that outside the modern world conspicuous consumption is a mechanism that can refer to integration rather than differentiation. Conspicuous consumption can be seen as the epitome of the material identity of a group and not necessarily of the elite individual who possess it, and as such may be used to send out social messages to other groups (Roscoe 2009). For example, conspicuous architecture is a mechanism for integrating a social group into building a message through collective practice and material means (Roscoe 2012). Archaeologically, detailed work in consumption patterns has also shown that an exotic origin does not warrant the use of the item for conspicuous consumption strategies (Legarra Herrero 2011a; Tykot 2011).

The implications for the study of interaction and social change in the Mediterranean are far reaching. Stress becomes laid on cultural context and this opens our understanding of agents of change to a broader social spectrum. Post-colonial theory has shown that long-distance connections would be differently adopted and adapted by local populations depending on their existing social structures and on the nature of these connections (van Dommelen 1997). Responses are not just limited to acceptance or resistance; there are far more complex ways of linking new external influences to internal social trends. Such rich interpretation of the past can only benefit by adding more non-elite voices to the picture. A corollary to this is that changes at such a broad social scale are better understood as medium and long-term socio-political dynamics with very different histories in each Mediterranean region.

A case study: Crete and the beginning of the Middle Bronze Age (2000–1700 BCE)

Middle Bronze Age Crete represents a well-known and long-discussed case of socio-political change in the Mediterranean. At the beginning of the Middle Bronze Age, we encounter a series of major changes in the archaeological record that indicate profound socio-political transformations: rapid growth at the most important settlements, in the case of Knossos from 3,000–4,000 people to 18,000–20,000 people (Whitelaw 2011); large central buildings appear at major settlements, normally referred to as palaces (Macdonald 2011); and the new administrative use of seals and the script known as Linear A are first documented in this period (Watrous 1994). It is also in this period that we can securely identify a number of Egyptian items and local imitations in the record for first time (Legarra Herrero 2011a), as well as a few technical innovations with an east Mediterranean origin, such as the fast potter's wheel (Knappett 1999).

At this point of the discussion one should not be surprised that the major focus of study has been on the role of elites in bringing about new changes, by exploiting the newly-developed exchange networks with Egypt and the east Mediterranean. Currently, the main explanation of the rapid changes seen at the beginning of the Middle Bronze Age argues that material and ideological links with the east Mediterranean are immediately seized upon by local elites to start a process of differentiation that allows them to lead Cretan society along the path of state formation (Parkinson and Galaty 2007; Manning 2008; Cherry 2010; Schoep 2010; Watrous 2012). In a classic deployment of the model explained above, exotica are thought to have been used by existing privileged individuals to mark out further ideological differences and to gain control over resources that can be used to participate in the new exchange links with the east Mediterranean. Competition between different regional elites to control resources and imported materials may have also accelerated changes all through the Middle Bronze Age on Crete (Schoep and Knappett 2004; Schoep 2006; Sbonias 2011). The use of this notion of elites is normally based on the study of the mechanisms that they used to gain power (Adams 2006; Schoep 2006) but the elites are never embodied in specific social agents, and it is therefore still unclear who these elites were, and how they related to the broader population. Only recently has a 'house society' been suggested for the island by Jan Driessen, where elites are placed at the head of corporate social groups organised around residential units (Driessen 2011; see also Hamilakis 2002a; Knappett 2009). However, a clearer definition of the elite has not made an impact on explanations of social change, and the causality of social change has not been expanded to incorporate a broader demographic spectrum (Wright 2004).

Individuals or small group of elites are not easily spotted in the archaeological record. Recent studies of mortuary data (Legarra Herrero 2011b) have challenged the traditional interpretation of socio-economic differences being clearly marked in Middle Bronze Age cemeteries on Crete (Manning 2008). Quite the contrary, communal use of the cemeteries and a collective ethos in mortuary ritual seems to dominate mortuary behaviour at the beginning of the Middle Bronze Age (Legarra Herrero 2011b). In this period, cemeteries underwent major transformations but these stressed collective interment and group ritual within centuries-old burial grounds. For example, large tombs in the cemeteries of presumed early palatial sites such as Archanes or Mallia are surrounded by paved areas associated with large deposits of cups and jugs that speak of group ritual, and seem to constitute new focal points for a growing community (Figure 2.1). These tombs share their collective interment practice with every other tomb on Crete, where bones and material were randomly scattered in the tombs in mixed deposits. This communal interment type had almost exclusively been the burial tradition on Crete for a thousand years and supports the idea that individual identities were diluted in the group ethos of the tomb, even during periods of profound change (Legarra Herrero 2011b). These powerful mortuary arenas speak of change, but they remain curiously silent about the elite.

The role of exotica in Middle Bronze Age Cretan society also needs revision. While authors have interpreted this material as evidence of new influences from Egypt (Watrous 1998; Aruz 2008; Wiener 2013), careful investigation of the material reveals strong local patterns of consumption that do not necessarily fit well with ideas of either conspicuous consumption or emulation (Legarra Herrero 2011a). Newly-imported items, or objects made in imported materials are few in number and represent a narrow and strange selection of items, mainly scarabs (actual imports and local imitations) and a limited range of Egyptian stone vessel types. Local imitations of these two types of items are a little more common, but do not register a significantly different pattern of deposition. Neither scarabs nor the type of stone vessels found on Crete are popular in Egypt during this period, but they are linked to two types of items that become

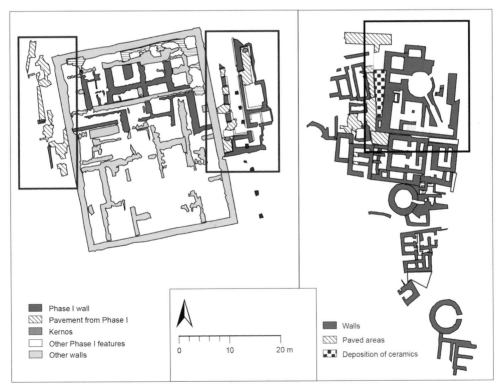

Figure 2.1: Chrysolakkos I (EM III/MM IA) cemetery at Mallia and Archanes cemetery (MM IA) with areas used for group ritual highlighted (redrawn by author).

prevalent in the Cretan archaeological record at the beginning of the Middle Bronze Age: seals and stone vessels. The increased appearance of seals in the record has been interpreted as relating to the growing importance of group identity in the regional administration of goods (Relaki 2011; Sbonias 2011), and the fact that scarabs are found mainly around certain geographical areas (Pini 2000) may indicate that a particular choice of seal was preferred by certain communities to express their identities. Scarabs continue a long history of zoomorphic sealstones on Crete (Karytinos 2000), and in some cases imported scarabs are found engraved with local Cretan motifs, which further supports the idea that scarabs were being used as seals. Similarly, stone vessels became much more popular in the archaeological record during this period, and the few imitations found usually uncovered in conjunction with significant depositions of local types of stone vessels (Figure 2.2; Legarra Herrero 2011a). Only at Hagia Triada was an imported stone vessel found in a peculiar depositional context although even here it appeared inside a communal tomb (Bevan 2004).

These trends in the deposition of items with off-island links do not support traditional views of such items being used to mark the differential status of certain

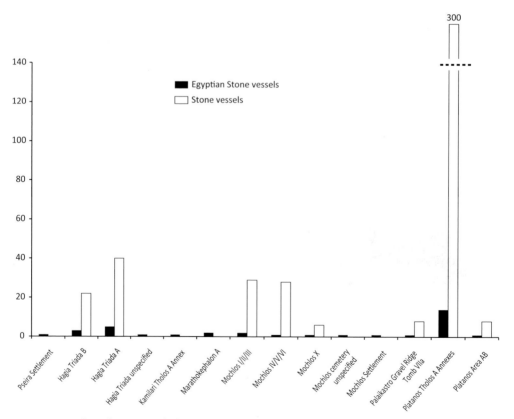

Figure 2.2: *Number of stone vessels found in MM I tombs. Only tombs with Egyptian imitations included.*

individuals; rather they seem to have been incorporated into existing local patterns of production and consumption. This may be explained in part by most of these items reaching the island after a long trip around the east Mediterranean and do not necessarily indicate direct links with Egypt. Available sailing techniques in MM I coupled with prevailing winds and currents make a direct trip from Egypt to Crete extremely difficult (Agouridis 1997). It is possible that Cretan populations chose to use certain items that were being traded across the Mediterranean because they fit in with existing consumption patterns, materials and ideological structures on the island (Legarra Herrero 2011a). These items may have lost many of their original meanings along the long chain of trade from their places of origin to Crete (Stein 1998), and were open to being imbued with new meanings by Cretan populations. While Crete may have opened up to new trade routes, it seems the Cretans were the ones choosing what kind of items to trade and that these were adapted to the local culture.

Without easily-recognisable elites, valuable exotica and clear emulation processes, change on Middle Bronze Age Crete is in need of new explanations. I have already mentioned that cemeteries underwent major transformations that encouraged social practices and group activities, and that new sealing systems seem to indicate regional community identities. Similar social trends can be traced in other newly-created social arenas, such as peak sanctuaries (Figure 2.3); open areas located on certain

Figure 2.3: Yuktas peak sanctuary (photograph by author).

mountain tops where ritual seems to have been open to large groups of people the large number of simple clay figurines that characterise their deposits (Nowicki 2008). This open social practice at peak sanctuaries would reinforce their role as geographical beacons for the establishment of group identity in the landscape (Peatfield 1987; Haggis 1999). The appearance of palatial buildings in central Crete, with their open courts, may well present similar new arenas for group ritual (Figure 2.4; Manning 2008).

Social dynamism on Middle Bronze Age Crete cannot be explained solely through the agency of a few, or the influence of external interactions. Changes seem to have been driven by large social groups that are emphasising new collective identities, such as co-residential communities in a new regional competitive framework. The main changes in the record do not refer to the appearance of distinctions but to the redefinition of significant social groups and identities, and the appearance of new regional arenas of interaction. While privileged individuals would have gained new social positions in this process, and it is most likely that in some large cemeteries certain small groups may have acquired greater importance (Legarra Herrero 2011b), there is no indication in the record that they were able to construct a new language

Figure 2.4: West court and west façade at Knossos palace (photograph by author).

of differentiation that set them apart from the rest of society, nor that they were the principal agents of change. Privileged individuals or successful groups would still find themselves torn between new opportunities and the continuing limitations set by the collective-oriented cultural context. The adherence to old traditions such as collective burials, may have been a key mechanism for wrapping change in a socially-acceptable language that may at the same time have set clear boundaries to intra-society differentiation dynamics.

And so the emphasis of study may be better focused on new group identities that brought advantages to large parts of the population, rather than on the rise of aggrandizers or leaders. This basic characterisation of Middle Bronze Age Crete leaves many questions unanswered. How did new social identities differ from older ones? What does this mean for the fluid relationship between influential individuals and the rest of the society? Why was there such an acute change at this point in Cretan history? Changing our approaches may not bring immediate answers, but it presents more pertinent questions to match the archaeological record.

A social history of the Mediterranean: Bringing in new paradigms

The collective nature of social change on Crete seems not have been a unique phenomenon. Authors have started to recognise such dynamics in other parts of the world (Blanton and Fargher 2008; Blanton 2010; Bernbeck 2012; Carballo, Roscoe, and Feinman 2012) as well as in the Mediterranean (Kolb 2005, 2012), and this implies that Crete could provide an extensively-investigated archaeological scenario that can facilitate our understanding of several other Mediterranean cultures in the Bronze Age.

On a purely archaeological level, monumental architecture attached to collective mortuary rituals on Crete has strong correlations in the central and west Mediterranean such as the temples of Malta (Malone and Stoddart 2009) and the communal Chalcolithic tombs in southeast Iberia (Lomba Maraundi, López Martínez, and Ramos Martínez 2009). The materialisation of group identity in the landscape through highly visible structures such as palaces finds parallels in Pre- and Nuraghic Sardinia (Blake 2002; Dyson and Rowland 2007; Russell 2010), Argaric Spain (Arribas Palau *et al.* 1974), and Talayotic Balearic Islands (Gili *et al.* 2006). Even in the more 'advanced' case of the southern Levant, central 'palaces' in early urban centres may not be the seat for powerful individuals but the focal point of a community (Greenberg 2011: 239), and these communities are increasingly being investigated from a collective point of view (Chesson 2003). Such large architectural programmes may indicate cases of conspicuous construction in which local group identities are reinforced at larger social scales as connectivity and interaction become more developed.

The dynamism that linked connectivity with constant social change was not necessarily solely the work of privileged individuals, aggrandizers or very clever individual agents; there were many other complex interactions between the different components of each culture, the outside influences, and the old histories and traditions that marked each Mediterranean population. The connected nature of the Mediterranean added to the range of strategies that social groups had at their disposal in the negotiation of social, economic and ideological identities. Connectivity does not reflect a meaningful activity *per se* but a constant reference point in the Mediterranean social landscape that is entangled in each cultural framework in a different manner. The development of connectivity by sea and land challenged social groups to enter new social scales of interaction. The development of the sail is not only important because it allows new products to travel, but also because it creates significant new links between social groups on a scale unknown before (Broodbank 2010). In the Bronze Age and Early Iron age, people were increasingly concerned not only with their immediate neighbours, but also with groups hundreds or even thousands of miles away. In these new circumstances, it is only natural that local groups needed to re-organise themselves to face these new challenges.

The way in which connectivity affected the basic cultural structure of populations and made it change can only be understood through a myriad of social identities, from gender to community, from individual practices to cultural identities, all overlapping in constant flow. In the particular case of the overuse of the notion of elites, an extreme focus on this type of social position means that the agency of the multiple social groups that form a culture, the practices by which they asserted and negotiated their agency, and the ways in which they shaped the development of social and ideological transformations are poorly understood. There are many cultural mechanisms in which the relational nature of power is negotiated. Heterarchy was one of the first approaches that highlighted alternative avenues of social interaction with regards to social change, and recent approaches to local agency and social networking are discovering new aspects of the complex relationship between interaction and change in the Mediterranean. Only when elites lose some of their privileged theoretical position and they are better located in relation to other social agents, the intricate connection in the Mediterranean between the materialisation of social identities, resource acquisition, travel, cultural interaction, settlement patterns, and ideological representations can be fully explored.

Conclusion

The sheer complexity of Mediterranean history will always thwart scholars' attempts at analysis. In our quest to draw even a simple sketch that alludes to that complexity, we find ourselves forced to resort to generalisations and theoretical shortcuts. The elite is a good example of the problems that arise when a useful term is applied without a clear theoretical framework. The indiscriminate use of the term can lead it to lose much of its explanatory power and to misunderstandings of the inner workings of social organisation and change in the Mediterranean. To study the dynamism of the Bronze and Iron Age Mediterranean, a more encompassing social approach is needed, one that studies the complex relationship between elites, group agency, ideology and connectivity in a clearly defined cultural context and through precise definitions of the terms based on archaeological evidence.

The problem is not that by focusing on elites we are losing the crucial perspective of a social history; but that it is precisely the social depth of connectivity that makes the Mediterranean unique. Connectivity is so significant for Mediterranean studies because it permeates every stratum of society. The narrower the social focus of our approaches, the less exceptional the Mediterranean appears.

References

Abulafia, D.
2011 *The Great Sea. A human history of the Mediterranean*. London: Allen Lane.

Agouridis, C.
1997 Sea routes and navigation in the third millennium Aegean. *Oxford Journal of Archaeology* 16(1): 1–24.

Ahrens, A.
2011 Strangers in a Strange Land? The Function and Social Significance of Egyptian Imports in the Northern Levant during the 2nd Millennium BC. In K. Duistermaat and I. Regulski (eds.), *Intercultural contacts in the Ancient Mediterranean. Proceedings of the International Conference at the Netherlands-Flemish Institute in Cairo, 25th to 29th October 2008* (Orientalia Lovaniensia Analecta 20): 285–308. Leuven: Uitgeverij Peeters en Departement Oosterse Studies.

Alberti, M.E.
2013 Aegean trade systems: Overview and observations on the Middle Bronze Age. In M. E. Alberti (ed.), *Exchange networks and local transformations. Interaction and local change in Europe and the Mediterranean from the Bronze Age to the Iron Age*: 22–43. Oxford: Oxbow Books.

Antonaccio, C.
2003 Hibridity and the Cultures within Greek Culture. In C. Dougherty and L. Kurke (eds.), *The cultures within Ancient Greek Culture: Contact, Conflict, Collaboration*: 57–74. Cambridge: Cambridge University Press.

Arribas Palau, A., E. Pareja López, F. Molina González, O. Arteaga Matute and F. Molina Fajardo
1974 *Excavaciones en el poblado de la Edad del Bronce del Cerro de la Encina (Monachil, Granada). El corte estratigrafico nº 3* (Excavaviones Arqueológicas en España 81). Madrid: Ministerio de Cultura.

Aruz, J.
2008 *Marks of distinction. Seals and cultural exchange between the Aegean and the Orient (ca. 2600–1360 B.C.)* (Corpus der Minoischen un Mykenischen Siegel Beiheft 7). Mainz Am Rhein: Verlag Philipp von Zabern.

Barceló, J.A.

2005 Patriarchs, Bandits and Warriors. An Analysis of Social Interaction in Bronze Age South-Western Iberian Peninsula, *Eliten in der Bronzezeit. Ergebnisse Zweier Kolloquien in Mainz und Athen. Teil I*: 223–244. Mainz: Verlag des Römischen-Germanischen Zentralmuseums.

Bell, C.

2012 The merchants of Ugarit: oligarchs of the Late Bronze Age trade in metals? In V. Kassianidou and G. Papasavvas (eds.), *Eastern Mediterranean Metallurgy and Metalwork in the Second Millennium BC. A conference in honour of James D. Muhly*: 180–187. Oxford: Oxbow Books.

Bernbeck, R.

2012 Multitudes before Sovereignty: Theoretical Reflections and a Late Neolithic Case. In T. Kienlin and A. Zimmermann (eds.), *Beyond Elites. Alternatives to Hierarchical Systems in Modelling Social Formations. International Conference at the Ruhr-Universität Bochum, Germany, October 22-24, 2009. Teil 1*: 147–167. Bonn: Habelt.

Bevan, A.

2004 Emerging Civilized Values? The Consumption and Imitation of Egyptian Stone Vessels in EMII-MMI Crete and its Wider Eastern Mediterranean Context. In J. C. Barrett and P. Halstead (eds.), *The Emergence of Civilisation Revisited* (Sheffield Studies in Aegean Archaeology 6): 107–126. Oxford: Oxbow Books.

Blake, E.

2002 Situating Sardinia's Giants' Tombs in Their Spatial, Social and Temporal Contexts. In H. Silverman and D. B. Small (eds.), *The Space and Place of Death* (Archaeological Papers of the American Anthropological Association, No. 11): 1191–1127. Arlington: American Anthropological Association.

2013 Social Networks, Path Dependence, and the Rise of Ethnic Groups in pre-Roman Italy. In C. Knappett (ed.), *Network Analysis in Archaeology: New Approaches to Regional Interaction*: 203–222. Oxford: Oxford University Press.

Blake, E. and A.B. Knapp (eds.)

2005 *The Archaeology of Mediterranean Prehistory, Blackwell studies in global archaeology*. Oxford: Blackwell.

Blanton, R.E.

2010 Collective Action and Adaptative Socioecological Cycles in Premodern States. *Cross-Cultural Research* 44 (1): 41–59.

Blanton, R.E. and L.F. Fargher

2008 *Collective Action in the Formation of Pre-Modern States*. New York: Springer.

2011 The collective logic of pre-modern cities. *World Archaeology* 43(3): 505–522.

Bourdieu, P.

1977 *Outline of a theory of practice, Cambridge studies in social anthropology 16*. Cambridge: Cambridge University Press.

Braudel, F.

1949 *La Méditerranée et le monde Méditerranéen à l'époque de Philippe II*. Paris: Colin.

Broodbank, C.

1993 Ulysses without sails: trade, distance, knowledge and power in the early Cyclades. *World Archaeology* 24(3): 315–331.

2000 *An Island Archaeology of the Early Cyclades*. Cambridge: Cambridge University Press.

2010 'Ships a-sail from over the rim of the sea': Voyaging, Sailing and the Making of Mediterranean Societies c. 3500–800 BC. In A.J. Anderson, J.H. Barrett and K.V. Boyle (eds.), *The global origins and development of seafaring*: 249–264. Cambridge: McDonald Institute for Archaeological Research.

2013 *The Making of the Middle Sea. A history of the Mediterranean from the beginning to the Emergence of the Classical world*. London: Thames and Hudson.

Brysbaert, A.

2008 *The power of technology in the Bronze Age Eastern Mediterranean. The case of the Painted Plaster* (Monographs in Mediterranean archaeology 12). London: Equinox.

Carballo, D., P. Roscoe and G. Feinman.

2014. Cooperation and Collective Action in the Cultural Evolution of Complex Societies. *Journal of Archaeological Method and Theory* 21 (1): 98–133.

Chapman, R.

2005 Changing Social Relations in the Mediterranean Copper and Bronze Ages. In E. Blake and A.B. Knapp (eds.), *The Archaeology of Mediterranean Prehistory* (Blackwell studies in global archaeology): 77–101. Oxford: Blackwell Publishing.

Cherry, J.F.

1986 Polities and Palaces: some problems in Minoan State formation. In J.F. Cherry and C. Renfrew (eds.), *Peer polity interacting and socio-political change*: 19–45. Cambridge: Cambridge University Press.

2010 Sorting Out Crete's Prepalatial Off-Island Interactions. In W.A. Parkinson and M.L. Galaty (eds.), *Archaic State Interaction. The Eastern Mediterranean in the Bronze Age* (School for Advanced Research Advanced Seminar Series): 107–140. Santa Fe: School for Advanced Research Press.

Chesson, M.S.

2003 Households, Houses, Neighborhoods and Corporate Villages: Modeling the Early Bronze Age as a House Society. *Journal of Mediterranean Archaeology* 16(1): 79–102.

Crumley, C.L.

2003 Alternative forms of social order. In V.L. Scarborough, F. Valdez and N.P. Dunning Jr (eds.), *Heterarchy, political economy, and the ancient Maya. The Three Rivers Region of the East-Central Yucatan Peninsula*: 136–145. Tucson: The University of Arizona Press.

Daloz, J.-P.

2010 *The sociology of elite distinction. From theoretical to comparative perspectives*. Basingstoke: Palgrave Macmillan.

Demand, N.H.

2011 *The Mediterranean Context of Early Greek History*. Chichester: Wiley-Blackwell.

Dietler, M.

1990 Driven by drink: The role of drinking in the political economy and the case of Early Iron Age France. *Journal of Anthropological Archaeology* 9 (4): 352–406.

1998 Consumption, Agency and Cultural Entanglement: Theoretical Implications of a Mediterranean Colonial Encounter. In J.G. Cusick (ed.), *Studies in Culture Contact. Interaction, Culture Change, and Archaeology* (Occasional Paper 25): 288–315. Carbondale: Center for Archaological Investigations, Southern Illinois University.

Dietler, M. and I. Herbich
2001 Feasts and Labor Mobilization: Dissecting a Fundamental Ecnonomic Practice. In M. Dietler and B. Hayden (eds.), *Feasts. Archaeological and ethnographic perspectives on food, politics, and power*: 240–264. Washington: Smithsonian Institution Press.

Dougherty, C.
2003 The Aristonothos krater: competing stories of conflict and collaboration. In C. Dougherty and L. Kurke (eds.), *The Cultures within Ancient Greek Culture: Contact, Conflict, Collaboration*: 35–56. Cambridge: Cambridge University Press.

Driessen, J.
2011 A Matrilocal House Society in Pre- and Protopalatial Crete? In I. Schoep, P. Tomkins and J. Driessen (eds.), *Back to the Beginning: Reassessing Social and Political Complexity on Crete during the Early and Middle Bronze Age*: 358–383. Oxford: Oxbow Books.

Dyson, S.L. and R.J.J. Rowland
2007 *Archaeology and History in Sardinia from the Stone Age to the Middle Ages: Sheperds, Sailors & Conquerors*. Philadelphia: University of Pennsylvania Museum of Archaeology and Anthropology.

Eckstein, A.M.
2009 *Mediterranean Anarchy, Interstate War, and the Rise of Rome*. Berkeley: University of California Press.

Galaty, M.L., W.A. Parkinson, J.F. Cherry, E.H. Cline, P.N. Kardulias, R. Schon, S. Sherratt, H. Thomas and D. Wengrow
2010 Interaction amidst Diversity: and Introduction to the Eastern Mediterranean Bronze Age. In W.A. Parkinson and M.L. Galaty (eds.), *Archaic State Interaction. The Eastern Mediterranean in the Bronze Age* (School for Advanced Research Advanced Seminar Series): 29–52. Santa Fe: School for Advanced Research Press.

Gili, S., V. Lull, R. Micó, C. Rihuete and R. Risch
2006 An island decides: megalithic burial rites on Menorca. *Antiquity* 80: 829–840.

González Wagner, C.
2013 Tartessos and the Orientilizing Elites. In M.C. Berrocal, L. García Sanjuán and A. Gilman (eds.), *The Prehistory of Iberia. Debating Early Social Stratification and the State*: 337–356. New York: Routledge.

Greenberg, R.
2011 Travelling in (World) Time: Tranformation, Commoditization, and the Beginnings of Urbanism in the Southern Levant. In T. Wilkinson, S. Sherratt and J. Bennet (eds.), *Interweaving worlds: systemic interactions in Eurasia, 7th to 1st millennia BC. Papers from a conference in memory of Professor Andrew Sherratt. What Would a Bronze Age World System Look Like? World systems approaches to Europe and western Asia 4th to 1st millennia BC*: 231–242. Oxford: Oxbow Books.

Haggis, D.C.
1999 Staple Finance, Peak Sanctuaries, and Economic Complexity in Late Prepalatial Crete. In
A. Chaniotis (ed.), *From Minoan farmers to Roman traders. Sidelights on the economy of ancient Crete*:
53–85. Stuttgart: Franz Steiner Verlag.

Halstead, P.
1989 The economy has a normal surplus: economic stability and social change among early farming
communities of Thessaly, Greece. In P. Halstead and J. O'Shea (eds.), *Bad year economies: cultural
responses to risk and uncertainty*: 68–80. Cambridge: Cambridge University Press.
2004 Life After Mediterranean Polyculture: The Subsistence Subsystem and the Emergence of
Civilisation Revisited. In P. Halstead and J.C. Barrett (eds.), *The Emergence of Civilisation Revisited*
(Sheffield Studies in Aegean Archaeology 6): 189–206. Oxford: Oxbow Books.

Hamilakis, Y.
2002a Too Many Chiefs?: Factional competition in Neopalatial Crete. In J. Driessen, I. Schoep and
R. Laffineur (eds.), *Monuments of Minos. Rethinking the Minoan Palaces. Proceedings of the International
Workshop "Crete of the Hundred Palaces?" held at the Université Catholique de Louvain, Louvain-la-Neuve,
14-15 December 2001* (Aegaeum 23): 179–199. Liège: Université de Liège. Histoire de l'art et
archéologie de la Gréce antique.
2002b What Future for the 'Minoan' Past? Re-thinking the Minoan Archaeology. In Y. Hamilakis
(ed.), *Labyrinth Revisited. Rethinking 'Minoan' Archaeology*: 2–29. London: Oxbow Books.

Hayden, B. and S. Villeneuve
2010 Who benefits from complexity? A view from Futuna. In T.D. Price and G.M. Feinman (eds.),
Pathways to power. New perspectives on the emergence of social inequality (Fundamental issues in
archaeology): 95–146. New York: Springer.

Helms, M.W.
1994 Chiefdom rivalries, control, and external contacts in lower Central America. In E. M. Brumfiel
and J.W. Fox (eds.), *Factional competition and political development in the New World*: 55–60. Cambridge:
Cambridge University Press.

Hodos, T.
2010 *Globalization and Colonization:* A View from Iron Age Sicily. *Journal of Mediterranean Archaeology*
23(1): 81–106.

Hopkins, K.
1983 *Death and renewal*. Cambridge: Cambridge University Press.

Horden, P. and N. Purcell
2000 *The Corrupting Sea. A Study of Mediterranean History*. Oxford: Blackwell.

Iacono, F.
2013 Westernizing Aegean of LH IIIC. In M.E. Alberti (ed.), *Exchange networks and local transformations.
Interaction and local change in Europe and the Mediterranean from the Bronze Age to the Iron Age*: 60–79.
Oxford: Oxbow Books.

Isaksen, L.
2013. 'O what a tangled web we weave' – towards a practice that does not deceive. In C. Knappett (ed.), *Network Analysis in Archaeology: New Approaches to Regional Interaction*: 43–67. Oxford: Oxford University Press.

Izzet, V.
2007 *The Archaeology of Etruscan Society*. Cambridge: Cambridge University Press.

Jung, R.
2009 Pirates of the Aegean: Italy – The East Aegean – Cyprus. In R. Karageorghis and O. Kouka (eds.), *Cyprus and the east Aegean. Intercultural contacts from 3000 to 500 BC. An international Archaeological Symposium held at Pythagoreion, Samos, October 17th-18th 2008*: 72–93. Nicosia.

Karytinos, A.
2000 Οι ζωομορφικές σφραγίδες των Αρχανών, *Πεπραγμένα Η' Διεθνούς Κρητολογικού Συνεδρίου. Ηράκλειο, 9-14 Σεπτεμβρίου 1996. Τόμος Α2. Προϊστορική και Αρχαία Ελληνική Περίοδος*: 37–50. Ηράκλειο: Εταιρεία Κρητικών Ιστορικών Μελετών.

Kienlin, T.L.
2012 Beyond Elites: An Introduction. In T. Kienlin and A. Zimmermann (eds.), *Beyond Elites. Alternatives to Hierarchical Systems in Modelling Social Formations. International Conference at the Ruhr-Universität Bochum, Germany, October 22-24, 2009. Teil 1*: 15–32. Bonn: Habelt.

Knapp, A.B. and P. van Dommelen.
2010 Material connections: mobility, materiality and Mediterranean identities. In P. van Dommelen and A.B. Knapp (eds.), *Material connections in the Ancient Mediterranean. Mobility, materiality and identity*: 1–18. Oxford: Routledge.

Knappett, C.
1999 Tradition and innovation in pottery forming technology: wheel throwing at Middle Minoan Knossos. *Annual of the British School at Athens* 94: 101–130.
2009 Scaling Up: From Household to State in Bronze Age Crete. In S. Owen and L. Preston (eds.), *Inside the City in the Greek World. Studies of Urbanism from the Bronze Age to the Hellenistic Period* (University of Cambridge Museum of Classical Archaeology Monograph no. 1): 14–26. Oxford: Oxbow Books.
2011 *An archaeology of interaction : network perspectives on material culture and society*. Oxford: Oxford University Press.

Kohl, P.L.
2011 World-Systems and Modelling Macro-Historical Processes in Later Prehistory: an Examination of Old and a Search for New Perspectives. In T. Wilkinson, S. Sherratt and J. Bennet (eds.), *Interweaving worlds: systemic interactions in Eurasia, 7th to 1st millennia BC. Papers from a conference in memory of Professor Andrew Sherratt. What Would a Bronze Age World System Look Like? World systems approaches to Europe and western Asia 4th to 1st millennia BC*: 77–86. Oxford: Oxbow Books.

Kolb, M.J.
2005 The Genesis of Monuments among the Mediterranean Islands. In E. Blake and A.B. Knapp (eds.), *The archaeology of Mediterranean prehistory*: 156–179. Oxford: Blackwell.
2012 The genesis of monuments in island societies. In M.E. Smith (ed.), *The comparative archaeology of complex societies*: 138–164. Cambridge: Cambridge University Press.

Legarra Herrero, B.

2011a New kid on the block: the nature of the first systemic contacts between Crete and the eastern Mediterranean around 2000 BC. In T. Wilkinson, S. Sherratt and J. Bennet (eds.), *Interweaving worlds: systemic interactions in Eurasia, 7th to 1st millennia BC. Papers from a conference in memory of Professor Andew Sherratt. What Would a Bronze Age World System Look Like? World systems approaches to Europe and western Asia 4th to 1st millennia BC*: 266–281. Oxford: Oxbow Books.

2011b The Construction, Deconstruction and Non-construction of Hierarchies in the Funerary Record of Prepalatial Crete. In I. Schoep, P. Tomkins and J. Driessen (eds.), *Back to the Beginning: Reassessing Social and Political Complexity on Crete during the Early and Middle Bronze Age*: 325–357. Oxford: Oxbow Books.

2013 Modern political views and the emergence of early complex societies in the Bronze Age Mediterranean. *Antiquity* 87(335): 245–249.

Lomba Maraundi, J., M.V. López Martínez and F. Ramos Martínez

2009 Un excepcional sepulcro del calcolítico: Camino del Molino (Caravaca de la Cruz). In J.A. Melgares Guerrero, P.E. Collado Espejo and J.A. Bascuñana Coll (eds.), *Jornadas de Patrimonio Cultural de la Región de Murcia*. Murcia: Ediciones Tres Fronteras.

López Padilla, J.A.

2009 El irresistible poder de la ostentación: la artesanía del marfil en la época del Argar. *Alberca: Revista de la Asociación de Amigos del Museo Arqueológico de Lorca* 7: 7–23.

Macdonald, C.F.

2011 Palatial Knossos: the Early Years. In I. Schoep, P. Tomkins and J. Driessen (eds.), *Back to the Beginning: Reassessing Social and Political Complexity on Crete during the Early and Middle Bronze Age*: 81–113. Oxford: Oxbow Books.

Malkin, I.

2002 A colonial middle ground: Greek, Etruscan and local elites in the Bay of Naples. In C. Lyons and J. Papadopoulos (eds.), *The Archeology of Colonialism: Issues and Debates*: 151–181. Los Angeles: Getty Research Insitute.

Malone, C. and S. Stoddart

2009 Conclusions. In C. Malone, S. Stoddart, A. Bonanno and D. Trump (eds.), *Mortuary customs in prehistoric Malta. Excavations at the Brochtorff Circle at Xaghra (1987-1994)*: 361–384. Cambridge: McDonald Institute for Archaeological Research.

Manning, S.

2008 Formation of the Palaces. In C.W. Shelmerdine (ed.), *The Cambridge Companion to the Aegean Bronze Age*: 105–120. Cambridge: Cambridge University Pres.

Maran, J.

2011 Lost in Translation: The Emergence of Mycenaean Culture as a Phenomenon of Glocalization. In T. Wilkinson, S. Sherratt and J. Bennet (eds.), *Interweaving worlds: systemic interactions in Eurasia, 7th to 1st millennia BC. Papers from a conference in memory of Professor Andew Sherratt. What Would a Bronze Age World System Look Like? World systems approaches to Europe and western Asia 4th to 1st millennia BC*: 282–294. Oxford: Oxbow Books.

Marcus, G.

1983 "Elite" as a Concept, Theory, and Research. In G. Marcus (ed.), *Elites: Ethnographic Issues*: 7–28. Alburquerque: University Of New Mexico Press.

Mattingly, D.J.
2011 *Imperialism, power, and identity: experiencing the Roman empire.* Oxford: Princeton University Press.

Nowicki, K.
2008 Some Remarks on New Peak Sanctuaries in Crete: The Topography of Ritual Areas and their Relationship with Settlements. *Jahrbuch des deutschen archäilogischen Instituts* 122: 1–32.

Parkinson, W.A. and M.L. Galaty
2007 Secondary States in Perspective: An Integrated Approach to State Formation in the Prehistoric Aegean. *American Anthropologist* 109(1): 113–129.

Patsiaouras, G. and J.A. Fitchett
2012 The evolution of conspicuous consumption. *Journal of Historical Research in Marketing* 4(1): 154–176.

Patton, M.
1996 *Islands in Time: Island Sociogeography and Mediterranean Prehistory.* Oxfod: Routledge.

Peatfield, A.A.D.
1987 Palace and Peak: the political and religious relationship between palaces and peak sanctuaries. In R. Hägg and N. Marinatos (eds.), *The Function of the Minoan Palaces. Proceedings of the Fourth International Symposium at the Swedish Institute in Athens, 10-16 June, 1984* (Skrifter Utgivna av Svenska Institutet i Athen, 4°, XXXV): 89–93. Stockholm: Svenska Institutet i Athen.

Pini, I.
2000 Eleven Early Cretan Scarabs. In A. Karetsou (ed.) *Κρήτη - Αίγυπτος. Πολιτισμικοί δεσμοί τριών χιλιετιών*: 107–113. Αθήνα: Υπουργείο Πολιτισμού - Αρχαιολογικό Μουσείο Ηράκλειου.

Relaki, M.
2011 The Social Arenas of Tradition. Investigation Collective and Individual Social Strategies in the Prepalatial and Protopalatial Mesara. In I. Schoep, P. Tomkins and J. Driessen (eds.), *Back to the Beginning: Reassessing Social and Political Complexity on Crete during the Early and Middle Bronze Age*: 290–324. Oxford: Oxbow Books.

Renfrew, C.
1986 Introduction: peer polity interaction and socio-political change. In C. Renfrew and J.F. Cherry (eds.), *Peer polity interacting and socio-political change*: 1–18. Cambridge: Cambridge University Press.

Riva, C.
2010 *The urbanisation of Etruria: funerary practices and social change, 700-600 BC.* New York: Cambridge University Press.

Roscoe, P.
2000 New Guinea Leadership as Ethnographic Analogy: A Critical Review. *Journal of Archaeological Method and Theory* 7(2): 79–126.
2009 Social Signaling and the Organization of Small-Scale Society: The Case of Contact-Era New Guinea. *Journal of Archaeological Method and Theory* 16(2): 69–116.
2012 Before elites: the political capacities of Big Men. In T. Kienlin and A. Zimmermann (eds.), *Beyond Elites. Alternatives to Hierarchical Systems in Modelling Social Formations. International Conference at the Ruhr-Universität Bochum, Germany, October 22-24, 2009. Teil 1*: 41–54. Bonn: Habelt.

Rowlands, M.
2010 Concluding thoughts. In P. van Dommelen and A.B. Knapp (eds.), *Material connections in the Ancient Mediterranean. Mobility, Materiality and identity*: 233–247. London: Routledge.

Russell, A.
2010 Foreign materials, islander mobility and elite identity in Late Bronze Age Sardinia. In P. van Dommelen and A.B. Knapp (eds.), *Material connections in the Ancient Mediterranean. Mobility, materiality and identity*: 106–126. Oxford: Routledge.

Savage, M. and K. Williams
2008 Elites: remembered in capitalism and forgotten by social sciences. In M. Savage and K. Williams (eds.), *Remembering elites*: 1–24. Oxford: Blackwell publishing.

Sbonias, K.
2011 Regional Elite-Groups and the Production and Consumption of Seals in the Prepalatial period. A Case-Study of the Asterousia Region. In I. Schoep, P. Tomkins and J. Driessen (eds.), *Back to the Beginning: Reassessing Social and Political Complexity on Crete during the Early and Middle Bronze Age*: 236–272. Oxford: Oxbow Books.

Schoep, I.
2006 Looking Beyond the First Palaces: Elites and the Agency of Power in EM III-MM II Crete. *American Journal of Archaeology* 110: 37–64.
2010 Making Elites: Political Economy and Elite Culture(s) in Middle Minoan Crete. In D.J. Pullen (ed.), *Political Economies of the Aegean Bronze Age. Papers from the Langford Conference, Florida State University, Tallahassee, 22-24 February 2007*: 66–85. Oxford: Oxbow Books.

Schoep, I. and C. Knappett.
2004 Dual Emergence: Evolving Heterarchy, Exploding Hierarchy. In J.C. Barrett and P. Halstead (eds.), *The Emergence of Civilisation Revisited* (Sheffield Studies in Aegean Archaeology 6): 21–37. Oxford: Oxbow Books.

Scott, J.
2008 Modes of power and the re-conceptualization of elites. In M. Savage and K. Williams (eds.), *Remembering elites*: 25–43. Oxford: Blackwell Publishing.

Sherratt, A.G. and S. Sherratt.
1998 Small Worlds: Interaction and Identity in the Ancient Mediterranean. In E.H. Cline and D. Harris-cline (eds.), *The Aegean and the Orient in the Second Millennium: Proceedings of the 50th Anniversary Symposium, Cincinnati, 18-10 April 1997* (Aegaeum 18): 329–343. Liège: Université de Liège. Histoire de l'art et archéologie de la Grèce antique.

Sherratt, S.
1998 'Sea Peoples' and the economic structure of the late second millennium in the eastern Mediterranean. In S. Gitin, A. Mazar and E. Stern (eds.), *Mediterranean peoples in transition: thirteenth to early tenth centuries BCE*: 292–313. Jerusalem: Israel Exploration Fund.
2003 The Mediterranean economy: 'Globalization' at the end of the second millennium BCE. In W.G. Dever and S. Gitin (eds.), *Symbiosis, Symbolism, and the Power of the Past: Canaan, Ancient Israel, and Their Neighbors, from the Late Bronze Age through Roman Palaestina*: 37–62. Winona Lake: Eisenbrauns.

Shore, C.
2002 Introduction: towards an anthropology of elites. In C. Shore and S. Nugent (eds.), *Elites Cultures. Anthropological perspectives*: 1–21. London: Routledge.

Slootjes, D.
2011 Local Elites and Power in the Roman World: Modern Theories and Models. *Journal of Interdisciplinary History* 42(2): 235–249.

Smith, A.T.
2003 *The Political Landscape. Constellations of Authority in Early Complex Societies*. Berkeley: University of California Press.

Stein, G.J.
1998 World System Theory and Alternative Modes of Interaction in the Archaeology of Culture Contact. In J.G. Cusick (ed.), *Studies in Culture Contact. Interaction, Culture, Change, and Archaeology* (Occasional Paper No. 25): 220–255. Carbondale: Center for Archaeological Investigations, Southern Illinois University.

Stockhammer, P.W.
2012 Conceptualizing Cultural Hybridization in Archaeology. In P. W. Stockhammer (ed.), *Conceptualizing Cultural Hybridization* (Transcultural Research – Heidelberg Studies on Asia and Europe in a Global Context): 43–58. Springer Berlin Heidelberg.

Stockhammer, P.W.
2013 From Hibridity to Entanglement, from Essentialism to Practice. *Archaeological Review from Cambridge* 28 (1): 11–28.

Tomkins, P.
2011 Behind the Horizon: Reconsidering the Genesis and Function of the 'First Palace' At Knossos (Final Neolithic IV-Middle Minoan IB). In I. Schoep, P. Tomkins and J. Driessen (eds.), *Back to the Beginning: Reassessing Social and Political Complexity on Crete during the Early and Middle Bronze Age*: 32–80. Oxford: Oxbow Books.

Tronchetti, C. and P. van Dommelen
2005 Entangled Objects and Hybrid Practices: Colonial Contacts and Elite Connections at Monte Prama. *Journal of Mediterranean Archaeology* 18 (2): 183–208.

Tykot, R.
2011 Obsidian Finds on the Fringes of the Central Mediterranean: Exotic or Eccentric Exchange? In A. Vianello (ed.), *Exotica in the Prehistoric Mediterranean*: 33–44. Oxford: Oxbow Books.

Van Bremen, R.
2007 Networks of Rhodians in Karia. *Mediterranean Historical Review* 22(1): 113–132.

Vianello, A. (ed.)
2011 *Exotica in the Prehistoric Mediterranean*. Oxford: Oxbow Books.

Van Dommelen, P.
1997 Colonial Constructs: Colonialism and Archaeology in the Mediterranean. *World Archaeology* 28(3): 305–323.

2011 One Sea for All: Intercultural, Social and Economic Contacts in the Bronze Age Mediterranean. In K. Duistermaat and I. Regulski (eds.), *Intercultural contacts in the Ancient Mediterranean. Proceedings of the International Conference at the Netherlands-Flemish Institute in Cairo, 25th to 29th October 2008* (Orientalia Lovaniensia Analecta 20): 411–426. Leuven: Uitgeverij Peeters en Departement Oosterse Studies.

Voskos, I. and A.B. Knapp
2008 Cyprus at the End of the Late Bronze Age: Crisis and Colonization or Continuity and Hybridization? *American Journal of Archaeology* 112(4): 659–684.

Watrous, L.V.
1994 Crete from earliest prehistory through the Protopalatial period. *American Journal of Archaeology* 98: 698–753.
1998 Egypt and Crete in the Early Middle Bronze Age: A Case of Trade and Cultural Diffusion. In E.H. Cline and D. Harris-cline (eds.), *The Aegean and the Orient in the Second Millennium: Proceedings of the 50th Anniversary Symposium, Cincinnati, 18–10 April 1997* (Aegaeum 18): 19–28. Liège: Université de Liège. Histoire de l'art et archéologie de la Grèce antique.
2012 An overview of secondary state formation on Crete: the Mirabello region during the Bronze Age. In E. Matzourani and P.P. Betancourt (eds.), *Philistor. Studies in Honor of Costis Davaras* (Prehistory Monograph 36): 273–282. Philadelphia: INSTAP Academic Press.

Whitelaw, T.M.
2011 The Urbanisation of Prehistoric Crete: Settlements Prespectives on Minoan State Formation. In I. Schoep, P. Tomkins and J. Driessen (eds.), *Back to the Beginning: Reassessing Social and Political Complexity on Crete during the Early and Middle Bronze Age*: 114–176. Oxford: Oxbow Books.

Wiener, M.H.
2013 Contacts: Crete, Egypt, and the Near East circa 2000 B.C. In J. Aruz, S.B. Graff and Y. Rakic (eds.), *Cultures in Contact. From Mesopotamia to the Mediterranean in the Second Millennium B.C.*: 34–45. New York: The Metropolitcan Museum of Art.

Wiessner, P.
2002 The Vines of Complexity. Egalitarian Structures and the Institutionalization of Inequality among the Enga. *Current Anthropology* 43(2): 233–269.
2009 The Power of One? Big Men Revisited. In K.J. Vaughn, J.W. Eerkens and J. Kantner (eds.), *The evolution of Leadership. Transitions in Decision Making from Small-Scale to Middle-Range Societies* (School for Advanced Research Advanced Seminar Series): 195–222. Santa Fe: School for Advanced Research Press.

Wright, J.C.
2004 The Emergence of Leadership and the Rise of Civilization in the Aegean. In J.C. Barrett and P. Halstead (eds.), *The Emergence of Civilisation Revisited* (Sheffield Studies in Aegean Archaeology 6): 64–89. Oxford: Oxbow Books.

Chapter 3

Scales and Modes of Interaction in and beyond the Earlier Neolithic of Greece: Building Barriers and Making Connections

Paul Halstead

The aim of this volume is to explore how and why people share materials, objects and ideas on various social scales – and whether the answers to these questions differ over the course of time. The present chapter explores these issues with reference to the earlier (Early and Middle) Neolithic of Greece: the earlier Neolithic for the sake of brevity and Greece because much of the previous scholarship reviewed below has a similar focus (not because modern state borders had meaning in the Neolithic).

Regional and inter-regional similarities in material culture have long been a focus of studies of the Neolithic in Greece, as the basis for building regional relative and absolute chronologies and for explanations of culture change (most persistently, for initial neolithisation) in terms of diffusion – often involving human migration. More recently, archaeometric analyses have demonstrated long-distance movement of a growing range of materials and objects, while biogeographical and genetic studies have confirmed the diffusion from southwest Asia to southeast Europe of livestock and crop species. On the other hand, prehistorians have also become more sensitive to the role of material culture in *negotiating* human cultural identities, rather than merely *reflecting* their biological and geographical origins. This chapter is arranged more or less historiographically. First, it briefly outlines how culture-historical studies interpreted regional and inter-regional similarities of Greek earlier Neolithic material culture *before* the advent of C^{14} dating. Secondly, it considers the implications, for this approach, of subsequent empirical and methodological developments in the field. Thirdly, it attempts to interpret spatial patterning in earlier Neolithic material culture in a more contextualised manner and at several complementary social scales.

The chapter critically evaluates the empirical evidence and arguments underpinning persistent claims that colonists from southwest Asia introduced farming to Greece. Consistent with the focus of this volume, however, it does *not* attempt to resolve the 'origins' (*i.e.* agents) of the neolithisation of Greece, let alone to argue *for* adoption by indigenous foragers. Rather it argues that models of origins have provided at best a very partial explanation of the spatially and temporally diverse material culture of the earlier Neolithic in Greece and have discouraged its investigation as the dynamic product of a range of social practices, identities, relationships and tensions.

Connecting the Neolithic of Greece

In *The Dawn of European Civilization*, Childe's sketch of early Neolithic culture in Greece emphasised its far-flung connections to the north, east and west. He regarded ceramics impressed with *Cardium* shell, found in the second phase of the Early Neolithic at Otzaki in central Greece (Figure 3.1), as "the symbols of the earliest Neolithic farmer-colonists throughout the Balkans and round the West Mediterranean too," while some "still earlier cultivators in South-Western Asia... did decorate their pottery with *Cardium* impressions" (Childe 1957: 58). Items of Greek Early (EN) or Middle Neolithic (MN) material culture as varied as stone studs or 'labrets', bone spoons, clay stamps, and painted pottery with decoration inspired by basketry provided further links eastwards and/or northwards. A plethora of such stylistic links established a persistent culture-historical view of the earlier Neolithic of Greece (*e.g.* Clark 1977; Champion *et al.* 1984; Perlès 2001; Scarre 2005) as an integral part of a Balkan early Neolithic culture group, extending through Bulgaria and the former Yugoslavia to southern Hungary and Romania; as "the westernmost outpost of the South-West Asiatic province" (Childe 1957: 62); and as a cultural stepping-stone from southwest Asia to central Europe and the northwest Mediterranean.

Even the last edition of the *Dawn* effectively preceded the 'radiocarbon revolution' (1957: xiii), so Childe necessarily used the material culture traits cited above both to establish inter-regional relative chronology for the Neolithic and to sketch out the development of Europe's first farming societies. Starting from the premise that "[f]arming must of course have started in South-west Asia" (Childe 1957: 16), he perhaps inevitably saw early Neolithic material culture as spreading thence into Europe via Greece and the northern Balkans (1957: 341). As to the means by which it spread, he concluded that the first farmers on Crete, in the absence of earlier evidence for hunter-gatherers, "were immigrants who brought their Neolithic equipment with them" (Childe 1957: 18). On the mainland of Greece, where Palaeolithic remains *were* known, Childe presciently suspected that the lack of Mesolithic sites might be due to a failure to look hard enough, but he again considered the first farmers to be colonists from southwest Asia because shared female figurines and incipient tell formation indicated a common ideology and rural economy (Childe 1957: 58).

As Childe made clear, study and definition of the Early Neolithic in Greece were still at an early stage in the mid-1950s. Accordingly, his case for linking the earlier Greek Neolithic to southwest Asian origins drew significantly on generic similarities in painted decoration of pottery between the *Middle* Neolithic of central Greece and

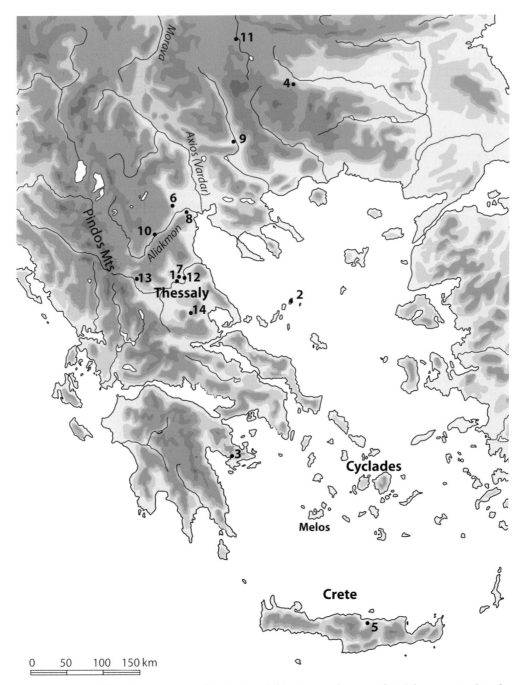

Figure 3.1: Map of southeast Europe showing Neolithic sites and geographical features cited in the text: 1. Argissa; 2. Cyclops cave; 3. Franchthi cave; 4. Kapitan Dimitrievo; 5. Knossos; 6. Nea Nikomedia; 7. Otzaki; 8. Paliambela-Kolindrou; 9. Promachonas; 10. Servia; 11. Slatina; 12. Soufli; 13. Theopetra cave; 14. Tsangli.

widely dispersed contexts in southern Turkey, Cyprus, Syria, and northern Iraq and Iran (Childe 1957: 58–62; for similar observations on the neolithisation of the central and north Balkans, see Budja 2009) that are now considered to be of varying – in some cases incompatible – date. The case for neolithisation of Greece by colonisation was not based, therefore, on compelling demonstration of detailed similarities of material culture with a specific source area, but rather on the belief that this was the most plausible way of accounting for the seemingly rapid appearance of a wholly new way of life. In fact, as Childe made explicit for the north Balkans, he suspected two successive waves of colonists from southwest Asia, that brought first incised or impressed and later painted pottery, and he contemplated the contribution of some early Neolithic cultural elements and perhaps even local domestication by indigenous north Balkan foragers. He also saw the development of an initially uniform culture into "distinct local cultures in the several natural subdivisions of the province" as the consequence of a mobile or migrating population settling down into local self-sufficient isolation (1957: 88). These nuances made his model compatible with the rather ambiguous material cultural record then available, but did so by tacitly abandoning its claim to provide a mechanism for rapid and wholesale cultural change.

Childe was of course a prisoner of the evidence available to him and anyway was in large measure synthesising previous scholarship conducted within a similar conceptual framework and under similar methodological constraints. The previous paragraphs have dwelt on his views set out in the *Dawn* because this great work of synthesis – but *without* Childe's nuances and expressions of uncertainty – has arguably shaped how many European prehistorians have viewed especially the earlier Neolithic of Greece. Even Marek Zvelebil, a leading proponent of an active role for indigenous European foragers in *adopting* (and to a limited extent domesticating) early crop and livestock species, accepted that colonising farmers were the agents of neolithisation through Greece and the Balkans into central Europe (*e.g.* Zvelebil 1986: 184 fig. 10). Acceptance of the colonisation model still drives interpretations of other data sets (*e.g.* the spatio-temporal distribution of crop taxa in southwest Asia and southeast Europe – Colledge *et al.* 2004) that strictly shed no light on the contributions of farming colonists and foraging natives to neolithisation.

Disconnecting the Neolithic of Greece

In the nearly six decades since the last edition of the *Dawn*, understanding of Greek Neolithic culture history has undergone some dramatic changes. First, thanks to calibrated radiocarbon dating, the period is now known to have spanned from shortly after 7000 BC (Facorellis and Maniatis 2013; Karamitrou *et al.* 2013; Perlès *et al.* 2013) to about 3000 BC – probably twice to four times as long as Childe would have guessed, though he was characteristically explicit regarding the uncertainties of his own chronology (1957: 342). Secondly, subsequent excavations have largely filled in the very discontinuous cultural sequence from early twentieth-century excavations on which Childe was dependent, so that an apparently short-lived Neolithic with radical disjunctions in material culture has given way to a long period of much more gradual transformation. For example, the seemingly sudden rupture between the MN Sesklo and Late Neolithic (LN) Dimini cultures of Thessaly, that Childe tentatively attributed to 'infiltration of new colonists' from the north Balkans (1957: 62–64; or alternatively from southwest Asia and the southern Aegean *to* the north Balkans, via central Greece – 1957: 66), is now replaced by a millennium of more gradual development. Likewise, the Early Neolithic in Greece now spans almost a millennium and begins with an initial largely *aceramic* phase, at least at Knossos on Crete, and an earliest ceramic phase, both at Knossos and on the mainland, with very small amounts of simple pottery (*e.g.* Evans 1973; Wijnen 1982; Papadakou *et al.* in press). The latter exhibits rather more generic similarities (few simple shapes and surface finishes) with southwest Asian counterparts than those that Childe highlighted (*e.g.* Thissen 2000: 143).

Thirdly, as Childe anticipated, appropriately targeted prospection *has* located Mesolithic sites in Greece (*e.g.* Runnels *et al.* 2005), while in excavations at Franchthi cave on the southern mainland a hiatus of just a few generations between the latest Mesolithic and earliest Neolithic levels (Perlès *et al.* 2013) is apparently bridged by continuity in lithic technology (Perlès 1990a) and shellfish exploitation (Shackleton 1988). On the other hand, archaeobotanical and zooarchaeological research has strongly confirmed Childe's vision of rapid and wholesale inception of farming at the beginning of the Neolithic in Greece. Plant and animal remains in late Mesolithic levels at Franchthi seem exclusively to be of wild species (Hansen 1991; Stiner and Munro 2011), while a few domesticates in Mesolithic levels at Theopetra and Cyclops caves are probably intrusive (*e.g.* Newton 2003; Kyparissi-Apostolika and Kotzamani 2005). Conversely, the earliest Neolithic levels at Franchthi cave and at open-air villages from Knossos on Crete to Argissa in central and Paliambela-Kolindrou in northern Greece have yielded remains dominated by domestic crop (Hansen 1991; Halstead 1994; Sarpaki 2013) and livestock species (Halstead and Isaakidou 2013). Moreover, current biogeographical and genetic evidence strongly supports the view that all these domesticates were introduced to Greece from southwest Asia (*e.g.* Burger and Thomas 2011). In the 1960s, however, when domestic cattle, pigs, bread wheat and perhaps barley from EN Knossos, Argissa and Nea Nikomedia seemed to be amongst the earliest known anywhere, some scholars considered Greece an integral part of a broad southwest Asian-southeast European hearth of domestication (Theocharis 1967; Higgs and Jarman 1969). Rodden saw support for this argument in material culture traits that Childe had considered of southwest Asian origin: EN sites from central Greece to the central Balkans comprised free-standing rectangular houses, unlike the agglomerated structures of southwest Asia, and shared a suite of similar portable items that were encountered piecemeal further east (Rodden 1965). Although independent domestication in southeast Europe now seems improbable, Rodden highlighted how the EN material culture of southeast Europe, if divorced from westward expansion of domesticates, did not necessarily indicate wholesale introduction by colonists from southwest Asia.

Fourthly, as Nandris noted (1970: 195), one unfortunate by-product of pre-C[14] chronology-building was the playing down of *observed* regional and local (and also contextual – Kotsakis 2006) variation in favour of temporal developments *presumed* to be synchronous on a regional and supra-regional scale. For example, as Childe had recognised (1957: 85–88), some forms of early Neolithic material culture (Nandris 1970: 203–204 figs. 1–2) were distributed widely across southeast Europe (*e.g.* labrets, 'Rod Head' figurines), while others were restricted to the 'natural subdivisions' thereof (*e.g.* 'Integral Seat' figurines in the lowlands of Thessaly or 'Black Arcaded Barbotine' pottery in the Axios/Vardar and Aliakmon drainages to the north). Yet other forms, however, spanned two or more such subdivisions (*e.g.* 'Chocolate-on-light' pottery along the northern Vardar and southern Morava). Nandris enigmatically attributed these overlapping stylistic distributions, each spanning 100–400 km, to the gradual adaptation of early farmers to the north Balkan temperate environment, but they plainly imply rather more complex social networks than Childe's tentative proposal of colonising farmers settling down into self-sufficient isolation.

Decorative styles or wares of earlier Neolithic fine ceramics are shared over distances of perhaps 50–100 km in Greece (*e.g.* Washburn 1983; Jacobsen 1984; Rondiri 1985), while petrographic analysis suggests that even some of the unremarkable plain ceramic vessels at EN Knossos, indistinguishable by eye from local products, had been brought 50–60 km from eastern Crete (Tomkins and Day 2001). On the other hand, archaeometric analysis has confirmed EN movement of Melian obsidian (*e.g.* Renfrew *et al.* 1965; Milić 2014; Perlès *et al.* 2011), anticipated by Childe on the basis of macroscopic recognition, over 150 km to Knossos on Crete, more than 300 km to the eastern shores of the Aegean and more than 400 km to the northern Aegean, thus indirectly linking regions that display relatively few ceramic affinities. Within the Aegean, therefore, obsidian at least was transported over distances far exceeding the overlapping distributions of shared fine ceramic styles, but far less than the 1000–2000 km over which Childe sought southwest Asian parallels (and origins) for items of portable material culture like labrets, bone spoons and clay stamps.

As regards this wider southwest Asian context of Greek EN material culture, Perlès recently acknowledged, as did Childe implicitly and Rodden explicitly, that "the artefactual analogies between Greece and the Near East... are *selective*... and... come from different regions and even different periods" within the latter (2001: 58). Nonetheless, she favoured the introduction of farming to Greece by long-distance colonisation from the east Mediterranean and attributed the eclectic nature of artefactual similarities to the colonists being "small groups of adventurous individuals," rather than whole communities, and following different pathways westwards from their original homes (2001: 62). In a later study, focussing on inter-regional *differences* as well as *similarities* in the seventh millennium BC, she argued that colonists spread both by sea, from the east Mediterranean to southern and central Greece, and overland, from Turkey to Bulgaria and northern Greece. Along both routes, the material traits transmitted westwards omitted the cult buildings associated with PPNB 'mega-sites' in southwest Asia, because social integration was more easily maintained in the modest EN villages of southeast Europe. After arrival, the two sets of colonists borrowed traits both from each other and from indigenous foragers (Perlès 2005). This model, however, of two corridors of east-west contact, is equally compatible with the dispersal of farming by colonisation or adoption and, to accommodate colonisation to available evidence, introduces several additional ingredients – including an element of indigenous adoption. On a more positive note, in considering the social contexts of use of both retained and discarded material culture traits, Perlès points forward to the next section of this chapter.

Re-connecting the Neolithic of Greece

The preceding sections have debated the material 'connections' of the Greek Neolithic in broadly culture historical terms of their degree of similarity and their distribution in time and space. A fundamental problem with this approach, whether used to support or to reject migrationist explanations of culture change, is that it treats material culture as passively reflecting unambiguous human identities, values and social relations. It is now widely accepted that humans may maintain multiple – perhaps contradictory – identities, values and social relations, which they actively shape rather than passively inherit and which they may promote, conceal or misrepresent through the medium of material culture (*e.g.* Hodder 1982). Material culture thus carries more diverse and complex meanings than Childe envisaged, making its 'reading' much more challenging but potentially far more rewarding.

Because potential interpretations of material culture are multiple, the following paragraphs attempt to model likely forms and scales of social interactions and identities by considering the practicalities of early farming life in Greece. It must be emphasised that this tactic is employed, not because the writer believes that subsistence or demography or cranial capacity determined the configurations of Neolithic social and cultural life, but because it makes sense in tackling a problem so complex to proceed, as we do in excavation, by working from the (more or less) known to the unknown.

Neolithic farming and the emergence of the household

The overwhelming predominance of domestic plants and animals leaves little room for doubt that the inhabitants of known Neolithic sites in Greece were largely sustained by farming. Most known EN-MN settlements take the form of 'villages', inhabited by somewhere between several tens and a few hundred persons (*e.g.* Isaakidou 2008: 102 table 6.1; Bogaard and Isaakidou 2010: 196 fig. 18.5). In the absence of intensive dairying, which seems precluded by available mortality data for domestic sheep, goats and cattle (*e.g.* Isaakidou 2006; Halstead and Isaakidou 2013: 131–133), feeding a farming community of this size primarily on 'carnivorous' pastoralism would have necessitated herding on a scale large enough to be of questionable viability in terms of both animal carrying capacity and human labour – especially given the predominance of sheep, which was the early livestock species least suited to ranging widely in a more or less wooded landscape. Alternatively, and far more viably, such a community could primarily have subsisted on grain crops grown on a very modest scale – a strategy compatible with available evidence for human diet and health (Papathanasiou 2003; Papathanasiou *et al.* 2013) and intensity of crop husbandry (Bogaard 2005; Bogaard *et al.* 2013).

Dependence on highly seasonal grain crops will have necessitated reliance on year-round storage, coupled with intensive labour for clearance and cultivation months in advance of harvest and consumption. With such 'delayed-return' food procurement and storage, among both hunter-gatherers (Barnard and Woodburn 1991) and farmers (Flannery 1972), producers tend to maintain control of food – in contrast with a generalised obligation to share among immediate-return foragers not dependent on storage. EN-MN settlements in Greece are aggregations of dwellings, each large enough to have sheltered something like 5–10 persons. Houses destroyed by fire at MN Tsangli in Thessaly contained the complete Neolithic toolkit (Wace and Thompson 1912), while others at MN Servia in northern Greece (Ridley and Wardle 1979) and across the Bulgarian border at EN Kapitan Dimitrievo and Slatina (Marinova 2007) contained burnt stores of grain. Direct evidence for domestic storage is scarce, but this may simply be due to poor preservation, while there is no evidence whatsoever for collective storage (pace Tomkins 2007: 189; *cf.* Halstead 2011: 141). Following Flannery, these dwellings may plausibly be considered to represent small 'households' units of shared residence, labour and consumption. Whereas Childe identified rectangular mud-and-post houses as typical of these early dwellings, subsequent excavations have revealed a mixture of round, often semi-subterranean 'huts' and rectangular above-ground 'houses', with the latter ranging from flimsy wattle-and-daub to more solid mudbrick structures. Whether a temporal trend towards more solid structures is discerned (Pappa 2008) or not, the effort invested in isolating these 'households' was highly variable and throughout the four millennia of the Neolithic was offset by variable counter-investment in the solidarity of the wider village community.

Vulnerable households and village solidarity
The constituent 'households' had two very strong practical rationales for investing in collective village solidarity. First, initial clearance of land is widely undertaken collectively, even when subsequent cultivation and harvest are the responsibility of individual households (*e.g.* Brown 1978: 78–81; García Fernández 1988: 135–136). In the case of earlier Neolithic Greece, emerging evidence for long-term labour-intensive husbandry suggests that individual households are likely to have retained use rights to particular cultivation plots (*cf.* Bogaard 2004) and this, in turn, implies that the village collectively ensured such rights within the community and defended them against

neighbouring communities. Similarly, the development of some settlements into very long-lived tells presupposes that, in the face of the inevitably variable reproductive success of different households, collective mechanisms existed to redistribute unused land to landless inhabitants (Isaakidou 2008: 106). Secondly, individual households of 5–10 (or even 20) persons were viable only in the short term (Sahlins 1974) and will frequently have depended on neighbours and kin in a range of contexts: for labour in the event of illness or injury and at unfavourable points in the generational cycle of changing balance between workers and mouths to feed; for practical or ritual expertise, perhaps monopolised by the elderly, on occasions such as childbirth, sowing, or the beginning of harvest; for food in the event of temporary scarcity; and for political support in disputes over damage to crops by livestock, theft of tools, accusations of witchcraft, and the like.

On the other hand, collective solidarity in Neolithic villages faced some significant challenges. First, households that sought more or less to ring-fence basic resources for internal use will have limited needy neighbours' access to food and so undermined the principle of collective solidarity (*cf.* Kent 1993). Secondly, year-round storage and repeated re-use of cultivation plots will have been strong disincentives to the fluidity of group membership by which inevitable inter-personal friction is defused in bands of mobile, non-storing hunter-gatherers. Thirdly, if the number of inhabitants was on the order of several tens to a few hundreds at tell villages (estimation is even more problematic for flat-extended sites), many EN-MN settlements may have reached a size where webs of close kinship and personal acquaintance gave way to competition or hostility between rival factions (Forge 1972; Chagnon 1979; Hill and Dunbar 2003). Indeed, apparent regularity in the upper size range of Neolithic tell villages in Thessaly (Bogaard and Isaakidou 2010: 196 fig. 18.5) may be the outcome of communities growing to this threshold and then fissioning.

The magnet of collective solidarity is particularly clear in the densely inhabited villages that developed into tells, but both these and the more recently recognised 'flat-extended' settlements seem to have been surrounded by ditches and perhaps palisades, and at least some of these ditches (*e.g.* at Thessalian EN Soufli and north Greek MN Paliambela-Kolindrou) served as collective burial grounds (Triantaphyllou 2008). While Neolithic tells typically extend over something like one hectare or even less, flat-extended settlements may cover tens of hectares and so have far longer ditches. Conversely, available evidence suggests that tells may be associated with relatively solid houses and flat-extended settlements with flimsier huts (Kotsakis 1999; 2006). Tell and flat-extended settlements thus represent greater investment in household independence and collective solidarity, respectively, and the contrasting patterns of residential stability (with tell houses, but not flat-extended huts, often rebuilt several times on the 'footprint' of preceding structures) arguably represent an emphasis on domestic versus collective control of land (Kotsakis 1999; Halstead 2011).

A hint of solidarity between close neighbours comes from the distribution of hearths both within EN-MN dwellings and in the spaces between, with the latter implying cooking in public view and thus increased pressure to share with neighbours. Cooking facilities do not seem to be placed in indoor kitchens or secluded outdoor yards until the Final Neolithic and Early Bronze Age, adding support to the view that the development of relatively autonomous households was a very gradual, long-term process (Halstead 1995).

There are other strong hints that commensality played an important role in social integration. At Neolithic Knossos, anatomically adjacent bones that tend not to be separated during butchery (*e.g.* radius and ulna) are routinely found together, but not so those that are often parted during dismembering (*e.g.* humerus and radius). At Paliambela-Kolindrou, EN pits contained restorable pots that suggest the pits were filled rapidly, but within these features animal bones included very few fragments that could have been derived from the same animal. Both at Knossos and Paliambela-Kolindrou, therefore, it seems that animal bones were largely dispersed *before* discard (Halstead and Isaakidou 2013). Moreover, at these and other Neolithic settlements, domestic animals were slaughtered throughout the year, including the hotter months when storage of meat is least feasible, and many if not most were killed at an age when they were too large to be consumed fresh by a single household, implying that many livestock were reared *for* commensality (Halstead 2007). The use of EN ceramics primarily for serving and consumption, rather than storage or cooking (Vitelli 1989), and the increasingly elaborate decoration of a minority of this tableware through the Early and Middle Neolithic also underlines the social significance of commensality. The persistent uniformity of tableware through the Early Neolithic at Knossos suggests that it played a role in commensal reinforcement of solidarity at the village level (Tomkins 2007), while on the mainland close regional similarities in the shape and decoration of fine tableware surely indicate that commensality also oiled social relationships *between* settlements. Either way, the broadening repertoire of tableware shapes and wares through the Early and Middle Neolithic (Papathanassopoulos 1996: 110–111 fig. 36) suggests increasing care to distinguish between different forms and perhaps contexts of commensality. Neolithic households would have faced a contradiction between the benefits of hoarding food for domestic use and the need to promote communal solidarity through commensality and, judging by the faunal and ceramic records, they partly resolved this, and increasingly so over time, by defining certain occasions as appropriate for wider commensality.

Within these early farming villages, however, food probably served to promote competition as well as cohesion (*e.g.* Urem-Kotsou and Kotsakis 2007; Halstead and Isaakidou 2011). If food was hoarded for domestic use, giving it to outsiders probably imposed an obligation to reciprocate – unlike with the generalised obligation to share among non-storing hunter-gatherers. Where the grain supply of one household was in surplus and that of another in deficit, members of the latter may simply have joined the former, achieving a balance between available food and mouths to feed, while creating or exacerbating an imbalance in available labour. Where all households had sufficient grain, some might still have sought, given the finite 'shelf-life' of stored grain, to expend surplus by converting it to the added-value form of fattened carcasses or perhaps beer and then using hospitality to recruit labour or create obligations of future reciprocity. Alternatively, surplus grain could be fed to draught cattle, greatly easing the task of thorough tillage for timely sowing and thus improving the prospects of a successful following harvest (Isaakidou 2008). Whether surplus grain was used to strengthen draught animals, to support neighbours in need or to provision feasting, it had the potential to exacerbate productive inequalities between households, while its use in feasting, at least, had a strong propensity to competitiveness. There are hints of such competition in early farming villages in Greece, in the variable investment of labour in dwellings (within as well as between settlements) and in the striking differences in size (from young lambs to adult cattle) of the livestock slaughtered for commensality (*e.g.* Pappa *et al.* 2004). Indeed, these two indices of competition may well have been linked, if animals were slaughtered to mobilise labour for house building. Whatever the context of consumption, animal heads seem to have been displayed on house facades at LN Promachonas in northern Greece (Trantalidou and Gkioni 2008) and a MN house model from Thessaly suggests that this custom was rather older (Toufexis 2003), although apparent exposure of animal and human skulls along a MN ditch at Paliambela-Kolindrou implies that, in this probably mortuary context, inter-household competitive display could alternatively be subordinated to collective solidarity.

Mates, alliances, and gift exchange

An intermarrying human population needs a minimum of approximately 175–475 members for long-term reproductive viability (*e.g.* Wobst 1974). On this basis, many – perhaps most – early farming settlements in Greece were not reproductively self-sufficient and occasional inter-settlement exchanges of livestock were also probably necessary to avoid deleterious inbreeding (Halstead 1992). On the other hand, a viable inter-marrying population need not have encompassed more than – at most – a handful of settlements and, at least in the relatively well researched and densely settled lowlands of eastern Thessaly, enough potential mates (and, likewise, breeding livestock) could have been found within a radius of a few kilometers – over distances far shorter than those spanned by shared styles of fine ceramics. Indeed, if these ceramic style zones do represent networks of marriage exchanges, their spatial scale is more compatible with sparse hunter-gatherer than denser early farming populations. Following Childe's approach to interpreting material culture, therefore, these style zones might be taken as evidence that early farmers in Greece were in large measure descendants of indigenous hunter-gatherers rather than southwest Asian colonists (*cf.* Dennell 1983: 157, 167–168).

Early farmers used chipped- and ground-stone tools for a wide range of functions and not all settlements will have had access to nearby sources of suitable stone, even as water-rolled cobbles in local streams or rivers, but technological need alone does not account for the distances over which raw materials or artefacts were moved. For example, the EN inhabitants of Argissa in eastern Thessaly acquired cores of obsidian from the island of Melos in the southern Aegean, cores of grey flint probably from the Pindos mountains to the west, and blades of honey flint perhaps from Bulgaria (cf. Gurova 2008), as well as making expedient use of poorer-quality local stone (Perlès 1990b). The rationale for procurement of this range of exotic material must be sought in the central role of gift exchange as a means of initiating and maintaining positive social relationships, both those within the settlement and especially those with outsiders that were not reinforced by frequent face-to-face contact (Mauss 1970). Gift-exchange relationships with outsiders will have fulfilled many roles, providing access to a wider pool of marriage partners, channels for procurement of items such as resin (Urem-Kotsou et al. 2002) or salt (Urem-Kotsou this volume), a place of refuge in the event of intra-communal dispute, or a source of hospitality in the event of local crop failure. In each of these cases, distant exchange relationships will have enhanced the likelihood of successful outcomes, while procurement of exotica for exchange would in turn have provided a strong motive for social interaction beyond the distances demanded by access to mates or practically essential raw materials. Light may also be shed on regional or sub-regional stylistic zones and long-distance movement of materials by considering further the internal economic, social and political dynamics of Neolithic village communities.

If community fission was a recurrent factor in the proliferation of early farming villages, this was sometimes probably accompanied by conflict, favouring the re-settlement of splinter groups at a safe distance. The *earlier* Neolithic of Greece has not yet yielded skeletal evidence for mass violence and, in eastern Thessaly at least, the close spacing and longevity of villages is arguably incompatible with endemic warfare such as occurred recently in Amazonia or highland New Guinea, but it is likely that some of the burnt horizons recognised in excavated settlements are the result of raiding rather than accidents or ritual closure (cf. Runnells et al. 2009). Indeed, EN-MN tell villages in Thessaly may exhibit a fairly consistent minimum extent of about 0.5 ha because smaller communities were vulnerable to raiding (cf. Forge 1972). If raiding was a concern, villages doubtless sought defensive alliances – and probably not with their nearest neighbours with whom they may have competed for resources such as pasture or game. Alliance building may have involved feasting, exchange of marriage partners, and perhaps shared rites of passage marking the transition from childhood to adulthood. The last would certainly fit with Mina's argument that anthropomorphic figurines differentiate between girls and women in broadly similar ways from Crete to northern Greece (Mina 2008).

The organisation of inter-village raids, alliances and feasts would have offered opportunities for aspiring 'big men' to compete for prestige, while all households probably sought to exchange gifts and mates with partners well placed to offer other benefits, such as subsistence help. The procurement of exotic gifts may also have been an important avenue for competition. Obsidian must have been carried from

Melos partly by boat and arguably, given the lack of evidence for earlier Neolithic habitation in the Cyclades (Broodbank 1999), by seafarers from the coasts of eastern mainland Greece, western Turkey and northern Crete. The skill required both to prepare cores for transport and then to produce technologically uniform blades at EN-MN Neolithic villages in eastern mainland Greece suggests that some of these sea-farers were also expert knappers and themselves carried obsidian to its points of consumption (Perlès 1990b). The obsidian from EN Knossos is technologically rather different (Conolly 2008), suggesting independent procurement (probably over longer stretches of open sea) perhaps by less specialised knappers from Crete. Whether undertaken by specialised 'middlemen' or non-specialised prospective consumers, therefore, the distribution of obsidian around EN-MN eastern peninsular Greece and Crete seems to have involved long-distance expeditions. Some exotica doubtless reached their eventual point of 'consumption' (*i.e.* archaeological discovery) by being passed from hand to hand 'down the line', as perhaps in the case of flint brought to sites in Thessaly as skillfully manufactured blades, although two caches, each of several hundred pristine flint blades, farther north at EN Nea Nikomedia (Rodden 1964) rather suggest long-distance expeditions – whether by producers, middlemen or consumers. The unusually large structure in which both caches of flint blades were found, together with two exceptionally large greenstone axes, has variously been interpreted as a village shrine/'clubhouse' or the residence of a prominent family, with divergent implications for access to the imports. In either case, individuals or small groups seem to have undertaken long and hazardous journeys in search of exotic material culture and perhaps arcane knowledge, much like the maritime adventurers of the Early Bronze Age Cyclades (Broodbank 1993).

Synthesis: Modelling social and material connections

The rich material world of the earlier Greek Neolithic can plausibly be understood in terms of observed or predictable social connections and divisions. The distinctive investment in 'domestic' architecture occurred in the context of developing household independence, while ditched 'flat-extended' and especially compact tell settlements highlight a countervailing commitment to collective solidarity at the village level. Fine ceramic tablewares and faunal evidence for carcass processing highlight the importance of commensality in promoting alliances, both within individual villages and between villages 50–100 km apart that shared similar styles of ceramic decoration. The overlapping (or perhaps diachronically shifting) social networks revealed by these ceramic style zones may account for more generic similarities of ceramic typological development across southeast Europe and for hints of shared rites of passage at least across Greece. On the other hand, if movement of raw materials such as obsidian and fine flint involved long-distance expeditions rather than down-the-line exchange, then some of these more generic stylistic similarities may be the fruit of direct social interaction over distances of a few hundred kilometres. The distribution of stone studs, clay stamps, and bone spoons is particularly unlikely to be due to direct social interaction over the great distances of space (from southeast Europe to Iran) and perhaps time involved. These items, all potentially for personal use or adornment, might more plausibly have been diffused through the overlapping social networks reflected in fine ceramic styles and the suggested expeditions to procure and distribute lithic materials. At any rate, it seems likely that material connections on very different spatial scales reflect different forms of social interaction rather than a single process such as migration.

Conclusion: Barriers and connections

In the first half of the twentieth century, attempts to establish a chronological framework for the Greek Neolithic focussed attention on long-distance material 'connections' eastwards and northwards and laid the foundations for the model, popularised by Childe, according to which southwest Asian colonists introduced farming and settled village life to Greece and thence the north Balkans and, eventually, the rest of Europe. Subsequent research has confirmed that domesticates spread from southwest Asia to southeast Europe, but has also established that Neolithic material culture developed in the latter region over a much longer period of time and with greater spatial variability than Childe recognised and that some of the similarities he identified between the two regions are fortuitous. Despite its empirical weaknesses, some of which Childe acknowledged, the colonisation model continues to exercise such a hold over European prehistorians that it drives the interpretation of artefactual and bioarchaeological datasets that are equally compatible with neolithisation by adoption of domesticates (and perhaps of farming know-how and some items of material culture). Analysis of ancient human DNA may eventually demonstrate that the earliest farmers in southeast Europe *were* colonists from southwest Asia, but the colonisation model offers at best a partial explanation of the development of Neolithic society and material culture in Greece (and elsewhere in Europe) and its uncritical acceptance has tended to divert scholarly attention from these important processes.

Starting from the premise that early farmers actively manipulated their material culture for a variety of purposes, rather than passively reproducing that of distant forebears, this chapter has attempted an outline model of their social and material world in the earlier Neolithic in Greece. The exercise is inevitably somewhat speculative and much of the detail is probably incorrect, not least in failing to accommodate the inevitable spatial and temporal variability in these early farmers' social interactions and their material expression (*cf.* Parkinson 2006). Arguably, however, the exercise has shown that much of the distinctive form and spatial organisation of earlier Neolithic material culture in Greece can plausibly be understood in terms of the predictable or archaeologically inferable economic, demographic, social and political dynamics of these farming communities – and regardless of their members' ultimate biological and geographical origins. It accommodates far more of the available evidence for complex material cultural connections at several different social and spatial scales (the focus of this volume) than do models of exogenous or indigenous *origins* and also, arguably, offers a far richer understanding of the early farming societies of Greece.

Acknowledgements

Valasia Isaakidou, Barry Molloy, Dushka Urem-Kotsou and an anonymous reviewer kindly provided more or less critical comments on a draft of this chapter. I hope this revised version is clearer!

References

Barnard, A. and J. Woodburn
1991 Property, power and ideology in hunting and gathering societies: an introduction. In T. Ingold, D. Riches and J. Woodburn (eds.), *Hunters and Gatherers, 2: Property, Power and Ideology*: 4–31. Oxford: Berg.

Bogaard, A.
2004 *Neolithic Farming in Central Europe: An Archaeobotanical Study of Crop Husbandry Practices*. London: Routledge.
2005 'Garden agriculture' and the nature of early farming in Europe and the Near East. *World Archaeology* 37: 177–196.

Bogaard, A., R. A. Fraser, T.H.E. Heaton, M. Wallace, P. Vaiglova, M. Charles, G. Jones, R.P. Evershed, A. K. Styring, N. H. Andersen, R.-M. Arbogast, L. Bartosiewicz, A. Gardeisen, M. Kanstrup, U. Maier, E. Marinova, L. Ninov, M. Schäfer and E. Stephan
2013 Crop manuring and intensive land management by Europe's first farmers. *Proceedings of the National Academy of Sciences* 110: 12589–12594.

Bogaard, A. and V. Isaakidou
2010 From mega-sites to farmsteads: community size, ideology and the nature of early farming landscapes in western Asia and Europe. In B. Finlayson and G. Warren (eds.), *Landscapes in Transition*: 192–207. Oxford: Oxbow.

Broodbank, C.
1993 Ulysses without sails: trade, distance, knowledge and power in the early Cyclades. *World Archaeology* 24: 315–331.
1999 Colonization and configuration in the insular Neolithic of the Aegean. In P. Halstead (ed.), *Neolithic Society in Greece*: 15–41. Sheffield: Sheffield Academic Press.

Brown, P.
1978 *Highland Peoples of New Guinea*. Cambridge: Cambridge University Press.

Budja, M.
2009 Early Neolithic pottery dispersals and demic diffusion in southeastern Europe. *Documenta Praehistorica* 36: 117–137.

Burger, J. and M.G. Thomas
2011 The palaeopopulationgenetics of humans, cattle and dairying in Neolithic Europe. In
    R. Pinhasi and J.T. Stock (eds.), *Human Bioarchaeology of the Transition to Agriculture*: 371–384.
    Chichester: Wiley.

Chagnon, N.A.
1979 Mate competition, favoring close kin, and village fissioning among the Yanomamo Indians. In
    N.A. Chagnon and W. Irons (eds.), *Evolutionary Biology and Human Social Behavior: an Anthropological
    Perspective*: 86–132. North Scituate: Duxbury.

Champion, T., C. Gamble, S. Shennan and A. Whittle
1984 *Prehistoric Europe*. London: Academic Press.

Childe, V.G.
1957 *The Dawn of European Civilisation*. London: Routledge and Kegan Paul.

Clark, G.
1977 *World Prehistory in New Perspective*. Cambridge: Cambridge University Press.

Colledge, S., J. Conolly and S. Shennan
2004 Archaeobotanical evidence for the spread of farming in the Eastern Mediterranean. *Current
    Anthropology* 45 Supplement: 35–47.

Conolly, J.
2008 The knapped stone technology of the first occupants at Knossos. In V. Isaakidou and P. Tomkins
    (eds.), *Escaping the Labyrinth: the Cretan Neolithic in Context*: 73–89. Oxford: Oxbow.

Dennell, R.W.
1983 *European Economic Prehistory*. London: Academic Press.

Evans, J.D.
1973 Sherd weights and sherd counts - a contribution to the problem of quantifying pottery studies.
    In D.E. Strong (ed.), *Archaeological Theory and Practice*: 131–149. New York: Seminar Press.

Facorellis, Y. and Y. Maniatis
2013 Radiocarbon dates from the Neolithic settlement of Knossos: an overview. In N. Efstratiou,
    A. Karetsou and M. Ntinou (eds.), *The Neolithic Settlement of Knossos in Crete: New Evidence for the
    Early Occupation of Crete and the Aegean Islands*: 193–200. Philadelphia: INSTAP Academic Press.

Flannery, K.V.
1972 The origins of the village as a settlement type in Mesoamerica and the Near East: a comparative
    study. In P.J. Ucko, R. Tringham and G.W. Dimbleby (eds.), *Man, Settlement and Urbanism*: 23–53.
    London: Duckworth.

Forge, A.
1972 Normative factors in the settlement size of neolithic cultivators (New Guinea). In P.J. Ucko,
    R. Tringham and G.W. Dimbleby (eds.), *Man, Settlement and Urbanism*: 363–376. London: Duckworth.

García Fernández, J.
1988 *Sociedad y Organización Tradicional del Espacio en Asturias*. Gijón: Silverio Cañada.

Gurova, M.
2008 Towards an understanding of Early Neolithic populations: a flint perspective from Bulgaria. *Documenta Praehistorica* 35: 111–129.

Halstead, P.
1992 From reciprocity to redistribution: modelling the exchange of livestock in Neolithic Greece. *Anthropozoologica* 16: 19–30
1994 The North-South divide: regional paths to complexity in prehistoric Greece. In C. Mathers and S. Stoddart (eds.), *Development and Decline in the Mediterranean Bronze Age*: 195–219. Sheffield: J.R. Collis.
1995 From sharing to hoarding: The Neolithic foundations of Aegean Bronze Age society? In R. Laffineur and W.-D. Niemeier (eds.), *Politeia: Society and State in the Aegean Bronze Age*: 11–20. Liège: University of Liège.
2007 Carcasses and commensality: investigating the social context of meat consumption in Neolithic and Early Bronze Age Greece. In C. Mee and J. Renard (eds.), *Cooking Up the Past: Food and Culinary Practices in the Neolithic and Bronze Age Aegean*: 25–48. Oxford: Oxbow.
2011 Farming, material culture and ideology: repackaging the Neolithic of Greece (and Europe). In A. Hadjikoumis, E. Robinson and S. Viner (eds.), *The Dynamics of Neolithisation in Europe: Studies in Honour of Andrew Sherratt*: 131–151. Oxford: Oxbow.

Halstead, P. and V. Isaakidou
2011 Political cuisine: rituals of commensality in the Neolithic and Bronze Age Aegean. In G.A. Jiménez, S. Montón-Subías and S. Romero (eds.), *Guess Who's Coming to Dinner. Feasting Rituals in the Prehistoric Societies of Europe and the Near East*: 91–108. Oxford: Oxbow.
2013 Early stock-keeping in Greece. In S. Colledge, J. Conolly, K. Dobney, K. Manning and S. Shennan (eds.), *The Origins and Spread of Stock-keeping in the Near East and Europe*: 129–144. Walnut Creek: Left Coast Press.

Hansen, J.M.
1991 *The Palaeoethnobotany of Franchthi Cave*. Bloomington and Indianapolis: Indiana University Press.

Higgs, E.S. and M.R. Jarman
1969 The origins of agriculture: a reconsideration. *Antiquity* 43: 31–41.

Hill, R.A. and R.I.M. Dunbar
2003 Social network size in humans. *Human Nature* 14: 53–72.

Hodder, I. (ed.)
1982 *Symbolic and Structural Archaeology*. Cambridge: Cambridge University Press.

Isaakidou, V.
2006 Ploughing with cows: Knossos and the 'secondary products revolution'. In D. Serjeantson and D. Field (eds.), *Animals in the Neolithic of Britain and Europe*: 95–112. Oxford: Oxbow.
2008 The fauna and economy of Neolithic Knossos revisited. In V. Isaakidou and P. Tomkins (eds.), *Escaping the Labyrinth: The Cretan Neolithic in Context*: 90–114. Oxford: Oxbow.

Jacobsen, T.W.
1984 Seasonal pastoralism in southern Greece: a consideration of the ecology of Neolithic urfirnis pottery. In P.M. Rice (ed.), *Pots and Potters: Current Approaches in Ceramic Archaeology*: 27–43. Los Angeles: UCLA Institute of Archaeology.

Karamitrou-Mentessidi, G., N. Efstratiou, J.K. Kozłowski, M. Kaczanowska, Y. Maniatis, A. Curci, S. Michalopoulou, A. Papathanasiou and S.M. Valamoti
2013 New evidence on the beginning of farming in Greece: The Early Neolithic settlement of Mavropigi in western Macedonia (Greece). *Antiquity* 87. http://antiquity.ac.uk/projgall/mentessidi336/ (last accessed 23-3-14).

Kent, S.
1993 Variability in faunal assemblages: the influence of hunting skill, sharing, dogs, and mode of cooking on faunal remains at a sedentary Kalahari community. *Journal of Anthropological Archaeology* 12: 323–385.

Kotsakis, K.
1999 What tells can tell: social space and settlement in the Greek Neolithic. In P. Halstead (ed.), *Neolithic Society in Greece*: 66–76. Sheffield: Sheffield Academic Press.
2006 Settlement of discord: Sesklo and the emerging household. In N. Tasić and C. Grozdanov (eds.), *Homage to Milutin Garasanin*: 207–220. Belgrade: Serbian Academy of Sciences and Arts, Macedonian Academy of Sciences and Arts.

Kyparissi-Apostolika, N. and G. Kotzamani
2005 Worlds in transition: Mesolithic/Neolithic lifestyles at the cave of Theopetra, Thessaly/Greece. In C. Lichter (ed.), *How Did Farming Reach Europe? Anatolian-European Relations from the Second Half of the 7th through the First Half of the 6th Millennium Cal. BC*: 173–182. Istanbul: Deutsches Archäologisches Institut Istanbul.

Marinova, E.
2007 Archaeobotanical data from the early Neolithic of Bulgaria. In S. Colledge and J. Conolly (eds.), *The Origins and Spread of Domestic Plants in Southwest Asia and Europe*: 93–109. Walnut Creek: Left Coast Press.

Mauss, M.
1970 *The Gift*. London: Routledge and Kegan Paul.

Milić, M.
2014 PXRF characterisation of obsidian from central Anatolia, the Aegean and central Europe. *Journal of Archaeological Science* 41: 285–296.

Mina, M.
2008 Figurin' out Cretan Neolithic society: anthropomorphic figurines, symbolism and gender dialectics. In V. Isaakidou and P. Tomkins (eds.), *Escaping the Labyrinth: the Cretan Neolithic in Context*: 115–135. Oxford: Oxbow.

Nandris, J.
1970 The development and relationships of the earlier Greek Neolithic. *Man* 5: 192–213.

Newton, S.
2003 The Mesolithic fauna from Theopetra Cave. In N. Galanidou and C. Perlès (eds.), *The Greek Mesolithic: Problems and Perspectives*: 199–205. London: British School at Athens.

Papadakou, T., D. Urem-Kotsou and K. Kotsakis
in press Keramiki tis arkhaioteris neolithikis apo ta Paliambela Kolindrou. *To Arkhaiologiko Ergo sti Makedonia kai Thraki*.

Papathanasiou, A.
2003 Stable isotope analysis in Neolithic Greece and possible implications on human health. *International Journal of Osteoarchaeology* 13: 314–324.

Papathanasiou, A., T. Theodoropoulou and S.M. Valamoti
2013 The quest for prehistoric meals: towards an understanding of past diets in the Aegean integrating stable isotope analysis, archaeobotany and zooarchaeology. In S. Voutsaki and S.M. Valamoti (eds.), *Diet, Economy and Society in the Ancient Greek World: Towards a Better Integration of Archaeology and Science*: 19–31. Leuven: Peeters.

Papathanassopoulos, G.A. (ed.)
1996 *Neolithic Culture in Greece.* Athens: N. P. Goulandris Foundation.

Pappa, M.
2008 Organosi tou Khorou kai Oikistika Stoikhia stous Neolithikous Oikismous tis Kentrikis Makedonias: D. E. Th - Thermi - Makriyalos. PhD dissertation, Aristotle University of Thessaloniki.

Pappa, M., P. Halstead, K. Kotsakis and D. Urem-Kotsou
2004 Evidence for large-scale feasting at Late Neolithic Makriyalos, N Greece. In P. Halstead and J.C. Barrett (eds.), *Food, Cuisine and Society in Prehistoric Greece*: 16–44. Oxford: Oxbow.

Parkinson, W.A.
2006 Tribal boundaries: stylistic variability and social boundary maintenance during the transition to the Copper Age on the Great Hungarian Plain. *Journal of Anthropological Archaeology* 25: 33–58.

Perlès, C.
1990a *Excavations at Franchthi Cave, Greece, 5: Les industries lithiques taillées de Franchthi (Argolide, Grèce), 2: les industries du Mésolithique et du Néolithique Initial.* Bloomington and Indianapolis: Indiana University Press.
1990b L' outillage de pierre taillée néolithique en Grèce: approvisionnement et exploitation des matières premières. *Bulletin de Correspondance Hellénique* 114: 1–42.
2001 *The Early Neolithic in Greece.* Cambridge: Cambridge University Press.
2005 From the Near East to Greece: let's reverse the focus - cultural elements that didn't transfer. In C. Lichter (ed.), *How Did Farming Reach Europe? Anatolian-European Relations from the Second Half of the 7th through the First Half of the 6th Millennium Cal. BC*: 275–290. Istanbul: Deutsches Archäologisches Institut Istanbul.

Perlès, C., A. Quiles and H. Valladas
2013 Early seventh-millennium AMS dates from domestic seeds in the Initial Neolithic at Franchthi Cave (Argolid, Greece). *Antiquity* 87: 1001–1015.

Perlès, C., T. Takaoğlu and B. Gratuze
2011 Melian obsidian in NW Turkey: evidence for early Neolithic trade. *Journal of Field Archaeology* 36: 42–49.

Renfrew, C., J.R. Cann and J.E. Dixon
1965 Obsidian in the Aegean. *The Annual of the British School at Athens* 60: 225–247.

Ridley, C. and K.A. Wardle
1979 Rescue excavations at Servia 1971–1973: a preliminary report. *Annual of the British School at Athens* 74: 185–230.

Rodden, R.J.
1964 Recent discoveries from prehistoric Macedonia: an interim report. *Balkan Studies* 5: 109–124.
1965 An Early Neolithic village in Greece. *Scientific American* 212: 82–92.

Rondiri, V.
1985 Epifaniaki keramiki neolithikon theseon tis Thessalias: katanomi sto khoro. *Anthropologika* 8: 53–74.

Runnels, C., E. Panagopoulou, P. Murray, G. Tsartsidou, K. Mullen and E. Tourloukis
2005 A Mesolithic landscape in Greece: testing a site-location model in the Argolid at Kandia. *Journal of Mediterranean Archaeology* 18: 259–285.

Runnels, C.N., C. Payne, N.V. Rifkind, C. White, N.P. Wolff and S.A. LeBlanc
2009 Warfare in Neolithic Thessaly: a case study. *Hesperia* 78: 165–194.

Sahlins, M.
1974 *Stone Age Economics*. London: Tavistock Publications.

Sarpaki, A.
2013 The economy of Neolithic Knossos: the archaeobotanical data. In N. Efstratiou, A. Karetsou and M. Ntinou (eds.), *The Neolithic Settlement of Knossos in Crete: New Evidence for the Early Occupation of Crete and the Aegean Islands*: 63–94. Philadelphia: INSTAP Academic Press.

Scarre, C.
2005 Holocene Europe. In C. Scarre (ed.), *The Human Past: World Prehistory and the Development of Human Societies*: 392–431. London: Thames and Hudson.

Shackleton, J.
1988 *Marine Molluscan Remains from Franchthi Cave*. Bloomington and Indianapolis: Indiana University Press.

Stiner, M.C. and N.D. Munro
2011 On the evolution of diet and landscape during the Upper Paleolithic through Mesolithic at Franchthi Cave (Peloponnese, Greece). *Journal of Human Evolution* 60: 618–636.

Theocharis, D.R.
1967 *I Avgi tis Thessalikis Proistorias: Arkhi kai Proimi Exelixi tis Neolithikis*. Volos: Filarkhaios Etairia.

Thissen, L.
2000 Thessaly, Franchthi and western Turkey: clues to the neolithisation of Greece? *Documenta Praehistorica* 27: 141–154.

Tomkins, P.
2007 Communality and competition: the social life of food and containers at Aceramic and Early Neolithic Knossos, Crete. In C. Mee and J. Renard (eds.), *Cooking Up the Past: Food and Culinary Practices in the Neolithic and Bronze Age Aegean*: 174–199. Oxford: Oxbow.

Tomkins, P. and P. Day
2001 Production and exchange of the earliest ceramic vessels in the Aegean: a view from Early Neolithic Knossos, Crete. *Antiquity* 75: 259–260.

Toufexis, G.
2003 Animals in the Neolithic art of Thessaly. In E. Kotjabopoulou, Y. Hamilakis, P. Halstead, C. Gamble and P. Elefanti (eds.), *Zooarchaeology in Greece: Recent Advances*: 263–271. London: British School at Athens.

Trantalidou, K. and G. Gkioni
2008 Promachon-Topolnica. Ta voukrana tou megalou uposkafou khorou: zoologikos prosdiorismos kai politismika parallila apo tin anatoliki Mesogeio. *To Arkhaiologiko Ergo sti Makedonia kai Thraki* 20: 217–228.

Triantaphyllou, S.
2008 Living with the dead: a re-consideration of mortuary practices in the Greek Neolithic. In V. Isaakidou and P. Tomkins (eds.), *Escaping the Labyrinth: the Cretan Neolithic in Context*: 136–154. Oxford: Oxbow.

Urem-Kotsou, D. and K. Kotsakis
2007 Pottery, cuisine and community in the Neolithic of north Greece. In C. Mee and J. Renard (eds.), *Cooking Up the Past: Food and Culinary Practices in the Neolithic and Bronze Age Aegean*: 225–246. Oxford: Oxbow Books.

Urem-Kotsou, D., B. Stern, C. Heron and K. Kotsakis
2002 Birch-bark tar at Neolithic Makriyalos, Greece. *Antiquity* 76: 962–967.

Vitelli, K.D.
1989 Were pots first made for food? Doubts from Franchthi. *World Archaeology* 21: 17–29.

Wace, A.J.B. and M.S. Thompson
1912 *Prehistoric Thessaly*. Cambridge: Cambridge University Press.

Washburn, D.K.
1983 Symmetry analysis of ceramic design: two tests of the method on Neolithic material from Greece and the Aegean. In D.K. Washburn (ed.), *Structure and Cognition in Art*: 138–164. Cambridge: Cambridge University Press.

Wijnen, M.
1982 *The Early Neolithic I Settlement at Sesklo: An Early Farming Community in Thessaly, Greece*. Leiden: Leiden University Press.

Wobst, H.M.
1974 Boundary conditions for Palaeolithic social systems: a simulation approach. *American Antiquity* 39: 147–178.

Zvelebil, M.
1986 Mesolithic societies and the transition to farming: problems of time, scale and organisation. In M. Zvelebil (ed.), *Hunters in Transition*: 167–188. Cambridge: Cambridge University Press.

Chapter 4

Impressed Pottery as a Proxy for Connectivity in the Neolithic Aegean and Eastern Mediterranean

Çiler Çilingiroğlu

The different regions of the Mediterranean are connected not by the water, but by the peoples of the sea. This may seem obvious, but it is worth saying in an area that has attracted so many bewildering formulas and descriptions (Braudel 1972: 276).

Introduction

Connectivity in the prehistoric Aegean is best exemplified by the obsidian exchange network that spanned every corner of the Aegean Basin. It is common knowledge that Melian obsidian was acquired by prehistoric communities on both sides of the Aegean Sea at least since the Upper Paleolithic period (Perlès 2001: 35). Especially in the 7–6th millennia BC, Melian obsidian is found at every excavated site, suggesting that both direct and indirect social-cultural bonds were established in the entire Aegean world (Milić this volume). The long-term persistence of this exchange network can be construed as a manifestation of a vibrant social and economic environment where many archaeologically invisible commodities, animals, plants, technologies, and cosmologies of diverse origins were in constant movement. Accordingly, islands and seascapes were presumably visited for fishing, hunting, grazing, plant collecting, exploring and settling. Considering the great antiquity of seafaring in the Aegean and Mediterranean, going back to the Lower/Middle Paleolithic (Kopaka and Matzanas 2009; Strasser *et al.* 2010; see Broodbank 2013: 95 for a cautionary view), it is no wonder that navigational skills, nautical know-how and technology were well-enough developed to sustain social and economic networks by 6000 BC.

This contribution will build on a previous paper (Çilingiroğlu 2010) and will incorporate new archaeological evidence. The author argues that a category of ceramics known as 'impressed pottery' can be implemented as an archaeological proxy to discern connectivity in the Aegean around 6000 BC (Figure 4.1).

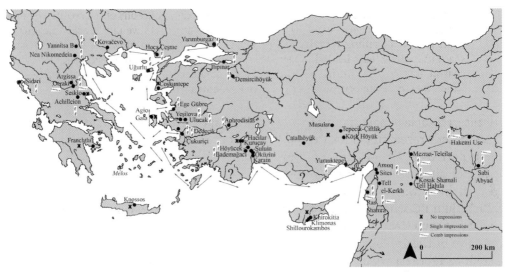

Figure 4.1: Distribution of impressed pottery in the Eastern Mediterranean around 6100-6000 BC. Two-sided, short arrows meant to indicate constant, short-range, spontaneous and unorganized nature of 'Neolithic slow-motion seafaring' facilitating diverse forms of mobility involving humans, animals, plants, raw materials, ceramics, ideas and fashions. The question marks indicate areas where impressed pottery is expected but not found so far due to poor research or inundation of sites.

Labelled in the literature as 'impressed pottery', 'impressed wares' or 'impresso' this specific type of pottery is actually defined by its decoration, rather than its fabric or vessel form. Usually impressions appear on different sorts of ceramic fabrics at a single site. Therefore, this contribution will refer to this group generically as 'impressed pottery'. Having a mainly coastal distribution in the Mediterranean, the widespread and sudden appearance of Neolithic impressed pottery can well be associated with maritime engagements. Enabled through constant short-range and occasional long-range sea-bound movements, this pottery decoration dispersed quickly in the eastern Mediterranean, around 6100–6000 BC. By referring to Braudel and his views on slow-motion shipping, I will suggest that Early Neolithic slow-motion seafaring 'has untiringly spun threads' around the Eastern Mediterranean in prehistory.

Early Neolithic slow-motion seafaring

Fernand Braudel introduced the term 'slow-motion shipping' in his seminal book *The Mediterranean and the Mediterranean World in the age of Philip II*. Braudel uses this term to broadly define small-scale, spontaneous and unorganised yet constant coastal seafaring in all sorts of directions which, according to him, decidedly laid the true foundations for connectivity in the Mediterranean alongside more organised and long-range seafaring. He (1972: 105–108) introduces the term as follows:

This slow-motion shipping, if we can call it, governed the geography of the coastal regions, in the sense that for one big ship capable of by-passing ports we must reckon dozens of boats and small sailing vessels that were processionary by vocation... Along the coastal sea routes, daily halts led to the remarkably regular establishment of villages... Everyday coastal shipping has untiringly spun threads connecting the different areas of the sea which may pass unnoticed in the great movements of history.

Despite a total lack of seafaring imagery before the Final Neolithic and Early Bronze Ages, recent research demonstrated that seafaring was not an emergent feature of those periods in the Aegean (Broodbank 2013: 327). Luckily we have circumstantial evidence showing maritime involvements in earlier periods. For instance, regular tuna fishing was evidently practiced by Franchthi foragers in the early 8th millennium BC where almost half of the animal bones were composed of blue fin variety of tuna (Jacobsen 1981: 307). Similarly, 9th–8th millennia BC occupations at the Cave of the Cyclops on Youra in the northern Aegean contained large amounts of fish vertebrae as well as bone fish hooks, indicating regular engagement with the sea (Sampson 1998: 13–14). The Aegean was navigated not only by Upper Paleolithic and Mesolithic foragers, but also by Lower/Middle Paleolithic foragers who arrived to Crete's southern coast from an unknown locale of departure, perhaps from mainland Greece, southwestern Turkey or northern Africa (Kopaka and Matzanas 2009; Strasser *et al.* 2010). Crete, although in favourable conditions visible from Kythera and Karpathos, was never connected to mainland (van Andel and Schackleton 1982: fig. 2; Agouridis 1997: 16). Consequently, it required longer hours spent on the open sea although halts at some islands to acquire shelter, water and food were most probably part of the voyage; unless the groups arrived from Africa. Nevertheless, non-coastal seafaring with reed-bundle crafts and dug-out canoes was evidently conducted in the Aegean, perhaps more than 130,000 years ago (Kopaka and Matzanas 2009; Strasser *et al.* 2010).

Current archaeological work on Cyprus substantiates the evidence from the Aegean. Recent studies at Klimonas and Asprokremnos demonstrate that people not only occasionally visited the island for various reasons but also organised voyages to found new settlements (Vigne *et al.* 2012). Organisation of such a voyage requires substantial planning and to survive the first year upon arrival on the island one needs enough food, animals and people. Cypriot evidence demonstrates well that around *c.* 9000 BC, seafaring and navigation technology were developed enough to organise successive voyages carrying people, animals and plants involving open-sea crossings of around 75–100 km (Broodbank and Strasser 1991; Broodbank 2013: 177).

The knowledge of the weather, winds, currents, seascapes, coasts, coastal landmarks, islands as well as the technology to build sea vessels, must have accumulated and been transmitted over generations, not only in the Aegean but in the entire Eastern Mediterranean Region. By the time the first settlements appeared, cult centres were being built, cereals and animals had been domesticated in Southwest

Asia, water transport (both maritime and riverine) must have already become an integral part of daily life. Presumably, seafaring knowledge and technology did not develop following a linear pattern of progress. There must have been times when the intensity and scale of maritime connections vacillated, the best example being Cyprus's growing insularity following the Pre-Pottery Neolithic period (Steel 2004: 62–63). Nevertheless, archaeological data increasingly encourages us to acknowledge the engagement of prehistoric people with water transport in our attempts to reconstruct major historical process like neolithisation, animal-plant dispersals and movements of people (Korfmann 1987; Guilaine 2007; King *et al.* 2008; Zeder 2011: 231; Broodbank 2013; Çilingiroğlu and Çakırlar 2013; Hughey *et al.* 2013; Rowly-Conwy *et al.* 2013).

Recognising the capacity for mobility over distances of prehistoric seafarer foragers and farmers is important, but we need to develop our tools and evidence to reconstruct seafaring technology and navigation techniques. Moreover, we need to be able to reconstruct the Early Neolithic coastal topography and sea level changes. Contrary to the Early Bronze Age world where depictions of long boats are occasionally made on various kinds of objects, Early Neolithic imagery is silent about any kind of water transport. The only tangible evidence of paddle propelled boats dating to the early 6th millennium BC was recovered during the Yenikapı salvage excavations in Istanbul, where two wooden paddles with a length of 1.35 and 1.13 m were found preserved in situ in the muddy deposits of a water channel (Kızıltan and Polat 2012: fig. 31).

Additional pre-Bronze Age evidence for seafaring appears in different parts of the Old World (McGrail 2001). Perhaps the earliest depiction of a boat in the Eastern Mediterranean originates from a site called 16-D-5 on the west bank of the White Nile, 25 km south of Omburman in Sudan, where in the Mesolithic layers dating to the early 7th millennium BC, a depiction of a so-called Nile boat was found engraved onto a granite pebble (Usai and Salvatori 2007). Yet another early depiction and positive evidence for reed-bundle boats was unearthed at the Ubaid site H3 in modern Kuwait. Dating to *c.* 5500–5000 BC, a ceramic boat model, remains of bituminous amalgam with reed impressions and barnacle encrustations as well as a painted ceramic disk depicting a boat with two masts were identified at the site, providing insights about the maritime travel and exchange activities around the Persian Gulf area during the middle of the 6th millennium BC (Carter 2006). According to Carter, the masts may be indicating the use of sails in southern Mesopotamia and Persian Gulf region.

In the Aegean, however, we lack such representations, not to mention archaeological evidence for actual boats. Besides, the earliest indications for the use of sails is attested on the late Early and Middle Minoan seals (Liritzis 1988) while the earliest use of sails in the Mediterranean is attested on an Egyptian vase from Naqada dating to *c.* 3100 BC (Agouridis 1997; McGrail 2001). Thus, there is no reason to assume that sail boats were in use during the Neolithic period around the Aegean.

Long boats, on the other hand, are commonly considered an emergent feature of Early Bronze II world, although their potentially earlier appearance cannot be simply ruled out (Broodbank 2000: 99; Papadatos and Tomkins 2013: 355). A recent experimental study on the Early Bronze Age long boats showed that such vessels functioned best when the wind blew from behind with a speed of 2 to 4 beaufort and wave height of half to one metre. Experimentally built long boats travelled with the help of 18–26 paddles and one steersman, depending on the length of the boat (Erkurt 2011). Although helpful to Early Bronze Age nautical archaeology, it remains unsolved how applicable these figures to the Early Neolithic seafaring practices. Another experimental study using reed bundle craft with six paddlers is more relevant for the purpose of this paper. This experimental voyage successfully reached Melos from Attica in fourteen days following an island hopping route. The voyage was delayed due to bad weather conditions between Kythnos and Seriphos implying that shorter travel times were possible for the same distance (Broodbank 2013: fig. 5.3).

To sum up, I am inclined to believe that reed-bundle crafts and/or dug-outs operated by human-power must have been in use during the Neolithic period. Consequently, Early Neolithic seafaring, because it most probably used paddled boats, was very much susceptible to local weather and sea conditions and therefore required considerable navigation and seafaring knowledge, which the Eastern Mediterranean people had been collecting and transmitting perhaps since the Middle Paleolithic. Undoubtedly, many voyages did not have a successful ending, but enough success was achieved to keep at least some people on the sea looking for new lands, raw materials, grazing grounds and fishing areas. A Neolithic-type of slow-motion seafaring was dictated by weather susceptibility, human power, frequent stops, coastal voyages, movement that preferred land visibility, a lot of traffic in all sorts of directions and transport of animals, plants, humans and all sorts of raw materials and finished products. Presumably it involved rituals and taboos at every step; from boat building to the voyaging itself, as ethnographic record suggests (*cf.* Malinowski 1984). The complicated nature of surface currents and powerful North winds in winter and Meltemia during summer must have forced Neolithic seafarers to plan voyages with constant land visibility or breaking-down of longer distances by island hopping. Islands were presumably both used as intermediary stops and also as shields protecting the vessels from strong North winds. The Cyclades, in this respect, must have played a key role in trans-Aegean encounters, already in the Neolithic, although most were not permanently settled before the 5th–4th millennium BC (Liritzis 1988: 243; Broodbank 2013: 213). Larger islands closer to the Anatolian mainland, such as Chios and Imbros (Gökçeada), were demonstrably settled already in the 7th–6th millennium BC; suggesting more regular interactions in many directions allowing for seafaring knowledge to grow further (Hood 1981; Erdoğu 2013). Neolithic (or for that matter, pre-sailing) navigation cannot be compared in scale, intensity and economic function to the Bronze Age maritime endeavours. Nevertheless, one can suggest that thriving economic and social networks were made possible for millennia preceding the Bronze Ages thanks to the accumulated knowledge of navigational know-how.

Impressed pottery in the Aegean

Our archaeological body of knowledge from the Eastern and Western Aegean suggests that analogous life-ways were prevalent in both areas. Much has been published about the common and non-common elements in the settlement patterns, settlement organisation, building techniques, subsistence and material culture in the Early Neolithic Aegean (Thissen 2000; Perlès 2003, 2005; Çilingiroğlu 2005; Özdoğan 2008; Reingruber 2011). The Aegean world in the late 7th and 6th millennium BC is characterised by sedentary, food-producing communities without institutionalised social differentiation, sharing similar symbolic expressions as exemplified in fine red slipped pottery, clay figurines, and stamps (Demoule and Perlès 1993; Perlès 2001: 62–63; Reingruber 2008: 603–604; Çilingiroğlu 2009, 2012; Lichter 2011). Resemblances in the archaeological record reflect common ways in which people perceived and interpreted their natural and social environments.

The same can be stated about pottery production. Highly comparable morphological features and surface treatments point to common production techniques that resulted in ceramics that held similar functions in daily life. For instance, the majority of pottery from the Early Neolithic Aegean is composed of fine-medium, carefully slipped and burnished wares (Wijnen 1982; Reingruber 2008; Çilingiroğlu 2012). Vessels showing bright red surfaces are commonly found on both sides of the Aegean. Vessel morphology is equally analogous. In the 7th millennium BC the forms are simple and sizes are small. Hole-mouth jars, convex-sided bowls, bowls with 's' profiles and globular jars with short necks are typical for both the Eastern and Western Aegean (Reingruber 2008; Çilingiroğlu 2012). Such vessels were used for cooking, serving and storing little amounts of food. With the beginning of the 6th millennium BC, vessel morphology becomes more diverse with carinated forms, pedestal bases and large storage jars (Demoule and Perlès 1993; Çilingiroğlu 2012). One very interesting common feature is related to the near-absence of coarse wares in the 7th–6th millennia BC in both regions (Demoule and Perlès 1993: 377; Vitelli 1989; Yiouni 1996; Reingruber 2008: 189). Instead more time and energy was invested in the production of visually appealing vessels at this stage (Çilingiroğlu 2012: 180). Another striking similarity is the rareness or complete absence of handles, especially in the ceramic assemblages before 6000 BC (Reingruber 2008: 165; Çilingiroğlu 2012: 75), as an important indication of similar handling and carrying preferences on both sides of the Aegean. All these similarities reflect a common attitude towards ceramic containers both technologically and socially.

Despite strong correlations, one should not overemphasise the similarities at the expense of differences. A closer look demonstrates that we are not confronted with identical cultural expressions. For instance, painted pottery, a trait of post-6000 BC Neolithic sites in Thessaly, is never adapted in the Eastern Aegean. Although a handful of painted sherds have been discovered at sites around Izmir and during surveys, they do not comprise a well-defined tradition of painted pottery at the beginning of 6th millennium BCE (Çilingiroğlu 2012: 63). In this respect, it suffices here to note that co-appearance of red-on-buff pottery in Thessaly and Lakes District may imply yet another maritime connection which, however, remains outside of the scope of this paper (see Furholt 2011: 23; Çilingiroğlu 2012: 181). There are other morphological features that are not shared in all areas around the Aegean. The sharply outturned rim types from Thessalian sites are not known in the Eastern Aegean (see Reingruber 2008: Taf. 19). The thin and long, separately attached tubular lugs of the Eastern Aegean do not appear in same form in the western Aegean. Horizontally placed lugs, known from Franchthi, are likewise absent in the eastern Aegean (Phelps 1975: 98–99). The so-called 'black-topped' pottery of mainland Greece does not appear in the Eastern Aegean (Reingruber 2008: 522). Or else, high pedestal bases and tulip shaped vessels, although sporadic appearances are recorded at Ege Gübre near Izmir (Ozan 2013), do not comprise a typical morphological feature in the Eastern Aegean (Çilingiroğlu 2012: Table 6.1).

As a result, although structural similarities in the material conditions of life can be detected in the archaeological record and we can begin to identify the diverse social networks that bonded people together, a closer inspection of diverse aspects of material culture will demonstrate that local features were also created and maintained by each community.

Impressed Pottery in the Eastern Aegean

Every excavated site in the Eastern Aegean dating to late 7th–early 6th millennium BC produced impressed pottery. Sherds with impressions constitute 1% or even less of the ceramic assemblages (Sağlamtimur 2012: 200; Çilingiroğlu 2012: 59; Herling *et al.* 2008: 21). Their preservation is usually poor, *i.e.* complete vessels rarely appear. Most impressed pottery is represented by small sized bodysherds. In the Eastern Aegean, impressed pottery is found at Ulucak on Kemalpaşa Plain, Yeşilova on Bornova Plain, Ege Gübre near Nemrut Bay and Çukuriçi on Küçük Menderes Plain (Çilingiroğlu 2010; Derin 2012; Sağlamtimur 2012; Horejs 2012). These are all investigations carried out on *höyüks* (settlement mounds) around modern Izmir, but there is reason to assume that many more sites contained impressed pottery in the area. Indeed, small-scale excavations and surface collections yielded occasional impressed sherds (Lichter 2002; Derin 2006; Caymaz 2008; Herling *et al.* 2008). Interestingly, no impressed pottery was found in ceramic assemblages from Agio Gala Lower Cave on Chios and Coşkuntepe in the southern Troad, which can be a function of small-scale research or their chronological horizon (*cf.* Hood 1981; Seeher 1990; Takaoğlu 2005). Uğurlu's (Imbros/ Gökçeada) and Kovačevo's Early Neolithic deposits, in the northern Aegean, however, did reveal impressed pieces with single impressions (Erdoğu 2013: fig. 37; Salanova 2011: fig. 3) and sporadic appearances of impressed pottery are also recorded at late seventh–early 6th millennium BC sites in Northwest Turkey (Çilingiroğlu 2010).

Impressed pottery shows common attributes within the Izmir region. Looking at the general characteristics, the impressions are applied on the outside of a pot, covering the whole outer surface except the rim area. The impressions may appear on red slipped, burnished or unslipped and not burnished surfaces. Impressions are executed using different tools which left different types of shapes on the vessel surface. Triangles, finger-nail impressions, circles, thin-horizontal lines and half circles are commonly found on the vessels.

In the Izmir Region, impressed pottery makes its first appearance around 6000 BC. The long stratigraphical sequence at the site of Ulucak allows a reconstruction of the evolution of ceramic fabrics and morphology from the middle 7th millennium BC to c. 5700–5600 BC. In what follows, the evolution of ceramic assemblages at Ulucak will be introduced.

At Ulucak, the early 7th millennium BC deposits, Level VI, is followed by the fifth settlement that consisted of multiple single-roomed, rectilinear, wattle-and-daub houses (Çilingiroğlu et al. 2012). At Ulucak, the earliest sizeable pottery assemblage appears in this level, dated to c. 6400–6200 BC. Ulucak V pottery assemblage is composed of mainly mineral tempered, plain burnished wares with a broad range of surface colours resulting from both open firing techniques and the application of different types of slips. The quantity of pottery recovered is much lower than that excavated in the younger levels at Ulucak implying that ceramic containers were still a novel element in the daily lives of early farmers with low production rates in this stage. Dark brown, brown, light brown, red, orange and cream surface colours are very common. Slip and burnishing is frequently applied. Decoration is confined to a few painted sherds. The vessel morphology is limited to a few shapes. Hole-mouth jars and bowls with 'S' and convex profiles constitute the majority of the assemblage. In the consequent building layers at Ulucak, one observes that the amount of red slipped and burnished wares increase and pottery with dark brown and brown surface colours decrease in frequency (Çilingiroğlu 2012). Impressed pottery makes its first appearance around 6000 BC in Level Va, and does not disappear until the end of the continuous settlement history around 5700/5600 BC when the site is abandoned for an uncertain period of time following a conflagration. In these few centuries when impressed pottery was in use, there were no changes in the quality, quantity and morphological features of impressed pottery (Çilingiroğlu 2012).

Impressions are detected on different sorts of ware groups. They are associated with red, cream, brown slipped and burnished and gray-brown unburnished wares. Among these groups, only gray unburnished wares can be highlighted as a novel feature appearing in conjunction with the impressed pottery. The other ware groups already existed at the site before the emergence of impressed decoration. And this last group may be potentially non-local which needs to be demonstrated by archaeometric analyses. I would like to mention here that at Achilleion impressed pottery had a similar appearance, medium-coarse and porous, where they were identified as 'imports' (Winn and Shimabuku 1989: 92). At Neolithic Knossos and the west Mediterranean littoral, circulation of non-local pottery is very well demonstrated

(Barnett 2000; Tomkins 2004) implying that mobility of ceramics is also thinkable for the Izmir Area, which remains to be tested in future.

Impressed pottery at Ulucak, although usually occurring as small bodysherds, is associated with closed forms. Globular jars with short necks or hole-mouth jars with horizontal lugs on the shoulders are typically related to impressed pottery (Çilingiroğlu 2012: Pl. 52, 58). As described above, the impressions are applied to different type of surfaces and impressions cover the whole outer surface. There is no standardisation of the shapes and density of the motifs but they are always made out of single impressions. Continuous impressions are not observed on the pots from this region (Çilingiroğlu 2010).

Impressed pottery in the Western Aegean

The distribution of impressed pottery in Greece is confined to regions around Argissa (Argissa, Achilleion, Otzaki, Gendiki), western Thessaly (Prodromos, Theopetra, Magulitsa, Kefalvrysi), the Macedonian district (Yannitsa B, Nea Nikomedeia, Mavropigi) and the west coast of Greece (Sidari, Asfaka) (Reingruber 2008: 253; Alram-Stern 1996: Abb. 43; Otto 1995: Taf. 2; Karamitrou-Mentessidi et al. 2015). In mainland Greece, impressed pottery is not found at every Early Neolithic site. At Sesklo, for instance, no impressed pottery is documented (Wijnen 1982: 37). Recent excavations at Mavropigi suggests production of impressed pottery around 6400 BC (Karamitrou-Mentessidi et al. 2015), which stands as a singularity in the whole eastern and western Aegean so far. Impressed ceramics from Achilleion Levels IV-III, Otzaki and Argissa (Winn and Shimabuku 1989: 92; Reingruber 2008: Tab. 3.3 and 4.7) make their first appearance just around or after 6000 BC and importantly this date concurs with their first appearance in the Eastern Aegean. Their amount in ceramic assemblages varies considerably and it is not possible to reach a typical figure for this region at the moment. At Achilleion, only 62 sherds carried impressions as opposed to 115,000 recorded pottery sherds, which means only 0.05% of the whole carried impressed motifs (Reingruber 2008: 288). On the other hand, out of 944 sherds analysed by Reingruber from Argissa, 154 displayed impressed decoration (Reingruber 2008: 159), constituting c. 16%, which is a huge proportion compared to Eastern Aegean sites and Achilleion. It is also reported that impressed pottery constitutes a dominant feature in Otzaki ceramic assemblage (Furholt 2011: 24).

In mainland Greece, most impressions, both the motifs and the arrangements, are identical to the Eastern Aegean motifs. Triangles, half circles, thin lines and finger nail impressions are found on the outer surface of the pots. The only difference is the presence of comb impressions leaving long dotted lines in the western Aegean which do not appear in the Eastern Aegean.

Among the western Aegean Early Neolithic sites, the most detailed published is the site of Argissa which provides a complete picture of ceramic development in Thessaly (Reingruber 2008). At this site the earliest pottery is characterised by the presence of red coloured pottery with a wash-like slip and simple vessel forms. In the following stage, *c.* 6200–6000 BC, painted, shell-tempered and 'blacktopped' pottery types are introduced. Around 6000 BC, the first examples of impressed pottery which are mostly defined by finger-nail impressions, appear. Following 6000 BC, impressed pottery is accompanied by red-on-white painted wares. Impressions are recorded mostly on medium and medium-coarse wares with smoothed or burnished surfaces having brown, grey, reddish brown and brownish grey colours (Reingruber 2008: 209). Here too the preservation of impressed pottery is very poor. Impressions are to a great extent observed on small sized body sherds. A brief look at the impressed pottery from Argissa shows dotted continuous lines appear on the pots alongside single impressions. The comb impression technique produces dotted lines and is recorded on 33 out of 154 impressed sherds (Reingruber 2008: 209–210). Another characteristic is that these continuous impressions are in some cases combined with painted red bands (Reingruber 2008: Taf. 29, 34).

As a result, the simultaneous and sudden appearance of impressed pottery with very similar motifs and arrangements around 6000 BC strengthens the tightly connected image of Aegean prehistoric societies. I believe this fact alone implies connectivity in the Aegean around 6000 BC. Nevertheless, the appearance of comb impressions in the western Aegean and their total absence in the Eastern Aegean remains difficult to explain (see Discussion below). The ceramic development at Argissa suggests that comb impressions appear slightly later than finger-nail impressions. A comparable developmental scheme is not observed in the Eastern Aegean where sites dating to 5700/5600 BC produced impressed pottery solely with single impressions. This observation and rather sudden appearance of impressed wares in the Aegean led me to investigate the wider distributional pattern of impressed wares in the Eastern Mediterranean.

Impressed Pottery in the Eastern Mediterranean

Impressed pottery has a widespread distribution across the entire Mediterranean. Starting from around 6000 to 5000 BCE, variations of impressed pottery were produced by early farmers along the Mediterranean coast from the Levant to Portugal including the North African coast. Called by different names in the archaeological literature like 'impresso', 'impressa' or 'cardial', impressed pottery accompanied by domestic livestock and plants came to be key proxies for identifying the earliest farmer-herders in the Mediterranean basin (Korfmann 1987; Guilaine 2007; also see Coward *et al.* 2008; Zeder 2008).

Aegean communities were not isolated from societies beyond their shores. As a matter of fact, Aegean societies arguably did not consider themselves to be inhabitants of a distinct geographic entity separate from the East Mediterranean. Braudel famously stated (1972: 277) that anything entering Mediterranean would be caught up in movement and washed ashore somewhere to be taken up and passed on endlessly. The situation with impressed pottery can only support this view.

Looking at the temporal framework, we observe that impressed pottery appeared around 6100–6000 BC not only in the Aegean, but also at Levantine, Syrian and south-eastern Anatolian sites. In those regions, river systems, especially the Euphrates and Orontes Basins, seemingly played decisive roles in the widespread distribution of impressed pottery. I would like to mention here specifically the site with the most refined radiocarbon evidence, Tell Sabi Abyad, a prehistoric mound in the Balikh Valley, to demonstrate that the appearance of impressed pottery in the Levant and the Aegean were more or less synchronous events. At Tell Sabi Abyad, the impressed pottery appears in the pre-Halaf period around 6100 BC and disappears with the transitional phase to Halaf around 5950 cal. BCE (Nieuwenhuyse 2007: Tab. 3.4.1). It appears that in the Eastern Mediterranean, impressed pottery was a short-lived phenomenon, whereas in the Aegean and in the Western Mediterranean impressed pottery continued to be produced and evolve until 5000 BC (Guilaine 2007).

What is more interesting, however, is the apparent resemblance between the impressed decorations from Eastern Mediterranean and Western Aegean sites (Figure 4.2). A closer look at the impressed pottery from Tell Sabi Abyad shows that dotted lines and comb impressions combined with red bands are commonly applied on the pots. The same decoration technique is widespread throughout the whole neighbouring region. Late 7th millennium sites in south-Eastern Turkey, Mezraa Teleilat (Urfa) and Hakemi Use (Diyarbakır), for instance, revealed similar impressed pottery with single and comb impressions (Özdoğan 2011; Tekin 2011: fig. 8). Similar to the Aegean sites, here impressions appear on different kinds of fabrics. For instance, at Mezraa Teleilat, impressions are associated with buff straw tempered pottery, red slipped wares and dark faced burnished wares (Özdoğan 2007: Figs. 53–58). Other contemporary sites in northern Syria, such as Halula, Kosak Shamali, Tell el Kerkh and Ras Shamra, also contained impressed pottery showing dotted lines as well as single impressions (Balossi-Restelli 2006).

As a result, impressed pottery with single and comb impressions appear at late seventh-early sixth millennia sites in the upper Euphrates/Tigris Basins and along the Syrian coast. Similar to the Aegean sites, the quantity of impressed wares in the overall ceramic assemblage is low. One big difference with the Aegean and western Mediterranean sites is that the impressed pottery phenomenon lasts very short in the Levant, *c.* 150 years as opposed to *c.* 300–400 years in the Aegean and 1,000 years in the western Mediterranean. With the inception of Halafian elements in the material culture, impressed pottery disappears in the Levant and Syria (Nieuwenhuyse 2007: Tab. 3.4.1).

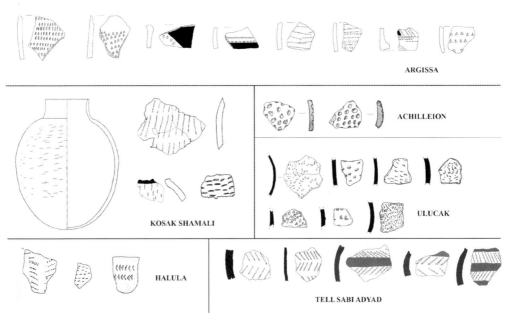

Figure 4.2: Various impressed pottery from sites in the Eastern Mediterranean and Aegean. Drawings after Reingruber 2008: Taf. 29 (Argissa); Balossi-Restelli 2006: Fig. 11.4 (Kosak Shamali); Balossi-Restelli 2006: Fig. 11.5 (Halula); Nieuwenhuyse 2007: Pl. 48 and 52 (Sabi Abyad); Gimbutas 1989: Fig. 5.69 (Achilleion); Çilingiroğlu 2012: Pl. 23 (Ulucak).

The Levant–Greece connection as a recurring pattern

The distribution of impressed pottery is mostly confined to coastal regions but in some areas inland its distribution is common as well. Most interestingly, one notices that central Anatolia remains out of the distribution area and this cannot be a function of poor research as central Anatolia is one of the best investigated areas in Turkey with respect to the Neolithic period (Özdoğan *et al.* 2012). The impressed pottery is either found in the coastal regions or at inland sites with contacts to the coastal areas. The distribution pattern of impressed pottery across the Eastern Mediterranean has implications for understanding the by then well-established maritime network of the Neolithic that includes the Levant, the southern Anatolian coast and the Aegean. The radiocarbon dates from key sites in all those regions (*i.e.* Tell Sabi Abyad, Ulucak, and Argissa) suggest that impressed pottery might have appeared a hundred years or so earlier in the Levant than in the Aegean, which suggests that the origins of this specific type and arrangement of decoration may be located in the East Mediterranean. What strikes one the most is the similarities in the arrangement and execution of designs between the Levantine and Thessalian sites (notably Argissa, Achilleion and Otzaki). Interestingly, comb impressions, occasionally combined with red bands, are attested in both regions whereas in the Izmir Area comb impressions are not known at all.

The connection between the Levant and Greece that by-passes the Anatolian landmass has already been recognised by other scholars for different time periods. Runnels (1995: 725), drawing on the lithic evidence, suggested that the Epi-Paleolithic of mainland Greece is more related to the southwest Asian traditions than to local Paleolithic cultures. Similarly, Perlès (2005: 286) postulated that the appearance of early farmer-herders in Greece has more to do with a maritime colonisation from the Levant and the southern Anatolian coast than the eastern Aegean littoral. Studying different time periods and archaeological data, both scholars reached similar conclusions about how established maritime routes functioned to link the Levant and Western Aegean in a more direct fashion than the Levant and eastern Aegean coasts despite geographical proximity.

Material culture offers striking patterns pertaining to these observations. Coffee-bean eyed figurines, for example, are found at contemporary Yarmoukian sites in the Levant and Thessaly, and do not appear in the Eastern Aegean (Perlès 2001: fig. 4.5). We see this pattern also in periods beyond the Neolithic. One striking example pointing towards this pattern of connection is the distribution of administrative seals and sealings during the Early Bronze Age. These objects appear at multiple Levantine sites and sites along the Euphrates as well as on Crete and in mainland Greece. Administrative seals and sealings from the Early Bronze Age do not appear on the eastern Aegean coast (Umurtak 2010; Broodbank 2013: fig. 7.50). Very interestingly, they appear at Bademağacı in southwestern Turkey, a site reachable by the natural pass of Çubuk Beli, en route to the coast (Umurtak 2010). It is not my intention to propose that Eastern Aegean, or Western Anatolia in general, remained outside of maritime interactions. There is ample evidence to suggest otherwise, especially during the EBA II-III period when west Anatolian coastal societies were in direct contact with their Cycladic contemporaries (Liritzis 1988; Şahoğlu 2005; Broodbank 2013). It seems rather that maritime interactions between Levantine and eastern Aegean coasts were more sporadic than the Levantine-Greek mainland traffic via the Cycladic Islands as optimal intermediary stops through the ages.

The story with impressed pottery follows a similar pattern whereby the Anatolian landmass is by-passed and interaction with the Eastern Aegean is less visible than the Western Aegean. Impressed pottery with similar motifs and arrangements appear all across the Aegean around the same time. The most striking observation is the parallel decoration techniques in the Levant and the Western Aegean. Interestingly, comb impressions are absent at the contemporary sites in the Eastern Aegean. It is unfortunate that the dearth of archaeological evidence from the southern Anatolian coast does not allow us to link the Levantine and Aegean sites on a firmer basis. Up until now, ongoing documentation of early 6th millennium BC pottery from the cave sites Öküzini, Karain and Suluin near Antalya has failed to produce impressed sherds (personal communication Metin Kartal and Ayşegül Aykurt). Fifty-five to 75 km north of those sites, however, impressed sherds are recorded from the Early Neolithic sites of Bademağacı and

Höyücek, demonstrating that the north of Antalya, which is connected to the coast via a natural pass, was part of the area in which this pottery was used (Duru and Umurtak 2005: 31; Duru 1996: lev. 14). Further research will hopefully provide a more nuanced picture of the distribution of this pottery.

Discussion

The distribution of impressed pottery implies that a prehistoric version of slow-motion seafaring was operating in the Levant, southern Anatolian coast and the Aegean. Considering that sail ships were not in use during the Neolithic period, what we envisage should be much smaller in scale and intensity than the Bronze Age networks. Although visual representations are lacking from the Neolithic body of evidence, prototypes of Aegean long-boats, paddled boats and dug-outs are potential forms of vessel we could expect to be a part of Neolithic sea-faring. Neolithic slow-motion shipping carried finished goods, animals, raw material, and people in all sorts of directions and engendered social interactions in many forms, fostering exchange of items, ideas, techniques, customs, fashions *etc*. The voyages were most probably not intended to start from a site in the Levant and end in Thessaly or near Izmir. The connections between these regions were provided by constant and intense short-range engagements (fishing, shellfish collecting, inter-societal meetings, exchange activities, transport of animals *etc*.) and low-density long-distance mobility (colonisation, leapfrogging, open-sea fishing, procurement and distribution of obsidian and adventurous exploration of new lands). This vital and mobile social world, enacted through easy and fast coastal travel, labeled by Broodbank (1999) as 'seafaring nurseries', functioned like a web that linked the East Mediterranean with the Aegean world. Through this complicated, spontaneous and unorganised chain, a trait like impressed pottery may have been transferred easily and quickly. I would like to compare here the neolithisation paces of inland and coastal regions to demonstrate the time and energy coastal transport saves people. It is striking to acknowledge the fact that inland neolithisation of Anatolia from East to West took almost 3,000 years whereas coastal neolithisation of the entire Central and Western Mediterranean happened in merely a few centuries (Schoop 2005: 53; Guilaine 2007). The radiocarbon evidence indicates that impressed pottery was first produced in the Levant and Euphrates Basin from where it might have dispersed towards the west (although it could be the other way around if earlier impressed pottery gets found around the Aegean).

One fascinating thing about the development of impressed pottery is that its rapid distribution coincides with the foundation of new sites. Sites in the northern Aegean such as Nea Nikomedia, Anzabegova, Yannitsa B and in Bulgaria (Polyanitsa-Platoto and Koprivets) have impressed pottery from their earliest strata onwards (Alram-Stern 1996; Çilingiroğlu 2010; Stefanova 1996; Todorova 1990: fig. 2). This brings to mind that impressed pottery was adapted by long-established farmer-herders in the Aegean as a new fashion, but that there was also a substantial amount of human mobility, including the establishing of new villages, at this time which facilitated the rapid dispersal of this type of decoration. Presumably, the continuous nature of maritime activities resulted in the foundation of new villages at advantageous positions along these routes or on alluvial coastal plains optimal for farmer-herders. Therefore, I am not offering a model where impressed pottery emerges solely as a trendy feature quickly adapted by potters, but suggesting that human mobility, along with potential mobility involving ceramics, had also played a key role in the dispersal of this decoration type in the Aegean and perhaps in the Eastern Mediterranean as well. All these mechanisms seem to have contributed to the rapid and almost synchronised dispersal of similar types of impressed pottery in these regions.

The simultaneous appearance of impressed wares on both sides of the Aegean is noteworthy. Judging by the different types of impressed pottery in the Aegean it seems plausible that different routes were taken by preference, one reaching the eastern and the other the western shores. A route entering from southern Anatolian coast into the Aegean may have followed the summer sea currents from southern Rhodes keeping the Dodecanese on the right, reaching the southern Cycladic islands, via Astypalaia and Amorgos. The diverging routes in the Aegean, perhaps caused by a strong North wind or sea currents, may have resulted in the non-matching decoration techniques observed in different parts of the Aegean. Levantine impulses entailing the comb impressions may have been picked up by Thessallian communities due to more successful traffic in this direction. Alternatively, the Izmir region potters simply did not prefer to decorate the vessels with comb impressions. One can suggest that deviating features in the type of impressions used speak for different choices on the part of the potters across the Aegean as they adapted this style. Creating designs with fingertips, a comb or a shell is technically very simple and therefore is unlikely to be beyond the technical capabilities of any potter. Apart from this, it is hard to imagine that one area was unaware of different pottery designs used by the other in a social environment where communities are in constant interaction via social and economic networks (Perlès 1992; Broodbank 2013). Therefore, it can be also suggested that the potters of the Eastern Aegean did not choose to decorate the pots with comb impressions or any other tool that may have left continuous patterns on the surface. Still, this non-matching feature is very intriguing and requires further research to be resolved.

A relative dearth of prehistoric research, coupled with sea-level rise in the early Holocene submerging coastal sites, impedes the identification of coastal Neolithic sites in many places, especially the southern Anatolian coast. This further prevents us from identifying the route of distribution of different types of impressed pottery. Nevertheless, archaeological materials, such as impressed pottery or obsidian betray the constant state of connectivity or using Braudel's words 'untiringly spun threads' generated by prehistoric seafarers in the Eastern Mediterranean.

Prospects

Many questions concerning the sudden appearance and coastal distribution of impressed pottery remain unsolved. The discussion following the presentation of this paper in Sheffield gave birth to new directions of research for the impressed pottery phenomenon. Kristian Kristiansen asked whether the archaeological record allows us to discern other objects and/or commodities accompanying the impressed wares, especially economic goods like domestic animals. Related to this, another question that arose was whether the impressed pottery is locally produced or was imported as vessels carrying certain contents. Certainly, as mentioned, the gray unburnished pottery with impressions, a novel fabric type related to impressed decoration, is worth analysing to discern whether these may be non-local wares. John Papadopoulos remarked that since sail ships were not in use during the Neolithic, the distributional patterns of different sorts of impressions should have to do with the currents and winds in the Aegean. Susan Sherratt made remarks and asked whether it is possible to identify the tools used by Neolithic potters to produce these decorations. Future research on impressed wares may focus on these aspects to gain a more fine-tuned image of the connectivity around 6000 BCE in the Eastern Mediterranean.

Acknowledgements

I would like to thank Barry Molloy, the organiser of the 2013 Aegean Round Table, and the Archaeology Department at Sheffield University, especially John Bennett and Paul Halstead, for their kind invitation to this truly enjoyable and fruitful meeting. I am very thankful for the comments and suggestions on an earlier manuscript by Barry Molloy, Marina Milić and Peter Tomkins which substantially improved the focus of this paper. I am also grateful to Agathe Reingruber and Martin Furholt for their help concerning distribution of ceramics in mainland Greece. All mistakes herein, of course, remain mine.

This paper is dedicated to the enduring memory of young lives lost during the Gezi Resistance in June/July 2013: Mehmet Ayvalıtaş, Abdullah Cömert, Ali İsmail Korkmaz, Mustafa Sarı, Ethem Sarısülük and Medeni Yıldırım.

References

Alram-Stern, E.
1996 *Die Ägäische Frühzeit, 1. Band, Das Neolithikum in Griechenland*. Wien: Verlag der Österreichischen Akademie der Wissenschaften.

Agouridis, C.
1997 Sea Routes and Navigation in the Third Millennium Aegean. *Oxford Journal of Archaeology* 16(1): 1–24.

Balossi-Restelli, F.
2006 *The Development of 'Cultural Regions' in the Neolithic of the Near East, BAR International Series 1482.* Oxford: Archaeopress.

Barnett, W.K.
2000 Cardial Pottery and the Agricultural Transition in Mediterranean Europe. In T.D. Price (ed.), *Europe's First Farmers*: 93–116, Cambridge: Cambridge University Press.

Braudel, F.
1972 *The Mediterranean and the Mediterranean World in the Age of Philip II.* London: Fontana/Collins.

Broodbank, C.
2000 *An Island Archaeology of the Early Cyclades.* Cambridge: Cambridge University Press.
2006 The Origins and Early development of Mediterranean Maritime Activity. *Journal of Mediterranean Archaeology* 19(2): 199–230.
2013 *The Making of the Middle Sea. A history of the Mediterranean from the Beginning to the Emergence of the Classical World.* London: Thames & Hudson.

Broodbank, C. and T.F. Strasser
1991 Migrant farmers and the Neolithic colonization of Crete. *Antiquity* 65: 233–245.

Carter, R.
2006 Boat remains and maritime trade in the Persian Gulf during the sixth and fifth millennia BC. *Antiquity* 80: 52–63.

Caymaz, T.
2008 Urla Yarımadası Prehistorik Yerleşimleri. *Arkeoloji Dergisi* XI: 1–56.

Coward, F., S. Shennan, S. Colledge, J. Conolly and M. Collard
2008 The spread of Neolithic plant economies from the Near East to northwest Europe: a phylogenetic analysis. *Journal of Archaeological Science* 35: 42–56.

Çilingiroğlu, A., Ö. Çevik and Ç. Çilingiroğlu
2012 Towards understanding early farming communities of West-Central Anatolia: Contribution of Ulucak. In M. Özdoğan, N. Başgelen and P. Kuniholm (eds.), *Neolithic in Turkey: New Excavations and New Research. Volume 4: Western Turkey*: 139–175. Istanbul: Arkeoloji ve Sanat Yayınları.

Çilingiroğlu, Ç.
2005 The concept of 'Neolithic Package': Considering its meaning and applicability. *Documenta Praehistorica* 32: 1–13.
2009 Of Stamps, Loom Weights and Spindle Whorls: Contextual Evidence on the Functions of Neolithic Stamps from Ulucak, İzmir, Turkey. *Journal of Mediterranean Archaeology* 22(1): 3–27.
2010 Appearance of Neolithic Impressed Pottery in Aegean and Its Implications for Maritime Networks in the Eastern Mediterranean. *Türkiye Bilimler Akademisi Arkeoloji Dergisi TÜBA-AR* 13: 9–22.
2012 *The Neolithic Pottery at Ulucak in Aegean Turkey. Organization of Production, Interregional Comparisons and Relative Chronology. BAR International Series 2426.* Oxford: British Archaeological Reports.

Çilingiroğlu, Ç and C. Çakırlar
2013 Towards configuring the Neolithization of Aegean Turkey. *Documenta Praehistorica* 40: 21–29.

Demoule, J.-P. and C. Perlès
1993 The Greek Neolithic: A New Review. *Journal of World Prehistory* 7(4): 355–416.

Derin, Z.
2006 İzmir'den İki Yeni Prehistorik Yerleşim Yeri: Yassıtepe Höyüğü, Çakallar Tepesi Höyüğü. *Arkeoloji Dergisi* 2006/1: 1–12.
2012 Yeşilova Höyük. In M. Özdoğan, N. Başgelen and P. Kuniholm (eds.), *Neolithic in Turkey: New Excavations and New Research. Volume 4: Western Turkey*: 177–195. Istanbul: Arkeoloji ve Sanat Yayınları.

Duru, R.
1996 Bademağacı Höyüğü (Kızılkaya) Kazıları. 1993 Yılı Çalışma Raporu. Belleten LX: 783–800.

Duru, R. and G. Umurtak
2005 *Höyücek, 1989-1992 yılları arasında yapılan kazıların sonuçları.* Ankara: Türk Tarih Kurumu.

Erdoğu, B.
2013 Uğurlu. A Neolithic Settlement on the Aegean Island of Gökçeada. In M. Özdoğan, N. Başgelen and P. Kuniholm (eds.), *Neolithic in Turkey: New Excavations and New Research. Volume 5: Northwestern Turkey and Istanbul*: 1–33. Istanbul: Arkeoloji ve Sanat Yayınları.

Erkurt, O.
2011 Deneysel Arkeoloji: Kiklad Tekneleri Canlandırma Projesi. In V. Şahoğlu and P. Sotirakopoulou (eds.), *Karşıdan Karşıya.MÖ 3. Bin'de Kiklad Adaları ve Batı Anadolu*: 178–185. Istanbul: Kitap Yayınevi.

Furholt, M.
2011 Zeichensysteme nach der Sesshaftwerdung. Keramik als Symbolträger und Vermittler sozialen Wandels in ägäischen Früh- und Mittelneolithikum. *Eurasia Antiqua* 17: 21–44.

Guilaine, J.
2007 Die Ausbreitung der neolithischen Lebensweise im Mittelmeerraum. In Badisches Landesmuseum Karlsruhe (ed.), *Vor 12.000 Jahren in Anatolien, die ältesten Monumente der Menschheit*: 166–176. Stuttgart: Konrad Theiss Verlag.

Herling, L., K. Kasper, C. Lichter and R. Meriç
2008 Im Westen nichts Neues? Ergebnisse der Grabungen 2003 und 2004 in Dedecik-Heybelitepe. *Istanbuler Mitteilungen* 58: 13–65.

Hood, S.
1981 *Excavations in Chios 1938-1955, Prehistoric Emporio and Ayio Gala.* Oxford: British School of Archaeology at Athens.

Horejs, B.
2012 Çukuriçi Höyük. A Neolithic and Bronze Age Settlement in the Region of Ephesos. In M. Özdoğan, N. Başgelen and P. Kuniholm (eds.), *Neolithic in Turkey: New Excavations and New Research. Volume 4: Western Turkey*: 117–131. Istanbul: Arkeoloji ve Sanat Yayınları.

Hughey, J.R., P. Paschou, P. Drineas, D. Mastropaolo, D.M. Lotakis, P.A. Navas, M. Michalodimitrakis, J.A. Stamatoyannopoulos and G. Stamatoyannopoulos
2013 A European population in Minoan Bronze Age Crete. *Nature Communications* 4, number 1861. DOI: 10.1038/ncomms2871.

Jacobsen, T.W.
1981 Franchthi Cave and the Beginning of Settled Village Life in Greece. *Hesperia* 50(4): 303–319.

Karamitrou-Mentessidi, N. Efstratiou, M. Kaczanowska and J.K. Kozlowski
2015 Early Neolithic Settlement of Mavropigi in Western Greek Macedonia. *Eurasian Prehistory*
    12 (1-2): 47–116.

Kızıltan, Z. And M.A. Polat
2013 The Neolithic at Yenikapı Marmaray-Metro Project Rescue Excavations. In M. Özdoğan,
    N. Başgelen and P. Kuniholm (eds.), *Neolithic in Turkey: New Excavations and New Research. Volume*
    5: Northwestern Turkey and Istanbul: 113–165. Istanbul: Arkeoloji ve Sanat Yayınları.

King, R., S. Özcan, T. Carter, E. Kalfoglu, S. Atasoy, K. Triantiphyllidis, A. Kouvatsi, A. Lin, C. Chow,
    L. Zhivotovsky, M. Tsopanomichalou and P. Underhill
2008 Differential Y-chromosome Anatolian influences on the Greek and Cretan Neolithic. *Annals*
    of Human Genetics 72: 205–214.

Kopaka, K. and Matzanas, C.
2009 Palaeolithic industries from the island of Gavdos, near neighbour to Crete in Greece. *Antiquity*
    83(321). Project Gallery: http://www.antiquity.ac.uk/antiquityNew/projgall/kopaka321/

Korfmann, M.
1988 East-West Connections throughout the Mediterranean in the Early Neolithic Period. *Berytus*
    36: 9–25.

Lichter, C.
2002 Central-Western Anatolia- key region in the neolithization of Europe? In F. Gérard and
    L. Thissen (eds.), *The Neolithic of Central Anatolia: Internal Developments and External Relations*
    during the 9th-6th millennia cal BC: 161–170. Istanbul: Ege Yayınları.
2011 Neolithic stamps and the neolithization process. A fresh look at an old issue. In R. Krauss
    (ed.), *Beginnings-New Research in the Appearance of the Neolithic between Northwest Anatolia and the*
    Carpathian Basin. Studien aus den Forschungsclustern des Deutschen Archäologischen Instituts: 35–46.
    Rahden: Verlag Marie Leidorf.

Malinowski, B.
1984 *Argonouts of the Western Pacific*. Long Grove: Waveland Press.

McGeehan Liritzis, V.
1988 Seafaring, craft and cultural contact in the Aegean during the 3rd millennium BC. *The*
    International Journal of Nautical Archaeology and Underwater Exploration 17(3): 237–256.

McGrail, S.
2001 *Boats of the world from the stone age to medieval times*. Oxford: Oxford University Press.

Nieuwenhuyse, O.
2007 *Plain and Painted Pottery: The rise of Neolithic ceramic styles on the Syrian and North Mesopotamian*
    Plains. Turhout: Brepols.

Otto, B.
1985 *Die verzierte Keramik der Sesklo- und Diminikultur Thessaliens*. Philipp von Zabern: Mainz am
    Rhein.

Ozan, A.

2013 Kıyı Ege Neolitik Çağ Çömlekçiliğinde Halka Dip Geleneği. *Cedrus* 1: 1–19.

Özdoğan, M.

2007 Mezraa-Teleilat. In M. Özdoğan and N. Başgelen (eds.), *Türkiye'de Neolitik Dönem*: 189–202. Istanbul: Arkeoloji ve Sanat Yayınları.

2008 An Alternative Approach in Tracing Changes in Demographic Composition: The Westward Expansion of the Neolithic Way of Life. In J. Bocquet-Appel and O. Bar-Yosef (eds.), *The Neolithic Demographic Transition and its Consequences*: 139–178. Heidelberg: Springer.

2011 Mezraa-Teleilat. In M. Özdoğan, N. Başgelen and P. Kuniholm (eds.), *Neolithic in Turkey: New Excavations and New Research. Volume 2: The Euphrates Basin*: 203–260. Istanbul: Arkeoloji ve Sanat Yayınları.

Özdoğan, M., N. Başgelen and P. Kuniholm (eds.)

2012 *The Neolithic in Turkey. New Excavations and New Research. Volume 3: Central Turkey*. Istanbul: Arkeoloji ve Sanat Yayınları.

Papadatos Y. and P. Tomkins

2013 Trading, the Longboat, and Cultural Interaction in the Aegean during the late fourth millennium BCE: The view from Kephala Petras, East Crete. *American Journal of Archaeology* 117(3): 353–381.

Perlès, C.

2001 *The Early Neolithic in Greece*. Cambridge: Cambridge University Press.

2003 An alternate (and old-fashioned) view of Neolithization of Greece. *Documenta Praehistorica* 30: 99–113.

2005 From the Near East to Greece: let's reverse the focus- Cultural elements that did not transfer. C. Lichter (ed.), *How did farming reach Europe? Anatolian-European relations from the second half of the seventh through the first half of the sixth millennium cal BC. (Byzas 2)*: 275–290. Istanbul: Ege Yayınları.

Phelps, W.W.

1975 The Neolithic pottery sequence in southern Greece. PhD dissetation, University of London PhD thesis, University of London.

Reingruber, A.

2008 *Die Argissa-Magula. Das frühe und das beginnende Mittlere Neolithikum im Lichte Transägäischer Beziehungen, Beiträge zur Ur- und Frühgeschichtlichen Archäologie des Mittelmeer-Kulturraumes, Band 35*. Bonn: Verlag Dr. Rudolf Habelt.

2011 Early Neolithic settlement patterns and exchange networks in the Aegean. *Documenta Praehistorica* 38: 291–305.

Rowly-Conwy, P., L. Gourichon, D. Helmer and J.-D. Vigne

2013 Early Domestic Animals in Italy, Istria, the Thyrrhenian Islands and Southern France. In S. Colledge, J. Conolly, K. Dobney and K. Manning (eds.), *The Origins and Spread of Domestic Animals in Southwest Asia and Europe*. 161–194. Walnut Creek: Left Coast.

Runnels, C.

1995 Review of Aegean Prehistory IV: The Stone Age of Greece from the Paleolithic to the Advent of the Neolithic. *American Journal of Archaeology* 99(4): 699–728.

Sağlamtimur, H.
2012 The Neolithic Settlement of Ege Gübre. In M. Özdoğan, N. Başgelen and P. Kuniholm (eds.), *Neolithic in Turkey: New Excavations and New Research. Volume 4: Western Turkey*: 117–131. Istanbul: Arkeoloji ve Sanat Yayınları.

Şahoğlu, V.
2005 The Anatolian Trade Network and the Izmir Region during the Early Bronze Age. *Oxford Journal of Archaeology* 24(4): 339–361.

Salanova, L.
2011 Ceramic assemblages and chronology: Problems and Solutions for the Early Neolithic settlement of Kovačevo (Bulgaria). *Studia Praehistorica* 14: 21–33.

Sampson, A.
1998 The Neolithic and Mesolithic Occupation of the Cave of Cyclope, Youra, Alonnessos, Greece. *The Annual of the British School at Athens* 93: 1–22.

Schoop, U.-D.
2005 The late escape of the Neolithic from the Central Anatolian Plain. In C. Lichter (ed.), *How did Farming Reach Europe?*: 41–58. Istanbul: Ege Yayınları.

Seeher, J.
1990 Coşkuntepe, Anatolisches Neolithikum am Nordostufer der Ägäis. *Istanbuler Mitteilungen* 40: 9–15.

Steel, L.
2004 *Cyprus before History. From the earliest settlers to the end of the Bronze Age*. London: Duckworth.

Stefanova, T.
1996 A comparative analysis of pottery from the 'Monochrome Early Neolithic Horizon' and 'Karanovo I Horizon' and the Problems of the Neolithization of Bulgaria. *Documenta Praehistorica* 23: 15–38.

Strasser, T., E. Panagopoulou, C. Runnels, P. M. Murray, N. Thompson, P. Karkanas, F. W. McCoy and K. W. Wegmann
2010 Stone Age Seafaring in the Mediterranean. Evidence from the Plakias Region for Lower Paleolithic and Mesolithic Habitation of Crete. *Hesperia* 79: 145–190.

Takaoğlu, T.
2005 Coşkuntepe: An Early Neolithic Quern Production Site in NW Turkey. *Journal of Field Archaeology* 30(4): 419–433.

Tekin, H.
2011 Hakemi Use. A Newly Discovered Late Neolithic Site in Southeastern Turkey. In M. Özdoğan, N. Başgelen and P. Kuniholm (eds.), *Neolithic in Turkey: New Excavations and New Research. Volume 1: The Tigris Basin*: 151–172. Istanbul: Arkeoloji ve Sanat Yayınları.

Thissen, L.
2000 Thessaly, Franchthi and Western Turkey: Clues to the Neolithization of Greece. *Documenta Praehistorica* 27: 141–154.

Todorova, H.

1990 Das Frühneolithikum Nordbulgariens im Kontext des ostbalkanischen Neolithikums. In Schweizerisches Landesmuseum (ed.), *Die ersten Bauern*: 71–76. Zurich: Schweizerisches Landesmuseum.

Tomkins, P.

2004 Filling in the Neolithic Background: Social Life and Social Transformation in the Aegean before the Bronze Age. In J.C. Barrett and P. Halstead (eds.), *The Emergence of Civilization Revisited. Sheffield Studies in Aegean Archaeology 6*: 38–63. Oxford: Oxbow Books.

Umurtak, G.

2010 Questions arising from a bulla found in the EBAII settlement at Bademağacı. *Adalya* XIII: 19–28.

Usai, D. and S. Salvatori

2007 The oldest representation of a Nile boat. *Antiquity* 81. Issue 314 Project Gallery online publication. http://antiquity.ac.uk/ProjGall/usai/index.html

Van Andel, T.H. and J.C. Shackleton

1982 Late Paleolithic and Mesolithic Coastlines of Greece and the Aegean. *Journal of Field Archaeology* 9(4): 445–454.

Vigne, J.-D., F. Briois, A. Zazzo, G. Willcox, T. Cucchia, S. Thiébault, I. Carrère, Y. Franel, R. Touquet, C. Martin, C. Moreau, C. Comby and J. Guilaine

2012 First wave of cultivators spread to Cyprus at least 10,600 y ago. *Proceedings of National Academy of Sciences* 109(22): 8445–8449.

Vitelli, K.D.

1989 Were pots first made for food? Doubts from Franchthi. *World Archaeology* 21: 17–29.

Wijnen, M. H.

1982 *The Early Neolithic I Settlement at Sesklo: An Early Farming Community in Thessaly, Greece*. Leiden: Universitaire Pers Leiden.

Winn, S. and D. Shimabuku

1989 Pottery. In M. Gimbutas, S. Winn and D. Shimabuku (eds.), *Achilleion, a Neolithic Settlement in Thessaly, Greece, 6400-5600 BC, Institute of Archaeology, Monumenta Archaeologica 14*: 75–164. Los Angeles.

Yiouni, P.

1996 The Early Neolithic Pottery: Technology. In K.A. Wardle (ed.), *Nea Nikomedeia I: The Excavation of an Early Neolithic Village in Northern Greece 1961-1964, Supplemantary Volume No 25*: 55–78. London, British School at Athens.

Zeder, M.A.

2008 Domestication and early agriculture in the Mediterranean Basin: Origins, diffusion, and impact. *Proceedings of the National Academy of Sciences* 105.33: 11597–11604.

2011 The Origins of Agriculture: New Data, New Ideas. *Current Anthropology* 52(4): 221–235.

Chapter 5

A Question of Scale? Connecting Communities through Obsidian Exchange in the Neolithic Aegean, Anatolia and Balkans

Marina Milić

Introduction

This paper will explore interaction between Neolithic societies in the Aegean and in the southern Balkans. Specifically, I will use provenance data for obsidian as an indicator of key aspects of scales and modes of interactions in this broad region. The appearance of obsidian in archaeological contexts has long been used as a key indicator for inter-regional exchange and long-distance movement of people, objects and know-how. The circulation of this chipped stone resource in prehistory is well attested, being carried through various means of exchange, across seas and inhospitable landscapes for hundreds of kilometres from sources to sites. It is well established that the consumption of obsidian in the Aegean basin is related primarily to the exploitation of sources on the island of Melos, where two geographically and chemically distinct sources are located, one at Adamas (also known as Sta Nychia) and the other at Demenegaki. On the basis of chemical and technological studies, it has been argued that the exchange of obsidian from these sources was largely maintained amongst the groups that lived on the Aegean islands and the surrounding mainland (Renfrew *et al.* 1965; Perlès 1990; Carter 2009) (Figure 5.1).[1]

This leads to the purpose of this paper, which will reconsider the consumption traditions of Aegean Neolithic societies, focussing primarily on sites located on the 'edges' of obsidian circulation zones where other types of stone were in, typically more common, use also, rather than those communities close to the sources that consumed Melian obsidian as their major raw material (Renfrew *et al.* 1965; Torrence 1986; Perlès 1990; Carter 2009).

While material from Melos forms the main Aegean obsidian resource, the use of other obsidian sources is documented in regions bordering the Aegean. To the east, material from the central Anatolian sources is widely used throughout Anatolia,

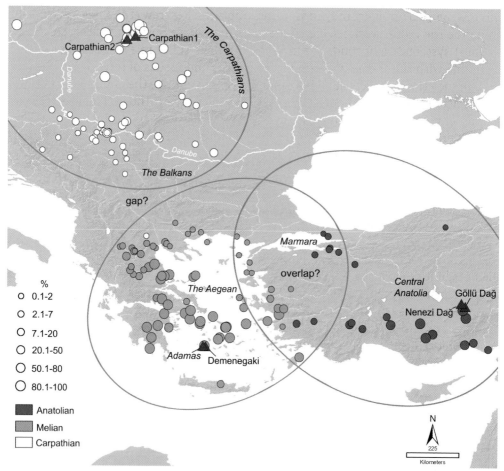

Figure 5.1: Obsidian sources and their distribution within Neolithic sites. The map is showing the relative proportion of obsidian within chipped stone assemblage at each site with colour scheme marking the dominant obsidian source.

reaching the Aegean coast in the west (Figure 5.1). To the north, in central Europe, obsidian from the Carpathian sources was exploited, reaching the Balkans and the northern fringes of the Aegean mainland to the south. As Figure 5.1 shows, the distribution zones of three obsidian source regions, Melian, Anatolian and Carpathian are neighbouring, but they also overlap in the Aegean. Melian and central Anatolian material 'overlap' in the eastern and north-eastern Aegean, while there is limited evidence for both Melian and Carpathian sources being utilised in the southern Balkans (Greek Macedonia). The sites studied in this paper are located in these 'peripheral' areas. These typically lie far from the sources, often a few hundred kilometres away from the quarries and as a result contain only small proportions of this raw material in their chipped stone assemblages (Renfrew *et al.* 1968; Perlès 1990). To define the more precise scale of the consumption of obsidian from each source, we must systematically conduct compositional analyses of relevant assemblages.

In line with the theme of this volume – scales and modes of interaction between Aegean societies and their neighbours – my aim is to explore the nature and intensity of contacts between the Aegean based communities with those that lived outside of this environment. To the east, these are contacts with the inland Anatolian communities and, to the north with the Balkan regions. Whilst, this study is based on obsidian exchange alone, it largely benefits from the distinguish characteristic of the ability to accurately trace the geological origin of this raw material. This is a component of a larger research program that integrates technological and contextual analyses of obsidian (Milić 2015), which is being prepared for publication currently. In this study, the chemical characterisation that links artefacts to sources is conducted using a pXRF device, following a relevant methodology widely employed in obsidian studies (*e.g.* Frahm *et al.* 2014; Milić 2014). The major advantage of this technique is the possibility to analyse large, even entire assemblages which enables us to develop a more complete picture about the exact number of each obsidian source represented at a given site (Milić 2014). Once the origin of obsidian has been established, the quantity and the form of artefacts found at sites could be plotted in relation to their geographical distance (as-the-crow-flies) from the source. These parameters are used as indicators of mode and scale of interaction between Aegean societies and their neighbours.

The major obsidian sources of central Anatolia, the Aegean, and Balkans: Product

The consumption of obsidian is particularly useful for demonstrating contact between different regions in Neolithic times, because its use was at its widest distribution in this epoch. Obsidian artefacts represent one of our most convincing media (easily recognised and in turn accurately provenanced) to trace trading activities, particularly in and around the Aegean (Perlès 1992; Carter and Kilikoglou 2007; Carter 2009). My main focus will be on the activities of those communities on the edges of distribution zones of the sources for this wider region, particularly as we occasionally find overlapping consumption of products from different sources (Figure 5.1). In the following section, I will outline the distribution of obsidian from each of the source regions as documented through recovery from archaeological contexts.

Central Anatolia

The central Anatolian volcanic complex is located in the Anatolian plateau, in Cappadocia, of which Göllü Dağ and Nenezi Dağ in the south are the most important archaeologically. Throughout the Neolithic obsidian procured by distant communities was initially preformed and/or completely reduced at specialist quarry-based workshops (Cauvin *et al.* 1998; Binder and Balkan-Atlı 2001; Binder 2002). Both Göllü Dağ and Nenezi Dağ sources had been exploited by distant groups since the later Palaeolithic at least, with small quantities of their products documented extending from the Antalya region of Mediterranean Anatolia to the southern Levant, some 380 km and 800 km distant respectively (Chataigner 1998: fig. 7a; Slimak *et al.* 2008; Carter *et al.* 2011). The major expansion in the circulation of these materials occurred during the Aceramic/Pre-Pottery Neolithic and Early Neolithic (9th–7th millennia BC), with the material being mainly consumed by populations in central Anatolia, Cyprus and throughout the Levant (Cauvin and Chataigner 1998; Carter *et al.* 2005a). From the late 7th millennium BC (early Pottery Neolithic) we start to see small quantities of Cappadocian (Göllü Dağ and Nenezi Dağ) obsidian being procured by communities in north-western Anatolia *c.* 500 km from the sources and the eastern and north-eastern Aegean, *c.* 700–800 km distant from the sources in Cappadocia. This western distribution will be addressed below.

The Aegean

In the Aegean, the Adamas and Demenegaki outcrops on the island of Melos (Figure 5.1). Due to the proximate nature of are *c.* 12 km apart, so that Torrence (1986: 96) considered them to be 'a single source'. They are however geochronologically and geochemically distinct (Shelford *et al.* 1982; Arias *et al.* 2006), and archaeologically there are suggestions that the two sources were possibly exploited and consumed in different ways and in different trips or periods (Carter 2008: 225; Carter and Kilikoglou 2007; Perlès *et al.* 2011: 47). We know that the earliest procurement of Melian obsidian took place in the late Upper Palaeolithic (11th millennium BC), as attested by small quantities recovered from the Franchthi Cave on the Argolid (Perlès 1987; Renfrew and Aspinall 1990). This discovery provided important – indirect – evidence for early maritime activity, a journey of *c.* 120 km in one direction (Broodbank 2006: 209). In the Mesolithic period (9th–8th millennia BC), Melian obsidian is reported from not only mainland sites, but also a number of other insular locations in the Cyclades and Crete (Sampson *et al.* 2002: 52–53; Kaczanowska and Kozłowski 2013; Carter *et al.* forthcoming). Melian obsidian was circulated in greater quantities and over greater distances from the Early Neolithic onwards (7th millennium BC), reaching its height of consumption in the Late Neolithic (5th millennium BC). At this time it was the dominant raw material at most sites in the Cyclades, Crete and Peloponnese (coastal sites in particular), while not insignificant quantities were consumed by communities in Thessaly (Perlès 1990) and the west Anatolian littoral. Tiny amounts made their way to populations in Macedonia and Thrace. Unlike other obsidian sources, the extensive use of Melian obsidian in the Early Bronze Age is relatively uninterrupted especially in the Cycladic islands and Crete (Carter 2009).

The Carpathians

The archaeologically most important obsidian sources of the Carpathians are located at the northern edges of the Great Hungarian Plain (Figure 5.1), in what today are Slovakia (Carpathian 1), and Hungary (Carpathian 2). Carpathian 1 (C1) was a better quality material and tended to be preferred to Carpathian 2 (C2) as a resource for chipped-stone tools, and it was also more widely distributed spatially (Williams-Thorpe et al. 1984; Bíró 2014). The earliest use of these sources dates to the Middle Palaeolithic (Dobosi 2011), with peak consumption occurring in the Middle to Late Neolithic period (6th-5th millennia BC) during which the long-distance movement and development of complex social processes through which obsidian was exchanged appears to have emerged (Bíró 1998). The distribution of these raw materials is predominantly riverine, with concentrations of obsidian at sites close to the main rivers (Kaczanowska and Kozłowski 2008; O'Shea 2011); the most intensive communication appears along the Tisza and Danube rivers (Williams-Thorpe et al. 1984; Bíró 1998). Carpathian obsidians were most widely used in Hungary, Slovakia and Romania, although small quantities have been documented at sites on the Black Sea to the east, west to Austria and Germany, north to Poland and south into Croatia and Serbia (Williams-Thorpe et al. 1984). The most southerly extension of C1 obsidian is reported in two sites from northern Greece (western Macedonia), material that I return to in detail below.

Modelling exchange

Thanks to 60 years of archaeometric research, archaeologists are now able to source the raw materials used to make obsidian tools they find on their excavations and surveys (Pollard and Heron 2008). Perhaps the most important aspect of this research is not simply documenting source histories and the movement of obsidian in its own right (as raw material and/or end-product), but our ability to use the data as a proxy to reconstruct human actions. Obsidian characterisation studies have thus been applied to a variety of major social science questions from reconstructing hunter-gatherer mobility (Perlès 1987; Carter et al. 2011), to using obsidian circulation as an index of Neolithisation (Carter et al. 2013), to interrogating the nature of supra-regional socio-economic interaction (Carter and Kilikoglou 2007). When we talk about charting mobility, obsidian trade routes have been used to assess the spread of farming and migrations from the Near East to Anatolia (Cauvin 2000: 93–95; Sherratt 2005). Similarly, the circulation of obsidian within the Mediterranean is indirectly but notably used to reconstruct maritime voyages and seafaring know-how (e.g. Broodbank 2006; Farr 2006; Ammerman 2011). In general, modelling obsidian procurement has had a large influence on theoretical discourses of exchange/trade/network/interaction between individuals or groups in archaeology (Renfrew et al. 1968; Perlès 1992; Carter and Kilikoglou 2007; Çilingiroğlu this volume).

In the 1960s Renfrew, Cann and Dixon demonstrated that obsidian sourcing studies can serve as an important tool for reconstructing inter-regional and cross-cultural contacts (Cann and Renfrew 1964; Renfrew *et al.* 1968). Since then, a large number of research programs in the Mediterranean and beyond have employed obsidian characterisation studies to detail source histories and to reconstruct people's activities and interactions. Models for understanding these interactions originally emerged in two obsidian-using regions, Anatolia and the Aegean (Renfrew *et al.* 1965; 1968) with further models subsequently developed for the central Mediterranean and Carpathian obsidian exchange networks (Hallam *et al.* 1976; Ammerman 1979; Williams-Thorpe *et al.* 1984).

This project's first stage involved the analysis of obsidian from a Neolithic number of sites throughout Anatolia and the Near East, considering two main variables: (a) the relative proportion of obsidian in the community's chipped stone assemblage, and (b) the linear (as-the-crow-flies) distance of that site from the source (as detailed by the characterisation study). On the basis of these data, Renfrew and his colleagues were able to chart the dissemination of obsidian throughout the region, recording in the process what appeared to be a regular fall-off in the relative quantity of central and/or eastern Anatolian obsidian in direct relationship to distance from source. Within this fall-off there was however a 'tipping point', between what Renfrew termed the 'contact' and 'supply' zones. The former comprised those communities where approximately 80% of the chipped stone tools were made of obsidian, the sites all laying within *c.* 300 km of the sources, where people were capable of travelling to the sources themselves to procure obsidian. Beyond this zone, the quantity of obsidian decreases on the basis of reciprocity as some communities keep a proportion of obsidian, while exchanging the rest with the neighbours farther *down-the-line* (Renfrew *et al.* 1968). While the above scenario refer to the Neolithic data, Renfrew detailed how one might view different kinds of fall-off curves at different times (or in different places), the distinction in these curves' shape corresponding to different forms of socio-economic interaction, exchange mechanism or the value of products in a range of societies (Renfrew 1975; 1984).

Modelling the nature of interaction on the basis of fall-off curves was similarly applied to the study of the Carpathian sources. Here, the fall-off graphs contained some 'outliers', that is, the sites that contain more obsidian in their assemblages than predicted by modelling, and these were described as redistribution centres (Williams-Thorpe *et al.* 1984) or sites with preferential access to the sources (Chapman 1981: 81) from which obsidian was further exchanged to other communities (*e.g.* the site of Vinča-Belo Brdo is located over 400 km from the Carpathians and contained 70% obsidian in one phase of its Neolithic history).

This general model for the distribution of obsidian has undergone considerable critique (*e.g.* Hodder and Orton 1976) and revision in line with developments in the field, both theoretical and scientific, taking account of different environmental, cultural and material factors. It is presented here as a general background to the current regional-scale analyses, parts of which are presented in this paper.

The application of exchange models to the circulation of obsidian within the Aegean

Turning to the Neolithic of the Aegean, it becomes clear that here the concepts of 'supply' and 'contact' zones could not be simply applied due to the lack of known settlements in the vicinity of the sources on the island of Melos during the Early and Middle Neolithic period. At this time, southern Greece and Thessaly received high quantities of obsidian (50–95%) representing areas in which the distribution of obsidian is believed to have been mediated by specialists/middleman who obtained obsidian directly from the sources. Perlès (1990) suggested that the distribution of Melian obsidian corresponded with Renfrew's freelance middleman trade in which the 'middleman has an effective area of operation outside of which he does not normally travel' (Renfrew 1975: 49). Beyond Thessaly, in Macedonia and Thrace, there is an abrupt fall-off of this material (often representing less than 1%) which lies in the jurisdiction of an itinerant trader, in Perlès' terminology (Perlès 1990; 1992; see also Renfrew 1975). During the Late and Final Neolithic, the islands in the vicinity of the Melian sources became inhabited and formed a direct 'supply zone' with over 95% of obsidian in their lithic assemblages. In this model, Thessaly and the Peloponnese became an intermediate zone that acquired obsidian as semi-finished products in relatively large amounts, like in previous periods, with no noticeable decrease as one moved farther away from the sources. Perlès would see the exchange of obsidian in Macedonia and distant Thrace as remaining in the hands of traders, receiving only a handful of obsidian, about 5% and less (Perlès 1992).

Obsidian as *exotica*

To again refer to Perles' (1992) study on the Aegean Neolithic exchange, she proposed the co-existence of three exchanges systems: exchange of utilitarian goods that may be widely distributed; exchange with social function amongst the groups in a smaller geographic region; and the exchange of 'prestige goods' limited to certain groups or individuals. The areas and sites discussed in this paper contain very small quantities of obsidian, usually brought from very distant sources. When archaeologists discuss exchange, in situations in which we find 'rare' objects they are often characterised as 'exotica' on the basis of their uncommon appearance. Such items have been interpreted according to the concept of gift exchange or as status symbols, because they are expected to be well made (elaborated jewellery, shell and stone ornaments, stone vases; *e.g.* Perlès 1992; Renfrew 1993; Chapman 2008) and/or they would be deposited within special archaeological contexts (burials, hoards, foundation or abandonment deposits of buildings). Recently, Tykot (2011) discussed the issues of using *exotic* in this manner in exchange studies, and favoured the introduction of the term *eccentric* for objects marking those unusual and odd occurrences. Some of characteristics of eccentric obsidian artefacts would be that these appear in very small numbers, they are not of the same origin as the more common obsidian type, and their shape/production is unusual (Tykot 2011: 35). Obsidian from the distant areas – Macedonia in the case of Melian distribution, western Anatolia in the case of the circulation of Anatolian material or the southern Balkans in the spread of obsidian from the Carpathians – is rare and travels long-distances. Nonetheless, we must still question whether we can correctly label obsidian as a prestige item or not, and by extension characterise it, meaningfully, as exotica.

It has been previously observed (Renfrew 1993) that certain objects should be a marker of 'communication' rather than of 'trade' and this involves contacts and activities that are less to do with material purposes (economic) and more closely linked to symbolic and ritual purposes (exchange gift or travel tokens). Cauvin (2000: 93) argued that obsidian does not have any technological but cultural value and its very long-distance transport had more symbolic than utilitarian significance. Indeed, the processes that brought an artefact to the site (seafaring know-how, travel into unfamiliar worlds, *etc.*), seem to be increasingly appreciated in determining the value than the actual artefact in itself (Helms 1988; Broodbank 1993; Perlès 2005; Ammerman 2011). The procurement and use of obsidian might be seen to represent technological and social choices, whereby distant resources are accessed to undertake activities that cannot, or would not, be pursued using locally available materials. Communities are, essentially, in particular circumstances not using freely available materials but are actively seeking a specific one through different chains of social relations. If it is a material fall-out from interaction for other purposes (Renfrew 1993), it is also possible that obsidian is a material echo of certain forms and purposes of long-distance interaction involving groups closer to the sources, though better contextual data is required to explore this possibility systematically.

Tracing connectivity: The key studies

The consumption of obsidian has been documented amongst Neolithic communities in the Aegean, Anatolia and the Balkans, in particular those dated to period between late 7th until mid-5th millennium BC. My intention here is to deal with areas that should have small assemblages predicted by modelling; ones that have been formed as a part of long-distance exchange. Surrounding the Aegean, the study areas are placed on the interface with the neighbouring regions of Anatolia and the Balkans, specifically: a) the eastern Anatolian coast and the 'overlap' of Aegean and Anatolian obsidian distribution zones; b) the northern Greek mainland (Macedonia), with the 'gap' between the Carpathian and Melian circulation (Figure 5.1). With this in mind, the purpose here is to explore the meaning of obsidian finds in these areas, including analyses of artefact type and technological categorisation in tandem with provenancing.

To better understand the social context of obsidian procurement and consumption in these liminal areas (of circulation), my project involved a targeted analysis of numerous assemblages from sites that fell within these so-called boundary and border zones. Elemental characterisation of significant quantities of artefacts was undertaken using a portable XRF spectrometer (hereafter pXRF). The technique allows non-destructive and fast analyses but, perhaps more importantly, it is well-suited to mass-sampling assemblages, in this case the study of over one thousand artefacts. The specifics of the method used to collect and analyse the data in the discussion below are discussed elsewhere (Milić 2014). The methodological benefits of using pXRF lie in defining the relative proportions of obsidians from different sources at each single site. In the case of newer excavations we can additionally sub-divide the distribution by contextual analyses on an intra-site level by placing material into stratigraphic and micro-regional contexts, and this can in turn be related back to macro-regional analyses.

Overlap? Eastern and north-eastern Aegean

The distribution of central Anatolian products in western Anatolia and the Aegean has only been recognised due to the findings of new excavations conducted in the last 20–30 years. The work of Renfrew et al. (1966, 1968), had originally established a boundary of the 'supply' zone for Göllü Dag and Nenezi Dag products at c. 250 km from sources. Beyond this, the distribution curve abruptly drops, containing sites that have only around 10% of obsidian in their overall lithic assemblages, as for example sites in the Anatolian Lake District, located c. 380 km from the central Anatolian sources. Recently, we have been able to learn more about the settlements in central-western (Izmir) and north-western (Marmara) regions. Excavations have revealed small amounts of central Anatolian obsidian at these sites, particularly in the central-western regions, and this present research reveals that the same sites were also supplied with obsidian from Aegean sources (Figure 5.1). This links many of these sites, to varying degrees, into two directionally distinct exchange systems.

The sites under consideration date to the late 7th/beginning of the 6th millennia BC or the Late Neolithic-Early Chalcolithic (LN-EC) in Anatolian terms, and the Early Neolithic in Aegean terms (Brami and Heyd 2011; Karul 2011 Çilingiroğlu 2012). The material came from a number of tell sites around the modern town of Izmir, in central-western Anatolia (Ulucak, Ege Gübre, Yeşilova, Dedecik-Heybelitepe, Çukuriçi Höyük) plus the broadly contemporary site of Ayio Gala cave on the nearby island of Chios (Çilingiroğlu 2012). To the north-east (Figure 5.2), obsidian is reported from a smaller number of sites including Coşkuntepe (Troad), Hoca Çeşme (Thrace) and Uğurlu on the island of Gökçeada/Imbros. Finally, in north-western Anatolia, obsidian has been documented at a group of Fikirtepe Culture settlements around the Sea of Marmara (Pendik, Fikirtepe, Menteşe, Barcın Höyük, Ilıpınar, Aktopraklık and Yenikapı; Özdoğan 2011; Milić 2015).

As discussed, previous research has demonstrated that the relative proportion of obsidian to other lithics in each of the source areas shows diverse patterning, largely due to geographical settings of the sources and, therefore, different distribution mechanisms. In the western Anatolian LN-EC period, obsidian from Cappadocian sources reached the areas of the Sea of Marmara and the Aegean coast. In the same region, we also have evidence for the consumption of Melian obsidian in various frequencies. When looking out into the edges of these distributions, the image that emerges reveals patterning on a micro-regional level. Sites located in the Izmir region contain very different quantities of obsidian (Table 5.1). The provenancing of artefacts from these sites showed a strong predominance of Melian obsidian (often *c.* 99%) with only a very few pieces of central Anatolian types. Furthermore, the Melian Adamas and Demenegaki sub-sources were equally represented in all mentioned cases in this region. On the other hand, even though central Anatolian types appear as one or two artefacts per site, Göllü Dağ and/or Nenezi Dağ are represented. Macroscopic examination of Ayio Gala obsidian has shown the presence of two small bladelet fragments of Cappadocian material (possibly Göllü Dağ) amongst an otherwise Melian assemblage (Figure 5.2).

We must consider what these *percentages* mean when it comes to their form and use. Melian obsidian is present in the form of blade cores reduced on sites into regular pressure-flaked blades, and this appears to be a pattern that we can identify across a wide area. The assemblages contained exhausted blade cores and number of rejuvenation flakes (Figure 5.3). The majority are regular unipolar blades probably manufactured by a knapper *in situ* at the settlements. The tradition of consumption of Melian obsidian in the form of regular blades is a characteristic phenomenon in this region. At Çukuriçi Höyük, Melian obsidian is the major raw material (over 80% of all chipped stone) and this community could have served as a centre for obsidian supply and redistribution in the region (Horejs, this volume). On the other hand, usually one

Table 5.1. *The relative proportion of obsidian in knapped stone assemblages and percentages of represented obsidian source groups (specific outcrops are not detailed)*

Site	Obsidian %	Melian	Cappadocian
Ege Gübre	*c.* 1%	>99%	<1%
Ulucak	*c.* 15%	>99%	<1%
Yeşilova	*c.* 40%	>99%	<1%
Çukuriçi Höyük[1]	>80%	100%	none
Dedecik-Heybelitepe[2]	50%	>99%	<1%
Uğurlu	*c.* 0.5%	*c.* 90%	*c.* 10%
Hoca Ceşme	*c.* 0.5%	*c.* 80%	*c.* 20%
Çoşkuntepe[3]	*c.* 0.5%	*c.* 95%	*c.* 5%

1 = B. Horejs, this volume; 2 = Herling *et al.* 2008; 3 = Perlès *et al.* 2011

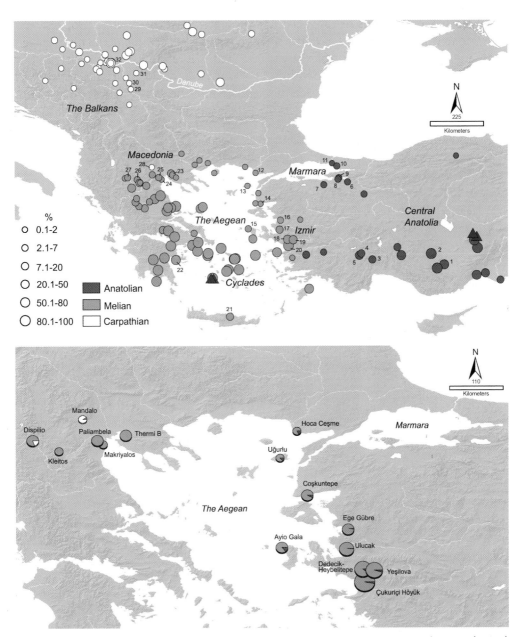

Figure 5.2: Relative proportion of obsidian at each site with marked sites mentioned in text (upper). Pie charts are showing the proportion of different obsidian types within study assemblages (bottom). Figure 5.2 sites: 1. Can Hasan; 2. Çatalhöyük; 3. Höyücek; 4. Kuruçay Höyük; 5. Hacilar; 6. Barcın Höyük; 7. Aktopraklık; 8. Menteşe; 9. Ilıpınar; 10. Pendik; 11. Fikirtepe; 12. Hoca Ceşme; 13. Uğurlu; 14. Coşkuntepe; 15. Ayio Gala; 16. Ege Gübre; 17. Ulucak; 18. Dedecik-Heybelitepe; 19. Yeşilova; 20. Çukuriçi Höyük; 21. Knossos; 22. Franchthi cave; 23. Thermi B; 24. Makriyalos; 25. Paliambela; 26. Kleitos; 27. Dispilio; 28. Mandalo; 29. Drenovac; 30. Slatina 31. Belovode; 32. Vinča-Belo Brdo.

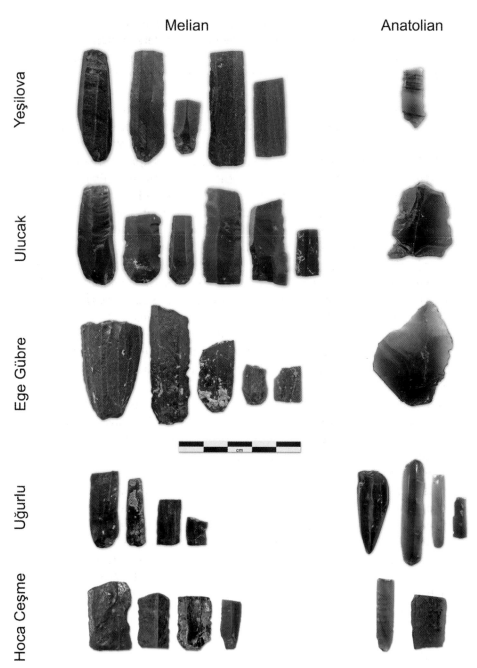

Figure 5.3: Obsidian from Melian and Anatolian sources found at eastern Aegean sites of Yeşilova, Ulucak and Ege Gübre, and northern Aegean sites of Uğurlu and Hoca Ceşme (photographs by author).

or two artefacts of central Anatolian origin (some 650 km away) occur in the entire assemblage and in the form of flakes or irregular bladelets, which is virtually the opposite of the Melian tradition in terms of how the material is consumed. (Figure 5.3). On the basis of current evidence they cannot be associated with the knapping of a core at the site.

Moving north into the north-eastern Aegean, obsidian is sparse (*c.* 1% of assemblages) but Melian material still dominates assemblages at Uğurlu, Hoca Çeşme and Çoşkuntepe. Notable is the increase in central Anatolian obsidian, particularly the Göllü Dağ source (Figure 5.2). The two Melian sources appear in equal numbers, typically in the form of finished blades and occasionally as flakes which might indicate that they were exchanged as preformed cores or finished blades (Figure 5.3). When Cappadocian obsidian is found, unlike the eastern Aegean sites, it seems to have been exchanged as very fine blades, and these rarely show evidence of use.

Farther north, in the Marmara region, the overall quantity of obsidian ranges from approximately 2–5% of chipped stone tools. The characterisation of obsidian revealed that material from central Anatolian sources is dominant for obsidian artefacts.[2] This material seems to have been exchanged as prepared bullet cores which were then reduced on site into fine pressure blades and bladelets (Gatsov 2009; Milić 2015). While it is possible to plot instances of obsidian according to their geological point of origin, this consideration of technological characteristics demonstrates complexity in the social practices through which different obsidians were procured and consumed.

It is noticeable that in all these micro-regions, blades and flakes were the only type of artefacts that circulated. In Anatolian core areas, production and consumption of a wide range of objects seems to be restricted to those communities that use obsidian as their major raw material (*e.g.* Çatalhöyük, Can Hasan) (Carter *et al.* 2005b). When Anatolian obsidian is exchanged, even to intermediary communities, i.e. sites in the Lake District (10%-40% at Kuruçay Höyük, Höyücek and Hacilar), it was always in the form of cores and blades (Mellaart 1970; Duru 1994; Balkan-Atlı 2005). This is how it also reached the Marmara region and the northern Aegean. On the other hand, in the Izmir region, despite the Melian dominance, one or two Anatolian pieces occur at each of the sites examined. The pieces that were examined in this study were often in the form of flakes or irregular bladelets. Melian obsidian, on the other hand, circulated around the Aegean, usually as prepared cores knapped into prismatic blades.

Gap? Macedonia

The next focus will be on the nature of contacts between the Late Neolithic (second half of 6th and 5th millennia BC) communities in the northern Aegean (Greek Macedonia) with those farther to the north in the Balkans. There was a 'gap' in this region characterised by the lack of obsidian exchange between the circulations of Melian sources on the one hand, and Carpathian to the north, on the other. The consumption of Melian obsidian drops with distance, and in Macedonia or Thrace, it is only present as less than 1%. Similarly, Carpathian obsidian represents only a tiny proportion of stone tools (often less than 0.5%) at settlements south of the Danube (Figure 5.2), while north of this river it can be relatively frequent (*cf.* Williams-Thorpe *et al.* 1984). The provenancing of obsidian from several sites in Macedonia (Makriyalos, Paliambela, Thermi B, Kleitos) confirmed that only obsidian from Melian sources was exchanged in this band, close to the Aegean Sea.

In the same region, in western Macedonia, two cases of Carpathian obsidian have been identified in an area otherwise dominated by Melian material within the small obsidian assemblages. Kilikoglou *et al.* (1996) identified pieces of Carpathian 1 obsidian at tell site of Mandalo. Interestingly, ten obsidian pieces associated with its LN phase (4600 and 4000 BC [Kotsakis *et al.* 1989]), the period considered in this paper, were brought from Carpathian, not Melian, sources. Another site with Carpathian 1 obsidian identified through this current research is the lake site of Dispilio. The site was occupied during MN, LN and FN periods (*c.* 5500–4500 BC), but the exact stratigraphic location of obsidian finds is currently not available. Here, Melian sources comprise 80% while Carpathian 1 was used for 20% of obsidian artefacts (Figure 5.2). Once more, just as in the eastern Aegean, the question is - what was the form of these Carpathian obsidian pieces and how this will help us to better understand their appearance 900 km away from the source. Melian obsidian usually represents <1% of assemblages in this region but it appears in a variety of production stages, which may or may not indicate one-off *in situ* production. The character of Carpathian objects was far from what one might expect to be 'exotic' in appearance or function. It is remarkable that at both Mandalo and Dispilio, Carpathian 1 obsidian is mainly found in the form of irregular blades and flakes (Figure 5.4). Even if this is only a part of the much larger, unexcavated assemblage, would it be correct to characterise this as a production deposit?

Mandalo and Dispilio assemblages can fruitfully be compared with assemblages found at the sites that should have been intermediary communities in the central and northern Balkans. In the early phase of the Late Neolithic period (second half of the 6th millennium BC), the site of Vinča-Belo Brdo in the middle Danube region, obsidian represents 70% of its chipped stone. This suggests that people there had had preferential access to the sources and/or the site acted as an obsidian redistribution centre (Chapman 1981: 81; Williams-Thorpe *et al.* 1984). Raw material was brought from the Carpathians to Vinča in semi-prepared cores and worked into micro-cores which could be used to produce fine pressure flaked blades, presumably by skilful craftsmen (Radovanović *et al.* 1984; Tripković and Milić 2008). The obsidian artefacts that are thus far found at sites in the central Balkans (*e.g.* Belovode, Slatina, Drenovac), between the Danube and the Aegean, revealed that the obsidian exchanged was, often found in the form of flakes or irregular blades, and not as the fine pressure-flaked blades produced at Vinča-Belo Brdo (Figure 5.4). This is strikingly similar to the situation

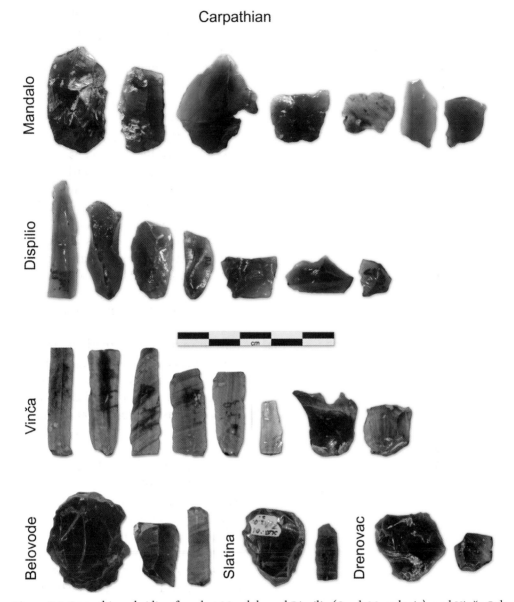

Figure 5.4: Carpathian obsidian found at Mandalo and Dispilio (Greek Macedonia), and Vinča-Belo Brdo, Belovode, Slatina and Drenovac (Serbia) (photographs by author).

at Mandalo and Dispilio. In light of this it is important to note that, in the case of Mandalo, we know that the absolute dates belong to the second half of 5th millennia (Kotsakis *et al.* 1989). Most of Dispilio Carpathian obsidian could also be dated to the FN phase (*c.* 4700–3300 BC) of the site. This appears to equate with the Vinča D period in the Balkans, when obsidian was only occasionally found at sites south of the Danube, including Vinča-Belo-Brdo itself (Tripković and Milić 2008; Borić 2009). It is, therefore, possible that these central-southern Balkan settlements belong to a sub-network in which sporadic obsidian artefacts were exchanged, amongst other more desirable objects of the 5th millennium BC, copper being one of the possible (obvious) candidates.

Discussion: Connected communities or communities with connections

According to the basic trade models outlined above and typically applied to the distribution of obsidian in the Neolithic, the communities on the edges of distribution zones should receive obsidian down-the-line via intermediary and/or 'redistribution' centres. These outlying communities were naturally not dependent on obsidian as a primary raw material. When we take into account quantity, provenance, technology, use-wear and contextual data (where possible) as primary parameters, then the varying roles that obsidian played in Neolithic social relations appears diverse, and value (whether high or low) was not strictly dependant on the sole factor of physical distance from sources. In many cases, rare pieces of obsidian in remote communities may certainly be related to the drop-off in obsidian being moved from its area of major consumption. This could mainly relate to relations with the groups that are in geographical intermediary positions, though we cannot ignore the capacity for longer distance movements relating to circumstances beyond trade or exchange. Apart from the quantifying objects as relatively asocial indicators of things moving, however, the other way of understanding the exchange process is in reconstruction of the *chaîne opératoire*, i.e. the form in which the material occurs at each site (Torrence 1986; Carter and Kilikoglou 2007; Perlès 2007). According to that principle, sites close to the sources would contain products from different stages of the production chain (nodules, cores, debris, blades), while farther away we should find products that are probably produced somewhere else and brought as finished artefacts to a site. On the other hand, if we find other categories of the production chain (*e.g.* waste flakes), should we regard this as an on-site manufacture even when obsidian is only represented by a handful of pieces and characterise this as limited knapping (Carter and Kilikoglou 2007: 130)? Many of the assemblages that have been examined contain relatively small amounts of obsidian, making it difficult to ascribe too much meaning to their presence given the unexceptional technological and often contextual characteristics of the finds.

Returning to Perlès' work, she emphasises that there is never a single exchange network which brings exogenous goods into a community (Perlès 1992: 117). Even if we centre our focus on obsidian only and the forms in which it circulates, we see that in the overlap regions that receive obsidian from two sources, we are inclined to envisage at least two exchange systems. Despite the fact that only general source areas rather than individual sources are considered, we can still typically talk about two different exchange networks and two directions of the connections.

In areas of the Aegean far from the sources, the circulation of obsidian implies that we are dealing with two practices – 'communication' and 'trade'. Melian obsidian in central-western Anatolia appears since the mid-7th millennium BC at least, while at Ulucak, small quantities are documented from its earliest habitation (level VI) dated to the beginning of the 7th millennium (Milić 2015). In the Neolithic, prepared blade cores were imported, redistributed and worked at settlements into regular blades. Blades remained the major form in which Melian obsidian was exchanged farther to the north-east on the Aegean coast (Uğurlu, Hoca Çeşme and Coşkuntepe). The uniform 'trade' between the Izmir region and Melos was occasional but it was continually carried out by generations of inhabitants, as evidenced by the stratigraphic distribution of obsidian. Obsidian was brought from a distance (around 400 km as-the-crow-flies) but its acquisition had a social and economic role likely imposed by its functional qualities.

If Melian obsidian together with the local flint could satisfy all functional needs, can one or two Anatolian pieces be considered as exotic items? Pieces of central Anatolian obsidian (both Göllü Dağ and Nenezi Dağ) are very rare although they appear at every site in the region. If the intensity of exchange is measured by the frequency of obsidian, then this communication would certainly not be extensive and organised. These very rare pieces (Perlès includes ornaments, metals and stone vessels), which are often considered as non-utilitarian performing social functions in which visual display is crucial. In turn, we must ask if it would be realistic to consider pieces of Cappadocian obsidian in the Aegean as being such 'special' objects. This is problematic because in no known case do they hold any aesthetic/functional nor contextual value that differentiates them from other chipped stone artefacts. The contacts that brought Cappadocian obsidian to Izmir might be part of exchange of other objects or through social relations, possibly even associated with personal mobility and not a desire for obsidian *per se*.

However, one case, rare in archaeological context, can stimulate our imagination; this being a life-sized stone statue from Urfa in eastern Turkey, dated to *c.* 10,000 BC (Schmidt 2007: 287–288). The eyes of the statue were made of two obsidian blade fragments inserted into eye sockets. If found in an isolated context, the character of these broken obsidian fragments would certainly not point to such a non-utilitarian use. For now, we can suggest that there is no economic need for Anatolian obsidian in Izmir region, but its appearance might have similar decorative function or alternatively it could reflect social relationships that certain groups maintained with the inland Anatolia (predecessors and possible eastern origin).

Looking to the second case-study in an area where obsidian is rare when present at all, we have observed that there was limited consumption of Melian obsidian in Macedonia. The appearance of Carpathian 1 obsidian in two locations was unexpected but could it has been considered to serve as an indicator of interactions between two distant regions (the Aegean and the central and northern Balkans), as has been emphasised. Ten Carpathian artefacts from Mandalo served as a link with Vinča culture in central Balkans some 450 km farther to the north (Kilikoglou *et al.* 1996; Tomas 2010). At the same time, none of the obsidian artefacts from the LN period at this site were from the Melian source. In the case of Displio, Melian obsidian is the main type, although the amount of Carpathian obsidian is significant (Figure 5.2). We see once more that the exchange of Melian obsidian consistently is in line with other communities farther to the south (*e.g.* Kleitos, Paliambela, Makriyalos) that bring similar products to Dispilio, including finished blades and flakes. Carpathian pieces, even though brought from a great distance, are of questionable technological/ morphological function. This is not unique, however, and such morphologies can be traced throughout the central Balkans where the regular micro-blades that would be found at this time in sites to the north of the Danube, are not yet known. The evidence we currently have from the excavated sites in Serbia suggests that amorphous flakes dominate the assemblages there. The initial thought might be that the fine fragile blades were hard to transport, and as a result obsidian is not used for its functional properties as a tool, in consideration of the presence of other good quality raw materials. Here, it has been argued that procurement of obsidian from the Carpathians is, just like Melian obsidian in Macedonia in general, a part of exchange that included other resources. Due to the traceability of obsidian, it is used as the key marker that provides the backbone for a perceived trade of less visible commodities (*e.g.* salt; Urem-Kotsou, this volume). But this is a house of cards. It could be proposed that the procurement of Melian obsidian was organised by the community and tied into uniform distribution amongst groups of villages in Macedonia. The acquisition of Carpathian obsidian, on the other hand, could be one-off events related to an individual or a household that briefly were in contact with the people in the north and this could be a sign/token of this journey whatever its purpose may have been. In this sense, we could polarise the situation by suggesting it was a symbol of the distant unknown rather than representing established knowledge of groups and resources, though reality is likely to lie somewhere between these positions. Exchange with groups having access to Carpathian obsidian is different and so drawing distribution lines need to represent a regular flow of contact but potentially singular events. This may be reflected in the 'gap' in distribution and the lack of intermediary sites identified to date (Figure 5.1). The appearance of Carpathian obsidian at Mandalo and Dispilio, but also at sites south of the Danube, is peculiar and it appears that the material was not fulfilling particular technological or functional purposes and if there is any significance, it is probably related to the raw material itself. The interaction with other communities alone is of great importance and it might be less relevant precisely what goods were exchanged. It is perhaps significant that the practices in which this morphology/technology of obsidian would have found meaning had a degree of shared relevance in these distinct areas. Obsidian could have been a symbol of irregular but familiar contacts rather than exchange of know-how technology.

Conclusions

Through mass-sampling of obsidian assemblages and employing an integrated approach to the raw material and technology, this paper has examined the role that obsidian played in long-distance connections in the Neolithic. The results showed that in different regions, the interactions are not necessarily uniform, allowing variations on micro-regional scales, as was particularly clear at sites in western Anatolia and western Macedonia. The amount of obsidian that is found at these sites is so small that it could hardly represent a major object of trade, to the extent that in many cases it could simply mark occasional or one events rather than exchange and established long-term interaction. At the very least, however, it represents knowledge of those other groups, and potentially relationships that were maintained over considerable time, perhaps many generations. It could be said that obsidian is a poor proxy for establishing the precise character or frequency of these relationships within the timeframes of individual lives. The rare pieces are tantalising because they reveal this connectivity and knowledge, but they are the product more of eccentric rather than systemic interaction. Indeed, in some cases the lack of statistically valid or clear patterning forms a pattern in itself as it reflects irregular and non-systematic modes of interaction.

In any of these medium or long distance movements we do not see the exchange of arrow or spear-heads, visually and technologically sophisticated tools, but in the best case scenario, we can observe the exchange of pressure-flaked blades. Indeed, some of the objects recovered could hardly have been exchanged for their aesthetics or functionality as they were irregular and not very useful as tools. Furthermore, unless these objects are hoarded or accidentally buried *in situ* due to some house or site being destroyed or embedded as part of other objects like Urfa statue, they are rarely found in primary contexts that might reveal their economic or symbolic value. The opposite may be the case even, whereby it was preferable to dispose of sharp obsidian objects off-site and thing like projectiles may have been used and lost in remote locations. For now, it can be suggested that outlier or eccentric pieces in Anatolia and Macedonia could be a part of an alternative or irregular route relating to movement of different goods, but also including the movement of individuals for the many reasons that lay outside the realm of expected reciprocal exchange mechanisms. They demonstrate occasional contacts that may not have been memorised (or repeated) amongst the successors of those involved in the exchange. Equally, they could be mnemonics of relationships, and kept those journeys and friendships conceptually alive in the community. In such cases, obsidian need not be moved through trade and it need not be related to regular journeys. Conversely, Melian obsidian circulated in western Anatolia and in Macedonia for centuries, somewhat subverting its potential 'foreign' or distant attributes.

Acknowledgements

I would like to thank Barry Molloy for inviting to participate in the Sheffield Aegean Round Table. I am grateful to Tristan Carter, Çiler Çilingiroğlu and Barry Molloy who commented on an earlier version of this text. Many people kindly helped me with the study the material included in this paper including Özlem Çevik, Çiler Çilingiroğlu, Zafer Derin, Burcin Erdoğu, Kostas Kotsakis, Haluk Sağlamtimur and Duška Urem-Kotsou.

This paper arises from research conducted during my PhD (UCL) and I thank my supervisors Andrew Bevan, Cyprian Broodbank and Todd Whitelaw for their support during the course of this research. All errors remain my own. The research was funded by UCL Overseas Research Scholarship, a Wenner-Gren Wadsworth International Fellowship and an Open Society Scholarship.

Notes

1. Some isolated examples of the Melian obsidian outside the Aegean have been confirmed, only in exceptional cases, *e.g.* in inland western Anatolia, 5th millennium Aphrodosias (Blackman 1986). In central Mediterranean, several pieces of Melian obsidian have been recently identified on the island of Palagruža in the Adriatic (Tykot 2013).
2. Previous provenancing work on small number of pieces from Ilipinar and Pendik have identified presence of north-western Anatolian sources called Galatia X (Keller and Seifried 1990; Bigazzi *et al.* 1998), however this was only a small sample and the elemental data is not available. In this work, I was not able to analyse geological reference material from Galatia X although their presence in archaeological assemblages is plausible.

References

Ammerman, A.J.
1979 A Study of Obsidian Exchange Networks in Calabria. *World Archaeology* 11: 95–110.
2011 The paradox of early voyaging in the Mediterranean and the slowness of the Neolithic transition between Cyprus and Italy. In G. Vavouranakis (ed.), *Seascapes in Aegean Prehistory*: 31–50. Athens: Danish Institute of Athens.

Arias, A., M. Oddone, G. Bigazzi, A. Di Muro, C. Principe and P. Norelli
2006 New Data for the Characterization of Milos Obsidians. *Journal of Radioanalytical and Nuclear Chemistry* 268(2): 371–386.

Balkan-Atlı, N.
2005 Yontmataş Endüstrisi. In R. Duru and G. Umurtak (eds.), *Höyücek, 1989-1992 Yılları Arasında Yapılan Kazıların Sonuçları*: 130–137. Ankara: Türk Tarih Kurumu.

Bellot-Gurlet, L., O. Pelon and M.L. Séfériadès
2008 Détermination de provenance d'une sélection d'obsidiennes du palais minoen de Malia (Crète). *Comptes Rendus Palevol.* 7: 419–427.

Bigazzi, G., G. Poupeau, L. Bellot-Gurlet and Z. Yezingili
1998 Provenance Studies of Obsidian Artefacts in Anatolia Using the Fission-track Dating Method: An overview. In M.-C. Cauvin, A. Gourgaud, B. Gratuze, N. Arnaud, P. Poupeau, Poidevin J.-L., and C. Chataigner (eds.), *L'Obsidienne au Proche et Moyen Orient: Du Volcan à l'Outil* (BAR International Series 738): 69–89. Oxford: British Archaeological Reports.

Binder, D.
2002 Stones Making Sense: What Obsidian Could Tell Us About the Origins of the Central Anatolian Neolithic. In F. Gérard and L. Thissen (eds.), *The Neolithic of Central Anatolia: Internal Developments and External Relations During the 9th - 6th Millennia Cal BC* (Proceedings of the International CANeW Table Ronde, Istanbul, 23–24 November 2001): 79–90. British Institute of Archaeology at Ankara/Malcolm and Carolyn Wiener Laboratory for Aegean and Near Eastern Dendrochronology at Cornell University.

Binder, D. and N. Balkan-Atlı
2001 Obsidian exploitation and blade technology at Komürcü-Kaletepe (Cappadocia, Turkey). In I. Caneva, C. Lemorini, D. Zampetti, and P. Biagi (eds.), *Beyond tools*: 79–90. Berlin: SENEPSE.

Biró, K.T.
1998 Stones, Numbers - History? The Utilization of Lithic Raw Materials in the Middle and Late Neolithic of Hungary. *Journal of Anthropological Archaeology* 17: 1–18.
2014 Carpathian Obsidians: State of Art of Central European Obsidian Research. In M. Yamada & A. Ono (eds.), *Lithic Raw Material Exploitation and Circulation in Préhistory. A Comparative Perspective in Diverse Palaeoenvironment*: 45–67. Liège: ERAUL.

Biró, K.T., I. Pozsgai and A. Vladar
1986 Electron Beam Microanalyses of Obsidian Samples From Geological and Archaeological Sites. *Acta Archaeologica Academiae Scientiarun Hungaricae* 38: 257–278.

Blackman, M.
1986 The provenience of obsidian artifacts from Late Chalcolithic levels at Aphrodisias. In M. Jaukowsky (ed.), *Prehistoric Aphrodisias: An Account of the Excavations and Artifact Studies*: 279–285. Providence: Brown University, Center for Old World Archaeology and Art.

Borić, D.
2009 Absolute Dating of Metallurgical Innovations in the Vinča Culture of the Balkans. In T.L. Kienlin and B.W. Roberts *(eds.), Metals and Societies. Studies in honour of Barbara S. Ottaway*: 191–245. Bonn: Verlag Dr. Rudolf Habelt GmbH.

Brami, M. and V. Heyd
2011 The origins of Europe's first farmers: the role of Hacılar and Western Anatolia, fifty years on. *Praehistorische Zeitschrift* 86(2): 165–206.

Broodbank, C.
1993 Ulysses without Sails: Trade, Distance, Knowledge and Power in the Early Cyclades. *World Archaeology* 24(3): 315–331.
2006 The Origins and Early Development of Mediterranean Maritime Activity. *Journal of Mediterranean Archaeology* 19(2): 199–230.

Cann, J.R. and C. Renfrew
1964 The Characterisation of Obsidian and its Application to the Mediterranean Region. *Proceedings of the Prehistoric Society* 30: 111–133.

Carter, T.
2008 The Consumption of Obsidian in the Early Bronze Age Cyclades. In N. Brodie, J. Doole, G. Gavalas, and C. Renfrew (eds.) *Horizon: A colloquium on the prehistory of the Cyclades*: 225–236. Cambridge: McDonald Institute Monographs.
2009 L'obsidienne Égéenne: Caractérisation, Utilisation et Culture. In M.-H. Moncel and F. Frohlich (eds.). *L'Homme et le Precieux. Matières Minérales Précieuses de la Préhistoire à Aujourd'hui* (BAR International Series 1934): 199–212. Oxford: British Archaeological Reports.

Carter, T., F.-X., Le Bourdonnec, M. Kartal, G. Poupeau, T. Calligaro and P. Moretto
2011 Marginal Perspectives : Sourcing Epi-Palaeolithic to Chalcolithic Obsidian from the Öküzini Cave (SW Turkey). *Paléorient* 37(2): 123–149.

Carter, T. and V. Kilikoglou
2007 From Reactor to Royalty? Aegean and Anatolian Obsidians from Quartier Mu, Malia (Crete). *Journal of Mediterranean Archaeology* 20(1): 115–143.

Carter, T. and M. Milić
2013 The Chipped Stone Industry from Dhaskalio. In C. Renfrew, O. Philaniotou, N. Brodie, G. Gavalas, and M. Boyd (eds.), *The Settlement at Dhaskalio. The Sanctuary at Keros and the Origins of Aegean Ritual*: 531–556. Cambridge: McDonald Institute Monographs.

Carter, T., G. Poupeau, C. Bressy and N.J.P. Pearce
2005a From Chemistry to Consumption: Towards a History of Obsidian Use at Çatalhöyük through a Programme of Inter-laboratory Trace-elemental Characterization. In I. Hodder (ed.), *Changing materialities at Çatalhöyük: reports from the 1995-1999 seasons*: 285–305. Cambridge: McDonald Institute for Archaeological Research.

Carter, T., A. Spasojević and J. Conolly
2005b The Chipped Stone. In I. Hodder (ed.), *Changing materialities at Çatalhöyük: reports from the 1995-1999 seasons*: 221–283. Cambridge: McDonald Institute for Archaeological Research.

Carter, T., S. Grant, M. Kartal, A. Coşkun and V. Özkaya
2013 Networks and Neolithisation: Sourcing obsidian from Körtik Tepe (SE Anatolia). *Journal of Archaeological Science* 40(1): 556–569

Carter, T., D. Mihailović, Y. Papadatos and C. Sofianou
Forthcoming The Cretan Mesolithic in context: New data from Livari Skiadi (SE Crete). *Antiquity*

Chapman, J.
1981 *The Vinča Culture of South-east Europe: Studies in Chronology, Economy and Society*. Oxford: British Archaeological Reports.
2008 Approaches to trade and exchange in earlier prehistory (Late Mesolithic – Early Bronze Age). In A. Jones (ed.) *Prehistoric Europe. Theory and practice*: 333–355. Oxford: Wiley-Blackwell.

Cauvin, J.
2000 *The Birth of the Gods and the Origins of Agriculture*. Cambridge: Cambridge University Press.

Cauvin, M.-C. and C. Chataigner
1998 Distribution de l'Obsidienne Dans les Sites Archéologiques du Proche et Moyen Orient. In
M.-C. Cauvin, A. Gourgaud, B. Gratuze, N. Arnaud, P. Poupeau, Poidevin J.-L., and C. Chataigner
(eds.), *L'Obsidienne au Proche et Moyen Orient: Du Volcan à l'Outil* (BAR International Series 738):
325–350. Oxford: British Archaeological Reports.

Cauvin, M.-C., A. Gourgaud, B. Gratuze, N. Arnaud, G. Poupeau, J.-L. Poidevin and C. Chataigner
1998 *L'Obsidienne au Proche et Moyen Orient: Du Volcan à l'Outil* (BAR International Series 738). Oxford:
British Archaeological Reports.

Chataigner, C.
1998 Sources des Artefacts Néolithiques. In M.-C. Cauvin, A. Gourgaud, B. Gratuze, N. Arnaud,
P. Poupeau, Poidevin J.-L., and C. Chataigner (eds.), *L'Obsidienne au Proche et Moyen Orient: Du
Volcan à l'Outil* (BAR International Series 738): 273–324. Oxford: British Archaeological Reports.

Çilingiroğlu, Ç.
2012 The Neolithic pottery of Ulucak in Aegean Turkey: organization of production, interregional
comparisons and relative chronology (BAR international series 2426). Oxford: British
Archaeological Reports.

Dobosi, V.
2011 Obsidian use in the Palaeolithic in Hungary and adjoining areas. *Natural Resource Environment
and Humans* 1: 83–95.

Duru, R.
1994 *Kuruçay Höyük I. 1978-1988 Kazılarının Sonuçları, Neolitik ve Kalkolitik Çağ Yerleşmeleri* (Vol. 1).
Ankara: Türk Tarih Kurumu.

Farr, H.
2006 Seafaring as social action. *Journal of Maritime Archaeology* 1(1): 85–99.

Frahm, E., R. Doonan and V. Kilikoglou
2014 Handheld Portable X-Ray Fluorescence of Aegean Obsidians. *Archaeometry* 56: 228–260.

Gatsov, I.
2009 *Prehistoric Chipped Stones, E Thrace & S Marmara, 7th-5th mill. B.C.* (BAR International Series 1904).
Oxford: British Archaeological Reports.

Hallam, B.R., S.E. Warren and C. Renfrew
1976 Obsidian in the Western Mediterranean: Characterization by Neutron Activation Analysis and
Optical Emission Spectroscopy. *Proceedings of the Prehistoric Society* 42: 85–110.

Helms, M.W.
1988 *Ulysses' sail: an ethnographic odyssey of power, knowledge, and geographical distance.* Princeton:
Princeton University Press.

Herling, L., K. Kasper, C. Lichter and R. Meriç
2008 Im Westen nichts Neues? Ergebnisse der Grabungen 2003 und 2004 in Dedecik-Heybelitepe.
Istanbuler Mitteilungen 58: 13–65.

Hodder, I. and C. Orton
1976 *Spatial Analysis in Archaeology*. Cambridge: Cambridge University Press

Kaczanowska, M. and J.K. Kozłowski
2008 The Körös and the early Eastern Linear Culture in the northern part of the Carpathian basin: a view from the perspective of lithic industries. *Acta Terrae Septemcastrensis Journal, Proceedings of the International Colloquium: The Carpathian Basin and its Role in the Neolithisation of the Balkan Peninsula VII*: 9–37.
2013 Mesolithic Obsidian Networks in the Aegean. In E. Starnini, (ed.), *Unconformist Archaeology: Papers in honour of Paolo Biagi* (BAR International Series 2528): 17–26. Oxford: British Archaeological Reports.

Karul, N.
2011 The Emergence of Neolithic Life in South and East Marmara Region. In R. Krauß (ed.), *Beginnings - New Research in the Appearance of the Neolithic between Northwest Anatolia and the Carpathian Basin* (Papers of the International Workshop 8th - 9th April 2009, Istanbul): 57–65. Istanbul: Deutsches Archäologisches Institut.

Keller, J. and C. Seifried
1990 The Present State of Obsidian Source Identification in Anatolia and the Near East. In C. Albore Livadie and F. Wideman (eds.), *Volcanologie et Archéologie PACT 25*: 58–87. Strasbourg: Conseil de l'Europe.

Kilikoglou, V., Y. Bassiakos, A.P. Grimanis, K. Souvatzis, A. Pilali-Papasteriou and A. Papanthimou-Papaefthimiou
1996 Carpathian Obsidian in Macedonia, Greece. *Journal of Archaeological Science* 23(3): 343–349.

Kotsakis, K., A. Papanthimou-Papaefthimiou, A. Pilali-Papasteriou, T. Savopoulou, Y. Maniatis and B. Kromer
1989 Carbon-14 dates from Mandalo, W Macedonia. In Y. Maniatis (ed.), *Archaeometry, International symposium on archaeometry*: 679–685. Amsterdam: Elsevier.

Mellaart, J.
1970 *Excavations at Hacılar*. Edinburgh: Edinburgh University Press.

Milić, M.
2014 PXRF characterisation of obsidian from central Anatolia, the Aegean and central Europe. *Journal of Archaeological Science* 41: 285–296.
2015 Obsidian exchange and societies in the Balkans and the Aegean from the late 7th to 5th millennia BC. PhD dissertation, University College London.

O'Shea, J.
2011 A River Runs Through It: Landscape and the Evolution of Bronze Age Networks in the Carpathian Basin. *Journal of World Prehistory* 24(2–3): 161–174.

Özdoğan, M.
1999 Northwestern Turkey: Neolithic Cultures in Between the Balkans and Anatolia. In M. Özdoğan and N. Başgelen (eds.), *Neolithic in Turkey: The cradle of civilization: new discoveries*: 203–224. Istanbul: Arkeoloji ve Sanat Yayinlari.

2011 Archaeological Evidence on the Westward Expansion of Farming Communities from Eastern Anatolia to the Aegean and the Balkans. *Current Anthropology* 52(S4): 415–430.

Perlès, C.
1987 *Les industries lithiques taillées de Franchthi (Argolide, Grèce). I. Presetation gènérale et industries paléolithiques (Excavations at Franchthi Cave, Greece, Fascicle 3).* Bloomington: Indiana University Press.
1990 L'outillage en pierre taillée néolithique en Grèce: approvisionnement et exploitation des matières premières. *Bulletin de Correspondance Hellénique* 114: 1–42.
1992 Systems of Exchange and Organisation of Production in Neolithic Greece. *Journal of Mediterranean Archaeology* 5(2): 115–162.
2005 Réflexion sur les échanges dans le Néolithique de Grèce. In Ph. Clancier, F. Johanns, P. Rouillard, and A. Tenu (eds.), *Autour de Polanyi, Vocabulaires, théories et modalités des échanges*: 201–215. Paris: De Boccard.
2007 Echanges et technologie : l'exemple du Néolithique. In J. Evin (ed.), *Un siècle de construction du discours scientifique en Préhistoire* (III: Aux conceptions d'aujourd'hui. Congrès du centenaire de la Socété préhistorique française / XXVIe Congrès préhistorique de France, Avignon, 21–25 septembre 2004): 53–62. Paris: Socété Préhistorique Française.

Perlès, C., T. Takaoğlu and B. Gratuze
2011 Melian obsidian in NW Turkey: Evidence for early Neolithic trade. *Journal of Field Archaeology* 36(1): 42–49.

Pollard, A.M. and C. Herron
2008 *Archaeological Chemistry*. Cambridge: The Royal Society of Chemistry

Radovanović, I., M. Kaczanowska, J.K. Kozlowski, M. Pawlikowski and B. Voytek
1984 *The chipped stone industry from Vinča*. Belgrade: Centar za arheološka istraživanja, Filozofski Fakultet.

Renfrew, C.
1975 Trade as Action at a Distance: Questions of Integration and Communication. In J.A. Sabloff and C.C. Lamberg-Karlovsky (eds.), *Ancient Civilisation and Trade*: 3–60. Albuquerque: University of New Mexico Press.
1984 Trade as action at distance. In C. Renfrew (ed.) *Approaches to Social Archaeology*: 86–134. Cambridge, Massachusetts: Harvard University Press.
1993 Trade Beyond the Material. In Scarre, C. and F. Healy (eds.) *Trade and Exchange in Prehistoric Europe*: 5–16. Oxford: Oxbow Monographs.

Renfrew, C. and A. Aspinall
1990 Aegean Obsidian and Franchthi Cave. In C. Perlès (ed.), *Les Industries Lithiques Tatllees de Franchthi (Argolide, Grece). Tome II: Les Industries du Mesolithique et du Neolithique Initial*: 257–270. Bloomington and Indianapolis: Indiana University Press.

Renfrew, C., J.E. Dixon and J.R. Cann
1965 Obsidian in the Aegean. *Annual of the British School of Archaeology at Athens* 60: 225–247.
1968 Further Analysis of Near Eastern Obsidians. *Proceedings of the Prehistoric Society* 34: 319–331.

Sampson, A., J.K. Kozlowski, M. Kaczanowska and B. Giannouli
2002 The Mesolithic settlement at Maroulas, Kythnos. *Mediterranean Archaeology & Archaeometry* 2(1): 45–67.

Schmidt, K.
2007 Katalog 94: Überlebensgroße ithyphallische Steinfigur. In Badisches Landesmuseum Karlsruhe (ed.) *Vor 12.000 Jahren in Anatolien. Die ältesten Monumente der Menschheit. Exhibition catalogue.* Theiss, Stuttgart.

Sherratt, A.
2005 ArchAtlas: The Obsidian Trade in the Near East, 14,000 to 6500 BC.

Slimak, L., S.L. Kuhn, H. Roche, D. Mouralis, H. Buitenhuis, N. Balkan-Atlı, D. Binder, C. Kuzucuoğlu and H. Guillou
2008 Kaletepe Deresi 3 (Turkey): Archaeological Evidence for Early Human Settlement in Central Anatolia. *Journal of Human Evolution* 54(1): 99–111.

Tomas, H.
2010 The world beyond the northern margin: the Bronze Age Aegean and the east Adriatic coast. In W.A. Parkinson and M.L. Galaty (eds.), *Archaic State Interaction: The Eastern Mediterranean in the Bronze Age*: 181–212. Santa Fe: School for Advanced Research Press.

Torrence, R.
1986 *Production and Exchange of Stone Tools.* Cambridge: Cambridge University Press.

Tripković, B. and M. Milić
2008 The origin and exchange of obsidian from Vinča-Belo Brdo. *Starinar* 58: 71–86.

Tykot, R.H.
2011 Obsidian Finds on the Fringes of the Central Mediterranean: Exotic or Eccentric Exchange? In A. Vianello (ed.), *Exotica in the Prehistoric Mediterranean*: 33–44. Oxbow Books.
2013 Material Movement Modes in the Mediterranean: Obsidian Sourcing Using PXRF Instruments. In J. Jurek (ed.), *Abstracts of the 19 Annual Meeting of the European Association of Archaeology, September 4-8, Pilsen, Czech Republic*: 418. Pilsen: University of West Bohemia.

Williams-Thorpe, O., S.E. Warren and J.G. Nandris
1984 The Distribution and Provenance of Archaeological Obsidian in Central and Eastern Europe. *Journal of Archaeological Science* 11: 183–212.

Chapter 6

Salting the Roads: Connectivity in the Neolithic Balkans

Dushka Urem-Kotsou

The North Aegean and the Balkans appear to have been connected throughout the Neolithic, from the very beginning of the period to at least its late phases – that is, from approximately 6500 to 3500 BC. Shared characteristics of pottery from Thessaly to the Danube testify to continuity in communication for more than 3,000 years. During the course of this long period, the intensity, modes, scale and routes of communication between sub-regions of the Balkan interior, on the one hand, and between the Balkan interior and the Aegean, on the other, must have varied. This paper discusses some evidence for communication between the sub-regions of the Balkans and the north Aegean. The production and circulation of raw materials and various categories of material culture, such as chipped and polished stone tools, marble vessels, and stone and marine shell ornaments, indicate diverse and well-differentiated forms of exchange network throughout the whole of the Neolithic. Archaeologically less visible commodities, salt in particular, will be also discussed in some detail in order to illustrate the complexity of communication and its role in social change in Neolithic communities across this vast area.

Traditionally, pottery style has been used as evidence for close relationships between sub-regions of southeastern Europe, including the Aegean, and Anatolia. It is worthy of note that pottery exhibits common characteristics from the beginning of the Neolithic and shows similar trends through the Neolithic throughout the Balkans and north Aegean. For example, during the earlier phases of the Neolithic, potters must have shared similar ideas which resulted in vessels of similar technology and style (*e.g.* red-slipped ware, painted and impresso wares). Although regional variations are obvious, pottery also displays striking inter-regional similarities. In the late 6th millennium BC, remarkable changes in pottery manufacture and overall style occurred not only in the Aegean but also in the whole of the Balkans, and apparently over a short period of time. The light-coloured pottery of earlier periods (i.e. red-slipped plane and decorated wares) was replaced by ceramics of dark colour, and similar new decorative techniques were adopted all over the Balkans including the north Aegean. Vessel style thus suggests shared ideas, not only in particular periods of the Neolithic, but throughout the whole period, indicating continuous communication between sub-regions of the Balkans and the Aegean. Pottery was not the sole vehicle by which these ideas were carried, however, since petrographic analysis suggests that vessels did not travel over long distances.

The movement of people, carrying with them their own pottery tradition, has often been used in the past, and to some extent is still used, to explain such phenomena. While large-scale movement of populations is a possibility at least in some periods of the Neolithic, and is compatible with emerging genetic evidence, I would argue that mobility of both individuals and small social groups over varying distances, in various directions, and for various reasons, must have played a dynamic role in the shared expressions observed in pottery. For example, micro-scale mobility of at least some inhabitants within a site catchment and between communities for reasons such as gathering food, fuel or other raw materials, working in the fields or hunting must have been quite regular (Halstead 2005: 39). Residential longer term displacement of craftsmen including potters, and any movement of itinerant specialists (*e.g.* knappers) or middlemen would have further enhanced the connectivity between Neolithic communities (Perlès 1992; Urem-Kotsou in press). Social gatherings on an inter-community level should be also taken into account, as the remains of large-scale feasting at Late Neolithic (LN) Makriyalos suggest (Pappa *et al.* 2004; Urem-Kotsou and Kotsakis 2007; Halstead 2011). Long-term residence of individuals or groups at more distant sites as a result of exogamy, conflict and fission, or subsistence failure has also been suggested (Halstead 1989; 2005). Furthermore, short-term occupation of settlements for a single habitation phase, suggesting at least local movement of whole communities, also appears to have been fairly widespread during the earlier phases of the Neolithic (*e.g.* the Starčevo culture) in the Balkan interior (Garašanin 1979: 120–121) and in some regions of Macedonia, north Greece (Kotsos 2014). This phenomenon also recurred during the later phases of the Neolithic, at least in certain regions of central and western Macedonia where some LN settlements seem to have been short-lived (Kotsakis 1999; 2014; Hondrogianni-Metoki 2001; Pappa 2008; Kotsos 2014).

Despite the potential of genetic and isotopic research, the movement of people is still, to a great extent, archaeologically 'visible' through the mobility of various forms of material culture. Although the quantity and quality of information on the movement of raw materials and objects varies between different regions of the Balkans, an interesting picture emerges from the available evidence.

Mobility of various forms of material culture in the Balkans

Evidence of production and circulation is available for several categories of material culture such as chipped, polished and ground stone tools, stone and ceramic vessels, and marble and marine shell ornaments. Each category exhibits variability in the organisation of production and distribution.

Ornaments made of marine shell (i.e. *Spondylus gaederopus* and *Glycymeris* sp.) are attested in settlements in the Balkans from the earlier phases of the Neolithic, but more frequently in the LN. Their production has been recognized on several sites in the northern Aegean, in both Thessaly and Macedonia. Not surprisingly, the majority of 'production centres' of marine shell ornaments are located near the coast, such as Stavroupoli in Thessaloniki (Karali 2004), Makriyalos in central Macedonia (Pappa and Veropoulidou 2011) or Dimini in Thessaly (Tsouneki 1989). Some, however, are situated at some distance from the coast such as Sitagroi, which is 25–30 km inland (Nikolaidou 2010). Both long- and short-distance networks have been proposed for the distribution of the finished products in northern Greece. It has also been proposed that particular settlements were engaged in the production and distribution of marine shell ornaments, while other sites played a role in their onward distribution.

Marine shell ornaments also probably reached the Balkan interior, whether through long-distance movement of special individuals or through a series of local inter-community exchanges (Chapman *et al.* 2011), by several 'trade-routes'. Finished products of Aegean marine shells could have reached settlements in the Balkan interior via the Axios/Vardar and southern Morava rivers or through Eastern Thrace, while the latter route was probably used for marine shell ornaments found in Bulgaria and Romania (Kyparissi 2011). The origin of at least some such ornaments in the Balkan interior and western provinces of northern Greece could alternatively have been the eastern Adriatic coast (Dimitrijević and Tripković 2006; Ifantidis 2011; but see Bajnóczi *et al.* 2013).

Diverse exchange networks are further supported by the evidence for movement of 'exotic' lithic objects including ornaments, vessels, chipped- and to a lesser extent ground- and polished-stone tools (Tsoraki 2011a, 2011b). The production of chipped-stone tools in northern Greece shows a rather complex picture since different systems may have been active in different provinces, while the distance that various products travelled varied considerably (Perlès 1992). A large proportion of chipped-stone tools was manufactured locally, presumably by local residents, but some tools of high quality flint were probably produced by itinerant specialists and others exchanged as finished products, while raw materials also travelled at various scales and in various directions (Perlès 1992; Dimitriadis and Skourtopoulou 2003; Tringham 2003; Skourtopoulou 2004). There may be considerable differences in stone procurement strategies between sites within a single area, and between regions in northern Greece, while the degree to which Neolithic communities relied on local or non-local sources also varied. It has been proposed that chipped-stone tools made of high quality materials were procured from networks of regional and interregional scale (Dimitriadis and Skourtopoulou 2003; Tringham 2003).

The distances that various goods travelled and the scale of the exchange network for stone tools may be illustrated by the distribution of obsidian. Most of the obsidian found in northern Greece is of Melian origin, and examples have been found as far away as Neolithic Passo di Corvo in the southern Italian Tavoliere (Perlès 1992). Obsidian tools of Carpathian origin found at a few Neolithic sites in Macedonia show that northern Greece also received some obsidian from other sources (Kilikoglou et al. 1996; Tringham 2003; Milić 2014; this volume). It is interesting to note that Carpathian obsidian reached northern Greece, but Melian obsidian is yet to be found in the Balkan interior (Milić 2014), even though Aegean *Spondylus* ornaments regularly reached this area. Furthermore, at Sitagroi in eastern Macedonia, a piece from Cappadocia in central Turkey has been identified along with Melian obsidian. Cappadocian obsidian testifies to relations between northern Greece and Anatolia, while Carpathian obsidian links northern Greece with the Balkan interior (Tripković and Milić 2008) and, together with honey flint and *Spondylus* ornaments, indicates a complex network with goods travelling in various directions: from south to the north, from east to the west, and vice versa.

In addition to Melian obsidian, stone ornaments and marble vessels also linked northern Greece with the Cyclades. Stone vessels found at LN Limenaria on the island of Thasos in the north Aegean were made from Cycladic marble, from Naxos and Paros (Maniatis *et al.* 2009), even though Thasos is itself rich in marble suitable for the production of vessels. The distance that Cycladic goods travelled in northern Greece is highlighted by stone jewelry found at Neolithic Dispilio in the mountainous interior of western Macedonia, far from the north Aegean coast (Ifantidis 2008; Ifantidis and Papageorgiou 2011).

A different scale of mobility is displayed by ceramic containers, most of which circulated on an intra-regional rather than inter-regional level (Pentedeka 2009; Saridaki 2011; Dimoula 2013). Pottery seems to have travelled somewhat greater distances in the later phases of the Neolithic when particular categories of ceramic wares (usually tableware) are found to have crossed regional boundaries (*e.g.* Hitsiou 2003; Kilikoglou *et al.* 2007; Pentedeka 2009).

The production and distribution patterns of stone tools, ornaments, and vases thus show that northern Greece was connected, as both provider and recipient of a variety of goods, with the Balkan interior, Cycladic islands, Anatolia and probably Adriatic coast through diverse exchange systems. Various networks coexisted and certain differences between regions seem to have existed. Furthermore, exchange networks and modes of exchange vary with the category of goods. As various materials discussed above illustrate, however, individual settlements within a single region played various roles in exchange networks. Thus, some settlements were important centres of production, distribution and redistribution, while others were less actively involved in regional exchange – at least of archaeologically visible materials and objects.

Exchange must have also encompassed other goods, the origins of which are more difficult to demonstrate, such as resins and tars. Research on these products in north Greece shows that among the taxa available to Neolithic people birch alone was systematically exploited to produce tar (*e.g.* Urem-Kotsou *et al.* 2002, Mitkidou *et al.* 2008). Exceptional occurrences of pine resin and pitch in LN amphorae indicate that this taxon too was occasionally exploited (Mitkidou *et al.* 2008). In contrast to the widespread distribution of pine, however, the occurrence of birch in northern Greece was very restricted as the pollen record and the analysis of charcoal from Neolithic settlements show (Gerasimidis and Athanasiadis 1995; Gerasimidis 1996; Ntinou and Badal 2000). Moreover, chemical analysis of birch bark tar found on Neolithic pottery indicates possible reuse of tar implying that it was precious to the inhabitants of the area under discussion. In spite of its scarcity, birch was favored throughout the Neolithic for the production of resinous substances, which were widely used for a variety of purposes (Mitkidou *et al.* 2008). These investigations thus show that resins and tars might not always have been available locally, implying movement of some people to procure raw material and to provide resin and tar lumps to communities distant from the sources.

Various ingredients and commodities less visible archaeologically, such as salt, must have also played a dynamic role in connecting Neolithic people in the Balkans. The rest of this paper focusses on salt, which must have been important to early farmers. The importance of salt for prehistoric communities was already recognized by Gordon Childe (1929) and many scholars have related this vital commodity to the initial accumulation of wealth and early social stratification in the Balkans.

Salt

It is likely that salt was appreciated very early in prehistory, possibly already from the Paleolithic period (Chapman *et al.* 2001), but its importance as a vital commodity has been related to the shift from hunting and gathering to agriculture and food production. Among the uses of salt that have been suggested as vital to Neolithic economies, its role in human and animal diet, food preservation and tanning are usually underlined. From a nutritional point of view, it is argued that a certain amount of salt is essential for both humans and animals. The quantity of salt needed to satisfy physiological needs has been conservatively estimated as 2–5 g per person per day or at least a kilogram per year (Tasić 2000: 36; Mitewa and Kolev 2012: 343). In the case of human diets based on a sufficient quantity of raw or roasted meat and fish there is no physiological necessity for additional salt, but additional salt is needed for human diets based on food of plant origin (cereals, pulses, vegetables), as was the case in the Neolithic. For animals, a varied diet drawn from a large area of pasture ensures sufficient salt intake. In the case of restricted variety, however, as may be the case for domesticated animals in particular seasons of the year (notably in winter), additional quantities of salt are required. For example, the estimated annual need for a cow is at least 10.3 kg and for a sheep or goat 3.6 kg per head (Tasić 2000: 36; see also Chapman *et al.* 2001: 11). Accepting even the most conservative estimates, it appears that early farming communities would have required a considerable quantity of salt annually to satisfy human and animal dietary needs. To this should be added the use of salt for other practical purposes like preservation of food, tanning, and curing or for more symbolic ends (*e.g.* Moga 2009). It seems likely, therefore, that the changes in subsistence pattern and dietary habits, which characterize the shift from hunting and gathering to farming and sedentism (*e.g.* Barker 2006), required the production and exchange of salt from early in the Neolithic period.

It is important to note that salt sources are distributed rather unevenly in space and differ in terms of form and accessibility. Apart from salt of marine origin available in coastal zones, in continental Europe sources of salt are restricted to particular regions where it occurs as a mineral in the form of rock-salt, dissolved as brine in salt springs, lakes and marshes, or as salty soils with halophyte vegetation. Not all salt sources were easily accessible to early farmers, since salt deposits could naturally occur at considerable depth. Given that salt is necessary for human and animal physiology it is reasonable to expect that early farmers that settled in regions devoid of salt sources were forced to procure salt from salt-rich regions. In spite of its character as an essential commodity, methodological problems in recognizing salt production, trade and use have been a serious obstacle to the investigation of its role in early farming communities. Because of the scarcity of reliable material evidence for the early exploitation of salt sources and particularly for its trade, scholars often turn to ethnography as an alternative method for better understanding the processes involved and the material evidence related to these activities.

On the basis of ethnographic data and historical sources, various modes of production of salt have been proposed (*e.g.* Adshead 1992; Chapman *et al.* 2001; Moga 2009; Cavruc and Harding 2012). Depending on the type of source exploited, these involve two entirely different salt winning techniques: evaporation of brine and mining of rock-salt. Archaeological visibility of salt-making depends on the mode, scale and purpose of salt production (*e.g.* for household consumption or for trade). However, the exploitation of salt sources does not always require sophisticated techniques and specialized equipment which would leave recognizable material evidence in the archaeological record. Just a supply of salt and fuel, or even manual labour, with minimal if any equipment for harvesting salt from naturally evaporating salt lakes, might suffice to obtain a considerable quantity (Adshead 1992; Moga 2009) while leaving hardly any archaeological trace.

Production and trading of salt in prehistory

The practical and symbolic use, importance and value of salt are well documented in history. For prehistory, however, such information was until recently almost entirely lacking. To some extent this is because the significance of salt in European prehistory only fairly recently emerged as an important issue. Archaeological investigations in recent decades have brought to light the first reliable evidence for early exploitation of salt sources in prehistory, but this has mainly shed light on the methods and techniques applied in early salt production, and on the material traces and artifacts related to these activities, while the movement of salt as an exchange commodity is still inferred indirectly as will be discussed below. Also, for prehistory, the exploitation of continental sources of salt is far better known than that of marine sources.

One of the earliest methods of obtaining salt documented archaeologically, at least in central and northern Europe, appears to have been the evaporation of dissolved rock-salt by the briquetage technique, which involves boiling of brine in ceramic vessels. This was followed by rock-salt mining, which in turn preceded the growing evidence for sea-salt extraction in later periods in this part of Europe (Saile 2012: 233). The earliest briquetage found in central Europe dates to the Middle Neolithic (mid-5th millennium BC) (Saile 2012, 229). In the western Mediterranean the earliest evidence of salt making also dates to the Middle Neolithic (end of the 5th millennium BC), but is related to rock-salt mining (Weller 2002). Remains of briquetage have been reported from several sites in this area dated to the Bronze Age (Guerra-Doce *et al.* 2011; 2012; Attema and Alessandri 2012). In the eastern Mediterranean, evidence of the exploitation and use of salt is dated as early as the Neolithic in Anatolia (7th millennium BC) and the Bronze Age in the Aegean. Clear evidence of the techniques applied in the early exploitation of salt in Anatolia is yet to be found. Collecting surface crystallized salt from an evaporating salt lake was suggested for the area around lake Tuz Gölü in central Anatolia (Atalay and Hastorf 2006; Erdogu and Özbasaran 2008). Collecting sea salt from natural salterns (*e.g.* rock pools by the sea) and brine evaporation in pots have been suggested for the single firm evidence of salt exploitation and use in the Aegean reported so far (Kopaka and Chaniotakis 2003). In southeastern Europe, as will be discussed in more detail below, the earliest salt making is dated to the Early Neolithic (end of the 7th millennium BC). The techniques used in this early salt production are still not fully understood, but seem not to have involved briquetage (Weller and Dumitroaia 2005).

There is increasing archaeological evidence, therefore, which testifies to the importance of salt for early farming communities in Europe. Direct archaeological evidence for the exploitation of salt sources, in the form of tools for mining rock salt and distinctive ceramic vessels for boiling brine, indicates that several techniques were applied during prehistory. The most widely attested technique is briquetage, although it should be noted that this technique is more easily recognizable archaeologically due to the large volume of distinctive ceramics that it generates. Ordinary household pottery might also have been used to process brine, particularly in the earlier phases of the Neolithic, but this type of salt production would be more difficult to confirm archaeologically. Other techniques, which do not require particular equipment and so are not readily recognizable archaeologically, must also have been used by early farmers, like collecting crystallized salt from the surface, as the cases of Tuz Gölü in Anatolia and the Bronze Age Aegean suggest.

Several authors have pointed to settlement patterns as indirect evidence for the exploitation of salt and its importance to early farmers. Thus, settlements close to salt sources may be unusually numerous, long lasting or wealthy, inviting the suggestion that salt is the cause of their success (*e.g.* Weller 2002; Tasić 2009; Cavruc and Harding 2012; Perić 2012; Bánffy 2013). Likewise, exotic objects found within salt-producing regions have been taken as an indication of the production of salt and of its high value as an exchange commodity (*e.g.* Weller 2002; Nikolov 2012). For example, some authors relate *Spondylus* objects directly to trade in salt between inland areas and coastal sites of salt production in the Mediterranean (Saile 2012: 232). The reconstruction of salt exchange networks has also been attempted by tracking other types of exotic objects, such as marble ornaments (Zapotocka 1984) or exotic lithic materials including radiolarite and obsidian (Kalicz 2011; Saile 2012: 232–233). Similarly, it has been suggested that the same trade network brought salt and obsidian to the Neolithic settlement of Çatalhöyük in Anatolia (Atalay and Hastorf 2006).

In the present state of research into salt, the study of production is more firmly based than that of exchange, for two principal and interrelated reasons. On the one hand, investigations have so far focussed on likely sources of salt and the sometimes abundant evidence for methods of salt production. On the other hand, the exchange of salt is extremely difficult to document archaeologically. The probability that salt was traded in perishable containers (*e.g.* leather, textile, baskets) is a serious obstacle, but, even if ceramic vessels were used, it would be difficult to confirm that they carried salt, despite the progress in scientific analysis of pottery contents. For the earlier phases of the Neolithic, Weller (2002) and Tasić (2009) suggest that salt was freely exploited and not reserved for a small number of local specialists, which implies movement of individuals and groups from different places to the sources of salt, small-scale production and perhaps short-chain exchange. In the later phases of the Neolithic and particularly in the Bronze Age, there is increasing evidence for specialized production and trade in salt. Recent finds from Bulgaria and Romania are particularly enlightening in this respect (Nikolov 2008; 2010; 2012; Cavruc and Harding 2012).

Salt production, exchange and consumption in the Balkans

The central Balkans, the core area of the EN Starčevo and LN Vinča cultures, is poor in salt sources, as is Transdanubia (the Hungarian plain), which stretches immediately to the north. Together the two regions form a very extensive salt-poor territory. A few areas of salty soil, known as *Slatina*, provide the only available salt in the central Balkans and these could barely have met the needs of the numerous Neolithic settlements of the Starčevo and Vinča cultures that flourished in this region. Conversely, some neighbouring regions are rich in salt. Apart from the Adriatic and northern Aegean coasts, there are particular areas of the Balkan interior where salt is available as a rock mineral or as a crystalline product collected from brine springs or streams. The closest inland sources of salt to the salt-poor central Balkans are located in Bosnia and Transylvania (Romania). If additional salt was a neolithic dietary necessity or at least highly desired to flavour bland grain-based dishes, then early farmers in this vast area must, arguably, have depended on salt obtained from salt-rich regions, suggesting that some kind of exchange of salt must have existed from the Early Neolithic. Until recently, however, there was extremely limited evidence for the production of salt in the prehistoric Balkans.

The earliest reliable evidence comes from the recently excavated site of Poiana Slatinei at Lunca in Romania, where Early Neolithic pottery and radiocarbon dates point to the exploitation of a salt spring by the end of the 7th millennium BC. Huge amounts of ash, charcoal and burnt soil without evidence of briquetage points to the exploitation of salt by a technique which involved fire without pottery, or at least without typical briquetage vessels. The exploitation of the spring was facilitated by the exceptionally strong natural concentration of salt, six times that of sea water (Weller and Dumitroaia 2005). The scale of this early production, which might point to exchange of salt, is yet to be determined. Further evidence of early exploitation of salt comes from the salt-rich site near modern Tuzla in northeast Bosnia. Until recently, this was the only known site of Neolithic salt production in the Balkans. Conical vessels, found in the vicinity of the salt sources and related to the evaporation of brine (Tasić 2009), are unique to this site, implying that they were made for organized production of salt.

Although still extremely limited, these findings suggest that salt was also of some importance for Neolithic communities in the Balkans. The distribution of Neolithic settlements in relation to presently known salt sources in the Middle Morava valley in central Serbia further indicates the importance of salt for early farmers. Although this area is not rich in salt sources, modern *Slatina* toponyms suggest that salt might have been available in the form of salty soil with halophyte vegetation. Early farmers could easily have identified such saline soils by observing the distinctive halophytic vegetation that grew in the vicinity of salt springs, or by observing the behaviour of grazing animals. Some 86 Neolithic settlements, many belonging to the Early Neolithic (EN), have been recorded so far in an area 45 km × 25 km in extent and most are located in the vicinity of salty soils. A few of the sites were inhabited throughout the Neolithic period and were unusually large, covering 20–50 ha (Perić 2012). Perić relates the lifespan and size of these settlements, at least to some extent, to proximity to salt sources. A similar concentration of Neolithic settlements in relation to salty soils has been observed in central Bosnia (Perić 2012).

Indirect evidence for the exploitation of salt in the Balkan interior during the earlier phases of the Neolithic is also seen in the striking mixture of contemporaneous cultures in salt-rich zones, including the Starčevo-Körös area to the north, the Starčevo-Criș area in salt-rich Transylvania to the northeast, and the salt-rich region around Tuzla in Bosnia, at the westernmost edge of the Starčevo culture. This phenomenon has been interpreted as an indication that salt, as an important commodity, brought different groups of people to areas rich in salt sources (Tasić 2000; 2009; 2012). Tasić interprets such a mixture of cultures in the earlier phases of the Neolithic as indicating a lack of monopoly over salt sources and thus the common interest of early farmers in this vital commodity. The scale of production and control over salt sources during the earlier phases of the Neolithic, however, certainly requires further investigation.

Recent discoveries from Romania and particularly Bulgaria provide information on production and exchange of salt in the later phases of the Neolithic (later 6th and

5th millennia BC) and in the Bronze Age. These finds suggest some changes in the production and exploitation of salt which may be related to social changes in the Late and Final Neolithic communities of the Balkan interior. Several scholars have observed that the richest material evidence for social inequality in this period in the Balkans is found in salt-rich areas, such as the so called Precucuteni and Cucuteni cultural complex in the Carpathian region and the Varna culture in northeast Bulgaria. They relate the prosperity of these societies to the systematic exploitation of salt for trade (Cavruc and Harding 2012; Nikolov 2012).

Excavations in the last few years at the Provadia tell site near Varna, dated to 5500–4200 BC, have brought to light direct evidence of large-scale production of salt in the later phases of the Neolithic (Nikolov 2012: 11–65). Provadia lies in the area of the richest salt deposits in SE Europe and was directly related to the production of salt. Throughout the settlement's lifespan, salt was produced by boiling brine in ceramic vessels made exclusively for this purpose, but the scale and mode of production changed through time. It has been estimated that the exploitation of salt sources already exceeded household needs from the initial phase of settlement, implying production of salt for trade. In particular, during the first phase (5500–5200 BC), salt was extracted in thin-walled vessels placed in special massive domed kilns located within the settlement. The estimated production capacity of each kiln was up to 10 tons annually, or 26–28 kg of purified hard salt per day (Nikolov 2012: 16–17). In the next phase (5200–4900 BC), brine continued to be boiled in a particular pottery type but in shallow pit installations near the settlement mound, which increased productivity to up to four times the capacity of the previous phase (Nikolov 2012: 22). Significant changes occurred from the following phase of the settlement dated to 4700 BC, when a large production complex was set up near the settlement and the technological process was again modified. Brine was boiled in numerous large ceramic vessels, but this time placed in deep, wide pits which enabled a further sharp increase in the scale of production, characterized by the excavator as 'industrial' (Nikolov 2012: 22).

The Provadia tell site is the only place in the Balkans identified so far where salt was produced on such a large scale that it could have been traded over long distances as early as the mid-6th millennium BC. The remarkable increase in production during the 5th millennium indicates that salt became a medium of exchange in long-distance trade (Nikolov 2012: 58). Provadia is directly related to the pronounced wealth of the society in the area of the Varna Lakes and has been linked to the famous cemetery of Varna with its exceptionally rich graves (Nikolov 2012: 26). The Varna culture (4700–4200 BC) has been considered a society with very early institutionalization of power and it is suggested that the economic prosperity of the Black Sea region, otherwise poor in natural sources, was based on the production and trade of salt in return for which various raw materials and luxury goods were acquired (Nikolov 2012: 58–62).

Recent investigations in Transylvania have brought to light other firm archaeological evidence for large-scale production of salt in later prehistory, involving mining of rock-salt and differing in many respects from the Provadia case. Investigations at the Băile Figa site have uncovered exceptionally well preserved wooden installations dating to the Bronze Age, which point to a complex system of sophisticated techniques for the extraction and exploitation of rock-salt sources. It is suggested that salt was produced in various forms, from cube shaped blocks and irregular lumps to shredded salt. The variability in salt form has been related to differences in the length of exchange, from long-distance (cubic blocks) to short-distance exchange (shredded salt) (Cavruc and Harding 2012). It is interesting to note that, despite the industrial character of salt production in this area, there is no trace of habitation close to loci of salt production, suggesting "that the producers paid regular visits to the production sites, but did not live there" (Cavruc and Harding 2012, 194). Cavruc and Harding further proposed that the salt sources in this area were exploited by people belonging to different cultures, implying that there was no monopoly of local sources of salt during the Bronze Age as was the case at Neolithic Provadia. They also underline a clear contrast between the observed continuity in technology and discontinuity in archaeological cultures in the area, leading them to propose 'supra-cultural' exploitation of salt (Cavruc and Harding 2012, 196).

The examples described above support the view that salt, already from the mid-6th millennium BC, was not only a dietary necessity produced for immediate household consumption and short-distance exchange, but also one of several highly valued goods circulating in middle- to long-distance exchange networks. Significantly, luxury goods such as gold ornaments, which appeared from the early 5th millennium BC, were found in salt-rich regions and not in the salt-less and salt-poor regions of the central Balkans, while the similarity of the gold pendants ('ring idols') found in this period in Anatolia, Greece, the Balkans and as far north as eastern Slovakia is striking (Zimmermann 2007; Zahos 2010). Less often these were also made of silver and lead, occasionally of clay or marble, and sometimes they were depicted as painted decoration on vessels (Zahos 2010: 88). Similarly, *Spondylus* ornaments, which represent luxury goods in the earlier phases of the Neolithic, reach their peak of popularity in the Late Neolithic all over the Balkans and up to central Europe (Séfériadès 2010).

Although there is direct evidence for Neolithic production of salt in southeast Europe only from the northern Balkans, salt must surely also have been produced on the Adriatic and Aegean coasts and might have been at least occasionally exchanged, along with other goods such as marine shell ornaments and lithics, to their northern neighbours.

To sum up, direct evidence for prehistoric salt production and exchange is still very scarce, but suffices to indicate that this commodity was important to early farmers. The striking mixture of earlier Neolithic cultures in the salt-rich regions of the Balkan Peninsula may indicate that salt brought different groups of people together and that none of these groups monopolized its production. In the Late and Final Neolithic there are indications of increased specialization in the production of salt and of longer-distance exchange in the northern part of the Balkans. Particular groups, such as the inhabitants of Provadia, probably had some control over the sources and production of salt. The increased significance of exotic commodities, such as marble and marine shell ornaments and a little later gold jewelry, all over the Balkans and northern Aegean in this period, may not be irrelevant to this issue.

Conclusions

Similarities in various forms of material culture indicate continuous communication between the regions of the Balkans and north Aegean throughout the Neolithic. Movement of material culture, in the form of finished or half-finished objects and raw materials, reveals rich and diverse networks of exchange. Some materials and objects travelled short and medium distances, while others were part of long-range exchange systems. The latter point to both long-distance travel by individuals or small groups and to enchained exchange through a series of local inter-community interactions. It is noticeable that larger amount of materials travelled long-distances particularly in the later phases of the Neolithic. Large-scale production of salt at this time coincided with long-distance movement of luxury items such as *Spondylus*, and with widespread sharing of material culture styles. Together these imply intensive movement of at least individual people and exchanges of ideas across the Balkans. Unequal access to production and exchange of exotic prestige goods and scarce commodities such as salt seems to have played an active role in the social changes observed in the Neolithic Balkans, of which the most prominent example is the early institutionalization of power testified in exceptionally rich graves at the cemetery of Varna.

Acknowledgements

I am grateful to Paul Halstead and Barry Molloy for stimulating discussions and comments on the paper. Nenad Tasić, Olga Perić and Drenovac project team are thanked for providing me with literature on salt in the region. Stavros Kotsos was a good source for new data on the Neolithic of the central Balkans. Maria Ntinou provided information on halophyte vegetation and Marina Milić on the circulation of obsidian in northern Greece and the Balkans.

References

Adshead, S.A.M.
1992 *Salt and Civilization*, New York: Palgrave Macmillan.

Atalay, S. and C. Hastorf
2006 Food, meals, and daily activities: food habitus at Neolithic Çatalhöyük. *American Antiquity* 71(2): 283–319.

Attema, P. and L. Alessandri
2012 Salt production on the Tyrrhenian coast in South Lazio (Italy) during the Late Bronze Age: its significance for understanding contemporary society. In V. Nikolov and K. Bacvarov (eds.), *Salt and Gold: The Role of Salt in Prehistoric Europe*: 287–300. Provadia, Veliko Tarnovo: Verlag Faber.

Bajnóczi, B., B. Schöll-Barna, N. Kalicz, Z. Siklósi, G.H. Hourmuziadis, F. Ifantidis, A. Kyparissi-Apostolika, M. Pappa, R. Veropoulidou and C. Ziota
2013 Tracing the source of Late Neolithic *Spondylus* shell ornaments by stable isotope geochemistry and cathodoluminescence microscopy. *Journal of Archaeological Science* 40: 874–882.

Bánffy, E.
2013 Tracing 6th-5th millennium BC salt exploitation in the Carpathian Basin. In A. Harding and V. Kavruk (eds.), *Explorations in Salt Archaeology in the Carpathian Zone* (Archaeolingua Alapítvány 49): 201–207. Budapest: Archaeolingua.

Barker, G.
2006 *The Agricultural Revolution in Prehistory*, Oxford: Oxford University Press.

Cavruc, V. and A. Harding
2012 Prehistoric production and exchange of salt in the Carpathian-Danube region. In V. Nikolov and K. Bacvarov (eds.), *Salt and Gold: The Role of Salt in Prehistoric Europe*: 173–200. Provadia, Veliko Tarnovo: Verlag Faber.

Chapman, J., B. Gaydarska, E. Skafida and S. Souvatzi
2011 Personhood and the life cycle of Spondylus rings: an example from Late Neolithic Greece. In F. Ifantidis and M. Nikolaidou (eds.), *Spondylus in Prehistory: New Data and Approaches – Contributions to the Archaeology of Shell Technologies* (BAR International Series 2216): 139–160. Oxford: British Archaeological Reports.

Chapman, J., D. Monah, G. Dumitroaia, H. Armstrong, A. Millard and M. Francis
2001 The exploitation of salt in the prehistory of Moldavia, Romania. *Archaeological Reports Universities of Durham and Newcastle-upon-Tyne* 23: 10–20.

Childe, V.G.
1929 *The Most Ancient East: The Oriental Prelude to European Prehistory*. New York: Alfred A. Knopf.

Dimitriadis, S. and K. Skourtopoulou
2003 Petrographic examination of chipped stone materials. In E. Elster and C. Renfrew (eds.), *Prehistoric Sitagroi: Excavations in Northeast Greece, 1968-1970, 2: The Final Report*: 127–132. Los Angeles: Cotsen of Archaeology, UCLA.

Dimitrijević, V. and B. Tripković
2006 *Spondylus* and *Glycymeris* bracelets trade reflections at Neolithic Vinča-Belo Brdo. *Documenta Praehistorica* 33: 237–252.

Dimoula, A.
2012 Proimi Keramiki Tekhnologia kai Paragogi. To Paradigma tis Thessalias. PhD dissertation, Aristotle University of Thessaloniki.

Dimoula, A., A. Pentedeka and K. Filis
in press Lete I. The pottery of a Neolithic site in central Macedonia 100 years after. In *Ekato Khronia Erevnas stin Proistoriki Makedonia*. Thessaloniki: Archaeological Museum of Thessaloniki.

Douka, K.
2011 The contribution of archaeometry to the study of prehistoric marine shells. In F. Ifantidis and M. Nikolaidou (eds.), *Spondylus in Prehistory: New Data and Approaches - Contributions to the Archaeology of Shell Technologies* (BAR International Series 2216): 171–180. Oxford: British Archaeological Reports.

Erdoğu, B. and M. Özbasaran
2008 Salt in prehistoric Central Anatolia. In O. Weller, A. Dufraisse and P. Pétrequin (eds.), *Sel, eau et forêt: d' hier à aujourd' hui. Actes du colloque international de la Saline Royale d' Arc-et-Senans*, octobre 2006 (Cahiers de la MSHE Ledoux 12): 163–174. Besançon: Presses universitaires de Franche-Comte.

Garašanin, M.
1979 Centralnobalkanska zona. In *Praistorija Jugoslavenskih zemalja II: Neolitsko doba*: 79–212. Sarajevo: ANU BiH.

Gerasimidis, A.
1996 Parelthon kai paron ton emfaniseon tis simidas (*Betula*) stin Ellada. In *Praktika 6' Epistimonikou Sunedriou, Paralimni-Kupros 6-11 Apriliou*: 126–132. Paralimni: Elliniki Votaniki Etairia, Viologiki Etairia Kuprou.

Gerasimidis, A. and N. Athanasiadis
1995 Woodland history of northern Greece from the mid Holocene to recent time based on evidence from peat pollen profiles. *Vegetation History and Archaeobotany* 4: 109–116.

Guerra-Doce, E., F.J. Abarquero-Moras, G. Delibes de Castro, J.M. del Val-Recio and A.L. Palomino-Lázaro
2012 Salt production at the Villafáfila Lake Complex (Zamora, Spain) in prehistoric times. In V. Nikolov and K. Bacvarov (eds.), *Salt and Gold: The Role of Salt in Prehistoric Europe*: 287–300. Provadia, Veliko Tarnovo: Verlag Faber.

Guerra-Doce, E., G. Delibes de Castro, F.J. Abarquero-Moras, J.M. del Val-Recio and A.L. Palomino-Lázaro
2011 The beaker salt production centre of Molino Sanchón II, Zamora, Spain. *Antiquity* 85: 805–811.

Halstead, P.
1989 The economy has a normal surplus: economic stability and social change among early farming communities of Thessaly, Greece. In P. Halstead and J. O'Shea (eds.), *Bad Year Economics: Cultural Responses to Risk and Uncertainty*: 68–80. Cambridge: Cambridge University Press.
2005 Resettling the Neolithic: faunal evidence for seasons of consumption and residence at Neolithic sites in Greece. In D. Bailey, A. Whittle and V. Cummings (eds.), *(un)settling the Neolithic*: 38–50. Oxford: Oxbow Books.
2011 Farming, material culture and ideology: repackaging the Neolithic of Greece (and Europe). In A. Hadjikoumis, E. Robinson and S. Viner (eds.), *Dynamics of Neolithisation in Europe*: 131–151. Oxford and Oakville: Oxbow Books.

Hitsiou, E.
2003 Production and Circulation of the Neolithic Pottery from Makrygialos (Phase II), Macedonia, Northern Greece. PhD dissertation, University of Sheffield.

Hondrogianni-Metoki, A.
2001 Egnatia odos, anaskafi stin proistoriki thesi 'Toumba Kremastis-Koiladas', Nomou Kozanis. *To Arkhaiologiko Ergo sti Makedonia kai Thraki* 13: 399–413.

Ifantidis, F.
2008 Lithinoi daktulioi apo to Dispilio. *Anaskamma* 1: 79–92.
2011 *Cosmos* in fragments: *Spondylus* and *Glycymeris* adornments at Neolithic Dispilio. In F. Ifantidis and M. Nikolaidou (eds.), *Spondylus in Prehistory: New Data and Approaches - Contributions to the Archaeology of Shell Technologies* (BAR International Series 2216): 123–137. Oxford: British Archaeological Reports.

Ifantidis, F. and P. Papageorgiou
2011 Sur un anneau néolithique en marbre fragmenté (Dispilio, Grèce). In F. Wateau, C. Perlès and P. Soulier (eds.), *Profils d'objets. Approches d'anthropologues et d'archéologues. VIIe colloque annuel de la Maison René-Ginouvès, Archéologie et Ethnologie*: 33–43. Paris: Éditions De Boccard.

Kalicz, N.
2011 *Méhtelek. The First Excavated Site of the Méhtelek Group of the Early Neolithic Körös Culture in the Carpathian Basin* (BAR/Archaeolingua, Central European Series 6). Oxford: British Archaeological Reports.

Karali, L.
2004 Anaskafi Stavroupolis: malakologiko uliko. In D. Grammenos and S. Kotsos, *Sostikes Anaskafes sto Neolithiko Oikismo Stavroupolis Thessalonikis, II (1998-2003)*: 527–603. Thessaloniki: Arkhaiologiko Instituto Vorias Elladas.

Kilikoglou, V., Y. Bassiakos, A.P, Grimanis, K. Souvatzis, A. Pilali-Papasteriou and A. Papanthimou-Papaefthimiou
1996 Carpathian obsidian in Macedonia, Greece. *Journal of Archaeological Science* 23: 343–349.

Kilikoglou, V., A.P. Grimanis, A. Tsolakidou, A. Hein, D. Malamidou and Z. Tsirtsoni
2007 Neutron Activation patterning of archaeological materials at the national center for scientific research 'Democritos': the case of black-on-red neolithic pottery from Macedonia, Greece. *Archaeometry* 49(2): 301–319.

Kopaka, K. and N. Chaniotakis
2003 Just taste additive? Bronze Age salt from Zakros, Crete. *Oxford Journal of Archaeology* 22(1): 53–66.

Kotsakis, K.
1999 What tells can tell: social space and settlement in the Greek Neolithic. In P. Halstead (ed.), *Neolithic Society in Greece* (Sheffield Studies in Aegean Archaeology 2): 66–76. Sheffield: Sheffield Academic Press.
in press Domesticating the periphery. New research into the Neolithic of Greece. In J. Bintliff (ed.), Recent Development in the long-term Archaeology of Greece. *Pharos. Journal of the Nederlands Institute at Athens*, Assen: Koninklijke Van Gorcum BV 2014. pp. 41–73.

Kotsos, S.
2014. Settlement and housing during the 6th millennium B.C. in western Thessaloniki and the adjacent Langadas province. In E. Stefani, N. Merousis and A. Dimoula (eds.), *A Century of Research in Prehistoric Macedonia 1912-2012*, pp. 315–322. Thessaloniki: Zitis.

Kyparissi-Apostolika, N.
2001 *Ta Proistorika Kosmimata tis Thessalias*. Athens: Ministry of Culture.
2011 *Spondylus* objects from Theopetra Cave, Greece: imported or local production? In F. Ifantidis and M. Nikolaidou (eds.), *Spondylus in Prehistory: New Data and Approaches - Contributions to the Archaeology of Shell Technologies* (BAR International Series 2216): 161–167. Oxford: British Archaeological Reports.

Maniatis, Y., S. Papadopoulos, E. Dotsika, E. Kavoussanaki and E. Tzavidopoulos
2009 Provenance investigation of Neolithic marble vases from Limenaria, Thassos: imported marble to Thassos? In Y. Maniatis (ed.), *Asmosia 7* (BCH supplement 51): 439–449. Athens: École française d'Athènes.

Milić, M.
2014 PXRF characterisation of obsidian from central Anatolia, the Aegean and central Europe. *Journal of Archaeological Science* 41: 285–296.

Mitewa, M. and H. Kolev
2012 Sodium Chloride: food and poison. In V. Nikolov and K. Bacvarov (eds.), *Salt and Gold: The Role of Salt in Prehistoric Europe*: 341–344. Provadia, Veliko Tarnovo: Verlag Faber.

Mitkidou, S., E. Dimitrakoudi, D. Urem-Kotsou, D. Papadopoulou, K. Kotsakis, J. Stratis and I. Stephanidou-Stephanatou
2008 Organic residue analysis of Neolithic pottery from North Greece. *Microchemica Acta* 160(4): 493–498.

Moga, I.
2009 Salt extraction and imagery in the ancient Near East. *Journal of Interdisciplinary Research on Religion and Science* 4: 175–213.

Nikolaidou, M.
2010 Kosmimata sti Neolithiki Makedonia. In N. Merousis, E. Stefani and M. Nikolaidou (eds.), *Iris*: 137–154. Thessaloniki: Ekdosis Kornilia Sfakianaki.

Nikolov, V.
2008 *Praistoriceski solodobiven centar Provadia-Solnitsata. Razkopki 2005-2007 g*. Sofia: NAIM-BAN.
2010 *Solta e Zlato. Praistoriceski solodobiven centar Provadia-Solnitsata*. Sofia: NAIM-BAN.
2012 Salt, early complex society, urbanization: Provadia-Solnitsata (5500–4200 BC). In V. Nikolov and K. Bacvarov (eds.), *Salt and Gold: The Role of Salt in Prehistoric Europe*: 11–67. Provadia, Veliko Tarnovo: Verlag Faber.

Ntinou, M. and E. Badal
2000 Local vegetation and charcoal analysis: an example from two Late Neolithic sites in Northern Greece. In P. Halstead and C. Frederick (eds.), *Landscape and Land Use in Postglacial Greece* (Sheffield Studies in Aegean Archaeology 3): 38–52. Sheffield: Sheffield Academic Press.

Pappa, M.
2008 Organosi tou Khorou kai Oikistika Stoikhia stous Neolithikous Oikismous tis Kentrikis Makedonias. PhD dissertation, Aristotle University of Thessaloniki.

Pappa, M. and R. Veropoulidou
2011 The Neolithic settlement at Makriyalos, northern Greece: evidence from the *Spondylus gaederopus* artifacts. In F. Ifantidis and M. Nikolaidou (eds.), *Spondylus in Prehistory: New Data and Approaches - Contributions to the Archaeology of Shell Technologies* (BAR International Series 2216): 105–121. Oxford: British Archaeological Reports.

Pappa, M., P. Halstead, K. Kotsakis and D. Urem-Kotsou
2004 Evidence for large-scale feasting at Late Neolithic Makriyalos, north Greece. In P. Halstead and J. Barrett (eds.), *Food, Cuisine and Society in Prehistoric Greece* (Sheffield Studies in Aegean Archaeology 5): 16–44. Oxford: Oxbow Books.

Pentedeka, A.
2009 Diktua Antallagis tis Keramikis kata ti Mesi kai Neoteri Neolithiki sti Thessalia. PhD dissertation, Aristotle University of Thessaloniki.

Perić, S.
2012 Die neolithischen Siedlungen in der mittleren Morava-Ebene und die Slatina-Toponymie. In V. Nikolov and K. Bacvarov (eds.), *Salt and Gold: The Role of Salt in Prehistoric Europe*: 219–224. Provadia, Veliko Tarnovo: Verlag Faber.

Perlès, C.
1992 Systems of exchange and organization of production in Neolithic Greece. *Journal of Mediterranean Archaeology* 5(2): 115–164.

Saile, T.
2012 Salt in the Neolithic of central Europe: production and distribution. In V. Nikolov and K. Bacvarov (eds.), *Salt and Gold: The Role of Salt in Prehistoric Europe*: 225–238. Provadia, Veliko Tarnovo: Verlag Faber.

Saridaki, N.
2011 *Apsalos-Grammi. I Analusi tis Keramikis upo to Prisma tis Petrografias.* MA dissertation, Aristotle University of Thessaloniki.

Séfériadès, M.
2010 Spondylus and long-distance trade in prehistoric Europe. In D.W. Anthony and J.Y. Chi (eds.), *The Lost World of Old Europe: The Danube Valley 5000-3500 BC*: 178–189. Princeton: ISAW and Princeton University Press.

Shackleton, N.J. and C. Renfrew
1970 Neolithic trade routes re-aligned by Oxygen isotope analysis. *Nature* 228: 1062–1065.

Skourtopoulou, K.
2004 I lithotekhnia apokrousmenou lithou ston oikismo tis Stavroupolis. In D. Grammenos and S. Kotsos, *Sostikes Anaskafes sto Neolithiko Oikismo Stavroupolis Thessalonikis, II (1998-2003)*: 361–476. Thessaloniki: Arkhaiologiko Instituto Vorias Elladas.

Tasić, N.N.

2000 Salt use in the Early and Middle Neolithic of the Balkan Peninsula. In L. Nikolova (ed.), *Technology, Style and Society* (BAR International Series 854): 35–41. Oxford: Archaeopress.

2009 *Neolitska kvadratura kruga*. Beograd: Zavod za udzbenike.

2012 New evidence on salt use in the Neolithic of southeast Europe. In V. Nikolov and K. Bacvarov (eds.), *Salt and Gold: The Role of Salt in Prehistoric Europe*: 213–218. Provadia, Veliko Tarnovo: Verlag Faber.

Tringham, R.

2003 Flaked stone. In E. Elster and C. Renfrew (eds.), *Prehistoric Sitagroi: Excavations in Northeast Greece, 1968-1970, 2: The Final Report*: 81–126. Los Angeles: Cotsen Institute of Archaeology, UCLA.

Tripković, B. and M. Milić

2008 The origin and exchange of obsidian from Vinča–Belo Brdo. *Starinar* 58: 71–86.

Tsoraki, Ch.

2011a Disentangling Neolithic Networks. Ground Stone Technology, Material Engagements and Networks of Action. In A. Brysbaert (ed.), *Tracing Prehistoric Social Networks through Technology. A Diachronic Perspective on the Aegean*: 12–29. London/New York: Taylor & Francis

2011b Stone-working traditions in the prehistoric Aegean: The production and consumption of edge tools at Late Neolithic Makriyalos. In V. Davis and M. Edmonds (eds.), *Stone Axe Studies III*: 231–244. Oxford: Oxbow Books.

Tsuneki, A.

1989 The manufacture of Spondylus shell objects at neolithic Dimini, Greece. *Orient* 25: 1–21.

Urem-Kotsou, D.

in press Changing pottery technology in the later Neolithic in north Greece. In C. Knappett and E. Kiriatzi (eds.), *Human Mobility and Technological Transfer in the Prehistoric Mediterranean*. Cambridge: Cambridge University Press.

Urem-Kotsou, D. and K. Kotsakis

2007 Pottery, cuisine and community in the Neolithic of north Greece. In J. Renard and C. Mee (eds.), *Cooking up the Past: Food and Culinary Practices in the Neolithic and Bronze Aegean*: 225–246. Oxford: Oxbow Books.

Urem-Kotsou, D., B. Stern, C. Heron and K. Kotsakis

2002 Birch-bark tar at Neolithic Makriyalos, Greece. *Antiquity* 76: 962–967.

Weller, O.

2002 The earliest rock salt exploitation in Europe. A salt mountain in the Spanish Neolithic. *Antiquity* 76(2): 317–318.

Weller, O. and G. Dumitroaia

2005 The earliest salt production in the world: an early Neolithic exploitation in *Poiana Slatinei-Antiquity* Lunca, Romania *Antiquity*. 79. http://antiquity,ac.uk/ProjGall/weller/index.html

Zahos, K.

2010 I Metallourgia stin Ellada kai sti NA Evropi kata tin 5' kai 4' Khilietia p.Kh. In N. Papadimitriou and Z. Tsirtsoni (eds.), *I Ellada sto Evrutero Politismiko Plaisio ton Valkanion kata tin 5' kai 4' Khilietia p.Kh*: 77–91. Athens: Mouseio Kikladikis Texnis and Idrima Goulandri.

Zápotocká, M.

1984 Náramky z mramoru a jiných surovin v mladším neolitu Čech a střední Evropy. *Památky archeologické* 75(1): 50–130.

Zimmerman, T.

2007 Anatolia and the Balkans, once again - ring-shaped idols from western Asia and a critical reassessment of some 'Early Bronze Age' items from İkiztepe, Turkey. *Oxford Journal of Archaeology* 26(1): 25–33.

Chapter 7

Aspects of Connectivity on the Centre of the Anatolian Aegean Coast in 7th Millennium BC

Barbara Horejs

Introduction

Any discussion of the scales and modes of interaction between prehistoric Aegean societies is of necessity based on the archaeological view of the Aegean as one broad cultural area, merely subdivided into different regions that are not homogeneous, either in time or in intensity (*e.g.* Renfrew 1972; Maran 1998: esp. 450–457; Broodbank 2000; Perlès 2001). The commonly invoked principle of *Aegean connectivity* forms one of the basic requirements for understanding Aegean archaeology.

The specific character of this basic connectivity and, moreover, its recognisability in prehistory call for an analysis of various phenomena, such as raw material networks, systems of trading and bartering in specific goods, social and political comparability and countless others. It is nonetheless difficult to reach complete or satisfactory results as a result of the sheer quantity of archaeological evidence available. Theories of archaeological connectivity offer at least a methodological tool to deal with these quantities and to model discrete networks.

Çukuriçi Höyük and the centre of the Anatolian Aegean coast

Çukuriçi Höyük on the centre of the Anatolian Aegean coast is located on the Küçük Menderes river delta opposite the island of Samos and is embedded in a sheltered basin that used to have direct access to the Aegean Sea in prehistoric times (Figure 7.1) (Brückner 1997; Kraft *et al.* 2001; Stock *et al.* 2013). The site is a tell with many phases of occupation spanning 7th to 3rd millennium BC, and its specific location at the Aegean coast as well as in one of the main river valleys in Western Anatolia highlights an important environmental feature for its enduring role in communities linking overlapping Aegean and Anatolian networks. The tell was settled during different periods with six distinct settlement phases excavated so far (Figure 7.2), including Pottery Neolithic, Late Chalcolithic and Early Bronze Age periods (Horejs *et al.* 2011; Galik and Horejs 2011; Horejs *et al.* 2015). The surrounding basin of *c.* 10 sq km and adjacent hills provided open areas in prehistory for farming and livestock husbandry as well as wooded areas and sources of fresh water for man and beast alike. Botanical and zoological studies have revealed each of these aspects of subsistence strategies in all prehistoric periods, although chronological variations in faunal and floral species reveal diversity, and the varying numbers of each can

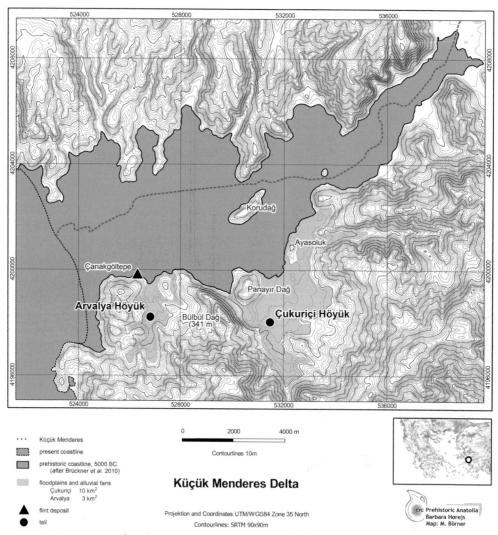

Figure 7.1: Reconstructed prehistoric environment around Çukuriçi Höyük (map by M. Börner/ERC Prehistoric Anatolia after Brückner 1997; Stock et al. 2013).

mainly be explained by cultural, climatic, and environmental changes over time. Alongside this, recent work has revealed the character of the latter two causes of change through pale geographical methods (Galik and Horejs 2011; Horejs *et al.* 2011: 50–60). Although changes in subsistence strategies and environmental conditions can be revealed clearly through various proxies, the point can be made that this micro-region offered all of the necessary scope for good living conditions and a high degree of self-sufficiency for prehistoric communities settled there.

Furthermore, geo-archaeological investigations have revealed a range of raw material sources in the immediate vicinity, such as sources of stone for polished tools or artefacts (*e.g.* serpentine, basalt, marble, quartz) or for use as building materials (marble, cist, limestone *etc.*) as well as chert suitable for producing knapped tools (Figure 7.1) (Wolf *et al.* 2012a; Wolf *et al.* 2012b). All these sources would have been known and utilised by Çukuriçi settlers at least since the 7th millennium BC, again with distinct variations in their significance and degree of active exploitation over time. In addition, imported raw materials which were used for the production of the same kind of objects and tools served very similar functions in practical, everyday terms. This has made it possible to shed light on the value of specific raw materials and exchange systems operating within this society and how this was integrated into a broader network.

Figure 7.2: Overview of Çukuriçi Höyük excavation with settlement phases (photo by N. Gail; illustration by F. Ostmann/ERC Prehistoric Anatolia).

Aspects of regional connectivity

The Neolithic societies of Çukuriçi Höyük can be seen as having been well integrated into a regional network through the material culture and the basic schemes and strategies for living in an early farming community. With the focus of recent research on prehistory on the centre of the Anatolian Aegean coast around modern Izmir, it is feasible for the first time to engage not only with single sites, but with a group of excavated settlements that all have horizons dating to the 7th millennium BC (Figure 7.3). The Neolithic settlements of Dedeçik Heybelitepe, Ege Gübre, Ulucak, Yeşilova and Çukuriçi Höyük make up a regional cluster that share more things in common than differences in many respects. Because detailed chronological debate should not be our ultimate objective, comparable settlement phases of this date can be extrapolated (if in a preliminary and tentative manner), on the basis of relative chronologies of the sites obtained by pottery studies (Çilingiroğlu 2012: 85 with modifications; Horejs 2012) and on radiocarbon dates recently published from those other sites (and Çukuriçi Höyük), allowing synchronisation of settlement horizons at each site.

Generally, the 7th millennium BC covers the Pottery Neolithic period in Anatolian chronology and can partially and only in some Anatolian regions be subdiveded in early and late phases (e.g. Özdoğan et al. 2007). Based on early history of research and east Anatolian and upper Mesopotamian chronologies, the Chalcolithic period is defined to start around 6000 BC (e.g. Schoop 2005). Although a real Copper Age in cultural sense does not exist in most part of Anatolia in these early stages and certainly not in western Turkey, the traditional basic frame work is (still) widely accepted. The recently excavated sites and their settlement phases at the centre of Anatolian Aegean coast are divided with Roman numerals, except Dedecik-Heybelitepe defining an older phase A followed by younger phase B (Herling et al. 2008).

The sites at the centre of Anatolian Aegean coast can be clustered in two main chronological Neolithic phases in 7th millennium: early (6700–6500 BC) and late (6500–5900/5800 BC). Detail studies of relative chronological links between them are not published yet; a preliminary chronological division of the distinct millennium is nonetheless possible based on various published studies, radiocarbon dates and summarising reports. They are nevertheless only representing chronological clusters, which should not be understood as cultural horizons at the moment.

The so far earliest Neolithic phase known in our region appears in Ulucak VI and Çukuriçi Höyük XIII (site-phase abbreviation: ÇuHö XIII), eventually also in Yeşilova III.8. Ulucak VI does not reveal any pottery; various concise radiocarbon-dates of Ulucak VI allow its fixing between 6760 and 6600 cal BC (Çilingiroğlu et al. 2012: 153).[1] Chronologically comparable is the foundation level of Çukuriçi Höyük XIII (Horejs et al. 2015, 298-301 Fig. 4); so far three radiocarbon dates of seeds from the settlement phase ÇuHö X indicating a slightly later dating.[2] In contrast to Ulucak VI, the settlement phase ÇuHö XIII contains pottery (four sherds). The founding of Yeşilova III.8 is not cleared yet.[3]

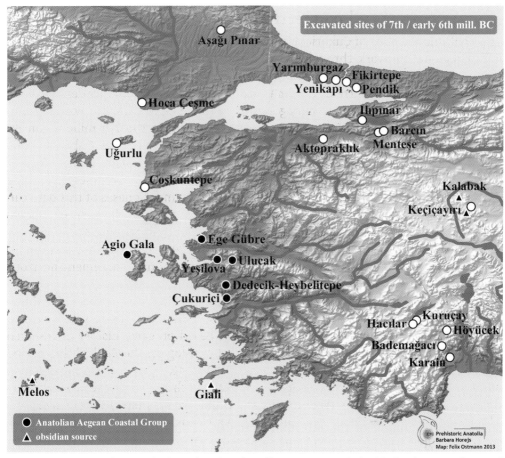

Figure 7.3: Excavated sites of 7th and early 6th millennium BC with highlighted group of Central Aegean coast (map F. Ostmann/ERC Prehistoric Anatolia).

From the mid of 7th millennium (6500–5900/5800 cal BC), these three tells are certainly settled. This late Neolithic phase is represented in Ulucak V–IV (Çilingiroğlu *et al.* 2012: esp. 153), Çukuriçi Höyük X-VIII[4] and Yeşilova III.7–6.3–5 (Derin 2012: 183). Although detailed studies of relative chronological links are a difficult endeavour particularly when excavations are ongoing, a distinction can be tentatively proposed at this juncture between these main chronological stages of Neolithic. Ulucak VI appears to be so far the earliest Neolithic phase, together with Çukuriçi Höyük XIII, dating around 6700 cal BC (Horejs *et al.* 2015, 298-301), cal BC, followed by phases XII and XI at Çukuriçi, where the occupation of the earliest Neolithic in Izmir region goes up to 6500 BC. Late Neolithic starts at around 6500 BC, when tells in Izmir region (Ulucak, Çukuriçi and Yeşilova) are certainly settled, and compiled by Ege Gübre IV (Sağlamtimur 2012: esp. 201–202) and Dedecik-Heybelitepe A (Herling *et al.* 2008; Lichter and Meriç 2012). Late Neolithic at Çukuriçi Höyük (ÇuHö

X-VIII) could be dated from 6500–5900/5800 BC. Even though the time after 6000 BC in chronological sense corresponds to the period of Early Chalcolithic (Schoop 2005), material culture of early 6th millennium at Çukuriçi Höyük seem to follow the Neolithic tradition until the 5900/5800 BC.

A strong intra-regional network between these communities can be postulated on the basis of the comparable assemblages of material, not only in stylistic, but also in technological and conceptual features. Especially the comparison of sites within the distinct chronological phases of early Neolithic (6700–6500) and late Neolithic (6500–5900/5800) let assume strong inter-regional links.

Ç. Çilingiroğlu's pottery studies have revealed strong similarities in classes, fabrics, shapes and principle concepts of pottery technologies, like the so-called Red Slipped Burnished (*RSB*) and Cream Slipped Burnished (*CSB*) wares, s-profile shaped jars, characteristic vertical tubular lugs, specific kind of ceramic temper *etc.* (Çilingiroğlu 2012: esp. 78–86) that are confirmed in recent publications of pottery from all relevant sites (Lichter and Meriç 2012; Derin 2012; Sağlamtimur 2012; Horejs 2012). These analogies in Neolithic pottery shapes, types, surface treatments, fabrics and classes represent a corresponding concept of pottery that can be defined as a strong marker for connectivity as well as characteristic 'regional style'.

Although our state of research does not offer a holistic picture of pottery in terms of 'provinces' at present, the region at the centre of the Anatolian Aegean coast obviously differs from other western Anatolian areas such as the Marmara Sea, where the so-called 'Fikirtepe horizon' has been proposed (*e.g.* Özdoğan 2006; Özdoğan 2013; Thissen 2001; Karul 2011). Late in the developmental sequence of Neolithic pottery, Impresso wares are recognizable at all sites in the last century of the 7th millennium and at the beginning of the 6th millennium BC (Çilingiroğlu 2010; Herling *et al.* 2008; Derin 2012; Horejs 2012; Sağlamtimur 2012). Although this phenomenon could have emerged as a result of a broader Mediterranean network, it is quite obvious that the whole region with each of its farming villages is caught up in this tangible manifestation of connectivity (Çilingiroğlu, in this volume).

The same can be said of the late Neolithic phases (mid- to end of the 7th mill. BC), when it came to polished stone axes, bone spatulae and bone tools, beads and other forms of portable artefact which seem to have correlations in the deployment of specific raw materials and in the suite of technological features employed in their manufacture and use. Although H. Sağlamtimur (2012: 201) describes the archaeological assemblage of Ege Gübre as 'quite distinctive from Ulucak', the so far published pottery and small finds seem to correspond very well with the other sites in the region and Ulucak IV particularly. Some differences could maybe be explained by chronological distinction, because most of the Pottery Neolithic phases at Ulucak (Ulucak Vf-c) are older than the horizons of Ege Gübre IV-III that seem contemporary with Ulucak Vb-a and IV.

For illustrating the regional material relations, the example of comparable sets of axes is salient. They are evident at all sites in the region being discussed and show strong analogies in size, shape, morphology and used raw materials. The axes appear at the same time as small-size, high-quality and polished mainly serpentine and basalt tools (likely to be trapezoids or narrow and elongated shapes like chisels). Alongside these we find heavy, large-size roughly polished types made of different coarse stones. Those from Çukuriçi have been geochemically analysed by D. Wolf (Wolf, in preparation), while the artefacts of the other sites are illustrated in published photos or drawings (Çilingiroğlu *et al.* 2012: 165 fig. 16; Derin 2012: 101, fig. 9; Sağlamtimur 2012: 223, fig. 28; Herling *et al.* 2008: 26–28). The assemblage of axes occurs in same types, raw materials and stylistic details in all settlements and seems to reflect a kind of corresponding 'regional style', already observed for the concept of pottery.

Aside from these obvious analogies between technologies, style and types in everyday materials, such as pottery and tools, strong links between these early farming communities are also detectable in the designs of early weapons. While lithic arrowheads were a rare occurrence around the region in late Neolithic period (one piece mentioned *e.g.* by Derin 2012: 182; for earlier examples s. Horejs *et al.* 2015, 308-309 Fig. 8), sling missiles seemed to be frequently deployed as assault weapons (Korfmann *et al.* 2007: 42; Özdoğan 2002) and are known in large quantities from Ulucak and Çukuriçi (Figure 7.4). They had obviously been stored in piles or deposited in hoards at both settlements (Ulucak: Çilingiroğlu *et al.* 2012, 147: 166–167; Çukuriçi: Figure 7.4). Although detailed studies are not over yet, the remarkable hoarding of these weapons on-site as well as their variety of shape (bi-conical, conical and globular), material (stone or clay) and diversified technologies ranging from the simply collected pebbles gathered to highly polished sling-stones or well-fired clay missiles are indicative of their comparable value and utility.

As it has been convincingly argued by M. Özdoğan (2002), sling missiles seem to replace the common flint or obsidian arrow points in Pre-Pottery Neolithic periods in Central Anatolia. While there is an overlapping span of time, where both – missiles and arrow points – occur in early Pottery Neolithic period, sling missiles become frequent at least in Late Pottery Neolithic of late 7th millennium BC. His observation does not only indicate cultural transformation from PPN to Pottery Neolithic (with potential social dimension as argued by Özdoğan 2002: esp. 443); it offers also a good point for the use of sling missiles as weapons.

In contrast to the use of rounded clay or stone balls to transfer heat to food and possibly also to rooms as discussed for assemblages at Çatalhöyük (Atalay 2005), the deposits of stone and clay missiles at Çukuriçi Höyük do not show traces of burning or boiling. Their function as boiling or cooking stones appears not plausible for the Çukuriçi assemblages. On the other hand, there are some indicators for the function of pottery bi-conical objects as weapons at other Neolithic settlements, summarized recently by L. Clare and B. Weninger (Clare and Weninger, in press). They interpret sling missiles in shape of bioncial clay objects[5] (like the Çukuriçi ones) recovered along a massive defensive wall in Hoca Çeşme in Turkish Thrace and a major conflagration of the settlement as hints for violent conflicts. Also in Höyücek in the Lake District in Western Anatolia, a large number of sling missiles

Figure 7.4: Building complex 10 of Çukuriçi Höyük during excavation with pile of slingshots deposited inside (photo M. Börner/ERC Prehistoric Anatolia).

on the floor of one destroyed building are seen as indicators for armed conflicts (Clare *et al.* 2008). And in the neighbouring site of Bademağacı in the Lake District, eight individuals including one with perimortem cranial trauma were found in burnt structures (Duru 2005; Erdal, Erdal 2012), taken as one argument in a broad discussion for general serious conflicts between 6600 and 6000 cal BC explained by economic and environmental stress (Clare *et al.* 2008). Taking these parallels of sling missiles in different contemporaneous contexts of destruction into account with the background of their potential replacement of lithic arrow points argued above as well as the absence of traces for domestic use at Çukuriçi like heating, their function as weapons appears most plausible at the moment.

As suggested by Ç. Çilingiroğlu (Çilingiroğlu *et al.* 2012) recently for Ulucak, hoarding of sling missiles inside the village may also suggest inter-regional tensions or even internecine conflicts that necessitated the storage of such in large numbers. With the comparable phenomenon of storing sling-stones en masse recently uncovered at Çukuriçi, there might be a counter part that supports this view on intra-regional conflicts, although hunting was another historically attested use for sling-stones that cannot be excluded and may also be a reason for their collection and storage on site. Deposits of obvious polished and prepared stone sling shots in context with ceramic-made ones and ordinary rounded pebbles at Çukuriçi indicates a comparable use for the latter, which are also known as single finds from other sites, like Dedecik-Heybelitepe (Herling *et al.* 2008). Also in Yeşilova there were 10 potential sling missiles recovered, but all except one are just rounded stones (Derin *et al.* 2009: fig. 31).[6]

Therefore it seems possible that these attacking weapons were also common in other sites in the region and have been preserved preferentially at Ulucak and Çukuriçi and in such numbers due to deposition conditions and a lack of later disturbance or taphonomic change. Even so, this category of weapon illustrates another trapping of the connectedness of practices and possessions between sites around the region.

Including the observations discussed above, an archaeological *Central Anatolian Aegean Coastal Group* is slowly taking shape for the 7th millennium BC. Strongly linked concepts of production, function, use and technology are not only detectable in pottery, tools and weapon practices, but also in subsistence strategies and rituals (see below). The proposed identification of a Neolithic archaeological Group in the region needs further investigation of detail relations between the single sites in the future, when details studies of partially ongoing excavations are published.

Regional diversities at the central Anatolian Aegean coast

At first sight, architectural details and settlement structures both reflect a general diversity rather than similarity in the important, permanent villages of what formed the proposed Central Anatolian Aegean Coastal Group. House structures with presumably held diverse, but core-meanings and values for first permanent settlements of the region (*e.g.* Samson 1990; Schachner 1999), and so this very marked diversity in the material conditions of inhabitation appears particularly noteworthy. The choice of technology used to build a house intended for permanent dwelling and use could be linked to experience, raw materials available, the communities' needs, climatic and environmental conditions as well as the community's local tradition, beliefs and social structure (Souvatzi 2008).

Looking at late Neolithic sites on the centre of the Anatolian Aegean coast (*c.* 6500–5900/5800 BC), their architecture is built using different technologies, although the environmental conditions seem comparable from the sources obtainable, such as wood and stone. The existence of both raw materials is indicated, first, by archaeological remains as postholes for wooden poles at all site sand, second, by reconstruction of woodland by faunal remains of game, at least at Ulucak and Çukuriçi (Çilingiroğlu *et al.* 2004: 3–8; Çakırlar 2012; Galik and Horejs 2011; Horejs *et al.* 2011) and first palynological results in the Küçük Menderes delta region.[7] Stone is also accessible throughout the region from neighbouring mountains as well as rivers and is an overt and obvious source of building material for houses. It was not used *en masse* and in bulk in earlier phases, but it was by the late Neolithic period around 6000 BC. As comparable access to building materials as well as similar climatic conditions can be assumed for the whole region, other aspects such as tradition and origin, experience, beliefs, social structures and necessity are therefore potential reasons for architectural diversity.

A look to the other side of the Aegean let us recognize a comparable phenomenon at the Neolithic Greek mainland. Convincingly analysed by S.G. Souvatzi, the relative uniform Neolithic culture with lots of shared key elements is contrasted by a high variability in households (Souvatzi 2008). The household in general forms the key unit in social structuring, but vary in morphology, ideology and social expression. Following Souvatzi's arguments for mainland Greece, this distinct diversity in households can also be seen as an expression how Neolithic communities and their households were structured and integrated. The variety moreover could reflect social identities on a local level. Projecting these results to the Anatolian Aegean coastal Group, its households diversities and differing spatial organization can be seen as regional expression of different local identities, perhaps originated in differing traditions? Anyhow, it is remarkable that this local variability seems to disappear at the end of the Neolithic period in the last centuries of 7th millennium.

Houses at Ulucak V (levels a.b.c.e.f) are built mainly using a wattle-and-daub technique with posts inserted without any stone foundations (Çilingiroğlu *et al.* 2012: 145–146), whilst contemporaneous buildings at Çukuriçi X-VIII are constructed with massive stone socles, partially with posts at regular intervals on top of the plinth for stabilizing the stamped mud walls (Figure 7.5: complex 3), a building method ostensibly comparable with the architecture of Yeşilova (Derin 2012: 180–181). This obvious technological diversity changes at the end of the Neolithic in the late 7th millennium when stone socles also become a regular feature at Ulucak IVk: maybe because of their better stability and resistance to damp and wet weather conditions?

Aside from different building technologies in the late Neolithic period (*c.* 6500–5900/5800 BC), potential local identities seem detectable in settlement organisation when it came to production, cooking, storage and living areas. Food production and cooking routinely used to be pursued inside and outside houses where hearths are located inside buildings as well as in courtyards or open areas in Çukuriçi phases IX and X (Figure 7.5 featuring complex 8 including red-marked hearths and different handcraft activities, pits and platforms). A contrasting scheme is observable tentatively at Yeşilova (Derin 2012: 181) and certainly at Ulucak V where various storage facilities, different kinds of production and cooking also including ovens and hearths are frequently situated *inside* the structures (Çilingiroğlu *et al.* 2012: 145). Although there are hitherto no detailed space-and-function analyses of those sites for the purposes of comparison, the main organizational scheme of domestic life and productive endeavour at the present stage of research appears diverse. Spatial analyses are also required for understanding the potential functional differentiation between agglutinated houses (*e.g.* Ulucak Va) and freestanding buildings with open courtyards, as observable at Çukuriçi IX and X as well as at Yeşilova. As argued above, the different systems of spatial organization reflect the local social organization of households with their preferences and identities. Aside from these general contrastive features, other more detailed characteristics of the Pottery Neolithic period are common, such as stone paving or lime-plastered floors and walls for example, (see Figure 7.5 with the lime-plastered area of an adjacent courtyard outside house complex 6).

To sum up, Ulucak, Yeşilova and Çukuriçi differ in some respects in terms of their building technology and the spatial organization within and around houses and areas of activity, what let us recognize differing social traditions and identities. They have in common the concept of rectangularity, not of necessity an obvious choice, which leads us finally to the special case of Ege Gübre. Rectangular buildings and circular structures (with stone socles as well as wattle and daub walls) are simultaneously used and grouped around one central courtyard for the settlement that had impressive dimensions. Hearth installations and facilities have been retrieved inside rectangular houses and from the courtyard. This area was partially used for cooking and tool production, but mainly as a 'refuse tip' as described by the excavator (Sağlamtimur 2012: 198–199). The huge courtyard as a village centre reflects not only a possible functional differentiation between diverse production zones as part of the villages' social and spatial organisation. It may also have served as an area for ritual activities, as indicated by a limestone stele (Sağlamtimur 2012: 210, fig. 8) and by the fact that the remains of game animals such as deer, boar and wild cattle were retrieved from that area only. Nonetheless, the courtyard dates back to late Neolithic, no earlier

Figure 7.5: Architecture and activity zones of settlement phase IX at Çukuriçi Höyük with different complexes (C). Note Complex 8 including hearths marked in red and areas of different craft activities, pits and platforms (plan M. Börner/ERC Prehistoric Anatolia)

than 6200 cal BC, and cannot be fitted into the regional tradition developed over the preceding centuries, as has been described for Ulucak V, Yeşilova III.7–3 and Çukuriçi X-IX. Although an autochthonous or independent initiative to erect round-plan structures cannot be ruled out for the Ege Gübre's community, their uniqueness also offers several signs of supra-regional contacts.

It should be pointed out that round or circular house structures are absent in the Aegean as well as in West and Central Anatolia. Therefore a foreign influence from Neolithic Cyprus through maritime interaction had already been suggested (Özdoğan 2011; Sağlamtimur 2012: 201). Combining these circular structures with the pottery impresso wares at the same time period, both together can be seen as indicators of a sphere of maritime interaction stretching at least from the Eastern Mediterranean to the Aegean at the end of the 7th millennium BC. Ç. Çilingiroğlu even proposes an interaction sphere from the Levant to Iberian Peninsula (Çilingiroğlu 2010 and in this volume). This speculative maritime network seems to have already been well-established by the late stages of a very dynamic and mobile part of the Neolithic period (*e.g.* Brami and Heyd 2011; Horejs *et al.* 2015), as suggested by other categories of evidence for Aegean connectivity.

Aegean connectivity in the Neolithic Age

Another important aspect of the subsistence strategies of farming communities was animal husbandry, which again exhibits a possible regional homogeneity, although this is currently based only on data from studies of two sites. Without pursuing specific details of Ç. Çakırlar's and A. Galik's analyses, the numbers of livestock at Çukuriçi and Ulucak obviously *do* reflect similar subsistence strategies in both communities predicated more on livestock and less on hunting (Çakırlar 2012; Galik and Horejs 2011; Horejs *et al.* 2011). Stock farming dominates the mammalian assemblage in both communities.

Simple quantification of domesticates and game remains may hamper the reconstruction of Neolithic consumption pattern (Halstead and Isaakidou 2011a; Halstead and Isaakidou 2011b; Isaakidou 2011) by various taphonomical as well as procedural uncertainties. At these two sites were high methodological excavation standards applied and the archaeozoological remains indicate domination in exploitation of sheep and goat and less intensity in the use of cattle and especially in pig not only by simple NISP based statistics but also by more sophisticated reflections in terms of bone weight and body part representation.

Beyond our confinement here to the regional level of the centre of the Anatolian Aegean coast, comparable volumes of livestock, interestingly enough, abound in other areas of the Aegean, particularly on mainland Greece and on Crete at the early to middle Neolithic sites of Nea Nikomedia, Knossos, Argissa Magoula, Agios Petros and Achilleion go to show, where sheep, goat and cattle can be observed in slightly fluctuating amounts with clearly dominating sheep and goat (Reingruber 2008: 514, tab. 5.6). In relation to the centre of the Anatolian Aegean coast, the subsistence strategies around Marmara Sea appear different as the archaeozoological results of Fikirtepe, Menteşe, Ilıpınar and Barcın Höyük suggest and illustrate moreover some intra-regional diversity (Boessneck, v.d. Driesch 1979; Buitenhuis 1994; Buitenhuis 2008; Gourichon and Helmer 2008; Würtenberger 2012).

Although there is a great need for detailed studies by specialists of modern faunal data, it can be stated that the Central Anatolian Aegean Coastal Group and the Greek mainland show some similarities in general life stock strategies in 7th millennium, whilst early villages around the Marmara Sea appear different. Thus, if animal husbandry is perceived as a key-element in the subsistence strategies of communities, then these cross-Aegean similarities might well be linked to cross-Aegean relations, even though the direct spread of subsistence strategies from East to West or vice versa cannot really be postulated at this juncture.

Yet from the particular perspective of Çukuriçi, its Neolithic communities exhibit clear signs of active use of the Aegean Sea and regular seafaring for a range of different reasons. Whilst a migration from inland areas of small groups during the first occupation of Ulucak has been plausibly argued by Ç. Çilingiroğlu (Çilingiroğlu 2011: 75; Çilingiroğlu and Çakırlar 2013), the coastal site of Çukuriçi Höyük may also have been settled by groups arriving via sea routes, as suggested by the procurement of raw materials and seafood consumed (Horejs *et al.* 2015). Both pursuits are detectable at least from the early–7th millennium BC and seem to play an important role in shaping local identities until the abandonment of the tell in the Early Bronze Age (Bergner *et al.* 2008; Horejs *et al.* 2011: 54–60). This specific local tradition was rooted back in the early occupation phases and, in my view, cannot really be ascribed to or linked with early farming communities originating from inland Anatolia.

When we look to the lithic industry of Neolithic Çukuriçi, then technology and morphology are the ways and means of fitting this into the scheme of regional characteristics. The presence of all categories from different stages of the production process is likely to support the theory of knapping tools on-the-spot, rather than importing pre-fabricated products, although a specific knapping workshop has not been identifiable hitherto (Horejs and Milić 2013). Blades were the favoured type of tool produced. Continuing technological studies might be able to demonstrate that the pressure technique was mainly used for blade production (on conical and semi-conical cores leading to the bullet cores) as would be typical to the general hallmarks of Neolithic lithic industries in the region.

The dominant use of bullet cores is frequently observable in this part of the centre of the Anatolian Aegean coast (Herling *et al.* 2008; Çilingiroğlu *et al.* 2012: 148; Derin 2012: 192–193; Sağlamtimur 2012: 200). From this perspective, it appears all the more extraordinary that the raw materials used for lithic production at Çukuriçi appear to be radically different from other sites. As mentioned above, local sources of chert were available, but used only in very small amounts, whereas obsidian was being imported and used on a much larger scale.

Obsidian clearly dominates the lithic assemblages of Çukuriçi totalling more than 80% at Neolithic occupation levels, whilst cherts were seldom used for chipped stones. Neutron Activated Analyses has been employed to determine the provenance of the obsidian, and the samples analysed thus far reveal that the Aegean island of Melos was the only obsidian source used for the products recovered.[8] Cappadocian sources known from later periods of the tell (4th and 3rd mill. BC) do not seem to have been imported in the Neolithic period (Bergner *et al.* 2008).

Turning to the amounts and varieties at other sites, not only in the region, but also throughout Western Anatolia, the high amount of Melian obsidian suggests a special impact of this specific raw material on the Çukuriçi's communities. They preferentially used this Aegean source instead of locally available flints. Even though significant quantities lithic raw materials remain unpublished for many sites, what we know so far indicates that they appear in what are fundamentally different relative proportions; obsidian usually occurs as a minority component in the assemblages of Ulucak, Yeşilova and Ege Gübre, where good-quality cherts and flints are numerically dominant (Çilingiroğlu *et al.* 2012: 148; Sağlamtimur 2012: 200; Lichter and Meriç 2012; Derin 2012: 182 – distinctive differing obsidian amounts for Yeşilova are mapped by M. Milić 2014). Other scientific obsidian analyses at Ulucak seem to show up even just small quantities of Melian obsidian in 7th millennium BC lithics assemblages (Çilingiroğlu *et al.* 2012: 148). New analyses by M. Milić by pXRF characterisation could show a huge predominance of Melian obsidian in Ulucak, Ege Gübre and Yeşilova with only a very few pieces of Anatolian types (Milić 2014 and this volume). As Milić correctly pointed out, the smaller amount of analysed artefacts at Çukuriçi with NAA could likely miss potential minor sources like the central Anatolian ones.[9]

When we take account of the amounts of obsidian that occur on the centre of the Anatolian Aegean coast as well as the strong regional Neolithic network argued for above, then a special role for the coastal site Çukuriçi is implicated in this exchange system, specifically in relation to obsidian from Melos. Material from the later periods (Early Bronze Age 1: early 3rd millennium BC) (Knitter *et al.* in print), maybe taken as comparative evidence for speculating that Çukuriçi's communities were quite active in procuring obsidian directly from the quarry sites. This would have been to provide raw material for regional exchange systems and could, besides, permit us to describe Çukuriçi as a 'gateway community' for obsidian in a broader Aegean context, at least in early EBA times (Knitter *et al.* in print). The rise and role of gateway communities in late 4th and early 3rd millennium BC have been recently discussed for coastal sites in Crete (Papadatos and Tomkins 2013). The authors could clearly demonstrate the specific dynamic and process linked with the system of gateway communities in the Aegean that cannot be transferred to former periods.

Whilst the agents and members of these distinct Early Bronze Age networks speculatively included various mediators between the sources of Adamas and Demenegaki on Melos (*e.g.* Broodbank 2000) and Çukuriçi, the Aegean islands between source and site were not feasible as possible agents of obsidian trade in the 7th millennium BC (cp. distribution in M. Milić 2014: 288, fig. 2, without Emporio and Tigani that seem to be not settled in that period, *e.g.* Hood 1981). Quite interesting for examining potential obsidian exchange networks in Neolithic are the results of the work of L. Herling in Dedecik-Heybelitepe farther inland (Herling *et al.* 2008), where around two thirds of the late 7th mill. BC assemblage was composed of obsidian. They suggested the importing of already prepared cores based on technological analyses in a 'down-the-line' system. Moreover, exhausted cores and complete exploitation of the material there was taken to indicate a scarcity of obsidian (Lichter and Meriç 2012: 134) in contrast to Çukuriçi datasets. This may encourage us to think of Çukuriçi's specific role in the exchange system of the centre of the Anatolian Aegean coast region.

Another particular feature of Neolithic Çukuriçi that can offer some clues to the potential principle agents in the supply of raw materials is indicated by patterns visible in their consumption of sea food. Although fish remains from Neolithic occupation phases have not been comprehensively analysed at the present stage of research, A. Galik's initial results give us clear evidence for fishing being a common activity that contributed to the communities' dietary practices. Over and above the predictable small and medium-size varieties of fish, there is also evidence of tuna (*Thunnusthynnus*) being caught, a fish that lives in open-seas, presumably being caught along its spawning routes that pass some distance from or along the coast (Stratouli 1996).

Freshwater fishing, surprisingly, does not appear to have been practiced. Diving for marine shells that lived in stony habitats appears to have been quite common, as shown, for example, by the large numbers of spondylus and arcanoae shells (Galik and Horejs 2011; Horejs *et al.* 2011). These same species are also known in higher amounts at the sites of Yeşilova and Ege Gübre in the late Neolithic period (Derin 2012: 181; Sağlamtimur 2012: 201). We can nonetheless suggest that Neolithic societies actively harnessed the Aegean Sea as a source of food using both fishing and diving techniques, and detailed analyses of species, rates and fishing techniques being studied by A. Galik will reveal more specific nuances on these traditions.

Fishermen can consequently be associated with shipping and seafaring. While there is no clear evidence of boats at Çukuriçi, many items from around the Mediterranean provide indirect and circumstantial evidence that have often been cited as proxies that support the existence of early shipping (*e.g.* Perlès 2001; Broodbank 2006). What is obvious is that mobile and peripatetic groups used to practise an early form of cabotage, travelling along the coast around the Aegean and also across the Sea, speculatively from island to island and from the coast in the Cyclades (*cf.* discussion by Çilingiroğlu, in this volume). As it is known so far, the islands as stopover were not settled in the 7th millennium, at least not permanently (Broodbank 2000). The relative abundance of sea-fauna at Çukuriçi points to a Neolithic society that frequently used the Aegean Sea for food supply and its members have been continuously moving within the Aegean Sea, most probably even voyaging into the open sea as far as the Cyclades, particularly the island of Melos.

The putative suppliers of obsidian to the centre of the Aegean coast of Western Anatolia can be tentatively identified within this fishing community, as indicated by the extremely high volumes of obsidian that appear to have played an exceptional part in forging local identities up until abandonment of the site in the 3rd millennium BC. Thus, Çukuriçi Höyük in the 7th millennium can also be viewed as a gateway for the supply of this raw material to the local and regional networks in Western Anatolia.

Interregional ritual connectivity

The striking mobility of Neolithic communities has often been referred to in supra-regional analogies that incorporate Anatolia, the Levant and the Aegean as taking part incomparable symbolic traditions, such as distinct types of figurines and pendants, clay stamps or red-plastered floors that have already been frequently discussed in these terms (*e.g.* Özdoğan 2007; Lichter 2005; Lichter 2011; Çilingiroğlu 2010; Perlès 2001; Hansen 2007; Hauptmann, Özdoğan 2007). These analogies reflect not only a high scale of mobility, but presumably also a kind of common perception of some specific ritual activities or an understanding of symbolism, such as the red plaster floors or sealing/marking/decorating objects with similar stamps. Returning to the Anatolian Aegean Coastal Group, its integration into these supra-regional networks has been discussed by C. Lichter (2006; 2011) and Ç. Çilingiroğlu (2009; 2010; 2012) in terms of red plaster, figurines, impresso wares or clay stamps. Also H. Sağlamtimur's (2012) interpretation of round structures at Ege Gübre as an Eastern Mediterranean architectural influence might possibly be included in those networks, if convincing and cogent analogies can be speculatively argued.

Recent results at Yeşilova and Çukuriçi offer another insight into inter-regional symbolic connectivity in the guise of the special ritual of leopard hunting. A femur fragment with *fossa patellaris* and *epicondylusmedialis* of a leopard (*panthera pardus*) was deposited in a late 7th millennium pit at Çukuriçi phase VIII (Galik *et al.* 2012). The assemblage deposited together with this bone includes pottery, obsidian blades, fragments of a spoon and a polished stone axe and a clay sling missile as well as domestic animal bones and seeds. The special preparation of the pit, its arrangement with flat stones on the pit-ground and its partially lime-plastered inner surface constitutes the special repository of the whole deposition.[10] The character of deposited objects and jars in context with burnt food remains (for details of the botanical and zoological analyses s. Galik *et al.* 2012) have been interpreted as the refuse from a feasting ritual. The combination with a leopard's femur let us assume a potential specific ritual role of the beast. It has to be pointed out that the very frequent depictions of leopards, in Neolithic Anatolia and Levant in particular, are in stark contrast with the very few animal remains recovered.[11] As argued convincingly by I. Hodder for Çatalhöyük (Hodder 2006), illustrations of leopards reflect a Neolithic society's conscious reference to a potentially dangerous - and possibly taboo -animal. The concept of Neolithic symbolism of wild leopards in relation to later objects, text sources and the results of ethnoarchaeological studies are discussed elsewhere (Galik *et al.* 2012), an here note that the beast seemed to play a distinct ritual role in Neolithic early farming communities. Especially, its expression as symbol of the wild dangerous sphere outside the protected and domesticated sphere inside the village is remarkable for Neolithic times.

A this point we can say that leopards appear to have been hunted at Çukuriçi Höyük and in one preserved case also deposited in a pit with special treatment and remains of a feasting ritual. In context of the symbolic meaning of the beast in Çatalhöyük and other Neolithic sites, we state a specific ritual connected to the hunting and feasting process. This femur bone demonstrates that leopards were not only brought to the region as fur, a potential consistent assumption due to one piece of a metatarsal found in Ulucak V (Çakırlar 2012: 22, tab. 3). A recently excavated jar with a depiction of a leopard in a relief in Yeşilova (Derin 2013) obviously shows that the beast was also known in reality and alive. It seems that the leopard was understood as symbolic expression in the Anatolian Aegean Coastal Group, too, although its manifestation differs from the Neolithic core zones in the east and southeast.

Conclusions

A rich variety of categories of evidence demonstrate that connectivity in the centre of the Anatolian Aegean coast in 7th millennium BC took the form of complex networks on regional as well as on interregional levels.

The clustering of more or less contemporary sites in one region shows strong linkages in terms of technology, style, morphology and use of material culture (in a broad sense). In addition, the way that sources of supply were used allows in my view a tentative, initial modelling of a regional group in Pottery Neolithic period. Strong regional relationships have been argued for, not only from direct comparison of material objects, but also by exploring overlapping ideas about subsistence strategies within these early farming and livestock communities. The use and design of weapons also indicate comparable policies about dealing with conflicts and/or hunting. On a broader scale, the uniformity of the discussed Neolithic sites in their material culture and ways of life is striking and let assume an Anatolian Aegean Coastal Group in 7th millennium BC.

Integrating the regional results into broader Aegean networks provides a strong basis to develop our understanding of the regional trading and bartering systems, as well. As proposed for the system of obsidian supply, the coastal site of Çukuriçi Höyük can be seen as a community with extensive regional exchange of this distinct raw material. That is why this community, which also appears to have participated regularly in fishing, presumably not only onshore, is identifiable in the region as one of the potential agents harnessing sources of supply. The integration of the Anatolian

Aegean Coastal Group into widespread Neolithic symbolic systems from the Levant, inner Anatolia and Mesopotamia links this part of the Aegean into this interregional network. We can also suggest, at the very least, that with the adaptation of Neolithic symbolism in a regional context with red-plastered floors, sealing systems and others, also the ritual role of leopards have been adopted and transformed by the local communities.

This regional homogeneity of cultural norms is striking in many respects, though this is set against an interesting contrast in the diversity noted at each site - mainly in terms of architectural technology on the level of households and the spatial organisation of settlements. These can hardly be explained by external factors or circumstances, such as differences in environment or access to necessary resources, but seems to reflect local traditions and identities as well as local social patterns. To attain a better understanding of the manner of connectivity in the region, further studies into their distinct diversity promise new answers about what may be the communities' different needs, traditions, beliefs, identities and maybe their origins, as well.

Acknowledgements

I would like to thank the organizers of the Sheffield Round Table for an inspiring workshop and Barry Molloy in particular for his great patience to written contribution. Moreover, I thank Mehmet Özdoğan, Çiler Çilingiroğlu and Raiko Krauß for fruitful discussions in the last years concerning Neolithization processes. Finally, my thanks go to the whole ERC project team and Bogdana Milić as well as Felix Ostmann particularly for their work with the Neolithic stratigraphy and chronology of Çukuriçi Höyük. I would also like to thank the European Research Council (ERC) for funding the project 'Prehistoric Anatolia' (263339) and the Austrian Science Fund (FWF) for financial support.

Notes

1. The summarily chronological tables and former reports suggested a dating of Ulucak VI up to 7000 BC in using two dates of charcoals (*e.g.* Özdoğan *et al.* 2012: 238; Çakırlar 2012); the excavators recently argued convincingly with five new short-lived samples that the earliest settlement was founded between 6760 and 6600 cal BC (Çilingiroğlu *et al.* 2012: 152–153).
2. MAMS 18320: ÇuHö12/1554/10/1: 2σ-range 6766–6592 cal BC; MAMS 18319: ÇuHö11/1362/10/3: 2σ-range 6682–6509 cal BC; MAMS 15270: ÇuHö 11/1398/11/1: 2σ-range 7020–6641cal BC.
3. The excavator Z. Derin published "*...the first result obtained from level III.7 is (one sigma) 6490 cal BC (7505 +/- 37 BP) and the finds from level III.8 suggest that it could go back a further 200 years*" (Derin 2012, 183).
4. One seed sample from house complex 6 (MAMS 18744: ÇuHö12/1637/10/1: 2σ-range 6437–6264 cal BC) is also proven by various samples from drilling cores corresponding to phase ÇuHö IX in height within a range of 6480 to 6210 cal BC.
5. Illustrated *e.g.* by Özdoğan 2002: 442, fig. 6.
6. My sincere thanks to Ç. Çilingiroğlu, who called my attention to these finds at Yeşilova.

7. Preliminary results have been presented by Maria Knipping (University Hohenheim) at the Geoarchaeological Workshop Ephesos at the Austrian Archaeological Institute (18.5.2013).
8. The former relatively small NAA programme of obsidians at Çukuriçi in the Curt Engelhorn Centre for Archaeometry in Mannheim, Germany, conducted by E. Pernicka has recently been integrated into a broader project of lithic raw materials as part of the ITN Marie Curie BEAN project-funding of the lithic studies of B. Milić starting in 2012.
9. I would like to thank M. Milić for this personal comment that will hopefully lead to further analyses of Çukuriçi assemblages in the near future.
10. For a detail description of the "leopard's pit" and its assemblage s. Galik *et al.* 2012, esp. fig. 2–9.
11. S. distribution map of excavated leopard bones from Paleolithic to End of Bronze Age in Galik *et al.* 2012: 274 fig. 11.

References

Atalay, S.
2005 Domesticating Clay: The Role of Clay Balls, Mini Balls and Geometric Objects in Daily Life at Catalhöyük. In I. Hodder (ed.), *Changing materialities at Catalhöyük: reports from the 1995-1999 seasons*(Catalhöyük Research Project Volume 5, BIAA Monograph 39): 139–168. Cambridge.

Bergner, M., B Horejs and E. Pernicka
2008 Zur Herkunft der Obsidianartefakte vom Çukuriçi Höyük. *Studia Troica* 18: 251–273.

Boessneck, J. and A. v. d. Driesch
1979 Die Tierknochenfunde aus der neolithischen Siedlung auf dem Fikirtepe bei Kadiköy am Marmarameer. Dissertation, University of Munich.

Brami, M. and V. Heyd
2011 The origins of Europe's first farmers: The role of Hacılar and Western Anatolia, fifty years on. *Prähistorische Zeitschrift* 86: 165–206.

Broodbank, C.
2000 *An island archaeology of the Early Cyclades*. Cambridge: Cambridge University Press.
2006 The Origins and Early Development of Mediterranean Maritime Activity. *Journal of Mediterranean Archaeology* 19: 199–230.

Brückner, H.
1997 Geoarchäologische Forschungen in der Westtürkei – das Beispiel Ephesos. In T. Breuer (ed.), *Geographische Forschungen im Mittelmeerraum und in der Neuen Welt. Festschrift für Klaus Rother* (Passauer Schriften zur Geographie 15): 39–51. Passau: Passauer Schriften zur Geographie.

Buitenhuis, H.
1994 Note on archaeozoological research around the Sea of Marmara. *Anatolica* 20: 41–144.
2008 Faunal remains from the late Neolithic and Early Chalkolithic levels. In J. Roddenberg and S. Alpaslan-Roddenberg (eds.), Life and Death in a Prehistioric Settlement in the Northwest Anatolia. *The İlıpınar Excavations* II: 205–218.

Çakırlar, C.
2012 The evolution of animal husbandry in Neolithic central-west Anatolia: the zooarchaeological record from Ulucak Höyük (*c.* 7040–5660 cal. BC, Izmir, Turkey). *Anatolian Studies* 62: 1–33.

Çilingiroğlu, Ç.

2009 Of stamps, loom weights and spindle whorls: Contextual evidence on the function(s) of stamps from Ulucak, İzmir, Turkey. *Journal of Mediterranean Archaeology* 22(1): 3–27.

2010 The Appearance of Impressed Pottery in the Neolithic Aegean and its Implications for Maritime networks in the Eastern Mediterranean. *Türkiye Bilimler Akademisi Arkeoloji Dergisi* 13: 9–22.

2011 The Current State of Neolithic Research at Ulucak, Izmir, in: R. Krauß (ed.) *Beginnings - New Research in the Appearance of the Neolithic between Northwest Anatolia and the Carpathian Basin. Papers of the International Workshop 8th-9th April 2009, Istanbul* (Menschen – Kulturen – Traditionen. Studien aus den Forschungsclustern des Deutschen Archäologischen Instituts 1): 67–76. Rahden/ Westfahlen: Menschen – Kulturen – Traditionen. Studien aus den Forschungsclustern des Deutschen Archäologischen Instituts.

2012 *The Neolithic Pottery of Ulucak in Aegean Turkey. Organization of production, interregional comparisons and relative chronology* (BAR International Series 2426). Oxford: British Archaeological Reports.

Çilingiroğlu, Ç. and Çakırlar, C.

2013 Towards configuring the neolitisation of Aegean Turkey. *Documenta Praehistorica* 40. doi:10.4312/ dp.40.3.

Çilingiroğlu, A., Ö. Çevik and Ç. Çilingiroğlu

2012 Ulucak Höyük. Towards Understanding the Early farmings Communities of Middle West Anatolia: Contribution of Ulucak. In M. Özdoğan, N. Basgelen and P. Kuniholm (eds.), *The Neolithic in Turkey. New Excavations and New Research* (Western Turkey 4): 139–175. Istanbul: Western Turkey.

Çilingiroğlu, A., Z. Derin, E. Abay, H. Sağlamtimur and İ. Kayan

2004 Ulucak Höyük. Excavations Conducted Between 1995 and 2002. *Ancient Near East Studies Supplement Series* 15.

Clare, L., E. J. Rohling, B. Weninger and J. Hilpert 2008

Warfare in Late Neolithic/Early Chalcolithic Pisidia, southwestern Turkey. Climate induced social unrest in the late 7th millennium calBC. *Documenta Praehistorica* 35: 65–92.

Derin, Z.

2012 Yeşilova Höyük. In M. Özdoğan, N. Basgelen and P. Kuniholm (eds.), *The Neolithic in Turkey. New Excavations and New Research* (Western Turkey 4): 177–195. Istanbul: Western Turkey.

2013 En yaşlı Anadolu Parsı. In *Kent Dergisi Bornova*, Mart 2013, Sayı 3: 22–27.

Derin, Z., F. Ay and T. Caymaz

2009 İzmir'inprehistorikyerleşimi, Yeşilova Höyüğü 2005–2006 yılıçalışmaları. *Arkeoloji Dergisi* 13: 1–52.

Duru, R.

2005 Bademğacı Kazıları 2002 ve 2003 yılları çalişma raporu. *Belleten* 68: 549–594.

Erdal, E.

2012 Organized violence in Anatolia: A retrospective research on the injuries from the Neolithic to Early Bronze Age. *International Journal of Paleopathology* (in print).

Galik, A. and B. Horejs
2011 Çukuriçi Höyük – Various Aspects of its Earliest Settlement. In R. Krauß (ed.), *Beginnings –*
New Research in the Appearance of the Neolithic between Northwest Anatolia and the Carpathian Basin.
Papers of the International Workshop 8th-9th April 2009, Istanbul (Menschen – Kulturen – Traditionen.
Studien aus den Forschungsclustern des Deutschen Archäologischen Instituts 1): 83–94. Rahden/
Westfahlen: Menschen – Kulturen – Traditionen. Studien aus den Forschungsclustern des
Deutschen Archäologischen Instituts.

Galik, A., B. Horejs and B. Nessel
2012 Der nächtliche Jäger als Beute – Zur prähistorischen Leopardenjagd. *Prähistorische Zeitschrift*
87(2): 261–307.

Gourichon, L. and D. Helmer
2008 Etude de la Faune Neolithique de Menteşe. In J. Roddenberg and S. Alpaslan Roddenberg
(eds.), Life and Death in a Prehistioric Settlement in the Northwest Anatolia.*The Ilıpınar*
Excavations II: 435–446.

Halstead, P. and V. Isaakidou
2011a A pig fed by hand is worth two in the bush: Ethnoarchaeology of pig husbandry in Greece and
its archaeological implications. In T. Wilkinson, S. Sherratt, J. Bennet (eds.) *Interweaving Worlds:*
Systemic Interactions in Eurasia, 7th to 1st Millennia BC(Oxbow Books): 160–174. Oxford: Oxbow Books.
2011b Revolutionary Secondary Products: the Development and Significance of Milking, Animal-
Traction and Wool-Gathering in Later Prehistoric Europe and the Near East. In T. Wilkinson,
S. Sherratt and J. Bennet, (eds.) *Interweaving Worlds: Systemic Interactions in Eurasia, 7th to 1st*
Millennia BC (Oxbow Books): 61–76. Oxford: Oxbow Books.

Hansen, S.
2007 *Bilder vom Menschen der Steinzeit. Untersuchungen zur anthropomorphen Plastik der Jungsteinzeit*
und Kupferzeit in Südosteuropa. Berlin: Archäologie in Eurasien 20. Philipp von Zabern Verlag

Hauptmann, H. and M. Özdoğan
2007 Die Neolithische Revolution in Anatolien. In *Die ältesten Monumente der Menschheit.*
Ausstellungskatalog Karlsruhe: 26–36.

Herling, L., K. Kasper, C. Lichter and R. Meriç
2008 Im Westen nichts Neues? Ergebnisse der Grabungen 2003 und 2004. *Istanbuler Mitteilungen*
58: 13–65.

Hodder, I.
2006 *Çatal Höyük. The Leopard's Tale, revealing the mysteries of Çatalhöyük.* London: Thames and
Hudson.

Hood, S.
1981 *Excavations in Chios 1938-1955. Prehistoric Emporio and Ayio Gala.* London: British school of
Archaeology in Athens Supplement Volume 15.

Horejs, B.
2012 Çukuriçi Höyük. A Neolithic and Bronze Age Settlement in the Region of Ephesos. In M. Özdoğan, N. Basgelen and P. Kuniholm (eds.), *The Neolithic in Turkey. New Excavations & New Research.* (Western Turkey 4): 117–131. Istanbul: Western Turkey.

Horejs, B., A. Galik, U. Thanheiser, and S. Wiesinger
2011 Aktivitäten und Subsistenz in den Siedlungen des Çukuriçi Höyük. Der Forschungsstand nach den Ausgrabungen 2006–2009. *Prähistorische Zeitschrift* 86: 31–66.

Horejs, B. and B. Milić
2013 *A 7th millennium BC house complex of Çukuriçi Höyük in the light of the lithic assemblage.* Poster presentation at the International Symposium on Chert and other Knappable Materials, Iaşi, Rumania, 20.-24.08.2013.

Horejs, B., B. Milić, F. Ostmann, U. Thanheiser, B. Weninger and A. Galik
2015 The Aegean in the Early 7th Millennium BC: Maritime Networks and Colonization, *Journal of World Prehistory* 28(4): 289–230.

Isaakidou, V.
2011 Farming regimes in Neolithic Europe: gardening with cows and other models. In T. Wilkinson, S. Sherratt, J. Bennet (eds.) *Interweaving Worlds: Systemic Interactions in Eurasia, 7th to 1st Millennia BC* (Oxbow Books): 90–112. Oxford: Oxbow Books.

Karul, N.
2011 The Emergence of Neolithic Life in South and East Marmara Region. In R. Krauß (ed.), *Beginnings - New Research in the Appearance of the Neolithic between Northwest Anatolia and the Carpathian Basin. Papers of the International Workshop 8th-9th April 2009, Istanbul* (Menschen – Kulturen – Traditionen. Studien aus den Forschungsclustern des Deutschen Archäologischen Instituts 1): 57–66. Rahden/Westfalen: Menschen – Kulturen – Traditionen. Studien aus den Forschungsclustern des Deutschen Archäologischen Instituts.

Knitter, D., B. Horejs, M. Bergner, B. Schütt and M. Meyer
In print *The importance of location in terms of Early Bronze Age 1 obsidian exchange in western Anatolia.*

Korfmann, M., F. Dedeoğlu and M. Erdalkıran
2007 Ulucak Höyük Neolitik Dönem Sapan Taneleri. In G. Umurtak, Ş. Dönmez, A. Yurtsever (eds.), *Refik Duru'ya Armağan*: 41–50. Istanbul: Zero Books.

Kraft, J.C., İ. Kayan and H. Brückner
2001 The Geological and Paleographical Environs of the Artemision. In U. Muss (ed.), *Der Kosmos der Artemis von Ephesos* (Sonderschriften des Österreichischen Archäologischen Institutes 37): 123–133. Wien: Sonderschriften des Österreichischen Archäologischen Institutes.

Krauß, R.
2011 *Beginnings - New Research in the Appearance of the Neolithic between Northwest Anatolia and the Carpathian Basin. Papers of the International Workshop 8th-9th April 2009, Istanbul* (Menschen – Kulturen – Traditionen. Studien aus den Forschungsclustern des Deutschen Archäologischen Instituts 1). Rahden/Westfalen: Menschen – Kulturen – Traditionen. Studien aus den Forschungsclustern des Deutschen Archäologischen Instituts.

Lichter, C.

2006 Zum Forschungsstand des Neolithikums und frühen Chalkolithikums in Westanatolien. In I. Gatsov and H. Schwarzberg (eds.), *Aegean - Marmara - Black Sea. The present state of research on the Early Neolithic. Proceedings held at EAA 8th Ann. Meeting at Thessaloniki, 28th Sept. 2002* (Schriften des Zentrums für Archäologie und Kulturgeschichte des Schwarzmeerraumes, 5): 29–46. Langenweissbach: Schriften des Zentrums für Archäologie und Kulturgeschichte des Schwarzmeerraumes.

2011 Neolithic Stamps and the Neolithization Process. A Fresh Look at an Old Issue. In R. Krauß (ed.) *Beginnings - New Research in the Appearance of the Neolithic between Northwest Anatolia and the Carpathian Basin. Papers of the International Workshop 8th-9th April 2009, Istanbul* (Menschen – Kulturen – Traditionen. Studien aus den Forschungsclustern des Deutschen Archäologischen Instituts 1): 35–44. Rahden/Westfahlen: Menschen – Kulturen – Traditionen. Studien aus den Forschungsclustern des Deutschen Archäologischen Instituts.

Lichter, C. (ed.)

2005 *How Did Farming Reach Europe? Anatolian–European relations from the second half of the 7th through the first half of the 6th Millennium Cal BC. Proceedings of the International Workshop Istanbul, 20–22 May 2004.* Istanbul: Byzas 2.

Lichter, C. and R. Meriç

2012 Dedecik-Heybelitepe. Excavations of a Neolithic Settlement in the Torbalı Plain. In M. Özdoğan 2012 (eds.), *International Earth Science Colloquium on the Aegean Region, IESCA-2012 1st -5th October 2012, İzmir, Turkey* (Abstracts Book): 308.

Maran, J.

1998 *Kulturwandel auf dem griechischen Festland und den Kykladen im späten 3. Jahrtausend v. Chr. Studien zu den kulturellen Verhältnissen in Südosteuropa und dem zentralen sowie östlichen Mittelmeerraum in der späten Kupfer- und frühen Bronzezeit.* Bonn: Universitätsforschungen zur Prähistorischen Archäologie 53.

Milić, M.

2014 PXRF characterisation of obsidian from central Anatolia, the Aegean and central Europe. *Journal of Archaeological Science* 41: 285–296.

Özdoğan, M.

2002 On Arrows and Sling Missiles: What Happened to the Arrows? In Aslan, R. (ed.), *Mauerschau. Festschrift für Manfred Korfmann*: 437–444. Verlag Bernhard Albert Greiner.

2006 Neolithic cultures at the contact zone between Anatolia and the Balkans. In I. Gatsov and H. Schwarzberg (eds.), *Aegean - Marmara - Black Sea: The present state of research on the Early Neolithic. Proceedings held at EAA 8th Ann. Meeting at Thessaloniki, 28th Sept. 2002* (Schriften des Zentrums für Archäologie und Kulturgeschichte des Schwarzmeerraumes ZAKS e.V. Band 5): 21–28. Halle (Saale): Zentrum für Archäologie und Kulturgeschichte des Schwarzmeerraumes e.V.

2007 Amidst Mesopotamia-centric and Euro-centric approaches: the changing role of the Anatolian peninsula between the East and the West. *Anatolian Studies* 57: 17–24.

2011 Archaeological Evidence on the Westward Expansion of Farming Communities from Eastern Anatolia to the Aegean and the Balkans. *Current Anthropology* 52 supplement 4: 415–430.

2013 Neolithic Sites in the Marmara Region. In M. Özdoğan *et al.* (eds.), *The Neolithic in Turkey. New Excavations and New Research.* Band 5: Northwestern Turkey and Istanbul: 167–269. Istanbul: Arkeoloji Ve Sanat Yayınları.

Özdoğan, M. and N. Başgelen (eds.)
2007 *Türkiye'de Neolitik Dönem. Yeni kazılar, yeni bulgular.* Istanbul: Arkeoloji ve Sanat Yayınları.

Özdoğan, M., N. Başgelen and P. Kuniholm (eds.)
2012 *The Neolithic in Turkey. New Excavations and New Research.* Band 4: Western Turkey. Istanbul: Arkeoloji ve Sanat Yayınları.
2013 *The Neolithic in Turkey. New Excavations and New Research.* Band 5: Northwestern Turkey and Istanbul. Istanbul: Arkeoloji Ve Sanat Yayınları.

Papadatos, Y. and P. Tomkins
2013 Tradings, the Longboat, and Cultural Interaction in the Aegean During the Late Fourth Millenium B.C.E.: The View from Kephala Petras, East Crete. *AJA* 117: 353–381.

Perlès, C.
2001 *Early Neolithic in Greece.* Cambridge: Cambridge University Press.

Renfrew, C.
1972 *The Emergence of Civilisation. The Cyclades and the Aegean in the Third Millennium B.C.* London: Methuen and Co. Ltd.

Reingruber, A.
2008 *Die Argissa-Magula II. Das frühe und das beginnende mittlere Neolithikum im Lichte transägäischer Beziehungen.* Bonn: Beiträge zur ur- und frühgeschichtlichen Archäologie des Mittelmeer-Kulturraumes 35.

Sağlamtimur, H.
2012 The Neolithic Settlement of Ege Gübre. In M. Özdoğan *et al.* (eds.), *The Neolithic in Turkey. New Excavations and New Research.* Band 4: Western Turkey: 197–225. Istanbul: Arkeoloji ve Sanat Yayınları.

Samson, R. (ed.)
1990 *The Social Archaeology of Houses*: Edinburgh: Edinburgh University Press.

Schachner, A.
1999 *Von der Rundhütte zum Kaufmannshaus. Kulturhistorische Untersuchungen zur Entwicklung prähistorischer Wohnhäuser in Zentral-, Ost- und Südostanatolien (BAR International Series 807).* Oxford: British Archaeological Reports.

Schoop, U.-D.
2005 *Das anatolische Chalkolithikum. Eine chronologische Untersuchung zur vorbronzezeitlichen Kultursequenz im nördlichen Zentralanatolien und den angrenzenden Gebieten.* Großschönau: Urgeschichtliche Studien 1.

Souvatzi, S.G.
2008 *A social archaeology of Neolithic households in Greece: An anthropological approach.* Cambridge: Cambridge University Press

Stock, F., A. Pint, B. Horejs, S. Ladstätter and H. Brückner
2013 In search for the harbours: New evidence of Late Roman and Byzantine harbours of Ephesus. *Quaternary International* 312: 57–69.

Stratouli, G.
1996 Die Fischerei in der Ägäis während des Neolithikums. Zur Technik und zum potentiellen Ertrag. *Prähistorische Zeitschrift* 71(1): 1–27.

Thissen, L.
2001 The Pottery of Ilıpınar, Phases X to VA. In J.J. Roodenberg and L.C. Thissen (eds.), The Ilıpınar Excavations II: 3–154.

Wolf, D., G. Borg and B. Horejs
2012a Geoarchäologische Untersuchungen zu den Erzvorkommen in Westanatolien. In F. Schlütter, S. Greiff and M. Prange (eds.), *Archäometrie und Denkmalpflege 2012* (Metalla Sonderheft 5): 143–144. Bochum: Metalla Sonderheft.
2012b Settlement walls of Çukuriçi Höyük – What stones could tell about prehistoric craftsman. In Ç. Helvacı *et al.* 2012 (eds.), *International Earth Science Colloquium on the Aegean Region, IESCA-2012 1st -5th October 2012, İzmir, Turkey* (Abstracts Book): 308.

Wolf, D.
in press Studien zur Geologie im Kaystros- und Kaikostal. Zur Nutzung von Lagerstätten und Rohstoffen in der Urgeschichte. PhD dissertation, Martin-Luther-University of Halle-Wittenberg.

Würtenberger, D.
2012 Archäozoologische Analysen am Fundmaterial des Barçın Höyüks im Vergleich mit ausgewählten Fundstellen Nordwest- und Westanatoliens des 7./6. Jahrtausends. Master's thesis, Universiy of Vienna.

Chapter 8

Kanlıgeçit – Selimpaşa – Mikhalich and the Question of Anatolian Colonies in Early Bronze Age Southeast Europe

Volker Heyd, Şengül Aydıngün and Emre Güldoğan

Setting the scene

This paper will explore changing patterns of settlement location, scale and complexity in the southeastern-most region of Europe - Thrace - in the third millennium BC. The purpose will be to define the contribution of local historical trajectories and 'foreign' cultural elements in the formation of social practices and material traditions, including material culture and the built environment. The character and role of exchange systems will be explored, and it is argued that influences from Anatolia were a spur to greater complexity of settlement systems and society in the study region during this period of the later part of the Early Bronze Age. We will assess the relevance of new archaeological data obtained from both excavation and survey projects for understanding these issues, and present them in light of our revised model for the trajectory of this region in prehistory and propose that a form of 'embryonic' colony can be identified, the first of its kind in Europe. In particular, we will focus on the sites of Kanlıgeçit and Selimpaşa in Turkish Thrace and Mikhalich in southeastern Bulgaria. We begin by establishing the historical scene and the specific questions to be addressed through this paper. In order to understand the social conditions and connections that provide the context for understanding these sites, we next provide a detailed analysis of high-status material culture, with a particular emphasis on those elements that both directly and indirectly attest to interaction and connectivity with elitist groups throughout the East Mediterranean, Anatolia and Europe more widely. Building on this framework, we then discuss the character of the key settlement sites that support the core arguments of this paper in relation to the role of interaction in the changing complexity of this region in the Early Bronze Age.

A somehow puzzling picture emerges when trying to compare the most southeastern corner of Europe, ancient Thrace[1], with northwestern Anatolia between the mid to later 4th and the first half of the 3rd millennia BC. On the one hand, we can recognise a similar ceramic inventory shared on both sides of the Bosphorus and the Dardanelles. These similarities - probably the first of its kind since the Neolithisation of the region - account in particular for pottery types of the second half of the 4th millennium BC (links between Cernavodă III and the so-called Fluted Wares of northwestern Anatolia: Gabriel 2001; Roodenberg and Thissen 2001; Nikolova 2008). This material culture link no doubt continues deep into the 3rd millennium BC when looking, for example, at its most iconic vessel form, the 'dark burnished plate/bowl with inverted thickened rim', which is the most numerous form at excavated and surveyed settlement sites (*e.g.*, Georgiev *et al.* 1979; Bertemes 1997; Frirdich 1997; Sarı 2009). On the other hand, this relationship is neither visible structurally in the archaeological features, such from the few known settlements or burials of this period, nor materially in the metal artefacts for example (Nikolova 1999: 287ff.; Efe and Fidan 2006).

Indeed, both regions go very different pathways culturally, with southeastern Europe becoming an integral part of the infiltration zone of Yamnaya populations from *c.*3050/3000 BC (Heyd 2011). These pastorally orientated populations originate from the north-Pontic/Caspian steppe lowlands. In Bulgaria their typical kurgans and burials can be found throughout the Thracian lowland regions. Geographically beyond, in Turkish and Greek Thrace, there is what we might perhaps consider a zone of influence that is revealed by the presence of some cord-decorated sherds from Kanlıgeçit in Turkish Thrace (Özdoğan and Parzinger 2012, Fig. 134), Dikili Tash in Greek Thrace or Pevkakia Magoula in Thessaly (Roman *et al.* 1992), and the anthropomorphic stelae of Skala Sotiros (Thassos Island) and Troy I, otherwise a typical northwest-Pontic Yamnaya feature (*cf.* Koukouli-Chrysanthaki 2005; Meyer-Todorieva 2010). The same cultural difference is true when looking at the settlement systems. In northwestern Anatolia, höyük (tell) sites were continuously occupied throughout the period in focus, and site sizes and complexity gradually increased, thus starting a development that would firstly see fortifications, outer-settlement areas, communal houses, shared storage facilities, workshop areas *etc.* and then eventually, in the second half of the 3rd millennium BC, strong indications for a pathway to urbanism (*e.g.* Steadman 2011; Sarı 2012; Kouka 2013).

In Thrace tell settlements are only re-settled in the latest 4th millennium BC, along with the Yamnaya infiltration, when people using a material culture (in the broadest sense) associated with the Ezero A culture (Georgiev *et al.* 1979; Schwenzer 2005). While this can perhaps be regarded as a first step in a demographic concentration and process of economic re-orientation, the settlements stay modest in size and organisation, and overall a relatively moderate level of social complexity prevails.

We have not as yet recovered any outstanding burials, lavishly equipped hoards, or precious metal objects beyond the size of a simple hair ring (Alexandrov 2009). Material culture of the Yamnaya group is still the dominating factor in assemblages dated to the first quarter of the 3rd millennium BC, and one might well envisage a relatively balanced exchange system to have been in place and a kind of symbiosis to have been established between predominantly agricultural societies using Ezero A and B1 material culture and inhabiting tell sites, and the pastoralists using Yamnaya material culture that were living in the wider landscapes around. However this situation changes in the second quarter of the 3rd millennium when Yamnaya-type kurgans and burials sharply diminish in numbers, and Ezero Tell sites expand regionally and locally.

So, while the first half of the 3rd millennium BC in Thrace is characterised by a (comparatively) moderate level of social and economic complexity and the ideological dominance of pastoral tribes of a north-Pontic origin, there is a real explosion in complexity in the period between 2400 and 2000 BC and the region becomes increasingly included within a much wider network that is now dominated by frequent and highly visible exchange and trade, and new forms of prestige and status expression, as to be detailed below.

The three following sections will try to explain this situation, firstly by highlighting and contextualising the dataset of several lavishly equipped graves and hoards, and prestigious and exotic single finds of this period, discovered mostly in Bulgaria in the last two decades. It will then describe the outstanding fortified settlement sites of Kanlıgeçit, Selimpaşa and Mikhalich, foreign in their design, construction and material culture compared to local settlements, before assessing the role of these sites in a discussion around exchange and trade; the relation between local elites and foreigners likely originating from Anatolia and the eastern Aegean; and the inclusion of this most southeastern corner of Europe in the wider Aegeo-Anatolian networks. Key objectives herein concern 1) demonstrating the degree of similarities amongst these outstanding settlement sites (despite the variability of data due to different intensities of research at each site); 2) characterisation of their interaction with the landscape around; and 3) development of an explanatory models that can help us understand the mechanisms behind the specific character of the region. It may not come as a surprise that this development is not so much explained by local evolution as it is by external factors, or a combination of both, which are far better suited to understanding the available records. The method to be applied is a structural comparison of the later Early Bronze Age situations on both sides of the Dardanelles and Bosphorus. The main outcomes shall give an idea about the geographical range of these interactions, about their quality and reach into, and effects on, local societies. We will also evaluate whether these outstanding settlement sites can be seen as Anatolian colonies, including a brief consideration of the wider question of what might constitute Early Bronze Age colonies. The emerging picture highlights the connections of Thrace as a pathway linking mainland Europe to Anatolia and the Aegean and this is set in the context of an overall high degree of connectivity characterising the second half of the 3rd millennium BC in the broader region.

Emerging complexity in Thrace from *c.*2400 BC

There can be no doubt that this new situation emerging after *c.*2400 BC, within the Early Bronze Age (EBA) III or *Sveti Kirilovo* phase in the Bulgarian chronological system, is due to influence from across the Bosphorus and Dardanelles, where exactly the same developments had happened several centuries earlier in a more gradual manner. In Thrace the change appears to have been more abrupt and levels of societal and economic complexity appear to rise rapidly, despite having here a prehistoric archaeology that is still struggling with its own inherent problems of an accurate chronological system. However, overall social complexity certainly did not reach the same level as northwestern Anatolia due to a further geographical distance to the alleged centres farther to the east/southeast and perhaps the lesser time span available to build up. Nevertheless, what is to be observed in the material record can be described with the same keywords of "organised settlement structures indicating the presence of a central authority"; "large settlements with citadels and lower towns"; "first introduction of wheel-made pottery (mass production)", "first examples of tin bronzes", *etc.* that had been used by, for example, Vasıf Şahoğlu (2005: 339) to describe northwest Anatolian EBA contexts.

A critical assessment of the archaeological record (Figure 8.1) reveals that this social development is materialised through new forms of settlement, imported pottery and imitations of this (to be discussed in the next section), lavishly equipped elite graves and precious-metal hoards, and in particular, certain specific artefacts deposited in these latter two contexts. This can be complemented by several outstanding single finds, which often lack specific find contexts because they come from burial mounds in Bulgaria that have been looted by criminal gangs in recent decades (Figure 8.2). The most important graves in this list are from the Dübene necropole (Plovdiv region), excavated since 2004 (Hristov 2012, with references), from Izvorovo (Haskovo region), excavated in 2008 (Borislavov 2010) and Rupite (Blagoevgrad region), looted in the early 1990s (Leshtakov 2011: 563–564, Fig. 2). All of these are burial mounds. Comparably lavishly equipped graves are not yet known from Turkish Thrace, Greek Thrace, or from Romania. These graves, hoards and special single finds shall be discussed in some detail here, before assessing the key settlement sites highlighted in the title, as they present important and recently, though often preliminarily, published datasets relevant to defining the cultural context of the sites. As a key component in the multi-faceted picture of emerging complexity, they represent an aspect of the local elites that held social positions and controlled resources to enable them to obtain prestigious and exotic artefacts. By focussing on new forms of precious-metal neck decoration that constitute an innovation of the period found in all graves

Figure 8.1: Map of key Early Bronze Age sites in southeast Europe (Bulgaria, Greece & Turkey) and northwest Anatolia mentioned in the text.

and most hoards, the connectivity and degree of internationalisation of these local elites becomes apparent.

The Dŭbene necropole

The site of Dŭbene, with its nearly 20,000 single gold objects, mostly tiny beads for compound necklaces, is outstanding and the quality and quantity of finds are only matched by the roughly contemporary material from Troy II and the Poliochni treasures (Bernabò Brea 1976; Sazcı 2007). In addition, the Dŭbene 'burial' treasure contains silver and copper/bronze objects, including a dagger, and other finds include blue faience/glass beads, as well as pottery and animal bones in abundance from the c.30 ritual features (pits, stone heaps, fireplaces) around a group of five larger tumuli. The largest single precious metal object is, however, a gold/electrum dagger of c.16

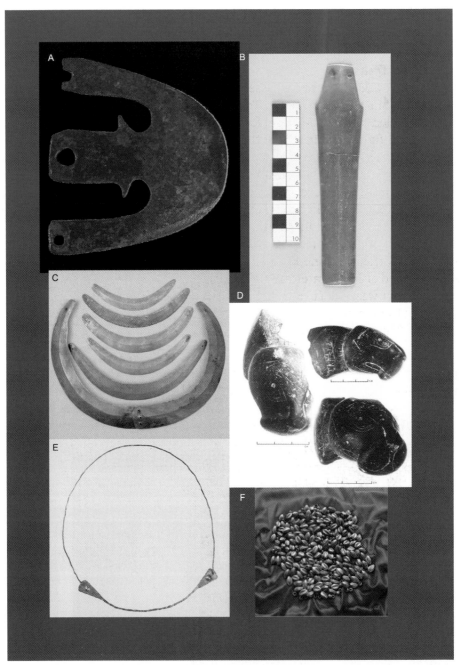

Figure 8.2: Selection of Early Bronze Age prestigious and/or exotic key finds from Bulgaria and Greek Thrace: A. Haskovo bronze axe (after Avramova & Todorieva 2005); B. Dŭbene electrum dagger (after Hristov 2007); C. Silver lunulae of Panayot Hitovo (after Fol et al. eds. 2004); D. Lionhead sceptre of Sitagroi (after Renfrew et al. eds. 1986); E. Golden neckring without provenance from ARES collection Sofia (after Fol et al. eds. 2004); F. Gold beads from Izvorovo (after Borislavov 2010).

cm length (Figure 8.2B), one of only two known from 3rd millennium BC Europe, the other coming from the Mala Gruda tumulus in Montenegro (Heyd 2013b, Fig. 10)[2].

The 'Haskovo Treasure'

The so-called 'Haskovo treasure', assembled before 1998, is likely to also originate from looted tumuli (Avramova and Todorieva 2005). This 'assemblage' is certainly not from a sealed context because, for example, the broad flat axe (Avramova and Todorieva 2005 fig. 2, left) in it is of the Altheim/Vinča type and belongs to the 4th millennium BC. The treasure is also not complete, as all the gold one might expect for such an exceptional find was in all probability sold to a dealer before approaching archaeologists in Sofia. There are nevertheless no real arguments to doubt it comes from southeastern Bulgaria or the environs of the town of Haskovo. Claims with respect to the iconic crescentic axe that the find, or parts of it, was made somewhere in the Near East or Turkey (Băjenaru 2013: 292), are based solely on this axe (Figure 8.2A), which is the only one of its kind in Europe. However, a handful of further crescent-shaped or fenestrated axes, also dating to later 3rd millennium BC contexts, are known from western Turkey (Efe and Fidan 2006, 24; Gernez 2007). It therefore makes sense to include the 10 × 10.7 cm wide/long Haskovo example to this cluster (Figure 8.3). This would accord well with Turan Efe's 'Great Canavan Route' (2007)

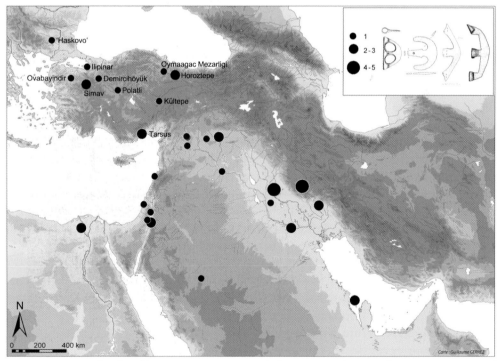

Figure 8.3: Map of 3rd millenium BC Crescentic and Fenestrated Axes after Gernez 2007 with additions. Named are 'Haskovo' and the Turkish specimens.

and Vasif Şahoğlu's 'Anatolian Trade Network' (2005) or Turan Efe's 'Great Caravan Route' (2007). These are the main theories used to explain the intensification in the cultural and economic relations of the Anatolian west and southwest with the interior, north Syria and Mesopotamia, respectively and between the north Aegean and Cilicia. These routes emerged gradually from the mid-3rd millennium BC, that is the EB III period in Turkey (see also Fig. 8.12 below). In relation to dating this collection of ojects, typologically the above mentioned axe is close to the Ilıpınar axe and both are rather late specimens, already predicting the development of the fenestrated axes. Guillaume Gernez (2007: 183f.) therefore equates it to the Levantine later 'Bronze Ancien IV', the period between 2200 and 2000 BC in absolute terms. Along with the axe, the triangular flat dagger deserves attention, as it is, with its 31.8 cm, not only one of the longest ever found in EBA southeastern Europe but is also described as having a 'tinned' surface. This is also said for the crescentic axe and similar observations were made for Anatolian bronzes (Muhly 2011: 866).

New precious forms of neck decoration

A link between all four burial sites comes in the form of the many small beads recovered at each of them. These occur in various forms and sizes and in silver (Haskovo) and gold (Dŭbene, Rupite, Izvorovo). They probably belong to neck chains and, based on the gold spacers found in Dŭbene (Tsintsov et al. 2009), and the quantity of gold beads in Izvorovo (altogether 344 pieces; here Figure 8.2F), they may have been from compound (crescentic) necklaces. These gold spacers connect the Dŭbene necklaces with similar ones from the Troy and Poliochni treasures. In Europe, another three specimens have been recorded from an exceptional burial found in Mound 1 of Bare (Rekovac, Pomoravlje district) in Central Serbia (Srejović 1976). Another findspot that is not securely dated to the 3rd millennium BC due to the early date of its discovery and poor contextual data, is the eastern Serbian site of Velika Vrbica (Kladovo, Bor district; Heyd 2013b: 31, Fig. 16A). These compound necklaces and the emphasis on the neck and the upper chest using splendid and brilliant ornamentation is another innovation of the mid 3rd millennium BC, probably firstly to be found in elite contexts of the Near East, Egypt and Anatolia and around the turn of the millennium, and to be subsequently copied throughout much of Europe (Heyd 2013a; see e.g., Frieman 2010: 189f. for the materialisation of the same idea in northwestern Europe).

Apart from these compound necklaces there are two other, closely connected groups of neck decorations to be found in EBA south-eastern Europe, that similarly were used to adorn the neck/upper chest body with a precious metal display: torques and lunulae. Stefan Alexandrov has recently (2011) published six golden torques from Bulgaria, all being single finds recovered by metal detectorists. A seventh, 15 cm wide, from the ARES collection in Sofia can be added (Fol et al. [eds.] 2004, no.108; here Figure 8.2E). Among them, only the specimen from Novae/Svishtov (Veliko Tarnovo region) is of the *Ösenhalsring*-type. It however finds its best connection in a further six golden *Ösenhalsring* torques from the recently (August 2011) discovered 'Svishtov treasure', dated by its other gold and bronze artefacts to around 2000 BC (pers. comm. S. Alexandrov). Two further gold torques have recently been published from Romania (Popescu 2013a), one of which (site of Cornăţel, jud. Sibiu) is of the *Ösenhalsring*-type, while the second (from a hoard at Răcătău, jud. Bacău) has braided loops. All other golden Bulgarian torques have simple eyelets or braided loops too. Some are combined with a special form of golden drop-shaped hair ring (similar to types ID and II in S. Alexandrov's list of 2009), widely known from the regions adjacent to the course of the Lower and Middle Danube (*cf.* Hänsel and Weihermann 2000). These kind of drop-shaped hair rings are also to be found in two other yet unpublished jewellery hoards of Provadiya (Varna region) and Yankovo Shumensko (Shumen region) (pers. comm. K. Leshtakov and V. Slavchev). Besides containing more than 30 gold and silver hair rings of various sizes, the hoard of Provadiya also yielded some silver beads, probably from one (or perhaps several) necklace(s) of the kind described above.

The Panayot Hitovo hoard

Another hoard, also dated to the later EBA with good arguments (pers. comm. K. Leshtakov; however for a Chalcolithic date see Popescu 2013b) is from Panayot Hitovo (Targovishte region). It was found in 2003 (Fol *et al.* 2004, no.150) and provides evidence for lunula-shaped neck ornamentations made of silver (and one of electrum), of which at least 10 were assembled in this treasure. Of particular interest is a larger composite lunula consisting of two halves that were put together by string or rivets (Figure 8.2C). This extraordinary treasure, originally deposited in a vessel, also contained 12 bracelets, 6 elongated metal strips (probably head decorations) and more than 50 hemispherical sheet buttons, all made of silver. Similar lunula-shaped pendants, again made of silver and electrum, were found at Bulgarian cave sites of Emen and Tabashka (Veliko Tarnovo region), where they were probably deposited as small hoards (Nikolova and Angelov 1961; Hristov 2000).

Altogether these precious metal neck ornaments from Bulgaria, whether chain, torque or lunula, form part of a wider cluster of highly prestigious and innovative gold or silver neck-ornamentation that occurs at some of the most iconic 3rd millennium BC sites in the Levant, Turkey and Greece such as Umm e-Marra, Byblos, Eskiyapar, Ikiztepe, Troy, Poliochni and Steno, with some outliers reaching into the Central Mediterranean (Figure 8.4). In Bulgaria, all named hoards seem, on the one hand, to date rather late within the 3rd millennium BC, perhaps covering only the last two centuries, *c.*2200–2000 BC. This makes them somewhat later at least than the Dŭbene graves. On the other hand, their distribution, and that of some interesting single finds, extends north of the Balkan mountain range and north and

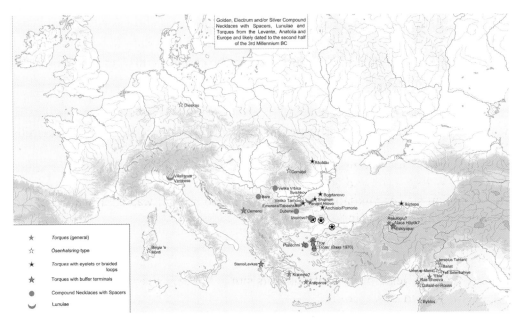

Figure 8.4: Map of Golden, Electrum and/or Silver Compound Necklaces with Spacers; and Lunulae and Torques from the Levante, Anatolia and Europe and likely dated to the second half of the 3rd millennium BC (note that the golden lunulae of northwest and northern Europe are not mapped here).

east adjacent to the above mentioned graves which are only known from southern Bulgaria so far.

Several other relevant objects can be mentioned briefly: some later shafthole axe hoards, such as from Ezero, level IV (Stara Zagora region; Georgiev *et al.* 1979: 179), Tutrakan (Silistra region; Chernikh 1978) and of unknown provenance recovered in 1996 (Avramova 2004); exotic finds like a rudimentary (?) slotted spearhead from Dolni Lukovit (Pleven region) (Chernikh 1978, Table 29,20 [find no.10710]); a tin-bronze miniature cup (3,6 cm high) from the site of Ovcharitsa II (Stara Zagora region; Fol *et al.* eds 2004, no.116); the lionhead stone sceptre from the 'Long House' at Sitagroi V (Renfrew *et al.* [eds.] 1986: 189, Fig. 8.4b; pl. XXV; herein Figure 8.2D). We can also mention more generally the many silver finds from later 3rd millennium BC Bulgaria, a region otherwise devoid of silver ores, but rich in gold (*cf.* Popov *et al.* 2011). We can also mention the presence of about 15 tin-bronze artefacts analysed so far (Heyd 2013b, fig. 12; *cf.* also Rahmstorf 2011: 104–106, fig. 9,1), and also tin-bronze dress pins from Assara, Mikhalich, Kanlıgeçit, Rupite, Golyamata Mogila, Mudrets and Gŭlŭbovo, can be compared with pieces from Küllüoba (Eskişehir province; Efe and Fidan 2006: 21, Tab. 4; Fidan 2012) and Seyitömer (Bilgen 2015). Taken together these, with little doubt, represent an innovative new dressing code with links to Anatolia, Syria and Mesopotamia (Klein 1992).

Outstanding Settlement Sites

Alongside these very special grave assemblages, hoards and single finds, there are also outstanding settlement sites of significance to the case presented in this paper. The investigation of these complex EBA sites in Turkish Thrace was part of a fieldwork program from 2006 to 2011 (Özdoğan *et al.* 2008; Aydıngün *et al.* 2010; Heyd *et al.* 2010; Güldoğan *et al.* 2011; Heyd and Skowranek 2012), carried out also in collaboration with Bulgarian archaeologists. During this program the outer settlement of Kırklareli-Kanlıgeçit (Kırklareli province) was investigated in 2006–2007; the settlement of Koyunbaba (Kırklareli province) in 2007; and the tell (höyük) site of Selimpaşa (Istanbul province) in 2007–2009 and 2012. In addition, information about the excavations at the Bulgarian site of Mikhalich-Baa Dere (Haskovo region) was obtained thanks to the co-excavator Krassimir Leshtakov (University of Sofia).

Kırklareli-Kanlıgeçit

Following many years of excavations, this site is becoming recognised as the most important known EBA site in the whole of Thrace. It was recently fully published by Mehmet Özdoğan and Hermann Parzinger (2012); therefore only a few key characteristics need to be summarised here. Originally this was a small Ezero-type Tell, constructed using wood and wattle-and-daub architecture. The existing settlement was entirely remodelled at some time around 2400 BC. This included the construction of a fortified citadel of *c*.0.4 hectares using stone and mudbrick architecture and a drystone glacis technique was employed for the wall. There was also a tower/gatehouse (?) built using ashlar masonry and within the citadel, there were megaron buildings up to 25 m long and encircled by temenoi walls with buttresses. In addition to this acropolis, there was an outer settlement of *c*.3–5 ha that stretched around its base. Typical Anatolian red-slip pottery ware and/or wheel-made pottery, all possibly locally made, constitute *c*.15% of the total pottery assemblage (Özdoğan 2011: 672). There are also specimens of the *International Anatolianising Pottery* (also called Lefkandi I-Kastri pottery in the western Aegean), in the form of depata, tankards and particularly Trojan plates. There are also very important signs of a specialised economy, in the form of horse breeding (up to 15% of all bones), wool-yarn production (many spindle-whorls) and, potentially, the exploitation of copper-ores from the near-by Strandza mountains.

It is in this context of economy and trade that we can discuss a wheel-made ceramic sherd that is made from a prehistoric fabric, and has a roller stamp impression on it. This was collected during our survey in the outer settlement, southwest of the citadel (field 6, *cf.* Özdoğan and Parzinger 2012, fig. 62), in August 2006 (Figure 8.5.1). However a question mark remains for this find, as it is a surface find, not stratified, and of a ware not common in Kanlıgeçit (pers. comm. Mehmet Özdoğan). This means that it cannot be fully excluded that the find is of a later date. Nevertheless, the best comparisons are with EBA II pithoi fragments, other (larger) pottery vessels and hearth decorations of the circum-Aegean region (see Rahmstorf 2006), with some examples from Lerna and Tiryns even exactly matching the decoration pattern of this sherd (Wiencke 1970 and Müller 1938). It is in this context of the use of stamps and seals that we draw attention to another sherd that has a clear round stamp impression (Figure 8.5.2). This comes from the Bulgarian settlement site of Gŭlŭbovo (Stara Zagora

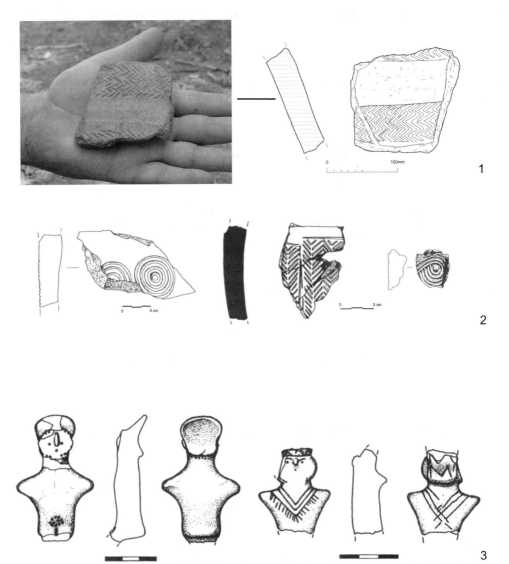

Figure 8.5: 1. Roller Impression sherd from the outer settlement of Kanlıgeçit; 2. sherds with stamps/ impressions from Gŭlŭbovo (Bulgaria, after Leshtakov 2002); 3. clay idols from the citadel of Kanlıgeçit (after Karul 2005; 2012).

region; Leshtakov 2002; in press), some 120 km away from Kırklareli, and this site contained a collection of *International Anatolianising Pottery* (depata, pilgrim flask, *etc.*), second in volume only to the assemblage from Kanlıgeçit. Gülübovo has also yielded a few further interesting stamp impressions on sherds, otherwise not known in the Bulgarian EBA or in Turkish Thrace.

There is yet another aspect in Kanlıgeçit that deserves attention. This refers to two clay figurines, described in detail by Necmi Karul (2005; 2012), featuring clear Anatolian features (Figure 8.5.3). There are no immediate comparisons to these in all of southeastern Europe and the few clay idols used in the Bulgarian EBA are characteristic of other traditions (Bertemes 2002). This leads to the fundamental issue of why would they copy the Anatolian clay idols, and perhaps the religious ideas standing behind them. Was this a local society, or perhaps its elite, imitating the trappings of civilization in northwestern Anatolia? The main Kanlıgeçit phase 2b is otherwise a near-perfect, albeit much smaller copy of the latest Troy II phases (IIc1-c3: Ünlüsoy 2011; see herein Figure 8.12), even displaying a very similar orientation of the Megara and the same slightly oval form of the citadel. One therefore wonders how a distinctively local elite should be capable of copying virtually everything from Troy IIc1-c3 without having a model of the architectural design, or the right people to command such an endeavour.

Similar observations also apply for the outer settlement, the focus of our survey and prospection in 2006/07 (Heyd and Skowranek 2012). We could not find any hint of a defensive ditch encircling it. It was probably never needed; the whole flatland is well watered and one might perfectly imagine a kind of protection to be given by various waterways, artificial lakes and swamps. High quality pottery was collected from many spots, particularly in the south and southwest to the citadel, including some of the best *International Anatolianising Pottery* pieces (*e.g.* Özdoğan and Parzinger 2012: 50–51 and Abb. 69, 7–8). Does this perhaps indicate the presence of some special quarters? At least it shows some 'inequality' in the outer occupation. Whatever the background, Kanlıgeçit represents a form of central place that can only be regarded as foreign in a regional environment still dominated by settlement mounds, wattle-and-daub architecture and hand-made dark burnished pottery. Interestingly now, such a local settlement is well-represented by our next site, only 12 km away from Kanlıgeçit.

Koyunbaba

This site is yet unpublished and a summary of our survey and prospection results of 2007 will be given here for the first time. Koyunbaba is certainly a tell site, however much flattened and extended over *c.*2–3 ha due to ongoing agricultural activities and also badly damaged by road construction. It is thus not clear whether there was a kind of outer settlement around the original (smaller) tell. Ideally located on a low and flat spur-like terrace encircled by three well-watered river valleys (Figure 8.6),

Figure 8.6: Koyunbaba (Kırklareli Province, Turkey): Photos showing the location of the site at a flat terrace over two gullies (photographs by authors).

just north of the modern village, the site yielded a rich surface pottery collection ranging in date from Chalcolithic through the Bronze to the Iron Age. However, the vast majority belong to the EBA, and are closely related in form and decoration, if not fully matching, the types of the Bulgarian Ezero B2 culture. This is also shown by the many bowls/plates with inverted rims and other ceramics with handles, decorated rims and applied notched ledges (Figure 8.7.1). More specifically, the majority of the EBA pottery assemblage probably finds its best comparisons with the latest Ezero layers III to I and Dyadovo layers IV to II, predates the EBA materials of the site of Drama (Yambol), and equates with an initial phase of Sveti Kirilovo or Bertemes' horizon group 4 (Bertemes 1997; 1998). This makes it concurrent with the pre-Anatolian occupation, and likely also the phase 2c of Kanlıgeçit. Contemporaneity and contact with this phase of Kanlıgeçit are indicated by two body sherds of Anatolian red-slip ware and one wheel-made plate, which were recovered during the survey (Figure 8.7.2). But caution needs to be applied as these are all surface finds.

The most exiting results, however, came from our extended geophysics prospection using the equipment and methods described in Heyd and Skowranek (2012). Detailed surface pottery counting revealed the presence of subterranean features that were also visible throug this geophysical work (Figure 8.8A and C). Not only could many pits be detected, which had already been badly ploughed, and some linear features, but most importantly a circular ditch system, comprising of an inner circle of c.60 m diameter and an outer one of c.120 m. Unlikely to be a purely defensive structure due to topography, the best comparisons come again from the Bulgarian Ezero culture and the sites of Cherna Gora (Leshtakov 2006) and particularly Drama (Figure 8.8B), where two interlinked ditches were also utilised and closely match the situation at Koyunbaba (Bertemes 2002). François Bertemes also cites such circular ditch systems, interpreted by him as open-air sanctuaries, from the sites of Yunacite, Karasura, Gerena, Dyadovo, Konyovo, Veselinovo (?) and Dana Bunar. Koyunbaba is thus the southernmost known of this Thracian phenomenon and the only known one of its kind in the region of modern-day Turkey.

It is important to note that this very local settlement is only 12 km away from the partly contemporary, but Anatolian-influenced, site of Kanlıgeçit. One needs to mention in this context that both sites are located in parallel, NNE-SSW running well-watered river valleys (the valley of the Teke Dere on the one hand and the Okluca Dere/ Haydadere river valley on the other hand), thus occupying different local catchment zones and probably being local population focal points also. Indeed, both sites seem to have similar origins in the form of rather small and typical tell sites of the Ezero culture. It is likely that Koyunbaba then became the more distinctive of the two by the construction of the possible open-air sanctuary as we have no evidence for such in Kanlıgeçit. But the transformation that Kanlıgeçit went through after some period of co-existence was even more fundamental when it became structured along very similar lines to the Anatolian-model. Koyunbaba seems to have been abandoned much earlier than Kanlıgeçit (it lacks diagnostic later Sveti Kirilovo phase materials) and it

Figure 8.7: Koyunbaba: Early Bronze Age pottery finds; 1. selection of survey potsherds; 2. special sherds from the survey, two wall sherds of Anatolian red-slip ware and a wheel-made plate rim sherd (photographs by authors).

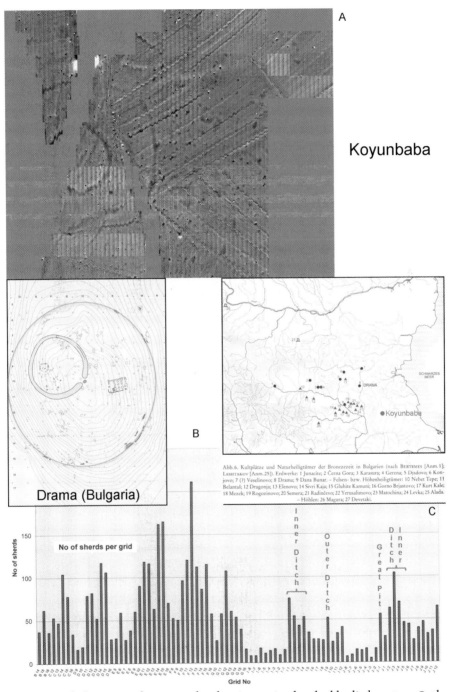

Figure 8.8: Koyunbaba: A. geophysics results showing a circular double ditch system; B. the Early Bronze Age site of Drama (Yambol, Bulgaria) as comparison, after Bertemes 1998 and 2002; C. pottery statistics from the site survey.

remains plausible that this occurred due to the transformation of Kanlıgeçit, which in turn progressed from being a local to a regional centre.

İstanbul-Selimpaşa Höyük

This site lies on an elevated area next to an 800 m long sandy bay in the Sea of Marmara, c.55 km west of the Bosphorus entry, thus making it probably the last safe harbour for any Bronze Age sea merchant wishing to enter the Black Sea. It is now the last remaining tell site on the northern side of the Sea of Marmara, and it was originally one of the largest mounds and it was certainly a regional centre on the basis that no other major settlement or tell are known within a distance of 15–20 km. The appearance and preservation of the site and the results of our survey and prospection there have been described in detail elsewhere (Heyd et al. 2010; Aydıngün 2014), and so a brief summary is provided here. The site (Figure 8.9) is c.150 m × 150 m wide, and has a maximum cultural deposit depth of 6–7 m. There is an upper plateau in the southeast which was originally c.60 × 60 m and it has steep sides towards the east and the south. The latter is the seafront where erosion and modern construction have cut away at least 10–20 meters of the tell. Geomagnetics and GPR have revealed an intensive occupation here and two to three semi-circular linear features around this acropolis, probably a defensive ring system made of stone walls. An outer settlement stretches to the north and west. The recovered material culture from our surveys ranges chronologically from the Chalcolithic and Troy I-Ezero to Troy II-III, Grey-Minyan, Troy VIIB2 and classical sherds. In the acropolis area, however, late EBA sherds were found close to the badly damaged surface without much intrusion of later materials, making it probable that the principal occupation here dates to the period between 2500 and 2000 BC. Although not yet excavated, these features make it very plausible that Selimpaşa Höyük's acropolis was similar in appearance to that of Troy II-III and Kanlıgeçit. Among the majority of EBA Ezero bowl/plate and cup sherds, there were also many sherds of Anatolian red-slip ware and several wheel-made Trojan plates and some red burnished/slipped pithoi fragments (Figure 8.10). At least one fragment of a little depas vessel was recovered also.

Selimpaşa Höyük is one of only four sites on the northern side of the Sea of Marmara in which EBA Anatolian red-slip and/or wheel-made pottery was described (the others being Kanallı [Kınallı] Köprü, Çatalca (potentially: Aydıngün et al. 2015: 423) and Karaagaçtepe). Interestingly, the immediate city centre of Istanbul - the potential key spot for crossing between northwestern Anatolia and Thrace - though excavation and survey has not yet delivered such pottery remains, despite other EBA pottery wares being found there (Dönmez 2006). But this might be due to chronological reasons. There is also a possibility that the whole social alignment of the groups inhabiting the Bosphorus land-bridge was more orientated to the Black Sea littoral and therefore these belonged to a cultural entity (see Efe 2004) different to the group at Selimpaşa, which in turn possessed closer links to the Dardanelles and Troy, at least in the second half of the 3rd millennium BC.

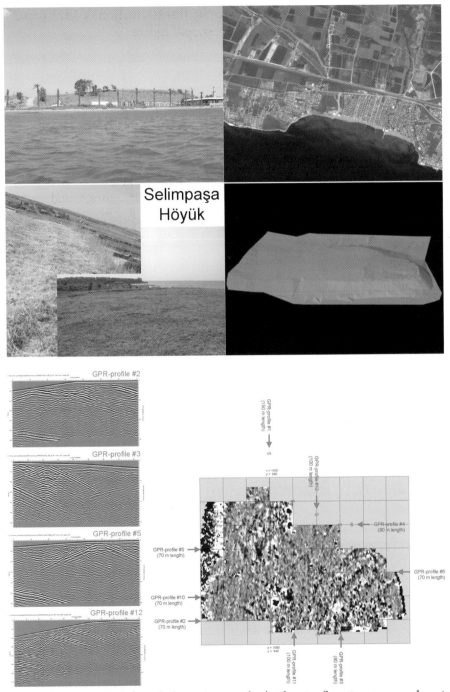

Figure 8.9: Selimpaşa Höyük (Istanbul Province, Turkey): The site (location, topography, pictures, GPR, geomagnetics), after Heyd et al. 2010.

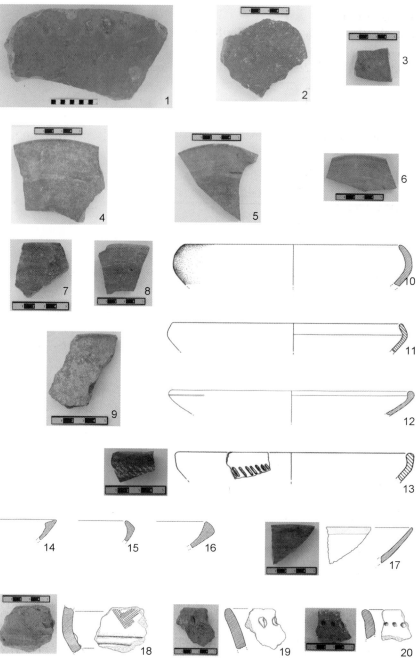

Figure 8.10: Selimpaşa Höyük: Early Bronze Age pottery finds (photos and drawings); 1. pithos wall sherd, wheel-made, reddish slip, c.2 cm thick; 2–3. Anatolian red-slip wares; 4–6. 8. 17. Troyan wheel-made plate rim sherds; 7. rim sherd of a higher form, hand-made; 9. bowls/plates; 11–16. bowls/plates with inverted and/or thickened rim, all hand-made; 18–20. decorated sherds, hand-made (photographs and illustrations by authors).

Mikhalich-Baa Dere

This site is about 70 km away from Kanlıgeçit, located in the south Sakar mountain region (Haskovo province), 1.5 km south of the modern village of the same name and not far away from the current Bulgarian-Turkish border. As in the previous cases of Kanlıgeçit and Selimpaşa, it consists of a fortified citadel in a naturally protected situation, this being a flat crest of a small hill with steep gullies to the south, east and west, and it had an extended outer settlement, stretching over some hectares apparently concentrated on two locations to the west/southwest and the northeast of the citadel (Figure 8.11). However, information about the outer settlement remains scanty and is confusing because it only comes from survey collections of pottery sherds and no excavation or detailed prospection has been conducted. The whole area is well-watered, with streams running close by and springs being within close proximity also. The first excavations in the citadel part of the site took place in the 1940s, but it was the excavations led by Morena Stefanova in the late 1990s and early 2000s that have significantly added to our understanding (see Stefanova 2004a with further references on previous expeditions). The citadel measures c.0.3–0.4 ha and has features that make it very similar to the one at Kanlıgeçit. Also having its origins as a small tell-like settlement in EBA II, it appears to be fortified during the second half of the 3rd millennium BC, when a 1.9–2.5 m wide dry-stone wall built of limestone, and preserved up to 1.2 m high, was constructed. The base was intentionally sloped and the upper part of this was built using mudbricks, as was the case in Kanlıgeçit. At least four occupation layers have been observed in the interior of this fortification, comprised of house, hearth and fireplace remains as well as settlement debris. Notable is a 130 m2 large burnt house from level 3–4 whose description, including mudbrick walls, reminds us of a megaron building (Stefanova 2004a: 178). More specific details, as with the houses of the later occupation at the site, remain unfortunately unclear at present.

What is clear, however, is the fact that the Depas *amphikypellon* cups, six altogether with three of them near-complete (Stefanova 2004b, Abb. 1; Leshtakov in press), did not come from the citadel but from the outer settlement. This is perhaps another interesting parallel to Kanlıgeçit, where the citadel has yielded only a few Depas-type sherds (see Özdoğan and Parzinger 2012, Abb. 82,2; Fig. 114,17; 115,11; 118,5; 121,14) while some of the thin and finely executed handles attributed to Depata-type come from the unpublished outer settlement survey collections. The difference is in their preservation, and the complete or near-complete specimens from Mikhalich come from a restricted number of locations, which casts doubt on their use and/or deposition as a normal element in the lives of the inhabitants of the outer settlement.

Other *International Anatolianising Pottery* or wheel-made and/or Anatolian red-slip ware pottery does not seem to have been recovered from Mikhalich so far, according to existing publications. These ceramics are, however, known in some quantity from the settlement site of Gülübovo (eg. Leshtakov 2002) some 55 km away from Mikhalich and explored in the 1990s. Here also a Depas cup was found, and several of these (one intact and six fragmented) were published from the site of Assara (Haskovo region;

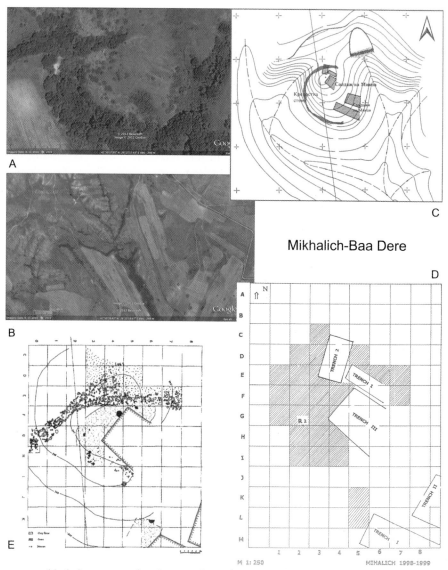

Figure 8.11: Mikhalich-Baa Dere (Haskovo, Bulgaria): The site (location, topography and excavation results); A–B. from GoogleEarth; C–E. after Stefanova 2004a.

Leshtakov 2003), 10 km away from Gülübovo. Wheel-made pottery is also mentioned for Tell Altan Tepe (Leshtakov 2002: 177, footnote 13) but not yet published (the examples also mentioned from Cherna Gora are in fact Iron Age in date). The same is true for one or two notable sherds found in pits from level V and VI of the eponymous Ezero Tell (Stefanova 2004b: 198). The dating of these to the EBA, we believe, is doubtful because their stratigraphical context appears too early to yield such pottery. While Gülübovo, Altan Tepe and Ezero are typical, albeit large Bulgarian tell settlements,

Assara is different in that it is a plateau site in a strongly fortified position next to the Maritsa river. This site was to later become a hillfort in the Iron Age, highlighting its strategic location. Much has already been written about the interpretation of these *International Anatolianising Pottery* finds in the Bulgarian EBA, whether it is their components, preservation, context, wheel-made or local imitations (eg., Leshtakov 2002; Stefanova 2004b; Rahmstorf 2006; Heyd 2013a: 51, Fig. 3.3; Leshtakov in press), and therefore does not need to be repeated here. However two aspects are important to take note of in the context of this present study: Ezero has only yielded one or two, if any, pieces of *International Anatolianising Pottery*; there are no such sherds in the well-excavated tell sites of Yunazite, Drama or Dyadovo. Taken together, these data suggest that the social processes through which these ceramics were brought to, or imitated, and consumed at, were limited in their geographical extend to the lower Maritsa region and adjacent Sakar mountain range.

Foreigners, Emporia, Colonies, Urbanism... Or All of Them: An Assessment

All three outstanding fortified settlement sites – Kanlıgeçit, Selimpaşa and Mikhalich – were roughly contemporary and seem to be very similar to each other and, despite having very different degrees of fieldwork exploring them, probably follow the same design and size model. The blueprint for these naturally protected citadels fortified using stone and mudbrick and having an extended outer settlement around, certainly has no local predecessors in Thrace. It has, however, its best comparisons in north-western Anatolia, where the sites of Troy and to some extent also Küllüoba (Efe 2007; Efe and Fidan 2008) and Seyitömer (Bilgen 2015) show the same model, and this had developed a few centuries earlier there. Kanlıgeçit, as the most intensively investigated of these sites, is structurally so close to Troy II/III, employing many details including architectural traditions along with potentially going much deeper into ideas of cult and religion, that one rightfully wonders how it is possible for a local elite to undertake this if they are only imitating an existing model. This leaves us in a position in which one has to seriously take into consideration an influx of foreign people. There is, admittedly, not a single individual identified by their household and possessions, or burial and customs, or using applied scientific methods (*e.g.* stable isotope analysis) that could attribute them to a specific Anatolian origin. The same conclusion of the existence of foreigners is also indicated by the use of many exotic and prestigious objects, often made of silver. This metal was not readily available in EBA Thrace. We can also note that tin-bronzes may have arrived into this region via Anatolia rather than Europe (Rahmstorf 2010: 683–685, fig. 6). In relation to artefacts associated with dress, adornment, and eating, drinking and feasting, we also observe that these are often not of autochthonous form. They all have their best comparisons in EBA north-western Anatolia and the eastern Aegean, and it is difficult to imagine how such a quantity and quality, and the imaginations and customs behind these, can be transferred to Europe without having individuals or groups of people carrying them, and the infrastructure to organise their transport and wider distribution (see also Leshtakov 2011).

Considering the evidence for foreigners at these sites does not, however, exclude local elites also trying to copy these innovations and achievements. It is even likely that the immediate reach of these foreign parties only includes the coastal zones of the Marmara and northern Aegean Seas along with the catchment area of the lower Maritsa river, with its tributaries Ergene, lower Tundza and Arda, up to a northern boundary near the mouth of the Sazliyka river at modern Simeonovgrad (Figure 8.12). This contact-zone would also embrace the resource-rich Strandza and Sakar mountains, but rule out some key sites located geographically beyond, such as Gülübovo, Ezero and Dübene. These would instead be within a kind of 'affected zone' hypothetically covering all of Thrace up to the Balkan mountains and also to include the coastal Black Sea area. Local elites were no doubt also present in the above named zone within immediate reach, as shown by their tumuli graves, and even if we have foreigners in this immediate zone, the majority or the population would surely still have been indigenous as shown, for example, by the mass of local pottery types in Kanlıgeçit.

The importance of the second settlement site described above, Koyunbaba can be seen in this context. Being only 12 km away from Kanlıgeçit and probably having a broadly similar origin, it was distinguished by the presence of a possible open-air sanctuary, though its development was perhaps cut short at the time of, or shortly

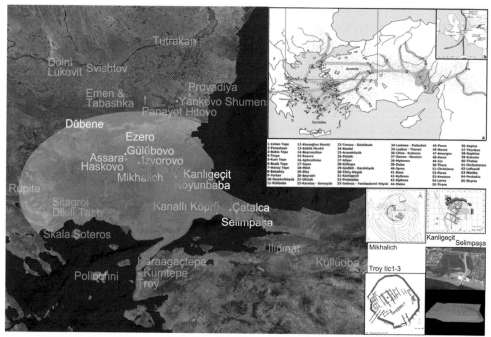

Figure 8.12: Thrace as integral part of the Early Bronze Age Anatolian Trade Network (image by authors).

after, the establishment of the Anatolian model-site of Kanlıgeçit. This suggests that the proposed influx of a foreign people was not a completely peaceful event. So while there is potential for conflict, the original foreigners can turn into locals after one or two generations, and alliances are built with the local elite, through the exchange of gifts, labour, goods, information and genes (see *e.g.* Tartaron 2005). Both sides benefit from such an interaction and subsequent symmetric cooperation. For the foreigners, they have the advantage of a social and economic autonomy securing the continuation of their exchange pattern with contact regions farther away, facilitating the influx of new foreigners of various backgrounds, while others were leaving. The local elites get fresh resources in their hands providing the means for the accumulation of wealth, for redistributional systems and creation of dependencies, and for peer-polity interaction in what might be a highly competitive social background. In consequence a 'contagious' process of conspicuous consumption develops with the result that the indigenous society is stimulated to advanced complexity; speaking generally, it is perhaps the incentive for the promotion from a *segmentary society* to *chiefdom level* (Heyd 2013a: 53–54; Kristiansen, 2014). Over time, an equilibrium might thus have been established, securing the existence of Kanlıgeçit, perhaps Selimpaşa and Mikhalich, and potentially other similar sites yet to be discovered, for some centuries.

There can be no doubt that the driving force behind this influx of goods and people is enhanced exchange and organised trade, and it is in no way an accident that concurrently the largest exchange network the world had seen up until then arrived at its peak. This network was centred in southern Mesopotamia, a region that had been fully urbanised for at least a millennium, and it stretched from as far away as western India on one side to southeast Europe on the other, and it also incorporated large parts of Central Asia (see Rahmstorf 2006; 2011). The effects of this network in terms of exchange, and social and economic progression in Anatolia and the eastern Aegean coast have already been considered nearly a decade ago when the seminal works of Vasıf Şahoğlu (2005) and Turan Efe (2007) were first published. Both have already included Kanlıgeçit and Turkish Thrace in their discussion, but were not considering the degree in which this most southeastern corner of Europe was part of this network. This needs to be adjusted. So from *c.*2400 BC and throughout the Early Helladic II/III or Anatolian EB IIIa/IIIb thresholds, conventionally dated to *c.*2200 BC (Maran 1998; Kouka 2013; Massa 2014), until the very late 3rd millennium BC (Parzinger and Özdoğan 2012: 268f.), Thrace was in no way a periphery, but an integral part of this commercial network, most probably due to its richness in natural resources. This may also be reflected in the integration of this region in later networks (*e.g.* in the Late Bronze Age: Leshtakov 2007; or in the classical periods). The strong Kanlıgeçit-Troy connection no doubt favours the predominance of the Dardanelles route (and subsequently the Maritsa river valley) for this network. However, also the Bosporus crossing needs to be seriously taken into account, despite its less investigated status, due to the distribution of the crescentic axes, the Kanlıgeçit clay idols, and other pottery evidence (Sarı 2012), while the maritime link is also significant for Selimpaşa.

Altogether it seems obvious that neither simple mechanisms of diffusion of information, ideas and goods are at work here, nor that the models of World Systems Theory (*e.g.* Wallerstein 2004; Harding 2013), as valuable as they are to describe the wider networks, can fully explain the situation in Thrace and therefore be easily applied. What exists is a much more complicated interference of ideological peripheries and traditional cultural boundaries, of acculturation processes, and seemingly contemporary different levels of complexity in this rather unstable contact zone region. Diffusion is traditionally rather seen as a more random process of transmission (see *e.g.* Elliot Smith *et al.* [eds.] 1927). However, with emerging societal complexity, this process becomes more targeted, and channelled via special 'agencies', or in our case some special sites in key networking, resource controlling or even politically dominating positions. It is exactly these sites that act here as hotspots of transmission for these new ideas, innovations and achievements. In this respect Kanlıgeçit, and perhaps Selimpaşa and Mikhalich, could well be seen as a kind of independent trading centres. However, it remains difficult to state whether the terms of 'Emporium' or 'Colony', or even 'Town', so loaded with backgrounds of classical Mediterranean civilisations, can readily be applied to this prehistoric situation of the later 3rd millennium BC. At least in Turkey one frankly considers the application of the term of 'towns' and 'early urbanisation' for the admittedly much larger, but structurally identical settlements there. Nevertheless, it is not easy to label a 4 ha large settlement with a 0.4 ha citadel a town. An Emporium is, by vague definition, an area within an existing settlement reserved for the merchandising business of foreigners. The situation at the Kültepe Kanesh Karum is the ideal analogue for this where we find definite evidence for foreign quarters within an established settlement (Kulakoğlu and Kangal 2010), in contexts only a few centuries later than ours. But here, this seems not to be the case; at least we have no evidence for such quarters beyond some uncertain inequalities at the outer settlements of Kanlıgeçit and Mikhalich, and the citadels cannot be considered to be part of the local tradition. A true colony in its classical sense (e.g. De Angelis 2009) is also not recognisable at first hand in Thrace. To argue for these, the political and to some extent also military background information on, for example, 'dependence on a mother town', 'privileged trade' or 'conquered/controlled territories' is completely missing. The same applies for any demographic pressure that stood behind the initiative. Nevertheless, what we have here might best be described as the colony idea at its very beginnings, virtually in its embryonic state, with only the basics of foreign traders, intrusive long-term settlements, negotiated or forced autonomy, merchandising network *etc.* in place (see also Stein 1999; Tartaron 2005). In such our sites would perhaps more resemble the Mesopotamian colonies, or 'trading posts', of northern Syria and southeastern Turkey dated to one millennium earlier, than the complex political institutions of the later periods. If acceptable, then Kanlıgeçit, Selimpaşa and Mikhalich might well be seen as the first of their kind, with a long list of more famous successors, on the European Continent.

Acknowledgements

We are grateful to our Bulgarian colleagues Stefan Alexandrov, Martin Hristov, Krassimir Leshtakov (all Sofia) and Vladimir Slavchev (Varna) for having us let unpublished manuscripts and presentations, and publications otherwise not easy accessible outside Bulgaria. Volker Heyd is particularly indebted to Hermann Parzinger (Berlin) and Mehmet Özdoğan (Istanbul) for having invited him to cooperate in the Kırklareli project and for introducing him to the outer settlement of Kanlıgeçit, the site of Koyunbaba and the Turkish Thracian landscape. He also wants to thank Mehmet Özdoğan for granting the permission to publish the roller stamped sherd from Kanlıgeçit some years ago. The paper has greatly benefitted from the comments of an anonymous reviewer and the corrections of the editor. We warmly appreciate this herewith.

Notes

1. That is modern Bulgaria south of the Balkan mountains, northern Greece east of the Nestos river (Greek Thrace), and the European part of Turkey, called Eastern or Turkish Thrace.
2. Interestingly in this context, the Varna Museum hosts another yet unpublished dagger made of precious metal, namely in silver, no doubt from Bulgaria but without provenance (pers. comm. V. Slavchev).

Bibliography

Alexandrov, S.
2009 Ukrashenija za kosa ot zlato i spevro prez bronzovata epocha v Severna Bulgaria (Gold and silver hair-rings from Bronze Age north Bulgaria). *Arheologija* (Sofia), 1–2: 5–18.
2011 Zlatni torkvi ot bronzovata epocha v Bulgarskite zemi (Bronze Age gold torques from Bulgaria). *Arheologija* (Sofia), 2: 7–15.

Avramova, M.
2004 The Hoarded Axes. In V. Nikolov and K. Bačvarov (eds.), *Von Domica bis Drama. Gedenkschrift für Jan Lichardus*: 163–169. Sofia: Arch. Inst. mit Museum der Bulgar. Akademie der Wissenschaften.

Avramova, M. and B. Todorieva
2005 A Bronze Age Metal Work Hoard from Southeastern Bulgaria. In: R. Laffineur, J. Driessen and E. Warmenbol (eds.), *The Bronze Age in Europe and the Mediterranean* (BAR International Series 1337): 69–73. Oxford: Archaeopress.

Aydıngün, Ş., E. Güldoğan, V. Heyd and H. Öniz
2010 2008 Yılı İstanbul Tarih Öncesi Çağlar Yüzey Araştırması. *27. Araştırma Sonuçları Toplantısı, 3. Cilt*: 273–288.

Aydıngün, Ş., V. Heyd, H. Öniz and E. Güldoğan
2014 İstanbul Tarih Öncesi Araştırmalarından Tunç Çağı Verileri. *Arkeoloji ve Sanat Dergisi* 145: 21–34.

Aydıngün, Ş., A.H. Eğilmez, H. Aydıngün, İ. Gürbüz, G. Gürbüz, M. Albukrek, G. Küçükali, E. Kuruçayırlı and B. Erdem

2015 Underground Structures From Istanbul Çatalca/Maltepe. In: *Hypogea 2015 - Proceedings of International Congress of Speleology in Artificial Cavities*. Rome, March 11–17 2015: 250–259.

Băjenaru, R.

2013 *Identități culturale, structui de putere și conflict militar în nordul Peninsulei Balcanice în mileniile IV-III a. Chr.* București: Editura Muzeului Național al Literaturii Române.

Bernabò Brea, L.

1976 *Poliochni - città preistorica nell'isola di Lemnos*, Vol. II,1. Roma: L'Erma di Bretschneider.

Bertemes, F.

1997 *Der mittelbronzezeitliche Kultplatz von Drama, Bez. Burgas, Bulgarien, und seine kulturhistorische Stellung im circumpontisch-nordägäisch-nordwestanatolischen Kontext*. Habilitation thesis, University of the Saarland.

1998 Der mittelbronzezeitliche Kultgraben von Drama und seine kulturhistorische Stellung in SE Europa. *Archäologisches Nachrichtenblatt* 3(4): 322–330.

2002 Heiligtum und Kultplatz in der thrakischen Ebene im 3. Jahrtausend v.Chr. *Berichte der Römisch-Germanischen Kommission* 83: 118–138.

Bilgen, A.N.

2015 *Seyitömer Höyük I*, İstanbul: Arkeoloji ve Sanat Yayınları.

Borislavov, B.

2010 The Izvorovo Gold. A Bronze Age Tumulus from Harmanli District, Southeastern Bulgaria. *Archaeologia Bulgarica* 14(1): 1–33.

Chernikh, E.N.

1978 *Gornoe delo i metallurgija v drevneischich Bolgarii*. Sofia.

De Angelis, F.

2009 Colonies and Colonization. In B. Graziosi, P. Vasunia and G. Boys-Stones (eds.), *The Oxford Handbook of Hellenic Studies*: 48–64. Oxford: University Press.

Dönmez, S.

2006 The Prehistory of the Istanbul Region: A Survey. *Ancient Near Eastern Studies* 43: 239–264.

Efe, T.

2003 Batı Anadolu Son Kalkolitik ve İlk Tunç Çağı. *ArkeoAtlas* 3, 94–129.

2004 Yassikaya, an Early Bronze Age Site near Heraclea Pontica (Kdz Ereğli) on the Black Sea Coast. In: B. Hänsel and E. Studeníková (eds.), *Zwischen Karpaten und Ägäis. Neolithikum und Ältere Bronzezeit. Gedenkschrift für V. Němejcová-Pavúková* (Studia Honoria 21): 27–37. Rahden/Westf.: Leidorf.

2007 The Theories of the 'Great Caravan Route' between Cilicia and Troy: The Early Bronze Age III in Inland Western Anatolia. *Anatolian Studies* 57: 47–64.

Efe, T. and E. Fidan

2006 Pre-Middle Bronze metal objects from inland western Anatolia: a typological and chronological evaluation. *Anatolia Antiqua* 14: 15–43.

2008 Complex II in the EB II Upper Town of Küllüoba Near Eskişehir. *Anatolica* 34: 67–102.

Elliot Smith G., B. Malinowski, H.J. Spinden and A. Goldenweiser (eds.)
1927 *Culture. The Diffusion Controversy*. New York: W.W. Norton & Company.

Fidan, E.
2012 İç Kuzeybatı Anadolu İlk Tunç Çağı Gözlü Süs İğneleri (*Toggle Pin*). *Colloquium Anatolicum* 11: 179–204.

Fol, A., J. Lichardus and V. Nikolov (eds.)
2004 *Die Thraker. Das Goldene Reich des Orpheus. Ausstellung in der Bundeskunsthalle Bonn*. Mainz: Von Zabern.

Frieman, C.
2010 Skeuomorphs and stone-working: elaborate lithics from the early metal-using era in coastal, northwest Europe. PhD thesis, University of Oxford.

Frirdich, C.
1997 Pinnacle E4/5 – Die Keramik der Periode Troia II im Vergleich. *Studia Troica* 7: 111–258.

Gabriel, U.
2001 Eine neue Sichtweise des "vor-trojanischen Horizontes". Ergebnisse der Ausgrabungen am Kumtepe 1993–1995. In P.I. Roman and S. Diamandi (eds.), *Cernavodă III-Boleráz. Ein vorgeschichtliches Phänomen zwischen dem Oberrhein und der Unteren Donau* (Studia Danubiana, series symposia 2): 84–87. Bucureşti: Institutul Român de Tracologie.

Gernez, G.
2007 *L'armement en métal au Proche et Moyen-Orient. Des origines à 1750 av. J.-C.* Thèse de doctorat, Université de Paris 1 Panthéon-Sorbonne (http://hal.archives-ouvertes.fr/docs/00/34/12/63/PDF/GERNEZ_Guillaume_-_These_Vol_I_Texte_.pdf).

Georgiev. G.I., N.Ya. Merpert, R. Katincharov and D.G. Dimitrov
1979 *Ezero. Rannobronzovoto selishte*. Sofia: Bulgarskata akademiya na naukite, archeologicheski institut.

Güldoğan, E., Ş. Aydıngün and V. Heyd
2011 2009 Yılı İstanbul Tarihöncesi Çağlar Yüzey Araştırması. *28 Araştırma Sonuçları Toplantısı, Cilt 1*: 355–363.

Hänsel, B. and P. Weihermann
2000 Ein neu erworbener Goldhort aus dem Karpatenbecken im Berliner Museum für Vor- und Frühgeschichte. *Acta Praehistorica et Archaeologica* 32: 7–29.

Harding, A.
2013 World Systems, Cores, and Peripheries in prehistoric Europe. *European Journal of Archaeology* 16, no. 3: 378–400

Heyd, V.
2011 Yamnaya burials and tumuli west of the Black Sea. In S. Müller-Celka and E. Borgna (eds.), *Ancestral Landscapes: Burial mounds in the Copper and Bronze Ages* (Travaux de la Maison de l'Orient et de la Méditerranée 61): 536–555. Lyon: Maison de l'Orient et de la Méditerranée.

2013a Europe 2500 to 2200 BC: Between Expiring Ideologies and Emerging Complexity. In H. Fokkens and A. Harding (eds.), *The Oxford Handbook of the European Bronze Age*: 46–67. Oxford: University Press.

2013b Europe at the dawn of the Bronze Age. In V. Heyd, G. Kulcsár and V. Serevenyi (eds.), *Transitions to the Bronze Age* (Archaeolingua Major Series 30): 9–66. Budapest: Archaeolingua.

Heyd, V., Ş. Aydıngün and E. Güldoğan

2010 Geophysical applications for ITA 2008: the example of the Selimpaşa Höyük. *25. Arkeometri Sonuçları Toplantısı*: 553–570.

Heyd, V. and C. Skowranek

2012 Geophysikalische Prospektion mit Fluxgate-Gradiometer. In M. Özdoğan and H. Parzinger, *Die frühbronzezeitliche Siedlung von Kanlıgeçit bei Kırklareli* (Studien im Thrakien-Marmara-Raum 3, Archäologie in Eurasien 27): 14–18. Berlin: DAI and Von Zabern.

Hristov, M.

2000 Bronze Age Gold and Electron Adornments from Tabashka Cave in the Osum River Drainage. In L. Nikolova (ed.), *Technology, Style and Society* (BAR International Series 854): 277–281. Oxford: Archaeopress.

2007 Necropolis and Ritual Structures from the Early Bronze Age near the Village of Dŭbene, Karlovo Region. 10 Apr. 2007. In B. Horejs and P. Pavúk (eds.), *Aegean and Balkan Prehistory*. http://www. aegeobalkanprehistory.net/article.php?id_art=3 (24 March 2013).

2012 A ritual structure from Balonv Gorun locality near the village of Dubene, Karlovo region. *Isvestija na natsionalnija istoricheski muzei* (*Proceedings of the National Museum of History*) 24: 9–32.

Karul, N.

2005 Anatolische Idole in Ostthrakien: Kirklareli-Kanlıgeçit. In B. Horejs, R. Jung, E. Kaiser and B. Terzan (eds.), *Interpretationsraum Bronzezeit. Bernhard Hänsel von seinen Schülern gewidmet* (Universitätsforschungen zur prähistorischen Archäologie 121): 117–121. Rahden/Westf.: Leidorf.

2012 Anthropomorphe Plastik. In M. Özdoğan and H. Parzinger, *Die frühbronzezeitliche Siedlung von Kanlıgeçit bei Kırklareli* (Studien im Thrakien-Marmara-Raum 3. Archäologie in Eurasien 27): 190–192. Berlin: DAI and Von Zabern.

Klein, H.

1992 *Untersuchung zur Typologie bronzezeitlicher Nadeln in Mesopotamien und Syrien* (Schriften zur vorderasiatischen Archäologie 4). Saarbrücken: Saarbrücker Druckerei und Verlag.

Kouka, O.

2013 Against the Gaps: The Early Bronze Age and the Transition to the Middle Bronze Age in the Northern and Eastern Aegean/Western Anatolia. *American Journal of Archaeology* 117: 569–580.

Koukouli-Chrysanthaki, Ch.

2007 Anthropomorphic Stelae from Greece. *Notizie Archeologiche Bergomensi* 12 (2005): 85–123.

Kristiansen, K.

2014 The decline of the Neolithic and the Rise of Bronze Age society. In C. Fowler, J. Harding and D. Hofmann (eds.), *The Oxford Handbook of the European Neolithic*. Oxford: University Press.

Kulakoğlu, F. and S. Kangal (eds.)
2010 *Anatolia's Prologue. Kultepe Kanesh Karum. Assyrians in Istanbul* (Kayseri Metropolitan Municipality Cultural Publications 78). Istanbul: ECOC Agency.

Leshtakov, K.
2002 Galabovo pottery and a new synchronisation for the Bronze Age in upper Thrace with Anatolia. *Anatolica* 28: 171–211.
2003 The Thracian Settlement at Assara (Constantia) near Simeonovgrad. *Isvestija na IM Haskovo* 2: 33–86.
2006 Structure, Function and Interpretation of Cherna gora 1 enclosure in Upper Thrace (Southeast Bulgaria). In M.-C. Frere-Sautot (ed.), *Des trous... Structures en creux pré- et protohistoriques* (préhistoires 12): 405–430. Montagnac: Mergoil.
2007 The Eastern Balkans in the Aegean Economic System During the LBA. Ox-Hide and Bun Ingots in Bulgarian Lands. In I. Galanaki, H. Tomas, Y. Galanakis and R. Laffineur (eds.), *Between the Aegean and the Baltic Seas. Prehistory Across Borders* (Aegaeum 27): 447–458. Liège: Univ. de Liège.
2011 Bronze Age mortuary practices in Thrace: A prelude to studying the long-term tradition. In S. Müller-Celka and E. Borgna (eds.), *Ancestral Landscapes: Burial mounds in the Copper and Bronze Ages* (Travaux de la Maison de l'Orient et de la Méditerranée 61): 561–571. Lyon: Maison de l'Orient et de la Méditerranée.

Leshtakov, K.
in press Troy and Upper Thrace: What Happened in the EBA 3? In: E. Pernicka, S. Ünlüsoy and S.W.E. Blum (eds.), *Early Bronze Age Troy: Chronology, Cultural Development, and Interregional Contacts.* An international conference held at the University of Tübingen, May 8–10, 2009 (Studia Troica Monographien 8). Bonn: Habelt.

Maran, J.
1998 *Kulturwandel auf dem griechischen Festland und den Kykladen im späten 3. Jahrtausend v. Chr.* (Universitätsforschungen zur Prähistorischen Archäologie 53). Bonn: Habelt.

Massa, M.
2014 Destructions, Abandonments, Social Reorganisation and Climatic Change in West and Central Anatolia at the End of the Third Millennium BC. *Arkeoloji'de Bölgesel Çalişmalar Sempozyum Bildirileri, YAS* 4: 89–123.

Meyer-Todorieva, B.
2010 Anthropomorphe Steinstelen aus dem Nordpontikum und dem Balkan vom 4. bis 2. Jt. v.Chr. In V. Becker, M. Thomas and A. Wolf-Schuler, *Zeiten - Kulturen - Systeme. Gedenkschrift für Jan Lichardus* (Schriften des Zentrum für Archäologie und Kulturgeschichte ds Schwarzmeerraumes 17): 217–230. Langenweissbach: Beier and Beran.

Müller, K.
1938 *Die Urfirniskeramik* (Tiryns IV). München: Bruckmann.

Muhly, J.D.
2011 Metals and Metallurgy. In G. McMahon and S. Steadman (eds.), *The Oxford Handbook of Ancient Anatolia (10,000-323 BCE)*: 858–876. Oxford: University Press.

Nikolova, Ja. and N. Angelova
1961 Razkopki na Emenskata peschtera. *Iswestija na archeologischeskija institut* 24: 297–316.

Nikolova, L.
1999 *The Balkans in Later Prehistory* (BAR International Series 791). Oxford: Archaeopress.
2008 Balkan-Anatolian Cultural Horizons from the Fourth Millennium BC and Their Relations to the Baden Cultural Complex. In M. Furholt, M. Szmyt and A. Zastawny (eds.), *The Baden Complex and the Outside World* (Studien zur Archäologie in Ostmitteleuropa 4): 157–166. Bonn: Habelt.

Özdoğan, M.
2011 Eastern Thrace: the Contact Zone Between Anatolia and the Balkans. In G. McMahon and S. Steadman (eds.), *The Oxford Handbook of Ancient Anatolia (10,000–323 BCE)*: 657–682. Oxford: University Press.

Özdoğan, M., E. Özdoğan, V. Heyd and H. Schwarzberg
2008. Türkiye'de 2006 Yilinda Yapilan araştırma ve kazilar (Archaeological surface survey and excavations in Turkey, 2006): Kırklareli yüzey araştırmaları (Kırklareli surface survey). *Türkiye Bilimler Akademisi Arkeoloji Dergisi (TÜBA-AR)* 10: 111–113.

Özdoğan, M. and H. Parzinger
2012 *Die frühbronzezeitliche Siedlung von Kanlıgeçit bei Kırklareli* (Studien im Thrakien-Marmara-Raum 3. Archäologie in Eurasien 27). Berlin: DAI and Von Zabern.

Popescu, A.-D.
2013a Considerații privind unele podoabe de aur din epoca bronzului de pe teritoriul României. *Arheovest* 1: 163–174.
2013b Cele mai timpurii obiecte de argint din Europa. In S.-C. Ailincăi, A. Țârlea and C. Micu (eds.), *Din Preistoria Dunării de Jos. 50 de ani de la începutul cercetărilor arheologice la Babadag*: 67–88. Brăila: Editura Istros a Muzeului Brăilei.

Popov, H., A. Jockenhövel and C. Groer
2011 Ada Tepe (Ost-Rhodopen, Bulgarien): Spätbronzezeitlicher-ältereisenzeitlicher Goldbergbau. In Ü. Yalçın (ed.), *Anatolian Metal V* (Der Anschnitt, Beiheft 24): 111–126. Bochum: Deutsches Bergbau-Museum.

Rahmstorf, L.
2006 Zur Ausbreitung vorderasiatischer Innovationen in die frühbronzezeitliche Ägäis. *Praehistorische Zeitschrift* 81(1): 49–96.
2010 Die Nutzung von Booten und Schiffen in der bronzezeitlichen Ägäis und die Fernkontakte der Frühbronzezeit. In H. Meller and F. Bertemes (eds.), *Der Griff nach den Sternen* (Tagungen des Landesmuseums für Vorgeschichte Halle 5): 675–697. Halle: Landesmuseum.
2011 Re-integrating 'Diffusion': the Spread of Innovations among the Neolithic and Bronze Age Societies of Europe and the Near East. In T. Wilkinson, S. Sherratt and J. Bennet (eds.), *Interweaving Worlds. Systemic Interactions in Eurasia, 7th to 1st Millennia BC. Papers from a conference in memory of Professor Andrew Sherratt*: 100–119. Oxford: Oxbow.

Renfrew, C., M. Gimbutas and E.S. Elster (eds.)
1986 *Excavations at Sitagroi: a prehistoric village in northeast Greece, Vol. 1* (Monumenta Archaeologica 13). Los Angeles: UCLA Institute of Archaeology.

Roman, P.I., A. Dodd-Opritescu and P. János
1992 *Beiträge zur Problematik der schnurverzierten Keramik Südosteuropas* (Heidelberger Akademie der Wissenschaften, Internationale Kommission, Erforschung der Vorgeschichte des Balkans 3). Mainz: Von Zabern.

Roodenberg, J.J. and L.C. Thissen (eds.)
2001 The Ilıpınar Excavations II (Pihans 93). Leiden: Nederlands Instituut voor het Nabije Oosten.

Sazcı, G.
2007 *The Treasures of Troia*. Istanbul: Aygaz.

Şahoğlu, V.
2005 The Anatolian Trade Network and the Izmir Region During the Early Bronze Age. *Oxford Journal of Archaeology* 24(4): 339–361.

Sarı, D.
2009 Late EB II pottery recovered in complex II of Küllüoba. *Anatolia Antiqua* 17: 89–132.
2012 İlk Tunç Çağı ve Orta Tunç Çağı'nda Batı Anadolu'nun Kültürel ve Siyasal Gelişimi. *MASROP e-dergi 7 (Küllüoba kazıları ve batı Anadolu tunç çağları üzerine yapılan araştırmalar)*: 112–249

Schwenzer, S.
2005 Zum Beginn der Frühbronzezeit in Bulgarien. In B. Horejs, R. Jung, E. Kaiser and B. Terzan (eds.), *Interpretationsraum Bronzezeit. Bernhard Hänsel von seinen Schülern gewidmet* (Universitätsforschungen zur prähistorischen Archäologie 121): 181–189. Rahden/Westf.: Leidorf.

Steadman, S.R.
2011 The Early Bronze Age on the Plateau. In G. McMahon and S. Steadman (eds.), *The Oxford Handbook of Ancient Anatolia (10,000-323 BCE)*: 229–259. Oxford: University Press.

Stefanova, M.
2004a Fortified settlement Mihalich; monumental construction and natural landscape (archaeological investigations in 2002). *Godishnik na Departament Archeologija NBU* 6(5–15): 175–180.
2004b Kontextuelle Probleme der Becher *depas amphikepellon* in Thrakien. In V. Nikolov and K. Bačvarov (eds.), *Von Domica bis Drama. Gedenkschrift für Jan Lichardus*: 197–201. Sofia: Arch. Inst. mit Museum der Bulgar. Akademie der Wissenschaften.

Stein, G.
1999 *Rethinking World Systems: Diasporas, Colonies, and Interaction in Uruk Mesopotamia*. Tuscon: University of Arizona Press.

Tartaron, T.F.
2005 Glykys Limin and the discontinuous Mycenaean periphery. In R. Laffineur and E. Greco (eds.), *Emporia. Aegeans in the Central and Eastern Mediterranean* (Aegaeum 25): 153–162. Liège and Austin: Univ. de Liège and Univ. of Texas.

Tsintsov, Z., M. Hristov, V. Karatsanova and S. Tsaneva
2009 Preliminary Results from the Study of Early Bronze Age Golden Artefacts from Ritual Structures by the Village of Dubene, Karlovo District, South Bulgaria. *Archaeologia Bulgarica* 13(3): 7–21.

Ünlüsoy, S.
2011 Die Stratigraphie der Burg von Troia II. *Archäologisches Nachrichtenblatt* 16(1): 65–74.

Wallerstein, I.
2004 *World-Systems Analysis – An introduction.* London: Duke Univ. Press.

Wiencke, M.H.
1970 Banded Pithoi of Lerna III. *Hesperia* 39: 94–109.

Chapter 9

The Built Environment and Cultural Connectivity in the Aegean Early Bronze Age

Ourania Kouka

Introduction

Archaeological research in the Aegean, since its beginnings in 1870 with the excavations of Heinrich Schliemann at Troy, has revealed a number of sites dating to what has been defined as the Aegean Early Bronze Age (henceforth EB), a period dating according to calibrated radiocarbon data from 3100–2000 BC (Manning 2010: Tab. 2.2; Kouka 2013: 570, fig. 1).

Data from extensive excavations and surveys in various geographical and climatological landscapes of the Aegean, such as in Mainland Greece, the Cyclades, Crete, Macedonia, Thrace, and the North and East Aegean including the West Anatolian littoral have been analysed using typological, sociological, anthropological and economic methods. As a result different rhythms in the interfaces and development of cultural process in these landscapes have been recognised. Cultural variability was distinct already in the Neolithic (6700–3100 BC), though in the Early Bronze Age, a period characterised by population growth, new settlement patterns can be identified. These are accompanied by changes in size and intra-site structure of settlements, the intensification of agriculture, craft specialization, industrial development (metallurgy of arsenical copper and bronze), the evolution of ship building technology, the expansion of trade, and increased evidence for social differentiation.

In this context, the built environment (domestic, funerary, and sacral) can be seen as a mental, social and economic product of human intentions, which in turn signifies the framework in which all aforementioned traits are implicated. Through the rich archaeological record we can seek to recognise communal identities within various micro-regions that we can define using both geographic and culturally specific factors, and leading from this we can furthermore seek to define cultural entities and to recognise diversities within and between these. Taken together, these form the basic components for writing a synchronic and/or a diachronic history of geographically fragmented regions such as the Aegean.

Taking this cultural diversity into account, some linked phenomena can still be traced in the various landscapes of the Aegean, as a result of our identification of land- and sea-trade networks in the 4th and 3rd millennium BC. The creation of limited or more extensive land or sea trade networks was closely related to the necessity for acquisition and exchange of raw materials (obsidian, metals) or finished products. Within this context of increased interaction, we find related phenomena of increased craft specialisation and changes to social organisation that include increased stratification within Aegean prehistoric communities (Renfrew 2004). It is also crucial to address the scale of sea-trade networks among various regions of the Aegean in relation to ship building technology. This includes the use of longboats since the late 4th millennium BC on the basis of evidence from Strophilas on Andros (Televantou 2008), and the knowledge of natural sea-routes and winds, that would enable the planning of a successful navigation network (Papageorgiou 2008).

Trade, though, should not be considered as a one-dimensional phenomenon in Aegean prehistoric economies, limited to the exchange of raw materials. It is better seen as a multidimensional event, in which technologies, goods or luxurious high-status objects, every-day practices (*e.g.* cooking), architectural or burial practices, symbolic actions and ideas of feasts either for the entire communities or just for an elite, and mentalities in general may also come together. Thus, an economic praxis, which may have been activated due to social forces within a community, may be seen to stimulate wider cultural interactions. In complex geographical contexts such as the Aegean, the varying intensities and motivations for these necessitate more than one reading of both material evidence and historical situations.

Following these introductory remarks, it will be suggested that connectivity can be manifested in a variety of ways, and using the case of architectural features, this paper will move beyond using these as indicators for chronology or of cultural diffusion, and it aims to:

1. To define and investigate cultural connectivity in the Early Bronze Age Aegean and the West Anatolian littoral based on specific levels of spatial analysis, such as characterisation of architectural units (houses, communal buildings, administrative buildings), settlement architectural plans and settlement patterns (central and satellite sites) (Konsola 1984; Pullen 1985; Kouka 2002).
2. To clarify the scale of connectivity in the successive chronological phases of the Early Bronze Age through a diachronic study of these levels from EB I through EB III within the wider cultural framework of each landscape.
3. To discuss questions such as objectives of connectivity, or the relationship between architectural tradition and connectivity.
4. To investigate connectivity as co-operative interaction *vs.* connectivity and conflict.
5. To define how or if networks of architectural connectivity may be related with economic networks.

It should be noted in advance, that the insular North and East Aegean and the West Anatolian littoral, considered to form a cultural entity (Kouka 2002: 301–302), offer the best datasets for such a discussion, since they deliver rich architectural evidence from EB I through EB III. Mainland Greece and the Cyclades will contribute with settlement data in particular from early and late EB II, while data from Crete, Macedonia and Thrace for reasons of space will not be considered in this paper. Finally, for the same reasons, the evidence from mortuary contexts will not be included in this discussion.

North and East Aegean and the West Anatolian littoral

The North and East Aegean and the West Anatolian littoral with their extensively excavated sites (Kouka 2002: Karte 1; Davis 2013, fig. 4) (Figure 9.1) form an excellent laboratory for studying degrees of interaction and competition within the same cultural zone. These relations are visible in settlement planning (settlement size typically ranges from 0.8 to 2 ha, with the exceptions of Heraion 3.5 ha and Liman Tepe 6.0 ha: Kouka 2002: Diagr. 2), the use of communal buildings such as fortification

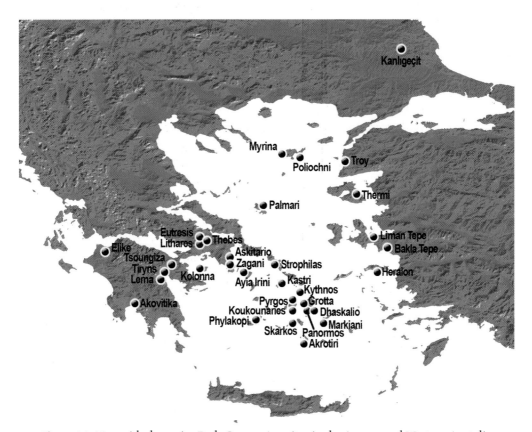

Figure 9.1: Map with the major Early Bronze Age sites in the Aegean and Western Anatolia.

systems, public buildings, administrative buildings or seats of the chiefs, the distribution of metallurgical workshops, and *exotica* from other Aegean landscapes, on hoarding of prestige objects, and the use of specific buildings or open spaces as arenas for expressing communal economic or social symbolism.

The Early Bronze Age I (3100/3000–2650 BC) in the northeast Aegean is a distinctive period with a totally different cultural profile compared with its Final Neolithic/ Late Chalcolithic past (henceforth FN, LCh). In the LCh large settlements consisting of circular and apsidal buildings without any planning are predominant (*e.g.* Myrina and Poliochni on Lemnos, Liman Tepe and Bakla Tepe in the Izmir region) (Kouka in press). In contrast, EB I is characterized by the development of new settlement patterns, including densely distributed settlements in landscapes such as the Troad, the regions of Izmir and Eskisehir (Tuncel 2009) and island landscapes such as Lemnos (Kouka 2002: 29–27, Karte 6, 7). Settlements are well planned, in many cases following the radiocentric system typical for this geographical region (*e.g.* Troy I: Ünlüsoy 2006: 133–135, fig. 1, 4; Thermi I-IIIB on Lesbos: Kouka 2002: 154, 170–171, 182–183, 196–197, Pl. 12, 15, 18, 21; Liman Tepe VI: Kouka 2013: 570, fig. 2 with earlier bibliography) (Figures 9.2a, 9.2b, 9.4) or the system organised in insulae (*e.g.* Poliochni: figure 3) both based on the use of rectangular long-room houses (Kouka 2002: 78–81, 98–99, Pl. 1, 3, 5, 7, 9). They are also strongly fortified with stone-built freestanding walls, supported by ramp-like terrace walls and well protected gates (Poliochni: Kouka 2002: 47–48, 64–65, 120–123, Pl. 3, 5; Thermi: Kouka 2002: 238–242, Pl. 12, 15, 18, 21; Liman Tepe: Kouka 2013: 570, fig. 2) (Figure 9.2a, 9.2b, 9.3, 9.4, 9.5, 9.7, 9.8), and have also communal buildings, such as communal storage buildings (Poliochni: Kouka 2002: 48–49; 2013, Heraion EB II-early: Kouka 2013: 576) and communal halls for most probably hosting political meetings or symbolic-religious feasts within the densely built settlements (*e.g.* Poliochni Blue-Yellow: Kouka 2002: 50) (Figure 9.2b, 9.7, 9.8). These buildings are different in form, size and construction than simple houses and are located either beside the fortifications or at important points within the settlements (centre, highest point of the hills, close to the harbours). They were in use over more than one architectural phase and had some modifications or radical rebuilding at the same place. Finally, for their erection, many members of communities were involved in, as was also the case in building fortifications. Micro-scale analysis of the island societies of the east Aegean and of Liman Tepe in the Gulf of Izmir has traced an interesting distribution of domestic and industrial activities, as well as the distribution of Aegean exotica. The presence of imported artefacts from the central and west Aegean occurs exclusively in workshops for the production of bronze jewellery, tools and weapons (workshops included crushing of copper ores, smelting and casting in moulds) imply the presence of a social group consisting of the families of metalworkers, apparently involved in the organisation of trade activities for covering the needs of their community in raw materials and non-local goods (Kouka 2002: 298; 2009a: 146, fig. 7, 8; Kouka and Şahoğlu in press; 2013: 570) (Figure 9.3, 9.7). Finally, on the basis of similarities in house architecture, in fortifications

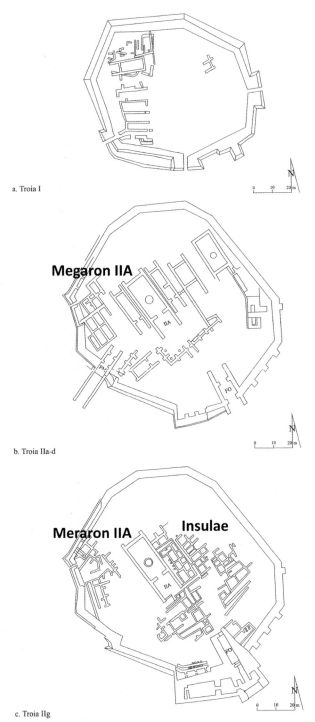

Figure 9.2: Plans of Troy: a. Troy I; b. Troy IIa-d; c. Troy IIg (based on Kouka 2002, Plan 54).

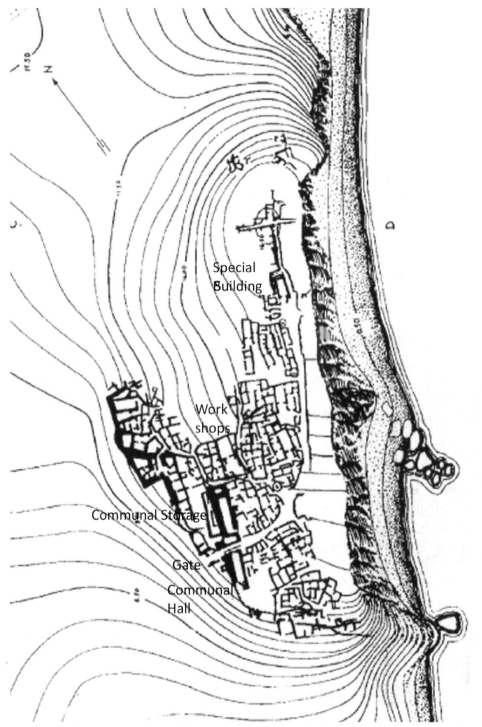

Special
Building

Work
shops

Communal Storage

Gate

Communal
Hall

Figure 9.3: Poliochni, Lemnos. Plan of phases Blue, Green, Red and yellow (based on Kouka 2002, Plan 1).

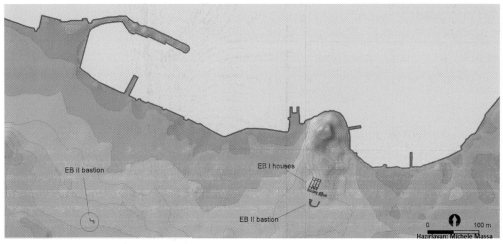

Figure 9.4: Liman Tepe. Topographical plan with the fortification and the radial arranged houses of the EBI and with the apsidal bastions of the fortified peninsula and the outer fortification of the EB II (Plan by Michele Massa).

Figure 9.5: Liman Tepe. The EB I fortification wall with the gate and the bastions from the southeast (Photo by V. Şahoğlu).

with rectangular or trapezoidal bastions, of the erection of communal buildings, of the types of local products (*e.g.* pottery, metal), and also of imported artefacts, I have postulated previously that a cultural *koine* operated in the east Aegean between 3000–2650 BC, as a result of an interaction between the East Aegean island settlements and those of Western Anatolia (Kouka 2002: 299–300; 2009a: 141).

Despite this cultural uniformity in EB I, some of these settlements only reached the zenith of their wealth by Early Bronze Age II (2700/2650–2300 BC). This may be due to their location on important trade-routes and their participation in sea and land trade networks (*Anatolian Trade Network*: Şahoğlu 2005, *Great Caravan Route*: Efe 2007). It is believed that these networks, as I have argued elsewhere (Kouka 2002, 299–301), were related to cultural processes surrounding bronze technology, the exchange and hoarding of prestige goods, new ceramic technologies, and the sharing of common symbolism (Kouka 2011). Settlements like Troy II, Liman Tepe V, Bakla Tepe in EB II-III, Poliochni Green-Yellow, Myrina, Thermi IV-V, Heraion I-V and Palamari II-III were extended following a new architectural plan that could better accommodate population growth (Figures 9.2, 9.2c, 9.3, 9.4). Apart from this, these sites were also reinforced by stronger fortifications, becoming in that way landmarks in their micro-regions. This was the case of Troy in the Troad and Liman Tepe in the Izmir Region, that both had a fortified upper and a fortified lower city (Kouka 2013: 577, fig. 2) (Figures 9.2b, 9.2c, 9.4, 9.6, 9.7). More specifically, Liman Tepe V possessed a new, well-planned fortification system with huge apsidal bastions (29 × 20 m) (Erkanal 1999: 240–241, Pl. LIII; Erkanal 2008a: 181–183, fig. 1, 7; Erkanal *et al.* 2009: 304, Pl. 1, Drawing 1, fig. 4–5), which protected the promontory and the harbour of the settlement, while the outer part of the settlement was also fortified with smaller apsidal bastions (Erkanal 1999: 241; Ersoy *et al.* 2001; Kouka 2013: 570–571, fig. 2–3) (Figures 9.4, 9.6, 9.7). Excavated EB II settlements also had communal buildings or building complexes either with an economic, political or even symbolic/religious character (*e.g* Megaron IIA in Troy II, Central Complex at Liman Tepe: Kouka 2002: 295–296; Kouka 2013: 571, fig. 3) (Figures 9.2b, 9.2c, 9.3, 9.4, 9.7). These had evidence also for craft specialisation, social stratification, and personal (*e.g.* the hoards of Troy and Poliochni, rich burial gifts in the pithos graves at Bakla Tepe) and communal (*e.g.* strong fortifications, communal buildings, buildings or complexes used as seats of chiefs) symbolism (Kouka 2011: 44–45). The above mentioned features are described on the basis of results of multi-criterion analyses, which have led to the designation of some specific settlements as having early urban features, or as centres of their micro-regions: these are Troy in the peninsula of the Troad, Liman Tepe in the Izmir Region, Poliochni in the east part of Lemnos. These sites may be compared to the fortified EH II settlements of Mainland Greece that have Corridor-Houses and with the well-fortified EC II settlements on specific Cycladic islands, as will be shown below.

Interaction reached its zenith in the East Aegean during late EB II (2500–2300 BC)-EB IIIA (2300–2200 BC), known in Mainland Greece and the Cyclades as the Lefkandi I-Kastri Phase. This phase is characterized by the following features: central politicoeconomic and religious architectural complexes (used for administration or hosting of feasts), the use of organised rich pithos cemeteries (*e.g.* at Bakla Tepe: Erkanal and Özkan 1999: 113–115, 124–125). We can also look to the development of new pottery technology and vessels for the consumption of wine by the elites (one-handled cup, bell-shaped cup, tankard, depas amphikypellon), the use of a new elite symbolism (Kouka 2011: 44–45), increased craft specialisation (particularly in the working of precious metals and bronzes) and the expansion of the scale of sea trade (Kouka 2002: 300). Apart from sea-routes, an inland trade route, called the *Great Caravan Route*, was established that linked south and south-east Anatolia through the central part with its western region. The *Great Caravan Route* introduced tin or tin alloys, craftsmen and artisans (goldsmiths), measuring systems for precious metals, and the potter's wheel in particular to western Anatolia (Kouka 2002: 299, 305). This route went beyond the Troad, up to Kanlıgeçit in Thrace, where a fortified settlement with a further fortified building complex within this, similar with that of Troy IIa-d has been excavated (Özdoğan and Parzinger 2012: 60, 267–278, fig. 26, 32, 37, 51, 54, 65, Heyd *et al.*, this volume) (Figures 9.1 and 9.2b). These expanded trade networks of the Aegean and Anatolia were not isolated, but were linked with those of the Eastern Mediterranean and the Near East. Cyprus also benefitted greatly due to its geographical location, and it is at this time that this copper-rich island entered its Early Bronze Age at *c.* 2400 BC. This was as a result of long, pre-Bronze Age interaction

Figure 9.6: Liman Tepe. The fortified peninsula with the apsidal bastion of the EB II from the south (Photo by Ch. Papanikolopoulos).

Figure 9.7: Liman Tepe from the northwest (Photo by H. Çetinkaya).

with the elites of the East Aegean islands and Western Anatolia and of a gradual colonisation from SW and S Anatolia, as visible in rectangular house architecture, metallurgical know-how, new pottery and weaving technology *etc.* (Kouka 2009b).

In Early Bronze IIIB (2200–2000 BC) serious socio-political changes seem to have taken place in many previously powerful settlements, as suggested by the decline of the once strong centres of western Anatolia (Troy II, Liman Tepe V) and by the contraction of the *Anatolian Trade Network*. What was still common in EB IIIB in the East Aegean and West Anatolian settlements was the disappearance of strong fortifications and communal buildings, a preference for simple house architecture, and strong communal symbolism represented by open settlement spaces rather than buildings. Feasts which may have been dedicated to fertility included the use of tortoise-shells as symbols and they also used depas cups and tankards of EB IIIB types for the consumption of wine. Evidence for this comes from the open communal space at Liman Tepe. Similar feasts must have also taken place in the Communal Building Complex at that site in late EB II, where stone phalloi were used as symbols of fertility. Therefore, at least in Liman Tepe a continuation in symbolism of life and fertility existed from the late EB II through EB IIIB periods (Kouka 2011: 47–49; 2013: 573–574).

Mainland Greece

The increase of population in the Early Helladic period (hereafter EH), particularly in southern Mainland Greece results in an increase in the number of settlements compared to the FN (Alram-Stern 2004: map with sites; Kouka 2008: fig. 27.2, 27.3, 27.4). The settlements are built on hills lying on fertile coastal plains. Most of the known settlements occupy 0.65 to 8 ha (Lerna 2.5, Lithares 3.5, Tiryns 5.9, Eutresis 8), while very few of them exceed 8 ha (Thebes-20, Manika-45) (Konsola 1984: 94–5, tabl. 1, 2) (Figure 9.1).

Well preserved settlement architecture from Mainland Greece dates in particular to EH II-III (2650–2100/2050 BC) and varies in preservation from site to site (Weiberg 2011). Konsola undertook a multi-criterion analysis and classified the best known settlements of the EH II-III in three categories (Konsola 1984, 165–173). As early urban settlements (Category I), or perhaps more approriately centres of their microregions, have been identified Kolonna on Aegina, Lerna, Tiryns, Zygouries, Thebes and Eutresis (Figure 9.9). Konsola used the following criteria, which are similar to those set out above for the East Aegean and Western Anatolia: town planning, arrangement of stone paved roads and squares for public use, existence of fortification systems and buildings with special functions, craft specialisation and the existence of metallurgical or obsidian workshops (trade, control of production and distribution of agricultural production, use of seals, concentration of wealth (jewellery, gold vases) and the existence of organised cemeteries (Konsola 1984).

Many sites consist of densely built rooms organised in irregular insulae, that are separated by roads and narrow paths following an agglutinative architectural system (*e.g.* Zygouries, Askitario: Konsola 1984: pl. 10. 13; Weiberg 2011: fig. 6, 7). Sites with circular or apsidal buildings (Thebes, Orchomenos-EH II, Tiryns-EH III, Lerna IV-EH III: Konsola 1984: pl. 2, 6, 17, 19; Rutter 1995: 4–10, pl. III-IV Heath-Wiencke 2000a: pl. 3–8; 2000b: 641–653) have irregular arrangements. More rarely, buildings flank a central road which runs through the whole settlement following a linear settlement plan (Lithares: Konsola 1984: pl. 5; Tzavella-Evjen 1984: pl. 5b; 1985: fig. 5). Finally, the radiating arrangement of building blocks consisting of long-room houses identical with the ones known from the East Aegean and separated by parallel streets is visible in the EB II-III site at Kolonna on Aegina Phase V (Walter and Felten 1981: 28–46, Pl. 7–8) (Figure 9.9).

Some EH settlements have preserved parts of fortification walls of a simple (Zagani in EH I: 3100–2650 BC) or complex form. Apsidal bastions of much smaller size than those of Liman Tepe V have also been used in the fortifications of Palamari-Phase II-III (5–9X5–9 m) (Theochari and Parlama 1997; Parlama 2007), Lerna IIIC-D (*c.* 4X4 m) (Heath-Wiencke 2000a: 91–124, Pl. 5–7; 2000b: 646–647), as well as in the EH III fortifications of Kolonna on Aegina-Phase V-VI (5.5–7 m wide) (Walter and Felten 1981: 28–33, 43–50). More specifically, the fortification of Lerna included a double stone wall, with chambers in between (casemate walls), and is reinforced by horseshoe-shaped

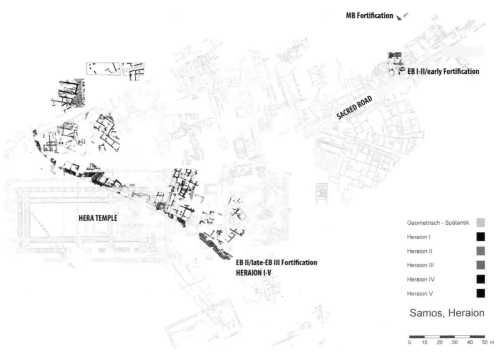

Figure 9.8: Heraion, Samos. Plan of the EB I–III settlement phases (Plan by H. Birk, O. Kouka, A. Clemente, N. Hellner, A. Tanner and K. Ragkou).

towers (Weiberg 2011: fig. 9, 10). The settlement of Aegina V is protected by a wall with alternate apsidal towers and gates and a rampart built at 3 metres from the wall.

Special EH II buildings, as the rectangular, two-storied 'Corridor Houses' (147–300 sqm) with central stamped-decorated hearths at Thebes, Aegina, Helike, Zygouries, Tsoungiza, Lerna, Akovitiva, as well as the 'Rundbau' of Tiryns (Kilian 1986: 68, fig. 56–59; Weiberg 2011: 56, fig. 9) are associated with the economic and social changes of the EB II period and have been interpreted as political-administrative (seat of the 'chief') and economic centres of the EH communities (overview in Alram-Stern 2004: 238–243; Katsonopoulou 2011: 67–68, fig. 6–7). These buildings are freestanding and located either in the centre of the settlement or near the fortification wall (Weiberg 2011: fig. 7, 9, 10). The best examples so far identified are the 'Building BG' of Lerna IIIC middle-late (Heath-Wiencke 2000a: 185–197, Pl. 6), the 'House of the Tiles' of Lerna IIID (Heath-Wiencke 2000a: 213–243, Pl. 8, 32), the 'Haus am Felsrand' in Kolonna II on Aegina (Walter and Felten 1981: 12–13, Pl. 4), the 'Weisses Haus' in Kolonna III (Walter and Felten 1981: 14–22, Pl. 5), and the 'Fortified Building' in Thebes (Aravantinos 1986). The significance of buildings of this category is best evidenced in Lerna III, where the communal area occupied by 'Building BG' and by its successor 'House of the Tiles', in which 143 clay sealings were found in one room, has been symbolically covered in Phase Lerna IV of the EH III by a monumental tumulus with a diameter of 18.75 m

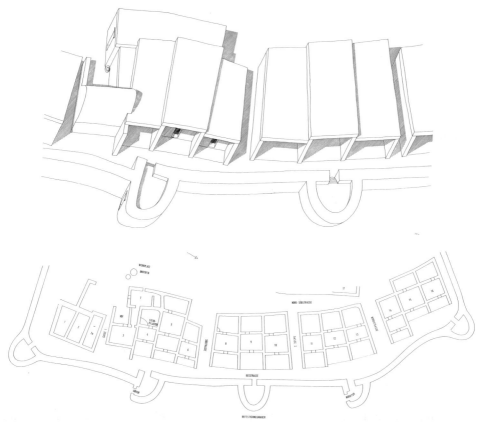

Figure 9.9: Aegina, Kolona V. Plan and isometric reconstruction (Walter and Felten 1981, Abb. 21–22).

(Heath-Wiencke 2000a: 297, fig. I.107b, I.108a, Section 22, 25), to 'commemorate the death of the House of the Tiles, of its occupants or of the community in which it stood?' (Heath-Wiencke 2000a: 297). Finally, the 'Sanctuary of the Bulls' of the EH II settlement at Lithares in Boeotia has been interpreted as a communal building, which might have been a place for religious feasts, as indicated by numerous clay figurines of bulls found in it (Tzavella-Evjen 1984: 21–22, pl. 5b, 82–84; 1985, 20, fig. 5).

The pottery associated with the 'Corridor Houses' included in the EH II-early and EH II-mature timeframe (2650–2500 BC) are exceptional, and a standard drinking set, consisting of sauceboats and saucers may have been used during feasts organised by the EH residents around hearths with rich stamped decoration in and/or close to these distinguished buildings (Pullen 2013: 550). This set, has been identified only at some EH sites (excluded Corinthia and Argolid: Pullen 2013: 550–551) and was replaced in the EH II-late or Lefkandi I-Kastri Phase (2500–2200 BC) (Davis 2013; Rutter 2013) by a new set consisting of two-handled tankards, one or two handled bell-shaped cups, depas cups, cut-away spouted jugs with globular body, shallow bowls and/or wheel-made plates (Pullen 2013: 545, fig. 1). These include East Aegean/Western Anatolian ceramic types of the EB II late-EB IIIA which are thought to be have been used there by local elites during feasts organised either in central buildings or in communal, open spaces (Kouka 2013: 573–574).

Significant for understanding the scale of connectivity between Mainland Greece on the one hand and the East Aegean and the West Anatolia littoral on the other, is the occurrence only in specific settlements of Mainland Greece of fortifications with apsidal bastions at Kolonna and Lerna, which were economic centres in their micro-regions (Figure 9.9) (*cf.* Liman Tepe V and Palamari on Skyros: Figure 9.6). We can also take account of the replacement of arsenical bronzes with tin bronzes, the hoarding of jewellery (EB III Aegina (2250–2100/2050 BC): Reinhold 2008: 24, 84–85, Taf. 3, 4; Elike: Katsonopoulou 2011: 81, fig. 20), the adaption and production of 'Anatolianising pottery' (up to Elike in the NW Peloponnese: Katsonopoulou 2011: 76–81, fig. 17, 18) and the first use or the potter's wheel (Kouka 2008: 318–319, fig. 27.4).

The Cyclades

Our knowledge about the built environment of the Early Cycladic period (henceforth EC) is limited due to strong erosion of the rocky ground of the islands, as well as due to destructions through intensive habitation of some of these settlements until the end of the Bronze Age (*e.g.* Ayia Irini on Keos, Phylakopi on Melos, Akrotiri on Thera). (Broodbank 2002: fig. 90; Kouka 2008: fig. 27.2, 27.3, 27.4). Excavated sites dating to EC I (3100–3000 BC) and the transitional EC I/EC II Kampos Phase (2900–2650 BC [Manning 2010: fig. 2:2]) are dramatically few (Markiani on Amorgos, Grotta on Naxos; Kouka 2008, fig. 27.3). Evidence of the EC IIA (Keros-Syros Culture: 2650–2500 BC) and of the EC IIB (Kastri Phase: 2500–2200 BC) from Ayia Irini on Keos, Phylakopi on Melos, Kastri on Syros, Kynthos on Delos, Pyrgos and Koukounaries on Paros, Grotta on Naxos and Markiani on Amorgos (Kouka 2008: 316–318; Stampolidis and Sotirakopoulou 2011) has been recently enriched through extensive excavations at Skarkos on Ios (Marthari 1997; 2008) and Dhaskalio on Keros (Renfrew *et al.* 2008; Renfrew *et al.* 2012), as well as by limited, though important, EC finds beneath the Late Cycladic I settlement at Akrotiri on Thera (Doumas 2008). The EC III period (Phylakopi I: 2200–2000 BC) and the transition to the Middle Cycladic is still a much debated phase (Broodbank 2013; Rutter 2013), due to the abandonment of settlements of the Kastri phase (Ayia Irini, Kastri, Panormos), the different cultural evolution on each Cycladic island after this phase and the ceramic evidence excavated at Phylakopi, Akrotiri and Dhaskalio (for recent overviews see Renfrew 2013; Broodbank 2013; Rutter 2013) (Figure 9.1).

The EC settlement patterns show at least one settlement on certain small islands, and more on the bigger islands located usually on low promontories or on high hills in the coastal zones and rarely in the inland regions of islands. Their size measures between 0.3–1.1 ha and the buildings consist of stone, mainly one-storey structures with small rooms, usually organised in houses or insulae of irregular form and size (Stampolodis and Sotirakopoulou 2011).

The settlements follow mostly the agglutinative architectural arrangement. Settlements like Dhaskalio (Renfrew *et al.* 2012: fig. 6), Kastri and Skarkos follow the natural topography or existing terraces of the ground. Skarkos, in particular, is the most well planned settlement of the EC period excavated to date, with distinct insulae of independently built, two-storey houses of similar plan; the insulae were separated by streets, that follow a radiating arrangement, which recalls the settlement plan of Thermi I-IIIB, coupled with the insulae arrangements of Poliochni (Marthari 1997). Furthermore, the site of Kastri displays a radiating or concentric settlement scheme, consisting of three concentric stone enclosures (Stampolidis and Sotirakopoulou 2011: 34–35, fig. 1).

Of importance for our discussion are the EC IIB fortifications with apsidal bastions, such as at Kastri on Syros, Panormos on Naxos and Markiani on Amorgos (Broodbank 2000: fig. 105), that are contemporary and similar with the aforementioned ones of Kolonna on Aegina, Lerna in the Argolid, Palamari on Skyros and Liman Tepe in the Izmir Region (Figures 9.6, 9.9).

The EC settlements did not reveal any central building equivalent with the EH 'Corridor Houses', or with the above mentioned EB 'Central complexes' at Troy and Liman Tepe, or with buildings with a political function (seats of the chiefs) similar to those found at Poliochni, Thermi and the Heraion of Samos (herein Figure 9.8; see also Kouka 2013: 575–576, online fig. 1 ajaonline.org/imagegallery/1647). An exception due to its unusual size may be the 'Hall' at Dhaskalio, namely a tripartite building measuring 16 × 4 m (Stampolidis and Sotirakopoulou 2011: 38, Renfrew *et al.* 2013).

The erection of fortifications with apsidal bastions is a strong architectural indication for connectivity between Western Anatolia, the Cyclades and the EH Mainland Greece. The occurrence at Kastri and Panormos, besides these exceptional bastions, of 'Anatolianising' pottery, and of the craft activities at the metallurgical workshop in Kastri which used alloys identical to the ones used at Troy and Thermi, underline connections between particular settlements in the Aegean, as also noted above.

Discussion and conclusions

The aforementioned presentation has focussed on specific aspects of the Aegean Early Bronze Age built environment. I have placed emphasis on hierarchy of settlements and within these the role of settlement planning, with particular reference to architectural forms and how these relate to the functions of houses, communal buildings or administrative buildings in the East Aegean-Western Anatolia, the Greek Mainland and the Cyclades. This has demonstrated that differences can be identified in the modes and scales of connectivity among these geographical regions taking place in the successive phases of the Early Bronze Age. For this reason, a high level of connectivity can be observed within each of the above discussed geographical regions of the Aegean from EB I through EB III. The scale of such a connectivity leads to the identification of a cultural *koine* in each of the investigated geographical regions: the EB I-III East Aegean-Western Anatolian *koine*, the Early Helladic I-III *koine*, and the Early Cycladic I-IIB *koine*. The North and East Aegean islands and the western Anatolian littoral form an excellent laboratory for studying a high level of cultural interaction and competition in EB I and early EB II within the same geographical region, visible in using the multiple proxies outlined above.

During EB I and in the earlier part of EB II the stratified societies of the North and East Aegean and the Greek Mainland develop similar political and economic structures (visible in specific buildings and 'Central Complexes' that are most probably seats of the chiefs, and in the use of 'Corridor Houses'), while the above mentioned areas share prestige goods as Melian obsidian, Cycladic metals, EC pottery (frying pans, incised, stamped and dark-on-light painted decorated pottery), EC marble vases (Liman Tepe, Bakla Tepe, Demircihüyük, Iasos), zoomorphic figurines (Çeşme-Boyalık), the use of cist-graves at the cemeteries of EB I Bakla Tepe and EB I-II Iasos, as well as EC chamber tombs at Çeşme-Boyalık indicate (Kouka 2002: 299–300: 2008: 315–318; 2009a: 146, fig. 9).

Specific modes of contact within the Aegean occuring during EB I and early EB II – the time of Renfrew's 'international spirit' – were employed even more during the Western Anatolian EB II-late and EB IIIA (as seen through the development of the *Anatolian Trade Network* and *Great Caravan Route*), that is synchronous with the Aegean Lefkandi I-Kastri Phase. During this period many East Aegean, Western Anatolian and EH settlements were expanded and reinforced with complex fortification systems with apsidal bastions, which became landmarks in their micro-regions. Meanwhile, some EC settlements that were located on high hills in coastal zones were also fortified with similar bastions. A distinctive feature, which links the areas discussed is the choice to reinforce only specific settlements with apsidal bastions (Liman Tepe, Palamari on Skyros, Kolonna on Aegina, Lerna, Kastri on Syros, Panormos on Naxos). Şahoğlu has proposed that specific settlements, made distinctive through apsidal bastions, were participating in the strongest links within his *Anatolian Trade Network* (Şahoğlu 2005: 354–355). Thus, a very high level of connectivity and interaction is evident in the methods of protecting communal wealth using such fortifications at late EB II Aegean settlements that were located on crucial sea-trade routes. This crucial architectonic feature provides an important indication for the reconstruction of an extensive, very well organized economic network. This may well have been employed by the EB Aegean elites who partook in settlement organisation. It can be speculated that these were involved in both trading and metalworking, and that these same people introduced new eating and drinking habits in the context of the established commensal feasts to the Central and the West Aegean. Tankards and depas cups reached a wide geographic region from eastern Thrace (the colony of Troy at Kanlıgeçit) to Tarsus,

Syria and North Mesopotamia. Technological novelties such as the intensive use of bronze alloys or the use of the potter's wheel, and luxurious jewellery displays were all strong elements of the economic network of the late EB II (Kouka 2008: 318–319; 2013: 577; *cf.* Broodbank 2000: 309–319). By EB III, a more restricted scale of interaction is evident among the various Aegean land- and sea-scapes, due to environmental, political and social crises, which led to the decline of the *Anatolian Trade Network*. Finally, the fortifications with apsidal bastions may be considered also as signs of conflict at some sites within the same cultural region, i.e. Cyclades or Mainland Greece.

The abovementioned survey has illustrated the built environment as an important parameter for the detection of both modes and scales of connectivity among specific areas of the geographically fragmented Aegean in the Early Bronze Age. Even if architecture considered a useful resources for the reconstruction of connectivity and cultural interaction, this study demonstrated that futher parameters of material culture (*e.g.* raw materials, technology, every-day practices, burial habits) hosted in the built environment should be considered in order to reconstruct modes and scales of connectivity.

Acknowledgements

I would like to express many thanks to Barry Molloy for the kind invitation to contribute to such an interesting topic and to congratulate him for an excellent organization. Furthermore, many thanks go to all participants of the Round Table for constructive discussions and comments. Last but not least many thanks to Barry Molloy and the unknown reviewers for useful comments.

Bibliography

Alram-Stern, E.
2004 *Die Ägäische Frühzeit 2. Band-Teil 1 & 2. Die Frübronzezeit in Griechenland.* Vienna: Verlag der Österreichischen Akademie der Wissenschaften.

Aravantinos, V.L.
1986 The EH II Fortified Building at Thebes: Some notes on its architecture. In R. Hägg and D. Konsola (eds.), *Early Helladic Architecture and Urbanization* (Studies in Mediterranean Archaeology 76): 57–63. Göteborg: Paul Åström.

Broodbank, C.
2000 *An Island Archaeology of the Early Cyclades.* Cambridge: Cambridge University Press.
2013 "Minding the gap": Thinking about change in Early Cycladic island societies from a comparative perspective. *American Journal of Archaeology* 117(4): 535–543.

Davis, J.L.
2013 "Minding the gap": A problem in Eastern Mediterranean chronology, then and now. *American Journal of Archaeology* 117(4): 527–533.

Doumas, C.G.

2008 Chambers of mystery. In N.J. Brodie, J. Doole, G. Gavalas and C. Renfrew (eds.), *Horizon – Orizon: A Colloquium on the Prehistory of the Cyclades, Cambridge, 25th-28th March 2004* (McDonald Institute Monograph Series): 165–175. Cambridge: McDonald Institute for Archaeological Research.

Efe, T.

2007 The theories of the 'Great Caravan Route' between Cilicia and Troy: The Early Bronze Age III period in inland western Anatolia. *Anatolian Studies* 57: 47–64.

Erkanal, H.

1999 Early Bronze Age fortification systems in Izmir Region. In P.P. Betancourt, V. Karageorghis, R. Laffineur and W.-D. Niemeier (eds.), *Meletemata: Studies in Aegean Archaeology presented to Malcolm H. Wiener as he enters his 65th year. Volume 1, (Aegaeum 20)*: 237–242. Liège and Austin: Université de Liège and University of Texas.

2008a Liman Tepe: New light on prehistoric Aegean cultures. In H. Erkanal, H. Hauptmann, V. Şahoğlu and R. Tuncel (eds.), *The Aegean in the Neolithic, Chalcolithic and the Early Bronze Age, Proceedings of the International Symposium, October 13th-19th 1997, Urla-Izmir (Turkey)* (Ankara University – Research Center for Maritime Archaeology (ANKÜSAM), Publication No: 1): 179–190. Ankara: Ankara University.

2008b Die neuen Forschungen in Bakla Tepe bei Izmir. In H. Erkanal, H. Hauptmann, V. Şahoğlu and R. Tuncel (eds.), *The Aegean in the Neolithic, Chalcolithic and the Early Bronze Age, Proceedings of the International Symposium, October 13th-19th 1997, Urla-Izmir (Turkey)* (Ankara University – Research Center for Maritime Archaeology (ANKÜSAM), Publication No: 1): 165–177. Ankara: Ankara University.

2011 Early Bronze Age settlement models and domestic architecture in the coastal region of Western Anatolia. In V. Şahoğlu and P. Sotirakopoulou (eds.), *Across: the Cyclades and Western Anatolia during the 3rd Millennium BC*: 130–135. Istanbul: Sabanci University Sakip Sabanci Museum.

Erkanal, H. and T. Özkan

1999 Excavations at Bakla Tepe. In T. Özkan and H. Erkanal (eds.), *Tahtalı barajı kurtarma kazızı projesi (Tahtalı dam area salvage project)*: 108–138. İzmir, Simedya.

Erkanal, H., M. Artzy and O. Kouka

2003 2001 Yılı Liman Tepe Kazıları. *24. Kazı Sonuçları Toplantısı 1*: 423–436.

2004 2002 Yılı Liman Tepe Kazıları. *25. Kazı Sonuçları Toplantisi 2*: 165–178.

Erkanal, H., V. Şahoğlu, R. Tuncel, O. Kouka, L. Keskin and İ. Tuğcu

2009 2007 Yılı Liman Tepe Kazıları. *30. Kazı Sonuçları Toplantısı*: 299–322.

Ersoy, Y., Ü. Güngör, and H. Cevizoğlu

2011 2009 Yılı Klazomenai Kazısı. *32. Kazı Sonuçları Toplantısı*. Vol. 4: 169–171.

Heath-Wiencke, M.H.

2000a *Lerna. A Preclassical Site in the Argolid. Volume 4: The Architecture, Stratification and Pottery of Lerna III. Part 1: Architecture and Stratification*. Princeton: American School of Classical Studies at Athens.

2000b *Lerna. A Preclassical Site in the Argolid. Volume 4: The Architecture, Stratification and Pottery of Lerna III. Part 2: The Pottery. Part 3: Summary.* Princeton: American School of Classical Studies at Athens.

Jablonka, P.
2001 Eine Stadtmauer aus Holz. Das Bollwerk der Unterstadt von Troia II. In Archäologisches Landesmuseum Baden-Württemberg *et al.* (ed.), *Troia. Traum und Wirklichkeit*: 391–394. Stuttgart: Archäologisches Landesmuseum Baden-Württemberg.

Katsonopoulou, D.
2011 A proto-urban Early Helladic settlement found on the Helike Delta. In D. Katsonopoulou (ed.), *Helike IV. Arkhaia Eliki kai Aigialeia. Protoelladika: I Notia kai Kentriki Ellada, Praktika D΄ Diethnous Epistimonikou Synedriou, Nikolaïïka Diakoptou, 1-3 Septemvriou 2007*: 63–88. Athina: Ekdoseis Diktynna E.P.E.

Kilian, K.
1986 The Circular Building at Tiryns. In R. Hägg and D. Konsola (eds.), *Early Helladic Architecture and Urbanization* (Studies in Mediterranean Archaeology 76): 65–71. Göteborg: Paul Åström.

Konsola D.
1984 I Proimi Astikopoïïsi stous Protoelladikous Oikismous. *Systimatiki Analysi ton Kharaktiristikon tis.* Athens: S. Athanasopoulos-S. Papadimas-G. Zacharopoulos.

Korfmann, M.
1998 Troia-Ausgrabungen 1997. *Studia Troica* 8. 49–56.

Kouka, O.
2002 *Siedlungsorganisation in der Nord- und Ostägäis während der Frühbronzezeit (3. Jt. v.Chr.)* (Internationale Archäologie 58). Rahden/Westfalen: VML Verlag Marie Leidorf GmbH.
2008 Diaspora, presence or interaction? The Cyclades and the Greek Mainland from the Final Neolithic to Early Bronze II. In N.J. Brodie, J. Doole, G. Gavalas and C. Renfrew (eds.), *Horizon - Orizon: A Colloquium on the Prehistory of the Cyclades, Cambridge, 25th-28th March 2004* (McDonald Institute Monograph Series): 311–319. Cambridge: McDonald Institute for Archaeological Research.
2009a Third millennium BC Aegean chronology: old and new data under the perspectives of the third millennium AD. In S. Manning and M.J. Bruce (eds.), *Tree-Rings, Kings, and Old World Archaeology and Environment: Papers Presented in Honor of Peter Ian Kuniholm*: 133–149. Oxford and Oakville: Oxbow Books.
2009b Cross-cultural links and elite identities: the Eastern Aegean/Western Anatolia and Cyprus from the early third millennium through the early second millennium BC. In V. Karageorghis and O. Kouka (eds.), *Cyprus and East Aegean: Intercultural Contacts from 3000 to 500 BC, Proceedings of the International Archaeological Symposium - Pythagoreion Samos, 17th-18th October 2008*: 31–47. Nicosia: A.G. Leventis Foundation.
2011 Symbolism, ritual feasting and ethnicity in Early Bronze Age Cyprus and Anatolia. In V. Karageorghis and O. Kouka (eds.), *On Cooking Pots, Drinking Cups, Loomweights and Ethnicity in Bronze Age Cyprus and Neighbouring Regions: An International Archaeological Symposium Held in Nicosia, November 6th-7th, 2010*: 43–56. Nicosia: A.G. Leventis Foundation.

2013 "Minding the gap": Against the gaps: The Early Bronze Age and the transition to the Middle Bronze Age in the Northern and Eastern Aegean/Western Anatolia. *American Journal of Archaeology* 117(4): 569–580.

2014 Past stories – Modern narratives: cultural dialogues between East Aegean islands and the West Anatolian Mainland in the 4th Millennium BC. In B. Horejs and M. Mehofer (eds.), *Western Anatolia before Troy. Proto-Urbanisation in the 4th Millennium BC?*: 43–63 Wien: Österreichische Akademie der Wissenschaften.

Kouka, O. and V. Şahoğlu

in press New data on the Aegean Early Bronze Age I – Early Bronze Age II (early) chronology from Liman Tepe, Izmir. In Doumas, Ch.A., A. Giannikouri and O. Kouka (eds.), *The Aegean Early Bronze Age: New Evidence, International Conference, Athens, April 11th–14th*. Athens: Ministry of Culture – Archaeological Institute of Aegean Studies.

Manning, S.W.

2010 Chronology and terminology. In E.H. Cline (ed.) *The Oxford Handbook of the Bronze Age Aegean (ca. 3000–1000 BC)*: 11–28. Oxford: Oxford University Press.

Marthari, M.

1997 Apo ton Skarko stin Poliokhni. Paratiriseis gia tin koinonikooikonomiki anaptyksi ton oikismon tis Proimis Epokhis tou Khalkou stis Kyklades kai ta nisia tou boreioanatolikou Aigaiou. In Doumas and La Rosa: 362–382.

2008 Aspects of pottery circulation in the Cyclades during the Early EB II period: fine and semi-fine imported ceramic wares at Skarkos, Ios. In N.J. Brodie, J. Doole, G. Gavalas and C. Renfrew (eds.), *Horizon – Orizon: A Colloquium on the Prehistory of the Cyclades, Cambridge, 25th–28th March 2004* (McDonald Institute Monograph Series): 71–84. Cambridge: McDonald Institute for Archaeological Research.

Mylonas, G.

1959 *Aghios Kosmas. An Early Bronze Age Settlement and Cemetery in Attica*. Princeton: Princeton University Press.

Papageorgiou, D.

2008 Sea routes in the prehistoric Cyclades. In N.J. Brodie, J. Doole, G. Gavalas and C. Renfrew (eds.), *Horizon – Orizon: A Colloquium on the Prehistory of the Cyclades, Cambridge, 25th–28th March 2004* (McDonald Institute Monograph Series): 9–11. Cambridge: McDonald Institute for Archaeological Research.

Parlama, L.

2007 Palamari Skyrou. Paratiriseis stin ekseliksi tou oikismou kata tin 3i p.X. xilietia kai provlimata astikopoiïsis. In A.A. Laimou, L.G. Mendoni, N. Kourou and E. Simantoni-Bournia (eds.), *AMYMONA ERGA. Timitikos tomos gia ton kathigiti Basili K. Lambrinoudaki*: 25–48. Athens: Periodiko "Arkhaiognosia" ar. 5.

Pullen, D.J.

1985 Social Organization in the Early Bronze Age Greece: A Multidimensional Approach. PhD dissertation, Indiana University.

2013 "Minding the gap": Bridging the gaps in cultural change within the Early Bronze Age Aegean. *American Journal of Archaeology* 117.4: 545–553.

Renfrew, C.
2004 Rethinking the *Emergence*. In J.C. Barrett and P. Halstead (eds.) *The Emergence of Civilisation Revisited* (Sheffield Studies in Aegean Archaeology): 257–274. Oxford: Oxbow Books.

Renfrew, C., C. Doumas and L.I. Marangou, G. Gavalas,
2008 *Keros, Dhaskalio Kavos: Volume 1: The Investigations of 1987-1988.* Cambridge: McDonald Institute Monographs.

Renfrew, C., O. Philaniotou, N. Brodie, G. Gavalas, and M.J. Boyd (eds).
2013 *The settlement at Dhaskalio* (The sanctuary on Keros and the origins of Aegean ritual practice: the excavations of 2006–2008. Volume I). Cambridge: McDonald Institute Monographs.

Reinholdt, Cl.
2008 *Der frühbronzezeitliche Schmuckhortfund von Kap Kolonna: Ägina und die Ägäis im Goldzeitalter des 3. Jahrtausends v. Chr.* (Österreichische Akademie der Wissenschaften-Denkschriften der Gesamtakademie 46. Ägina – Kolonna Forschungen und Ergebnisse 2). Wien: Verlag der Österreichischen Akademie der Wissenschaften.

Renfrew, C., M. Boyd and C.B. Ramsey
2012 The oldest maritime sanctuary? Dating the sanctuary at Keros and the Cycladic Early Bronze Age. *Antiquity* 86: 144–160.

Rutter, J.B.
1995 *Lerna. A Preclassical Site in the Argolid. Volume 3: The Pottery of Lerna IV.* Princeton: American School of Classical Studies at Athens.

Şahoğlu, V.
2005 The *Anatolian Trade Network* and the Izmir region during the Early Bronze Age. *Oxford Journal of Archaeology* 24.4: 339–361.

Sampson, A.
1988 *Manika II. O Protoelladikos Oikismos kai to Nekrotafeio.* Athens: Ekdosi Dimou Khalkideon.

Stampolidis, N.C. and P. Sotirakopoulou
2011 Early Cycladic architecture. In V. Şahoğlu and P. Sotirakopoulou (eds.), *Across: the Cyclades and Western Anatolia during the 3rd Millennium BC*: 32–40. Istanbul: Sabanci University Sakip Sabanci Museum.

Televantou, C.
2008 Strofilas: A Neolithic settlement on Andros. In N.J. Brodie, J. Doole, G. Gavalas and C. Renfrew (eds.), *Horizon - Orizon: A Colloquium on the Prehistory of the Cyclades, Cambridge, 25th-28th March 2004* (McDonald Institute Monograph Series): 43–53. Cambridge: McDonald Institute for Archaeological Research.

Theochari, M. and Parlama, L.
1997 Palamari Skyrou: i okhyromeni poli tis Proimis Khalkhokratias. In C.G. Doumas and V. La Rosa (eds.) *Poliokhni kai i Proimi Epokhi tou Khalkou sto Boreio Aigaio/Poliochni e l'Antica età del Bronzo nell'Egeo Settentrionale, Diethnes Synedrio, Athina, 22-25 Apriliou 1996/Convegno Internazionale, Atene, 22-25 Aprile 1996*: 344–356. Athens: Panepistimio Athinon - Scuola Archeologica Italiana di Atene.

Tuncel, R.

2009 IRERP survey program: new prehistoric settlements in the Izmir Region. In H. Erkanal, H. Hauptmann, V. Şahoğlu and R. Tuncel (eds.), *The Aegean in the Neolithic, Chalcolithic and the Early Bronze Age, Proceedings of the International Symposium, October 13th–19th 1997, Urla-Izmir (Turkey)* (Ankara University – Research Center for Maritime Archaeology (ANKÜSAM), Publication No: 1): 581–592. Ankara: Ankara University.

Tzavella-Evjen, C.

1984 *Lithares*. Athens: Ypourgeio Politismou: Ekdosi Tameiou Arkxaiologikon Poron kai Apallotrioseon.

1985 *Lithares. An Early Helladic Settlement in Boeotia*. Occasional Paper 15. Los Angeles: Institute of Archaeology, University of California, Los Angeles.

Ünlüsoy, S.

2006 Vom Reihenhaus zum Megaron - Troia I bis Troia III. In M. Korfmann (ed.), *Troia - Archäologie eines Siedlungshügels und seiner Landschaft*: 133–144. Mainz am Rhein: Philipp von Zabern.

Walter, H. and F. Felten

1981 *Alt-Ägina 3, 1. Die vorgeschichtliche Stadt. Befestigungen. Häuser. Funde*. Mainz am Rhein: Philipp von Zabern.

Weiberg, E.

2011 Topography and settlement: perception of the bounded space. In D. Katsonopoulou (ed.), *Helike IV. Helike IV. Arkhaia Eliki kai Aigialeia. Protoelladika: I Notia kai Kentriki Ellada, Praktika D′ Diethnous Epistimonikou Synedriou, Nikolaïïka Diakoptou, 1–3 Septemvriou 2007*: 45–61. Athens: Ekdoseis Diktynna E.P.E.

Chapter 10

Emerging Economic Complexity in the Aegean and Western Anatolia during Earlier Third Millennium BC

Lorenz Rahmstorf

Introduction

Sealing and weighing were highly relevant economic procedures during the Bronze Age. The history of seal-use started already in the Early Pottery Neolithic (Pre-Halaf Neolithic) during the late seventh millennium BC in the Near East (Duistermaat 2010), while the first firm archaeological evidence for weighing is to be connected with the very beginning of the Bronze Age in Mesopotamia (*e.g.* Speiser 1935: 89–96, pl. XLII, 15, XLIII, a) and Egypt (*e.g.* von der Way 1997: 153, 162–163, 204, pl 70, 9; XXII, 8; Mollat 2007: 2046 Abb. 1) around 3000 BC or very early in the third millennium BC. We will focus here on the Early Bronze Age (EBA) Aegean and western inland Anatolia approximately as far east as the course of the Kızılırmak/Halys River, especially in the earlier part of the period between *c.* 3000–2500 BC. Sealing is directly connected with the concept of property, and its protection and management, and the documentation of authenticity of products or (later) of written documents. The first Neolithic seals in Syria were probably used only to protect private property against tampering (Duistermaat 2010; Duistermaat 2012), whereas the later Copper Age seals from the Near East were part of administrative control systems, for example well-documented examples at Değirmentepe near Malatya in eastern Anatolia during the late Obeid period in the 5th millennium BC (Esin 1994), nearby Arslantepe during the later 4th millennium (Fiandra *et al.* 2007) or near contemporary Tepe Gaura in northern Mesopotamia (Rothman 2007). The chronological and spatial diversity of the development of sealing and weighing nonetheless contains an element of commonality in terms of conception and practice, and so present very useful criteria for measuring the scales and modes of interaction that this volume seeks to address.

Weighing determines socially and economically negotiated value and is applied in the production and exchange of objects which eventually became commodities. The appearances of both practices were indeed very large conceptual steps in human social development. In regard to weighing, one has first to formulate a notion of measure and of a unit of measure. Considering the high degree of abstraction needed (Morley and Renfrew 2011: 3) and some mathematical knowledge (of multiples and fractions) it is may not be so surprising that it first occurred during the flourishing of the first civilisations in Mesopotamia and Egypt. For these reasons it is of primary importance to consider when such notions came to be materialised for the first time, especially outside the realm of the Euphratus/Tigris and the Nile. The identification of both practices – sealing and weighing – depends on the definition of clear archaeological evidence.

In this chapter, I will discuss the earliest appearance of seal- and weight-use in the Aegean and Western Anatolia. Archaeological investigations of early seal and weight use are still few in number for the Aegean, and even less are available for Anatolia. For example, recent overviews of the prehistory of Anatolia (Sagona and Zimansky 2009; Düring 2011) did not mention their relevance for understanding the EBA. Sealing and weighing are considered here as signs of emerging economic complexity. Of course these are not the only strategies that might lead to an increase in the complexity of economic and social practices, but I will limit myself to an assessment of impact of these two practices in this study. The term (cultural) 'complexity' is very popular in the archaeological literature, although it is rarely precisely explained what is meant by this. Morris (2009: 519) has proposed a minimal definition of cultural complexity being 'the scale of practices (settlement, energy capture, monument-building, inequality and heterogeneity, and communication) characterizing societies'. However, in Morris' all-embracing definition of 12 forms of cultural complexity (Morris 2009: tab 2.1) neither administrative devices (sealing) nor metrology (weighing) surface directly as expressions. However, one could allocate both very broadly under the heading of communication in his definition as both are expressing an agreed concept between parties. As both practices are sophisticated phenomena in my understanding, they demonstrate an important structural component in non-literate societies especially. In the following discussion, I will trace the early history of the use of sealing in the Aegean and Western Anatolia and this will be followed by a similar analysis of weights. The intention of this undertaking is:

1. to demonstrate that we have archaeological evidence of seal use in the first half of the third millennium through a small number of seal impressions on clay lumps which were intended to seal something, probably in a similar way as we know occurred at sites such as Lerna in the second half of the third millennium BC;
2. to use this and the increasing evidence of the later third millennium to argue that seal use became an important part of the economic organisation of the EBA societies in the Aegean;
3. to establish that the first evidence for the use of weights started during this same broad period of time in the earlier third millennium BC;
4. to emphasise the fact that both economic strategies are frequently found together at EBA settlements.

Sealings

The term seal impressions or sealings, also called *cretulae* (Fiandra and Frangipane 2004), the apparent Latin expression for them, is applied here for any intentional impressions made on clay covering a container (such as a vessel, a box or a chest) or the knob of a door. I do not consider direct impressions on artefacts, for example on pottery, as sealings and will exclude those from the discussion here. Seal impressions on breakable unburned clay inform us that an object, a seal, was utilised to impress them. Sometimes 'decorative stamps' or 'pintaderas' known from the Neolithic and Copper Age in Europe, especially from South East Europe (including Greece), are also called seals. However, there is no evidence that clearly demonstrates that these were used to function as seals. Despite the many burnt layers where accidental or intentional firing could have baked any potential sealings in the tell settlements of the Carpathian Bassin, the Balkans and the Aegean, there are simply no sealings form these periods. It seems that these 'decorative stamps' were not meant to be impressed on clay as they are simply do not work well as such a tool (Krzyszkowska 2005: 33). The situation was to change dramatically during the subsequent EBA in the Aegean and Western Anatolia, when we know of about 25 sites with sealings (Figure 10.1). Yet, it should be remembered that sealings normally survive deposition during site formation processes only when they were (accidentally) baked.

Lemnos and Cyclades

Finds in recent years have demonstrated that there is reliable evidence for seal use in EBA communities before the beginning of Lerna IIIC or Lefkandi I-Kastri horizon that began as early as the 26th/25th centuries BC in the EBA II in the Aegean (Maran 1998: pl. 80; Manning 2010: 21, Tab.2.2.). The earliest site with such evidence is Myrina on Lemnos (Archontidou-Agyri and Kokkinoforou 2004a; Archontidou-Agyri and Kokkinoforou 2004b). The architecture of the first phase (Blue Period) of Myrina has been called monumental due to the size of one megaroid building and due to the size of the building material used (Achilara 1997: 310). In the Kasoli plot, a fragment of a sealing (Figure 10.2.1a-b) was found in a storage room of a house which is dated as being contemporary to an early phase of the Blue Period of the Poliochni sequence (Achilara 1997: 301, fig. 3, 3; CMS V Suppl. 3, 1: 333, 335, no. 210). While only a few vessels from this context have been published so far, the assignment of the pottery to this phase by the excavators appears reasonable (compare also Traverso 1997). The earlier part of the Blue Period is dated to *c.* 2950–2850 BC (Kouka 2002: tab. 1). The fragment from the Kasoli plot appears to have been directly placed on the corner of the sealed object. An imprint of fabric might be visible on the backside but this was largely covered by a very hard green substance, as it was described (L. Achilara in CMS V Suppl. 3: 337). Unfortunately, no image of this side is presented in the publication. The find from the Kasoli plot is of particular importance as it proves the knowledge of seal-use already in the early third millennium BC, a few hundred years before

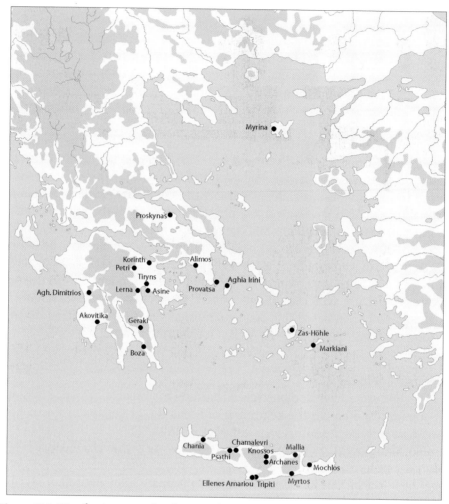

Figure 10.1: Distribution map of sealings in the Aegean from third millennium BC contexts.

most other Aegean sites with sealings can be dated. A second sealing from Myrina (Figure 10.2.2) with cord impressions on the back surface came to light in a later context dating to Poliochni Red or the transition from Poliochni Green to Poliochni Red (Dova 2003: 114; CMS V Suppl. 3, 1: 333–334, no. 209). This could be roughly placed around 2500 BC. According to I. Pini the impressions on the back side point to the use of a bag-like container, probably made of leather. These finds from Myrina are most important as they demonstrate with hard evidence the long assumed seal-use in the Northeast Aegean during the EBA.

Until recently it was speculated whether seal impressions were used only for decorative purposes on pottery and hearth structures in the Cyclades (Pullen 1994: 51). With the change of focus to including settlement archaeology (as well as cemeteries) in the Cyclades, it is becoming evident that seal use was also widespread in the islands,

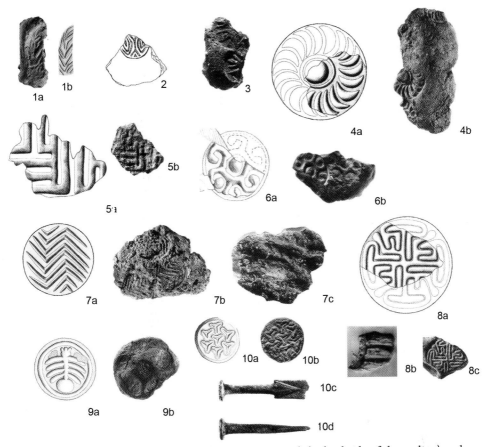

Figure 10.2: Sealings (drawing/picture of the impression and the backside of the sealing) and a seal from the Early Bronze Age Aegean: 1–2 Myrina; 3 Aghia Irini; 4 Zas-Cave; 5 Mochlos; 6 Corinth; 7 Leondari/Provatsa; 8 Akovitika; 9 Tiryns; 10 Aplomata. (1 and 5 from CMS VS.3; 2 from Dova 2003; 3 from Wilson 1999; 6 and 8 from CMS VS.1A; 7 and 9 from CMS VS.1B. objects not to scale).

even though only a handful of sealings are as yet known and come from just three sites. These include sealings from Aghia Irini on Kea (Figure 10.2.3; Caskey 1964: 319–320, pl. 48, j; Wilson 1999: 166, pl. 102, SF-409), the Zas-Cave on Naxos (Figure 10.2.4a-b; Zachos and Dousoungli 2008: 90–91, fig. 10.10.a) and Markiani on Amorgos (Angelopoulou 2006: 221–222, fig. 8.25: 069, 847, 1802/032; CMS V Suppl. 3: no. 46–47). One sealing from Markiani (Angelopoulou 2006: 221–222, fig. 8.25: 847) was found in the 'fissure' of Trench 1,1 (Marangou *et al.* 2006: 61, Tab 4.4) and belongs to the Markiani phase III which is dated to the earlier part of EC II between 2800–2500 BC (Renfrew *et al.* 2006: 79, fig. 5.6.). Unfortunately, the fragment with a hardly discernible motif is very worn and probably therefore its back side was not depicted. There are also a few sealings (Angelopoulou 2006: 221–222, fig. 8.25: 069, 1802/032) from Markiani phase IV which is contemporary with the Lefkandi I-Kastri horizon (*c.* 2500–2200 BC). The sealing from the Markiani phase III context demonstrates that the use of seals was known in the Cyclades already *c.* 2800–2500 BC. The dating evidence obtained from a series of new C[14]-dates from Markiani is in this instance of special importance as it brings the discussion about the chronological placement of the Lefkandi I-Kastri assemblage within the EBA Aegean finally to an end. Recently published radiocarbon dates from Markiani (Renfrew *et al.* 2006) clearly suggest that it began during the middle of the third millennium, around 2500 BC, as J. Maran, S. Manning and E. Christmann had argued during the mid-1990s in their assessment of EBA Aegean chronology (Maran 1998: 154, Taf. 80 with further references).

Prepalatial Crete

The number of EBA sites in Crete from which sealings have been recovered has risen considerably since the early 1990s. In the decades before only a few sites with sealings like Mochlos (Figure 10.2.5) were known. In addition to the sites mentioned by I. Schoep and C. Knappett (2004: 26), we can add now recently published material from Knossos (Wilson 2010: 149, fig. 36–37; Hood and Cadogan 2011: 234–235, fig. 9, 3), Archanes (CMS II, 6: no. 151, dated to MM IA) and Ellenes Amariou (Relaki 2009: 365–366, tab. 1). Still it seems that the EM IIA dating of two sealings from the West Court House at Knossos (CMS II, 8: 758–759, Add. 1–2) remains problematic. D. Wilson (2010: 149) suggests that "a very small amount of later MM pottery (*c.* 3% of the total by weight) found in this deposit, however, leaves open the possibility of a MM date for one or both of these examples. I. Pini (2002: 5) would date both, but especially the second sealing (CMS II, 8, 2: Add. 2) to MM II on stylistic grounds. Indeed, the motif of the seal images would seem strange within the known repertoire of imagery used in EBA II Crete. Against this position, P. Tomkins and I. Schoep have recently argued that "restudy of context and associated pottery argues in favor of the original EM IIA date" (Tomkins and Schoep 2010: 71). I would add that it should be not surprising to have sealings in EM IIA, considering the early examples from Myrina and Markiani. It is not possible to date other sites with sealings in Crete more precisely than within EM II (Myrtos, Malia, Ellenes Amariou?), and others must be dated to EM II/III (Chania, Trypiti), EM III or EM II-MM I (Chamalevri, Psathi, Knossos, Archanes, Palikastro, see Pini 1990; Vlasaki-Andreaki and Hallagher 1995; Schoep 2004; Relaki 2009). Yet there are only a little over a dozen sealings known from the whole EM I-MM IA-period. There is variation in the types of sealings, most are direct objects sealings but there is also a probable nodulus from Mallia.

The southern Greek mainland

So far there there are no sealings known from the mainland from contexts of EH IIA (= Lerna A and B) or even EH I date, but from contexts contemporary with later EH II phase (= Lerna C and D), the situation changes drastically. In all cases from the Aegean islands and Crete, sealings are either single finds or were found with very few other examples in the same assemblage or at other find spots at the same sites (Figure 10.3). It is only on the mainland at Lerna (CMS V: no. 43–119), Petri (Koustoula 2000; Kostoula 2004) and Geraki (Weingarten *et al.* 1999; Weingarten 2000; Weingarten *et al.* 2011) that we find high find numbers of sealings. It is not possible to give exact numbers from these sites because sealings are most often found in a fragmented condition. The numbers given in Figure 10.3 for these three sites should therefore not be taken as highly precise. For example, M. Kostoula (2000: 138) calculated that the 250 fragments from the site of Petri alone represent *c.* 100 sealings. Apart from the sporadic finds from excavations that took place many decades ago at sites such as Corinth (Figure 10.2.6; Waage 1949: 421, pl. 63; CMS V Suppl. 1 A: no. 398) and Asine (CMS V: no. 519–522; CMS XI: no. 310), single sealings have been published or mentioned more recently in reports

Site	Relative Date	Absolute Date	Approximate number of sealings
Aghia Irini	EH II B (Aghia Irini III)	2400–2200	1 sealing
Aghios Dimitrios	EH III B	2500–2200	1 sealing
Akovitika	EH II	2700–2200	1 sealing
Alimos	EH II	2700–2200	1 sealing
Archanes	MM IA	2050–1950	1 sealing
Asine	EH II	2700–2200	3 sealings
Boza	EH II	2700–2200	1 sealing
Chamalevri	EM III/MM IA	2200–2050	1 sealing
Chania	EM II/EM III	2700–2050	1 sealing
Corinth	EH II	2700–2200	1 sealing
Ellenes Amariou	EM II?	2700–2200	1 sealing
Geraki	EH II B (Lerna C–D)	2500–2350	259 sealings (?)
Knossos	EM II A; EM IIB; EM III	2700–2050	4 sealings
Leondari-Provatsa	EH II	2700–2200	1 sealing
Lerna	EH II B (Lerna III C–D)	2500–2200	217 sealings (?)
Mallia	EM II B	2500–2200	1 sealing
Markiani	EC II (Markiani III and IV)	2800–2200	2 sealings
Mochlos	LM I (context)	–	1 sealing
Myrina	EBA I (Poliochni Blue, early);	2900–2800	1 sealing
	EBA II (Poliochni Green–Red)	2600–2500	1 sealing
Myrtos	EM II B	2500–2200	1 sealing
Petri	EH II B (Lerna C–D)	2500–2200	250 fragments = c. 100 sealings
Proskynas	EH II	2700–2500	1 sealing
Psathi	EM II B or EM III-MM IA	2500–1900	1 sealing (?)
Tiryns	EH II	2700–2200	5 sealings
Trypiti	EM II–EM III	2700–2050	1 sealing
Zas-Cave	EC II B	2500–2200	8 sealings

Figure 10.3: Sealings from EBA Aegean sites: their approximate number and date.

of excavations at sites such as Leondari/Provatsa on Makronissos (Figure 10.2.7; CMS V Suppl. 1 B: no. 33), Boza in the southern Peloponnese (Zavvou 2007: 418–421, fig. 15), Aghios Dimitrios in the western Peloponnese (CMS V Suppl. 1 B: no. 146; Zachos 2008: 78, pl. 53, b), Alimos in Attica (Blackman 2000/01: 10) and Proskynas in Boeotia (Zachou 2004: 1271, pl. 1, b).

It is hard to interpret any pattern in the very different amounts of sealings known from all of these mainland sites. Does this reflect functional differences at sites of different rank in a supposed settlement hierarchy or are the numbers just depending on the chance of preservation (through accidental fires) and modern recognition in the trench as well as on the strategy of excavation? The second scenario appears to be more plausible, even if we cannot rule out functional differences in the investigation of sites as having relevance also. The increasing tendency to recover sealings on more recent excavations (using more sophisticated recovery practices) may suggest that it is not a vagary of past practices that creates the patterns we have to work with. In many excavations it has only more recently become standard procedure to dig slowly and careful, and to use sieves to process dry soils and to collect all artefacts from each layer. With such recovery procedures applied, the chance to excavate crumbled pieces of sealings increases considerable – see for example the comments by M. Prent with regard to the recently excavated site of Geraki in Lakonia (M. Prent in Weingarten *et al.* 2011: 162). Nevertheless, on present evidence, it is also tempting to identify some parts of the southern Greek mainland – especially the northeast Peloponnese – as culturally more advanced in regard to socio-economic and technological developments (Maran 1998: 432) and hence more receptive for large complexes of sealings.

In light of this, intensive seal-use might seem to be connected with special sites such as those that had Corridor Houses like Lerna, Kolonna, Akovitika and Thebes and special redistributive economic systems (Pullen 2008: 34–35). In saying this, it is due to the above mentioned changes in recovery strategies that we have so many sealings from Lerna, while we apparently have just one from Akovitika (Figure 10.2.8) and none at all from Kolonna. This being despite the fact these are all extensively excavated sites with Corridor Houses. From the largely unpublished settlement of Petri, similar numbers of sealings to that known from Lerna have been found in the excavated parts of the site, though no Corridor Houses have been documented. Also at the site of Geraki such monumental architecture is missing so far. This might reflect just the vagaries of excavation. At present, however, the evidence available from the mainland and other parts of the Aegean suggests that the appearance of sealings, and particularly their appearance in large numbers, was not confined to sites with monumental architecture such as the Corridor Houses (Lerna, Akovitika, Kolonna, Thebes) or the unique circular building ('Rundbau', Figure 10.4.1–3) at Tiryns (Figure 10.2.9).

Another significant obstacle for the analysis of early Aegean seal use, especially on the mainland, is the apparent lack of actual seals. By this I mean the kind of seals with sharp trefoil, loop and spiraloid motifs that you need to impress the sealings in such a crisp way as we find at Lerna and other sites. It could be suggested that this was done by metal seals, though these are only preserved in a very few cases, for example the lead stamp-seal from Aplomata on Naxos (Figure 10.2.10). This seal is dated by J. Rambach to earlier EC II A, his Aplomata-Group (Rambach 2000a: 150; Rambach 2000b: Beilage 10: 81; Beilage 15). This dating gives further weight to the idea of seal use in the Cyclades before the middle of the third millennium BC. The face of this seal is decorated with a trefoil design which finds good parallels in the motifs of the impressions at Lerna (Krzyskowska 2005: 40, fig. 69). The relative value of the metal and the mutability of the medium (recycling) are possible reasons for why we know little about these earliest seals in lead and copper and maybe also in precious metal (silver or gold?). Another explanation (Maran 1998: 235) might be the use of fine grained hardwood (M. H. Wiencke in CMS V: 28) and ivory/bone (Younger 1991: 37) as potential materials. Yet, as O. Krzyskowska (2005: 40) pointed out, ivory and bone are normally not perishable and should have survived even destructions by fire, as at Lerna.

Western Anatolia

At the site of Demircihüyük near Eskisehir a single sealing with fabric imprints on the back was found in a pit in Room 200 of the Phase F2 (Obladen-Kauder 1996: 321, pl. 136, 5). This phase could be paralleled with Troy Ib, according to Efe (1988: 117, fig. 98). The imprint of the seal shows a row of squares which were rolled or impressed on the clay (Obladen-Kauder 1996: 286). Finally, a sealing came to light at Emalı-Karataş in south-western Anatolia in a trench between a small fortified hill (with just a large single-room building) and the settlement. It belongs to Level III of the site (Mellink 1972, 258–259, pl. 55, 5). Karataş III is dated by J. Warner to the EBA Ib of M. Mellink chronological scheme. This would imply an approximate absolute date around the 28th or 27th century BC (Warner 1996: 7–10, chart 11; Efe and Türkteki 2011: 190, Tab.). The motif of an angle-filled cross appears to be impressed on a sealing from Boz Höyük-Dinar near Kusura (Mellaart 1954: 216, 239, fig. 466). It is a surface find but at this site Chalcolithic and EBA pottery was found (Mellaart 1954: 181, 192, fig. 2–3). With Alişar Höyük we are already in central Anatolia. There, a 'fragmentary sun-dried mud brick' (von der Osten 1937: 81–82, fig. 87, e 1974) was excavated in layers of the 'Copper Age' of the site's sequence. Unfortunately, the amorphous object has not been published, but on its backside there appears to be an image that may be a potential sealing. On the same plate in the publication several seals with the angle-filled cross motif are illustrated (von der Osten 1937: 81–82, fig. 87, c 576). A total of only four EBA sites with sealings in Western and Central Anatolia might appear as weak evidence for an assumed reconstruction of a widespread seal-use, but one has to remember that much fewer Anatolian sites of this period have been published in comparison to the Aegean.

Seals discussion

On the basis of the evidence currently available, one can conclude that the idea to apply a chunk of clay on a container and to seal it with a specific tool was first taken up the Aegean by the early third millennium BC, at least as far as the northeast Aegean is concerned. The material evidence for this period is still meagre, and only one site (Myrina) can be dated to the earliest phase (EB I/IIA), but the site of Markiani, and possibly Knossos, produced sealings that can be dated to the subsequent phase (EB II) between 2800/2700–2500 BC. But it is only by the middle of the third millennium that the number of sites with sealings sharply increases, even if we concede that our dataset belongs more to later EBA II than to its early part. Apparently it is with the Lefkandi I-Kastri phase and contemporary phases in the Aegean islands and southern Greek mainland that seal-use became a more common practice. Strangely no sealings are known from the EBA phases of Troy and Poliochni, despite the abundance of fire destructions at both sites (Maran 1998: 422–423). The early date of the main excavations at both sites is a potential reason for the lack of sealings because the excavators may not have been aware of the possible existence of crumbling clay objects with faint impressions on them.

How can we explain the emergence of seal-use in the Aegean in late EBA I/II? It is commonly held assumption that sealstones in the Aegean are not an indigenous invention (*e.g.* Schoep 2012: 423, n. 2) and the practice of marking containers through sealings was adopted from Near Eastern state-societies (*e.g.* Bintliff 2012: 97, 117), where the practice had a good pedigree. This is implied by the fact that seal-use in the Aegean and Western Anatolia started at approximately the same point in time during the early third millennium BC, whereas farther east, in eastern Anatolia and the upper Euphrates seals had been in use for several millennia before. Only with the beginning of the Bronze Age does this economic strategy begin to appear farther west, even if one has to confess that EBA sealings are still rare finds in Western and Central Anatolia. Nevertheless the early dates of sealings in Demircihüyük and Karataş-Semajük around 2800 BC might indicate the period in the early third millennium BC when seal use became transmitted from Eastern to Western Anatolia and ultimately the Aegean. The foreign influences on the Aegean islands north of Crete and the Greek mainland during the EBA II were mainly coming from the east over Anatolia, as it appears from the evidence of the pottery and various small finds (Şahoğlu 2005; Rahmstorf 2006a). In the case of Crete again foreign stimulus must be taken into account: "it cannot be coincidence that seals first appear at approximately the same time as the first materials from Egypt and/or the Levant appear" (Schoep 2012: 423, n. 2).

Further supporting evidence of a Near Eastern origin for seal-use is the fact that while the Aegean EBA glyptic imagery is surely unique in many instances, it also incorporates motifs known from Anatolia and farther east. One of the best known EBA examples is probably the angle-filled cross-motif (Aruz 2008, 28–29; Rahmstorf 2010a, 682–683, fig. 5). The motif is simple and it appears in earlier and later periods in Western and Middle Asia and even farther afield, but it is the impressive concentration of seals and impressions of this kind in the EBA II Aegean (*e.g.* most recently from Markiani: Angelopoulou 2006: 219–222, fig. 8.25, 317) and especially EBA III Anatolia (Umurtak 2002) that rule out any coincidence. Other authors have emphasised already that the popularity of the motif must have spread from Anatolia into the Aegean (Pini 1972: 183; Warren 1970, 36, n. 22). Also the few cylinder seals in the EBA Aegean (Genz 2003: 49–50 with further reference) are Aegean imitations of Near Eastern originals, although in a few cases like the cylinder seal from Poliochni (E. Porada in Bernabò-Brea 1976: 300–302) they appear to be imports. The recent find of 10 Mesopotamian, presumable Akkadian cylinder seals in EBA III layers of a central building at Seyitömer Höyük near Kütahya in inland Western Anatolia, together with objects of gold, underlines the Near Eastern contribution (Bilgen 2011: 210–212; Sari 2013). If this cache of finds might hint to the physical presence of Syro-Mesopotamian traders in this region is of course a matter of debate, yet seals seem to have been individual artefacts providing some kind of personal signature of the seal keeper. These finds are especially interesting in the light of the later textual evidence (Frayne 1993: 28–29) referring to a Mesopotamian military expansion during the Akkad Period into Anatolia. The historicity of this military campaign has however been questioned (Bachhuber 2013: 504–506 with further references). Finally, one could also point to the Aegean EBA II practice of impressing large jars with roller stamps, a practice also found in the EBA in Syria, the southern Levant, parts of Anatolia and the Aegean eastern Mediterranean (Rahmstorf 2006a: 62–67, fig. 8–9 with further references). Despite some difference in detail between the examples from the Levant and eastern Anatolia on the one hand and the Aegean on the other, a connection must have existed, even if "its exact nature remains obscure" (Krzyskowska 2005: 56).

What kind of economic complexity does the early seal-use in the Aegean imply? This is indeed a tricky question as we only have the archaeological context of the finds to gain insights into how they might have functioned. In many cases the precise contextual information on the sealings has not yet been published or the single occurrences of such finds may rather highlight the vagaries of slow site formation processes which are not helpful in reconstructing any processes in the use of seals. Only the few well published cases where we have concentrations of sealings and/or their association which sudden destruction horizons are giving insights into possible scenarios. This leaves as the basis of our interpretation mainly the evidence from Lerna and to a lesser extent the not yet fully published site of Geraki. By far the largest concentration of sealings at Lerna comes from the small Room XI only accessible from the exterior of the house, which could not have stored bulk foodstuff in any quantity (Wiencke 2000: 302). Besides the sealings, the room contained primarily fine ware pottery, mainly dozens of saucers and a few sauceboats and just one fragment of a pithos (Wiencke 2000: 479–488, fig. II.63–66). There are at least two possibilities for the meaning of the sealings in Room XI, which are complicated by the fact that is unclear how many containers had been sealed by the persevered sealings. In the first explanation the sealings have been "prised off by looters, eager to get at the commodities within" (Krzyskowska 2005: 50) before the House of the Tiles was burned down – most of the sealings were broken before they were burned (Wiencke 2000: 302). In this case we would expect some remains of ceramic containers but many if not all sealings might have been places on perished wooden boxes. Or secondly, the sealings have been deliberately saved for 'archival purposes' "in order to preserve the identities of the individuals involved in the transactions that the sealings represented" (Pullen 2008: 34; Pullen 2011b: 199 with further references).

Since the ground-breaking studies of E. Fiandra in the 1960s (*e.g.* Fiandra 1968; Fiandra and Ferioli 1990) it has often been assumed that large concentrations of sealings represent 'archives before writing' (Ferioli *et al.* 1994). The first sealings were applied, then after a certain period of time, were broken but retained and stored in an archive room and finally, after an audit, the broken sealings were discarded. For all these three stages it is of course hard to find clear archaeological evidence at any single site. The site of Arslantepe on the Upper Euphrates in eastern Anatolia with its late Chalcolithic phase in the late 4th millennium BC might offer one of the best preserved and studied cases for tracing such a model (Frangipane *et al.* 2007). In the Aegean numerous studies of the past 10 years or so have emphasised the role of communal consumption and feasting, thereby downplaying the economic significance of seal use. In a recent study O. Peperaki made the point that the number of vessels from Room XI stands in rough correspondence to the number of individual seals (Peperaki 2004: 223). This could be a sign of communal consumption. She assumes that provisions for a feast were sealed in jars of moderate size and kept together with the drinking vessels. While this interpretation rightly puts importance on the social component and emphasises the role of Lerna as a social gathering-place, it largely discounts the economic role of the sealing practice which is hard to imagine in the light of seal use elsewhere in the ancient world (see below).

To a certain extent similar discussions (Relaki 2009: 353, n. 1 and 4 with further literature) have occurred on the topic of the reasons behind seal-use in EM II–MM I Crete. Assemblages of sealings found in the same context are lacking so far, probably reflecting the chances of preservation and recovery. At all prepalatial sites all sealings are solitary finds, and it is only at Knossos that four have come to light (Figure 10.3), albeit in different contexts. Using such evidence, any interpretation is much hindered, as discussed above. They seem to be in all cases direct object sealing, one early nodulus might be preserved from Mallia from MM I A level (Hue and Pelon 1992: 31–33, figs. 33–34; Krzyskowska 2005: 78, n. 51). A recently published MM IB clay sealing from the Southwest Houses at Knossos is the earliest securely dated pommel/peg sealing on Crete (Macdonald 2012: 93, fig. 3.6), whereas such sealings are already common at EH II Lerna (however, the EM II sealing from Myrtos might have been a door knob sealing as well: Warren 1972: 226; Relaki 2009: 364). Pommel or peg sealings which secured door knobs (even it cannot be completely excluded that they were applied on knobs on boxes and chests), and therefore regulated access to rooms, are a clear sign of some kind of administration and so far only known from sites dating to MM I B–MM II.

Generally, the sealings from Prepalatial Crete might indicate small-scale storeroom administration at a village-level or household management as in the case of the single preserved sealing from Myrtos (Warren 1972: 226). It is interesting to note that the seal used in this case has an angle-filled cross, which is so typical for the middle and later EBA in the Aegean and Anatolia as mentioned above.

In recent years the concept of radical changes taking place during MM I leading the emergence of the palaces during that time has been considerable undermined (several papers in Schoep *et al.* 2012). Some elements like the emergence of court buildings and crucial social reconfigurations are now thought to have appeared much earlier, probably already during the later EM II (Schoep 2012: 422; Tomkins 2012: 75). Yet, a clear indication for an earlier take-off of Cretan palaces should include signs for administration of stored goods, lacking so far from EM II–MM IA contexts. However, we should not forget that most of the EM II levels of the most promising sites, Mochlos and Vasiliki, were excavated in the beginning of the 20th century AD when such things as crumbling sealings might have been easily overlooked. All in all, it is still hard to tell to what extent economic complexity can be reflected by the use of seals during the EM II and EM III. In a recent study the Prepalatial sealing practices have not been explained as a sign of administration but as "a ritualised activity that had to be performed in front of an audience in order for claims on specific resources to be validated" (Relaki 2009: 368). This provides the important observation that seals did not only have an economic role, but also social and symbolic components as markers of privilege and difference (Tomkins and Schoep 2010: 71–72 with further references). This complements their primary function in protecting and managing property, which may be inevitable in view of the history of seal use from prehistory to the modern world (see various contributions in Collon 1997).

We must also assess if we can connect the existence of seals to any specific types of sites in the EBA Aegean and western Anatolia. At sites with monumental architecture like Corridor Houses or the central mound building at Emalı-Karataş, large numbers of sealings might not be too surprising. On the other hand, we have small rural sites like Markiani (Renfrew 2006, 254) that had sealings. This undermines any expectation that such practices were only possible at 'proto-urban centers' such as Tiryns and Lerna. Weingarten's belief that "every settlement in the EH II world had learned, and taken to heart, this method of marking and protecting property" (Weingarten *et al.* 1999: 369; see also Weingarten *et al.* 2011: 155) is increasingly attractive – and one should add also to this the settlements of the Aegean islands. The safeguarding and protection as well as the possible manipulation of goods through regulation of access via sealings seems to have been much more common in the Aegean and probably also Western inland Anatolia and "point to a wider proto-bureaucracy" (Binliff 2012: 88). It is still hard to quantify the role that long-term storable agricultural products like oil and wine played in the economy of the EBA. Not only is direct proof often difficult to obtain, but also an in-depth study of storage and storage vessels of the EBA is rendered difficult for reasons such as "very few centers have been explored fully" (Christakis

2011: 199) on Prepalatial Crete or "no EH pithos has been measured for its capacity" (Pullen 2011b: 187). At least at Lerna from House DM (Wiencke 2000: 142) and at Geraki from Trench 17/11i (Crouwel *et al.* 1997: 60–62, fig. 5, pl. 6–8; Crouwel *et al.* 1998: 96–99, fig. 3, pl. 1–2) pithoi are preserved together with larger assemblages of pithos and jar sealings, although the mobility of agricultural products is considered to have been on a limited scale (Pullen 2011b: 189) in contrast with later palatial complexes. The sealings from Room XI of the House of the Tiles show also they often sealed smaller containers of ceramic, reed and wood. This implies that "limited quantities of items of higher value" (Pullen 2011b: 189) were also stored. One attractive suggestion which has however not yet any archaeological proof has been proposed by Weingarten (1997): that silver was also sealed at Lerna. The following chapter on potential weights in EBA Aegean and Anatolia puts some indirect credibility to this suggestion.

Weights

Weight metrology is the second novelty in the Aegean and Western Anatolian EBA that contributed to the economic complexity of the period. Some years ago I suggested that so-called 'pestles' or 'spools' made of stone and spondylus, in a few cases also in metal, mainly lead, are in fact balance weights (Figures 10.4.4–8; 10.5; 10.6.3; 10.7.5). This was based at that time on the interpretation of three such objects from Tiryns which had some markings. These markings reflected a logical relationship with the mass of the objects. In 2003 I was aware of *c.* 200 such objects from some 34 Aegean and Anatolian sites (Rahmstorf 2003: 298–299). Intensive study of the literature and primary study of further material in recent years has expanded the known number to up to 480 objects from currently 72 sites from the Aegean and Anatolia. At *c.* 50 of the sites, these objects have been excavated in clear EBA layers (Figure 10.5). At the remaining sites, these were found in layers of later periods (but each of these sites also has EBA occupation) or the circumstances of discovery remain obscure. One of the aims of my work has been to figure out whether all 'spools' are in fact weights or whether only some were used for this purpose reflecting possible chronological or regional differences. For example, they could have been used at certain points in their life-cycle or in certain regions as balance weights while others may also have indeed used as pestles or grinders for pigments. The whole group of these artefacts is therefore called 'spool-shaped potential balance weights' (SSPBW) as it might be difficult to prove that they were used as balance weights in every case.

Defining EBA balance weights

In all there are nine indications why it is likely these objects were utilised as weights. These points will be discussed briefly below. The complete evidence will be presented in much greater detail in a publication currently prepared for press which will include the relevant data from all sites:

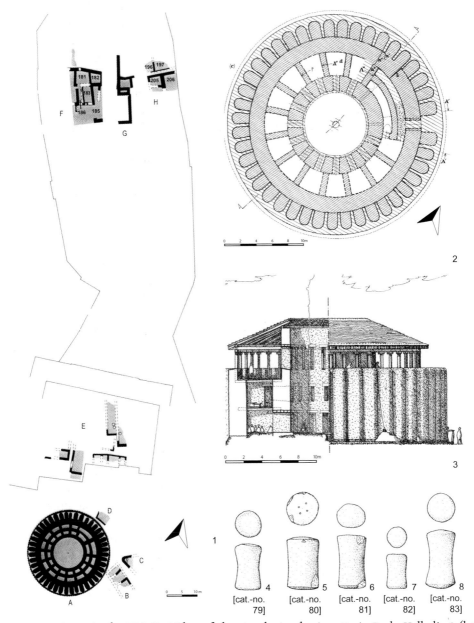

Figure 10.4: Tiryns in the EBA II: 1 Plan of the site during horizon 7a in Early Helladic 2 (later Mycenaean palace is given in outline). – Reconstructed plan of the circular building ("Rundbau"). – 3 One possible reconstruction of the circular building ("Rundbau"). – 4-8 Spool-shaped potential balance weights (SSPBW) from the Upper Citadel (1 from Maran 2000; 2-3 from Marzolff 2009; 4-8 author; objects not to scale).

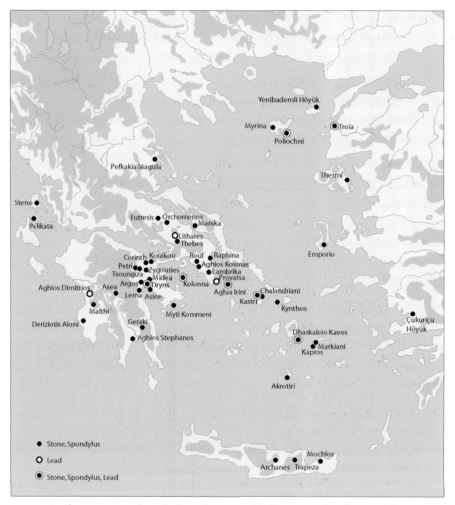

Figure 10.5: Distribution map of spool-shaped potential balance weights (SSPBW) from EBA Aegean sites and their material.

1. Specific type

They form a distinctive and easily recognisable class of artefacts. They are more or less symmetrical and have a well smoothed or polished surface. Only in a very few cases is it difficult to separate them from simple pestles. This homogeneity makes it difficult to accept that some should have functioned as balance weights and others not.[1]

2. Size and mass

They have a considerable range in size and mass. The lightest objects weigh *c.* 2 g like examples from Dhaskalio Kavos (Scarre 2007: 360–362, fig. 9, 9–12, No. 437, No. 085), the heaviest reach nearly 4 kg (3790 g; Caskey 1986: pl. 2, f; Wilson 1999: 150, 197, pl. 38, SF-115; pl. 96, SF-115). Most objects are however lighter than 100 g.

3. Material
They are made of deliberately chosen material, often attractive colourful stone. They are carefully worked and shaped and their surface is often polished. This investment in manufacture stands in notable contrast to the most often assumed function as pestles. In addition very few show any clear traces of abrasion.

4. Markings
Up to eleven (not just four, *cf.* Haas-Lebegyev and Renfrew 2013: 503) SSPBW have markings on their surface that consist of straight parallel incisions or small circles. Five, possibly six, are known from Tiryns (Figure 10.4.5; Rahmstorf 2010b: fig. 8.1.) and respectively one from Petri Nemeas (unpublished, pers. com. M. Kostoula) and from Kolonna on Aegina (Felten *et al.* 2008: 74, fig. 33, 15). One from Tarsus in Cilicia in southern Anatolia (Goldman 1956: 275, fig. 420, 110; Rahmstorf 2010b: fig. 8.2.5) seems to have one incision. Finally there is a 'spool' from the settlement of Dhaskalio in the Cyclades (Figure 10.6.3; Renfrew *et al.* 2007: 124, fig. 15, 12; Haas-Lebegyev and Renfrew 2013a: 491, 495, 502–503, figs. 25.4–5: no. 5741, pl. 12b: no. 5741) and from Lithares on the Greek mainland (Tzavella-Evjen 1984: 141, no. 6689). The last two mentioned are made of lead, the others are made of stone. There are a few others finds where the evidence is ambiguous as to whether they had intentional marking. Eleven marked weights out of *c.* 480 objects might appear to be a small number (2.2%), but it can be observed that also in the Near East and Egypt (*c.* 4.4% according to Cour-Marty 1991: 142) that only a very small percentage of the corpus of known weights is marked or even inscribed. Due to the lack of interest in such objects in these regions it seems likely that this percentage must be reduced as preliminary marked or even inscribed balance weights become published. Hence, the small percentage of weights is not an argument against their potential use as potential balance weights. In addition, we do not know whether the SSPBW might have been marked in a much more degradable way, for example with painted parallel lines, as Early Cycladic marble figurines (Hendrix 2003) were for much different reasons.

5. Adjustment of weight
One SSPBW from Tsoungiza from an EH IIA context (Pullen 2011a: 146, Krattenmaker 2011: 735) has been calibrated by the addition of metal. In a crack in the surface of the stone object, a rectangular small copper or bronze plate has been forcibly inserted. Strangely this highly interesting detail was not mentioned in the final publication of the small finds in stone from the site (Krattenmaker 2011: 735, GS 63). Calibrating (or manipulating) the exact mass of stone weights through small inclusions of metal is also evident on some second millennium balance weights, for example at Ulu Burun (Pulak 2000: 254, fig. 17.2, W104). This specific SSPBW from "Tsoungiza EH II Developed

Phase 1" is dated contemporary to "Lerna III phase late A-early B" (Pullen 2011a: 15, Tab. 1.2.) and this may give a rough estimate for its absolute chronology of around 2600 BC or even in the 27th century BC.

6. Concentrations

They have been found in concentrations, at least in some cases (*e.g.* Tiryns, Kastri). This may hint at their assumed function as sets of weights, each representing different multiples of a supposed basic unit. A 5th dynasty relief from Sakkara in Egypt is showing a (wooden?) box with weights placed next to each other (Michailidou 2005: 46, fig. [no number]). Possibly they were stored similarly in the Aegean. Nevertheless it is the exception to find them in concentrations. In the third millennium BC, weights were found only in rare cases in graves where you might expect larger samples. In the Aegean and Anatolia this occurs only in four secure cases (Steno, Aghios Kosmas, Chalandriani, Kapros) out of the 72 sites with SSPBW. This lack of balance weights in graves is not only typical for the Aegean but also in general for EBA weights in Western and Southern Asia and Egypt. During this period weights are normally found in settlements. Only by the second millennium specific grave assemblages with sets of weights become more common.

Settlement remains, however, are only very rarely preserved in the 'Pompeii-situation'. At settlements with balance weights in Egypt, Mesopotamia, the Arabian Gulf and the Indus region, they are also rarely found in concentrations. In exceptional cases they were located in destructions and later largely untouched tumble layers like in the case of the EBA Royal Palace at Ebla (Ascalone and Peyronel 2006: 186–189) or – even more uncommon – in caches/hoards of weights like as at Akkadian Nippur (McMahon 2006: 135, pl. 165, nos. 8–33). In the Aegean an example for a settlement destruction with suddenly collapsed walls or floors is especially illustrated by the dozen SSPBW found together in the Room 198 (late EH II) in the Lower Citadel of Tiryns (Kilian 1982: 420–421; Kilian 1983: 315, fig. 45; Rahmstorf 2006b: 25–26, fig. 4). One SSPBW found nearby in Room 197 is marked by a circle. A cache of SSPBW together with metal working tools represents the case of the SSPBW from Kastri, Room 11 (Bossert 1967: 61–63, fig. 1). The rather distributed spread of weights of settlements illustrates often the complex site formation processes with are responsible for the actual find spot where we excavate the objects and rarely fully (can) understand. In other cases, it might indicate the singulary use of just one weight in similar processes of production.

7. Balances

Contemporary scale beams made of bone are known from the Northeast Aegean and Western Anatolia at Poliochni, Troy, Küllüoba and Bozhöyük (Rahmstorf 2006a: 72, fig. 10, 24–27). A further previously unidentified fragment of scale beam is exhibited in the Archaeological Museum at Chora on Naxos, reflecting also the existence of such objects in the Southern Aegean. A sixth potential part of a scale is a peculiar three-arm lead object from Aghia Irini (Wilson 1999: 146, pl. 94, SF-26). In this case, however, its function must remain so far unproven and controversial as it is fragmented.

8. Units and weighing system

The 5–6 marked SSPBW from Tiryns are implying a basic unit of slightly above 9 grams, possibly the intended unit was 9.4 g, but through minimal abrasion through use (Mollat 2011) and possibly intentional cheating balance weights tend to be in general lighter than the assumed unit. This unit of *c.* 9.4 g is confirmed by the SSPBW from other sites. For example the four 'spools' from Tsoungiza weigh 8.8 (-) g (1 × *c.* 9.3 g; Krattenmaker 2011: 735, fig. 12.2., GS 64 – slightly chipped, dated to Lerna III B late), 27.9 g (3 × 9.3 g; Krattenmaker 2011: 735, fig 12.2., GS 65 – mentioned above), 43.9 (-) g (original surface largely missing; possibly 5 × *c.* 9.3 g; unpublished, Tsoungiza 1336-8-2, context dated to LH I) and 93.3 g (10 × 9.33 g; unpublished, Tsoungiza 93-8-12, EH III? – I would like to thank J. Wright and D. Pullen for permissions to study these finds). Nevertheless, there are other site series where the 'spools' cannot be attributed to such a unit. For example, the piece with parallel incisions marked SSPBW from Kolonna (Felten *et al.* 2008: 74, fig. 33, 15) weighs 34.5 g. This implies a unit of 11.5 g (I would to thank W. Gauß who has weighed the object), but this is slightly chipped and maybe it was intended to be set a bit bigger, maybe at 11.75 g. The object itself was found possibly as kick-up in a Mycenaean layer as EH II layers are extensive in Kolonna and include also the remains of two Corridor Houses. Finally, there are also indications for a third unit slightly below 8 g. This is especially exemplified by EBA I weights from Çukuriçi Höyük near Ephesus (see below). These three different units, when placed exactly at 7.83, 9.4 and 11.75 stand in a relation of 1, 1.2 and 1.5 or 100%, 120% and 150%. Their first common denominator of these three units is 47 (6 × 7.83, 5 × 9.4 and 4 × 11.75) and indeed many SSPBW are concentrated around and especially below this mass.[2] The three units are all fractions as they are expressed in our modern unit of weight: in gram. The ancient people did use of course natural numbers for their units. It is possible to convert the units expressed in grams to the real numbers used by the EBA people. The key to do this is the understanding of their relation 100%, 120% and 150% and the first denominator at 47 which is 600%. Hence the numbers 10, 12 and 15 and the denominator 60 emerge and make this weighing system fully sexagesimal (Rahmstorf 2010b: 101–102, tab. 8.4–5 for further details). It is possible that the larger unit within this system was placed at 470 g (= 600), however there are few heavy SSPBW preserved, but many represent fractions of 470 g, like a 1/3, 1/2, 1/5 of it (Rahmstorf 2006a: fig. 17).

Nevertheless, there are indications that other units might have been in use as well. The SSPBW from Lerna are especially difficult to understand. Some may indicate the use of a unit slightly above 8 g (8.45 g, Banks 1967: 190, no. 358, Wiencke 2000: 100; 33.15 g (4 × 8.29 g), Banks 1967, 190, no. 357; Wiencke 2000: 101; 101.8 g (12 × 8.48), Banks 1967, 190, no. 360, Wiencke 2000: 196), maybe what is known in Near Eastern archaeology as the Mesopotamian shekel of *c.* 8.4 g. Other SSPBW from Lerna could be understood as multiples of the three interrelated units just discussed. Hence it is indeed not always easy to argue solely on metrological grounds from small series of 'spools' at specific sites that they were used as balance weights. But this is also the case for Near Eastern balance weights where their use as such objects is not questioned due to characteristic shape (*e.g.* sphendonoid) or the characteristic material (iron rock oxide stones like hematite). This is exemplified by EBA weights from Ebla in Syria which are often difficult to assign to any specific units (Ascalone and Peyronel 2006). As the assumed units are placed so close to each other and there is a considerable margin in error it becomes an often difficult task and different interpretations of potential multiples or fractions are possible. The simple reason behind this fact is the contemporaneous use of different units at the time which render the metrological analyses as difficult (Alberti, this volume). In general, it is a justified criticism (Pakkanen 2011: 161–162, n. 44) that the weight data of the SSPBW need more detailed discussion with the statistically relevant methods like cosine quantogram analysis.

9. Similar weight units in Syro-Mesopotamia

Some if not all of the reconstructed units are also known in EBA Syro-Mesopotamia. For example, a weight from Tell Brak has five parallel incisions and weighs 46.92 g (5 × 9.38 g; Oates *et al.* 2001, 619, fig. 485, no. 35), another one with three incisions weighs 25.03 g (3 × 8.34 g; Oates *et al.* 2001, 619, fig. 485, no. 35), apparently the Mesopotamian shekel. Both came to light in the Akkadian temple complex of Area SS at Tell Brak. A weight (68.7 g) with six incisions from Ebla might point to the 11.5–11.75 g-unit (6 × 11.45 g; Ascalone and Peyronel 2006: 521, pl. 2, 5), others which are not marked can be interpreted as weights representing shared multipes of the three interrelated units of 7.83, 9.4 and 11.75, respectively of the mina (*e.g.* 45.4 g; 95.67 g; 141.9 g; 467.5 g; 930 g; 938 g; 946; 951.5 g; Ascalone and Peyronel 2006: passim). A weight inscribed in Akkadian with 'one mina' from Tell es-Sweyhat weighs 472.2 g (Holland 2006, 231, fig. 163, nos. 2–3, pl. 123, b-c). There three interrelated units (7.8 g; 9.4 g and 11.75 g) with a shared mina of 470 based on a sexagesimal system are most likely a Syro-Mesopotamia invention taking into account the importance of the number 60 in Uruk-Period accounting and metrology (Englund 1998: 111–120). The fact that different units were used at the same time complicates the picture and might call into question the whole credibility of the assumed function of 'spools' as balance weights. But the contemporaneous use of different units is well paralleled among the weight metrological systems in the Near East (*e.g.* Parise 1984) and Egypt (*e.g.* Mollat 2007: 2051). Only the Harappans had just one weight unit (*c.* 13.7 g; Hendrickx-Baudot 1972: 15–16) during the whole period of their civilisation. For this reason, only in the Indus Valley do we not find any balance weights which are marked. Hence markings on weights are in fact indications that different units were in contemporary use.

Nevertheless, it is of course not possible to prove without any doubt that all 'spools' were balance weights. Most recently in the discussion of 'spools' from the EC settlement of Dhaskalio, dated to 2750–2200 BC (Renfrew *et al.* 2012: fig. 8), J. Haas-Lebegyev and C. Renfrew contested the interpretation of the spools as balance weights, at least of the ones from Dhaskalio. Their argumentation will be reviewed below. It is of particular interest to figure out if the earliest of these 'spools' can be considered as balance weights. Our first examples of SSPBW appear in contexts of the later EBA I and the transitional phase to EBA II. Artefacts which are datable to this time window are however few in number. After Dhaskalio, I will therefore briefly discuss early examples known from Poliochni and Çukuriçi Höyük.

Dhaskalio Kavos

Most recently Haas-Lebegyev and Renfrew have published what they term 'spools', herein SSPBW, from the excavations between 2006 and 2008 on Dhaskalio which is today a tiny island opposite the site of Kavos on the Cycladic island Keros (Figure 10.6.1–2). This publication represents the first publications of 'spools' in the sufficient detail necessary to assess their potential functions. This has set a new standard for how such objects should be published in the future, which includes a detailed presentation of stratigraphy, contexts and all other finds (Renfrew *et al.* 2013a). The only improvement might be the use of a weighing scale with a precision of 0.1 g which is necessary for weight studies, rather than one with whole units (1 gram) correct to no decimal places. In the functional discussion of the objects they reject the use of the 'spools' from Dhaskalio as balance weights and interpret them very generally as "prestige objects, used with a variety of functions depending on the context and on the immediate needs of their users" (Haas-Lebegyev and Renfrew 2013a: 504). First I will discuss the points they made which in their view contradict an interpretation of the objects as balance weights. After that I will present additional arguments based on the evidence from Dhaskalio Kavos – possible only through the magnificant detailed publication – suggesting that the 'spools' from Dhaskalio were indeed balance weights.

'Spools' and the pestle function

There are three points to consider: first, the usual pestles; second traces of colour; and, third traces of wear. First of all, it is indeed as J. Haas-Lebegyev and C. Renfrew write: "stone objects found together with marble bowls, and thus most likely functioning as pestles, are, however, usually of different shape, clearly differing from the usual spool- or cyclindrical-shaped objects: they are either of a larger cone-shape, or less frequently of another shape" (Haas-Lebegyev and Renfrew 2013a: 502). Real pestles look different. Secondly, it is hard to find either 'spools' with traces of pigments or clear contextual association of SSPBW with equipment like stone bowls or mortars where pigments could have been crushed with the 'spools'. The evidence from the SSPBW from Aghios Kosmas in fact does not really support a functional understanding of them as grinders for pigments as proposed by G. Mylonas.[3] In addition, in contrast to Haas-Lebegyev and Renfrew I could not observe any colour pigments on one of the SSPBW (5952) from Dhaskalio, as they write.[4] Nevertheless there is at least one clear instance[5] for the definitive use of 'spools' as pestles. A dozen SSPBW found together in the destruction horizon mentioned already above in Room 198 (late EH II) in the Lower Citadel of Tiryns (Kilian 1982: 420–421; Kilian 1983: 315, fig. 45) is the most obvious indication for the use of the spools as weights which is also implied by the metrological analysis of the objects and the SSPBW found nearby weighing 9.2 g marked with a circle (Rahmstorf 2006b, 25–26, fig. 4). However, from this complex comes a roughly shaped 'spool' with traces of colour pigment on one circular end. This colour traces are similar to the ones on a marble bowl from the same context (Kilian 1982: fig. 46) so that they clearly represent a pestle and a grinding bowl. So, we have the best evidence for their weight use together with an indication of the use of a spool as a pestle! Yet, one should notice that this 'spool' (Kilian 1982: 422, fig. 45 [third row left]) exhibited in the Archaeological Museum at Nafplion (NM 31418) has clear traces of wear on the circular end with the reddish pigments. It is not really symmetrical but twisted to one side and has a larger breakage surface which had calc-sinter implying that it had already a long history of use. One might think of a different explanation for this: a piece selected because of its shape, secondary use, or even an interchangeable use.[6] Here we are coming to the third point to consider: traces of wear, which are rarely visible on the circular ends of the SSPBW. Where it has been documented, it is perfectly plausible that this is indicating in several cases secondary use, indeed as pestles. For example, at Dhaskalio, it is important to note that only SSPBW from Phase C and surface layers are generally much more chipped and show breakages. Some show intensive wear, the spondylus 'spools' from surface or tumble layers are in some cases heavily eroded (5140, 12431). This is especially likely also for SSPBW found in MBA and LBA kitchen or storage assemblages like at Akrotiri (Birtacha 2008: 359, fig 35.21. 3474; 35.25. 3474; Devetzi 2008: 141–142, fig. 15.15. 3474) or Midea (Demakopoulou *et al.* 1997/98: 66, fig. 50): probable pick-ups from earlier (EBA) layers at these sites and became reused in a suitable way.

Metrological analysis of the 'spools' from Dhaskalio
Haas-Lebegyev and Renfrew argue that some of the 'spools' from Dhaskalio could fit well the proposed units while others 'do not conform readily to the proposed weight units' (Haas-Lebegyev and Renfrew 2013a: 503). First of all, one can easily observe that six have more or less the same mass: three weighing 4 g and three weighing 58/59 g. Such concentrations are a first hint. The statistical chance that such a distribution is just random is extremely small. It becomes especially interesting when we consider the five completely preserved examples (5952, 10171, 10160, 10174, 5135) from Trench I in Phase B (see Haas-Lebegyev and Renfrew 2013a: Tab. 25.1). Four could well be fractions of a mina of 470 g (1/8: 58 g and 59 g and 1/5: 92 g and 94 g) and eight times the unit of 9.4 g (73 g). This assignment applies also for the

SSPBW weighing 92 g and 94 g (10 × 9.4 g). The only one from Phase A (10209) fits again this unit (18 g: 2 × 9 g) as also the largest one persevered (5202) from Phase C (380 g: 40 × 9.5 g; 4/5 of 470 g). This latter unstratified piece might show already some secondary use. It is important to note that only with Phase C most SSPBW show intensive wear and possible secondary use. The above mentioned spondylus 'spools' from surface and tumble layers are in some cases heavily eroded (5140, 12431) and should therefore not be included in metrological calculations. As already mentioned above (see *1. Specific type*) 5438 is not belonging to the class of 'spools' or SSPBW. Excluding these three the metrological results become consistent, even another two are a bit too light (10703: 43 g, 12090: 44 g) to be assignable nicely to the common multiple at 47 g mentioned above (see *8. Units and weighing system*). 10743 (107 g) fits rather well (12 × 8.9 g). All in all, the sample from the Dhaskalio settlement can be assigned quite well to the assumed unit of 9.4 g and fractions of the mina of 470 g.

The lead weights from Dhaskalio
Two SSPBW made of lead were found at Dhaskalio. They are known from several other EBA II sites in the Aegean (Figure 10.5). One (144 g: 3 × 48 g; 12 × 12 g; 15 × 9.6 g; 18 × 8 g) from Dhaskalio is heavily weathered and maybe over-weight (for environmental effects on lead weights see Pakkanen 2011: 143), the other (138 g) is well persevered bears at one end nine pierced holes arranged in 'U'-shape (Figure 10.6.3). Dividing its mass by nine suggests a unit of 15.38 g. Another lead SSPBW Lithares on the mainland dated to EH II Early (Maran 1998: 67–68) with five incised dots weighs 178 g resulting in 35.9 g. According to the authors "these values do not, however, seem to follow any of the weight units proposed by Rahmstorf" (Haas-Lebegyev and Renfrew 2013a: 503). Nevertheless, they rather well represent multiples of the assumed units (15.38 ÷ 2 = 7.69 g; 35.9 ÷ 4 = 8.98 g). It has to be emphasised that a contemporary EH II Early SSPBW from phase A of the settlement of Aghios Kosmas (Mylonas 1959: 18, fig. 166, 6) already mentioned above weighs exactly also 35.9 g. Nevertheless, the markings of the two lead 'spools' are indeed difficult to comprehend. However, the markings on contemporary Syrian balance weights are similarly not always easy to understand and again seem to represent multiples and fractions of the units. This for example the case for specifically marked weights from the Royal Palace E of Ebla (Ascalone and Peyronel 2006: 115, 119, pl. 14: 49, pl. 15) or small hematite weights from Tell Beydar (Milano 2004, 2–3, fig. 1 [2634-M-1], fig. 3 [13139-M-2]). One from Beydar (2634-M-1) is very small weighing only 2.6 g but has 6 parallel incisions. This might rather indicate that the weight is referring to the sixth part of 15.6 g – maybe again the double 7.8 g unit as in the case of the Dhaskalio lead 'spool' (see also below: Çukuriçi Höyük). The 'U'-shape of the marking on one of the Dhaskalio SSPBW (Figure 10.6.3) implies a very specific meaning which is not understood so far.

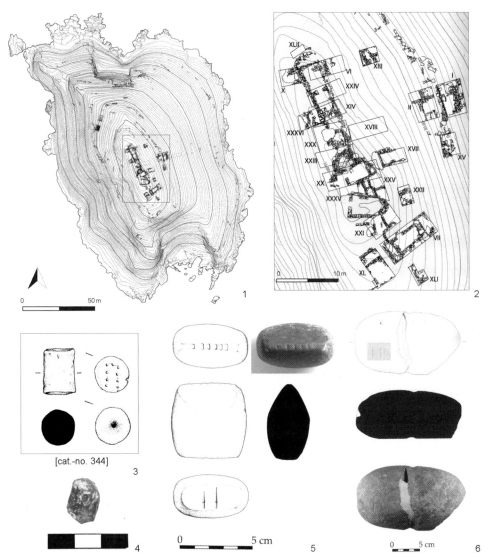

Figure 10.6: Dhaskalio during the EBA: 1 Plan of the island, showing walls recorded from the survey and the excavation trenches, contours at 0.5 m and 5 m. - 2 Plan of the trenches on the summit. - 3 Spool-shaped potential balance weight (SSPBW) made of lead from Trench VI, Phase C. - 4 Presumable small lapis lazuli chunk? from C. Doumas' excavations in 1963 (subsequent Trench XVII). - 5-6 Presumable stone balance weights from C. Doumas' excavations in 1963 (subsequent Trench XVII), possible intentional markings highlighted in 6 (1 from Renfrew et al. 2009; 2 from Renfrew and Boyd 2011; 3 after Renfrew et al. 2007; 3 not to scale, 4-6 from Doumas 2013 and supplementary material on CD in Renfrew et al. 2013a).

The shape of the spools

It has been argued that that "weights usually have at least one flat and stable surface to be placed firmly in a scale pan" (Haas-Lebegyev and Renfrew 2013a: 503; also J. Crouwel in Crouwel *et al.* 2005: 18). However, this is only true for weights from the second millennium BC, especially the Near Eastern type of sphendonoid weights. During the third millennium BC sphendonoids have not yet a flat surface (*e.g.* the hematite weights from Poliochni, see Bernabò-Brea 1976: 304–305, pl. CCLVII, 1–7), the flat surface is a later development of the shape. Spherical weights are very typical for the third millennium BC (Nippur: McMahon 2006: 135, pl. 165, nos. 8–33), for example at Ebla they are the most common type (Ascalone and Peyronel 2006: 71, pl. 8–13). It seems indeed that the scale pans were made of made of perishable material. Metal scale plates from the third millennium BC are only preserved from a couple of Mesopotamian sites (Müller-Karpe 1993: pl. 65–66), but not one scale beam has been published so far from the same period in Mesopotamia. In Western inland Anatolia, the Northeast Aegean and possibly also in the Southern Aegean a couple of scale beams made of bone and copper/bronze are documented (see above), however, no metal scale plates are known. The balances in the third millennium BC were largely made of perishable material like wood, which is suggested also by Old Kingdom depictions of very large scales. These balances have sometimes hooks where the plates, baskets or bowls were mounted (Davies 1902, pl. 13; Michailidou 2005: 46, fig. [no number]). When looking at these depictions from Egypt (e. g. Mogensen 1921: 43, fig. 42; Ducros 1910, 245, fig. 51) these containers hanging at either end of the balance beams may have been not only made of copper but also of leather, textile or basketry. One SSPBW (K. Birtacha in Marangou 1990: 80, no. 73) in the Archaeological Museum of Naxos (Mus. Inv. No. 4458), possibly from Dhakalio Kavos, has a surface structure on one of its circular ends which could be the petrified impression of a textile.

Weights and a small chunk of lapis lazuli (?) from C. Doumas excavations

One additional argument for the identification of the objects as balance weights also at Dhaskalio is the stone object found in the first excavations of C. Doumas on the island. In his Building B which is located within the subsequent Trench XVII of the excavations from 2006–2008 Doumas found "on the floor, mixed with ashes, a small schematic marble figurine, various stone tools, a fragment of blue glass paste as well as a number of sea shells" (Doumas 2013: 83). The highly interesting 'blue glass paste' is also described as "bluish stone (?) or glass, slightly translucent" (Doumas 2013: 86, DF22) but unfortunately not illustrated or further analysed in the printed publication. On the supplementary material provide on an enclosed CD several coloured photographes of the bluish stone are included[7] (Figure 10.6.4). From this illustration it is possibly a very small chunk of lapis lazuli mainly consisting of lazurite with a few embedded particles of whitish calcite. To this EC II assemblage, considering the typical ground stone tools and the figurine, belongs also a wedge-shaped object of pale green stone (Figure 10.6.5). It has "six shallow parallel incisions along the edge and [two] small grooves across the flat surface opposite [which] may reflect a measuring unit" (Doumas 2013: 84, fig. 7.9. DF12). Unfortunately it has not been weighed. In view of the incisions the inevitable guess would be that it is a balance weight, even if I cannot quote any parallel to such an object yet. The two sets of parallel incisions at opposite sides might even point to its reference to two different units of weight. As far as I could see the object is not mentioned anywhere else again in the publication of the settlement of Dhaskalio. Finally, a broken "large hammer of ovoid form" (Doumas 2013: 83, fig. 7.8. DF9) has three parallel shallow incisions (Figure 10.6.6) – again it is possible that this is a balance weight.

Metallurgy and weights

SSPBW have been found in association with metallurgical activities. At several sites, for example Aghios Dimitrios, Kastri, Thermi, Poliochni, they were excavated in direct or close association with metalwork. Also assemblages from Dhaskalio support this. Most SSPBW from Dhaskalio were found in surface or 'tumble layers', but some were found on, above and between floor layers and were considered to form part of primary contexts (Haas-Lebegyev and Renfrew 2013a: 493). These are six SSPBW in Trench I (Phase B), two in Trench VII (Phase C) and single finds in Trench XXIII and XXV. Trench I yielded the most examples and the most complete contextual information indicating some functional correlation with tools for metal production and SSPBW.[8] Georgakopoulou states "for Phase B, all metallurgical finds were recovered from trench I" (2013: 690, with the exception of two single finds from Trench II and V) and all six SSPBW known from Phase B were found in Trench I (for the seventh questionable 'spool' from Phase B at Dhaskalio see above). This emphasises a relationship between the SSPBW and metallurgy. This applies also for the few from Phase C which are considered to be found in primary contexts. Two SSPBW (10743, 10765) derive from a rich Phase C context (Layer 32) in Trench VII which was situated in the middle and western part of a room may "suggest a period of abandonment and initial phases of house decay" including a "period when the deposit was 'open to the elements'" (Renfrew and Loughlin 2013: 234). The assemblages include also at least six hammers/ pounders and modified/worked cobbles (Rowan *et al.* 2013: 578, 580, fig. 29.13, 10754). East and west of that room in trench VII metallurgical remains were found. In the east a tuyère, metallurgical ceramics and slag, in the west a litharge fragment were excavated (Georgakoulou 2013: 687, 690).

Of special interest is the coincidence of silver production by cupellation and the appearance of SSPBW, which might be also indicated by the last mentioned context at Dhaskalio. Cupellation, the metallurgical process in which silver is extracted from silver-rich lead metal, can be identified in the archaeological record through finds of litharge, the lead oxide by-product of cupellation. At many EBA sites where litharge was excavated such as Lambrika (Kakavogianni *et al.* 2008: 51–57, fig. 12–15), Aghia Irini (Wilson 1999: 146, 171, 173, 197–198, pl. 94, SF 28–31), Leondari/Provatsa (Spitaels 1983: 63, fig.) and Dhaskaleio Kavos (Georgakopoulou 2007: 396), we also know of SSPBW; in some documented cases from the same archaeological context. An important detail in this regard might be the fact that the largest SSPBW known come from these sites. Large SSPBW are generally were rare, as there only five from two sites (Dhaskelio, Aghia Irini) that weigh more than 300 g.[9] At present there are 11 sites with litharge finds known from the Aegean which can be dated to the Final Neolithic/EBA. Besides Limenaria on Thasos (Papadopoulos 2008) all these sites are situated in Attica and the Cyclades (Makronissos, Kea, Siphnos, Dhaskalio/Keros). In the case of Lambrika an apparent workshop for silver extraction has recently been excavated (Kakavogianni *et al.* 2008). The nexus of the emergence of silver metallurgy, the precise assessment of value (and equivalence) and the emerging weight metrology can be observed in the textual records from third millennium Syro-Mesopotamia (*e.g.* Postgate 1992: 69, 95, 101, 125, 193, 201–203, 227, Text 3:5, 5:4, 5:9, 6:7, 10:2, 10:11–12, 12:2). It could be the case that similar nexus existed in the EBA Aegean (*cf.* Rahmstorf 2015, 164–166 fig. 12).

Concluding remarks on the significance of Dhaskalio and Kavos

1. The problematic issue of the functional interpretation of the SSPBW from Dhaskalio was discussed here at some length for several reasons. First of all, the commendable publication of the finds by J. Haas-Lebegyev and C. Renfrew is the first detailed discussion of their interpretation as balance weights (and its rejection) published so far. Secondly, no other site (Dhaskalio *and* Kavos) in the Aegean and Anatolia has generated this number of SSPBW, *c.* 110.[10] Thirdly, the SSPBW retrieved from the special deposits of Kavos received the same treatment as Cycladic marble figurines or stone bowls: they were intentionally broken or even sawn into pieces (Renfrew *et al.* 2007b: 127, fig. 15, 6 (only SF 1317); Scarre 2007: 360–362; fig. 9, 9–10, No. 570). This emphasises the importance of the SSPBW in the life of EBA people and also speaks rather against a mundane function as a pestle. Fourthly, Dhaskalio seems to have been a key trading site in the Aegean. The tiny rocky island of Dhaskalio was connected by a landbridge (Dixon and Kinnaird 2013: 52, figs. 4.6–7) during the EBA with the main island of Keros and this reminds one of other gateway communities (Branigan 1992) with such topography like Mochlos on Crete or Tyre in the Lebanon: communities which had indeed a maritime specialisation (Broodbank 2013: 323, 329, figs. 7.43, 9.30). The recently published small finds from Dhaskalio give a glimpse of trade relations, especially with the east.
2. There is Central Anatolian (Cappadocian) obsidian, only known so far from a few other EBA Aegean sites (Agrilia, Mallia and Platanos B (?): Carter and Milić 2013: 541, 543).
3. An elongated biconical and small biconical carnelian beads (Haas-Lebegyev and Renfrew 2013b: 663–664, figs. 31.20–21, 12562) have their closest parallels in Treasure E from Troy (Tolstikow and Trejster 1996: 111, cat.-no.121–122) and from the Kolonna hoard from Aegina (Reinholdt 2008: 117, pl. 3) as Lebegyev and Renfrew refer to and in the hoard from Eskiyapar near Boğazköy in Central

Anatolia (Özgüç and Temizer 1993: 616, 624, fig. 22–26). Their shape, and in one case the decoration (etching), material and the tools required to produce them leave as the best explanation that they are objects imported from the Near East.[11]

4. There are only four spindle whorls from the whole site, but three of them find their best parallels in shape and incised linear decor at EBA sites in Western inland, Central and Southern Anatolia (see Gavalas 2013: 650, figs. 31.9–10, 5484, 11167, 12854 – more typological parallels could be quoted from other published EBA Anatolian sites). As there are no loom weights from the sites, textile production was apparently not existing at this site with Dhaskalio focusing on trade and Kavos on related ritual activities (*cf.* Rahmstorf 2015, 153–157 fig. 5–6).

5. The possible small lapis lazuli chunk (Figure 10.6.4) from Christos Doumas' 1963 excavations at Dhaskalio mentioned above would be first known EBA piece from the Aegean, with the exception of the famous and unparalleled lapis lazuli axe from Troy Treasure L (Tolstikow and Trejster 1996: 152, cat.-no. 169) being one of the largest lapis lazuli artefacts (L 27.8 cm) known from the whole Bronze Age. EBA lapis lazuli in Anatolia is rare,[12] while there are some 130 sites with lapis lazuli between Syria and western India.

6. Finally it was not only an eastern orientation which is visible in the small finds: a stone bracer from a Phase C context (Haas-Lebegyev and Renfrew 2013b: 663–664, figs. 31.22–23) in Dhaskalio has good contemporary parallels in the Bell Beaker world[13] (*cf.* Rahmstorf 2015, 161, 164, fig. 11).

Poliochni

In the early Blue Period spools were recovered during investigations by Italian archaeologists before the Second World War at Poliochni on Lemnos. Near to the fortification wall a "somewhat concave cylinder of marble streaked white and yellowish, perfectly smooth" (Bernabò-Brea 1964: 160, Inv.-no. 4409) came to light which appears to be a well-made example of our artefact type. It was not illustrated in the volume by Bernabò-Brea, but I have studied it in the Archaeological Museum on Lemnos. It has a mass of 54.7 g, with minimal chips on the surface, and it is typical for the (later) SSPBW as it could represent a multiple of the 9.2–9.4 g-unit. An absolute date in the 29th century BC is likely for this artefact on the basis of its dating to the early Blue Period. From the same area, but from an advanced stage of the Blue Period, a cylindrical stone object made from orange-brown sandstone was excavated. Its surface is highly porous and neither smoothed nor polished (Bernabò-Brea 1964: 157, Inv.-no. 4635, pl. CIII, 13). This is one of the very few 'spools' whose affinity to our group remains questionable. The object weighs 86.2 g and is preserved to *c.* 95%. The original weight could have been slightly above 90 g which would again roughly agree with the 9.2–9.4 g-unit. It derives from an area where metal working appears to have been carried out, demonstrated by finds of slag (Kouka 2002: 63). Farther north in a deep sounding in Insula XIII, in the so-called Megaron 832, two spool-shaped objects were found. One has a very irregular shape. It must be considered as a pestle indeed (Bernabò-Brea 1964: 112, Inv.-no. 6100/12, pl. CIII, 16). The other spool-shaped object however fits very well with our group of objects. It is broken, and a large portion from the middle is lacking (Bernabò-Brea 1964: 112 Inv.-no. 6100/12, pl. CIII, 14). In addition to an abundance of pottery, there are again finds of slag and a tuyère (Bernabò-Brea 1964: 112, pl. LXXXIII, r). One C^{14}-date from a carbonised fig found in layers of building phase 2 of Megaron 832 provides a date range between 2910–2672 BC (1-sigma, Begemann *et al.* 1992: 220–221: 4145 +/-70 BP). Also in the northern part of Poliochni Blue in Insulae I-II, two spool-shaped objects were found. One of these, described as a cylindrical spool made of red stone with yellow veins (Bernabò-Brea 1964: 268, Inv.-no. 5010, pl. CIII, 15), could unfortunately not be located in the museum. This is the third object from Poliochni Blue that should be assigned to our group. Furthermore, there is another 'spool' with a very rough surface treatment (Bernabò-Brea 1964: 268, Inv.-no. 5007, pl. CIII, 17). It is slightly chipped and weighs 97.9 g. Again, compared to the very well-made SSPBW manufactured from carefully chosen materials in later centuries, this object does not fit into our group. Both 'spools' from the northern insulae cannot be connected to any specific assemblage. But again metal was possibly worked there due to the finding of six pieces of slag (Bernabò-Brea 1964: 266). L. Bernabò-Brea already wondered whether the coarse 'spools' had a similar function as the fine, well-worked 'spools.' These latter most probably were made of imported stone, as he remarked (Bernabò-Brea 1964: 607). For the present, one has to conclude that the earliest datable 'spools' from the 29th and 28th centuries are not a homogenous group, at least if one includes also the coarse cylinders. When considering only the well-worked 'spools' made of attractively veined stone, it is impressive to see how much similar they are to later SSPBW. But is it realistic to think of them as functioning already as balance weights? In regard to the very small sample and the often fragmented state of preservation of the objects it cannot be proven that they were balance weights.

Çukuriçi Höyük

The 100 m × 80 m large tell of Çukuriçi Höyük (see Horejs in this volume) close to ancient Ephesus has a 4 m depth of stratigraphy from the Late Neolithic/Early Copper Age to the beginning of the EBA. The upper EBA layers of the settlement, the Phases ÇuHu IV–III (Figure 10.7.1) are contemporary to parts of the sequence at Troy I. Typical Troy II vessels like the Depas or wheel turned plates, which are part of the Lefkandi I-Kastri assemblage on the Aegean islands, are not encountered in the top layers at the site (Horejs *et al.* 2011: 42–43). In absolute terms the Phases ÇuHu IV–III are dated to 2850–2750 BC through a sequence of 10 C^{14}-dates (Horejs *et al.* 2011: 43). It is well documented throughout the EBA phase at Çukuriçi Höyük that metal working was one of the most important activities of its inhabitants. At this site numerous kilns were excavated. An intriguing assemblage was found in Room 1 of ÇuHu III, directly at the modern escarpment in the middle of tell settlement. The contents must have belonged to a metallurgical workshop (Figure 10.7.2 a–l; Horejs 2009: 364–365, fig. 6). It includes also a small copper-silver alloy artefact (Figure 10.7.4; Horejs *et al.* 2010, fig. 6.2) excavated not far from Room 1. Presumable its appearance may to some degree imitate gold. Also different metal working tools (Figure 10.7.2 r–t, v–z), and needles (Figure 10.7.2 m–q, u) have been excavated at the site. In 2008 a rectangular weight made of basalt was found in a levelled layer between ÇuHu IV–III (Figure 10.7.6; Horejs 2009: 365–366, fig. 8). Weights of this kind find good parallels in EBA sites in the Near East for example at Ebla (Ascalone and Peyronel 2006: passim) or at Troy and Poliochni Phase Yellow (Bernabò-Brea 1976: 304–305, pl. CCLVII). One year later a 'spool' of salmon coloured stone came to light in the layers of ÇuHu IV (Figure 10.7.5; B. Horejs pers. com. 30.11.2009). The object and its context are so far unpublished and I thank B. Horejs that I can present it here. In the excavations in 2011 two further weights were found: a small oblong and a larger oblong weight both made of dark stone (pers. com. B. Horejs). The above mentioned basalt weight (Figure 10.7.6) has a mass of 15.67 g, the large oblong weight weighs twice this: 31.2 g. The SSPBW has a mass of 3.78 g but a very tiny fragment has been broken off. The weight ratio between the three objects is therefore 1 – 4 – 8. It seems more likely that the intended ratio was ½ – 2 – 4, based on the unit of *c.* 7.8 g mentioned above was in use from the third millennium in Syro-Mesopotamia, especially at the site of Ebla (Ascalone and Peyronel 2006: 92–95: the so-called 'siclo eblaita' or 'siclo siriano'). Addendum 2016: This is confirmed by two most recent finds (Horejs 2016, fig. 4, 4–5): a fragmented cylinder in argillaceous shale (5.6 g; ca. 2/3 preserved – 1 × c. 7.8 g) and a flat rounded peridotite stone (39.79 g; 5 × 7.96), further strengthening the nexus of early weights and metal production.

Concluding remarks on EBA weight use in the Aegean and Western Anatolia

It is possible to draw some conclusions from the presented data on the emergence of weight metrology in the Aegean. This can be presented in three successive periods from 2900–2200 BC, and not thereafter from 2200 onwards.

2900–2700 BC: The evidence of the earliest 'spools' from Poliochni Blue and the Aghios Kosmas cemetery (above: *'Spools' and the pestle function*) might not seem to support an interpretation of them as balance weights. Yet, the new results from the recent excavations at Çukuriçi Höyük confirm that weight metrology was already practised in the Aegean, at least on the eastern coast, at an early stage around 2850–2750 BC. With the earliest definite weights in Egypt and Syro-Mesopotamia datable to around 3000 BC and the early third millennium BC this is impressive data for the adoption of this important innovation in the Aegean and Western Anatolia. The find at Çukuriçi Höyük of a 'spool' in the same level as stone weights of Near Eastern type and its fit to the assumed unit (in this case of the unit of 7.8 g) is a strong indication that the 'spools' might have also been used already as weights at other Aegean and

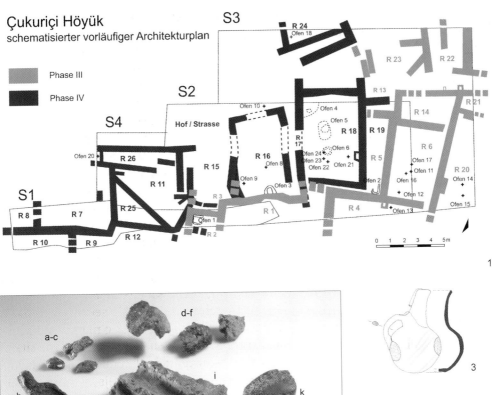

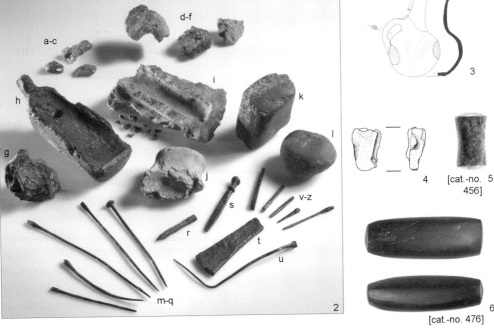

Figure 10.7: Çukuriçi Höyük in EBA I: 1 Plan of the trenches S1–S4 in the phases IV and III (state of excavation in 2010). – 2 Metalurgical finds from the site. – 3 Jug. – 4 Metal object of a silver-copper alloy. – 5 Spool-shaped potential balance weight (SSPBW). – 6 Oblong basalt weight (1–2 from Horejs 2010; 3–4 from Horejs et al. 2010; 5 unpublished, courtesy: B. Horejs; 6 from Horejs 2009; objects not scale).

Anatolian sites. Their shape represents a local Aegean choice. Only at sites in the Northeast Aegean (Poliochni) and Anatolia (Troy, Çukuriçi Höyük, Tarsus) have both oblong dark stone weights of Near Eastern type and 'spools' been found together. Çukuriçi Höyük lucidly illustrates the nexus between metallurgy involving precious metals and special alloys and balance weights.

2700–2550/2500 BC: In the earlier part of the EBA II not many SSPBW can be dated. These however already show the application of a unit of 9.4 g or slightly lighter. This is demonstrated by single of SSPBW from Aghios Kosmas settlement phase A, Lithares (lead), Lerna III B, Aghios Dimitrios (lead) and Tsoungiza. A SSPBW from EH II Early at Tsoungiza was also calibrated using a piece of metal. The lead 'spool' from Lithares bears markings, maybe relatable to a unit of 9 g. These objects indicate an established weight metrology on the Greek mainland clearly before any Lefkandi I-Kastri influence is recognisable.

2550/2500–2200: Most SSPBW can be dated to this period and on current evidence it appears that excavation of every settlement site of this period has revealed some of them. A contextual link between metallurgy and weight use, especially in the case of silver extraction, seems to be indicative at several sites. SSPBW are especially found in large numbers at sites with strong affiliation to trade (Aghia Irini, Dhaskalio) and have monumental architecture (Tiryns, Kolonna). Secondary use of SSPBW as pestles is observable in some cases (*e.g.* Tiryns).

2200–2000: It is hard to demonstrate that any SSPBW were still produced during this period because the stratified SSPBW from EBA III (*e.g.* Aghia Irini, Kolonna) could be explained as kick-ups from earlier EBA II layers. It is possible that weight metrology was given up and lost (as seal use) in most parts of the Aegean, as seems to have happened also to seals. Only on Crete these economic procedures continued (in the case of the seals) or were re-invented (in the case of the weights: the disc weights[14]). Apparently the first 'civilisation' emerged then on Crete and not on the Greek mainland.

Conclusions

The 'exceptional character' (Nakou 1997: 637) of the Northeast Aegean with sites like Troy and Poliochni (and now also Myrina) is well documented already during the third millennium. The richness of the metallurgy, the splendour of the hoards ('treasures') and as well as outstanding buildings with apparent special functions (like the 'Bouleuterion' at Poliochni or the Megara at Troy) give the material culture a quality not encountered before. These sites also provide the first evidence for signs of economic complexity at the beginning of the Bronze Age. However, it was not only the North Aegean that "were in receipt of diverse influence at least as far back as the early third millennium through indirect interaction with the state societies of Mesopotamia" (Nakou 1997: 648) but other parts of the East Aegean coast and Western Anatolia also. The littoral of western Anatolia and its hinterland surely still veil more sites like Çukuriçi Höyük. Excavations at Liman Tepe suggest this might be another candidate, when the results will be published in detail. During the early centuries of the third millennium BC we get the first, yet still meagre, evidence for the presence of seal-use and weight metrology. A possible guess is that both practices were connected: small amount of material were precisely weighed out and could then be secured into sealed containers. There is not yet any clear contextual indication for such practices from a destruction horizon, yet the overall distribution of sealings and SSPBW in the Aegean demonstrates that both practices are often encountered at the same site (compare Figure 10.1–10.5). Recently skepticism has been raised (Haas-Lebegyev and Renfrew 2013a: 503) regarding an earlier claim (Rahmstorf 2003: 296) about the association of the use of weights and seals in the EBA II. More recently published data (from Geraki, Petri, Myrina, Markiani, Mochlos) has however confirmed this. From all sites on the mainland and the islands where sealings have been reported (and also the small finds have been at least partially published) we know also of SSPBW: Aghios Kosmas, Geraki, Lerna, Tiryns, Asine, Petri, Corinth, Provatsa, Aghia Irini, Myrina, Markiani, Archanes, Mochlos. Only on Crete where SSPBW appear only at northern sites with *Cycladica*, sealings have been found at sites where no balance weights are known. As Crete remains largely outside the distribution of the SSPBW, it is possible that other not yet identified weights were used on the island before the disc weights became common in the second millennium BC.

As has been shown, for several reasons it is unlikely that the twin innovations of seal-use and weight metrology, were autochthonous inventions. This is indicated by the earlier existence of both of them in the lands east of the Aegean and Western Anatolia (Eastern Anatolia, Syria, Mesopotamia). Both innovations left their first traces in the earlier third millennium BC during the late EBA I and during the transition from EBA I to EBA II, before the Lefkandi I-Kastri horizon emerged around the middle of the third millennium BC. Indeed, the Lefkandi I-Kastri horizon, as well as the Philia horizon on Cyprus, have been characterised by intensive contact phases that merely represent the culminations of longer-term processes (Peltenburg 2007). However, the nature of changes taking place during the 29th–26th centuries, are still difficult to explain. Excavated and well-documented settlements of this period are few, at least in comparison with the wealth of sites known from the middle and later third millennium BC. The purpose of this paper has been to underline that the impressive developments visible in many regions of the Aegean and Western Anatolia around the middle of the third millennium, *e.g.* during the period of the Corridor Houses on the Southern Greek mainland, are to no small extent the outcome of the implementation of important innovations, 'escaped technologies' from the East during the earlier third millennium BC which became adapted but changed to local preferences. Derivatives, if not somewhat independent interpretations of the foreign practices are especially perceptible in the Aegean. For example, in the Anatolian EBA and the Northeast Aegean the oblong dark stone ('haematite') weights were popular and were similar to ones from Syria. In the Aegean, however a distinctive new shape was created in the early third millennium BC – the spool-shaped weight. In addition to this, the glyptic expressions in the Aegean are to a certain measure autonomous inventions – such as the use of roller stamps for decorating large clay hearths. These important developments started early in the third millennium – shortly after the conventional beginning of the Bronze Age in this region. Silver appears to have already played an important role during this early period when we consider the first metal vessels made out of silver from Aegean islands and the evidence for silver extraction. Mining (e. g. on Siphnos: Wagner and Weisgerber 1985), production (e. g. at Lambrika in Attica: Kakavogianni *et al.* 2008) and consumption (*e.g.* bowls, bracelets) of silver is already well known in the earlier third millennium BC. Real bronze, however, did not yet play a substantial role in economic life during the earlier half of the third millennium and even during the latter half of that epoch, its impact was limited because arsenical copper was still much more in use. Hence to call the early third millennium BC already an *Early Bronze Age* seems to be a misnomer, rather the *Age of Accountancy and Metrology* had started.

Acknowledgements

I would like to thank Barry Molloy for the invitation to speak at the Round Table, Sue Sherratt for her kind hospitality during the snowy stay in Sheffield and Barry, Emanuela Alberti and anonymous reviewer for their comments on an earlier draft which help to focus more precisely on the theme. Barry's careful editing of the text much improved its readability. All possibly remaining faults are my responsibility. Most of the spool-shaped potential balance weights (SSPBW) could only be studied in a postdoctoral (habilitation) research through the help and support of many colleagues, Institute of Classical Studies, London and Fritz Thyssen-Stiftung, Cologne.

Notes

1. However, this specific class of objects are still published together with objects which can be considered as pestles indeed. For example some "spools" from Dhaskalio or Aghia Irini (Haas-Lebegyev and Renfrew 2013a: 494, fig. 25.2, 5438; 25.3, 5438; Wilson 1999: pl. 38, SF-120, pl. 96, SF-120) seem to be indeed pestles because they are of different shape with just one side for grinding.
2. Pelikata on Ithaka (45 g; Heurtley 1934/35: 37, pl. 9, no. 178), Tiryns (46,3 g, Kilian 1982: 422, fig. 45 [2. row, right]; 46.15 g, Kilian 1982, 422 Abb. 45 [3. row, third from left]), Corinth (45 g, Corinth Museum MF 4874), Geriza (47.45 g, Blegen 1928: 198, fig. 186 [mid left]), Kolonna (46.25 g, Walten and Felten 1981: 102, 143, 179, pl. 127, no. 508, X; 47.85 g; Lang 2003: 131, pl. 42, no. 11), Aghios Kosmas (45.2 g, Mylonas 1959, 30, fig. 166, no. 5), Aghia Irini (45.6 g, Davis 1986: pl. 68, AP-3; 45.7 g, K7.227, CM 1347; 46.9 g, Wilson 1999: 151, 198, pl. 38, SF-126; 96, SF-126), Dhaskalio Kavos (c. 44 g, Haas-Lebegyev and Renfrew 2013a: 491–493, 495, 499, figs. 25.2–3: no. 12090, pl. 12b: no. 12090; 45.7 g, 4457, unpublished) Amorgos (44.7 g [surface very worn], Sherratt 2000: 175, cat.-no. 8.30., pl. 219), Akrotiri on Thera (45.9 g, ΤΑΦΡΟΣ 68–69, unpublished), Lesbos on Lesbos (44.5 g, Lamb 1936: 195, pl. XXIII, no. 30.56), Tarsus, Southern Anatolia (45.8 g, slightly chipped, Goldman 1956: 275, fig. 420, no. 109).

3. Four from Aghios Kosmas are reported to have pigments on one of their circular ends (Mylonas 1959: 84, 99, 142–143, fig. 166, nos. 2, 5, 8, 11; Haas-Lebegyev and Renfrew 2013a: 501). I could study these finds in the National Museum at Athens in November 2005. One of them with blue pigment from Grave 21 (Mylonas 1959, 99, 143, fig. 166, 11) has an irregular shape and widens suddenly at the point where it is broken (?). It seems to be indeed a pestle and is not belonging to our group. The SSPBW from graves 7 (Mylonas 1959, 87, fig. 166, 8) had no traces of color as described by Mylonas when I studied it in the National Museum, but maybe they had disappeared over time. If the object belongs to the grave assemblage (what is not fully clear) it can be dated to the Kampos Phase, roughly around 2800 BC, and would be the earliest datable SSPBW on the Greek mainland. Its mass is 9.9 g, not fitting to the later units. The second spool from Grave 9 (Mylonas 1959: 89, fig. 166, 10) weighs 7.2 g, again an assignation to the later units seems difficult. Two from the settlement phase B of Aghios Kosmas dated to EH II Late (Maran 1998: 81, pl. 81) are reported to have traces of color on top (Mylonas 1959: 143, fig. 166, 2, 5), but again I could not find any traces on them in 2005. The mass of the SSPBW from the settlement confirms rather nicely the assumed units (mainly 9.4 g-unit). Two were found in Bothros 3 of phase A of the settlement (EH II Early and maybe even EH I Late: Maran 1998: 81–82), hence possibly contemporary with the cemetery. One of these two is fragmented, the other weighs 35.9 g (4 × 8.98 g). The other five SSPBW from the later Phase B of Aghios Kosmas (Rahmstorf 2006a: figs. 16) fit well to this unit (Mylonas 1959: fig 166, 2, 4–5, 7: 9.2 g; 36 g; 45.2 g; 64.1 g), only two (Mylonas 1959: fig. 166, 1, 3: 15.3 g; 16.8 g) might be assignable to other units (2 × 7.8 g?; 2 × 8.4 g?).

4. The well preserved SSPBW 5952 from Trench I of phase B is reported to have "most probably remains of red pigment embedded in the marble" (Haas-Lebegyev and Renfrew 2013a: 493), later in the functional discussion the probable aspect is left away: "with traces of pigments" (Haas-Lebegyev and Renfrew 2013a: 501). On the excellent additional colour photographs supplied on the supplementary material of the enclosed CD no pigment traces are visible in my judgement. It is only that the cream-coloured marble has slight spots with more intensive orange-brownish color components, visible in the small recent breakage areas at the edge of one circular end.

5. Level XVIIb at Beycesultan in southwestern inland Anatolia two "spools" were associated with two marble bowls in the "shrine" (Lloyd and Mellaart 1962: 35, 276, pl.32, 7–8). The two objects are however not symmetrical: one circular end is convex, the other roughly flat. Therefore they cannot be easily attributed to our class of "spools" or SSPBW.

6. Compare Petruso 1992, 4: "It is not uncommon to observe persons in the Mediterranean today using brass scale weights as nutcrackers, hammers, pestles and the like, for which purposes, it must be admitted, they are admirably suitable".

7. It is not possible to open many folders on original CD enclosed with the publication. I would like to thank Michael Boyd for sending me a replacement.

8. Layer 15/25 which is interpreted as the result of a ceiling collapse which probably appeared "quite soon after this part of the site was abandoned (Renfrew *et al.* 2013b: 103). This event sealed an interesting assemblage on Floor P: 3 SSPBW (10160, 10711, 10174), 4 tuyères, a copper-based spill, a unifacial marble grinding slab, one rubber and one pestles and five stones discs of much different size. One floor further down another SSPBW (5952) was found together with several stone tools and a piece of slag (Renfrew *et al.* 2013b: 107) suggesting metallurgical practices were undertaking in this trench (Renfrew *et al.* 2013b: 103). The other two SSPBW (5135, 10174) were found in tumble layers further above, still together with some metallurgical finds (Renfrew *et al.* 2013b: 100).

9. Unfortunately two (Dhaskalio 10765 and 11805) of three from the settlement of Dhaskalio are very badly fragmented but their diameter implies a mass in both cases of half a kilo of even more. Dhaskalio 5202 is weighing 380 g, fitting very well the assumed units (4/5 of 470 g;

40 × 9.5 g; 50 × 7.6 g). Two very large SSPBW are also known from Aghia Irini. One the "giant pestle" (Caskey 1986: pl 2, f; Wilson 1999: 150, 197, pl. 38, SF-115; pl. 96, SF-115) from Period III (late EC II) Deposit BO, a rich debris level above floor of House ED, room 4 (Wilson 1999: 196–197) which "appears to be made up of debris from the collapse and/or dismantling of its upper mudbrick story" (Wilson 2013: 395, Tab. 2), is over 18 cm large and weighs 3790 g. Its weight fits again rather well the assumed units (8 × 473.8 g; 320 × 11.8 g; 400 × 9.5; 480 × 7.9 g). This debris includes also three other SSPBW, the very large litharge piece and the potential lead scale mentioned above. Two second large SSPBW is again a fragmented example found in the early MBA context CM at Aghia Irini (Overbeck 1989, 171, pl. 83, CM-15). It is still weighing 411 g and may have had a weight of *c.* 500 g.

10. When the settlement Dhaskalio and the finds from the special deposits from Kavos are taken together and conceivably SSPBW from Dhaskalio Kavos in the Naxos Archaeological Museum and the Goulandris Museum are included as well the absolute number might amount to 110 SSPBW. Tiryns (74), Aghia Irini (*c.* 41), Kolonna (40), Lerna (13), Akrotiri (13), Poliochni (12) and Kastri (11) follow already with considerable distance in numbers.

11. Both, the Kolonna hoard and the treasures from Troy are well known for their explicit inclusion of objects of Near Eastern origin or imitations of such. Noteworthy is especially the etched carnelian bead from the Kolonna hoard, a type which is found otherwise only in regions between modern day Iraq and western India (distribution map: Rahmstorf 2011, 148 [bottom]). The Aegean short elongated biconical beads seem to be a faint and distant reflections of the much longer, sometimes over 10 cm long carnelian beads found with a similar distribution (Possehl 1996: 159–160, fig. 13). The very hard carnelian stone (7 on Mohs scale) is not found in the Aegean, Anatolia or Mesopotamia, but only in regions farther east. This extreme hard metamorpheous stone could be only perforated through the use of a specific stone: "Ernestit", named after Ernest J. H. Mackay, the excavator of Mohenjo-daro by M. Kenoyer (Kenoyer 1998: 161, fig. 8.32). It was very time consuming (Roux 1995). (*cf.* now Ludvik et al. 2015; Rahmstorf 2015, 159–163 figs. 9–10).

12. There is a mace head from EBA Bozhöyük, some 40 km northwest of Eskişehir in Western inland Anatolia, not depicted in the publication, but described as being "very beautiful blue stone (lapis lazuli?)" (Körte 1899: 16). At EBA Kültepe near Konya in South Central Anatolia, three cylindrical lapis lazuli beads found in a grave together with 71 gold and 56 carnelian beads in layer 13 at late EBA Kültepe (Özgüç 1986: 43, fig. 3, 41) and four lapis lazuli cylinder seals stylistically dated to the later third millennium BC (Özgüç 1986: 45, fig. 3, 42–43). This combination of blue (lapis lazuli), red (carnelian) and yellow (gold) beads is highly typical of the Mesopotamian colour palette of jewellery in the third millennium BC.

13. J. Maran (2007: 13–14, pl. 4, 1–5) suggested that for the first time a few years ago. Later publications of such finds from the EBA Aegean (Kolonna: Rahmstorf 2008: 160–161, fig. 5) and Western and Southern Balkans (Heyd 2007) underlined the fact that such finds are found in some numbers outside the Bell Beaker pottery distribution in the later third millennium BC between 2300–2100 BC (EH III Lerna and Kolonna). J. Haas-Lebegyev and C. Renfrew (2013b: 663–664) referred also to allegedly earlier and later parallels from the Neolithic, earlier EBA or the MBA. These are however neither parallels as they have only one perforation at one side and/or are round in diameter (*e.g.* Rambach 2000a: pl. 3, 5) nor are their archaeological contexts indicating pre- or post-late EBA dating: a stone bracer was found at Prodomos in Thessaly, a site which has not only Neolithic but also BA layers (Alram-Stern 1996: 344 with further references).

14. A possible Anatolian connection is highly interesting in the case of the Minoan disc weights which find typological parallels at several Middle Bronze Age sites in Asia Minor. See Alberti, this volume.

References

Achilara, L.
1997 Μύρινα οι μνημειακές εγκαταστάσεις του οικοπέδου Ευτ. Καζώλη. In C. G. Doumas and V. La Rosa (eds.), *Η Πολιόχνη και η πρώιμη εποχή του Χαλκού στο Βόρειο Αιγαίο/Poliochni e l'Antica Eta del Bronzo nell' Egeo Settentrionale*, Πρακτικά Διεθνούς Συνεδρίου, Αθήνα 22–25 Απριλίου 1996: 298–310. Athens: Scuola Archeologica Italiana di Atene.

Alram-Stern, E.
1996 *Die ägäische Frühzeit. Serie 2: Forschungsbericht 1975-1993. Band 1: Das Neolithikum in Griechenland mit Ausnahme von Kreta und Zypern* (Veröffentlichungen der Mykenischen Kommission 16). Vienna: Verlag der Österreichischen Akademie der Wissenschaften.

Angelopoulou, A.
2006 The lead seal and clay sealings. In L. Marangou, C. Renfrew, C. Doumas and G. Gavalas (eds.), ΜΑΡΚΙΑΝΗ ΑΜΟΡΓΟΥ – *Markiani, Amorgos. An Early Bronze Age fortified settlement. Overview of the 1985-1991 investigations* (British School at Athens, Supplementary Volume 40): 219–222. London: British School at Athens.

Archontidou-Agyri, A. and M. Kokkinoforou (eds.)
2004a *Myrina in the Early Bronze Age.* Mytilene: Υπουργείο Πολιτισμού.
2004b *Η Μύρινα της πρώιμης εποχής του Χαλκού/Myrina in the Early Bronze Age.* Mytilene: Υπουργείο Πολιτισμού.

Aruz, J.
2008 *Marks of distinction: Seals and cultural exchange between the Aegean and the Orient* (Corpus der Minoischen und Mykenischen Siegel, Beiheft 7). Mainz: Philipp von Zabern.

Ascalone, E. and L. Peyronel
2006 *I pesi da bilancia del Bronzo Antico e del Bronzo Recente* (Materiali e Studi Archeologici di Ebla VII). Rome: Università degli Studi di Roma "La Sapienza".

Bachhuber, C.
2013 Sumer, Akkad, Ebla and Anatolia. In H. Crawford (ed.), *The Sumerian world*: 498–516. London: Routledge.

Banks, E.
1967 *The Early and Middle Helladic Small Objects from Lerna.* Diss. University of Cincinnati.

Begemann, F., S. Schmitt-Strecker and E. Pernicka
1992 The metal finds from Thermi III–V: a chemical and lead-isotope study. *Studia Troica* 2: 219–239.

Bernabò–Brea, L.
1964 *Poliochni. Città preistorica nell'isola di Lemnos. Vol.I.* Rome: L'Erma di Bretschneider.
1976 *Poliochni. Città preistorica nell'isola di Lemnos. Vol.II.* Rome: L'Erma di Bretschneider.

Bilgen, A.N.
2011 Seyitömer Höyük. In Şahoğlu, V. and P. Sotirakopoulou (eds.), *Across: The Cyclades and Western Anatolia During the 3rd Millennium BC*: 208–212. Istanbul: Sakıp Sabancı Museum.

Bintliff, J.

2012 *The complete archaeology of Greece: From Hunter-Gatherers to the 20th Century A.D.* Malden, MA, Oxford, Chichester: Wiley-Blackwell.

Birtacha, K.

2008 'Cooking' installations in LC IA Akrotiri on Thera: a preliminary study of the 'kitchen' in the Pillar Shaft 65. With appendices by E. Asouti, A. Devetzi, D. Mylona, A. Sarpaki & K. Trantalidou. In N. Brodie, J. Doole, G. Gavalas and C. Renfrew (eds.), *Horizon - Ὁρίζων. A colloquium on the prehistory of the Cyclades*: 349–376. Cambridge: McDonald Institute of Archaeological Research.

Blackman, D.

2000/01 Archaeology in Greece. *Archaeological Reports* (London) 47: 1–144.

Blegen, C.W.

1928 *Zygouries. A prehistoric settlement in the Valley of Cleonae.* Cambridge/Mass.: Harvard University Press.

Bossert, E.-M.

1967 Kastri auf Syros: Vorbericht über die Untersuchung der prähistorischen Siedlung. *Archaiologikon Deltion* 22, Meletai 1: 53–76.

Branigan, K.

1992 Mochlos – an Early Aegean "Gateway community"? In R. Laffineur and L. Basch (eds.), *Thalassa: L'Égée préhistorique et la mer* (Aegaeum 7): 97–105. Liège: Université de Liège.

Broodbank, C.

2013 *The making of the Middle Sea. A history of the Mediterranean from the beginning to the emergence of the Classical world.* London: Thames and Hudson.

Carter, T. and M. Milić

2013 The chipped stone industry from Dhaskalio. In C. Renfrew, O. Philaniotou, N. Brodie, G. Gavalas, M. J. Boyd. *The settlement at Dhaskalio* (The sanctuary of Keros and the origins of Aegean ritual practice 1): 531–556. Cambridge: McDonald Institute for Archaeological Research.

Caskey, J.L.

1964 Excavations in Keos, 1963. *Hesperia* 33: 314–335.

1986 Did the Early Bronze Age end? In G. Cadogan and J.L. Caskey (eds.), *The End of the early Bronze Age in the Aegean*: 9–30. Leiden: E.J. Brill.

Christakis, K.S.

2011 Redistribution and political economies in Bronze Age Crete. *American Journal of Archaeology* 115: 197–205.

CMS II, 6

1999 *Corpus der minoischen und mykenischen Siegel. Band II, Teil 6. Die Siegelabdrücke von Aj. Triada und anderen zentral- und ostkretischen Fundorten unter Einbeziehung von Funden aus anderen Museen.* Nach Vorarbeiten von N. Platon bearbeitet von W. Müller & I. Pini. Berlin: Mann.

CMS II, 8
2002 *Corpus der minoischen und mykenischen Siegel. Band II, Teil 8. Die Siegelabdrücke von Knossos*. Nach Vorarbeiten von N. Platon bearbeitet von M. A. V. Gill, W. Müller und I. Pini. Mainz: Philipp von Zabern.

CMS V
1975 *Corpus der minoischen und mykenischen Siegel. Band V. Kleinere griechische Sammlungen. Bearbeitet von I. Pini*. Berlin: Mann.

CMS V Suppl. 1 A
1992 *Corpus der minoischen und mykenischen Siegel. Band V Supplementum 1A. Kleinere griechische Sammlungen. Bearbeitet von I. Pini*. Berlin: Mann.

CMS V Suppl. 1 B
1993 *Corpus der minoischen und mykenischen Siegel. Band V Supplementum 1B. Kleinere griechische Sammlungen. Bearbeitet von I. Pini*. Berlin: Mann.

CMS V Suppl. 3
2004 *Corpus der minoischen und mykenischen Siegel. Band V Supplementum 3, 1–2. Neufunde aus Griechenland und der westlichen Türkei. Bearbeitet von I. Pini mit Beiträgen zahlreicher Autoren*. Mainz: Philipp von Zabern.

CMS XI
1988 *Corpus der minoischen und mykenischen Siegel. Band XI. Kleinere europäische Sammlungen. Bearbeitet von Ingo Pini, J. H. Betts, M.A.V. Gill, D. Sürenhagen, & H. Waetzoldt*. Berlin: Mann.

Collon, D. (ed.)
1997 *7000 years of seals*. London: British Museum Press.

Cour-Marty, M.-A.
1991 Weights in ancient Egypt. A method of study. In *Akten des Vierten Internationalen Ägyptologenkongresses München 1985, 4. Geschichte, Verwaltungs- und Wirtschaftsgeschichte, Rechtsgeschichte, Nachbarkulturen* (Studien zur altägyptischen Kultur, Beiheft 4): 137–143. Hamburg: Buske.

Crouwel, J., M. Prent, J. Fiselier and J.A.K.E. de Waele
1997 Geraki, an acropolis site in Lakonia. Preliminary report on the third season (1997). *Pharos. Journal of the Netherlands Institute in Athens* 5: 49–83.

Crouwel, J., M. Prent, R. Cappers and T. Carter
2008 Geraki, an acropolis site in Lakonia. Preliminary report on the fourth season (1998). *Pharos. Journal of the Netherlands Institute in Athens* 6: 93–118.

Crouwel, J., M. Prent, S. MacVeagh Thorne, J. van der Vin and L. Smits
2005 Geraki, an acropolis site in Lakonia. Preliminary report on the eleventh season (2005). *Pharos. Journal of the Netherlands Institute in Athens* 13: 3–28.

Davies, N. de G.
1902 *The rock tombs of Deir el Gebrawi*. London: Egypt Exploration Fund.

Davis, J.L.
1986 *Ayia Irini: Period V* (Keos V). Mainz: Philipp von Zabern.

Demakopoulou, K., N. Divari-Valkou, P. Åström, and G. Walberg
1997/98 Excavations at Midea 1995–1996. *Opuscula Atheniensia* 22–23: 57–90.

Devetzi, A.
2008 Akrotiri, Thera: stone vessels and implements of the Early Bronze Age – a preliminary report. In N. Brodie, J. Doole, G. Gavalas and C. Renfrew (eds.), *Horizon - Ὁρίζων. A colloquium on the prehistory of the Cyclades*: 135–147. Cambridge: McDonald Institute of Archaeological Research.

Dixon, J. and T. Kinnaird
2013 Sea-level change and the Early Bronze Age topography. In C. Renfrew, O. Philaniotou, N. Brodie, G. Gavalas and M.J. Boyd. *The settlement at Dhaskalio* (The sanctuary of Keros and the origins of Aegean ritual practice 1): 45–55. Cambridge: McDonald Institute for Archaeological Research.

Dova, A.
2003 Οι φάσεις εξέλιξης του προϊστορικού οικισμού στην Μυρίνα Λήμνου. In A. Blachopoulos and K. Birtacha (eds.), *Αργοναύτης. Τιμητικός τόμος για τον Καθηγητή Χρίστο Γ. Ντούμα από τους μαθητές του στο Πανεπιστήμιο Αθηνών (1980-2000)*: 101–125. Athens: Καθημερινή.

Ducros, H.
1910 Deuxieme étude sur les balances égytiennes. Annales du Service des antiquités de l'Égypte 10: 240–253.

Düring, B.S.
2011 *The prehistory of Asia Minor. From complex hunter-gatherers to early urban societies*. Cambridge: Cambridge University Press.

Duistermaat, K.
2010 Administration in Neolithic societies? The first use of seals in Syria and some considerations on seal owners, seal use and private property In Müller, W. (ed.), *Die Bedeutung der minoischen und mykenischen Glyptik* (CMS Beiheft 8): 167–182. Mainz: Philipp von Zabern.
2012 Which came first, the bureaucrat or the seal? Some thoughts on the non-administrative origins of seals in Neolithic Syria. In I. Regulski, K. Duistermaat and P. Verkinderen (eds.), *Seals and Sealing Practices in the Near East. Developments in Administration and Magic from Prehistory to the Islamic Period*. Proceedings of an International Workshop at the Netherlands-Flemish Institute in Cairo on December 2-3, 2009 (Orientalia Lovaniensia Analecta): 1–15. Leuven: Peeters.

Efe, T.
1988 *Demircihüyük III,2. Die Keramik 2. C Die frühbronzezeitliche Keramik der jüngeren Phasen*. Mainz: Philipp von Zabern.

Efe, T. and M. Türkteki
2011 Inland western Anatolian region: Introduction. In Şahoğlu, V. and P. Sotirakopoulou (eds.), *Across: The Cyclades and Western Anatolia During the 3rd Millennium BC*: 186–191. Istanbul: Sakıp Sabancı Museum.

Englund, R.K.
1998 Texts from the Late Uruk Period. In J. Bauer, R. K. Englund and M. Krebernik, Mesopotamien. *Späturuk-Zeit und Frühdynastische Zeit* (Annäherungen 1; Orbis Biblicus et Orientalis 160/1): 15–233. Freiburg/Switzerland, Göttingen: Universitätsverlag, Vandenhoeck & Ruprecht.

Esin, U.
1994 The Functional Evidence of Seals. In P. Ferioli, E. Fiandra, G.G. Fissore, M. Frangipane (eds.) *Archives before Writing. Proceedings of the International Colloquium, Oriolo Romano, October 23-25, 1991:* 59–81. Rome: Ministero per i Beni Culturali e Ambientali.

Felten, F., C. Reinholdt, E. Pollhammer, W. Gauß and R. Smetana
2006 Ägina-Kolonna 2005. *Jahresheft des Österreichischen Archäologischen Instituts* 75: 9–38.

Ferioli, P., E. Fiandra, G.G. Fissore and M. Frangipane (eds.)
2004 *Archives before Writing. Proceedings of the International Colloquium, Oriolo Romano, October 23-25, 1991.* Rome: Ministero per i Beni Culturali e Ambientali.

Fiandra, E.
1968 A che cosa servivano le cretule di Festòs. In *Proceedings of the Second International Cretological Congress* 1: 385–395. Athens: Archaeological Society.

Fiandra, E. and P. Ferioli
1990 The Use of Clay Sealings in Administrative Functions from the 5th to 1st Millennium B.C. in the Orient, Nubia, Egypt and the Aegean: Similarities and Differences. In T.G. Palaima (ed.), *Aegean Seals, Sealings and Administration. Proceedings of the NEH-Dickson Conference of the Program in Aegean Scripts and Prehistory of the Department of Classics, University of Texas at Austin, January 11-13, 1989* (Aegaeum 5): 221–232. Liège: Université de Liège.

Fiandra, E. and M. Frangipane
2004 Controllo dell'economia e nascita della burocrazia. Le cretulae: un efficace strumento di potere nelle mani delle prime elites di governe. In M. Frangipane (ed.), *Alle origine del potere. Arslantepe, la collina dei leoni:* 77–81. Milano: Mondadori/Electa.

Frangipane, M., P. Ferioli, E. Fiandra, R. Laurito and H. Pittman
2007 *Arslantepe cretulae. An early centralised administrative system before writing* (Arslantepe 5). Rome: Università di Roma La Sapienza.

Frayne, D.
1993 *Sargonic and Gutian Periods (2334-2113 BC). The Royal Inscriptions of Mesopotamia, Early Periods 2.* Toronto: University of Toronto Press.

Gavalas, G.
2013 Spindle whorls and related objects. In C. Renfrew, O. Philaniotou, N. Brodie, G. Gavalas and M.J. Boyd. *The settlement at Dhaskalio* (The sanctuary of Keros and the origins of Aegean ritual practice 1): 649–652. Cambridge: McDonald Institute for Archaeological Research.

Genz, H.
2003 *Ritzverzierte Knochenhülsen des dritten Jahrtausends im Ostmittelmeerraum: eine Studie zu den frühen Kulturverbindungen zwischen Levante und Ägäis* (Abhandlungen des Deutschen Palaestinavereins 31). Wiesbaden: Harrassowitz.

Georgakopoulou, M.
2007 The metallurgical remains. In C. Renfrew, C. Doumas, L. Marangou and G. Gavalas (eds.), *Keros, Dhaskalio Kavos. The investigations of 1987-1988. Κέρος, Κάβος Δασκαλιου* (Keros 1): 382–403. Cambridge: McDonald Institute of Archaeological Research.

2013 Metal artefacts and metallurgy. In C. Renfrew, O. Philaniotou, N. Brodie, G. Gavalas and M.J. Boyd. *The settlement at Dhaskalio* (The sanctuary of Keros and the origins of Aegean ritual practice 1): 667–692. Cambridge: McDonald Institute for Archaeological Research

Goldman, H.
1956 *Excavations at Gözlü Kule, Tarsus. Volume II. From the Neolithic trough the Bronze Age.* Princeton: University Press.

Haas-Lebegyev, J. and C. Renfrew
2013a The spools from Dhaskalio. In C. Renfrew, O. Philaniotou, N. Brodie, G. Gavalas and M.J. Boyd. *The settlement at Dhaskalio* (The sanctuary of Keros and the origins of Aegean ritual practice 1): 491–504. Cambridge: McDonald Institute for Archaeological Research.
2013b Other finds of stone. In C. Renfrew, O. Philaniotou, N. Brodie, G. Gavalas and M.J. Boyd. *The settlement at Dhaskalio* (The sanctuary of Keros and the origins of Aegean ritual practice 1): 662–665. Cambridge: McDonald Institute for Archaeological Research.

Hendrix, E.A.
2003 Painted Early Cycladic figures. An exploration of context and meaning. *Hesperia* 72: 405–446.

Hendrickx-Baudot, M.P.
1972 The weights of the Harappa-Culture. *Orientalia Lovaniensia Periodica* 3: 5–34.

Heurtley, W.A.
1934/35 Excavations in Ithaca, II. The Early Helladic settlement at Pelikáta. Annual of the British School at Athens 35: 1–44.

Heyd, V.
2007 When the West meets the East: The Eastern periphery of the Bell Beaker phenomenon and its relation with the Aegean Early Bronze Age. In I. Galanaki, H. Tomas, Y. Galanakis and R. Laffineur (eds.), *Between the Aegean and Baltic Seas. Prehistory across borders. Proceedings of the International Conference: Bronze and Early Iron Age interconnections and contemporary developments between the Aegean and the regions of the Balkan peninsula, Central and Northern Europe, University of Zagreb, 11-14 April 2005* (Aegaeum 27): 91–107. Liège: Université de Liège.

Hood, S. and G. Cadogan
2010 *Knossos Excavations 1957-1961: Early Minoan* (Annual of the British School at Athens Suppl. Vol. No. 46). London: British School at Athens.

Horejs, B.
2009 Metalworkers at the Çukuriçi Höyük? An Early Bronze Age mould and a "Near Eastern weight" from Western Anatolia. In L. Kienlin and B. Roberts (eds.), *Metals and societies. Studies in honour of Barbara S. Ottaway* (Universitätsforschungen zur prähistorischen Archäologie): 358–368. Bonn: Habelt.
2016 Neue Gewichtssysteme und metallurgischer Aufschwung im frühen 3. Jahrtausend - ein Zufall. In M. Bartelheim, B. Horejs and R. Krauss (eds.), *Von Baden bis Troia. Ressourcennutzung, Metallurgie und Wissenstransfer. Eine Jubiläumsschrift für Ernst Pernicka. Oriental and European Archaeology* 3: 251–272. Rahden/Westfalen: Leidorf.

Horejs, B., M. Mehofer and E. Pernicka
2010 Metallhandwerker im frühen 3. Jt. v. Chr. – Neue Ergebnisse vom Çukuriçi Höyük. *Istanbuler Mitteilungen* 60: 7–37.

Horejs, B., A. Galik, U. Thanheiser and S. Wiesinger
2011 Aktivitäten und Subsistenz in den Siedlungen des Çukuriçi Höyük. Der Forschungsstand nach den Ausgrabungen 2006–2009. *Prähistorische Zeitschrift* 86: 31–66.

Hue, M. and O. Pelon
1992 La sale à piliers du palais de Malia et ses antécédents. *Bulletin de Correspondance Hellénique* 116: 1–36.

Kakavogianni, O., K. Douni and F. Nezeri
2008 Silver metallurgical finds dating from the end of the Final Neolithic Period until the Middle Bronze Age in the Area of Mesogeia. In I. Tzachili (ed.), *Aegean metallurgy in the Bronze Age. Proceedings of an international symposium held at the University of Crete, Rethymnon, Greece, November 19-21, 2004*: 45–57. Athens: Ta Pragmata Publications.

Kenoyer, M.
1998 *Ancient cities of the Indus Valley civilization.* Oxford: Oxford University Press.

Kilian, K.
1982 Ausgrabungen in Tiryns 1980. *Archäologischer Anzeiger*: 393–430.
1983 Ausgrabungen in Tiryns 1981. *Archäologischer Anzeiger*: 277–328.

Körte, A.
1899 Kleinasiatische Studien. Ein altphrygischer Tumulus bei Boz-öjük. *Mitteilungen des Deutschen Archäologischen Instituts* 24: 1–45.

Kostoula, M.
2000 Die frühhelladischen Tonplomben mit Siegelabdrücken aus Petri bei Nemea. In I. Pini (ed.), *Minoisch-mykenische Glyptik. Stil, Ikonographie, Funktion. V. Internationales Siegel-Symposium Marburg, 23-25.9. 1999* (Corpus der Minoischen und Mykenischen Siegel, Beiheft 6): 135–148. Berlin: Mann.
2004 Die Ausgrabungen in der frühhelladischen Siedlung von Petri bei Nemea. In E. Alram-Stern, *Die ägäische Frühzeit. 2. Serie Forschungsbericht 1975-2002. 2. Band. Die Frühbronzezeit in Griechenland mit Ausnahme von Kreta* (Österreichische Akademie der Wissenschaften. Philosophisch-historische Klasse. Veröffentlichungen der mykenischen Kommission 21): 1135–1157. Wien: Akademie der Wissenschaften.

Kouka, O.
2002 *Siedlungsorganisation in der Nord- und Ostägäis während der Frühbronzezeit* (Internationale Archäologie 58). Rahden: Leidorf.

Krattenmaker, K.
2011 The ground stone tools. In D. J. Pullen, *The Early Bronze Age village on Tsoungiza Hill* (Nemea Valley Archaeological Project, Volume 1): 727–740. Princeton: American School of Classical Studies at Athens.

Krzyszkowska, O.
2005 *Aegean seals: an introduction* (Bulletin of the Institute of Classical Studies Suppl. 85). London: Institute of Classical Studies, University of London.

Lamb, W.
1936 Excavations at Thermi in Lesbos. Cambridge: Cambridge University Press.

Lang, F.

2003 Artefakte aus Felsgestein von den neuen Grabungen in Ägina/Kolonna. In B. Asamer and W. Wohlmayr (eds.), *Akten des 9. Österreichischen Archäologentages am Institut für Klassische Archäologie der Paris Lodron-Universitär Salzburg, 6.-8. Dezember 2001*: 129–134. Wien: Phoibos-Verlag.

Lloyd, S. and J. Mellaart

1962 *Beycesultan, Vol. I: The Chalcolithic and Early Bronze Age levels* (Occasional Publications of the British Institute of Archaeology at Ankara 6). London: the British Institute of Archaeology at Ankara. Ludvik, G., Kenoyer, J. M., Pieniążek, M. and W. Aylward 2015 New perspectives on stone bead technology at Bronze Age Troy. Anatolian Studies 65: 1–18.

Macdonald, C.F.

2012 Palatial Knossos: the early years. In I. Schoep, P. Tomkins and J. Driessen (eds.), *Back to the beginning. Reassessing social and political complexity on Crete during the Early and Middle Bronze Age*: 81–113. Oxford: Oxbow.

Manning, S.W.

1995 *The absolute chronology of the Aegean Early Bronze Age: Archaeology, radiocarbon and history* (Monographs in Mediterranean Archaeology 1). Sheffield Academic Press.

1997 Troy, radiocarbon and the chronology of the NE Aegean in the Early Bronze Age. In C.G. Doumas and V. La Rosa (eds.), *Η Πολιόχνη και η πρώιμη εποχή του Χαλκού στο Βόρειο Αιγαίο/Poliochni e l' Antica Eta del Bronzo nell' Egeo Settentrionale*, Πρακτικά Διεθνούς Συνεδρίου, Αθήνα 22–25 Απριλίου 1996: 498–520. Athens: Scuola Archeologica Italiana di Atene.

2010 Chronology and terminology. In E. Cline, (ed.), *The Oxford Handbook of the Aegean Bronze Age*: 11–28. Oxford: Oxford University Press.

Maran, J.

1998 *Kulturwandel auf dem griechischen Festland und den Kykladen im späten 3. Jahrtausend v. Chr. Studien zu den kulturellen Verhältnissen in Südosteuropa und dem zentralen sowie östlichen Mittelmeerraum in der späten Kupfer- und frühen Bronzezeit* (Universitätsforschungen zur prähistorischen Archäologie 53). Bonn: Habelt.

2007 Sea-borne contacts between the Aegean, the Balkans and the Central Mediterranean in the 3rd millennium BC – The unfolding of the Mediterranean world. In I. Galanaki, H. Tomas, Y. Galanakis and R. Laffineur (eds.), *Between the Aegean and Baltic Seas. Prehistory across borders. Proceedings of the International Conference: Bronze and Early Iron Age interconnections and contemporary developments between the Aegean and the regions of the Balkan peninsula, Central and Northern Europe, University of Zagreb, 11-14 April 2005* (Aegaeum 27): 3–21. Liège: Université de Liège.

McMahon, A.

2006 *The Early Dynastic to Akkadian transition: the area WF sounding at Nippur* (Nippur 5, Oriental Institute Publications 129. Chicago: Oriental Institute.

Mellaart, J.

1954 Preliminary report on a survey of pre-classical remains in southern Turkey. *Anatolian Studies* 4: 175–240.

Mellink, M.J.

1972 Excavations at Karataş-Semayük and Elmalı, Lycia, 1971. *American Journal of Archaeology* 76: 257–269.

Michailidou, A.
2005 *Weight and value in pre-coinage societies. An introduction* (Κέντρον Ελληνικής και Ρομαϊκής Αρχαιότητος. Εθνικόν Ἴδρυμα Ερεύνων. Μελετέματα 42). Athens: Εθνικόν Ἴδρυμα Ερεύνων.

Milano, L.
2004 Weight stones from Tell Beydar/Nabada. *Kaskal* 1: 1–7.

Mogensen, M.
1921 *La mastaba égyptien de la Glyptothèque Ny Carlsberg.* Copenhagen: Gyldendal.

Mollat, H.
2007 Zur Metrologie der Gewichtsstücke Alt-Ägyptens. *Maß und Gewicht* 84: 2045–2077.
2011 Wiegen – aber richtig interpretieren. Märchen um Gewichte. *Maß und Gewicht* 98: 2411–2414.

Morley, I. and C. Renfrew
2011 Introduction. Measure: Towards the construction of our world. In I. Morley and C. Renfrew (eds.), *The archaeology of measurement. Comprehending heaven, earth and time in ancient societies*: 1–4. Cambridge: Cambridge University Press.

Morris, I.
2009 Cultural complexity. In B. Cunliffe, C. Gosden and R.A. Joyce (eds.), *The Oxford Handbook of Archaeology*: 519–554. Oxford: Oxford University Press.

Müller-Karpe, M.
1993 Metallgefäße im Iraq: von den Anfängen bis zur Akkad-Zeit (Prähistorische Bronzefunde 2, 14). Munich: Steiner.

Mylonas, G.
1959 *Aghios Kosmas. An Early Bronze Age settlement and cemetery in Attica.* Princeton: Princeton University Press.

Nakou, G.
1997 The role of Poliochni and the North Aegean in the deveopment of Aegean metallurgy. In C.G. Doumas and V. La Rosa (eds.), *Η Πολιόχνη και η πρώιμη εποχή του Χαλκού στο Βόρειο Αιγαίο/ Poliochni e l' Antica Eta del Bronzo nell' Egeo Settentrionale*, Πρακτικά Διεθνούς Συνεδρίου, Αθήνα 22–25 Απριλίου 1996: 634–648. Athens: Scuola Archeologica Italiana di Atene.

Oates, D., J. Oates and H. McDonald
2001 *Excavations at Tell Brak. Vol. 2: Nagar in the third millennium BC.* Oxford: McDonald Institute for Archaeological Research.

Obladen-Kauder, J.
1996 Die Kleinfunde aus Ton, Knochen und Metall. In A. Baykal-Seeher and J. Obladen-Kauder, *Demircihüyük. Die Ergebnisse der Ausgrabungen 1975-1978. Band IV: Die Kleinfunde*: 207–383. Mainz: Philipp von Zabern.

Özgüç, T.
1986 New observations on the relationship of Kültepe with Southeast Anatolia and North Syria during the third millenium B.C. In J.V. Canby, E. Porada, B.S. Ridgway and T. Stech (eds.), *Ancient Anatolia. Aspects of change and cultural development. Essays in honor of Machteld J. Mellink* (Wisconsin Studies in Classics): 31–47. MadisonUniversity of Wisconsin Press.

Özgüç, T. and R. Temizer
1993 The Eskiyapar Treasure. In M.J. Mellink, E. Porada and T. Özgüç (eds.), *Aspects of art and iconography: Anatolia and its neighbors. Studies in honor of Nimet Özgüç*: 613–628. Ankara: Türk Tarih Kurumu Basimevi.

Overbeck, J.C.
1989 *Ayia Irini: Period IV. Part 1: the stratigraphy and the find deposits* (Keos VII). Mainz: Philipp von Zabern.

Pakkanen, J.
2011 Aegean Bronze Age weights, *chaînes opératoires* and the detecting of patterns through statistical analyses. In A. Brysbaert (ed.), *Tracing social networks through studying technologies: A diachronical perspective from the Aegean* (Routledge Studies in Archaeology 3): 143–166. New York, London: Routledge.

Papadopoulos, S.
2008 Silver and copper production practices in the prehistoric settlement at Limenaria, Thasos. In I. Tzachili (ed.), *Aegean metallurgy in the Bronze Age. Proceedings of an international symposium held at the University of Crete, Rethymnon, Greece, November 19-21, 2004*: 59–67. Athens: Ta Pragmata Publications.

Parise, N.F.
1984 Unità ponderali e rapporti di cambio nellla Siria del Nord. In A. Archi (ed.), *Circulation of goods in non-palatial context in the Ancient Near East* (Incunabula Graeca 82): 126–138. Rome: Edizioni dell'Ateneo.

Peltenburg, E.
2007 East Mediterranean interactions in the 3rd Millennium BC. In S. Antoniadou and A. Pace (eds.), *Mediterranean crossroads*: 141–161. Athens: Pierides Foundation.

Peperaki, O.
2004 The House of the Tiles at Lerna: Dimensions of 'Social Complexity. In J.C. Barrett and P. Halstead (eds.), *The Emergence of Civilisation Revisited* (Sheffield Studies in Aegean Archaeology 6): 214–231. Oxford: Oxbow Books.

Petruso, K.M.
1992 *Ayia Irini: The balance weights. An analysis of weight measurement in prehistoric Crete and the Cycladic islands* (Keos VIII). Mainz: Philipp von Zabern.

Pini, I.
1972 Weitere Bemerkungen zu den minoischen Fußamuletten. *Studi Micenea ed Anatolici* 15: 179–187.
1990 Eine frühkretische Siegelwerkstatt. In *Proceedings of the Sixth International Cretological Congress*: 115–127. Chania: Historical Society Crete.
2002 Einleitung. In M. A.V. Gill, W. Müller und I. Pini, *Corpus der minoischen und mykenischen Siegel. Band II, Teil 8. Die Siegelabdrücke von Knossos*: 1–23. Mainz: Philipp von Zabern.

Possehl, G.L.
1996 Meluhha. In J. Reade (ed.), *The Indian Ocean in antiquity*: 133–208. London, New York: Kegan Paul International.

Postgate, J.N.
1992 *Early Mesopotamia. Society and economy at the dawn of history*. London: Routledge.

Pulak, C.
2000 The balance weights from the Late Bronze Age shipwreck at Uluburun. In C.F.E. Pare (ed.), *Metals make the world go round. The supply and circulation of metals in Bronze Age Europe. Proceedings of a conference held at the University of Birmingham in June 1997*: 247–266. Oxford: Oxbow Books.

Pullen, D.J.
1994 A lead seal from Tsoungiza, Ancient Nemea, and Early Bronze Age sealing systems. *American Journal of Archaeology* 93: 35–52.
2008 The Early Bronze Age in Greece. In C.W. Shelmerdine (ed.), *The Cambridge Companion to the Aegean Bronze Age*: 19–46. Cambridge: University Press.
2011a *The Early Bronze Age village on Tsoungiza Hill* (Nemea Valley Archaeological Project 1). Princeton: The Amerian School of Classical Studies at Athens.
2011b Before the palaces: Redistribution and chiefdoms in Mainland Greece. *American Journal of Archaeology* 115: 185–195.

Rahmstorf, L.
2003 The identification of Early Helladic weights and their wider implications. In S.P. Foster and R. Laffineur (Hrsg.), *Metron. Measuring the Aegean Bronze Age. Proceedings of the 9th Aegean International Conference. 18.–21.4.2002, Yale University* (Aegaeum 24): 293–300. Liège: Université de Liège.
2006a Zur Ausbreitung vorderasiatischer Innovationen in die frühbronzezeitliche Ägäis. *Prähistorische Zeitschrift* 83/1: 49–96.
2006b In search of the earliest balance weights, scales and weighing systems from the East Mediterranean, the Near and Middle East. In M.E. Alberti, E. Ascalone and L. Peyronel (Hrsg.), *Weights in context. Bronze Age weighing systems of Eastern Mediterranean: chronology, typology, material and archaeological contexts. Proceedings of the International Colloquium, Rome 22-24 November 2004* (Studi e Materiali 13): 9–45. Rome: Istituto Italiano di Numismatica.
2008 The Bell Beaker Phenomenon and the Interaction Spheres of the EBA East Mediterranean: Similarities and Differences. In A. Lehoërff (ed.), *Construire le temps. Histoire et méthodes des chronologies et calendriers des derniers millénaires avant notre ère en Europe occidentale. Actes du XXXe colloque international de Halma-Ipel, UMR 8164 (CNRS, Lille 3, MCC), 7-9 décembre 2006, Lille* (Collection Bibracte 16): 149–170. Glux-en-Glenne: Bibracte, Centre archéologique européen.
2010a Die Nutzung von Booten und Schiffe in der bronzezeitlichen Ägäis und die Fernkontakte der Frühbronzezeit. In H. Meller and F. Bertemes (eds.), *Der Griff nach den Sternen. Wie Europas Eliten zu Macht und Reichtum kamen* (Tagungen des Landesmuseums für Vorgeschichte Halle 5): 675–697. Halle: Landesamt für Denkmalpflege und Archäologie Sachsen-Anhalt.
2010b The concept of weighing during the Bronze Age in the Aegean, the Near East and Europe. In I. Morley and C. Renfrew (eds.), *The archaeology of measurement. Comprehending heaven, earth and time in ancient societies*: 88–105. Cambridge: Cambridge University Press.
2011 Maß für Maß. Indikatoren für Kulturkontakte im 3. Jahrtausend. In *Kykladen. Lebenswelten einer frühgriechischen Kultur* [Exhibition Catalogue Karlsruhe]: 144–153. Karlsruhe, Darmstadt: Badisches Landesmuseum, Primus Verlag. 2015 The Aegean before and after c. 2200 BC between Europe and Asia: trade as a prime mover of cultural change. In H. Meller, H.W. Arz, R. Jung and R. Risch (eds.), *2200 BC - Ein Klimasturz als Ursache für den Verfall der Alten Welt. Tagungen des Landesmuseums für Vorgeschichte Halle 12/1*: 149–80. Halle: Landesamt für Denkmalpflege und Archäologie in Sachsen-Anhalt.

Rambach, J.

2000a *Kykladen I. Die frühe Bronzezeit. Grab- und Siedlungsbefunde* (Beiträge zur ur- und frühgeschichtlichen Archäologie des Mittelmeerraumes 33). Bonn: Habelt.

2000b *Kykladen II. Die frühe Bronzezeit. Frühbronzezeitliche Beigabensittenkreise auf den Kykladen. Relative Chronologie und Verbreitung* (Beiträge zur ur- und frühgeschichtlichen Archäologie des Mittelmeerraumes 34). Bonn: Habelt.

Relaki, M.

2009 Rethinking administration and seal use in third millennium Crete. *Creta Antica* 10: 353–372.

Reinholdt, C.

2008 *Der frühbronzezeitliche Schmuckhortfund von Kap Kolonna. Ägina und die Ägäis im Goldzeitalter des 3. Jahrtausends v. Chr. Mit einem Beitrag von A. G. Karydas und Ch. Zarkadas* (Ägina-Kolonna. Forschungen und Ergebnisse 2 = Contributions to the chronology of the Eastern Mediterranean 15 = Österreichische Akad. Wiss. Denkschriften der Gesamtakademie 46). Vienna: Verlag der Österreichischen Akademie der Wissenschaften.

Renfrew, C.

2006 Markiani in perspective. In L. Marangou, C. Renfrew, C. Doumas and G. Gavalas (eds.), ΜΑΡΚΙΑΝΗ ΑΜΟΡΓΟΥ – *Markiani, Amorgos. An Early Bronze Age fortified settlement. Overview of the 1985-1991 investigations* (British School at Athens, Supplementary Volume 40): 247–257. London: British School at Athens.

Renfrew, C. and M. Boyd

2011 Ein erstes regionales Zentrum. Das frühkykladische Heiligtum von Keros. In *Kykladen. Lebenswelten einer frühgriechischen Kultur* [Exhibition Catalogue Karlsruhe]: 164–174. Karlsruhe, Darmstadt: Badisches Landesmuseum, Primus Verlag.

Renfrew, C., M. Boyd and C. Bronk Ramsey

2012 The oldest maritime sanctuary? Dating the sanctuary at Keros and the Cycladic Early Bronze Age. *Antiquity* 86: 144–160.

Renfrew, C., G. Gavalas and P. Sotirakopoulou

2013b The development of the excavation: stratigraphy and phasing. In C. Renfrew, O. Philaniotou, N. Brodie, G. Gavalas and M.J. Boyd (eds.), *The settlement at Dhaskalio* (The sanctuary of Keros and the origins of Aegean ritual practice 1): 63–77. Cambridge: McDonald Institute for Archaeological Research.

Renfrew, C., R. Housley and S. Manning

2006 The absolute dating of the settlement. In L. Marangou, C. Renfrew, C. Doumas and G. Gavalas (eds.), ΜΑΡΚΙΑΝΗ ΑΜΟΡΓΟΥ – *Markiani, Amorgos. An Early Bronze Age fortified settlement. Overview of the 1985-1991 investigations* (Annual of the British School at Athens, Supplementary Volume 40): 71–80. London: British School at Athens.

Renfrew, C. and T. Loughlin

2013 The South Summit Area: Trenches VII, XLI, XL, XXI, XXII. In C. Renfrew, O. Philaniotou, N. Brodie, G. Gavalas and M.J. Boyd (eds.), *The settlement at Dhaskalio* (The sanctuary of Keros and the origins of Aegean ritual practice 1): 225–280. Cambridge: McDonald Institute for Archaeological Research.

Renfrew, C., O. Philaniotou, N. Brodie and G. Gavalas
2009 The Early Cycladic settlement at Dhaskalio, Keros: preliminary report of the 2008 excavation season. *Annual of the British School at Athens* 104: 27–47.

Renfrew, C., O. Philaniotou, N. Brodie, G. Gavalas and M.J. Boyd (eds.)
2013a *The settlement at Dhaskalio* (The sanctuary of Keros and the origins of Aegean ritual practice 1). Cambridge: McDonald Institute for Archaeological Research.

Renfrew, C., O. Philaniotou, N. Brodie, G. Gavalas, E. Margaritis, C French and P. Sotirakopoulou
2007 Keros: Dhaskalio and Kavos, Early Cycladic stronghold and ritual centre. Preliminary report of the 2006 and 2007 excavation seasons. *Annual of the British School at Athens* 102: 103–136.

Rothman, M.S.
2007 The archaeology of early administration systems in Mesopotamia. In E.C. Stone (ed.) *Settlement and society. Essays dedicated to Robert McCormick Adams*: 235–254. Los Angeles: Cotsen Institute of Archaeology.

Roux, V.
1995 Le travail des lapidaires. Atelier de Khambhat (Cambay): passé et présent. In F. Tallon (ed.), *Les pierres précieuses de l'Orient ancien des Sumériens aux Sassanides (Exposition-dossier du département des Antiquités orientales 49)*: 39–44. Paris: Réunion des Musées Nationaux.

Rowan, Y., J. Dixon and R. Dubicz
2013 The ground stone assemblage from Dhaskalio. In C. Renfrew, O. Philaniotou, N. Brodie, G. Gavalas and M.J. Boyd (eds.), *The settlement at Dhaskalio* (The sanctuary of Keros and the origins of Aegean ritual practice 1): 557–595. Cambridge: McDonald Institute for Archaeological Research.

Sagona, A. and P. Zimansky
2008 *Ancient Turkey*. London, New York: Routledge.

Şahoğlu, V.
2005 The Anatolian trade network and the Izmir region during the Early Bronze Age. *Oxford Journal of Archaeology* 24: 339–361.

Sari, D.
2013 The cultural development of Western Anatolia in the third and second millennia BC and its relationship with migration theories. In Mouton, A., Rutherford, I. and Yabubovich, I. (eds.), *Luwian identities: culture, language and religion between Anatolia and the Aegean*: 305–314. Leiden: Koninklijke Brill NV.

Sbonias, K.
2010 Diversity and transformation. Looking for meanings in the Prepalatial seal consumption and use. In Müller, W. (ed.), *Die Bedeutung der minoischen und mykenischen Glyptik* (Corpus der Minoischen und Mykenischen Siegel, Beiheft 8): 349–362. Mainz: Philipp von Zabern.

Scarre, C.
2007 Stone and shell pestles. In C. Renfrew, C. Doumas, L. Marangou and G. Gavalas (eds.), *Keros, Dhaskalio Kavos. The investigations of 1987-1988. Κέρος, Κάβος Δασκαλιου* (Keros 1): 360–363. Cambridge: McDonald Institute of Archaeological Research.

Schoep, I.
2012 Bridging the divide between the 'Prepalatial' and the 'Protopalatial' periods. In I. Schoep, P. Tomkins and J. Driessen (eds.), *Back to the beginning. Reassessing social and political complexity on Crete during the Early and Middle Bronze Age*: 403–428. Oxford: Oxbow.

Schoep, I. and C. Knappett
2004 Dual Emergence: Evolving Heterarchy, Exploding Hierarchy. In J.C. Barrett and P. Halstead (eds.), *The Emergence of Civilisation Revisited* (Sheffield Studies in Aegean Archaeology 6): 21–37. Oxford: Oxbow Books.

Schoep, I., P. Tomkins and J. Driessen (eds.)
2012 *Back to the beginning. Reassessing social and political complexity on Crete during the Early and Middle Bronze Age*. Oxford: Oxbow.

Sherratt, S.
2000 *Catalogue of Cycladic antiquities in the Ashmolean Museum. The captive spirit*. Oxford: Oxford University Press.

Speiser, E.A.
1935 *Excavations at Tepe Gawra, Vol. I: Levels I-VIII*. Philadephia: University of Pennsylvania Press.

Spitaels, P.
1983 The dawn of silver metallurgy in Greece. *London Illustrated News* 271 (No. 7020): 63–64.

Tomkins, P.
2012 Behind the horizon: reconsidering the genesis and function of the 'First Palace' at Knossos (Final Neolithic IV-Middle Minoan IB). In I. Schoep, P. Tomkins and J. Driessen (eds.), *Back to the beginning. Reassessing social and political complexity on Crete during the Early and Middle Bronze Age*: 32–80. Oxford: Oxbow.

Tomkins, P. and I. Schoep
2010 Crete. In E. Cline (ed.), *The Oxford Handbook of the Aegean Bronze Age*: 66–82. Oxford: Oxford University Press.

Traverso, A.
1997 Nuovi dati su Poliochni Azzuro. In C. G. Doumas and V. La Rosa (eds.), *Η Πολιόχνη και η πρώιμη εποχή του Χαλκού στο Βόρειο Αιγαίο/Poliochni e l' Antica Eta del Bronzo nell' Egeo Settentrionale*, Πρακτικά Διεθνούς Συνεδρίου, Αθήνα 22–25 Απριλίου 1996: 58–77. Athens: Scuola Archeologica Italiana di Atene.

Tzavella-Evjen, H.
1984 *Λιθαρές* (Δημοσιεύματα του Αρχαιολογικού Δελτίου 32). Athens: Tamio Archaiologikon Poron kai Apallotrioseon.

Umurtak, G.
2002 Some observations on a lead stamp seal from the Bademağaci excavations. *Anatolica* 28: 159–169.

Vlasaki-Andreaki, M. and E. Hallager
1995 Evidence for seal use in Pre-Palatial Western Crete. In W. Müller (ed.), *Sceaux minoens et mycéniens* (Corpus der Minoischen und Mykenischen Siegel, Beiheft 5): 251–270. Berlin: Mann.

von der Osten, H.H.
1937 *The Alishar Hüyük. Seasons of 1930–1932. Part I* (The University of Chicago Oriental Institute Publications 28. Researches in Anatolia 7). Chicago: University of Chicago Press.

von der Way, T.
1997 *Tell el-Farac în/Buto I. Ergebnisse zum frühen Kontext. Kampagnen der Jahre 1983–1989* (Archäologische Veröffentlichungen 83). Mainz: Phillip von Zabern.

Wagner, G.A. and G. Weisgerber (eds.)
1985 *Silber, Blei und Gold auf Sifnos. Prähistorische und antike Metallproduktion* (Der Anschnitt, Beiheift 3, Veröffentlichungen des Deutschen Bergbau-Museum Bochum 31). Bochum: Deutsches Bergbau-Museum.

Waage, F.O.
1949 An Early Helladic well near Old Corinth. *Hesperia Supplementum* 8: 415–422.

Walter, H. and F. Felten
1981 *Die vorgeschichtliche Stadt: Befestigungen, Häuser, Funde* (Alt-Ägina iiI, 1). Mainz: Philipp von Zabern.

Warner, J.L.
1994 *Elmali-Karataş. The Early Bronze Age village of Karataş.* Bryn Mawr: Bryn Mawr College.

Warren, P.
1970 The primary dating evidence for Early Minoan seals. *Kadmos* 11: 29–37.

Weingarten, J.
1997 Another Look at Lerna: An EH IIB Trading Post? *Oxford Journal of Archaeology* 16: 147–166.
2000 Early Helladic II sealings from Geraki in Lakonia: evidence for property, textile manufacture, and trade. In I. Pini (ed.), *Minoisch-mykenische Glyptik. Stil, Ikonographie, Funktion. V. Internationales Siegel-Symposium Marburg, 23–25.9. 1999* (Corpus der Minoischen und Mykenischen Siegel, Beiheft 6): 317–329. Berlin: Mann.
2010 Minoan seals and sealings. In E. Cline (ed.), *The Oxford Handbook of the Aegean Bronze Age*: 317–328. Oxford: Oxford University Press.

Weingarten, J., H.J. Crouwel, M. Prent and G. Vogelsang-Eastwood
1999 Early Helladic sealings from Geraki in Lakonia, Greece. *Oxford Journal of Archaeology* 18: 357–376.

Weingarten, J., S. Macveagh Thorne, M. Prent and H.J. Crouwel
2011 More Early Helladic sealings from Geraki in Lakonia, Greece. *Oxford Journal of Archaeology* 30/2, 131–163.

Wiencke, M.H.
2000 *The architecture, stratification, and pottery of Lerna III* (Lerna. A Preclassical site in the Argolid. Results of the excavations conducted by the American School of Classical Studies at Athens IV). Princeton: Princeton University Press.

Wilson, D.E.

1999 *Ayia Irini: Periods I–III. The Neolithic and Early Bronze Age settlements. Part 1: The pottery and small finds* (Keos IX). Mainz: Phillip von Zabern.

2010 Knossos 1955–1957: Early Prepalatial deposits from Platon's tests in the Palace. *Annual of the British School at Athens* 105: 97–155.

2013 Ayia Irini II–III, Kea. The phasing and relative chronology of the Early Bronze Age II settlement. *Hesperia* 82: 385–434.

Younger, J.G.

1991 Seals? From Middle Helladic Greece. *Hydra* 8: 35–54.

Zachos, K.

2008 *Ayios Dhimitrios. A prehistoric settlement in the southwestern Peloponnese. The Neolithic and Early Helladic periods* (BAR International Series 1770). Oxford: British Archaeological Reports.

Zachos, K. and A. Dousoungli

2008 Observations on the Early Bronze Age sealings from the cave of Zas at Naxos. In N. Brodie, J. Doole, G. Gavalas and C. Renfrew (eds.), *Horizon - Ὁρίζων. A colloquium on the prehistory of the Cyclades*: 85–95. Cambridge: McDonald Institute of Archaeological Research.

Zachou, E.

2004 Die frühbronzezeitliche Siedlung in Proskynas/Lokris. In E. Alram-Stern, *Die ägäische Frühzeit. 2. Serie Forschungsbericht 1975–2002. 2. Band. Die Frühbronzezeit in Griechenland mit Ausnahme von Kreta* (Österreichische Akademie der Wissenschaften. Philosophisch-historische Klasse. Veröffentlichungen der mykenischen Kommission 21): 1267–1283. Wien: Österreichische Akademie der Wissenschaften.

Zavvou, E.

2007 Νέα στοιχεία για τις Λακωνικές πόλεις της δυτηκής άκτης της Χερσονήσου του Μαλέα. In Πρακτικά του Ζ' Διεθνούς συνεδρίου Πελοποννησιακών Σπουδών: Πύργος, Γαστούνη, Αμαλιάδα 11-17 Σεπτεμβρίου 2005 Tomos Β: 413–451. Athens: Εταιρεία Πελοποννησιακών Σπουδών.

Chapter 11

Trade and Weighing Systems in the Southern Aegean from the Early Bronze Age to the Early Iron Age: How Changing Circuits Influenced Changing 'Glocal' Measures

Maria Emanuela Alberti

Measuring systems are fundamental in all practical aspects of life and are attested in many types of society. They are one of the most basic and 'embedded' elements of any culture and change accordingly to the social, political and economic history of the societies using them (Kula 1986). Their transformations through time can thus provide insights into the major cultural and economic changes that occurred in a given area. In particular, if different cultural and geographical areas share a common measuring system, their economic interaction has to be considered significant, and indeed it is usually documented by other types of evidence also, especially concerning trade activities. There is a 'special relationship' between trade and measuring systems because measuring devices are not only an administrative and productive tool but a trade *medium* in themselves. The aim of this paper is exactly to explore this 'special relationship' among southern Aegean societies during the Bronze Age and Early Iron Age.

Among pre-coinage societies, such as those of Bronze Age Mediterranean, weighing systems played a fundamental role in economic transactions. This ensured that comparison between different valuables/reference goods was possible. In this way it was possible to establish the relative value of measured goods. The weight (or the volume) of a commodity corresponded to a certain value in a chosen *medium*. This was generally, but not exclusively, metal, especially silver. It was therefore possible to correlate a certain amount of wool as corresponding to a specific amount of other things such as silver or cereals. Through this process, the measure gives the value (Milano and Parise 2003; Sorda and Camilli 2003). Each time an economic/value assessment was required, all kinds of commodities, no matter how standardised in shape or dimensions, were weighed or measured. The best examples in the Aegean are the Linear B texts of the series KN Oa (730–734), where both ingots (numbered) and their weight value (in talents) are recorded: indeed, no unequivocal direct relationship existed between weight value and ingots (Zaccagnini 1986). The system of measurement was the key for any economic transaction and we may expect that this would have been deeply embedded in the economy of a given society (Milano and Parise 2003; Sorda and Camilli 2003; Zaccagnini 2003; Clancier *et al.* 2005; Parise 2009; Gestoso Singer 2010; Ascalone and Peyronel 2011). If the economy of a certain region or state is strong and imposes itself on its neighbours, then this provides a mechanism whereby its own measuring system can expand abroad. Thus, when we study the weighing systems of pre-coinage societies, we can detect which were the strongest economies of certain periods and how they interacted. It is no surprise, therefore, that we see the trading history of the Bronze Age Mediterranean (that we know of from other sources) so systematically reflected in the history of regional and 'international' weighing systems. In this paper, I will primarily focus on the southern Aegean from the Early Bronze Age (EBA) – to the Early Iron Age (EIA), ca 2000–700, but reference will be made to the interconnections in the wider Aegean and around the Mediterranean.

According to recent scholarship, trading operated at different levels and through different modes or mechanisms contemporaneously in the Mediterranean during the Bronze Age. Within these, a large part of the exchange was carried out outside of the official system of 'gift exchange' and 'administrated trade' (Zaccagnini 1994; Liverani 1998, 58–64; Sherratt 1998; 1999; van Wijngaarden 2002). Palatial, elite, palace-sponsored, independent, 'private' trade enterprises operated alongside each other and overlaps existed to various degrees involving partnership, combination and independence (Milano and Parise 2003; Zaccagnini 2003; Sorda and Camilli 2003; Clancier *et al.* 2005; Routledge and McGeough 2009). When using Near Eastern written sources or Mediterranean archaeological evidence, it has not been possible to define a general formal schema or model of trade relationships because they are too complex and diversely articulated to allow for universal models, and so descriptions and definitions tend to work better on a case by case basis (Milano and Parise 2003; Zaccagnini 2003; Sorda and Camilli 2003; Clancier *et al.* 2005; Parise 2005; Peyronel 2008; Alberti 2011b).

Framing the analysis of southern Aegean interconnections

A multi-level trade system is the outcome of the multivariate trajectories of the societies involved, where a complex of internal and external factors comes into play. These combine elements of both staple and wealth economies (Renfrew 1972; Brumfiel and Earle 1987; Sherratt and Sherratt 1991; Scarre and Healy 1993; Sherratt 2010). In this contribution, the focus will be especially on proper trade elements, such as the various aspects and levels of import/export activities, and the diverse transcultural phenomena (spreading of various technologies, craftworks, administrative systems, architectures, languages, ideologies, religions, *etc.*), with particular attention to the history of weighing systems. However, trade interaction and networks are strongly linked to the type and dimensions of the economies of the various areas that come into play (Sherratt and Sherratt 1991; Sherratt 2010). In this sense, a full appreciation of the structure of trade systems in a given area and period should ideally also consider other elements, such as settlement patterns and infrastructures, scale of agriculture and craft-production, internal economic and social organisation (*e.g.* Kohl 2011; Faust and Weiss 2011; on a Mediterranean scale, Broodbank 2013). It is commonly agreed that the movement of people, things and ideas along trade routes strongly influenced social and economic trajectories in prehistoric societies, and played a fundamental role in the expanding Aegean economies (Knapp 1998; Sherratt 1999; Sherratt and Sherratt 1991; 1998; Broodbank 2000; 2004; Laffineur and Greco 2005; Broodbank and Kiriatzi 2007; Brodie *et al.* 2008; Macdonald *et al.* 2009; Parkinson and Galaty 2010; Maran and Stockhammer 2012; Alberti and Sabatini 2012; Broodbank 2013).

The history of trade in the Aegean has been largely and variously affected by the geographical configuration of the area. The study of winds and current patterns has underlined the different regimes of the northern and southern Aegean, and therefore their natural division (Agouridis 1997; Papageorgiou 2008; also Broodbank 2000; Sherratt 2001; Broodbank and Kiriatzi 2007; Davis 2008; Alberti 2012). This is a key point in Aegean history, where the two areas tended to normally follow different trajectories, with repercussions for the trading and interaction patterns in various periods. In particular, the NE Aegean (north of Samos and facing Anatolian coast, i.e. roughly ancient Lydia and Mysia) and the SE Aegean (between Samos and Rhodes and facing Anatolian coasts, i.e. roughly ancient Caria) seem to have belonged to quite different trade circuits throughout the Bronze Age: the former interacted more closely with ancient Thrace, Khalkidhiki and Thessaly, while the latter had a higher degree of interconnection with the central Aegean and Crete (Mountjoy 1998; Georgiadis 2003; Hope Simpson 2003; Broodbank 2004; Laffineur and Greco 2005: 129–278; Felten *et al.* 2007: 151–200, 257–360; Benzi 2009; Macdonald *et al.* 2009). Compare, for example, the divergent reception of Minoan and Helladic textile tools in the NE, SE and central Aegean sites (Pavúk 2012; Gleba and Cutler 2012; Cutler 2012). At present, the only known exception to this pattern is the evidence of significant Minoan materials in Samothrace from the MBA: much detailed information is needed to understand the phenomenon, though the hypothesis of a strategic initiative in connection with the exploitation of the metalliferous ores of the area is highly probable (Matsas 1991 and 2009; Girella and Pavúk 2015).

For the NE and SE Aegean respectively, the terms 'Upper' and 'Lower Interface' (with reference to an 'East Aegean – Western Anatolia Interface') were originally used (Mountjoy 1998) to define phenomena of the Mycenaean period, but can be usefully employed also for other periods, to underline the particularities of these areas (*e.g.* Davis and Gorogianni 2008). The same is true of for the terms 'Western String' (Keos,

Melos, Thera; Davis 1979) and 'Eastern String' (Kasos, Karpathos, Rhodes; Niemeier 1984), originally meant to identify dynamics in the late MBA – early LBA.

The distribution of land-masses and the wind and current patterns in the southern Aegean (Agouridis 1997; Papageorgiou 2008; Brodie *et al.* 2008: 83; Broodbank 2000: 1–105, 287–292; Alberti 2012) suggest that we should envisage a series of localised maritime circuits, which interfaced with one another, thus allowing the circulation of people, goods and ideas through a chain of segmented steps; longer voyages had to follow cyclical routes. Some major crossing routes assured stronger connections (see Figure 11.1; Alberti 2012 for further geographical details). From the perspective of the southern Aegean internal maritime routes, Miletus, Rhodes and Kythera lay at the articulation points with other external circuits (northern Aegean, eastern Mediterranean and southern mainland respectively): their strategic position can perhaps account for the particular intensity of their connections with Crete during the MBA and the early LBA (Broodbank 2004; Macdonald *et al.* 2009: 73–96, 121–166,

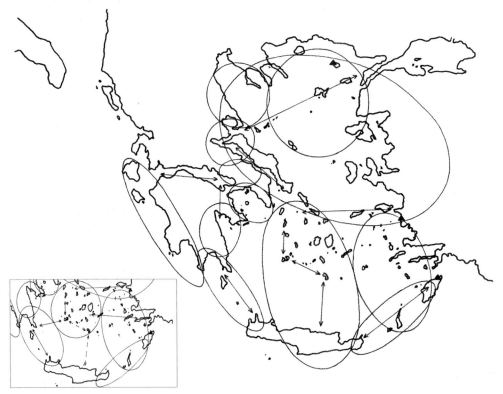

Figure 11.1: Aegean trade routes and circuits from MBA to LB I Early (LMIA) (main figure). During LB I Late, the direct connection between Crete and Thera gives place to a more indirect route from the Central Cyclades to Laconia and Kythera (box). (M. E. Alberti, F. Merlatti)

175–218; Warren 2009; Alberti 2012), in contrast with less involved neighbouring sites (*e.g.* Iasos in Caria or Seraglio on Kos, see respectively Momigliano 2012 and Vitale – Hancock 2012).

On the external side of Mediterranean maritime interaction, the principal currents and winds make an anticlockwise route more viable (Agouridis 1997; Sauvage 2012: 265–294; Broodbank 2013: 8–9). Taking a hypothetical point of departure in northern Syria, for a large part of the Bronze Age, the route continued to NE Cyprus, coastal Cilicia, Pamphylia and Lycia, Rhodes, Crete, then crossed the Mediterranean towards the Libyan coast, to return to the Nile Delta and coastal Syria – Palestine. In its full deployment during the advanced Late Bronze Age (see below), it also reached Sicily and Sardinia (Stampolidis and Karageorghis 2003: 15–117; Laffineur and Greco 2005: 313–472; Broodbank 2013: fig. 8.1).

Studies of Aegean trade and interconnection patterns are extensive: and it is increasingly acknowledged that interaction played a crucial role in forging the complex world of Aegean societies and in shaping their historical trajectories. Some analyses have underlined the importance of external contacts, within a 'world-systems' perspective (Sherratt and Sherratt 1991; Sherratt 2010). Other studies have focused on internal connections (Broodbank 2000; Felten *et al.* 2007; Berg 2007; Alberti 2012), either with a 'world-systems' approach (Berg 1999; Kardulias 2010; Parkinson and Galaty 2010) or stressing the role of 'networks' (Knappett *et al.* 2008; Knappett 2011: 123–145; Knappett and Nikolakopoulou 2014). For the present paper, internal and external interconnections are equally important, and a flexible approach is more desirable: different perspectives can provide useful insights, depending on the period and area under investigation and on the various scales of analysis (see, with much broader scope, Broodbank 2013; for a minimalist view, see Zurbach 2012).

Most recent reconstructions of the history of trade in the Bronze Age southern Aegean recognise the need to distinguish various chronological phases, each one showing a particular cultural flavour within different cycles of pulsing connectivity (Sherratt 2010; Broodbank 2013; Knappett and Nikolakopoulou 2014; phasing already in Sherratt and Sherratt 1991). This is especially linked to the spread of some cultural elements from the key economic area(s) in each period, such as fashions and technologies related to pottery, textile and prestige item manufacture, administrative equipment, and, more relevant for this paper, weighing systems. Other less tangible elements, such as iconographies, symbolisms, ideas and ideologies, and possibly cults, will not be taken into account here. As a result, there were diverse phenomena of reception, with wide evidence for selection, appropriation, re-elaboration, imitation and reverberation. Such aspects have been thoroughly studied in recent years, through the concepts of hybridisation and entanglement (Maran and Stockhammer 2012; also Voskos and Knapp 2008; Karageorghis and Kouka 2011; Stockhammer 2012a; 2012b). However, the co-occurrence of elements from both the external and the internal traditions in local assemblages is so multi-variate that again it is best to consider the evidence on a case by case basis. To give some examples related to pottery production, typical synthetic outcomes of multi-cultural influences are the EB IIB Kastri Group/ Lefkandi I assemblage (Rutter 2012), the MBA Lustrous Decorated ware of the coastal southern Peloponnese (Taylour and Janko 2008: 177–298; Kiriatzi 2010), the LoD/ DoL pottery from LB I Keos (Vitale and Hancock 2012), and the early LH Mainland Polychrome (and related productions) and Lustrous Painted ('Mycenaean') wares (Taylour and Janko 2008: 185–187; Mathioudaki 2010; Rutter 2012).

Considering other classes of materials, the same can be said for the LB IIIB Mycenaean weighing system (see below). On the other hand, a selective process is probably implied in the diffusion of only one type of Minoan loom-weight throughout the Aegean between the MBA and LBA (Cutler 2012). When trying to define transcultural phenomena on the basis of the archaeological record, however, we should also consider the generally high level of heterogeneity proper to each cultural area *per se* (both synchronically and diachronically) and to related cultural environments: see *e.g.* the diverse versions of a common Keros/Syros 'package' in the EB IIA Cyclades (Broodbank 2000: 202–205), or the complex patterns of MBA ceramic productions in the Cyclades and southern mainland (Felten *et al.* 2007: 81–150, 257–360), and the elements of regionalism of the decorated LBA Mycenaean wares in certain periods (Mountjoy 1999).

One of the most debated cases of waves of cultural influence is undoubtedly the so-called 'Minoanisation', i.e. the spreading of Minoan cultural traits into the Aegean regions, especially in the southern Aegean. It is characterised by the circulation and often adoption of specific forms of fine and coarse ware ceramics, weaving, weighing and administrative tools, ritual paraphernalia, and frescoes. After much debate (Hägg and Marinatos 1984; Hardy *et al.* 1990; for a wide range of perspectives see Laffineur and Greco 2005: 129–286), it is now regarded as consisting of a dynamic multi-faceted and highly variable phenomenon, underlying many different historical realities, based often on second-hand transmission and local circuits, and variously linked with trade routes, economic factors, fashion, emulation, re-interpretation, affiliation and identity negotiation (Broodbank 2004; Whitelaw 2005; Berg 2006; Davis and Gorogianni 2008; Knappett and Nikolakopoulou 2008; Macdonald *et al.* 2009; Momigliano 2012). It is also possible to pose the question of 'Minoanisation in Crete itself' (Broodbank 2004: 51). The same dynamism, complexity and multi-faceted patterns characterise the previous and following phases of transcultural phenomena. On the other hand, these are related to both to the economic structure of the Aegean as a whole and to the economic fortunes of its key-areas (Sherratt 2010: 88; see below). The intensity of these phenomena seems to have been related (*inter alia*) to the efficiency of the transport means used in each phase, and thus to have been higher after the introduction of sailing crafts between the 3rd and 2nd millennia (Broodbank 2000: 287–291, 341–349; Sherratt 2010; Legarra Herrero 2011). As a result, features of 'Minoanisation' (and 'Mycenaeanisation') appear more strongly in the archaeological evidence from the southern Aegean than the 'international' elements of the previous phases, be they from the Cyclades or the NE Aegean (Knappett and

Nikolakopoulou 2014). It is with this dynamism and complexity in mind that the various historical, cultural and trading phases will be considered in the following pages and the terms 'Minoanising', 'Mycenaeanising', 'Westernising' and 'Levantinising' will be used (Sherratt 2010; Knappett and Nikolakopoulou 2014). Each of these (trans-) cultural phases is closely connected to the others, and so together they create a form of continuous osmosis, that underpins Aegean history (Melas 2009). Thanks to this, Aegean cultures acquired their own particular blend of practices, different from those in other Mediterranean worlds.

General remarks on Eastern Mediterranean BA weighing systems

Beginning in the early third millennium at the latest, Near Eastern societies developed complex systems of measuring weight, volumes, lengths and land area. For the purpose of this present paper, I will concentrate on the measures of weight that were used to quantify metals, wool, textiles and other commodities. Larger units of weight measurement, such as the talent and the mina (and also the wool unit) are quite close, if not identical, in many areas, while the smaller units, called shekels in Anatolia, Syria and Mesopotamia, and *qdt* in Egypt, are more different to each other. In Anatolia and Syria-Palestine, there were various shekels, and these were linked to each other by mathematical proportion and thus easily convertible one into the other. This conversion system is documented in the third millennium at Ebla, Tell Brak, Tell Sweyhat, Tarsus and Troy (see L. Rahmstorf, this volume). Mesopotamian measures differed and were less easily convertible into the systems of Anatolia and Syria. Moreover, during the LBA Egypt adopted the Syrian ('Ugarit' series *s* = *qdt*) units (Milano and Parise 2003; Sorda and Camilli 2003; Clancier *et al.* 2005; Alberti and Parise 2005; Alberti *et al.* 2006; Ascalone and Peyronel 2007; Michailidou 2008a: 205–216; Alberti 2009; 2011a). The units used in the various areas can be summarised as follows (for each region, larger units are listed before the smaller ones):

Anatolia and Syria-Palestine:

multiples
1 **talent** =28,2 kg = 60 minas
1 **mina** 470 g = 40 **h** = 50 **s** = 60 **k** ('western mina')

shekels
1 shekel of Hatti 11.75 g (**h**)
1 shekel of Ugarit 9.4 g (**s**)
1 shekel of Karkemish 7.83 g (**kar**)
Conversion: 4 **h** = 5 **s** = 6 **kar** = 47 g

Mesopotamia:

1 **talent** 30.3 kg = 30 'double' minas
1 **'double' mina** 1,008 g = 30 minas
1 **mina** 504 g = 60 shekels
1 **shekel** 8.4 g (**mp**)

Egypt:

5 **dbn** 470 g = 1 'western mina'
1 **dbn** 90.95 g = 10 **qdt**
1 **qdt** 9.09 g = **s**

Aegean societies are also known to have had measures of weight, volume, land area. However, the evidence is not so consistently represented and we are generally limited to archaeological finds of balance weights. As we will see, in some periods weighing units of Near Eastern type were widely used in the Aegean, while in other periods it was local units that were mostly employed. The larger units of weights in the Aegean, the talent, the double mina, the mina and the half mina, were similar (in terms both of absolute and relative values) to those in use in the Near East. On the other hand, other Aegean units of lighter weight had no or only very problematic parallels in Anatolia and Syria, thus suggesting a possible Aegean origin for these units (see below). This is especially the case for the basic Minoan unit of 60–65 g, called **x**. Its fraction **k** of 20–22 g could more easily be converted into eastern shekels, but not without problems: actually, with some approximation it can be considered either twice the value of **s** (9.4 g) or **h** (11.4), but no correspondence is straightforward and the archaeological evidence not sufficiently abundant (see below; Michailidou 2004: 318; Alberti and Parise 2005; Alberti 2011a). During the Mycenaean period, the weighing system remains substantially the same as in Neopalatial times, with various modifications and an increased popularity of the **k** unit (possibly to be identified with the Linear B unit P, see below and Table 11.4), especially in the multiples of 10 and 20 (220 g and 440 g) (Petruso 1992; 2003; Alberti 2003; Alberti and Parise 2005; Michailidou 2008; Parise 2009; Alberti 2009; 2011a):

Aegean:

multiples

1 **talent** ca 30 kg = 30 double minas (Linear B **L**)
1 **double mina** ca 1 kg = 2 minas (Linear B **M**)
1 **mina** ca 500 g = 8 **x**
1 **half mina** ca 240–260 g = 4 **x** (Linear B **N**)

main unit
1 *x* 60–65 g
fraction
1 *k* 20 g (= 1/3 *x*) (Linear B *P*)

Most used during Mycenaean times:
10 *k* 220 g
20 *k* 440 g

The following overview of the history of the Aegean weighing systems is based on analysis of the weights found in the same findspot/context (weight group): if they really constitute a working set, their weights should have recognisable ratios between them and thus constitute a series. In addition, the marks that some of the weights happen to bear can indicate their relative value: *e.g.* one or two incised strokes (or dots, or circles) would theoretically indicate the value of one or two units (on all these topics, see Alberti *et al.* 2006; on marks, see Petruso 1992 and Michailidou 2008; for a statistical, non contextual approach, see Pakkanen 2011).

Late EBA – Full MBA: Networks, regionalism and first 'Minoanisation'; Near Eastern and Aegean weights

During the EB I-II, even with conspicuous changes throughout the period, the Aegean trading system appears to be structured as a complex network of interconnections between east and west, from Troy to Lerna and from western Greece to the Adriatic regions (see Kouka and Rahmstorf, this volume). In the southern Aegean, the major sites involved seem to act as 'peers' on trade routes, creatively sharing cultural codes and prestige assemblages: especially Kolonna (Aegina), Ayios Kosmas (Attica), Manika (Euboea), Ayia Irini (Keos), Grotta (Naxos), Chalandriani (Syros), Daskaleio-Kavos (Keros) and Skarkos (Ios). The strategic role played by Cycladic communities in the maritime network fosters the diffusion of Cycladic goods and taste in the area (especially in EB I-IIA; Broodbank 2000: 247–309; 2013: 257–346; Brodie *et al.* 2008: 61–298; Alram Stern 2011). After an initial phase of interaction, Crete appears to become somewhat separated from the rest of the Aegean (Brodie *et al.* 2008: 237–270; Legarra Herrero 2011). Because of the main maritime transport means used in this phase (paddled long-boats), travel distances and trade intensity were considerably lower than in the following periods, and necessitated many more trading posts along the routes: in this sense, the EB I-II constitutes, for the Bronze Age southern Aegean, quite a distinct (long) phase and one of the few periods (compare with LB IIIC, see below) in which internal trade interconnections could be described in terms of networks, without strong evidence of 'world-system' dynamics (Broodbank 2000: 180–210; Broodbank 2013: 308, 322; Knappett and Nikolakopoulou 2014). At the same time, on the external side, the Aegean area as a whole shows evidence of strong contacts with

Anatolia, sharing some common cultural traits, among which are sealings, weighing (see Rahmstorf, this volume), the introduction of tin bronze and, in the later part of the EB II, pottery fashions (see above, on the Kastri Group/Lefkandi assemblage; see Rahmstorf 2006a; 2006b and this volume; Kouka, this volume). From this point of view, some presence of 'world–system' mechanisms in external interaction cannot be excluded (Broodbank 2013: 337).

As for the Aegean EBA weighing systems, recent work by Rahmstorf indicates that during this period of intense interconnection, the Aegean and the Eastern Mediterranean shared a common weighing system, with Near Eastern units and systems of conversion (see above; Rahmstorf this volume; 2003; 2006a; 2006b; 2008b; 2010; 2011a; 2011b). This could suggest the existence of an economic asymmetry, with Anatolia and Syria acting as the main pole of attraction. What is very important to stress for the subsequent metrological developments is the use of units of ca 10 g and the use of multiples counted according to the decimal system (see Rahmstorf 2006a: fig. 4, multiples of 5 and 10 units *s* from Tiryns; this volume for Tzoungiza).

Throughout the later EBA and the very beginning of the MBA, important transformations occur in the Aegean region. Thanks also to the advent of sailing crafts, the linkage between Crete and the rest of the Aegean became progressively closer (Broodbank 2000: 320–361; Sherratt 2010; Legarra Herrero 2011; Knappett and Nikolakopoulou 2014). The trade network of peer-ranked centres begins to be disrupted, and the chain of interactions that defines the island network becomes restricted, becoming limited to Attica, the Saronic Gulf, the central Cyclades and Dodecanese; the presence of 'duck vases' can be seen as one of the main indicators of this (Broodbank 2000: 352, 355; Sherratt 2010: 94). It is also notable that new, stronger, and apparently directional, links are forged between Crete, Kythera and the southern Peloponnese (as evidenced by Minoanising material found in those places: *e.g.* Broodbank and Kiriatzi 2007 on Kythera; Taylour and Janko 2008 on Ayios Stephanos).

During the MBA, two contrasting cultural tendencies can be detected, one based on regional identities and the other on varying degrees of Minoanisation; the diverse dynamics between these two tendencies shape the cultural identities of communities in different parts of the Aegean (Broodbank 2000: 349–361; Felten *et al.* 2007; Macdonald *et al.* 2009; Philippa-Touchais *et al.* 2010; Voutsaki 2010; Alberti 2012 for a detailed discussion). We could broadly divide the southern Aegean into the following regional units of interaction: the central mainland, the north-east, southern and western Peloponnese, the Saronic Gulf with Aegina, the central Cyclades, the southern Dodecanese 'Lower Interface' and Crete. The systematic linkage with palatial societies in Crete might be seen to provide the system with a gravitational core and a more directional structure (dendritic system), with the progressive stabilisation of three main S-N routes (Figure 11.1): the Crete – Kythera – southern Peloponnese route, the 'Western String' and the 'Eastern String' (Broodbank 2000: 356–359; Whitelaw 2004a; 2004b; Brodie *et al.* 2008: 305–348). The system was fully in place by the middle of the MBA: see *e.g.* the re-foundation of Ayia Irini IV (Keos), well after the beginning of the

MBA (Overbeck and Crego 2008), and the progressive expansion of Phylakopi (Melos) during the MBA (Whitelaw 2004b; 2005). Within this framework, trade activities are carried out through segmented geographical circuits, by a restricted number of leading major centres (in the south-central Aegean especially Akrotiri on Thera, Phylakopi on Melos, Ayia Irini on Keos and Kolonna on Aegina), while other sites and areas play a decidedly more secondary role. Protopalatial Crete is indeed now fully linked to the rest of the Aegean and to the Eastern Mediterranean, and, with its impressive ecological, agricultural, demographic and social assets, imposes itself as a major actor on the scene and acts as a filter between the Aegean and external maritime connections (Broodbank 2000: 349–361; Watrous 2001; Felten *et al.* 2007: 257–360; Macdonald *et al.* 2009; Philippa-Touchais *et al.* 2010: 826–943).

During the MBA interaction with Egypt and the Levant becomes increasingly evident: the distribution of Minoan and Minoanising artefacts overseas and of eastern imports in the Aegean underlines the filter role played now by Crete and the existence of a circular 'long route' from Syria to Cyprus, Crete and Egypt (Cline and Harris Cline 1998: 13–27; Karetsou 2000; Brysbaert 2008; Phillips 2008; Barrett 2009; Højen Sørensen 2009; Cherry 2010; Sherratt 2010: 95–96; MacGillivray 2013; Broodbank 2013: 345–446).

Unfortunately, there are no detailed studies on MBA Aegean weights, and the course of developments is therefore difficult to detect. The only systematically studied and published assemblage comes from Malia (*Quartier Mu*, MM IIB; Alberti 2000). Analysis of that material suggests that in Crete a local weighing system was in use, characterised by local types (stone discs and lead discs, among others) and metrological standards that have possible correspondences with the later 'Minoan' units and with contemporary Near Eastern units. At the moment, however, it is impossible to say if these units and types are really new and local, because the documentation from EB III and MBA is so poorly known and understood.[1]

Late MBA – Early LBA: Minoanisation, the 'northern route' and Minoan/Aegean weights

In general terms, the last phases of the MBA and the early phases of the LBA in the southern Aegean (MM III – LM IB, MH III – LH IIA) are characterised by the continuation and intensification of previous dynamics of interaction, including a closer and fuller linkage of Mainland societies with those in the southern Aegean. The trade system starts to expand and to incorporate bordering areas that were previously not closely linked, such as the central Mediterranean, northern Greece and, more indirectly, the Black Sea area. Interconnections with the eastern Mediterranean increased, resulting in a strong economic stimulus for the Aegean as a whole (Muhly 2003; Broodbank 2004; Laffineur and Greco 2005: 175–226, 323–335, 429–472; 571–599; Brodie *et al.* 2008: 339–408; Sherratt 2010; Papadimitriou and Kriga 2012; Broodbank 2013: 368–372; Knappett and Nikolakopoulou 2014).

In the internal southern Aegean sphere, major trends notable in the mature MBA develop further in this phase, giving way to a more integrated and less regionalised system, with Neopalatial Crete and Minoanisation as the leading economic and cultural elements. The pattern of trade-circuits is substantially the same as in the previous phase (Figure 11.1), with an increasing weight of Crete at one extremity (reinforcing the dendritic aspects of the network) and the growing influence of the Helladic pole(s) on the other side (a precursor to the future gravitational reversal). Minoan cultural influence or Minoanisation (see above) which increased in the Aegean throughout the MBA, reaches its apogee in this period. What is becoming increasingly clear is that the spread of these Minoan and Minoanising traits is due not only to first-hand contacts, but, especially for the eastern Aegean and Helladic mainland, also to second-hand transmissions of cultural elements and to the creation of a Minoanising or hybrid *milieux* in each region (Laffineur and Greco 2005: 175–226; Felten *et al.* 2007: 257–360; Taylour and Janko 2008: 551–610; Macdonald *et al.* 2009; Philippa-Touchais *et al.* 2010: 847–884). In this phase, the presence of Minoan and Minoanising material culture in some strategic key-sites of the southern Aegean increases, especially at Kythera, Trianda (Rhodes) and Miletus (Caria) (see above).

Transcultural phenomena seem to play an important role, now as before, in shaping regional and local material culture: Cycladic, Helladic and Anatolian – Aegean 'Interface' worlds, were, each one in its own way and with many internal variations, the result of various intermingling traditions and influences (see above; Broodbank 2004; Laffineur and Greco 2005: 175–226; Whitelaw 2005; Berg 2007; Felten *et al.* 2007: 257–360; Brodie *et al.* 2008: 338–408; Macdonald *et al.* 2009: 59–96, 121–166; Philippa-Touchais *et al.* 2010: 603–633, 683–699). To give a most famous example, the offerings from the Mycenae Shaft Graves are a splendid case of a 'glocal' assemblage: imports from various areas accompany hybrids and typical local products, and Minoanising features seem to be filtered through the Cyclades or Aegina (Maran 2011). Interestingly, Early Mycenaean material culture shows a special multi-rooted character from its very beginnings, though the final combination(s) and the underlying substantial tradition are definitely (and variously) Helladic (Wright 2006; 2008; Schon 2010; Voutsaki 2010; Maran 2011; Rutter 2012; Broodbank 2013: 432).

By LB I, when complex Helladic societies begin to emerge, Early Mycenaean materials are increasingly attested in other Aegean areas. This is especially true for the Cyclades in the years (LM IB/LH IIA) following the Santorini eruption, when direct contacts with Crete appear reduced and relationships have to be conducted through the route linking the western Cyclades with the southern Peloponnese and Kythera or with the 'Eastern String' (Figure 11.1 box). In particular, Kythera and Melos seem to replace Thera within the system of trade-routes (compare figs 35a, 35b and 35c in Berg 2007; *ibidem*, 104; Davis and Cherry 1990; Davis and Gorogianni 2008; Knappett and Nikolakopoulou 2014; for routes, Agouridis 1997 and Mountjoy 2004). It is precisely in this framework that we can place some 'delocalisation' phenomena: the good quality LM IB style pottery produced in the Greek mainland and Aeginetan workshops apparently outnumbers the LM IB wares manufactured in Crete at sites such as Melos and Keos in the Cyclades (Mountjoy and Ponting 2000; Mountjoy 2008; Rutter 2012). Early Mycenaean pottery is also imported and imitated in the 'Lower Interface' (Mountjoy 1998; Marketou *et al.* 2006). It has to be stressed that from this advanced phase (LB I), the distinction between Cretan and Helladic/Cycladic fine ware starts to diminish, giving place to a more integrated stylistic and technological horizon. This is distinctly different from the EBA and MBA situation, and eventually will result in the homogeneous (though nonetheless regionalised) production of Mycenaean decorated pottery during the following centuries.

Aegean relationships with the eastern Mediterranean develop further in this phase (import/export evidence, Minoanising fashion and frescoes in the Levant and Egypt, representations of people from 'Keftiu' in tombs from Thebes, Egypt, 15th century: Gale 1991; Cline and Harris Cline 1998: 39–97; Laffineur and Greco 2005: 323–334, 429–472; Brysbaert 2008; Bennet 2011; Duistermaat and Regulski 2011: 183–380). Crete still seems to be acting as a filter between internal and external routes, though mainland Greece is probably in contact with western Anatolia through the north Aegean circuits (Schon 2010; Pavúk 2012). The distribution of imports in Cyprus, the Dodecanese, Crete, southern Italy and Sicily during LB I underlines the popularity of a northern sea-route: a continual series of overlapping networks can be traced from the north coast of Cyprus (Ayia Irini Paleokastro and Toumba tou Skourou), to Trianda on Rhodes, then on to the 'Eastern String' and the east and north coasts of Crete (Kato Zakros, Mochlos, Knossos, Poros – Katsambas, and Chania)[2]. From there the route continued on to the Ionian Sea, eastern Sicily and the Tyrrhenian Sea. Visits to the southern coasts, from Levant to southern Cyprus and Crete and then to southern Sicily, are not so numerous in this phase (see *e.g.* the low numbers of imports from Eastern Mediterranean and Aegean at Kommos for this phase, Shaw *et al.* 2006) and apparently mostly linked to Levantine initiatives (Cline 1994: 92; Graziadio 2005; Marazzi and Tusa 2005; Militello 2005; Soles 2005; Sauvage 2012: 265–294; Broodbank 2013: 346–347, fig. 8.1: 444).

As for weighing systems, this is the phase that has yielded the greatest evidence for the use of Minoan/Aegean balance weights. These have largely been recovered from Crete (Knossos, Mochlos, Zakros, and Haghia Triada) but also other locations in the Aegean: Ayia Irini (Keos), Akrotiri (Thera), Mikro Vouni (Samothrace), Heraion (Samos), Miletus (Caria), Vapheio (Laconia). The islands of the 'Western String' have yielded the largest assemblages, mostly sets of weights found in good archaeological contexts, thus pointing to the relevance of their economic (trading and production) activities. Most of these weights are made in lead which comes from Laurion (Stos-Gale and Gale 2006). The diffusion of these weights is considered one of the most important marks of Minoanisation and of the leading role of Minoan power in the Aegean (Parise 1986; Petruso 1992; Alberti 2003; 2011a; Akrotiri: Michailidou 1990; 2006; 2007; 2008a: 41–100; Ayia Irini: Petruso 1992: 21–36; Alberti 1995; Knossos: Evans 1906; Mochlos: Brogan 2006).

The most common weight type is the disc, both in lead and in stone, and it is typical of the Aegean. The basic Minoan/Aegean unit of measurement is x or 60–65 g. The talent (L), double mina (M), mina, wool unit (l), main unit (x), main sub-multiple (k) and other smaller units are used within a single series of fractions, even if each can function as a unit independently ('parallel units'). As far as the inferior units are concerned, the situation has still to be fully understood, since very few small weights are known for this period (Alberti and Parise 2005; Alberti 2011a: 22, table 5). The progressive division (Table 11.1) has a duodecimal or sexagesimal base (Parise 1986; Petruso 1992; Michailidou 2008; Alberti 2011a). Along with local Aegean weights (lead and stone discs, with relative values related to the main Minoan series), typical Near Eastern weights (especially haematite sphendonoid and domed ones, with relative values related to shekels, 'western mina' or even **deben**) have been recovered from sites in the Aegean (*e.g.* Akrotiri and Mochlos; see respectively Michailidou 2006 and Brogan 2006). In the most important groups of balance weights (MB III-LB I; Table 11.2), the best represented units and types are the Aegean ones, and only a minority of Near Eastern elements have been recognised (Michailidou 2006; Brogan 2006; Alberti 2009; 2011a).[3] Unfortunately, most of the main assemblages of balance weights from Neopalatial Crete come from early excavations, and are thus without a secure context (*e.g.* Knossos, Tylissos, Mochlos, Zakros; Petruso 1992). Recently, however, a group of weights has been published from Mochlos Building B.2 (LB I advanced – LM IB): they are four lead discs, with weights based on the main unit **x**: 1/2 **x**; 3/2 **x**; 2 **x**; 2 **x** (Brogan 2006).

As mentioned, the datasets of weights recovered from the large-scale excavations at Ayia Irini on Keos and from Akrotiri on Thera (LB I – LC I) are very large and informative. In particular, the finds from Ayia Irini have been one of the main sources for the identification of the Aegean weighing system. At that site, the weights from House A ground floor are all lead discs and they are calibrated to the main unit **x**: 1/4 **x**, 1/2 **x**, 1/2 **x**, 1 **x**, 1 **x**, 3/2 **x**, 3/2 **x**, 2 **x** (Petruso 1992: 21–36; Alberti 1995). Akrotiri yielded the largest and most impressive range of finds, which includes also heavier weights and the use of a standard related to the measurement of wool: see *e.g.* the case of the West House, where there were lead discs weighing up to 1, 3, 4 and 6 double minas, and submultiples of the wool unit (Michailidou 1990; 2006; 2007; 2008a: 41–100).

Table 11.1: *Simplified structure of the weighing system used during the Neopalatial period in the Aegean, reconstructed on the basis of the attested groups of weights. The wool* (**l**) *and textile* (**f**) *units and the smaller hypothetical fractions are not considered. For a detailed view, see Alberti 2011a.* Abbreviations: par – parallelpiped; d – disc; cb – cube; sf – sfendonoid; st – stone; ld – lead; br – bronze.

'Minoan' (Neopalatial) System MMIII-LMI				
1	L	30,000 g	480	
1/30	M			
	double mina	1,000 g	16	duodecimal and sexagesimal progressive fractions
1/60	Mina	500 g ca	8	
1/480	x	60–65 g	1	
1/1440 (1/1500)	k	20 g	1/3	

Table 11.2: Aegean weighing units and weight types during MBIII – LB I-II.

	Aegean Units							???	Eastern Units		Minas		Types			
	f 36 g	W 50 g	k 20 g	w 5 g	x 58-66 g	M/N	Wool (z, l)	Ae 6.6 g/ dbn 13.2 g	s = qdt 9.4 g	mp= 8.7 g	Western 470–480 g	Heavy 500–579 g	d st	d ld	others	Eastern weights
Haghia Triada		X	X		X	X	X	?					X	X		
Tylissos		X	X		X			X	X		X		X	X	X	
Malia					X									X		
Mochlos			X		X	X	X	X						X	X	X
Palaikastro					X								X	X		
Ayia Irini			X		X			X	X			X	X	X	X	
Akrotiri	X	X	X		X	X	X	?		X	X	X	X	X		X
Vapheio					X	X								X		

The same picture holds true for the restricted evidence available from mainland Greece. In the Vapheio tholos tomb (LB I advanced–LH IIA), among other gravegoods that exhibited a complex pattern of cultural influences (particularly a strong Minoanising flavour), an impressive assemblage of nine balance weights (lead discs) and ten bronze scale pans has been found. The set of weights is typically Minoan, both in shape and standards, with weights clearly arranged in a series based on x and M: 1 x; 2 x; 2 x; 3 x; 4 x = N; 8 x = N 2; 16 x = M; 16 x = M; 16 x = M. Every multiple from x to 4 M (64 x) can be composed (Alberti 2006; Michailidou 2008a: 156–178). Apparently, no echo of the previous EH weighing systems is discernible, although its absence does not prove the system was no longer in use. The absence is quite striking nonetheless, and can probably be seen as another example of shared Minoanising practices adopted by the Early Mycenaean leading groups.

The metrological evidence thus confirms the general historical picture for this period: the Aegean economy was quite interconnected, with a strong leading role being played by Crete. Connections with the Near East, though relevant, were of secondary importance in the structure of the internal economic system.

Advanced and mature LBA: Mycenaeanisation, 'globalisation', the southern route, the northern shift and 'glocal' weights

A different scenario can be reconstructed for the following Mycenaean palatial phase: first, the 'core' of the southern Aegean system moves from Crete to the Mainland; second, Aegean trade circuits are structurally connected to external *foci* of economic growth, such as the central Mediterranean and Cyprus (LB IIIA-B; general overview in Sherratt 2010: 96–98; Broodbank 2013: 402–414, 446–447, 464–465, fig. 8.1, 8.67, 9.1).

During LB IIIA-B early, internal Aegean trade routes are substantially similar to those in the preceding period (Figure 11.2). During the LB IIIA surviving Eastern Mediterranean imports are concentrated in Crete, especially Kommos (Cline 1994; 2007; Shaw *et al.* 2006; Day *et al.* 2011; van Wijngaarden 2012), suggesting that the island is still playing its role of interface or filter between the Aegean and Mediterranean routes. In the following LB IIIB Early period, the pattern of distribution of eastern imports start to change: their presence in Kommos is considerably reduced, while some clusters are attested at LH IIIB1 Mycenae and Thebes (Cline 1994; Tournavitou 1995; Shaw *et al.* 2006). A more internal entrance route for Eastern imports through our 'Interface' is probable, especially via Rhodes and across through the Cyclades (Mountjoy 1998; Hope Simpson 2003; Schon 2010). The first Western elements appear during the early part of LB IIIB (bronzes at Ulu Burun, Knossos; mould at Mycenae; Handmade Burnish Ware at Chania and Sardinian Handmade Burnished Ware at Kommos; Jung 2009; Lis 2009; Shaw *et al.* 2006). Many scholars consider that Mediterranean trade involvement formed a major economic basis for Mycenaean palatial societies (though see Molloy, this volume), but trading and diplomatic frameworks are both notoriously difficult to understand (Cline and Harris Cline 1998: 137–148, 291–299; Cline 2007; Alberti 2011b; Beckman *et al.* 2011; van Wijngaarden 2012).

Based on the long-term cultural osmosis of previous periods, and especially on the diffused Minoanising matrix, during LB IIIA and IIIB Early Mycenaean influence and fashions (*e.g.* fine and coarse pottery, prestige goods, funerary habits, ritual paraphernalia and, with respect to Crete only, administrative tools) spread out into the whole Aegean and beyond, in various combinations with preceding local traditions. The dynamics of Mycenaeanisation are as complex and variegated as the Minoanisation phenomena. What has to be stressed is that Mycenaeanisation is a dynamic process, both within mainland and island societies, resulting in strongly regionalised (and continuously transforming) identities in the framework of what has been termed a Mycenaean *koine* (Georgiadis 2003; D'Agata and Moody 2005; Mountjoy 2008; Langohr 2009; Knappett and Nikolakopoulou 2014; for decorated pottery, Mountjoy 1999). Pottery from various regions (especially the Argolid and western and southern Crete) circulates and there are local imitations and hybridisation phenomena at work (see *e.g.* for the 'Lower Interface', Mountjoy 1998; Laffineur and Greco 2005: 129–152, 199–286; Marketou *et al.* 2006; Benzi 2009). The presence of groups of Cretan transport stirrup

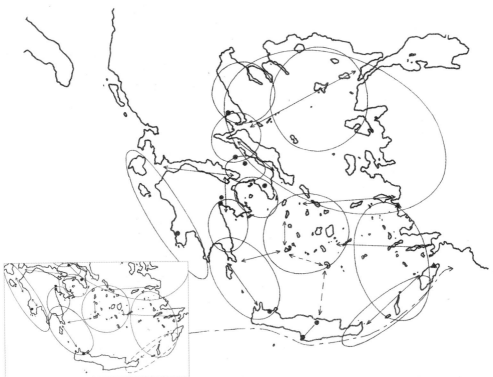

Figure 11.2: Aegean trade routes and circuits during the LBII-IIIB Early (main figure). During LB IIIB Advanced, the trade involvement of Southern and North-Central Crete diminishes, Chania being then the major trading centre of the island (box) (M. E. Alberti, F. Merlatti).

jars (probably containing olive oil) at Mycenae and Thebes in the first part of LB IIIB (Haskell *et al.* 2011) raises questions about the economic relationships and balance among the Aegean regions in this phase.

On the external Mediterranean side, the southern variant of the 'long route' between Syria and the central Mediterranean, also called the 'route of the isles', acquires renewed importance during the LB IIIA – IIIB Early (Broodbank 2013: 464–465, fig. 8.1, 8.67 and 9.1; Cline 1994: 92; Marazzi and Tusa 2005; Militello 2005), incorporating the south and east coasts of Cyprus (Enkomi, Kition, Kalavassos-Ayios Dimitrios, Alassa, Hala Sultan Tekke), the south coasts of Crete (Kommos), southern Sicily (Thapsos, Cannatello) and southern Sardinia (Antigori). In the anticlockwise pattern of Mediterranean circuits (see above), the return route from the Aegean towards Syria may have followed a series of already well-established ports on the Libyan (Marsa Matruh and Zawiyet Umm el-Rakham) and Syro-Palestinian coasts (Gaza, Ashkelon, Ashdod, Tel Nami, Tell Abu Hawam, Tel Akko, Tyre, Sarepta, Byblos), until it reached the important centre of Ugarit (Cline and Harris Cline 1998: 105–111, 137–148, 291–299; Stampolidis and Karageorghis 2003: 15–83; Laffineur and Greco 2005: 355–392). The strengthening of this more direct connection between the Levant and the central Mediterranean allows a further exchange of people, products and ideas in both directions, especially during the LB IIIA2 – B, with an intensity that gives a sense of 'globalisation', perfectly embodied by the variegated cargo of the Ulu Burun shipwreck (Sherratt 2003; Stampolidis and Karageorghis 2003: 15–83; Laffineur and Greco 2005: 355–392; Duistermaat and Regulski 2011: 183–380). On this southern route we may recognise above all materials from Cyprus, the Levant and, to a lesser extent, Crete and Sardinia (Hallager and Hallager 2003; Stampolidis and Karageorghis 2003: 15–35, 141–151; Militello 2005; Bell 2006; Shaw *et al.* 2006; Haskell *et al.* 2011; Maran and Stockhammer 2012: 32–120; Sauvage 2012). Though Mycenaean and Mycenaeanising wares become the 'fashion' of the period in the eastern Mediterranean, along with fine Cypriot tableware, it is now widely accepted that the greater part of the Aegean materials found in the Levant travelled more often via Cypriot or Levantine intermediaries rather than with Mycenaean ones (Yon *et al.* 2000; van Wijngaarden 2002; Sherratt 2003; Balensi *et al.* 2004; Laffineur and Greco 2005: 355–370). On the other hand, Levantine and Cypriot materials, though present, are less common on the northern paths of the route, especially in the Ionian and Adriatic Sea and eastern Sicily, where Aegean materials have the major share of imports / influence (Laffineur and Greco 2005: 473–652; Shaw *et al.* 2006; Blake 2008; Radina and Recchia 2010). A crucial element in fostering the growth is the full linkage of Cyprus and its export-oriented economy from the 13th century (Sherratt 2000; 2003; 2010; Gale 2011; Cadogan *et al.* 2012; Kassianidou and Papasavvas 2012). The metallurgical aspect of Cypriot production and trading initiatives has been seen as contributing to the spread of metallurgical innovations and the progressive intermingling and blending with technical traditions from the central Mediterranean and central Europe, which will take place more consistently in the following phases (Sherratt 2000; 2010; Jung 2009; Borgna 2009).

Some important changes in the internal structure of Aegean trade can be identified by the very end of the palatial period (LB IIIB2), possibly caused by definitive establishment of the core in the Mainland, and these hold true at least for the LB IIIC Early (Figure 11.2 box): judging from the distributions of imports in the Aegean for the late 13th century, the major internal sea routes seem to shift towards the north (Sherratt 2001; 2003), with the minor involvement of southern Crete (Rutter 2006), and a major role for western Crete (Chania; Hallager and Hallager 2000; 2003), the Argolid, which is as usual the hub of connection between north and south (Mycenae, Tiryns; Cline 1994; Vetters 2011; Maran 2012), and also Boeotia (Thebes; Alberti *et al.* 2012 with references) and Achaea (Giannopoulos 2008; Moschos 2009). Though Mycenae has its own share of imports in this late palatial phase, the most important

Table 11.3: *Simplified structure of the weighing system used during the Mycenaean period in the Aegean, reconstructed on the basis of the attested groups of weights. The wool unit (l) and the hypothetical smaller fractions are not illustrated.*

"Mycenaean" System (LBIIIA-B)					
	most used			*less used*	
1	L	30,000 g	1,500		
1/30	M				
	double mina	1,000 g	50		mixed counting system
1/60				Mina 500 g ca) (= 8 x = 24 k)	sexagesimal and decimal
1/70	20 k	400–440 g	20		(duodecimal only residual)
1/140	10 k	200–220 g	10		
				x 60–65 g (= 3k)	
1/1440 (1/1500)	k	20–22 g	1		

Table 11.4: *Measures of weight in Linear B. Some units known from the balance weights of the Neopalatial period (x c. 60 g, and mina c. 500 g) are not attested in the Mycenaean documents, though some examples of both are present among the LB IIIA-B weights. The absolute value of Q is still uncertain (see Alberti forthcoming for discussion). On 'light' and 'heavy' values, see Alberti 2005.*

Linear B	Lin.B Trascr.	Talent ratio	P ratio	"light" absolute value (g)	"heavy" absolute value (g)
AB *118 (talent)	L	1		29,088	31,329.6
*145 (wool unit)	LANA	1/10		2899	3132.96
*117 (double mina)	M	1/30		969.6	1044.32
*116 (half mina)	N = RO (02)	1/120	12	241	261.08
*115	P	1/1440	1	20.2	21.75
*114	Q	1/8640	1/12	3.36	3.62

concentrations of Eastern and Western items are found at the harbour-towns of Chania and Tiryns, both in pivotal positions within the trade routes (also Sherratt 2003; Jung 2009; Lis 2009; Iacono 2012). The intensification of the internal route to the central Mediterranean and Adriatic is paralleled by the increasing emergence of wealthy and warrior burials in western Achaea, which start to include imports from the Argolid, Crete and some 'Westernising' bronzes during LB IIIB2-C Early (Sherratt 2001; Rutter 2006; Borgna 2009; Moschos 2009; an alternative position is argued by Molloy, this volume). The circulation of decorated pottery from the Argolid decreases considerably, with the parallel growth of regional production (Mountjoy 1999; 2008; Georgiadis 2003; Knappett and Nikolakopoulou 2014), while the presence of Cretan transport stirrup jars on the mainland is still strong (especially at Tiryns and Mycenae, some at Thebes: Haskell *et al.* 2011). However, regional networks are affected by settlement shifts taking place in the Cyclades (Mountjoy 2008; Knappett and Nikolakopoulou 2014), the 'Interface' (Georgiadis 2003) and Crete (Wallace 2010; Borgna 2013).

During LB IIIB2/C Early, the shipwrecks of Cape Iria (Argolic Gulf) and Modi (Saronic Gulf) illustrate the importance of small- to medium- scale transport within regional circuits and, at the same time, the role of long-term connections (Phelps *et al.* 1999; Agouridis 2011). The similar case of Cape Gelidonya, off the south Anatolian coast, has been considered the best example of the widespread Mediterranean circulation and recycling of bronze in this phase (Bass 1967; Sherratt 2000; 2003).

Following the general economic trend, weighing standards become more 'international' or 'globalised' during the Mycenaean palatial period. In the Aegean, most balance weight groups of this period have both traditional Minoan/Aegean characteristics and innovative features and also include various weights representing Near Eastern units. The Mycenaean weighing system presents some innovations in relation to the Neopalatial tradition (Parise 1994; 1996; 2009; Petruso 2003; Alberti 2006; 2009; 2011a; Rahmstorf 2008a). A decimal accounting system for multiples is documented, along with the more traditional duodecimal and sexagesimal multiples and fractions of the main talent/x series. It is worth recalling that the decimal system of multiples was already in use during the EBA (see above). Major units used include the talent, the double mina, mina (only a few cases) and the wool unit, and are familiar from the previous phase. The unit x (60–65 gr) is found less frequently, while the series based on k (20 gr) becomes increasingly popular; especially as 10 k and 20 k and as fractions of k. This series based on k, integrated within the mina series, can be see to be the main series of the period (Table 11.3). This is a transformation *within* the Minoan system, more adapted to both the Helladic tradition and its Near Eastern counterpart (which was at the base of the Early Helladic weighing system, as we saw above). These new elements of the weighing system, as reconstructed from the balance weights, match from many points of view the measuring system attested in Linear B, where the unit x and the mina are not attested, and the unit used for measuring small quantities is P of *c.* 20 g (Table 11.4). The most important evidence for weights comes from Mycenae, Athens, Thebes, Tiryns and the area of Knossos. In most find groups from these sites, disc shaped weights have Aegean units, while the elongated/sphendonoid ones use Near Eastern units: see, for example, the evidence from LB IIIB Tiryns (Figure 11.3; Rahmstorf 2008a: 158–163). At Mycenae, however, beside typical Aegean weights, and a few typical Near Eastern ones, some groups of weights of Aegean type seem to be based on Near Eastern units (Alberti 2011a: 24–25, tables 10–11; Table 11.5).

One of the best examples of what may have been considered a (then) 'modern' set comes from Thebes: there, both traditional and innovative weighing assemblages are documented. The two lead discs from the 'Armoury' are not surprisingly based on the double mina **M**, according to the Minoan/Aegean tradition. On the other hand, the group of stone weights from the 'Ivory Workshop' includes one disc, two cubes and five sphendonoids: their metrological values can be ascribed respectively to the widely attested Mycenaean/Aegean **k** unit, to the main Minoan/Aegean unit **x** and to the Syrian shekel **s** (or egyptian **qdt**). However, if the group is to be seen as a working set, the mark incised on one sphendonoid seems to suggest a common unit of *c.* 20 g, i.e. again the unit **k** (Table 11.6). In this case, weights of different traditions would have been re-organised according to the local measuring system (Alberti and Aravantinos 2006).

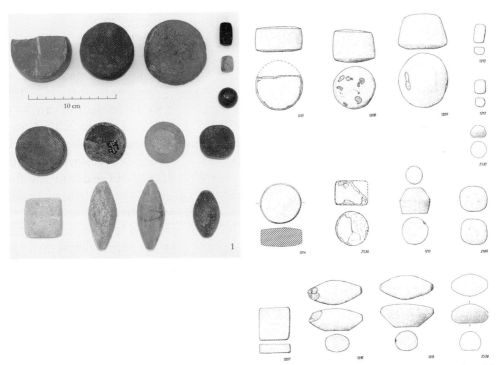

Figure 11.3: LH IIIB stone balance weights from Tiryns: disc-shaped, dome-shaped, cube, sphendonoids (elongated) (from Rahmstorf 2008 a, Taf. 57 and 93.1; courtesy of L. Rahmstorf).

Table 11.5: Aegean weighing units and weight types during LB IIIA-B.

	Aegean weights													Typology			Sets of Near Eastern weights
	Aegean units							???	Eastern units			Minas					
	f 36 g	W 50 g	k 20 g	w 5 g	x 58–66 g	M/N	Wool (z, l)	ae 6.6 g/ dbn 13.2 g	s = qdt 9.4 g	h = 11.4 g ?	mp = 8,7 g ?	Western 470–480 g	Heavy 500–579 g	d st	d ld	cb st	
Mycenae			x	x	x	x			x	?	?			x	x		x
Thebes			x	x	x	x								x	x	x	x
Tyrins					x										x		x
Athens			x		x			?	x						x	x	
Knossos					x									x			

Table 11.6: Thebes, the 'Ivory Workshop' weights as a whole set (modified from Alberti & Aravantinos 2006, Tab. V).

Weight	Type	Marks	Mass (g)	s	k	x
TH.01	sf st		4.9	½	¼	1/12
TH.02	sf st	One incised circle	19.5	2	1	1/3
TH.03	sf st		39.5	4	2	2/3
TH.04	sf st		39.7	4	2	2/3
TH.05	sf st		39.8	4	2	2/3
TH.06	cb st		57 (-)	6	3	1
TH.07	cb st		59.2 (-)	6	3	1
TH.10	d st		431.7	40	20	7

The complexity of the trading and weighing relationships of the period is reflected in the balance weights found in the two shipwrecks of Ulu Burun (end of the 14th *c.*) and Cape Gelidonya (end of the 13th *c.*). The weights from the former (Pulak 2000) include various sets based on the Syrian/Egyptian *s/qdt* (9.4 g), one set based on the Syrian *kar* (7.8 g) and another set based on the Mesopotamian *mp* (8.7 g). Two (or perhaps even four) examples can be probably considered as of Aegean type and standard, but they do not form a series (their possible values would be *k* and 3 *x*)[4]. Also interesting is the presence among the Syrian weights from Cape Gelidonya of various examples weighing 7 *s* (9.4 × 6 = 65.8 g). This is quite an unusual multiple, not commonly attested in Near Eastern sets: since the weight corresponds to the Minoan unit *x* (60–65 g), it can be suggested that these weights were expressly included because they were suitable for conversion between the Syrian and the Aegean system (Bass 1967; Parise 1971; Alberti and Parise 2005: table 11–12; Alberti 2011a).

LB IIIC–EIA: 'Western' fashions, Aegean networks and Near Eastern weights

The crisis of the Mainland palatial organisations at the transition from LB IIIB2 to LB IIIC Early, though affecting in many ways the settlement pattern and the political and socio-economic structures of Mainland polities (*e.g.* Deger-Jalkotzy and Zavadil 2003; 2007; Deger-Jalkotzy and Lemos 2006; Deger-Jalkotzy and Bächle 2009), does not seem to have had immediate repercussions on the main routes of the internal trade system, which apparently continued to be effective, with some internal modifications (Sherratt 2000; 2003; see below). In terms of cultural trends, the most characteristic trait of the period is the wide diffusion and imitation in the Aegean (and Levant) of Westernising elements (bronzes, Handmade Burnished Ware), leading to the progressive but definitive insertion of new fashions (especially for weapons and jewellery, but also pottery) into the regional codes of material culture (Harding 1984; Bouzek 1985; Sherratt 2003; Jung 2006 and 2009; Lis 2009; Rahmstorf 2011c; Iacono 2012; Molloy, this volume). The distribution of these 'Westernising' elements seems to follow a rather more diffuse and polycentric pattern than before, suggesting the existence of important settlement networks along the major trading routes: from Attica (Laurion ores still being a key-resource) the route heads west, through the Corinthian Gulf to Achaea with neighbouring regions and the Adriatic corridor (*e.g.* Aigeira, Nikoleika, Patras, Monodendri and Teichos Dymaion). The second segment of maritime activity is the sea-route from eastern Attica (*e.g.* Thorikos and Perati, very close to the Laurion/Thorikos silver sources) to the Euboean Gulf (*e.g.* from Perati to Mitrou and Kynos on the mainland side and Amarynthos and Lefkandi on the Euboean side) and the Pagasitic Gulf (Volos), all areas that were intensively settled and shared various elements of material culture (Deger-Jalkotzy and Zavadil 2003; 2007; Deger-Jalkotzy and Lemos 2006: 257–360, 465–664; Thomatos 2007; Giannopoulos 2008; Vlachopoulos 2008; Bachhuber and Roberts 2009: 22–60; Borgna and Càssola Guida 2009: 29–158; Deger-Jalkotzy and Bächle 2009; Iacono 2012; Broodbank 2013: 445–502). In many Aegean regions, settlement patterns changed throughout the period, especially in the Cyclades (Mountjoy 2008), the SE Aegean (Georgiadis 2003) and Crete (Wallace 2010; Borgna 2013): trade activities in these areas would probably vary accordingly, as has been suggested for Crete (Borgna 2013).

On the other hand, the pattern of Mediterranean interconnections that had emerged in the previous phase is substantially still valid in most aspects, even with some transformations. Cypriot, Levantine and Levantinising objects, Western and Westernising products, Mycenaean and Mycenaeanising, Late Minoan and Minoanising exports circulate along these segmented routes, engaging with the continuous transformation and hybridisation of local material cultures, in a complex mixing of strong regional identities and international blending, which paves the way to the Early Iron Age world (Sherratt 2003; Stampolidis and Karageorghis 2003: 83–101, 173–186; Borgna and Càssola Guida 2009; Karageorghis and Kouka 2011). Iron technology, though already practised on Cyprus, has only a minor role within the Aegean economy of this phase (Sherratt 2000; 2003).

In particular, during the LB IIIC Early southern Aegean internal trade circuits continue as before (Figure 11.4 box), but the involvement of Messenia diminishes in favour of the Argolid, Corinthian Gulf and Achaea (Sherratt 2001; 2003). The main trading centres are still Chania and Tiryns, which collect a number of Western and Westernising items and some Eastern imports (Hallager and Hallager 2000; Jung 2009; Rahmstorf 2011c; Vetters 2011). Westernising objects reach their widest Aegean diffusion in this phase, spreading in coastal and inland sites of the Peloponnese, Central Greece and Crete (Jung 2009; Lis 2009; Rahmstorf 2011c; Iacono 2012). The evidence from Chania is paralleled by other indicators of Cretan economic activity, such as the presence of a few Cretan transport stirrup jars at Tiryns (Maran 2005) and of a strong Cretan flavour in the pottery production of southern Italy (Borgna 2009; 2013).

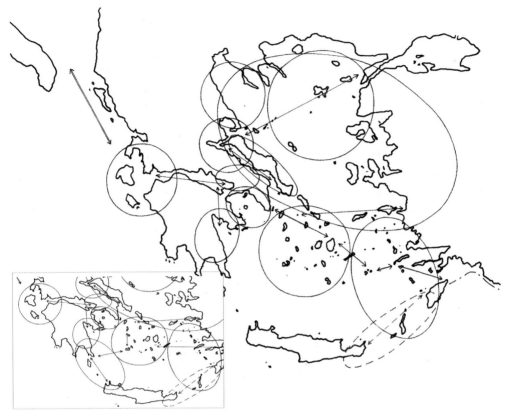

Figure 11.4: Aegean trade routes and circuits during the LB IIIB Late end the LB IIIC Early, when the involvement of Messenia diminishes in favour of the Corinthian Gulf and Achaea (box). Aegean trade routes and circuits during the LB IIIC Middle (main figure) (M. E. Alberti, F. Merlatti).

Following this period, major transformations take place during the transition to LB IIIC Middle, and are fully visible in its latest part (Advanced): the role of Crete in trading activity seems to diminish (Borgna 2009; 2013) and Cypriot connections are more evident, both in the Argolid and the south-east Aegean. The LB IIIC Middle evidence from Tiryns is a good example of this trend, with the continuing presence of Cypriot and other Eastern imports but the reduction of Cretan transport stirrup jars (Maran 2005; Vetters 2011). Southern Aegean circuits seem to acquire a new configuration (most probably following already existing routes), a network connecting Cyprus to Attica via Rhodes, Kos and Naxos, with various possible deviations (Figure 11.4). Along this route, major centres thrive and material culture is highly interconnected, especially pottery and funerary assemblages, while island products, Cypriot imports or Cypriote-related objects circulate, along with some Westernising bronzes (Cline 1994; Mountjoy 1998; 1999; Georgiadis 2003; 2009; Thomatos 2007; Vlachopoulos 2008; Benzi 2009; Knappett and Nikolakopoulou 2014). A Levantinising

Table 11.7: Aegean weighing units and weight types from LB IIIC to EIA.

	Aegean Units							???	NE Units			??	Types						
	f 36 g	*W* 50 g	*k* 20 g	*w* 5 g	*x* 58–66 g	M/N	Wool (z, l)	*ae* 6.6 g/ *dbn* 13.2 g	*s = qdt* 9.4 g	*h =* 11.4 g	*mp =* 8.7 g	*e/ necef*	d st	d ld	d br	cb st	cb br	sf st	sf br
Perati LHIIIC	?								x									x	
Lefkandi Xeropolis LHIIIC					x									x					
Lefkandi T. 79 SPGII									x		x	?						x	
Rhodes Kamiros 8th c.									x	?	x						x		x
Rhodes Kamiros 7th c.																x			
Pithekoussai 7th c.											x				x				

taste is particularly common along this route, and, assuming funerary repertoires are representative of broader trends in movement of material culture, it is quite well represented in the funerary assemblages, especially at Perati (Cypriot and Levantine pottery, jewellery, balance weights and seals and iron knives are attested), which has to be seen as one of the most important terminals or pivot-points of the Aegean trade in the period (Iakovidis 2003; Sherratt 2003). In Achaea, this is the main flourishing phase, with important long-range connections towards the central Mediterranean and the SE Aegean and a local production of Westernising bronzes (Moschos 2009).

After the end of LB IIIC Middle, evidence for trade becomes progressively rare, even though some areas are clearly still involved in regional and overseas interconnections (Sherratt 2003; Deger-Jalkotzy and Bächle 2009; Bachhuber and Roberts 2009: 22–60). When the data become sufficient again for us to begin to draw a more holistic picture, by the advanced EIA (end of the 9th and 8th c.), we again find Aegeans ('Greeks') and Cypriot-Levantines ('Phoenicians') acting on the same routes, using often the same ports (*e.g.* Kommos, Tharros, Sant' Imbenia, Carthage, and later on also Pithekoussai, Sulcis/S. Antioco, Toscano, Cadiz). By the 7th c., when proper colonisation in the central Mediterranean began according to widely accepted opinion, the previous division Aegeans/northern route and Levantines/southern route finds new archaeological visibility and territorial substance (Sherratt and Sherratt 1993).

Quite interestingly, almost no evidence for the survival of the Mycenaean weighing system is known for this (quite long) period, but Near Eastern weights do occur, even if in very low numbers, at the major Aegean trading centres. It seems then that local Aegean systems were essentially administrative tools, linked to the palatial administration, and/or that the process of evolution that had already started during Mycenaean palatial times ended with a complete 'Orientalisation' of the system. Types and units that are known are almost always of Near Eastern type, while traditional Aegean weights are not attested after LB IIIC. This may also be taken to support the suggestion that the economic leadership of the Mediterranean belonged to Cyprus, the Levant and then to Phoenicia (Table 11.7; Kroll 2008; Alberti 2011a).

It is in this framework that Greek weighing systems and then coinages were shaped in the first centuries of the 1st millennium BC. And so, it is highly possible that the origins of many Greek weighing measures, which are at the base of the subsequent coinages, are based on Near Eastern standards. We can see this, for example, in the balance weight from Pithekoussai, the first Greek settlement in the Central Mediterranean (from levels of the early 7th cent.). This is considered to be an 'Euboic stater', but, to our eyes, it is a Mesopotamian shekel (8.7 g) (Ridgway 1984: 108–109; Parise 2006). To some extent, then, a parallel can be traced with the history of the writing systems in the Aegean.

Explanatory note and acknowledgements

The present text is a short overview (with reduced references) of the most recent developments in the field of southern Aegean trade and metrology, ideally to be read alongside the contribution of L. Rahmstorf, this volume. For a wider discussion and full bibliography, see Alberti *et al.* 2006; Michailidou 2008; 2010; Alberti 2009; 2011a; 2011b; 2012. On measure and ancient societies, see recently Morley and Renfrew 2010. Relative chronological phases are mainly designed as EBA, MBA, LBA, to cover all the Aegean areas: however, in some cases regional chronologies are adopted as well (i.e. EC, EM, EH, *etc.*). All dates are Before the Common Era. The temporal and geographical scope of the paper has required the use of many iterances of '-isation' which are accepted as a debated concept, though it is impractical to place all posited terms in inverted commas.

I especially wish to thank Barry Molloy for his help with this text, both for the language and the contents, which considerably improved the final outcome. My thanks also go to John Bennet, Lorenz Rahmstorf and Susan Sherratt for their comments and suggestions on a first draft of this paper. I am also grateful to Elisabetta Borgna, Carl Knappett and Irene Nikolakopoulou for permission to read and quote from their unpublished works, to Lorenz Rahmstorf for the images of the Tiryns weights, and to Luca Girella and Peter Pavúk for valuable information on the Mikro Vouni excavation. I am obviously the only one responsible for any remaining errors.

Notes

1. I wish to thank Lorenz Rahmstorf for bringing to my attention the existence of lead discs at Old Assyrian (i.e. roughly contemporary with the Proto-palatial period) Karum Kanesh (Özgüç 1986: 77–78, figs. 62–63, pl. 130, 1–6; comments in Michailidou 2004). More study and reflection on this evidence is needed before any conclusion can be reached. On the Aegean side, the presence of at least one weight of 65 g from EB Tiryns, which from the context has to be interpreted as 7 *s*, may perhaps suggest that this mass was not unknown in the previous EB Aegean (Rahmstorf 2006a: 27, fig. 4). EB Cycladic documentation also needs re-examination.
2. See *e.g.* the import and local manufacture of Cypriot pottery in Trianda on Rhodes (Marketou *et al.* 2006), the metal ingots and other *exotica* from Kato Zakros (Platon 1971), Mochlos (Soles 2005) and Poros – Katsambas (Dimopoulou–Rethemiotaki 2004) on Crete.
3. In some cases, Aegean weights can be used also according to Near Eastern units: *e.g.* lead discs of 48 g are to be considered from the context as ¾ *x*, but they can mathematically also be 5 *s* (for such correspondences, see Alberti 2011a: 21, tab. 4).
4. Respectively lead discs W 60 and W 111 in Pulak 2000, where they are considered as Near Eastern multiples; other reported lead discs W 108 and W 109 are damaged. It would be quite significant to have a sample standard of the "Mycenaean" *k* among the ship weights, especially considering the few actual hints of the use of a double shekel (2 *s* or 2 *h*) in Ugarit at the same time (Bordreuil 2006: 222).

References
Agouridis, Ch. S.
1997 Sea-routes and Navigation in the Third Millennium Aegean. *Oxford Journal of Archaeology* 16(1): 1–24.
2011 The Late Bronze Age Shipwreck off the islet of Modi (Poros). *Skyllis* 11(2): 25–34.

Alberti, M. E.
1995 Ayia Irini : Les poids de balance dans leur contexte. *Quaderni Ticinesi di Numismatica e Antichità Classiche* 25: 9–37.
2003 Weighing and dyeing between East and West: weighing materials from funerary contexts in the Late Bronze Age Aegean. In Polinger Foster and Laffineur 2003: 277–284.
2005 I sistemi ponderali dell'Egeo nell'età del Bronzo. Studi, storia, pratica e contatti. *Annuario della Scuola di Atene* LXXXI, serie III, 3, 2003/II (2005): 597–640.
2006 Changing in time: some aspects of the Aegean and Cypriot balance weights. In Alberti *et al.* 2006: 315–340.
2009 Pesi e traffici: influenze orientali nei sistemi ponderali egei nel corso dell'età del bronzo. In F. Camia and S. Privitera (eds.), *Obeloi. Contatti, scambi e valori nel Mediterraneo antico. Studi offerti a Nicola Parise* (Tekmeria 11): 13–41. Paestum – Athens: Pandemos.
2011a La levantinizzazione dei sistemi ponderali nell'Egeo dell'età del Bronzo. In Ascalone and Peyronel 2011: 1–42.
2011b Redistribuzione e commercio? Il sistema di traffici miceneo, in N. Parise, M. E. Alberti, C. Martinelli, Reciprocità e ridistribuzione: modelli meccanici e modelli statistici. In V. Nizzo (ed.), *Dalla nascita alla morte: antropologia e archeologia a confronto, Atti dell'Incontro Internazionale di Studi in onore di Claude Lévi - Strauss, Roma 21 maggio 2010*: 346–359. Rome: Editoriale Service System s.r.l.
2012 Aegean Trade Systems. Overview and Observations on the Middle Bronze Age. In Alberti and Sabatini 2012: 22–43.
forthcoming *I sistemi di misura micenei*. In M. Del Freo and M. Perna (eds.), *Introduzione allo studio dei testi in lineare B*, Napoli, in press.

Alberti, M. E. and V. Aravantinos
2006 The balance weights from the Kadmeia, Thebes. In Alberti *et al.* 2006: 293–314.

Alberti, M.E., V. Aravantinos, M. Del Freo, Y. Fappas, A. Papadaki and F. Rougemont
2012 Textile Production in Mycenaean Thebes. A First Overview. In Nosch and Laffineur 2012: 87–105.

Alberti, M. E., E. Ascalone and L. Peyronel (eds.)
2006 *Weights in Contexts. Bronze Age Weighing Systems of Eastern Mediterranean. Chronology, Typology, Material and Archaeological Contexts. Proceedings of the International Colloquium Rome 22nd - 24th November 2004* (Studi e Materiali 13). Rome: Istituto Italiano di Numismatica.

Alberti, M. E. and N. Parise
2005 Towards a unification of mass-units between the Aegean and the Levant. In Laffineur and Greco 2005: 383–390.

Alberti, M. E. and S. Sabatini (eds.)
2012 *Exchange Networks and Local Transformations. Interaction and Local Change in Europe and the Mediterranean from the Bronze Age to the Iron Age*. Oxford: Oxbow.

Alram Stern, E.
2011 Kreta und die Kykladen. Zu den Außenbeziehungen Kretas wärend Frühminoische IB und II. In F. Blakolmer, C. Reinholdt, J. Weilhartner, and G. Nightingale (eds.), *Österreichische Forschungen zur Ägaischen Bronzezeit 2009. Akten der Tagung vom 6. Bis 7. März 2009 am Fachbereich Altertumswissenschaften der Universität Salzburg*: 31–40. Wien: Verlag der Österreichischen Akademie der Wissenschaften.

Ascalone, E., and L. Peyronel
2007 *I pesi da bilancia del bronzo antico e del bronzo medio* (Materiali e studi archeologici di Ebla VII). Rome: Università degli Studi di Roma La Sapienza.
2011 *Studi italiani di metrologia ed economia del Vicino Oriente Antico dedicati a Nicola Parise in occasione del suo settantesimo compleanno* (Studia Asiana 7). Roma: Herder.

Bachhuber, Ch. and R. G. Roberts (eds.)
2009 *Forces of Transformation. The End of the Bronze Age in the Mediterranean. Proceedings of an international symposium held at St. John's College, University of Oxford, 25-26th March 2006* (Themes from the Ancient Near East BANEA Publication Series, vol. 1). Oxford: Oxbow.

Balensi, J., J.-Y. Monchambert and S. Müller-Celka (eds.)
2004 *La céramique mycénienne de l'Egée au Lévant. Hommage a Vronwy Hankey* (Travaux de la Maison de l'Orient et de la Méditerranée 41). Lyon: Maison de l'Orient et de la Méditerranée.

Barrett, C. E.
2009 The perceived value of Minoan and minoanizing pottery in Egypt. *Journal of Mediterranean Archaeology* 22(2): 211–234.

Bass, G. F.
1967 Cape Gelidonya: A Bronze Age Shipwreck. *Transactions of the American Philosophical Society 57(8)*. Philadelphia: American Philosophical Society.

Beckman, G., T. Bryce and E.H. Cline
2011 *The Ahhiyawa texts. Writings from the Ancient World*. Atlanta, GA: Society of Biblical Literature.

Bell, C.
2006 *The Evolution of Long Distance Trading Relationships across the LBA/Iron Age Transition on the Northern Levantine Coast. Crisis, Continuity and Change. A Study Based on Imported Ceramics, Bronze and Its Constituent Metals* (BAR IS 1574). Oxford: British Archaeological Reports.

Bennet, J.
2011 The Geography of the Mycenaean Kingdoms. In Y. Duhoux and A. Morpurgo Davies (eds.), *A Companion to Linear B: Mycenaean Greek Texts and their World*, Vol. 2: 137–168. Leuven: Peeters.

Benzi, M.
2009 LB III Trade in the Dodecanese: An Overview. In Borgna and Càssola Guida 2009: 47–62.

Berg, I.
1999 The Southern Aegean System. *Journal of World - Systems Research*, vol. V.3: 475–484.
2007 *Negotiating island identities. The active use of pottery in the Middle and Late Bronze Age Cyclades* (Gorgias Dissertation 31 Classics 5). Piscataway NJ: Gorgias Press.

Bevan, A.
2002 The Rural Landscape of Neopalatial Kythera: A GIS Perspective. *Journal of Mediterranean Archaeology* 15(2): 217–255.

Blake, E.
2008 The Mycenaeans in Italy: a minimalist position. *Papers of the British School at Rome* 76: 1–34.

Bordreuil, E.
2006 Preliminary consideration for a typology of the weights of the Late Bronze Age discovered at Ras Shamra – Ugarit. Archaeological and textual data. In Alberti *et al.* 2006. 203–232.

Borgna, E.
2009 Patterns of bronze circulation and deposition in the Northern Adriatic at the close of the Late Bronze Age. In Borgna and Càssola Guida 2009: 289–309.
2013 Di periferia in periferia. Italia, Egeo e Mediterraneo orientale ai tempi della koinè metallurgica: una proposta di lettura diacronica. *Rivista di Scienze Preistoriche* 63: 123–151.

Borgna, E. and P. Càssola Guida (eds.)
2009 *Dall'Egeo all'Adriatico: organizzazioni sociali, modi di scambio e interazione in età postpalaziale (XII-XI secolo a.C.), Atti del Seminario internazionale (Udine, 1-2 dicembre 2006)* (Studi e ricerche di protostoria mediterranea 8). Rome: Quasar.

Bouzek, J.
1985 *The Aegean, Anatolia and Europe: Cultural Interrelations in the Second Millennium B.C.* (Studies in Mediterranean Archeology 29). Göteborg – Prague: Äström.

Brodie, N., J. Doole, G. Gavalas and C. Renfrew (eds.)
2008 *Horizon 'Ορίζων. A colloquium on the prehistory of the Cyclades* (McDonald Institute Monographs). Cambridge: McDonald Institute for Archaeological Research.

Brogan, T. M.
2006 Tipping the scales: evidence for weight measurement from the wider neopalatial community at Mochlos. In Alberti *et al.* 2006: 233–264.

Broodbank, C.
2000 *An Island Archaeology of the Early Cyclades*, Cambridge: Cambridge University Press.
2004 Minoanisation. *Proceedings of the Cambridge Philological Society* 50: 46–91.
2013 *The Making of the Middle Sea. A History of the Mediterranean from the Beginning to the Emergence of the Classical World.* London: Thames and Hudson.

Broodbank, C. and E. Kiriatzi
2007 The first Minoan of Kythera revisited: technology, demography, and landscape in the prepalatial Aegean. *American Journal of Archaeology* 111(2): 241–274.

Broodbank, C., E. Kiriatzi and J. Rutter
2005 From Pharaoh's feet to the slave-woman of Pylos? The history and cultural dynamics of Kythera in the Third Palace Period. In Dakouri-Hild and Sherratt 2005: 71–96.

Brumfiel, E.M. and T.K. Earle
1987 Specialization, exchange and complex societies: an introduction. In E.M. Brumfiel and T.K. Earle (eds.), Specialization, exchange and complex societies: 1–9. Cambridge: University Press.

Brysbaert, A.
2008 *The power of technology in the Bronze Age eastern Mediterranean: the case of the painted plaster* (Monographs in Mediterranean Archaeology 12). London – Oakville, CT: Equinox Publishing Ltd.

Cadogan, G., E. Hatzaki and A. Vasilakis (eds.)

2004 *Knossos: Palace, City, State. Proceedings of the Conference in Herakleion organised by the British School at Athens and the 23rd Ephoreia of Prehistoric and Classical Antiquities of Herakleion, in November 2000, for the Centenary of sir Arthur Evans's Excavations at Knossos* (BSA Studies 12): 311–321. London: British School at Athens.

Cadogan, G., M. Iacovou, K. Kopaka and J. Whitley (eds.)

2012 *Parallel lives. Ancient island societies in Crete and Cyprus. Papers arising from the Conference in Nicosia organised by the British School at Athens, the University of Crete and the University of Cyprus, in November-December 2006* (BSA Studies 20). London: British School at Athens.

Cherry, J.F.

2010 Sorting Out Crete's Prepalatial Off-Island Interaction. In Parkinson and Galaty 2010: 107–140.

Clancier, Ph., F. Joannès, P. Rouillard and A. Tenu (eds.)

2005 *Autour de Polanyi. Vocabulaires, théories et modalités des échanges.* Paris: de Boccard.

Cline, E. H.

1994 *Sailing the Wine-Dark Sea. International Trade and the Late Bronze Age Aegean* (BAR IS 591). Oxford: British Archaeological Reports.

2007 Rethinking Mycenaean international trade with Egypt and the Near East. In Galaty and Parkinson 2007: 190–200.

Cline, E. H. and D. Harris-Cline (eds.)

1998 *The Aegean and the Orient in the Second Millennium, Proceedings of the 50th Anniversary Simposium, Cincinnati 18-20 April 1997* (Aegaeum 18). Liège: Université de Liège.

Cutler, J.

2012 Ariadne's thread: the adoption of Cretan weaving technology in the wider southern Aegean in the mid-second millennium BC. In Nosch and Laffineur 2012: 145–154.

D'Agata, A. L. and J. Moody (eds.)

2005 *Ariadne's Threads. Connections between Crete and the Greek Mainland in Late Minoan III (LMIIIA2 to LMIIIC). Proceedings of the International Workshop held at Athens, Scuola Archeologica Italiana, 5-6 April 2003* (Tripodes 3). Athens: Scuola Archeologica Italiana di Atene.

Dakouri-Hild, A. and S. Sherratt (eds.)

2005 *Autochthon. Papers presented to O.T.P.K. Dickinson on the occasion of his retirement* (BAR IS 1432). Oxford: British Archaeological Reports.

Davis, J. L.

1979 Minos and Dexithea. Crete and the Cyclades in the Later Bronze Age. In J. L. Davis and J. F. Cherry (eds.), *Papers in Cycladic Prehistory*: 143–157. Los Angeles: University of California Press.

2008 Minoan Crete and the Aegean Islands. In Shelmerdine 2008: 186–208.

Davis J. L. and J. F. Cherry

1990 Spatial and temporal uniformitariansim in Late Cycladic I: perspectives from Kea and Milos on the prehistory of Akrotiri. In Hardy *et al.* 1990: 185–200.

Davis, J. L, and E. Gorogianni
2008 Potsherds from the Edge: The Construction of Identities and the Limits of Minoanized Areas of the Aegean. In Brodie *et al.* 2008: 339–348.

Day, P. M., P. S. Quinn, J. B. Rutter and V. Kilikoglou
2011 A world of goods: transport jars and commodity exchange at the Late Bronze Age harbor of Kommos, Crete. *Hesperia* 80(4): 511–558.

Deger-Jalkotzy, S. and A. E. Bächle (eds.)
2009 *LHIIIC Chronology and Synchronisms III. LHIIIC Late and the Transition to the Early Iron Age. Proceedings of the International Workshop held at the Austrian Academy of Sciences at Vienna, February 23rd and 24th, 2007.* Wien: Verlag der Österreichischen Akademie der Wissenschaften.

Deger-Jalkotzy, S. and I. S. Lemos (eds.)
2006 *Ancient Greece: from the Mycenaean Palaces to the Age of Homer* (Edinburgh Leventis Studies 3). Edinburgh: Edinburgh University Press.

Deger-Jalkotzy, S. and M. Zavadil (eds.)
2003 *LHIIIC Chronology and Synchronisms. Proceedings of the International Workshop held at the Austrian Academy of Sciences at Vienna, May 7th and 8th, 2001.* Wien: Verlag der Österreichischen Akademie der Wissenschaften.
2007 *LHIIIC Chronology and Synchronisms II. LHIIIC Middle. Proceedings of the International Workshop held at the Austrian Academy of Sciences at Vienna, October 29th and 30th, 2004.* Wien: Verlag der Österreichischen Akademie der Wissenschaften.

Dimopoulou-Rethemiotaki, N.
2004 Το επίνειο της Κνωσσού στον Πόρο – Κατσαμπά. In Cadogan *et al.* 2004: 363–380.

Duistermaat, K. and I. Regulski (eds.)
2011 *Intercultural Contacts in the Ancient Mediterranean. Proceedings of the International Conference at the Netherlands-Flemish Institute in Cairo, 25th to 29th October 2008* (Orientalia Lovaniensia Analecta 202). Leuven – Paris – Walpole MA: Peeters Publishers and Department of Oriental Studies.

Evans, A. J.
1906 Minoan Weights and Minoan Currency from Crete, Mycenae and Cyprus. In *Corolla Numismatica: Numismatic Essays in Honour of Barclay V. Head*: 336–367. Oxford.

Faust, A. and E. Weiss,
2011 Between Assyria and the Mediterranean world: the prosperity of Judah and Philistia in the seventh century BCE in context. In Wilkinson *et al.* 2011: 189–204.

Felten, F., W. Gauß and R. Smetana (eds.)
2007 *Middle Helladic Pottery and Synchronisms. Proceedings of the International Workshop held at Salzburg October 31st - November 2nd, 2004* (Ägina-Kolonna Forschungen und Ergebnisse I, Contributions to the Chronology of the Eastern Mediterranean XIV, ÖAW Denkschriften der Gesamtakademie XLII). Wien: Verlag der Österreichischen Akademie der Wissenschaften.

Galaty, M. L. and W. A. Parkinson (eds.)
2007 *Rethinking Mycenaean Palaces II* (The Cotsen Institute of Archaeology University of California, Los Angeles Monograph 60). Los Angeles: University of California.

Gale, N. H.
2011 Copper oxhide ingots and lead isotope provenancing. In Ph. P. Betancourt and S. C. Ferrence
    (eds.), *Metallurgy: Understanding How, Learning Why. Studies in Honor of James D. Muhly* (Prehistory
    Monographs 29): 213–220. Philadelphia PA: INSTAP Academic Press.

Gale, N.H. (ed.)
1991 *Bronze Age Trade in the Mediterranean. Papers presented at the Conference held at Rewley House,
    Oxford, in December 1989* (Studies in Mediterranean Archeology 90). Jonsered: Äström.

Georgiadis, M.
2003 *The South-Eastern Aegean in the Mycenaean period. Islands, landscape, death and ancestors* (BAR IS
    1196). Oxford: British Archaeological Reports.
2009 The South-Eastern Aegean in the LHIIIC Period: What do the tombs tell us? In Bachhuber
    and Roberts 2009: 92–99.

Gestoso Singer, G.
2010 Forms of payment in the Amarna Age and in the Ulu Burun and Cape Gelidonya shipwrecks.
    Ugarit Forschungen 42: 261–277.

Giannopoulos, Th. G.
2008 *Die letzte Elite der mykenischen Welt. Achaia in mykenischer Zeit und das Phänomen der
    Kriegerbestattungen im 12.-11. Jahrhundert v.Chr.* (Universität Forschungen zur prähistorischen
    Archäologie Heidelberg 152). Bonn: R. Habelt.

Girella, L. and P. Pavúk
2015 Minoanisation, Acculturation, Hybridisation: the evidence of the Minoan presence in the NE
    Aegean between Middle and Late Bronze Age. In N. Chr. Stampolidis (ed.), *Migration and Integration
    in the Aegean Islands and Western Anatolia during the Late Bronze and Early Iron Age. Istanbul 31 March – 3
    April 2011*: 387–340. Instanbul: Koç University Press.

Gleba, M. and J. Cutler
2012 Textile production in Bronze Age Miletus. First observations. In Nosch and Laffineur 2012:
    113–119.

Graziadio, G.
2005 The Relations between the Aegean and Cyprus at the beginning of Late Bronze Age: an overview
    of the archaeological evidence. In Laffineur and Greco 2005: I, 323–334.

Hägg, R. and N. Marinatos (eds.)
1984 *The Minoan Thalassocracy. Myth and Reality, Proceedings of the Third International Symposium at the
    Swedish Institute in Athens, 31 May-15 June 1982* (Skrifter utgivna av Svenska Institutet i Athen 4o
    32). Stockholm: Svenska Institutet i Aten.

Hallager, E. and B. P. Hallager (eds.),
2000 *The Greek-Swedish Excavations at the Agia Aikaterini Square, Kastelli, Khania, 1970-1987, Vol. II, The
    Late Minoan III C Settlement* (Skrifter utgivna av Svenska Institutet i Athen 4° 47/2). Stockholm:
    Svenska Institutet i Aten; Sävedalen: P. Åström.
2003 *The Greek-Swedish Excavations at the Agia Aikaterini Square, Kastelli, Khania, 1970-1987 and 2001.
    Vol. III, The Late Minoan IIIB:2 Settlement* (Skrifter utgivna av Svenska Institutet i Athen 4° 47/3 i-ii).
    Stockholm: Svenska Institutet i Aten; Sävedalen: P. Åström.

Harding, A. F.
1984 *The Mycenaeans and Europe*. London: Academic Press.

Hardy, D. A., C. G. Doumas, J. A. Sakellarakis, and P. M. Warren (eds.)
1990 *Thera and the Aegean World III. Proceedings of the Third International Congress, Santorini, Greece, 3–9 September 1989*: vol. I Archaeology. London: The Thera Foundation.

Haskell, H. W., R. E. Jones, P. M. Day and J. T. Killen (eds.)
2011 *Transport Stirrup Jars of the Bronze Age Aegean and East Mediterranean*. Philadelphia: INSTAP Academic Press.

Højen Sørensen, A.
2009 Approaching Levantine shores. Aspects of Cretan contacts with western Asia during the MM – LM I period. *Proceedings of the Danish Institute at Athens 6*: 9–56.

Hope Simpson, R.
2003 The Dodecanese and the Ahhiyawa question. *Annual of the British School at Athens 98*: 203–298.

Iacono, F.
2012 Westernizing Aegean of LH IIIC. In Alberti and Sabatini 2012: 60–79.

Iakovidis, Sp.
2003 Late Mycenaean Perati and the Levant. In M. Bietak (ed.), *The Synchronisation of Civilisations in the Eastern Mediterranean in the Second Millennium BC II, Proceedings of the SCIEM 2000 - Euroconference, Haindorf, 2nd of May - 7th of May 2001* (Contributions to the Chronology of the Eastern Mediterranean IV): 501–513. Wien: Verlag der Österreichischen Akademie der Wissenschaften.

Jung, R.
2006 *ΧΡΟΝΟΛΟΓΙΑ COMPARATA. Vergleichende Chronologie von Südgriechenland und Süditalien von ca. 1700/1600 bis 1000 v.u.Z.*, Wien.
2009 I 'bronzi internazionali' e il loro contesto sociale fra Adriatico, pensiola balcanica e coste levantine. In Borgna and Càssola Guida 2009: 129–157.

Karageorghis, V. and Ou. Kouka (eds.)
2011 *On Cooking Pots, Drinking Cups, Loomweights and Ethnicity in Bronze Age Cyprus and Neighbouring Regions: An International Archaeological Symposium held in Nicosia, November 6th-7th 2010*. Nicosia: A.G. Leventis Foundation.

Kardulias, N.
2010 World-Systems applications for understanding the Bronze Age in the Eastern Mediterranean. In Parkinson and Galaty 2010: 53–80.

Karetsou, A. (ed.)
2000 *Κρήτη-Αίγυπτος. Πολιτισμικοί δεσμόι τριών χιλιετιών*. Herakleion: Υπουργείο Πολιτισμού.

Kassianidou, V. and G. Papasavvas (eds.)
2012 *Eastern Mediterranean metallurgy and metalwork in the second millennium BC. A conference in honour of James D. Muhly, Nicosia, 10th-11th October 2009*. Oxford: Oxbow Books.

Kiriatzi, E.

2010 "Minoanising" Pottery Traditions in southwest Aegean during the Middle Bronze Age: Understanding the Social Context of Technological and consumption Practice. In Philippa – Touchais *et al.* 2010, 683–699.

Knapp, A. B.

1998 Mediterranean Bronze Age trade: distance, power and place. In Cline and Harris Cline 1998: 193–205.

Knappett, C.

2011 *An Archaeology of Interaction. Network Perspectives on Material Culture and Society.* Oxford: Oxford University Press.

Knappett, C., T. Evans, and R. Rivers

2008 Modelling maritime interaction in the Aegean Bronze Age. *Antiquity* 82: 1009–1024.

Knappett, C. and I. Nikolakopoulou

2008 Colonialism without colonies? A Bronze Age case study from Akrotiri, Thera. *Hesperia* 77(1): 1–42.

2014 Inside Out? Materiality and Connectivity in the Aegean Archipelago. In A. B. Knapp and P. van Dommelen (eds.), *Cambridge Handbook of the Mediterranean World in the Bronze-Iron Ages:* 25–39. Cambridge: Cambridge University Press.

Kohl, Ph. L.

2011 Worlds-systems and modelling macro-historical process in later prehistory: an examination of old and a search for new perspectives. In Wilkinson *et al.* 2011: 77–86.

Kroll, J. H.

2008 Early Iron Age balance weights at Lefkandi, Euboea. *Oxford Journal of Archaeology* 27 (1): 37–48.

Kula, W.

1986 *Measures and men.* Princeton; Guildford: Princeton University Press.

Laffineur, R. and E. Greco (eds.)

2005 *Emporia. Aegeans in the Central and Eastern Mediterranean, Proceedings of the 10th International Aegean Conference, Athens, Italian School of Archaeology, 14-18 April 2004* (Aegaeum 25). Liège and Austin: Université de Liège and University of Texas at Austin.

Langohr, Ch.

2009 *ΠΕΡΙΦΕΡΕΙΑ. Étude régionale de la Crète aux Minoen Récent II-IIIB (1450 - 1200 av. J.-C.) 1. La Crète centrale et occidentale* (Aegis 3). Louvain-la Neuve: Presses universitaires de Louvain.

Legarra Herrero, B.

2011 New kid on the block: the nature of the first systemic contacts between Crete and the Eastern Mediterranean around 2000 B.C. In Wilkinson *et al.* 2011: 266–281.

Lis, B.

2009 Handmade and Burnished pottery in the eastern Mediterranean at the end of the Bronze Age: towards an explanation for its diversity and geographical distribution. In Bachhuber and Roberts 2009: 152–163.

Liverani, M.
1998 *Uruk la prima città*. Rome-Bari: Laterza.

Lolos, Y. G.
2009 Salamis ca 1200 B.C.: connections with Cyprus and the East. In Borgna and Càssola Guida 2009: 29–46.

Macdonald, C. F., E. Hallager and W.-D. Niemeier (eds.)
2009 *The Minoans in the central, eastern and northern Aegean – new evidence. Acts of a Minoan Seminar 22-23 January 2005 in collaboration with the Danish Institute at Athens and the German Archaeological Institute at Athens* (Monographs of the Danish Institute at Athens 8). Athens: The Danish Institute at Athens.

MacGillivray, J. A.
2013 Absolute Middle Minoan III — the bigger picture: early Neopalatial Crete's relations with the ancient Orient in the mid-second millennium B.C. In C. F. Macdonald and C. Knappett (eds.), *Intermezzo. Intermediacy and Regeneration in Middle Minoan III Palatial Crete* (BSA Studies 21): 221–224. London: British School at Athens.

Maran, J.
2005 Late Minoan coarse ware stirrup jars on the Greek Mainland. A postpalatial perspective from the 12th century B.C. Argolid. In D'Agata and Moody 2005: 415–431.
2006 Coming to terms with the past: ideology and power in Late Helladic IIIC. In Deger-Jalkotzy and Lemos 2006: 123–150.
2011 Lost in translation: the emergence of the Mycenaean culture as a phenomenon of glocalization. In Wilkinson *et al.* 2011: 282–294.
2012 Ceremonial feasting equipment, social space and interculturality in Post-Palatial Tiryns. In Maran and Stockhammer 2012: 121–136.

Maran, J. and Ph. W. Stockhammer (eds.)
2012 *Materiality and Social Practice: Transformative Capacities of Intercultural Encounters*. Oxford and Oakville: Oxbow Books.

Marazzi, M. and S. Tusa
2005 Egei in Occidente. Le più antiche vie marittime alla luce dei nuoi scavi sull'isola di Pantelleria. In Laffineur and Greco 2005: II, 599–610.

Marketou, T.
2009 Ialysos and its neighbouring areas in the MBA and LBI period: a chance for peace. In Macdonald *et al.* 2009: 73–96.

Marketou, T., E. Karantzali, H. Mommsen, N. Zacharias, V. Kilikoglou, and A. Schwedt
2006 Pottery Wares from the prehistoric settlement at Ialysos (Trianda) in Rhodes. *Annual of the British School at Athens* 101: 1–55.

Mathioudaki, I.
2010 "Mainland Polychrome" Pottery: Definition, Chronology, Typological Correlations. In Philippa-Touchais *et al.* 2010, 621–633.

Matsas, D.
1991 Samothrace and the north-eastern Aegean: the Minoan connection. *Studia Troica* I: 159–180.
2009 The Minoan in Samothrace. Abstract and bibliography. In Macdonald *et al.*: 251.

Melas, M.
2009 The Afiartis Project: excavations at the Minoan settlement at Fournoi, Karpathos (2001–2004) –
     a preliminary report. In Macdonald *et al.* 2009: 59–72.

Michailidou, A.
1990 The Lead weights from Akrotiri: The archaeoogical record. In Hardy *et al.* 1990: 407–419.
2004 On the Minoan economy: a tribute to "Minoan weights and mediums of currency" by Arthur
     Evans. In Cadogan *et al.* 2004: 311–321.
2006 Stone balance weights? The evidence from Akrotiri on Thera. In Alberti *et al.* 2006: 233–263.
2007 Σταθμὰ. In Chr. G. Doumas (ed.), *Ακρωτήρι Θήρας. Δυτική Οικία. Τράπεζες – Λίθινα – Μετάλλινα –
     Ποικίλα*: 200–230. Athens: Η εν Αθήναις Αρχαιολογική Εταιρεία.
2008 *Weight and Value in Pre-Coinage Societies II. Sidelights on Measurement from the Aegean and the
     Orient* (ΜΕΛΕΤΗΜΑΤΑ 61). Athens: Athens: National Hellenic Research Foundation and Research
     Centre for Greek and Roman Antiquity.
2010 Measuring by weight in the Late Bronze Age Aegean: the people behind the measuring tools.
     In Morley and Renfrew 2010: 71–87.

Milano, L. and N. Parise (eds.)
2003 *Il regolamento degli scambi nell'antichità (III-I millennio a.C.)*. Rome – Bari: Laterza.

Militello, P.
2005 Mycenaean palaces and western trade: a problematic relationship. In Laffineur and Greco
     2005: II, 585–595.

Momigliano, N.
2012 Bronze Age Carian Iasos. Structures and Finds from the Area of the Roman Agora
     (*c.* 3000–1500 BC). Roma: Giorgio Bretschneider.

Morley, I. and C. Renfrew (eds.)
2010 *The Archaeology of Measurement: Comprehending Heaven, Earth and Time in Ancient Societies.*
     Cambridge: Cambridge University Press.

Moschos, I.
2009 Evidence of social re-organization and reconstruction in Late Helladic IIIC Achaea and
     modes of contacts and exchange via Ionian and Adriatic sea. In Borgna and Càssola Guida
     2009: 345–414.

Mountjoy, P. A.
1998 The East Aegean – West Anatolia Interface in the Late Bronze Age: Mycenaeans and the
     Kingdom of Ahhiyawa. *Anatolian Studies* 48: 33–69.
1999 *Regional Mycenaean Decorated Pottery*. Rahden/Westf: Leidorf.
2004 Knossos and the Cyclades in Late Minoan IB. In Cadogan *et al.* 2004: 399–404.
2008 The Cyclades during the Mycenaean period. In Brodie *et al.* 2008: 467–478.

Mountjoy, P. A. and M. J. Ponting
2000 The Minoan thalassocracy reconsidered: provenance studies of LH II A/LM I B pottery from Phylakopi, Ayia Irini and Athens. *Annual of the British School at Athens* 95: 141–184.

Mühlenbruch T.
2009 Tiryns – the settlement and its history in LHIIIC. In Deger-Jalkotzy and Bächle 2009: 313–326.

Muhly, J.
2003 Trade in Metals in the Late Bronze Age and Iron Age. In Stampolidis and Karagerorghis 2003: 141–150.

Niemeier, W. -D.
1984 The end of the Minoan Thalassocracy. In Hägg and Marinatos 1984: 205–214.

Nosch, M.-L. and R. Laffineur (eds.)
2012 *Kosmos. Jewellery, Adornment and Textiles in the Aegean Bronze Age. Proceedings of the 13th Aegean International Conference, University of Copenhagen, Danish National Research Foundation's Centre for Textile Research, 21-26 April 2010* (Aegaeum 33). Leuven: Peeters.

Overbeck, J. C. and D. M. Crego
2008 The commercial foundation and development of Ayia Irini IV (Kea). In Brodie *et al.* 2008: 305–310.

Özgüç, T.
1986 *Kültepe-Kaniş II. Eski yakındoğu'nun ticaret merkezinde yeni araştırmalar/ New researches at the trading center of the Ancient Near East* (Turk Tarih Kurumu Yayınları V. Dizi – Sa. 41). Ankara: Türk Tarih Kurumu Basimevi.

Pakkanen, J.
2011 Aegean Bronze Age Weights, Châines Opératoires and the Detecting of Patterns through Statoistical Analyses. In A. Brysbaert (ed.), *Tracing Prehistoric Social Networks through Technology: A Diachronic Perspective on the Aegean* (Routledge Studies in Archaeology 3): 143–166. London and New York: Routledge.

Papadimitriou, A.
2006 The Early Iron Age in the Argolid: Some new aspects. In Deger-Jalkotzy and Lemos 2006: 531–548.

Papadimitriou, N. and D. Kriga
2012 "Periphery versus core". The integration of secondary states into the World System of the Eastern Mediterranean and the Near East in the Late Bronze Age (1600–1200 BC). In Alberti and Sabatini 2012: 9–21.

Papageorgiou, D.
2008 Sea Routes in the Prehistoric Cyclades. In Brodie *et al.* 2008: 9–12.

Pare, C. F. (ed.)
2000 *Metals Make the World Go Round. The Supply and Circulation of Metals in Bronze Age Europe, Proceedings of a Conference held at the University of Birmingham in June 1997.* Oxford: Oxbow Books.

Parise, N. F.

1971 Un'unità ponderale egea a Capo Gelidonya. *Studi Micenei ed Egeo-Anatolici* 14: 165–170.

1986 Unità ponderali egee. In M. Marazzi, S. Tusa and L. Vagnetti (eds.), *Traffici micenei nel Mediterraneo. Problemi storici e documentazione archeologica, Atti del Convegno di Palermo (11-12 maggio e 3-6 dicembre 1984)*: 303–314. Taranto: Istituto per la storia e l'archeologia della Magna Grecia.

1994 Il sistema ponderale "miceneo". In M. Marazzi (ed.), *La società micenea*: 300–303. Rome: Bagatto.

1996 Fondamenti "minoici" delle misure "micenee". In E. De Miro, L. Godart and A. Sacconi (eds.), *Atti e Memorie del Secondo Congresso Internazionale di Micenologia, Roma-Napoli, 14-20 ottobre 1991*: III, 1269–1271. Rome: Ateneo.

2005 Metallo e moneta fra Oriente e Occidente. Intorno al dibattito su imprestiti orientali e innovazioni greche. In Clancier *et al.* 2005: 229–237.

2006 Equivalencias entre las antiguas unidades ponderales en Oriente y las primeras especies monetarias de Occidente. In A. Beltrán Martínez (ed.), *Actas del XII Congreso Nacional de Numismática, Madrid-Segovia 25-27 de octobre de 2004*: 15–22. Madrid.

2009 *Pesi e misure nel Mediterraneo orientale prima della moneta*. Roma: Edizioni Nuova Cultura.

Parkinson, W. and M. Galaty (eds.)

2010 *Archaic State Interaction: The Eastern Mediterranean in the Bronze Age*. Santa Fe: School for Advanced Research Press.

Pavúk, P.

2012 Of spools and discoid loom-weights. Aegean-type weaving at Troy revisited. In Nosch, and Laffineur 2012: 121–130.

Peyronel, L.

2008 *Storia e archeologia del commercio nell'Oriente antico*. Rome: Carocci.

Petruso, K. M.

1992 *Keos VIII. Ayia Irini: the balance weights*. Mainz on Rhine: Philipp von Zabern.

2003 Quantal Analysis of Some Mycenaean Balance Weights. In Polinger Foster and Laffineur 2003: 285–291.

Phelps, W., Y. Lolos and Y. Vichos (eds.)

1999 *The Point Iria Wreck: Interconnections in the Mediterranean ca. 1200 B.C. Proceedings of the International Conference, Island of Spetses, 19 September 1998*: 59–76. Athens: Hellenic Institute of Marine Archaeology.

Philippa-Touchais, A., G. Touchais, S. Voutsaki and J. Wright (eds.)

2010 *Mesohelladika. Μεσοελλαδικά: La Grèce continentale au Bronze Moyen. Η ηπειρωτική Ελλάδα στη Μέση εποχή του Χαλκού. The Greek Mainland in the Middle Bronze Age. Actes du colloque international organisé par l'École française d'Athènes, en collaboration avec l'American School of Classical Studies at Athens et le Netherlands Institute in Athens, Athènes, 8-12 mars 2006* (BCH Suppl. 52). Athens: École française d'Athènes.

Phillips, J.

2008 *Aegyptiaca on the Island of Crete in Their Chronological Context: A Critical Review*. (Contribution to the Chronology of the Eastern Mditerranean XVIII, OAW XLIX), vols. I-II. Wien: Verlag der Österreichischen Akademie der Wissenschaften.

Platon, N.
1971 *Zakros. The Discovery of a Lost Palace of Ancient Crete*. New York: Charles Scribner's Sons.

Polinger Foster, K. and R. Laffineur (eds.)
2003 *METRON. Measuring the Aegean Bronze Age. Proceedings of the 9th International Aegean Conference, New Haven, Yale University, 18–21 April 2002* (Aegaeum 24). Liège and Austin.

Popham, M., L.H. Sackett and Ph. Themelis
1980 *Lefkandi I. The Iron Age* (BSA Suppl. Vol. 11). Oxford: The British School of Archaeology at Athens, Thames and Hudson.

Pulak, C. M.
2000 The balance weights from the Late Bronze Age Shipwreck at Uluburun. In Pare 2000: 247–266.

Radina, F. and G. Recchia
2010 *Ambra per Agamennone. Indigeni e Micenei tra Egeo, Ionio e Adriatico nel II millennio a.C.*, Exhibition catalogue. Bari: M. Adda.

Rahmstorf, L.
2003 The identification of Early Helladic balance weights from Tiryns and their implications. In Polinger Foster and Laffineur 2003: 293–300.
2006a In search of the earliest balance weights, scales and weighing systems from the East Mediterranean, the Near and Middle East. In Alberti *et al.* 2006: 9–45.
2006b Zur Ausbreitung vorderasiatischer Innovationen in die frühbronzezeitliche Ägais. *Prähistorische Zeitschrift* 81: 49–96.
2008a *Tiryns XVI. Kleinfunde aus Tiryns. Terrakotta, Stein, Bein und Glas/Fayence vornehmlich aus der Spätbronzezeit*. Wiesbaden: Reichert Verlag.
2008b Early Bronze Age balance weights from Tarsus, Alişar Höyük and other sites, *Araştirma Sonuçlari Toplantisi* 26: 201–210.
2010 The concept of weighing during the Bronze Age in the Aegean, the Near East and Europe. In Morley and Renfrew 2010: 88–105.
2011a Re-integrating 'diffusion': the spread of innovations among the Neolithic and Bronze Age societies of Europe and the Near East. In Wilkinson *et al.* 2010: 100–119.
2011b Maß für Maß. Indikatoren für Kulturkontakte im 3. Jahrtausend. In *Kykladen. Lebenswelten einer frühgriechischen Kultur*: 144–153. Karlsruhe and Darmstadt: Badisches Landesmuseum and Primus Verlag.
2011c Handmade pots and crumbling loomweights: 'Barbarian' elements in the eastern Mediterranean in the last quarter of the 2nd millennium BC. In Karageorghis and Kouka 2011: 315–330.

Renfrew, C.
1972 *The Emergence of Civilisation. The Cyclades and the Aegean in the Third Millennium BC*. London: Methuen.

Ridgway, D.
1984 *L'alba della Magna Grecia*. Milano: Longanesi.

Routledge, B. and K. McGeough
2009 Just what collapsed? A network perspective on 'palatial' and 'private' trade at Ugarit. In Bachhuber and Roberts 2009: 22–29.

Rutter, J. B.

2006 Ceramic evidence for external contact: Neopalatial and Post-palatial. In Shaw *et al.* 2006: 859–863.

2012 Migrant drinking assemblages in Aegean Bronze Age settings. In Maran and Stockhammer 2012: 73–88.

Sauvage, C.

2012 *Routes maritimes et systèmes d'échanges internationaux au Bronze Récent en Méditerranée orientale* (Travaux de la Maison de l'Orient et de la Méditerranée 61). Lyon: Maison de l'Orient et de la Méditerranée.

Scarre, Ch. and F. Healy (eds.)

1993 *Trade and Exchange in Prehistoric Europe. Proceedings of a Conference held at the University of Bristol, April 1992.* Oxford: Oxbow Books, in association with the Prehistoric Society and the Société préhistorique françaises.

Schon, R.

2010 Think Locally Act Globally: Mycenaean Elites and the Late Bronze Age World-System. In Parkinson and Galaty 2010: 213–236.

Shaw, J. W, A. Van de Moortel and J. B. Rutter

2006 The harbor town and its international connections. In J. W. Shaw and M. C. Shaw (eds.), *Kommos V. The Monumental Minoan Buildings at Kommos*: 854–863. Princeton and Oxford, Princeton University Press.

Sherratt, S.

1998 'Sea Peoples' and the economic structure of the late second millennium in the Eastern Mediterranean. In S. Gitin, A. Mazar and E. Stern (eds.), *Mediterranean People in Transition. Thirteenth to Early Tenth Centuries BCE in Honour of Professor T. Dothan*: 292–313. Jerusalem: The Israel Exploration Society.

1999 *E pur si muove*. Pots, markets and values in the second millennium Mediterranean. In J.-P. Crielaard, V. Stissi, G. J. van Wijngaarden (eds.), *The Complex Past of Pottery. Production, Circulation and Consumption of Mycenaean and Greek Pottery (Sixteenth to Early Fifth Centuries B.C.). Proceeding of the ARCHON International Conference, held in Amsterdam, 8-9 November 1996*: 163–211. Amsterdam: Gieben.

2000 Circulation of metals and the end of the bronze age in the Eastern Mediterranean. In Pare 2000: 82–98.

2001 Potemkin palaces and route-based economies. In S. Voutsaki and J. Killen (eds.), *Economy and Politics in the Mycenaean Palace States. Proceedings of a Conference held on 1-3 July 17999 in the Faculty of Classics, Cambridge* (Cambridge Philological Society Suppl. 27): 214–238. Cambridge: The Cambridge Philological Society.

2003 The Mediterranean economy: 'globalization' at the end of the Second Millennium BCE. In W. G. Dever and S. Gitin (eds.), *Symbiosis, symbolism, and the power of the past: Canaan, ancient Israel, and their neighbors from the Late Bronze Age through Roman Palaestina. Proceedings of the Centennial Symposium, WF Albright Institute of Archaeological Research and American Schools of Oriental Research, Jerusalem, May 29-31, 2000*: 37–62. Winona Lake Indiana: Eisenbrauns.

2010 The Aegean and the wider world: some thoughts on a world-systems perspective. In Parkinson and Galaty 2010: 81–106.

Sherratt, A. and S. Sherratt
1991 From Luxuries to Commodities: The Nature of Mediterranean Bronze Age Trading Systems. In Gale 1991: 351–386.
1993 The growth of the Mediterranean economy in the early first millennium BC. *World Archaeology* 24/3 1993: 361–378.
1998 Small worlds. Interaction and identity in the ancient mediterranean. In Cline and Harris Cline 1998: 329–342.

Soles, J.
2005 From Ugarit to Mochlos – Remnants of an Ancient Voyage. In Laffineur and Greco 2005: I, 429–448.

Sorda, S. and L. Camilli (eds.)
2003 *Per una storia del denaro nel Vicino Oriente Antico. Atti dell'incontro di studio, Roma 13 giugno 2001* (Studi e Materiali 10). Roma: Istituto Italiano di Numismatica.

Stampolidis, N. Chr. and V. Karageorghis (eds.)
2003 *Πλόες. Sea Routes... Interconnections in the Mediterranean 16th-6th c. BC. Proceedings of the International Symposium held at Rethymnon, Crete, in September 29th-October 2nd 2002.* Athens: Museum of Cycladic Art.

Stockhammer, P.W. (ed.)
2012a *Conceptualizing cultural hybridization. A Transdisciplinary approach. Papers of the Conference, Heidelberg, 21st-22nd September 2009* (Transcultural Research. Heidelberg Studies on Asia and Europe in a Global context). Berlin and Heidelberg: Springer.
2012b Entangled pottery: phenomena of appropriation in the Late Bronze Age Eastern Mediterranean. In Maran and Stockhammer 2012: 89–103.

Stos-Gale, Z. and N. Gale
2006 The origin of metal used for the lead weights in Minoan Crete. In Alberti *et al.* 2006: 290–292.

Taylour, W. D. and R. Janko,
2008 *Ayios Stephanos. Excavations at a Bronze Age and Medieval settlement in southern Laconia* (BSA Suppl. Vol. 44). London: British School at Athens.

Thomatos, M.
2007 Koine and subsidiary Koines: coastal and island sites of the central and southern Aegean during the LHIIIC middle. In Deger-Jalkotzy and Zavadil 2007: 315–326.

Tournavitou, I.
1995 *The 'Ivory Houses' at Mycenae* (BSA Suppl. Vol. 24). London: The British School at Athens.

van Wijngaarden, G.J.
2002 *Use and appreciation of Mycenaean pottery in the Levant, Cyprus and Italy (1600-1200 BC).* Amsterdam: Amsterdam University Press.
2012 Trade goods reproducing merchants? The materiality of Mediterranean Late Bronze Age exchange. In Maran and Stockhammer 2012: 61–72.

Vetters, M.
2011 A Clay Ball with a Cypro – Minoan Inscription from Tiryns. *Archäologischer Anzeiger* 2011/2: 1–49.

Vitale, S. and T. A. Hancock Vitale
2012 The Minoans in the south-eastern Aegean? The evidence from the "Serraglio" on Kos and its main historical implications. In Alberti and Sabatini 2012: 44–59.

Vlachopoulos, A.
2008 A Late Mycenaean journey from Thera to Naxos: the Cyclades in the twelfth century B.C. In Brodie *et al.* 2008: 479–492.

Voskos, I., and A. B. Knapp
2008 Cyprus at the end of the Late Bronze Age. *American Journal of Archaeology* 112(4): 659–684.

Voutsaki, S.
2010 From the kinship economy to the palatial economy: The Argolid in the second millennium B.C. In D. Pullen (ed.), *Political Economies of the Aegean Bronze Age. Papers from the Langford Conference, Florida State University, Tallahassee, 22-24 February 2007*: 86–111. Oxford and Oakville: Oxbow Books.

Wallace, S.
2010 *Ancient Crete. From Successful Collapse to Democracy's Alternatives, Twelfth to Fifth Centuries BC*. Cambridge: Cambridge University Press.

Warren, P. M.
2009 Final summing up. In Macdonald *et al.* 2009: 263–265.

Wilkinson, T. C., S. Sherratt and J. Bennet (eds.)
2011 *Interweaving Worlds. Systemic Interactions in Eurasia, 7th to 1st Millennia BC. Papers from a conference in memory of Professor Andrew Sherratt "What Would a Bronze Age World System Look Like? World systems approaches to Europe and western Asia 4th to 1st millennia BC"*. Oxford and Oakville: Oxbow Books.

Whitelaw, T.
2004a Alternative pathways to complexity in the southern Aegean. In J. C. Barrett and P. Halstead (eds.), *The Emergence of Civilisation Revisited* (Sheffield Studies in Aegean Archaeology 6): 232–256. Oxford: Oxbow Books.
2004b The development of an island centre: urbanization at Phylakopi on Melos. In J. Cherry, Ch. Scarre and S. Shennan (eds.), *Explaining social change: studies in honour of Colin Renfrew* (McDonald Institute Monographs): 149–166. Cambridge: McDonald Institute for Archaeological Research.
2005 A tale of three cities: chronology and minoanisation at Phylakopi in Melos. In Dakouri–Hild and Sherratt 2005: 37–62.

Wright, J. C.
2006 The formation of the Mycenaean palace. In Deger-Jalkotzy and Lemos 2006: 7–52.
2008 Early Mycenaean Greece. In C. W. Shelmerdine (ed.), *The Cambridge Companion to the Aegean Bronze Age*: 230–257. Cambridge: Cambridge University Press.

Yon, M., V. Karageorghis, and N. Hirschfled
2000 *Céramiques mycéniennes d'Ougarit* (Ras Shamra – Ougarit 13). Paris – Nicosia: Éditions Recherche sur les civilisations.

Zaccagnini, C.

1986 Aspects of copper trade in the eastern Mediterranean during the late bronze age. In
M. Marazzi, S. Tusa, L. Vagnetti (eds.), *Traffici micenei nel Mediterraneo. Problemi storici e
documentazione archeologica, Atti del Convegno di Palermo (11-12 maggio e 3-6 dicembre 1984)*: 413–424.
Taranto: Istituto per la storia e l'archeologia della Magna Grecia.

1994 Les échanges dans l'antiquité: paradigmes théoriques et analyse des sources. In J. Andreau,
P. Briant and R. Descat (eds.), *Les échanges dans l'antiquité: le rôle de l'Etat. Entretiens d'archéologie
et d'histoire* : 213–225. Saint Bertrand de Comminges.

2003 *Mercanti e politica nel mondo antico*. Roma: Erma di Bretschneider.

Zurbach, J.

2012 Mobilités, réseaux, ethnicité. Bilan et perspectives. In L. Capdetray and J. Zurbach (eds.),
*Mobilités grecques. Mouvements, réseaux, contacts en Méditeranée, de l'époque archaïque à l'époque
héllenistique (Actes du colloque de Nanterre, juin 2012)* (Scripta Antiqua 46): 261–273. Bordeaux:
Ausonius; Paris: de Boccard.

Chapter 12

'Brave New Worlds': Islands, Place-making and Connectivity in the Bronze Age Mediterranean

Helen Dawson

"Islands are places of strikingly enhanced exposure to interaction."
(Horden and Purcell 2000: 76)

The exposure of island cultures to outside influences can be considered a key factor for explaining both their eclecticism and distinctiveness: alternating periods of increased interaction and relative isolation may be related to an islands' geographical configuration and/or to cultural processes and contingency, and cultural idiosyncrasy has been attributed both to natural and cultural factors (*e.g.* Copat *et al.* 2011; Rainbird 2007; Robb 2001; Tanasi and Vella 2014). On a practical level, maritime connectivity in Mediterranean prehistory was influenced by the islands' location and availability of resources along different routes, as well as boat technology (*e.g.* Castagnino-Berlinghieri 2003; Papageorgiou 2008; Anderson 2004). Yet, islands were much more than convenient 'stopovers.' The degree to which island communities participated in webs of interaction provides a measure of their agency and their ability to create their own cultural spaces and wider connections (*e.g.* Robb 2001; Knapp 2007). Shifting our focus, from viewing islanders as merely participating to being active players in such networks, can help us understand how interaction and connectivity came into being (*cf.* Knapp and van Dommelen 2010: 3).

The Middle to Late Bronze Age period (*c.* 1500–1200 BC) is widely regarded as a peak of cultural interaction at different scales within the Mediterranean region (Laffineur and Greco, eds. 2005). During this period, the small islands of the central Mediterranean were increasingly involved (whether directly or indirectly) in exchange networks with the Aegean and the Levant. Interaction ranged from the local, inter-island scale to the inter-regional, Mediterranean scale. Understanding these connections, their underlying causes and effects on different communities has been a common goal for many archaeologists, who (as we will see in the following section) have approached these questions adopting different theories and methods. In this paper, I will suggest that differential participation in these networks, as can be seen from the settlement and material record of the smaller central Mediterranean islands (*cf.* Bietti Sestieri 1982), had a transformative role on its communities, which resulted in the creation of new ideas about people and places, which in turn affected the range of interaction. "Regardless of whether people themselves arrived in a new place or encountered other people or objects coming from elsewhere, the process of *constructing a new world*, literally and mentally, holds the key to understanding mobility... the restructuring of existing identities and/or the formulation of new, hybrid identities" (Knapp and van Dommelen 2010: 6, my emphasis). What might connectivity have meant to different communities? How would interaction have affected people's perceptions of themselves and of others, of their expanding and contracting worlds and horizons? This paper will present some initial considerations on island identity, sense of place, and place-making, as possible ways of addressing connectivity and interaction in the Bronze Age Mediterranean.

Connectivity

The current range of publications on connectivity highlights the rich diversity of ways in which people interacted in the past. Studies of connectivity, especially those influenced by Wallerstein's (1974) 'World-Systems Theory' (WST), have emphasised usefully that societies do not develop in isolation and highlighted the importance of understanding 'intersocietal interaction' (Hall *et al.* 2011: 266). These approaches tend to investigate cultural flows and use their directionality to identify sites acting as cores, peripheries, semi-peripheries, and marginal areas. The original body of theory has been refined in recent decades, with newer approaches referred to as 'World-Systems Analysis' (WSA): this takes into account the implications of mutual interaction and places a greater focus on networks (Hall *et al.* 2011: 238–240). WSA has been applied extensively to the study of European prehistory, most notably by Sherratt (1993, 1994), and Kristiansen (1998).

Connectivity is also a key theme in network analysis and social network analysis (SNA) in particular (Knappett ed. 2013). These methods accord importance to sites on the basis on their 'centrality', defined in terms of the frequency, intensity and directionality of their connections (*e.g.* Rivers *et al.* 2013). In this approach, interactions are considered as primary and sites as secondary, in contrast to other approaches (such as 'central place theory' and Thiessen polygons) which tend to be site-centric. Proximal Point Analysis (PPA), as used by Broodbank (2000: 239) in his study of the Bronze Age Cyclades, also shifted the attention to the links, explaining why certain sites emerge on islands with few resources and host populations well over their carrying capacity.

The approaches mentioned so far can explain why large, so-called central sites emerged where they did; but, although they are able to factor in changes in the direction of interaction and other anomalies, graphic representations of networks are far removed from the actual experience of interaction, or what Horden and Purcell refer to as 'the alchemy of engagement' (2000: 230). Therefore, while WSA and network analysis can explain past connections in terms of factors or equations that make sense to us, they fail to capture the meaning of geography for people in the past. In fairness, this is not the aim of these approaches.

In terms of effects, connectivity can lead to hybridization, emulation, competition, and changes in group identity, to name but a few possibilities. Research has focused on 'orientalising', 'minoanising', 'mycenaeanising' – and occasionally 'westernizing' – elements. Islands are widely held to be ideal places to study these processes (*e.g.* Broodbank 2004; Bevan and Conolly 2013; Knapp and van Dommelen 2007) and thus, in certain ways, their role as 'laboratories' (Evans 1973) for the study of culture change persists in the literature. Post-colonial studies emphasise the mutual effects of connectivity in explaining processes of hybridisation (*e.g.* van Dommelen 2012), in terms of the 'transformative potential' arising from interaction (Maran and Stockhammer 2012: 1). This approach explores how new meaning is created through the integration of material culture within different communities (Maran and Stockhammer 2012: 1; Panagiotopoulous 2011). In comparison to WSA, which explains the rise of social complexity by focusing on the long-term and the broad regional scale, these other approaches tend to focus on more localised dynamics. They illustrate the role of material culture as 'generating' ideas in different contexts, rather than necessarily as 'representative' of culture (Maran and Stockhammer 2012: 2; *cf.* Cline 2005).

Ideas about space

In what way are geographies meaningful? In the case of islands, there is an ongoing debate on the correct emphasis to be placed on land and sea, and the various merits of focusing on islandscapes vs. seascapes, or the archaeology of islands vs. the archaeology of the sea (*e.g.* Berg 2010; Dawson in press; Rainbird 2007). These approaches have equal merit when applied in a complementary fashion and we should not simply replace one paradigm in favour of another. As we saw in the previous section, network analyses have succeeded in modeling different forms of interaction. In parallel to these approaches, we might also consider how ideas about places developed in the past: is it possible and worthwhile to approach interaction also in terms of perception?

In my own work on island colonisation in the prehistoric Mediterranean (Dawson 2011; 2014), I have noted that biogeography has some relevance in understanding the earliest patterns of island occupation, yet the subsequent divergence is such that cultural elements must be responsible for this variation. Cultural attitudes to space, resulting from changing perceptions of time, distance, and travel (*cf.* Helms 1988), may have been particularly relevant factors in this process. Reaching an unknown place, encountering different communities, getting hold of a coveted resource, learning about far-away places, would have been powerful experiences, which may have further encouraged people to 'brave' new worlds. If long-distance travelling was involved in gaining resources, places, such as islands, may have been considered to be special because they were so hard to reach. Places would have conferred status to the material, and ultimately objects may have been considered as 'pieces of places' (Bradley 2000: 87, 88). This could well be the case for obsidian, which was highly desirable as seen from its broad distribution in the Neolithic and could be obtained only on a few islands (Tykot 1996).

Phenomenological theory, as set out by Tilley and Thomas in the mid-1990s, was the first attempt in archaeology to grapple with the intangible qualities of places, arguing that they could be experienced by archaeologists through their direct engagement with landscapes and material culture. Although they have undergone much criticism, the value of phenomenological approaches has also been highlighted (*e.g.* Brück 2005). According to Tilley (1994; 1996) and Thomas (1996), archaeologists can unravel past ideas about places and objects by experiencing, i.e. moving through the landscape and describing things through texts, drawings and photographs. The main criticism to these theories has been that, while it is possible for archaeologists to identify meaningful relationships (i.e. patterns) between people, objects, and places, they cannot possibly gauge the original meaning of such associations (Brück 2005: 55, 64).

These criticisms have not put off the supporters of phenomenology, who claim that archaeology should entail 'direct engagement' and developing 'a feeling and sensibility for place' (Tilley 2004: 219). As a response, its practitioners are developing more rigorous fieldwork techniques. Such appraisals may record the character of a place (a well-established concept in architecture and planning), i.e. whether a place is wide/open, or narrow/enclosed, the presence of focal points, whether it is dark, shady, light, airy, and other ephemeral or transient aspects, such as smells and noises (*e.g.* Hamilton and Whitehouse 2006). Approaching archaeological sites in such way can effectively broaden our understanding of how people interacted with their landscape. Approaches that attempt to gauge past ideas about landscapes and places should not replace other established methods of landscape reconstruction (Bintliff 2009), but can provide a more humanised version of the past. The rethinking of the relationships between people and things (and, by extension, places) also lies at the heart of Hodder's theory of entanglement (2012) and other recent contributions on relational archaeologies (*e.g.* Watts, ed. 2013).

Although very different in their set aims and methodologies, network analyses and place-making theories (including phenomenology) can benefit from each other. As we have already seen, the former is especially suitable for reconstructing interaction at multiple scales. The latter can add important layers of meaning and introduce new parameters: small, remote sites, for example, may have special cultural characteristics that cannot be explained simply on the basis of spatial or economic features.

This will encourage new ways of thinking about space, ways which may have been more relevant to prehistoric people.

Islands and sense of place

In the context of islands, it seems logical to talk about 'sense of place.' In western popular culture it is taken almost for granted through the association of romantic ideas with islands (e.g. Billig 2010). Islands' distinct sense of place arises from their natural features, especially their being bounded by the sea, a feature which is more prominent on smaller islands, where present-day studies suggest that communities experience strong place-identification or an 'island identity' (Hay 2006: 22). Admittedly, insular and coastal sites share many common features, yet, unlike coastal locations which are an extension of the mainland, islands are physically separated by the sea and greater effort is required to create viable settlements and establish and maintain connections. Unsurprisingly, this leads to different types of cultural phenomena on small islands compared to the mainland. Indeed, Broodbank (2000: 20) has defined the ability of islanders to 'deviate from, lose entirely, or preserve certain cultural features from the mainland' as the 'island effect'. There is no equivalent term to insularity to explain the condition of living in coastal locations, and ultimately studying and comparing island cultures reveals a richer range of potential relationships between culture and space.

Bevan and Conolly (2013: 6) have recently highlighted the empirical value of the island unit in their field survey of the small island of Antikythera. This is a revival of an earlier idea: 'an island offers a clearly definable unit... excellent circumstances to compare indigenous and exogenous' (Broodbank and Strasser 1991: 233). Islands have clear boundaries; however, group identity may not be coterminous with that defined spatial unit. Viewing islands as convenient units of investigation has nothing to do with issues of isolation: rather in the prehistoric Mediterranean 'bounded cultures and well-defined populations with readily distinct identities may have been far less common than usually assumed' (Knapp and van Dommelen 2010: 1). The range of interaction, not just geography, is important: at the local, island scale; at the regional, archipelago scale; and at the broader, Mediterranean scale. Our task is therefore to identify and map these interactions and their extent, since these have a bearing on sense of place and identity.

The extensive literature on sense of place reflects its complexity. Classic studies (Tuan 1974; Relph 1976) highlight its multifaceted aspects, which comprise place distinctiveness, place continuity, place dependency, place attachment, loyalty, identification, and feelings of 'insideness' and 'outsideness'. Relph (1976) defined 'insideness' as a feeling of belonging to a place, leading to a person's identification with that place. The opposite is 'outsideness', a feeling of separation from a place, e.g. homesickness in a new place, or a feeling of alienation or not belonging to one's home after a long period of absence (Seamon and Sowers 2008). Sense of place arises from different practices, which link people physically and emotionally to specific locations (Erdoğu 2005: 99). It is integral to social memory, ancestry, and can foster community allegiance.

Can we determine the scale of sense of place or of place-related identification? Are people connected to a specific village, island, island group, or wider archipelago/ mainland region? Were these spatial and social categories meaningful in the past? Costantakopoulou's (2005) textual work on the Greek islands showed that, in the Classical and Hellenistic periods, the inhabitants of islands with more than one polis identified with their islands rather than with their individual cities; moreover, this island identity enabled islanders to overcome political fragmentation. She also discusses the 'netting' or capture of islands, as described by the ancient historian Herodotus (Costantakopoulou 2007: 126–127). When conquering an island, the occupiers would join hands forming a long line across the island and then march through the island to capture the inhabitants. She suggests that this 'netting' expresses 'the idea of an island as a well-defined place' clearly bounded by the sea.

Grasping prehistoric sense of place poses greater challenges. Nonetheless, archaeology provides the means to study sense of place in the distant past, through the development of quantitative and qualitative spatial approaches (*e.g.* Grima 2001, 2008; Rennell 2010). Within Malta, Grima has suggested that the iconography of the prehistoric temples reflects the domain of the land and of the sea, that the temples themselves were 'metaphors for islands' and that moving inside the temple was a 'metaphoric journey' (Grima 2001: 63). In the Outer Hebridean islands, Rennell (2010) identified different scales of place, on the basis of GIS analysis and visual and acoustic criteria, observing how the spatial configuration and sensory features of different Iron Age sites, located on islets within lochs, emphasized insularity, by way of nesting dwellings within islands (Rennell 2010: 57).

In the following section, I will explore how these alternative ways of thinking about space and place can shed different light on cultural interaction in the central Mediterranean islands in the Bronze Age.

Small islands, big worlds

The extensive research on connections between the eastern and central Mediterranean during the Bronze Age provides the ideal opportunity to explore some of the ideas discussed so far. Only a very short synthesis of this vast scholarly work is attempted here as way of background to the ideas explored in this paper, through brief sketches of the evidence in broad chronological order. Interactions between communities living, on the one hand, in peninsular Italy, Sicily, the Aeolian Islands, Malta, and Vivara (see Figure 12.1), and, on the other hand, in the Aegean and eastern Mediterranean areas, can be inferred from the distribution of pottery styles and prestige items (Bietti Sestieri 1988; Leighton 1999; Tusa 1994). It is harder to gauge the nature of these broad-ranging interactions and their effects, although the classification of pottery

Figure 12.1: Map of key locations mentioned in the text.

into imports, imitations and derivatives (Jones *et al.* 2006; 2014) is shedding some light on the possible mechanisms of interaction, in terms of the movement of goods vs. the movement of people (see Blake 2005 and Iacono 2015 for different perspectives on interaction).

How did contact take place between the communities of Sicily, the smaller islands, and Malta, and who did they interact with? Were there actual colonies or enclaves or a more casual intermingling of people and cultures? How might have this affected people's ideas of local and far-way places? Whether or not ideas about places were geographically accurate is not important: they still contributed to the process of interaction and may have influenced how it unfolded. Identities 'gain meaning through encounter with others and relate flexibly to *real and imagined space*' (Mac Sweeney 2009: 103, my emphasis).

Early Bronze Age (c. 2500–1500 BC, corresponding to EH II–MH III)

It is plausible that people from Malta and the Aeolian islands, with their expertise at navigation, were directly involved in initiating maritime connections at a regional scale in the Early Bronze Age (Cazzella and Recchia 2012: 1007). Presumably, exchange routes in the area had their origins in the circulation of Lipari obsidian, which, in the Neolithic, reached southern France (Tykot 1996, fig. 10). Starting from the 17th century BC, pottery from the Aeolian Islands, followed by that from the Aegean in the 16th century BC, is found in the Tyrrhenian Sea on the island of Vivara (Marazzi and Tusa 1994; Rizio 2005: 624). There is evidence for exchange between Sicily and Malta (Sicilian sulphur and flint in Malta and Tarxien Cemetery pottery in southern Sicily) (Castellana 1998; Cazzella and Recchia 2012: 1006). Sulphur and alum were also extracted from the island of Vulcano (Giustolisi 1995), which was the only island in the Aeolian archipelago never to be permanently settled, presumably because the volcanic landscape caused people to feel uneasy.

Small islands, such as the Aeolian Islands and Vivara, may have been perceived as being safer by outsiders compared to the mainland (Cazzella and Recchia 2012). Initially, at least, it seems that the islanders did not fear outsiders. A fragment of a drinking cup found at the site of Filo Braccio on the island of Filicudi, from a context dated to 1900–1800 BC, offers a possible glimpse of such a meeting of cultures. The cup shows what appears to be a human figure in the midst of zigzag lines, presumably symbolising the sea, and surrounded by crude representations of boats with oars (Capo Graziano culture, corresponding to Tarxien Cemetery phase on Malta) (Figure 12.2). The cup is of coarse fabric and the object does not appear to be a prestige item but it shows a scene that might commemorate the original arrival of the community to the island or another significant event, such as the encounter with another seafaring group (Martinelli *et al.* 2010: 308–312).

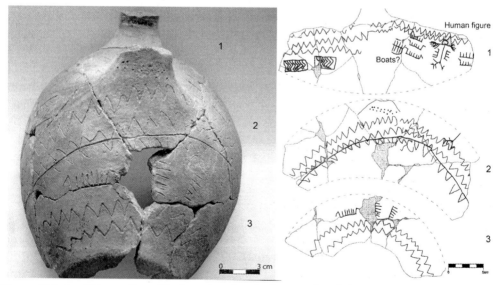

Figure 12.2: An EBA cup from Filo Braccio, Filicudi, decorated with boats, the sea, and a human figure (adapted from Martinelli et al. 2010, figs 15–16; reproduced with permission from the Museo Archeologico Regionale Luigi Bernabo Brea, Lipari).

Middle Bronze Age (c. 1500–1350 BC, corresponding to LHI-II-IIIA)

This network of interaction eventually accommodated a new element in a more regular fashion than could be previously seen. The existing local exchange system was gradually expanded to include long-distance relations with the Aegean and Levantine regions (Copat *et al.* 2010: 55). By this time, the Aeolian Islands and for the first time also Pantelleria were involved in the interactions, which now appear to exclude Malta (Tanasi 2008; Cazzella and Recchia 2012). In fact, only two Mycenaean sherds have been found on Malta so far and thus it is hardly likely that there was any direct contact between these cultures at this point (Bonanno 2008: 35). Nonetheless, the Maltese may have exported textiles and highly polished Borg-in-Nadur pottery, the latter found in great quantities at Thapsos in Sicily, where pottery of Cypriote-Mycenaean tradition was also produced using local coarse clay rich in volcanic grits, and a few tombs revealed metal objects of Cypriote influence and Mycenaean luxury items (Tusa 1983: 389–398; Tanasi 2008: 81; Alberti and Bettelli 2005: 554). Although Malta was still involved in trade with Sicily, it seems to have an increasingly marginal role during this period (Cazzella and Recchia 2012: 1009).

The inter-regional extent of this trade is evident: Levantine matt-painted type pottery has been found at the site at Mursia (17th-15th centuries BC) on Pantelleria, south of Sicily; similar pottery is also found on Vivara, in Sicily at Monte Grande, and at Tell el-Dab'a in the Nile Delta (Ardesia *et al.* 2006: 72). These small central Mediterranean islands became centres of an exchange network that for the first time did "not necessarily rely on locally available raw materials" (Copat *et al.* 2010: 52). Tanasi and Vella (2014: 62) consider that islands "were often places where encounters with 'foreignness' brought by sea travel took place, whether through migration or prospection by smaller groups". Fortifications and the proliferation of defensible locations at this time, as seen at Thapsos and Cannatello on Sicily, Mursia on Pantelleria, Punta Milazzese on Panarea (Figure 12.3), and Faraglioni on Ustica, were also a consequence of trade and connectivity (*e.g.* Holloway 2005): winds of change began to affect the islanders' perceptions of the outside world, with increasing maritime connections exposing them to greater threat than before (Broodbank 2013: 431; Tusa 2015: 272).

Late Bronze Age (Italian 'Bronzo Recente' 1350–1200 BC and 'Bronzo Finale' 1200–850 BC, corresponding to LH IIIB-C)

By the Late Bronze Age, Thapsos and other coastal centres in Sicily, such as Cannatello, were abandoned and in some cases destroyed, as was the case also on the islands (Cazzella and Recchia 2012: 1009; Militello 2005: 593). In fact, the overall number of known settlements on the Sicilian islands dropped drastically from some 15 in the EBA and MBA to just one in the LBA and FBA, when there is no evidence that any of the islands were settled apart from Lipari. This destruction is attributed to the arrival of so-called Ausonian groups from the Italian mainland (Bernabo Brea 1957;

Figure 12.3: The MBA village of Punta Milazzese on Panarea.

Bietti Sestieri 2010). This was also the time of the collapse of the Mycenaean palatial system and the demise of long-distance trade with the central Mediterranean. At Pantalica, the cemetery of 5,000 tombs produced a single Aegean-type pot (Vianello 2009: 48), although the site's central building, the *anaktoron*, bears similarities to Mycenaean architecture (Tanasi 2009: 53). Items still reached Sicily, possibly through the hands of migrant artisans, refugees, and mercenaries (Eder and Jung 2006: 486; Tanasi 2004, 2005; Vianello 2009). The so-called Sicilian 'internationalism' of the Middle Bronze Age was eventually replaced by regional fragmentation and a greater focus on peninsular Italy (Bietti Sestieri 1988, 2008: Tusa 1983: 457; Tanasi 2006). In a reversal to the earlier trend, Italic products now found their way into Aegean contexts (Vianello 2009, Iacono 2012).

Measuring intangible qualities of place in the Bronze Age

Some researchers acknowledge that small islands were key places for the establishment of interaction and "achieved a new significance" in the intense patterns of connectivity of this period (Copat *et al.* 2010: 59; see also Tusa 2015: 273). Despite their lack of resources and diminutive sizes, these islands supported permanent settlements which were capable of acquiring materials from different areas and exchanging them with other islanders or directly with foreign groups. Clearly, communities were not passively influenced by insularity: although islands pose specific challenges, such as lack of resources, limited space and farmland, islanders can benefit from their location.

"Networks install a series of two-way relations" and all parties involved "should bear the marks of this interaction" (Gosden 1993: 24). Whether or not exchange during the Bronze Age was frequent or sporadic, the arrival of material that was recognisably foreign to small islands would have altered people's perception of space. These encounters would have affected both local and incoming people, their ideas and perceptions of the islanders' own small worlds and of more distant lands, including the areas where resources were obtained, exchanged and ultimately consumed, and, by extension, ideas about people. How did these ideas translate in practical terms? Does the archaeological record bear any trace of these intangible qualities? If so, how can we access these different meanings?

I have been exploring these questions focusing on the small islands surrounding Sicily, integrating GIS-based spatial analysis and phenomenology (phase 1 of the study, recently completed), and network analysis (phase 2 of the study, just begun). This research is beginning to shed new light on the ways people used different parts of an island and archipelago in relation to both local and broader dynamics. As a starting point for phase 1, I considered that the setting and location of villages, burial sites, and ritual areas reflect community orientation in relation to the islands, mainland, and sea. To an extent, settlement and burial choices in the small islands mirrored similar trends in Sicily, but with distinct adaptations to local conditions. One peculiarity is the prolonged use of locations with special characteristics for ritual.

Whereas, in the Early Bronze Age, the preferred settlement location was within easy access to the coast, during the Middle Bronze Age, islanders moved to naturally defended headlands. The sites that have produced evidence at this time for contact with the eastern Mediterranean and the Aegean (such as Lipari Acropolis, Punta Milazzese on Panarea, and Mursia on Pantelleria) all occupied rocky outcrops rising above the sea with small plateaus at the summit and were also fortified towards the interior. Burial areas were closely associated to settlements, being often located on steep-sloping ground with commanding views above the settlements and surroundings. On the larger islands, such as Lipari and Salina, the interior was still dotted with farmsteads, which took advantage of the best landscapes. Thus, agriculture remained an important activity even when trade was more widely practised.

Islanders also met to carry out communal rituals. Ritual focused around secondary volcanic phenomena as seen on Lipari and Panarea (such as thermal springs and fumaroles) and cave sites with stillicide water (as seen on Ustica). An important point is that the ritual sites were used for considerably longer periods compared to contemporary settlements and burial areas. Over time, the islanders' beliefs would have changed, yet the location remained the same. Islanders developed an attachment to such locations, which were used over several generations, reinforcing community identity (Dawson in press). As people from neighbouring islands met at specific places to carry out ritual activities, community identity need not necessarily be confined to an individual island, but may extend to a whole archipelago. Different practices acted as vectors of identity and thus by studying the archaeological traces left by such practices we can discern different scales of community identity (Harris 2014).

The network analysis will address the islands' wider connections, on the basis of data from published archaeological surveys and excavations (local vs. non local material culture, architecture, burial, and ritual traditions). What was the extent of outside influences on the material culture, burial and settlement record of the small islands? Was the effect stronger or weaker on the smaller or larger islands, and how did the islands compare to the coastal sites on the Sicilian mainland? Small islands are considered especially vulnerable to outside influences; but, even at the height of maritime interaction, local cultural elements were maintained, indicating strong continuity and a sense of community identity (Tusa 2015: 273).

This study is work in progress and this paper admittedly raises many unanswered questions. In this contribution, I have presented the theoretical background, research questions, and methodological tools in my research. An important part of this project is to consider how both natural and cultural factors contribute to different degrees of connectivity as well as the development of sense of place and community identities. Such a study calls for an approach combining both quantitative and qualitative analysis.

Acknowledgements

I would like to thank Barry Molloy for inviting me to contribute to this volume without my being able to attend the actual workshop. Davide Tanasi kindly sent me a draft of his paper co-authored with Nicholas Vella. Emanuela Alberti, Naoise Mac Sweeney, and Barry Molloy offered detailed feedback on an earlier version of this paper and helped improve it considerably. My research is made possible through a grant from the EU (Marie Curie – PCOFUND-GA-2010-267228) (Phase 1) and the Gerda Henkel Research Foundation (Phase 2), with generous support from the Topoi Excellence Cluster, Freie Universität Berlin. This paper is work-in-progress; any comments will be gratefully received: helen.dawson@topoi.org

References

Alberti, L. and M. Bettelli
2005 Contextual problems of Mycenaean pottery in Italy. In R. Laffineur and E. Greco (eds.), *Emporia: Aegeans in the Central and Eastern Mediterranean*, Aegaeum 25: 547–560. Liège and Austin (TX): University of Liège and University of Texas at Austin.

Anderson, A.
2004 Islands of ambivalence. In S.C. Fitzpatrick (ed.), *Voyages of discovery: the archaeology of islands*. 251–274. Westport: Praeger Publishers.

Ardesia, V., M. Cattani, M. Marazzi, F. Nicoletti, M. Secondo and S. Tusa
2006 Gli scavi nell'abitato dell'età del Bronzo di Mursia, Pantelleria (TP). Relazione preliminare delle campagne 2001–2005. *Rivista di Scienze Preistoriche* 56: 1–75.

Berg, I.
2010 Re-capturing the Sea. The Past and Future of "Island Archaeology" in Greece. *Shima: The International Journal of Research into Island Cultures* 4(1): 16–26.

Bernabò Brea, L.
1957 *Sicily before the Greeks*. London: Thames and Hudson.
1966 Abitato neolitico e insediamento maltese dell'Età del Bronzo nell'isola di Ognina (Siracusa), e i rapport fra Sicilia e Malta dal XVI and XII sec. a.C. *Kokalos* 12: 41–69.

Bernabò Brea, L. and M. Cavalier
1968 *Meligunìs Lipára III. Stazioni preistoriche delle isole Panarea, Salina e Stromboli*. Palermo: Flaccovio.

Bevan, A. and J. Conolly
2013 *Mediterranean Fragility and Persistence. Antikythera's Island Communities*. Cambridge: Cambridge University Press.

Bietti Sestieri, A.M.
1982 Implicazioni del concetto di territorio in situazioni culturali complesse: le isole Eolie nell'età del Bronzo. *Dialoghi di Archeologia* 4: 39–60.
1988 The 'Mycenaean connection' and its impact on the central Mediterranean societies. *Dialoghi di archeologia* 6:23–51.
2008 L'eta del Bronzo finale nella penisola italiana. *Padusa* 44: 7–54.
2010 *L'Italia nell'Eta del Bronzo e del Ferro. Dalle palafitte a Romolo (2200-700 a.C.)*. Rome: Carocci.

Billig, V.
2010 *Inseln: Geschichte einer Faszination*. Berlin: Atthes & Seitz.

Bintliff, J.
2009 The Implications of a Phenomenology of Landscape. In E. Olshausen and V. Sauer (eds.) *Die Landschaft und die Religion. Stuttgarter Kolloquium zur Historischen Geographie des Altertums, 9, 2005*: 27–45. Geographica Historica Band 26. Stuttgart: Franz Steiner Verlag.

Blake, E.
2005 The Mycenaeans in Italy. A minimalist perspective. *Papers of the British School at Rome* 76: 1–34.

Bonanno, A.
2008 Insularity and isolation: Malta and Sicily in Prehistory. In A. Bonanno (ed.) *Malta in the Hybleans, the Hybleans in Malta. Malta negli Iblei, gli Iblei a Malta*: 27–37 Progetto KASA, Officina di Studi Medievali.

Bradley, R.
2000 *An Archaeology of Natural Places*. London: Routledge.

Broodbank, C.
2000 *An Island Archaeology of the Early Cyclades*. Cambridge: Cambridge University Press.
2004 Minoanisation. *Proceedings of the Cambridge Philological Society* 50: 46–91.
2013 *The Making of the Middle Sea. A History of the Mediterranean from the Beginning to the Emergence of the Classical World*. London: Thames and Hudson.

Broodbank, C. and T. Strasser.
1991 Migrant farmers and the Neolithic colonization of Crete. Antiquity 65: 233–245.

Brück, J.
2005 Experiencing the past? The development of a phenomenological archaeology in British prehistory. *Archaeological Dialogues* 12(1): 45–72.

Castagnino-Berlinghieri, E.F.
2003 *The Aeolian Islands: crossroads of Mediterranean routes. A survey on their maritime archaeology and topography from the prehistoric to the Roman periods* (BAR International Series 1181). Oxford: British Archaeological Reports.

Castellana, G.
1998 *Il santuario castellucciano di Monte Grande e l'approvvigionamento dello zolfo nel Mediterraneo nell'età del Bronzo.* Palermo: Regione Sicilia, Assessorato Beni Culturali e Ambientali e della Pubblica Istruzione.

Cazzella, A. and G. Recchia
2009 The 'Mycenaeans' in the central Mediterranean: a comparison between the Adriatic and the Tyrrhenian seaways. *Pasiphae* 3: 27–40.
2012 Sicilia, Eolie, Malta e le reti di scambio tra gli ultimi secoli del III e gli inizi del I millennio a.C. *Atti della XLI Riunione Scientifica. San Cipirrello (PA), 16-19 Novembre 2006*: 1001–1113. Firenze.

Cline, E.H.
2005 The multivalent nature of imported objects in the ancient Mediterranean world. In R. Laffineur and E. Greco (eds.), *Emporia: Aegeans in the Central and Eastern Mediterranean*, Aegaeum 25: 45–52. Liège and Austin (TX): University of Liège and University of Texas at Austin.

Copat, V., M. Danesi and G. Recchia
2010 Isolation and interaction cycles. Small Mediterranean Islands from the Neolithic to the Bronze Age. *Shima – The International Journal of Research into Island Cultures* 4(2): 41–64.

Constantakopoulou, C.
2005 Proud to be an islander: island identity in multi-polis islands in the Classical and Hellenistic Aegean. *Mediterranean Historical Review* 20(1): 1–34.
2007 *The Dance of the Islands. Insularity, Networks, the Athenian Empire, and the Aegean World.* Oxford: Oxford Classical Monographs.

Dawson, H.
2011 Island colonisation: settling the Neolithic question. In N. Phoca-Cosmetatou (ed.) *The first Mediterranean islanders: initial occupation and survival strategies*: 31–54. University of Oxford School of Archaeology: Monograph 74.
2014 *Mediterranean Voyages. The archaeology of island colonisation and abandonment.* London: Left Coast Press Inc. UCL (Institute of Archaeology Series 62).
in press Deciphering the elements: Cultural meanings of water in an island setting. *Accordia Research Papers* 15.

Di Stefano, G.
2008 Insediamenti e necropoli dell'Antico Bronzo dell'area iblea e Malta: contatti o influenze? In A. Bonanno (ed.) *Malta in the Hybleans, the Hybleans in Malta. Malta negli Iblei, gli Iblei a Malta*: 49–54. Progetto KASA, Officina di Studi Medievali.

Eder, B. and R. Jung
2006 On the character of social relationships between Greece and Italy in the 12th/11th c. BC. In R. Laffineur and E. Greco (eds.), *Emporia: Aegeans in the Central and Eastern Mediterranean*, Aegaeum 25: 485–495. Liège and Austin (TX): University of Liège and University of Texas at Austin.

Erdoğu, B.
2005 Visualizing Neolithic Landscape: Archaeological Theory in the Aegean Islands. In C. Lichter (ed.) *How Did Farming Reach Europe? Anatolian-European Relations from the Second Half of the 7th through to the First Half of the 6th Millennium Cal BC* (Proceedings of the International Workshop Istanbul, 20-22 May 2004. Byzas 2): 95–105. Istanbul: Ege Yayinlari

Evans, J.D.
1973 Islands as laboratories for the study of culture process. In A. C. Renfrew (ed.) *The Explanation of Culture Change: Models in Prehistory*: 517–520. London: Duckworth.

Giannitrapani, E.
1997 Rapporti tra la Sicilia e Malta durante l'Età del Bronzo. In S. Tusa (ed.) *Prima Sicilia, alle origini della società siciliana*: 429–444 Palermo: Ediprint.

Gosden, C.
1993 *Social Being and Time*. Oxford: Blackwell.

Giustolisi, V.
1995 *Vulcano: Introduzione alla Storia e all'Archeologia dell'Antica Hiera*. Palermo: Centro di Documentazione e Ricerca per la Sicilia Antica "Paolo Orsi".

Grima, R.
2001 An iconography of insularity: a cosmological interpretation of some images and spaces in the Late Neolithic Temples of Malta. *Papers from the Institute of Archaeology* 12: 48–65.
2008 Landscape, Territories, and the Life-Histories of Monuments in Temple Period Malta. *Journal of Mediterranean Archaeology* 21(1): 35–56.

Hall, T.D., P.N. Kardulias and Ch. Chase-Dunn
2011. World-Systems Analysis and Archaeology: Continuing the Dialogue. Journal of Archaeological Research 19(3): 233–279.

Hamilton, S. and R. Whitehouse
2006 Phenomenology in Practice: Towards a Methodology for a `Subjective' Approach. *European Journal of Archaeology* 9: 31–71.

Harris, O.J.T.
2014 (Re)assembling Communities. *Journal of Archaeological Method and Theory*. DOI: 10.1007/s10816-012-9138-3 (online first publication, print edition to follow).

Hay, P.
2006 A phenomenology of islands. *Island Studies Journal* 1(1): 19–42.

Helms, M.
1988 *Ulysses' sail: an ethnographic odyssey of power, knowledge and geographical distance*. Princeton: Princeton University Press.

Hodder, I.

2012 *Entangled. An Archaeology of the Relationships between Humans and Things.* Chichester: Wiley-Blackwell.

Holloway, R.R.

2005 Fortifications with towers in Bronze Age Sicily. In R. Gigli (ed.), *Megalai Nesoi. Studi dedicati a Giovanni Rizza per il suo ottantesimo compleanno* (2 vols.). Vol. 1: 299–305. Catania: Studi e materiali di archeologia mediterranea 2–3.

Horden, P. and N. Purcell

2000 *The Corrupting Sea: a study of Mediterranean History.* Oxford: Blackwell.

Iacono, F.

2015 Feasting at Roca: Cross-cultural encounters and society in the Southern Adriatic during the Late Bronze Age. *European Journal of Archaeology* 18: 259–281.

2012 Westernising LHIII C. In M.E. Alberti and S. Sabatini (eds.) *Exchange Networks and Local Transformations: Interactions and Local Changes in Europe and the Mediterranean between the Bronze Age and the Iron Ages*: 60–79. Oxford: Oxbow Books.

Jones, R.E., S.T. Levi and M. Bettelli

2006 Mycenaean pottery in the Central Mediterranean: Imports, Imitations and Derivatives. In R. Laffineur and E. Greco (eds.), *Emporia: Aegeans in the Central and Eastern Mediterranean*, Aegaeum 25: 539–546. Liège and Austin (TX): University of Liège and University of Texas at Austin.

Jones, R.E., S.T. Levi, M. Bettelli and L. Vagnetti

2014 *Italo-Mycenaean Pottery: The Archaeological and Archaeometric Dimensions*, Incunabula Graeca, CNR-ISMA Roma, 2014.

Knapp, B.

2007 Insularity and island identity in the prehistoric Mediterranean. In S. Antoniadou and A. Pace (eds.) *Mediterranean Crossroads*: 37–62. Oxford: Oxbow Books.

Knapp, A.B. and P. van Dommelen

2010 Material connections. Mobility, materiality and Mediterranean identities. In P. van Dommelen and A.B. Knapp (eds.) Material connections in the ancient Mediterranean: mobility, materiality and Mediterranean identities: 1–18. London: Routledge.

Knappett, C. (ed.)

2011 *An Archaeology of Interaction. Network Perspectives on Material Culture and Society.* Oxford: Oxford University Press.

Knappett, C., T. Evans and R. Rivers

2008 Modelling maritime interaction in the Aegean Bronze Age. *Antiquity* 82: 1009–1024.

Kristiansen, K.

1998 The emergence of the European world system in the Bronze Age: Divergence, convergence and social evolution during the first and second millennia BC in Europe. In K. Kristiansen and M. Rowlands (eds.) *Social transformations in archaeology: global and local perspectives.* 287–324. Routledge, London.

Leighton, R.
1999 *Sicily Before History. An Archaeological Survey from the Palaeolithic to the Iron Age.* London: Duckworth.

Mac Sweeney, N.
2009 Beyond Ethnicity: The Overlooked Diversity of Group Identities. *Journal of Mediterranean Archaeology* 22(1): 101–126.

Maran, J. and P.W. Stockhammer
2012 Introduction. In J. Maran and P.W. Stockhammer (eds.) *Materiality and Social Practice. Transformative Capacities and Intercultural Encounters.* Papers of the Conference, Heidelberg, 25th–27th March 2010: 1–3. Oxford: Oxbow Books.

Marazzi, M. and S. Tusa (eds.)
1994 *Vivara. Centro Commerciale mediterraneo dell'età del Bronzo. Vol. II. Le tracce dei contatti con il mondo egeo (scavi 1976-1982).* Bagatto Libri: Roma.

Martinelli, M.C., G. Fiorentino, B. Prosdocimi, C. d'Oronzo, S.T. Levi, G. Mangano, A. Stellati and N. Wolff
2010 Nuove ricerche nell'insediamento sull'istmo a Filo Braccio a Filicudi. Nota preliminare sugli scavi 2009. *Origini* 32: 285–314.

Panagiotopoulos, D.
2011 The Stirring Sea. Conceptualising transculturality in the Late Bronze Age Eastern Mediterranean. In K. Duistermaat and I. Regulski (eds.) *Intercultural contacts in the ancient Mediterranean*: 31–52. Leuven: Peeters.

Papageorgiou, D.
2008 Sea routes in the prehistoric Cyclades. In N. Brodie, J. Doole, G. Gavalas and C. Renfrew (eds.) *Horizon: a colloquium on the prehistory of the Cyclades*: 9–11. Cambridge: McDonald Institute Monographs.

Rainbird, P.
2007 *The Archaeology of Islands.* Cambridge University Press.

Relph, E.
1976 *Place and Placelessness.* London: Pion.

Rennell, R.
2010 Islands, islets, experience and identity in the Outer Hebridean Iron Age. *Shima: The International Journal of Research into Island Cultures* 4(1): 47–64.

Rivers, R., C. Knappett and T. Evans
2013 What makes a site important? Centrality, gateways and gravity. In C. Knappett (ed.) *Network analysis in archaeology. New approaches to regional interaction*: 125–150. Oxford: Oxford University Press.

Rizio, A.
2006 Vivara: An "International" Port in the Bronze Age. In R. Laffineur and E. Greco (eds.), *Emporia: Aegeans in the Central and Eastern Mediterranean*, Aegaeum 25: 623–628. Liège and Austin (TX): University of Liège and University of Texas at Austin.

Robb, J.

2001 Island identities: ritual, travel and the creation of difference in Neolithic Malta. *European Journal of Archaeology* 4(2): 175–201.

Seamon, D. and J. Sowers

2008 Place and placelessness, Edward Relph. In P. Hubbard, R. Kitchen and G. Vallentine (eds.) *Key Texts in Human Geography*: 43–51 London: Sage.

Sherratt, A.

1993 What would a Bronze-Age world system look like? Relations between temperate Europe and the Mediterranean in later prehistory. *Journal of European Archaeology* 1: 1–57.

1994 Core, Periphery, and Margin. In C. Mathers and S. Stoddart (eds.) *Development and Decline in the Mediterranean Bronze Age*: 335–345. Sheffield: J.R. Collis.

Tanasi, D.

2004 Per un riesame degli elementi di tipo miceneo nella cultura di Pantalica Nord. In V. La Rosa (ed.) *Le presenze micenee nel territorio siracusano*. Atti del Primo simposio siracusano di preistoria siciliana (Siracusa 15–16 dicembre 2003): 337–383. Padova: Aldo Ausilio Editore.

2005 Mycenaean pottery imports and local imitations: Sicily vs Southern Italy. In R. Laffineur and E. Greco (eds.), *Emporia: Aegeans in the Central and Eastern Mediterranean*, Aegaeum 25: 561–569. Liège and Austin (TX): University of Liège and University of Texas at Austin.

2006 *La Sicilia e l'arcipelago maltese nell'età del Bronzo Medio*. Kasa, Officina di Studi medievali.

2009 Sicily at the end of the Bronze Age: 'Catching the Echo'. In C. Bachhuber and R. Gareth Roberts (eds.) *Forces of Transformation. The End of the Bronze Age in the Mediterranean*. BANEA, vol. 1: 51–58. Oxford: Oxbow Books.

Tanasi, D. and N. Vella

2014 Islands and Mobility: Exploring Bronze Age Connectivity in the South–Central Mediterranean. In P. van Dommelen and B. Knapp (eds.) *The Cambridge Prehistory of the Bronze and Iron Age Mediterranean*: 53–73. Cambridge: Cambridge University Press.

Thomas, J.

1993 The politics of vision and the archaeologies of landscape. In B. Bender (ed.) *Landscape: Politics and Perspectives*: 19–48. Oxford and New York: Berg.

1996 *Time, culture and identity. An interpretive archaeology*. London.

Tilley, C.

1994 *A phenomenology of landscape. Places, paths and monuments*. Oxford and New York: Berg.

1996 The power of rocks. Topography and monument construction on Bodmin Moor. *World Archaeology* 28: 161–176.

2004 *The Materiality of Stone. Explorations in Landscape Phenomenology*. Oxford and New York: Berg.

Tuan, Yi-Fu

1974 *Topophilia: A Study of Environmental Perceptions, Attitudes, and Values*. Englewood Cliffs, New Jersey: Prentice-Hall.

Tusa, S.

1983 *La Sicilia nella preistoria*. Palermo: Sellerio.

1994 *Sicilia Preistorica*. Palermo: Dario Flaccovio.

2015 *Sicilia archeologica. I caratteri e percorsi dell'isola dal Paleolitico all'Età del Bronzo negli orizzonti del Mediterraneo*. Ragusa: Edizioni di Storia e Studi Sociali.

Tykot, R.
1996 Obsidian procurement and distribution in the central and western Mediterranean. *Journal of Mediterranean Archaeology* 9(1):39–82.

Van Dommelen, P.
2012 Colonialism and migration in the ancient Mediterranean. *Annual Review of Anthropology* 41: 393–409.

Van Dommelen, P. and A.B. Knapp (eds.)
2010 *Material connections in the ancient Mediterranean: mobility, materiality and Mediterranean identities.* London: Routledge.

Vianello, A.
2009 Late Bronze Age Exchange Networks in the Western Mediterranean. In C. Bachhuber and R. Gareth Roberts (eds.) *Forces of Transformation. The End of the Bronze Age in the Mediterranean.* BANEA, vol. 1: 44–50. Oxford: Oxbow Books.

Wallerstein, I.
1974 *The Modern World-System, vol. I: Capitalist Agriculture and the Origins of the World-Economy in the Sixteenth Century.* New York/London: Academic Press.

Watts, C. (ed.)
2013 *Relational archaeologies: Humans, animals, things.* London: Routledge.

Chapter 13

Nought may Endure but Mutability: Eclectic Encounters and Material Change in the 13th to 11th Centuries BC Aegean

Barry P. C. Molloy

Introduction

The year 1200 BC stands as a watershed moment in Bronze Age Europe and the Mediterranean. Within less than five decades either side of this point, settlement systems were dramatically transformed in far flung areas within a climate of intensified mobility. In the Carpathian Basin, long-established centres of habitation were abandoned and new fortified sites emerged alongside smaller open settlements (Artursson 2010). Terramare sites in Northern Italy were abandoned to be replaced by a smaller number of new settlements, and the design of many had defensibility firmly in mind (Bianchin Citton 2009; Kristiansen forthcoming). Sweeping changes in settlement pattern are seen east of the Adriatic also, where in parts of Slovenia, Dalmatia, Albania and Montenegro, the number of fortified sites increases and new domestic and mortuary practices emerge (Bulatović *et al.* 2003; Barbarić 2009; Galaty 2009; Teržan and Karavanić 2013). In the Balkan interior, increased agglomeration of settlements occurs along the Sava-Danube corridor (Jevtić and Vukmanović 1996) and many settlements along other major route-ways become fortified, notably the north–south arterial route of the Morava valley (Stojić 1996; Bulatović 2007; Kapuran 2009). Nowhere were settlement and demographic transformations felt more acutely than in the Aegean, where palatial culture collapsed in southern Greece and settlement density diminishes throughout much of the region (Andreou *et al.* 1996; Drews 1993; Souyoudzouglou-Haywood 1999; Tartaron 2004; Dickinson 2006). In a volume focusing on scales and modes of interaction, the relationship between changes taking place in the Aegean and these other regions could hardly have more potential drama.

This paper considers how increased intercultural mobility within these regions played a role in the emergence of artefacts of mixed heritage in the Aegean in the thirteenth to eleventh century BC. Specifically, the local transformations of types of bronze artefact with exogenous origin are considered in light of potential new meanings being attached to them and indigenous artefacts following The Catastrophe around 1200 BC (Drews 1993; Cline 2014). In order to address this, the concept of entanglement (Stockhammer 2012) is employed to account for changes in the appearance and functions of common artefact types. This approach considers the coming together of traditions through social encounters and interactions, and how changes to artefact forms can be material outcomes of these. The bronzework examined is primarily weaponry, which constitutes the material components of martial arts systems that were by definition highly social phenomena. This makes weaponry an ideal dataset for exploring entanglement. The ceramic record is briefly examined for the purpose of cross-referencing temporalities, intensities, and the character of connectivity between societies in parts of Italy and Greece.

Mobility, connectivity and change: 1200 BC

Romantic tales of migrating hordes of Dorians laying waste to Mycenaean palatial societies have been resigned by many to academic mythology (Maspero 2010; O'Brien 2013). While we may no longer seek evidence for mass permanent population movements, we nonetheless find echoes of new forms of mobility in the material culture of the Aegean and East Mediterranean from the thirteenth century (Harding 1984; Bouzek 1985; Dickinson 2006). As a result, sweeping models of migration have largely been displaced in favour of less all-or-nothing talk of mobility, which may includes movement of people, things and/or ideas (Chapman and Hamerow 1997: 2; Bergerbrandt 2013). Explaining this mobility at the time of palatial collapse has included large-scale raiding by Sea Peoples (Sandars 1985), movement of mercenaries (Catling 1961, 1956; Bettelli 2002; Jung and Mehoefer 2009), re-/displacement of elites (Bouzek 1994), economic entrepreneurship (Sherratt 2000; 2003; Dickinson 2006), cultural appropriation (Iacono 2013; Broodbank 2013: 462–464), or less closely defined exchanges (Harding 1984). There is general agreement that during the height of the Mycenaean palatial period in LH IIIB, a trickle of bronze weapons, new ceramic forms, and personal ornaments were introduced to Greece from Italy and the Balkans. Since LH IIIA, and to a degree since LH I, societies in the Aegean had maintained relationships with groups in neighbouring regions – visible primarily through ceramics in southern Italy, weaponry in the southern Balkans and amber in Greece (primarily in LH I-II).

The collapse of the palaces by LH IIIC would certainly have played a role in the changing character of long-standing regional social relations, although the question remains as to whether that collapse was a catalyst for, or a symptom/by-product of, these changing relationships. A useful review of the chronology, spatial extent and character of this collapse in the Aegean, sometimes dubbed 'the catastrophe', is provided by Drews (1993) and its initial aftermath by Dickinson (2006: 58–78; 2009) and Deger-Jalkotzy (1998; 2006). In general terms, this was characterised by the physical destruction of palatial centres in the decades around 1200 BC, and the loss of literacy and decline of economic networks. This primarily affected the Mycenaean heartlands and Crete, and while changes occurred in other parts of Greece, these did not tend to be as dramatic. Indeed, Mycenaean culture in any sense of the word must be seen as a complex phenomenon variably embraced by peoples in different parts of modern Greece[1] (Feuer, 2011; Boyd, this volume). In light of this, whether we believe in a united Mycenaean kingdom(s) or not during LH IIIA-B (Kelder 2005; 2010), it is clear that the peoples in different geopolitical regions of that ambit were not interacting as a single unit with the various contemporary societies in Italy and the Balkans (Figure 13.1). A zonal approach to regional space in which we speak of 'the Balkans', 'Italy' or 'the Mycenaean world' may be a useful shorthand, though the reductionist effect of thinking of these as meaningful 'blocks' should be kept firmly in mind if we are to take better account of diversity in each region.

Attempts to characterise inter-connections between societies within and around the Aegean have intensified in recent years, with studies refining the chronology, character, directionality and intensity of connectivity (*e.g.* Harding 2007; Horejs 2007; Strack 2007; Blake 2008; Jung *et al.* 2008; Borgna and Càssola Guida, 2009; Giannopoulos, 2009; Moschos 2009; Tomas, 2010; Sherratt 2012; Iacono 2013; Molloy and Doonan 2015). Recognition

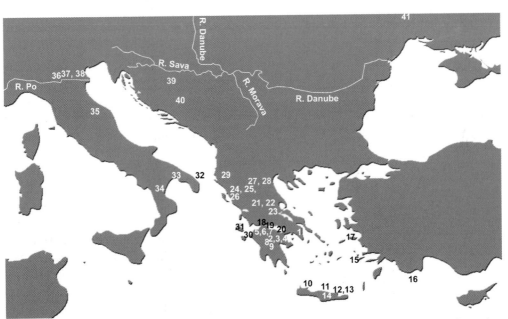

Figure 13.1: Places mentioned in the text: 1) Perati, 2) Mycenae, 3) Tiryns, 4) Midea and Dendra, 5) Voudheni, 6) Mitopolis and Monodendri, 7) Kangadhi, 8) Nemea, 9) Anthochori, 10) Chania, 11) Zapher Papoura and New Hospital Site, Knossos, 12) Chamaizi, 13) Mouliana, 14) Psychro cave, 15) Kangadha on Kos, 16) Uluburun shipwreck, 17) Samos, 18) Delphi, 19) Korakou, 20) Aigeira, 21) Kierion, 22) Agrilia, 23) Lamia, 24) Aiani, 25) Metaxata, 26) Konitsa, 27) Kastanas, 28) Polimistrias, 29) Kelkyre, 30) Teichos Dimaion, 31) Diakata on Kephalonia, 32) Roca Vecchia, 33) Scoglio del Tonno, 34) Broglio, 35) Casalecchio, 36) Peschiera, 37) Pila Del Brancón, 38) Fratessina, 39) Matijeviči, 40) Lučica, 41) Hordeevka.

of interaction with groups in southern Italy (including the islands) from LH IIIA-C–LH IIIC is dominated by the study of ceramics, although metalwork, amber, and ivory also changed hands. Explanations for the alleged increase in importance of the Adriatic to trade and economics in the East Mediterranean have focussed on expanding trading networks (Sherratt 2000; 2003; 2012; Eder and Jung 2005; Iacono 2013). A recurrent theme in this scenario is that the Mycenaeans were seeking new sources of metal in Italy, though empirical evidence is thin at best (Blake 2008: 6–9; Jung and Mehoefer 2013; Molloy and Doonan, 2015). Looking in the other direction, Bettelli (2002), Jung (2009a; 2009b) and Kristiansen (forthcoming) argue that Italian artefacts that appear in the East Mediterranean are evidence for the mobility of people, and they follow Catling (1956) in placing particular emphasis on the movement of warriors as mercenaries or raiders in later LH IIIB-C. Across the Adriatic in the Balkans, the lack of ceramic imports alone has been considered to reflect weaker social links, although it is fair to see ceramics as reflecting a limited and perhaps specific component of social interactions. The exchange of military technology and artefacts dominated interaction between societies in Greece and the southern Balkans, and may suggest again a bias towards particular forms of interaction. Notably, analyses of Balkan-Italian interaction at this time remain very rare.

When assessing scales and modes of connectivity, the functions of those artefacts that define the existence of networks also to no small degree define their purposes. In seeking to explain how and why artefacts from outside of the Aegean came to play roles in societies there, it is necessary to disentangle the social aspects of the networks that brought them. It is also important from this perspective to disaggregate exemplars of 'foreign' influence by focussing on their social contexts of consumption, such that weapons of violence are not conflated with domestic pots or occasional imported ornaments at our starting point. In so doing, we may well look from the time before the emergence of distinct phenomena and trace how they emerge as we move forward in time (Van der Leeuw 2013: 337) rather than retrospectively conflating socially or contextually poorly related materials to form a unifying narrative.

Urnfield or entangled bronzes?

Iacono (2013) has recently discussed the use of artefact types in Greece, particularly bronzework, with Italian and/or Balkan progenitors as *westernizing*, emphasising the role of local choice in using artefact forms of a distinctly non-native tradition. His position places strong emphasis on the aesthetic/symbolic qualities of those artefacts. Sherratt (2000: 85; 2003: 41) views this development as itinerant smiths 'naturalising' novel object types that were sought after and traded in the East Mediterranean due to their functional and aesthetic alterity, as well as their value in unregulated metal exchange. Jung and Mehoefer (2009; 2013) advocate a position of more direct introduction by Italian warriors, potentially as mercenaries, trading partners, and/or mobile warrior groups. In these cases the Mycenaean world and East Mediterranean are treated from a geographic perspective whereby groups there are engaging with, and receiving influence from, external Italian groups. Balkan influences on metalwork are not considered to be particularly significant in these studies. Some years ago Harding's (1984) analysis of the 'Mycenaeans and Europe' attempted to segregate Italian and Balkan influences in the Naue II swords in Greece, which he considered problematic because many artefacts were an indecipherable mix of morphological elements.

Drawing on the ambiguities of origins or influences noted by Harding, I propose in this paper that firstly we are not dealing with directional influences between points of cultural origin and reception, but rather groups developing artefact designs within a multicultural milieu, and secondly that for the majority of the land mass within the contemporary borders of Greece, Balkan influence is significantly better represented than Italian. It is argued that this influence was dominantly militaristic on the basis that weaponry is the most commonly shared artefact category. This sharing is considered to operate on two distinct levels, one deriving from short to medium range interactions by land (Balkan) and sea (Italian) and a second from long-range interactions of a maritime nature associated with the activities of sea borne men of fortune often dubbed the Sea Peoples (Sandars 1985).

In this latter context we may find groups from multiple origins, including Italy and the Balkans, with distinct ethnic backgrounds interacting in a new social environment. As evidence for mass migration is clearly lacking, we must look to contexts whereby smaller groups were moving across cultural boundaries. This may have been associated with a growing phenomenon of piracy, as defined by Hitchcock and Maeir (2014). In such circumstances, we may envisage a milieu whereby cultural multiple cultural traditions came together aboard ships divorcing them from the specific traditions of a given region and creating a novel and literal 'third space' for encounters (Fahlander 2007). This could lead to the entanglement of combat or martial art traditions that was materialised as a synthesis of functional and aesthetic aspects in bronze combat weaponry. It may also be manifested by smiths seeing novel objects and selectively adapting desirable components (*e.g.* the solid-cast sockets of spearheads). This process of mixing of traditions has been referred to as hybridisation or creolisation, though as Stockhammer (2012) has argued, these place unwarranted emphasis on the ultimate form of the object as opposed to the social conditions through which it emerged. The term entanglement is adopted in this paper as it reflects the coming together of both form and function in the development of new objects with a mixed or entangled heritage derived from more than one tradition along with novel developments (see also Fahlander 2007: 22). For this reason, we must consider that the symbolic value of the items may not have been defined by qualities of alterity or foreignness, but a reduced social distance between different cultural and ethnic groups making and using similar things.

The term 'Urnfield Bronzes' is often used to generically group artefacts that exhibit features related to metalwork to the north and west (Harding 1984; Sherratt 2000; Iacono 2013). This term of convenience, however, risks isolating the artefacts as inalienably foreign and detaching them from the new trajectories of development and meaning that exogenous traditions take on in new cultural environments (Panagiotopoulos 2012; Maran 2013: 147). The regular reproduction of distribution plots of 'Urnfield Bronzes' (*e.g.* Bouzek 1985: 143; Sherratt 2000: 86; Broodbank 2013:

463; Iacono 2013: 64) maintains this perpetual quality of foreignness. I propose that Entangled Bronzes is a more appropriate term for artefacts which have taxonomic characteristics that are ultimately of exogenous origin but which have distinctively local articulations in the East Mediterranean, alongside indigenous and wholly novel components. This reduces the implied directionality of the existing terminology and accounts more completely for the active role of local groups in the development of new synergistic artefact forms.

Leading from this, and as argued in detail below, many or even most of the 'Urnfield Bronzes' should not be treated as a class apart from the other bronzes in circulation because this masks the character of interaction underlying their development. While some imports and direct copies remain into LH IIIC, both these and entangled forms have regional distributions that can be defined. While it is conceded that on the above definition we should include all contemporary bronze weapons as being entangled, the use of term is intended to dispense with the 'foreign' connotations arising from the term Urnfield Bronzes, or more recently 'Italian type' (Jung and Mehoefer 2009; 2013), and so I use it here pragmatically to emphasise the multicultural aspects of development in local East Mediterranean contexts.

From beyond the pale: Italian and Balkan bronze types in the East Mediterranean

The chronology and description of artefacts of European origin and influence in the Aegean have been widely discussed, and include bronze weapons, fibulae, amber, ceramics and occasional finds such as rings, pins or pendants (Snodgrass 1964; Avila 1983; Harding 1984; 1995; Bouzek 1985; 1994; Czebreszuk 2007; 2011; Strack, 2007; Giannopoulos, 2009; Jung 2009a; 2009b). A complete 'package' is lacking in any particular context and finds are typically isolated, locally manufactured, and in assemblages dominated by Aegean material culture (Dickinson 2006; Moschos 2009). Dickinson (2006: 204; but see Iacono 2013) has noted that sites with bronze weaponry of entangled heritage are very rarely found with Handmade Burnished Ware (hereafter HBW) or amber, and the latter two rarely overlap (*e.g.* from different contexts at Tiryns, or one example of each in different graves at Perati in Attica). It is commonly accepted that most Entangled Bronze objects found in Greece were locally made, being derived from a presumed 'early horizon' of imports that catalysed this process (Harding 1984: 283; Bouzek 1985: 143; 1994; Sherratt 2000: 85; Jung 2009b). Known examples of these supposed progenitor artefacts remain exceptionally sparse, however, and are proportionately very rare in comparison with 'local' bronzework. This stands in contrast to the absolute and relative frequency of Entangled Bronze forms in LH IIIC. The *a priori* position that objects of the later date somehow emerged from the rare and spatially restricted earlier ones is predicated on an evolutionary logic. This fails to take proper account of the transformed social contexts in which weapons were acquired and used before and after the collapse of the Mycenaean palaces and their networks of interaction.

We can begin characterising the metalwork with an observation drawn from the systematically published thirteenth to eleventh century BC hoards from Slovenia (bridging Italy and the Balkans by land). Turk (1996) has demonstrated that weapons typically make up 5–15% of 'large hoards of mixed composition', and a very similar pattern is notable in Balkan hoards (Vinski-Gasparini, 1973; Basler *et al.* 1983; Jovanović 2010; pers. obs. 2012–2013). Accepting that hoards are constructed phenomena created to pursue specific social agendas (Brück and Fontijn 2013), it is nonetheless apparent that weapons represent a small proportion of the total metal artefacts in circulation in those lands. This is in marked contrast to the East Mediterranean where they represent the vast majority of Entangled Bronze artefacts. This implies that interaction involved the carriage of a highly selective yet functionally distinct range of artefacts, and by extension the likelihood that the agents moving these were those using them. This said, imports appear to be very rare in LH IIIC so we must ask how people in the Aegean were being exposed to the form of the weaponry during that particular period.

Metalwork

The chronological and spatial patterns particular to each category of metalwork make it preferable to treat them separately here.

Swords

Swords comprise a unique aspect of material culture, in that they are often seen as the intimate possessions of those individuals who played a strategic role in political power dynamics (Kristiansen 2002; Earle 2013; Sørensen 2013; *contra* Bruck and Fontijn 2013: 198–210). Found from the Levant to Britain, the Naue II sword has been the subject of several region-specific typological studies and has perhaps the most widespread distribution of any artefact type in prehistoric Europe, making it a particularly valuable proxy for measuring connectivity. The earliest dated examples of Naue II swords in Northern Italy derive from mid-thirteenth century contexts, closely contemporary to the first evidence for the form at Mycenae (Krzyszkowska 1997; Jung and Mehoefer 2009). The Naue II sword occurs widely in Greece in LH IIIC (Figure 13.2), although the reasons behind its success in that period are not agreed upon. A functionalist explanation contends that it was simply a superior weapon and so it displaced the Aegean sword tradition – a view most recently advocated in detail by Jung and Mehoefer (2009; 2013; Jung 2009b). I have argued elsewhere that this affords an unbalanced agency to an object form in itself and that the continued use of Aegean sword forms requires us to see it as one of many adaptive choices within an evolving martial system (Molloy 2005; 2010; 2011, 2010, 205). I can certainly agree with Jung and Mehoefer that the addition of the Naue II sword extended the range of choices within local systems, and its impact on the changing martial arts milieu appears to have been contributory rather than causal.

Figure 13.2: 1) Naue II sword with faux-midrib from Karditsa/Graditsa in Thessaly 2) Naue II sword from Sitia region, East Crete (Photographs by author and used courtesy of the Ashmolean Museum, Oxford).

In areas north of the Gulf of Corinth, a distinctive feature develops on Naue II swords that is rarely seen anywhere else in Europe – a stylised midrib flanked by two ridges (Figure 13.2.1). The appearance of this feature strongly echoes that of the older Type D tradition of Aegean swords on which the rib and ridge combination was a characteristic feature (Figure 13.3). It can be noted that most Naue II swords that possess these faux-midribs are notably longer and thinner than the 'original' design (Figure 13.4). This required them to be used in a manner that incorporates cutting techniques that had much in common with those employed with earlier Aegean midrib swords, like the Type D (Molloy 2008). Most were simply not suited to the robust slashing often postulated as being the defining characteristic of Naue II swords because they would bend or break if used in that manner. None so far are dated earlier than LH IIIC and they occur across much of Central and Northern Greece, Albania, Croatia, FYRO Macedonia and Bulgaria (Figure 13.5). Only one possible example from Italy is known to me (From Castellace in Calabria (Paccierelli 2006: Fig 2.32)). At least three examples (out of seventeen swords of this type) are known from Achaea (T. Papadopoulos 1999; Papazoglou-Manioudaki 1994; Moschos 2009: 386).

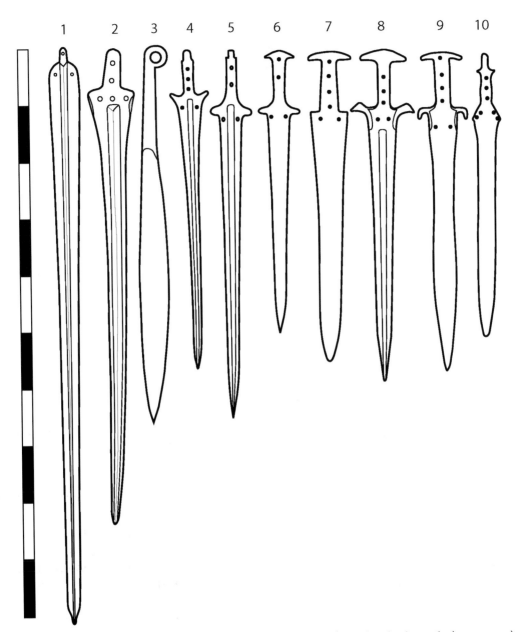

Figure 13.3: Typology of Aegean swords: 1) Type A; 2) Type B; 3) Single-edged sword; 4) Type C1; 5) Type Di; 6) Type Dii; 7) Type Fii; 8) Type Gi; 9) Type Gii; 10) Type Naue ii (drawn by author).

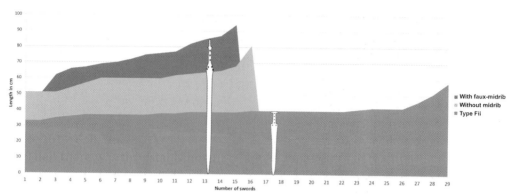

Figure 13.4: Comparative lengths of Naue II swords with faux-midrib, those without this feature, and Aegean Type Fii swords.

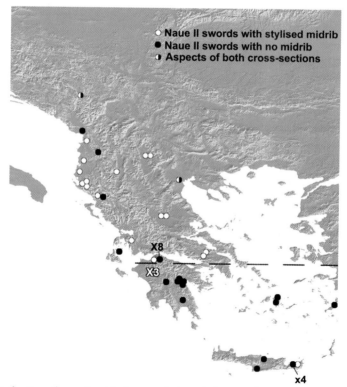

Figure 13.5: Distribution of swords with faux-midrib and those with 'classic' cross-section typical to earliest Naue II forms.

The areas north of the Mycenaean heartlands in which these forms of Naue II are found are exactly the same areas that had previously used Aegean midrib swords and had a notable penchant for modifying the design to suit local traditions (Kilian-Dirlmeier 1993: catalogue #81–87, 104–108; Harding 1995: catalogue #23–25). The distinctly Greek–South Balkan range of Naue II swords combined aesthetic and functional aspects of an already archaic tradition. The resultant changes in the weapon form may thus be seen as a materialisation of both craft and martial art practices combining two distinct traditions through which a new or entangled one emerged. We can also observe that the addition of a pommel spur to Naue II swords in the Aegean was probably derived from the native midrib sword tradition of the fifteenth to thirteenth century, as it did not occur on the more recent local types Dii, Fii and Gii swords (Catling 1961; Sandars 1963). This may further support the survival of the earlier sword tradition in certain locations and their role in the entanglement of traditions. In this we can see an archaic and a new tradition coming together and largely bypassing the more recent history of military material culture and associated practices.

In Crete, the picture is distinctly different from that on the mainland. While one example of the above faux-midrib form has been found at Mouliana, the more typical feature of Cretan Naue II swords is that they were produced with a much reduced length and weight in contrast to their 'progenitors' (Molloy 2010). It is notable that Aegean tradition swords (Type Fii and Gii) in East Crete are unusually long by contrast, suggesting a mixing of sword-fighting styles associated with the Type F and the Naue II, whereby the material components of combat practice (the swords) came to be made in more similar proportions, thus meeting at the dimensional extremity of both traditions.

South of the Gulf of Corinth Naue II swords are manufactured in proportions that are most similar to those in Italy. This is evident in their general design characteristics, notably the cross section and a distinct preference for swords in the range of 58–62 cm. The hilt forms equally have similarities to Italian examples, though on some the roundness of the shoulders, for example, implies local developments. Most of the swords we have from this period come from the cemeteries of Achaea, a region that maintained particularly close contacts with southern Italy for a long duration (Moschos 2009).

There had long been different contemporary designs of Aegean sword in use, stretching back to the types A and B and single-edged swords of the Shaft Grave era, so this diversity was indeed a hallmark of the Mycenaean martial ethos (Molloy 2010). In LH IIIC, the boundaries between Aegean types also became blurred, such that horned swords of Type Gii could have similar blades to Type Fii swords or the by-then archaic Type Dii tradition (compare Kilian-Dirlmeier 1993: #103 (Perati) with #104 (Mouliana) and #102 (Ithaka) with #147 (Kelkyre) or #202 (Chamaizi)). Nonetheless, the retention of the distinctive hilt forms of each type demonstrates that makers and users maintained these as meaningful differences. It is notable also that the adoption of multiple tiny ribs on the blades of these swords has close parallels on contemporary Levantine swords (Shalev 2004), hinting that these swords too were playing a role in intercultural encounters in the post-palatial period. With this variety of swords in circulation in LH IIIC, choice clearly extended beyond a simple dichotomy of exogenous vs. autochthonous traditions.

We are fortunate to have a well-published dataset relating to the metallurgy of late Mycenaean swords, making this group quite distinct amongst bronze artefacts. It can be observed that Naue II swords in the Aegean often followed the local smithing tradition whereby most had higher tin contents than we find in Italy or the Balkans (Trampuž-Orel 1996; Mangou and Ioannou 1999; Koui *et al.* 2006; Hook 2007; Giumlia-Mair *et al.* 2010; pers. obs. 2013). This tradition of higher tin content is probably related to an established preference for this level of tin, as seen in earlier Aegean sword forms (Mangou and Ioannou 1998; 1999). This was not merely an issue of workshop conservatism because it also affected the mechanical properties of the sword which in turn influenced combat practice, and higher tin also altered the colour of the finished artefact.

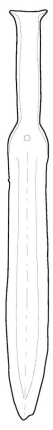

Figure 13.6: Peschiera type dagger (drawn by author).

Daggers

Daggers of Type Peschiera (also called Type Pertosa) represent a form with an Italian origin (Figure 13.6). The distinctive sub-group/variant Psychro dominates the Greek assemblage, though this is found in only two instances in Italy, at Scoglio del Tonno and at Peschiera. The earliest examples of this type in the Aegean come from LM/LH IIIB contexts at Zapher Papoura and Nemea (Th. Papadopoulos 1998: 29–30). The example from Teichos Dimaion is from a transitional LH IIIB / LH IIIC destruction context, and metallurgical analysis of this confirms that it is of local manufacture and not an import (Jung, Moschos and Mehoefer 2008; Moschos 2009). Another example comes from the site of Dodona in Epirus, from where a battle-axe with parallels in the Carpathian basin was recovered (Bouzek 1985: 142). Of the five contemporary dagger types defined by Bianco Peroni (1994), the Peschiera type is with one exception the only form in the Aegean. This suggests that the examples in the Aegean are the product of selective choices in the appropriation of daggers of a non-local form. Given the early LH IIIB date of the first pieces, the dominance of an otherwise rare variant, the native metallurgy of the Teichos Dimaion piece, and the dearth of other Italian forms of dagger, we can suggest that many of those known from Greece are the products of local workshops. The LH IIIC Middle double-edge dagger from Klauss in Achaea has close Italian parallels and may have ultimately originated there (Papadopoulos and Kontorli-Papadopoulou 2000: 144). The flow of actual objects may have been very irregular and infrequent. Unlike other Italian-type artefacts, the dated examples of Peschiera daggers are biased towards production in the palatial period, during which they outnumber dated examples of Naue II swords in Greece, but in LH/LM IIIC their use diminishes numerically and also proportionately with respect to other Entangled Bronze objects.

Spears

Spearheads of LH IIIB-C date in the East Mediterranean are particularly diverse, and include Aegean, Urnfield and Entangled forms, leading to wide disparities between the type-groups defined in the four studies of taxonomies published to date (Snodgrass 1964; Höckmann, 1980; Avila 1983; Cassola Guida 1992). In contrast to this, and although several forms are also known, there is greater regularity in the geometry, metrics and general appearance of spearheads in the Balkans and Italy (Vinski-Gasparini, 1973; Salzani, 1994; Pacciarelli 2006; Jovanović 2010). Only a small number of broadly 'Urnfield' tradition spearheads in the East Mediterranean find parallels in those other areas close enough to warrant considering them imports.

With multifarious typological nomenclature at our disposal, I prefer here to keep things descriptive and work with five broad groupings when speaking about spearheads with Entangled Bronze heritage, as this will serve to illustrate the points relevant to this paper (Figure 13.7). Spearheads with specifically Aegean progenitors (i.e. with a split socket) continue in use, and it is worth noting that Naue II swords in Achaea are found with this type in particular and never with Entangled Bronze spearheads (Moschos 2009: 387).

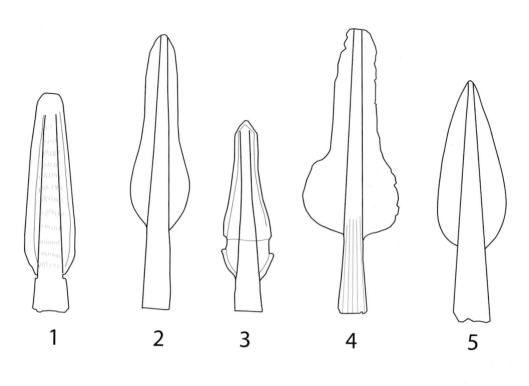

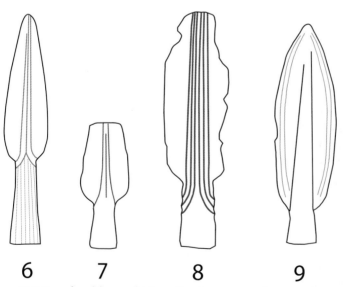

Figure 13.7: Spearhead forms: 1) Mitopolis, 2) Metaxata, 3) 'Crete', 4) Gribiani, 5) Argo, 6) Polemistrias. 7) Bela Crkva, 8) Delphi, 9) Near Lamia (re-drawn by author after Avila 1981 and Höckmann 1980. 7.7 drawn by author).

The first tradition is flame-shaped (Figure 13.7.1). These are amongst the earliest to develop and they continue into LH IIIC. At least two examples are known from the late fourteenth century Uluburun shipwreck (Pulak 1988), and another piece from Langadha on Kos is dated to around 1200 BC (Morricone 1967: 136–142). While similarities can be found, the actual type is unknown in the Balkans, and similar finds in Italy occur only in one instance each from the south (Paccierelli 2006: fig 2.14) and north (Jung 2009b: 73–74, Fig. 1.4). In Achaea, this form is particularly common. These trans-Adriatic contacts may account for the preference for the form specifically in Achaea, where it was manufactured locally. The results of analyses of three out of four pieces from Achaea (Jung 2009b: 75) show them to be made of metal compositions typically in use in the Aegean, the fourth piece is of metal consistent with that in circulation in Italy.[2] Similar pieces from Mycenae and Anthochori in the Peloponnese and Kierion in Thessaly may well be imports from Achaea, the last being the only published (possibly) Italian-inspired spearhead found north of the Gulf of Corinth.

The second tradition originates in the Balkans (Harding 1984: 167) and begins with a handful of probable imports (Figure 13.7.2) followed by the development of a distinctly local variation that is common in Albania and Epirus in particular, and north of the Gulf of Corinth more generally. This general group is defined by a distinctly 'violin-shape' or convex edges to the blade with a marked swelling in the profile in the third of the blade closest to the opening of the socket. The socket is invariably solid-cast and penetrates nearly to the tip of the blade. Examples of likely imports (or close copies thereof) are found at Metaxata in Kephallonia, Aiani in Epirus, and Mouliana in Crete, a possible import from 'Crete' (Figure 13.7.3) and another from Mitopolis in Achaea (Bouzek 1985: 135–142; Avila 1983). This last occurs alongside a late Type D sword in a later LH IIIB burial (Moschos 2009: 350). Good parallels for the 'Crete' and Mitopolis spearheads are rare, suggesting they may be local products, though some comparanda occur in Croatia (*e.g.* Vinski-Gasparini 1973, Figure 112. 3) and in Italy (*e.g.* Paccierelli 2006: Fig. 1.35; Fig. 3.6). Examples of this type from Corinth and Polis Cave in Ithaka are noteworthy in that they have the outline of this type, but the socket does not penetrate into the blade, marking them as local products (Avila 1983: 162C and 162D respectively). In general the origin of this second tradition in Greece appears Balkan where it is a dominant shape, and the occasional examples known in Italy (*e.g.* Pila Del Brancón [in Salzani 1994]) may well also prove to be imports from across the Adriatic. Examples of locally made spearheads derived from this general tradition are more common. These have a more pronounced swelling to their 'violin form' (Figure 13.7.4) and here are called Albano-Epirote on the basis of their dominant distribution. Recent excavations have increased the number of this type known to more than 15. Outliers occur in West Macedonia, Boeotia and Kangadhi in Achaea. The form is characterised by the swelling of the blade and by the faceted socket, though its importance also lies in the fact that the socket is cast and continues nearly to the point. This demonstrates that the technological know-how for casting this feature had been introduced from the north into Greece by the time these spearheads came into use. No examples of this Albano-Epirote type are known north of Albania, though the inspiration for the form clearly lies in that direction (compare Figure 13.8.1 and 13.8.2), as indicated by the small number of imports or close imitations. The date of its first production is unclear, but it appears to have been in common use by the middle of LH IIIC at least.

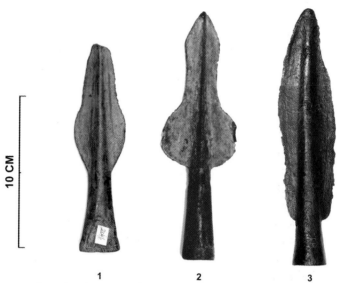

Figure 13.8: 1) Caransebeş, 2) "Thessaly", 3) Diakata on Kephallonia (Photos by author. 1 courtesy of Museum of Vršac, 2 courtesy of Ashmolean museum, Oxford, 3 courtesy of Argostoli Museum).

Figure 13.9: Spearhead mould fragments from Tiryns (courtesy of Lorenz Rahmstorf).

Spearheads with leaf-shaped blades form the third group (Figure 13.7.5). These are spatially and chronologically extensive, and so it is hard to use blade form to define directionality of influences. The cast socket suggests influence of 'Urnfield' craft traditions, though many diverge from the general proportions known in the Balkans or Italy. Certainly by LH IIIC leaf-shaped spearheads were being manufactured in various parts of Greece, as moulds from Kastanas in Macedonia and Tiryns (Figure 13.9) in the Peloponnese demonstrate (Hochstetter 1987; Rahmstorf 2008). Many of this group are small in size, particularly in Crete.

The fourth tradition of spearhead was also made locally, though it was more clearly derived from a type common to the Sava-Danubian area. These have moulded ribs along the socket/midrib. The piece from Polimistrias in Macedonia (Figure 13.7.6) has three ribs typical of Balkan types (*e.g.* Figure 13.7.7), but a faceted socket typical of the Albano-Epirote tradition, a feature unknown in the Balkans or Italy until the early first millennium BC.[3] A spearhead from Delphi can be added to this group (Höckmann 1980: G25), and is also likely to be an Iron Age interpretation of a Bronze Age Balkan import (Figure 13.7.8). Related to these is a spearhead from Agrilia in Thessaly (Volos museum inv. 2647) with ribs flanking the socket, and this was identified as being of distinctly Balkan form by Harding (1984: 167). The low trace element values from compositional analysis (*e.g.* Ni 0.04%, Sb 0.02%), however, suggest local manufacture using locally available metal (Mangou and Ioannou 1999; Molloy and Doonan 2015). These pieces further suggest that in areas north of the Gulf of Corinth, there was greater familiarity with Balkan than Italian forms, and that either imported objects were being copied or craftsmen familiar with both traditions were operating there. The winged-axe mould from Mycenae provides a further parallel for a craftsman knowledgeable about the Balkan-North Italian tradition being active on the Greek mainland (Stubbings 1954).

The final group of spearheads is rare (Figure 13.7.9), with pieces occurring near Lamia in Central Greece and Diakata on Kephallonia (Figure 13.8.3), both of which are likely to be direct imports from the north. These have short sockets and a regular curve to their elongated, leaf-shaped profile. The feature of incising lines along the edge may have been influential on pieces such as the above one from 'Crete' (Figure 13.7.3; Avila 1983), indicating perhaps a wider original distribution. The type is known in northern Italy and across the central to west Balkans (Vinski-Gasparini, 1973; Basler *et al.* 1983; Salzani 1994; Jovanović 2010).

Many of the artefacts manufactured in the Aegean, and more specifically those that are relatively *sui generis* and so not mentioned above (including most of the Cretan material, for example), are linked mainly through the method of casting solid sockets that penetrated into the blade, occasional aesthetic features (*e.g.* moulded ribs), and their general proportions. They are not, however, the products of attempts at faithful reproduction of Urfield weapons, as they possess elements selected from a jumbled stylistic and technological repertoire. Most of these objects do not look Italian or Balkan and indeed would appear distinctly out of place if they were excavated in either region. In the final analysis, these spearheads may be considered entangled but distinctively East Mediterranean because that is where they were created, which should lead us to dramatically depopulate the distribution maps of Urnfield Bronzes cited above. It is worth noting that the divide between regions north and south of the Gulf of Corinth appears to correspond with a division between Balkan and Italian influences respectively noted also for swords. While objects from Crete have been suggested to possess a dominantly Italian influence, most are either at the extremes of being unique or too generic to identify major points of influence, and appear to emerge from a far less directional sort of milieu.

Armour

The helmet from the New Hospital Site at Knossos (Hood and De Jong 1952) is dated to the early fourteenth century. Along with another unprovenanced piece believed to be from Greece, it is of a form known to occur in central Europe into the eleventh century at least (Clausing 2003a; Mödlinger 2013). The helmet from a sub-Mycenaean context at Tiryns, with its rosette decoration, lacks specific parallels in other areas of Europe, although Mödlinger sees the execution of the rosette decorative device as being more at home in Urnfield areas. It is difficult to say anything about corselets due to a dearth of finds, though general similarities in terms of manufacturing tradition, form and function can be noted on surviving artefacts and depictions of them from the Aegean and the Carpathian Mountains and Basin (Snodgrass 1964; 1971; Andrikou 2007; Mödlinger 2012; Molloy 2013).

The use of metal greaves was first seen alongside the Dendra corselet dated to c. 1400 BC. By the twelfth century BC, this form of armour is found in Greece, Italy, the Balkans and Central Europe (Clausing 2003b; Karavanić 2009; Mödlinger in preparation). The technology of manufacture, the dimensions and the general form (discoid) is good evidence that this type of armour had a shared craft as well as functional heritage. It is more difficult, however, to speak of the origin of specific forms or directionality in their adoption, apart from a general Greek origin for the concept. Decorative motifs vary considerably, although examples such as the eleventh century pair from the Athenian Acropolis have good parallels for the 'four-spoke-wheel' motif known in the Balkans and central Europe (Karavanić 2009).

Shields

Hencken (1950) noted that shields of round form and similar proportions to European types occur in Greek art at the same time as they become widespread across Europe – the later thirteenth century (see also Jung and Mehoefer 2009: 127–129; Molloy 2012: 128–129). Images such as that on the krater of Shield Bearers from Tiryns testify that representation, and by extension probably use, began by late LH IIIB (Vermeule and Karagheorgis 1982: 108–109, Fig. X.1) and a recent C14 dating program demonstrates that this form of shield was well established by 1200 BC in Europe (Needham et al. 2012). Round shields in both areas appear to be approximately 40–60 cm in diameter (Coles

1962; Molloy 2009; Uckelmann 2012). Because we rely exclusively on representational evidence, it is little wonder that discussion about European style shields in Greece has been brief in recent decades.

A find alleged to date to the Geometric period is, however, worth briefly reconsidering. This is a sheet bronze shield from Delphi, which cannot be dated by associated material and so its dating is primarily based on finds of broadly similar models of shields from the Geometric period at other sites (Homolle 1908; Hencken 1950; Uckelmann 2012: 63). The design of this shield is, however, notably different to the ceramic models it is compared with from Samos and possibly Rhodes, and bronze models from Cyprus, Delphi and Crete (Uckelmann 2012: 63). These latter pieces all have a v-notch characteristic of European shields, no doubt inspired by Herzsprung types, but the notch on most of the Mediterranean models penetrates into the boss thus marking them as divergent. The Delphi shield was different because it may have been a functional weapon. It had a true boss and, unlike the others, a handle was riveted in place. Furthermore, the application of the small bosses, rings and v-notch are devices found on two different, but related, types of European Late Bronze Age shields. The rings and bosses are definitive characteristics of Uckelmann's (2012: 14–21) Type Lommelev-Nyírtura and Group Plžen, both dated to *c.* 1300–1000 BC (Figure 13.10). Apart from one example in Denmark, the other (at least) five examples of Type Lommelev-Nyírtura shield are known from the Carpathian basin and Balkans – and these are the exclusive type of bronze shield yet known from this region. Only the Danish shield has the central area around the boss preserved, and while the v-notch motif was not used, it was known in that area of Europe (Uckelmann 2012: 50–73). We do not know what the central area of the other shields in this group looked like, and so we cannot rule out the presence of v-notches.

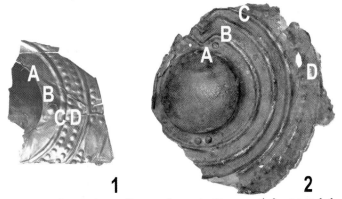

Figure 13.10: 1) Type Lommelev-Nyírtura from Nyírtura in Hungary (after M. Uckelmann); 2) Shield with v-notch and concentric rings and miniature bosses from Delphi (photograph by author). Shared features: A= Raised central boss with no interruptions to circuit, B= Rivet to secure handle, C= Uninterrupted embossed concentric ring, D= Concentric rows of bosses next to embossed ring.

In relation to the shield from Delphi, it may be that this is an entangled bronze weapon or a relatively faithful later copy of an original one, see for example Group Plzen shields (Uckelmann 2012). Shield 67 from the Idaean Cave in Crete (Hencken 1950: Figs. 8, 9), if we discount the small fragments alleged to come from it but not refitting with it, could equally be such a low-fidelity and crudely made near-contemporary piece. In both cases, three rings with v-notches are surrounded by concentric miniature bosses, suggesting they are of a single distinct (Aegean?) tradition or copying a distinct object. At the very least, we can be certain that the person who made the Delphi shield, and possibly the Cretan one, had a realistic knowledge of depicting the v-notch and/or what Lommelev-Nyírtura and/or Group Plzen shields actually looked like. Spearheads of LH IIIB-C date exhibiting Balkan influence are also known from Delphi (see above) and may lend support to the suggestion that this shield too is of Bronze Age date. A temporal divide between the use of functional artefacts with this v-notch and the reduction of this motif to a stylised symbol on models may explain the presence of the very un-European looking v-notch shield symbolism of the Iron Age in Greece. If this interpretation is correct, then the use of the motif in the Iron Age may be a much distorted survival from the Bronze Age and not a contemporary introduction with rapid stylisation towards the end of their period of use in Europe, as commonly argued (most recently Uckelmann 2012: 63–68).

Fibulae

Another category of bronze artefact frequently encountered is that of the bow-fibulae that emerge in the later thirteenth century. The earliest forms occur in Italy and along the Sava-Danube corridor and into the Morava valley (Vasić 1999; Teržan 2007; Lo Schiavo 2010). As with the other bronzes, a specific point of origin is difficult to pinpoint on the basis of numerical frequency alone, though it is clear that they emerged as part of the general shared milieu in parts of the Balkans and Northern Italy. They were most probably associated with specific forms of dress (cloaks?), and so form part of a larger, more visible social 'statement' than their small size in itself implies. That most were found on settlement sites as the product of unintentional deposition may suggest they were in quite wide circulation (Dickinson 2009). Given the simplicity of the form, ease of manufacture, and potential incidental diversity that emerges on this basis, it is difficult to use nuances of the form to discern regional variation, though their very existence and the parallel development of types in the Aegean and farther north suggest longevity to the clothing styles they represented. With this survey of the metalwork complete, we turn now to a very brief overview of the evidence for connectivity visible in the ceramic assemblages of Italy and Greece for comparative purposes.

Ceramics

Greece

The ceramic evidence is less clear cut than the bronzework, and the well-known 'barbarian' or 'Dorian' ware of old, more recently Handmade Burnished Ware (HBW), has been shown to have a very complex history. This class of pottery is not indigenous to Greece and is found occasionally in LH IIIB2 and more often, though still in small quantities, during LH IIIC. The inter-site variation in terms of forms and chronologies has been discussed in depth by Rutter (1990; 2012), Jung (2006) and Strack (2007) and detailed discussion goes beyond the parameters of this paper. It is important for the present discussion to recognise that no package of forms or functions was common to the sites where this pottery occurs. Furthermore, Strack (2007: 82) emphasises the marked heterogeneity in the manufacturing traditions at each site in terms of recipes, forming, surface treatment and firing techniques. This indicates that these are not the product of specific communities and perhaps not always made by specialist potters. The general picture is that there was no 'pure' and geographically specific point of origin. While the class, as well as the forms in which it was produced, has its roots generally in the Italian tradition, this does not account for the full range of stylistic and typological traits of artefacts found in Greece (Jung 2006; 2009b; Rahmstorf 2011: 318–319). Some exceptions occur, such as Kommos where imported Sardinian vessels occur, and Chania, where some possible imports are accompanied by locally made pieces that have close Italian parallels (Rutter 2012: 83 with refs). They occur at a restricted number of sites and always constitute a tiny minority in the overall assemblage (Rahmstorf 2011).

A key point raised by Strack (2007) is worth emphasising here: HBW had considerable longevity, despite the disparity in its spatial, chronological and typological patterning. The occurrence of these vessels was not a brief 'flash in the pan'. Indeed, new forms of objects including weights and figurines in the handmade tradition occur in LH IIIC Middle, long after the LH IIIB introduction of the ware (Rahmstorf 2011). Instances of its use appear to align with long-established maritime routes at sites along the Gulf of Corinth (Teichos Dymaion, Aigeira, Korakou) and down into the Argolid (Mycenae, Tiryns, Midea). It occurs at various sites in Crete where there is also regional variation within the island. There are also differences between forms on Cretan and the mainland sites, which makes it clear that different routes and perhaps mechanisms were responsible for its distribution within the Aegean region and as far afield as Cyprus and Tell Kazel in Syria (Strack 2007: 98; Boileau *et al.* 2010; Karageorgis 2011a, 2011b; Pilides and Boileau 2011). The superficial links between Levantine and Aegean-type sword blades mentioned above is perhaps salient again here. A single explanation for the manufacture of HBW in different times and places is unlikely. Its disparity and occurrence in otherwise local assemblages could suggest in some cases it is the product of local persons who had spent much time abroad. Counting it as a marker of immigration is thus problematic. This is compounded when we consider how individual immigrants may become 'more local than the locals themselves' in their consumption of material culture, influenced by the attractors that led them to settle and remain in Greece.

The finds of Grey Ware alongside HBW in the Argolid may provide a more direct link to Calabria and Apulia (Strack 2007: 100), although the quantity is too small to suggest anything of a commercial relationship, apart perhaps form Tiryns. It may, however, correspond with a known concentration of Mycenaean ceramic imports into those areas. The core issue for this paper is that on the basis of current evidence, the forms and distribution of both HBW and Grey Ware do not support the idea of either direct immigration from Italy or of direct acquisition of craft skills from there. It appears that the producers were circulating and living in the East Mediterranean. The use of exogenous ceramic traditions may have arisen from a combination of partial know-how, selectivity, and local developments and so it need not be indicative of geographic or ethnic origins of the makers.

Italy

The relationship of Aegean communities with those in the Adriatic has been the subject of renewed interest in recent years (Iacono 2013 for summary). Metalwork typical of Aegean traditions is extremely rare in Italy whereas ceramic imports can be identified at many sites (Blake 2008; Jung and Mehoefer 2013). It is notable that many imports into Italy in LH IIIA and IIIB came from Crete, West Greece, the Ionian Islands, and areas of the Peloponnese that were not in the heartlands of powerful palatial entities, so that communication with Apulia, Calabria, Sicily and Sardinia became linked into potentially expanding non-palatial networks (Sherratt 2003; Blake 2008). By LH IIIC, however, the range of imports into Italy dropped considerably and, where investigation has been sufficiently thorough, local imitations at most sites outnumbered imports (Blake 2008: 1, 5). Even at the height of the use of Aegean pottery at Italian sites, it represented a tiny minority in most assemblages, and was unlikely therefore to reflect acculturation, colonisation, trade, or indeed anything beyond sporadic encounters. An exception would be the site of Roca in Apulia because an unusually high density of Aegean type pottery was excavated there (Guglielmino 2009; Maggiulli 2009), almost equalling the *c.* 5600 sherds (or *c.* 1600 pots) from the 93 other Italian sites cited by Blake (2008). North of Apulia the story is markedly different, with Mycenaean sherds becoming increasingly rare, at many sites less than ten sherds have been recovered, many of which may have come via or directly from (meaning local manufacture) southern Italy. Those few sherds of alleged Mycenaean pottery known from the Balkans (see Tomas, 2010: 198–200 for a recent discussion) may well prove to be Italian or Macedonian, rather than Aegean imports.

Overall, the picture is of sporadic contacts operating at very specific levels of society in both the sending and the receiving communities, and not one of a systematic or continuous trading network (Iacono 2013). By LH IIIC Middle, Mycenaean imports drop off in most areas of Italy (Blake 2008; Moschos 2009: 380). Moschos (2009) has demonstrated that this was exactly the time that the deposition of metalwork of what he terms mixed Italian and Mycenaean heritage was at its height in Achaea. It may be that the increase in weaponry represents increased military actions that were interrupting the previous connections associated with the movement of ceramics. In any case, by LH IIIC we are looking at overlapping local networks linking West Greece and Apulia (and perhaps the Ionian islands), not Italians and Mycenaeans more generally. This throws into sharp relief the dearth of Entangled Bronze bronzes known from LH IIIB contexts and the large number in use by LH IIIC through to the Sub-Mycenaean period, even if it is accepted that weapons may have had a longer use-life than ceramics.

Discussion

It is clear that knowledge of Italian and/or Balkan forms of bronze artefacts was well established during the palatial period in southern Greece. Despite this, the influence of this knowledge on the forms and functions of products of the Aegean bronze industry was negligible throughout the century-long duration of LH IIIB. Equally, there is no notable increase in their presence until the decades following the collapse of the palaces. Even Peschiera daggers that were current for a long time as the virtually exclusive incarnation of the diverse range in contemporary Italy were not influenced by, nor did they influence, the local bronze industry. The widespread embracing of Entangled Bronze artefacts in LH IIIC might thus be seen as a deviation, not a progression, from the palatial reception of artefacts of exogenous origin or derivation. In this sense, metalwork better represents social discontinuity than continuity. It may reasonably be suggested that during LH IIIB, the Mycenaean palaces dominated interaction in their maritime networks such that the presence of foreign persons or objects in their territories was mediated on the basis of their intentions. With the collapse of the infrastructure of such networks, in LH IIIC this mediation must have become more diffuse through the intentions of more diverse and potentially multicultural groups.

At the risk of appearing to follow recent theoretical trends, my intention in using the term Entangled Bronze has not been to so much to introduce a categorisation but rather a descriptive/non-prescriptive phrasing that can simultaneously take account of exogenous influences and local contexts of material and social reproduction. This relates to object forms and the practices surrounding their use alike. I feel this could be truer to the material diversity than grouping together a disparate range of imports and derivative or loosely similar objects as 'Urnfield Bronzes', whether or not we place particular meaning in that or any other term. It is difficult in light of this to see the untidy mix of objects I have called Entangled Bronzes as a measure of long-distance trade or exchange, particularly as there is little evidence for imported metal as raw material or artefacts during LH IIIC. It is equally challenging to view areas of nominally more intense deposition of imports and/or entangled bronzes along sea-routes as representing the character of ancient routeways (Sherratt 2000:

86–88; Sherratt 2003: 41) rather than depositional practices of past communities or excavation biases today. This is especially the case if we consider the finds we have today as being the tip of the iceberg (Sherratt 2000: 84–88). Absolute numbers usually represent the vagaries of preservation and excavation (Needham 1993), and so a more useful measure of frequency in our case might be relative proportions in relation to artefacts of a more Aegean pedigree in the regions examined. This may be supported by consideration of particular functional or social categories of object, for example the predominance of Naue II versus Aegean forms of sword in Achaea. They thus stand in marked contrast to ceramics or burial practices, for example. In general, their forms and functions can be related to diversity in forms of fighting employed, and this in turn indicates that the systems in place were permeable enough to accommodate different practices alongside each other. The choices we see materialised are therefore important relative to each other and not in isolation from each other. Nonetheless, more of one form than any other does not detract from the reality that all forms were considered appropriate choices within an entangled and 'messy' whole.

With this in mind, if we cannot reasonably suggest that in LH IIIB there was a substantial influx of imported bronzes and by LH IIIC the vast majority of finds recovered had been locally produced, then how do we account for this major shift in metalworking and combat practices? It is clear that most bronzes that were moving, whether actual artefacts or ideas surrounding their use, were weaponry and personal dress, both related to personal mobility and the former especially to particular forms of social interaction. People were clearly moving into and around the East Mediterranean well into LH IIIC (Sherratt 2003; 2012; Broodbank 2013: 462–464) and on the basis of the evidence available, warriors were a significant or even dominant component of these groups. Any continued mercantile trade/exchange between the East and Central Mediterranean could at best have played a minor part in these interactions by LH IIIC because neither metalwork nor ceramics were any longer moving in bulk or with regularity. The intense fall-off in Aegean ceramics in Italy by LH IIIC is in contrast to a growth of the (substantially) minority tradition of HBW at sites in the Aegean, where deviation from (probable) Italian prototypes suggests a continuity of the tradition on East Mediterranean, even community specific, terms.

One final arena where identities were negotiated may be revealing in this discussion, and these are the LH IIIC tumuli found in certain parts of Greece. The well-published example from Chania near Mycenae is illustrative, particularly as this was the largest monument constructed there in LH IIIC. At that site, the cremated remains of nine people included both sexes and at least one child, and ceramic vessels were used to contain their remains (Palaiologou 2013: 249). Cremation was not native to the Aegean and was common in both Italy and the Balkans, but apart from one HBW vessel, all ceramics used in the burial rites were local Mycenaean. It is notable that the use of tumuli had been in decline or abandoned in Urnfield areas, and the actual structure of this tumulus itself was somewhat divergent from typical Italian or Balkan practices and finds its best parallels in Albania. Together with other tumuli in Greece containing mixed symbolic and material assemblages (Palaiologou 2013: 272–275), the monument represents an entanglement of traditions. We have no reason to presume these were first generation migrants being buried in a compromised fashion, and must presume that the practice is drawn from Urnfield traditions but modified in its new cultural setting. As with the HBW and Entangled Bronzes, there was a distinct memory of a (physically) distant tradition but it was much transformed in the Aegean context. It was also a short-lived phenomenon.

These burials take us back to the question of the actual origin, as well as identity, of people and objects expressing a mixed heritage. We have in recent years reflected upon such origins from a geographic perspective, and a directional one at that – with many looking to an Italian origin for foreign features in the Aegean. The entanglements that we see in metalwork and HBW might, however, have arisen from what may be considered horizontal transmissions of knowledge whereby copying was 'achieved without any richly-textured, high-fidelity knowledge' (Knappett 2010: 86). Considering such artefacts beyond the physical space and assemblages in which we find them, we must take account of the relational, cognitive space they inhabited where it was easier to establish and alter them. This is quite different from direct transmissions such as the reproduction of specific artefacts or practices based on possession of them or direct instructions by a person expert in that specific field of activity e.g. smithing. Finding the earliest examples of imports and associating them with specific places of origin is of limited use for understanding on-going and disjointed transformations spanning centuries. In this sense, the trend towards Italian inspiration for everything 'northern' is demonstrably inaccurate. Balkan influences are clear in the metalwork of many areas of modern Greece whose residents were interacting variably with other groups in the region, so tracing directionality becomes more than a little obfuscated. Explaining this in terms of peoples from diverse geographical origins interacting in a new space (the East Mediterranean), sometimes in pluralistic communities, giving rise to new ideas is certainly attractive.

For this reason we may briefly turn to the much debated, and much maligned, Sea Peoples (recently: Drews 1993; Wachsmann 2000; 2013; Dickinson 2006: 47; Jung 2009b; 2011; Yasur-Landau 2010; Broodbank 2013: 462; Hitchcock and Maeir 2014) to provide a potential explanation to draw the above discussion into a (partly) historical setting. On the basis of the predominantly military aspect of Entangled Bronzes and their distribution in the Aegean, Cyprus, Levant and Egypt (Sandars 1985), there appears a strong material argument to support some maritime movement of warriors, even if we need not of necessity believe the specific ethnic designations described by Egyptian sources (Broodbank 2013: 464; Cline 2014). Without the palaces controlling maritime and terrestrial routes, the door was opened for smaller scale movements for both voluntary and involuntary commercial interactions – trading and raiding (Sherratt 2000). These warriors on the move need not be construed as the migrating Dorians of old, but groups seeking to exploit vacillations in the political environment where rich lands and trade routes became less effectively protected by shifting alliances and maritime forces. In such contexts, established pathways of occasional trade could rapidly become highways of raiding and then soon revert, built upon strong knowledge of geographies and political changes or weaknesses. Perhaps the Makarska hoard in Dalmatia, or the finds of ingots (complete miniatures and fragments of typical sized ones) and other Cypriot metalwork in the Balkans (Tržan 1996; Sherratt 2012) can be seen as exactly the kinds of personal booty that an individual may return with as their share from raiding.

The force multiplier in this may well have been the widespread adoption and adaptation of the Mycenaean war galley proposed by Wachsmann (2013) that enabled a greater number of seaborne piratic groups to populate the waters. Hencken (1950) drew the useful comparison with the Visigoths who went from land-based raiders to a dominant force in the Central and West Mediterranean sea within a single generation. It is tempting to see the Entangled Bronzes in the same light as Mycenaean galleys as a material *lingua franca*, as many have, for the East Mediterranean piratic groups or Sea Peoples. The distinctive regional diversity in the forms of these artefacts, however, demonstrates that in practice many of the groups using them were fighting in different ways that represented different traditions. Returning to the mobility in Europe mentioned in the opening paragraph of this paper, it is notable that this was a hallmark of Hallstatt A1 more than Bronzezeit D – that is our metalwork evidence is dated to a mature phase of the former period in the 12th century BC and later. Significant interaction may have preceded this, but the rise of demographic pressures, and the massive increase in bronze deposition that we find in Italy and the Balkans (and Central Europe) were contemporaneous to LH IIIC.

Whether the collapse of the palaces and this transformation in Italy and the Balkans was serendipitous or inter-related, both situations led to changes in patterns of personal mobility between the thirteenth and twelfth century. This is not to suggest that we must subscribe to Bouzek's (1985) sequential waves of migration, but rather that we seek to define the distinct tempo or rhythms, as well as temporality, of these mobility phenomena. In this setting, any Sea Peoples may have been less a confederation and more a constellation of shifting groups venturing into the East Mediterranean along established routes on scales that may have varied year to year. This may certainly fit with the model of Chain or Career migration leading on from Circular migration proposed by Anthony (1997). The character of interaction that builds upon knowledge of places and routes in the latter model is transformed in this case from trading to raiding. Some such raiders may have returned home within a single year while others remained for longer periods.

Dickinson (2006: 47) critiques the Sea Peoples as being ahistorical because they lacked a visible base in the East Mediterranean, but it was perhaps precisely this lack of base that led them to be a periodic phenomenon (i.e. not directional migrants or part of a formal confederation). The interaction of these multi-ethnic groups in maritime contexts would leave little or no direct archaeological trace. If we consider these ephemeral maritime contexts as venues for 'third space encounters' of the post-colonial framework (Fahlander 2007; Knappett 2010; Stockhammer 2012; van Dommelen and Rowlands 2012) we find a very plausible mechanism for the horizontal transmission of the military traditions that we find so clearly in the material record.

In this way we can suggest an explanation for material patterns that are widespread based on regular cultural encounters rather than importing and badly emulating objects or wholesale migration and subsequent settlement of distinct cultural groups. We can furthermore consider, for example, the small handful of amber beads of (probable) northern Alpine style occurring typically as single finds in LH IIIB and IIIC (Czebreszuk 2011; Harding 2013) and the sporadic instances of other forms of personal ornament (Giannopoulos 2009) as indicative of the character of contacts. These can well be the outcomes of *ad hoc* 'trinket exchanges' between individuals moving along known maritime routes for any range of reasons beyond the transport of commodities via trade networks. Finds such as the Makarska hoard or the Carpathian-type battle-axe from Dodona suggest that interactions within the Balkans could be long-distance and not of necessity undertaken overland. We should nonetheless add to our Sea Peoples the many land-based interactions that could have occurred between neighbouring and distant groups in the southern Balkans. Such relationships need not lead to directional transmissions of technology in the grand diffusionist sense, but rather the creation of forums for interaction where people, things and ideas mingled with varying fidelity or intentionality.

From the local perspective, Maran (2006; 2011; 2012) has convincingly argued for the active manipulation of material cultural traditions and associated patterns of practice to suit the needs of the post-collapse elites. The legitimacy of the elites was seen to be based on (intentionally) entangled histories – palatial, non-palatial, foreign, subaltern, hegemonic, confederated, invented. In this revision of histories and reinterpretation of political mechanisms, potentially involving people of mixed origins, life-experiences and cultural beliefs, it is unlikely that objects as symbolically and practically potent as weapons would have remained uninvolved. It is for this reason that the smithing and fighting in a 'new old-fashioned way' in some parts of Greece is particularly relevant. It may be one example of how considerable social capital could be generated through objects and associated practices which could strategically relate to variegated 'histories' and contemporary politics. For such reasons, we might consider any attempt to define a coherent and measurable 'reality' that explains the receptivity and use of objects with mixed origins in blanket terms to be at odds with a social environment in which various competing visions of social reality were vying for recognition or facing refutation. As Barrett (1998: 24) argued, "such material does not speak for itself or represent an essential logic for archaeological scrutiny, rather it reminds us of the distance separating purposeful life and its residual consequences."

Conclusion

The history of interaction between societies in the Aegean and Italy, and between those in the Aegean and Balkans, has left distinctly different material traces. The high visibility of ceramics in the archaeological record and an historical bias in research towards sites in southern Greece has generally led to an emphasis on Italian connections. I have argued that the impact of military interactions with societies from north of Boeotia up to the Danube may have been equally influential though different in character. By considering military contacts as distinct from those instigated for other purposes, this paper has sought to distinguish between different modes and scales of interaction and to assess the specific impacts of these. In Greece I defined distinct regional patterns whereby societies north of the Gulf of Corinth have a strong Balkan influence, those in the Peloponnese a stronger Italian influence, and those on Crete pursued a more variable yet distinct set of traditions. Interaction between peoples in each of these parts of Greece would potentially constitute intercultural encounters of a form, even if indirectly by virtue of the different groups encountering objects which exhibited alternative balances of Italian, Balkan and/or distinct Aegean traditions.

Apart from linking artefacts to places of origin, it is clear that there is much to be gained by thinking in terms of changes in local developmental sequences arising through encounters within intercultural milieus. Personal artefacts exchanged between peers that are interacting for non-commercial reasons can best account for the disparity in *actual* 'northern' material culture being interred in otherwise Aegean cultural assemblages along with the development of entangled objects. This trinket exchange (or plunder?) could also arise from individual non-Aegean people, many probably being warriors, preferring not to return home and settling in the East Mediterranean as individuals within peer-groups (i.e. not group migrations or long-distance trading networks). By emphasising some micro-regional trends specific to bronze artefact forms and functions, the varying degrees of influence from Italian, Balkan and emergent East Mediterranean traditions have been shown to be socially meaningful. It is important in this regard that few regions 'faithfully' reproduce the weapons and complete combat panoplies, and by extension martial art and craft practices, from which they emerge. In this, the dialogues between stylistic tradition, craft know-how and interaction can be seen to be negotiated both in terms of the production and development of emergent traditions. Interpersonal violence, particularly various forms of warfare, may well be seen as a forum of interaction that left some of the most visible traces of intercultural interaction. In the renegotiation of social order in the post-palatial societies of southern Greece and the dissolution of a long-standing martial influence of these on groups in other parts of Greece and the southern Balkans, entanglement may arise as an incidental outcome of encounters and/or an intentional strategy for integrating traditions.

Speaking in terms of Entangled Bronzes is not without theoretical and practical complications (Galaty 2014), but this allows us to reduce the element of alterity or foreignness that pervades our understanding of objects related to Italian and Balkan traditions in Aegean contexts and the East Mediterranean more widely. This in turn encourages us to better account for the development of the bronze industry in terms of local contexts of interaction within a global milieu and in particular the influence of established craft and military practices on emergent traditions. For this reason I have sought to employ a clear definition of the social contexts and purposes of those interactions along with the mechanisms through which ideas were transmitted in practical workaday terms. Material categories such as metalwork, pottery or amber are thus not seen as simple proxies for generic 'interaction', but rather material traces of potentially distinct forms of social discourse. A social schism between LH IIIB and LH IIIC metalwork traditions was emphasised, particularly the receptivity and interpretation of Urnfield area inspirations. The often alleged dominance of Entangled Bronzes in this latter period was also contested by demonstration of the continued vibrancy of the (predominantly) Aegean tradition visible clearly in artefact numbers.

I have proposed that an entanglement of military traditions occurs both materially in some artefacts and socially through their correlate of martial art practices. This emerged from a combination of short and medium range interactions between neighbouring groups and long-range directional and purposeful movement of warriors to remote venues of interaction. The paper explored how the melding of martial traditions in the post-palatial world could serve to ground inter-regional 'ideas' within local material realities of life, though the social venues for negotiating such meanings may have occurred in a variety of locations, close or distant. By defining the nature of regional variation in Greece and suggesting mechanisms of entanglement, I have attempted a military explanation that links these material culture transformations to the known historical phenomenon of sea borne raiding and piracy in the thirteenth and twelfth centuries BC (Cline 2014). Following Hitchcock and Maeir (2014), I believe that these potential piratic groups were organised multi-ethnic confederations that were soluble, transient, archaeologically ephemeral but potentially sizable in both numbers and socio-political impact. As a phenomenon, their varying origins meant that they brought together diverse cultural practices, objects, and know-how and on fragmentation of the groups, these influences were carried away to far flung areas of the Mediterranean and Europe.

Acknowledgements

I would like to thank all those who participated in the Round Table and this paper has benefited from the discussions held during the event. I am very grateful to Roger Doonan for his collaboration in organising and running the event, and to John Bennet for all of his support during the event and for offering valuable advice on this paper. This chapter has benefitted very much from the suggestions of Jeremy Rutter, Marina Milic and Francesco Iacono, and the many discussions I have had over the years with Kristian Kristiansen, Ioannis Georganas and Alan Peatfield. All errors, omissions, theoretical *faux pas* or wild ideas remain my own responsibility, of course. The research was conducted during a Marie Curie Intra-European Fellowship held at the Department of Archaeology, University of Sheffield 2011–2013.

Notes

1. For clarity, modern national names and boundaries are used alongside geographic terms.
2. Jung, 2009b, Jung and Mehoefer, 2013 and Stavropoulou Gatsi *et al.*, 2012 argue that Greek artefacts with trace element and lead isotope signatures indicative of Italian origin equates to importation of finished artefacts, not trade in metal as a resource. In light of the significant trade in scrap metals, as well as ingots, and the likelihood of temporal shifts and irregular networks in LH IIIC, I prefer in this paper not to ascribe a specific mechanism for the import of all alleged instances of Italian metal in Greece. This is accentuated by the fact that, for example, the sword from Kouvaras that Stavropoulou-Gatsi *et al* 2012 consider an Italian import is of the fauxmidrib form I consider to be characteristic of the Central Greek – South Balkans general region in which it was recovered.
3. The Ha B-C spearheads from Matijevići in Croatia and Lučica in Bosnia (Basler *et al.*, 1983 T. XCVI.2; König, 2004: 96, T. 59. A1) have this feature, though a possible stylisation of it can be found on a spearhead from Brodski Varoš (Vinski-Gasparini, 1973: Fig. 61.20) and may hint at contemporary contact in LH IIIC.

References

Andreou, S., M. Fotiadis and K. Kotsakis
1996 Review of Aegean Prehistory V: The Neolithic and Bronze Age of Northern Greece. *American Journal of Archaeology* 100: 537–597.

Andrikou, E.
2007 New evidence on Mycenaean Bronze Corselets from Thebes, Boeotia and the Bronze Age Sequence of Corselets in Greece and Europe. In I. Galanaki, H. Tomas, Y. Galanakis and R. Laffineur (eds.), *Between the Aegean and Baltic Seas: Prehistory Across Borders* (Aegaeum 27): 401–409. Liège: Univeritè de Liège.

Artursson, M.
2010 Settlement Structure and Organisation. In T. Earle and K. Kristiansen (eds.), *Organising Bronze Age Societies*: 87–122. Cambridge: Cambridge University Press.

Avila, R.A.J.
1983 *Bronzene Lanzen- und Pfeil-spitzen der Griechischen Spätbronzezeit*, (Prähistorische Bronzefunde V.3). Munich: C.H. Beck.

Barbarić, V.
2009 Late Bronze Age in Dalmatia: State of research. In E. Borgna and P. Cassola Guida (eds.), *From the Aegean to the Adriatic: Social Organisations, Modes of Exchange and Interaction in Postpalatial Times (12th - 11th B.C.)*: 311–324. Rome: Quasar.

Barrett, J.
1998 The politics of scale and the experience of distance: The Bronze Age World System. In L. Larsson and B. Stjernquist (eds.), *The World-View of Prehistoric Man* (KVHAA Konferenser 40): 13–25. Stockholm: Natur Och Kultur.

Basler, D., B. Alojz, S. Gabrovec, M. Garašanin, N. Tasić, B. Čović and K. Vinski-Gasparini
1983 *Praistorija Jugoslavenskih zemalja IV: Bronzana Doba*. Sarajevo: "Svjetlost" OOUR Izdavačka djelatnost.

Bergerbrandt, S.
2013 Migration, innovartion and meaning: Sword depositions on Lolland 1600–1100 BC. In M.E. Alberti and S. Sabatini (eds.), *Exchange Networks and Local Transformations*: 146–155. Oxford: Oxbow Books.

Bettelli, M.
2002 *Italia meridionale e mondo miceneo. Ricerche su dinamiche di acculturazione e aspetti archeologici, con particolare riferimento ai versanti adriatico e ionico della penisola italiana, Grandi contesti e problemi della protostoria italiana.* Firenze: All'insegna del giglio.

Bianchin Citton, E.
2009 Il Veneto tra Bronzo Recente e Bronzo Finale: Popolamento e aspetti socio-economici di un'area di cerniera tra l'adriatico e l'Oltralpe. In E. Borgna and P. Cassola Guida (eds.), From the Aegean to the Adriatic: Social Organisations, Modes of Exchange and Interaction in Postpalatial Times (12th-11th BC): 257–272. Rome: Quasar.

Bianco Peroni, V.
1994 *I pugnali nell'Italia continentale* (Prähistorische Bronzefunde IV.1). Stuttgart: Steiner.

Blake, E.
2008 The Mycenaeans in Italy: a minimalist perspective. *Papers of the British School at Rome* 76: 1–34.

Boileau, M.C., L. Badre, E. Capet, R. Jung and H. Mommsen
2010 Foreign ceramic tradition, local clays: The Handmade Burnished Ware of Tell Kazel (Syria). *Journal of Archaeological Science* 37: 1678–1689.

Borgna, E. and P. Càssola Guida (eds.)
2009 From the Aegean to the Adriatic: Social Organisations, Modes of Exchange and Interaction in Postpalatial Times (12th–11th BC). Rome: Quasar.

Bouzek, J.
1985 *The Aegean, Anatolia and Europe: cultural interrelations in the second millennium B.C.* Göteborg: Paul Áströms Förlag.
1994 Late Bronze Age Greece and the Balkans: A Review of the Present Picture. *The Annual of the British School at Athens* 89: 217–234.

Broodbank, C.
2013 *The making of the Middle Sea: a history of the Mediterranean from the beginning to the emergence of the classical world.* London: Thames and Hudson.

Bruck, J. and D. Fontijn
2013 The myth of the chief: prestige goods, power and personhood in the European Bronze Age. In A. Harding and H. Fokkens (eds.), *The Oxford Handbook of the European Bronze Age*: 197–215. Oxford: Oxford University Press.

Bulatović, A.
2007 *Vranje: kulturna stratigrafija praistorijskih lokaliteta u Vranjskoj regiji.* Belgrade: Arheološki institute

Bulatović, L., P. Lutovac, T. Lauko, B. Ravnik-Toman, M. Guštin, J. Tratnik.
2003 *Zlatno doba Crne Gore/The golden age of Montenegro*. Podgorica: JU Muzeji i galerije.

Cassola Guida, M.
1992 *Nuovi studi sulle armi dei Micenei*. Rome: Edizioni dell'Ateneo.

Catling, H.
1956 Bronze Cut-and-thrust Swords in the Eastern Mediterranean. *Proceedings of the Prehistoric Society* 22: 102–125.
1961 A New Bronze Sword from Cyprus. *Antiquity* 35: 115–123.

Chapman, J. and H. Hamerow
1997 On the move again: Migrations and invasions in archaeological explanation. In J. Chapman and H. Hamerow (eds.), *Migrations and Invasions in Archaeological Explanation*: 1–10. Oxford: British Archaeological Reports

Clausing, C.
2003a Spätbronze- und eisenzeitliche Helme mit einteiliger Kalotte. *Jahrbuch des Römisch-Germanischen Zentralmuseum Mainz* 48: 199–225.
2003b Geschnürte Beinschienen der späten Bronze- und älteren Eisenzeit. *Jahrbuch des Römisch-Germanischen Zentralmuseum Mainz* 49: 149–187.

Cline, E.
2014 *1177 BC: The Year Civilization Collapsed*. Princeton: Princeton University Press.

Coles, J.
1962 European Bronze Age Shields. *Proceedings of the Prehistoric Society* 28: 156–190.

Czebreszuk, J.
2007 Amber between the Baltic and the Aegean in the Third and Second Millennia BC (An Outline of Major Issues). In I. Galanaki, H. Tomas, Y. Galanakis and R. Laffineur (eds.), *Between the Aegean and Baltic Seas: Prehistory Across Borders* (Aegaeum 27): 164–179. Liège: Univeritè de Liège.
2011 *Bursztyn w kulturze mykeńskiej: zarys problematyki badawczej*. Poznań: Wydawnictwo Poznańskie.

Deger-Jalkotzy, S.
1998 The last Mycenaeans and their successors updated. In S. Gitin, A. Mazar and E. Stern (eds.), *Mediterranean Peoples in Transition: Thirteenth to Early Tenth Centuries BCE*: 114–128. Jerusalem: Israel Exploration Society.
2006 Late Mycenaean Warrior tombs. In S. Deger-Jalkotzy and I. Lemos (eds.), *Ancient Greece from the Mycenaean Palaces to the Age of Homer* (Edinburgh Leventis Studies): 151–179. Edinburgh: Edinburgh University Press.

Dickinson, O.
2006 *The Aegean from Bronze Age to Iron Age: Continuity and Change Between the Twelfth and Eighth Centuries BC*. London: Routledge.
2009 Social development in the Postpalatial Period in the Aegean. In E. Borgna and P. Cassola Guida (eds.), *From the Aegean to the Adriatic: Social Organisations, Modes of Exchange and Interaction in Postpalatial Times (12th - 11th B.C.)*: 11–20. Rome: Quasar.

Drews, R.
1993 *The End of the Bronze Age*. Princeton: Princeton University Press.

Earle, T.
2013 The 3M: Materiality, Materialism and Materialization. In S. Sabatini and S. Bergerbrant (eds.), Counterpoint: Essays in Archaeology and Heritage Studies in Honour of Professor Kristian Kristiansen. British Archaeological Reports, Oxford, 353–360.

Eder, B. and R. Jung
2005 On the Character of Social Relations between Greece and Italy in the 12th/11th C. BC. In *Emporia. Aegeans in the Central and Eastern Mediterranean* (Aegaeum 25): 485–495. Liège: Univeritè de Liège.

Fahlander, F.
2007 Third space encounters: Hybridity, mimicry and interstitial practice. In P. Cornell and F. Fahlander (eds.), *Encounters/Materialities/Confrontations: Archaeologies of Social Space and Interaction*: 15–41. Newcastle: Cambridge Scholars Press.

Feuer, B.
2011 Being Mycenaean: A View from the Periphery. *American Journal of Archaeology* 115: 507–536.

Galaty, M.L.
2014 Review of J. Maran and P. Stockhammer (eds.) 2012 *Materiality and Social Practice: Transformative Capacities and Intercultural Encounters*. Oxford: Oxbow Books. *European Journal of Archaeology* 17(1): 162–167
2009 Albanian coastal settlement from prehistory to the Iron Age. In S. Forenbaher, (ed.), *A Connecting Sea: Maritime Interaction in Adriatic Prehistory*: 105–112. Oxford: British Archaeological Reports.

Giannopoulos, T.
2009 "One ring to bind them". The chamber tomb I of Monodendri in Achaea and the missing piece of an interesting puzzle. In E. Borgna and P. Cassola Guida (eds.), *From the Aegean to the Adriatic: Social Organisations, Modes of Exchange and Interaction in Postpalatial Times (12th–11th BC)*: 115–128. Rome: Quasar.

Giumlia-Mair, A., R.-M. Albanese Procelli and F. Lo Schiavo
2010 The Metallurgy of the Sicilian Final Bronze Age/Early Iron Age necropolis of Madonna del Piano (Catania, Sicily). *Trabajos de Prehistoria* 67: 469–488.

Guglielmino, R.
2009 Le relazioni tra l'Adriatico e l'Egeo nel Bronzo Recente e Finale. La testimonianza di Roca. In E. Borgna and P. Cassola Guida (eds.). *From the Aegean to the Adriatic: Social Organisations, Modes of Exchange and Interaction in Postpalatial Times (12th–11th BC)*: 185–204. Rome: Quasar.

Harding, A.
1984 *The Mycenaeans and Europe*. London: Academic Press.
1995 *Die Schwerter Im Ehemaligen Jugoslawien* (Prähistorische Bronzefunde IV.14). Stuttgart: Franz Steiner Verlag.
2007 Interconnections between the Aegean and Continental Europe in the Bronze and Early Iron Ages: Moving beyond Scepticism, In I. Galanaki, H. Tomas, Y. Galanakis and R. Laffineur (eds.). Between the Aegean and Baltic Seas: Prehistory Across Borders (Aegaeum 27): 47–56. Liège: Université de Liège.

2013 World systems, Cores and Peripheries in Prehistoric Europe. *European Journal of Archaeology* 16: 378–400.

Hencken, H.
1950 Herzsprung Shields and Greek Trade. *American Journal of Archaeology* 54: 294–309.

Hitchcock, L. and A. Maeir
2014 Yo-ho, yo-ho, a seren's life for me! *World Archaeology* 46(3). 624–640.

Hochstetter, A.
1987 *Kastanas: Ausgrabungen in einem Siedlungshügel der Bronze- und Eisenzeit Makedoniens, 1975-1979* (Prähistorische Archäologie in Sudosteuropa). Berlin: Spiess.

Höckmann, O.
1980 Lanze und Speer im spatminoischen und mykenischen Griechenland. *Jahrbuch des Römisch-Germanischen Zentralmuseums Mainz* 27: 13–158.

Homolle, T.
1908 *Fouilles de Delphes.* Athens: École française d'Athènes.

Hood, S. and P. De Jong
1952 Late Minoan Warrior-Graves from Ayios Ioannis and the New Hospital Site at Knossos. *Annual of the British School at Athens* 47: 243–277.

Hook, D.
2007 The Composition and Technology of Selected Bronze Age and Early Iron Age Copper Alloy Artefacts from Italy. In A.-M. Bietti Sestieri and E. Macnamara (eds.), *Prehistoric Metal Artefacts from Italy (3500-720 BC) in the British Museum*: 308–323. London: British Museum.

Horejs, B.
2007 Macedonia: mediator or buffer zone between cultural spheres? In I. Galana, H. Tomas, Y. Galanakis and R. Laffineur (eds.), *Between the Aegean and Baltic Seas: Prehistory Across Borders* (Aegaeum 27): 293–306. Liège: Université de Liège.

Iacono, F.
2013 Westernizing Aegean of LH IIIC. In M.E. Alberti and S. Sabatini (eds.), *Exchange Networks and Local Transformations*: 60–79. Oxford: Oxbow Books.

Jevtić, M. and M. Vukmanović
1996 Late Bronze and Early Iron Age in the Danube Valley from V. Gradište down to Prahovo. In N. Tasić (ed.), *The Yugoslav Danube Basin and the Neighbouring Regions in the 2nd Millennium BC*: 283–290. Belgrade: Arheološki Institut.

Jovanović, D.
2010 *Ostave Vršačkog Gorja: Markovac-Grunjac.* Vršac: Vršac Muzej.

Jung, R.
2006 *Chronologia comparata. Vergleichende Chronologie von Südgriechenland und Süditalien von ca. 1700/1600 bis 1000 v. u. Z.* Wien: Verlag der österreichischen Akademie der Wissenschaften.

2009a "Bronzi internazionali" ed il loro contest sociale fra Adriatico Peninsulo balcanica e coste Levantine. In E. Borgna and P. Cassola Guida (eds.), *From the Aegean to the Adriatic: Social Organisations, Modes of Exchange and Interaction in Postpalatial Times* (12th–11th BC): 129–159. Rome: Quasar.
2009b Pirates of the Aegean: Italy – the East Aegean – Cyprus at the end of the Second Millennium BC. In V. Karagheorgis and O. Kouka (eds.), *Cyprus and the East Aegean Intercultural Contacts from 3000 to 500 BC: An International Archaeological Symposium Held at Pythagoreion, Samos, October 17th–18th 2008*: 72–93. Nicosia: A.G. Leventis Foundation.
2011 Innovative cooks and new dishes: Cypriote pottery in the 13th and 12th centuries BC and its historical interpretation. In V. Karageorghis and O. Kouka (eds.), *On Cooking Pots, Drinking Cups, Loomweights and Ethnicity in Bronze Age Cyprus and Neighbouring Regions*: 57–86. Nicosia A.G. Leventis Foundation.

Jung, R. and M. Mehoefer
2009 A sword of Naue II type from Ugarit and the historical significance of Italian-type weaponry in the Eastern Mediterranean. *Aegean Archaeology* 8: 111–135.
2013 Mycenaean Greece and Bronze Age Italy: Cooperation, trade or war? *Archäologisches Korrespondenzblatt* 43: 175–192.

Jung, R.I., I. Moschos and M. Mehoefer
2008 Fonevontas me ton idio tropo: Oi eirinekes epafes yia ton polemo metaxi dutikis Elladas kai Italias kata ti diapkeia ton opsimon Mukinaikon xronon. In S.A. Paipetis and Ch. Giannopoulou (eds.), *Politismiki Allilogonimopoisi Notias Italia Kai Dutikis Elladas Mesa Apo Tin Istoria*: 85–107. Patras: Periphereia Ditikis Ellados.

Kapuran, A.
2009 *Arhitektura iz poznog bronzanog i starijeg gvozdenog doba u basenu Južne Morave / Late bronze and early iron age architecture in the Juzina Morava basin.* Belgrade: Univerzitet u Beogradu, Filozofski fakultet.

Karageorghis, V.
2011a What happened in Cyprus *c.* 1200 BC: hybridization, creolization or immigration? An introduction. In V. Karageorghis and O. Kouka (eds.), *On Cooking Pots, Drinking Cups, Loomweights and Ethnicity in Bronze Age Cyprus and Neighbouring Regions*: 19–28. Nicosia: A.G. Leventis Foundation.
2011b Handmade Burnished Ware in Cyprus and elsewhere in the eastern Mediterranean. In V. Karageorghis and O. Kouka (eds.), *On Cooking Pots, Drinking Cups, Loomweights and Ethnicity in Bronze Age Cyprus and Neighbouring Regions*: 97–112. Nicosia: A.G. Leventis Foundation.

Karavanić, S.
2009 *The Urnfield culture in continental Croatia.* Oxford: British Archaeological Reports.

Kelder, J.
2005 The chariots of Ahhiyawa. *Dacia* XLVIII-XLIX: 151–160.
2010 *The Kingdom of Mycenae: A Great Kingdom in the Late Bronze Age Aegean.* Potomac: Capital Decisions Ltd.

Kilian-Dirlmeier, I.
1993 *Die Schwerter in Griechenland (ausserhalb der Peloponnes), Bulgarien und Albanien* (Prähistorische Bronzefunde IV.12). Stuttgart: F. Steiner.

Knappett, C.

2010 Communities of Things and Objects: a Spatial Perspective. In L. Malafouris, and C. Renfrew (eds.), *The Cognitive Life of Things: Recasting the Boundaries of the Mind*: 81–90. Cambridge: MacDonald Institute for Archaeological Research.

König, P.

2004 *Spätbronzezeitliche Hortfunde aus Bosnien und der Herzegowina* (Prähistorische Bronzefunde XX.11). Stuttgart: F. Steiner.

Koui, M., P. Papandreopoulos, E. Andreopoulou-Mangou, L. Papazoglou-Manuoudaki, A. Priftaj-Vevecka and F. Stamati

2006 Study of Bronze Age copper-based swords of Type Naue II and spearheads from Greece and Albania. *Mediterranean Archaeology and Archaeometry* 6: 5–22.

Kristiansen, K.

Forthcoming Interpreting Bronze Age trade and migration. In E. Kiriatzi and C. Knappett (eds.), *Mobile Technologies across Dynamic Landscapes: Perspectives from Mediterranean Prehistory*. London: British School at Athens.

2002 The tale of the sword: Swords and swordfighters in Bronze Age Europe. *Oxford Journal of Archaeology* 21: 319–332.

Krzyszkowska, O.

1997 Cult and craft: Ivories from the Citadel House Area at Mycenae. In *Texni: Craftsmen, Craftswomen and Craftsmanship in the Aegean Bronze Age* (Aegaeum 16): 145–150. Liège: Université de Liège.

Lo Schiavo, F.

2010 Le Fibule dell'Italia meridionale e della Sicilia dall' età del bronzo recente al VI secolo A.C. (Prähistorische Bronzefunde XIV.14). Stuttgart: Franz Steiner Verlag.

Maggiulli, G.

2009 I ripostigli di Roca Vecchia (Lecce): analisi dei materiali e pro-blematiche archeologiche. In E. Borgna and P. Cassola Guida (eds.). From the Aegean to the Adriatic: Social Organisations, Modes of Exchange and Interaction in Postpalatial Times (12th–11th BC): 205–218. Rome: Quasar.

Mangou, E. and P.V. Ioannou

1998 On the Chemical Composition of Prehistoric Greek Copper-based Artefacts from Crete. *Annual of the British School at Athens* 93: 91–102.

1999 On the chemical composition of prehistoric Greek copper-based artefacts from Mainland Greece. *Annual of the British School at Athens* 94: 81–101.

Maran, J.

2006 Coming to terms with the past: Ideology and power in Late Helladic IIIC. In S. Deger-Jalkotzy and I. Lemos (eds.), *Ancient Greece from the Mycenaean Palaces to the Age of Homer* (Edinburgh Leventis Studies): 123–150. Edinburgh: Edinburgh University Press.

2011. Contested Pasts—The Society of the 12th c. B.C.E. Argolid and the Memory of the Mycenaean Palatial Period. In W. Gauss, M. Lindblom, A. Smith, J. Wright (eds.), *Our Cups Are Full: Pottery and Society in the Aegean Bronze Age*: 169–178. Oxford: British Archaeological Reports.

2012 Ceremonial feasting equipment, social space and interculturality in Post-Palatial Tiryns. In J. Maran and P. Stockhammer (eds.), *Materiality and Social Practice: The Transformative Capacities of Intercultural Encounters*: 121–136. Oxford: Oxbow Books.

Maspero, G.
2010 *The Struggle of the Nations: Egypt, Syria and Assyria* (1st edition 1896). Whitefish: Kessinger Publishing LLC.

Mödlinger, M.
2012 European Bronze Age cuirasses: Aspects of chronology, typology, manufacture and usage. *Jahrbuch des Römisch-Germanischen Zentralmuseums Mainz* 59: 1–49.
2013 From Greek boar tusk helmets to the first European metal helmets: New approaches on development and date. *Oxford Journal of Archaeology* 32(4): 391–412.
in press *Bronze Age European Armour*.

Molloy, B.P.C.
2005 The adoption of the Naue ii sword in the Aegean. In C. Briault, J. Green, A. Kaldelis and A. Stellatou (eds.), *Proceedings of Symposium on Mediterranean Archaeology 2003*: 115–127. Oxford: British Archaeological Reports.
2008 Martial arts and materiality: a combat archaeology perspective on Aegean swords of the fifteenth and fourteenth centuries BC. *World Archaeology* 40. 116–134.
2009 For Gods or Men? The use of European Bronze Age shields. *Antiquity* 83. 1052–1064.
2010 Swords and Swordsmanship in the Aegean Bronze Age. *American Journal of Archaeology* 114: 403–428.
2011 Use-wear analysis and use-patterns of Bronze Age swords. In M.Mödlinger and M. Uckelmann (eds.), *New Approaches to Studying Weapons of the Bronze Age*: 67–84. Oxford: British Archaeological Reports.
2012 Martial Minoans: War as social process, practice and event in Bronze Age Crete. *Annual of the British School at Athens* 107: 87–142.
2013 The origins of plate armour in the Aegean and Europe. *Talanta: Proceedings of the Dutch Archaeological and Historical Society* XLIV-XLV: 273–294

Molloy, B.P.C. and R. Doonan
2015 A moving story: Some observations on the circulation of metal, metalworking and metal users in the thirteenth to eleventh century BC Balkan and Apennine peninsulas. In P. Suchowska-Ducke and H. Vandkilde (eds.), *Mobility of Culture in Bronze Age Europe. Proceedings of an International Conference and the Marie Curie ITN "Forging Identities" at Aarhus University June 2012*: 235–244 Oxford: British Archaeological Reports.

Morricone, L.
1967 *Eleona e Langada: sepolcreti della tarda età del Bronzo a Coo*. ASAtene 43–44: 5–311.

Moschos, I.
2009 Evidence of Social Re-organization and Reconstruction in Late Helladic IIIC Achaea and Modes of Contacts and Exchange via the Ionian and Adriatic Sea. In E. Borgna and P. Cassola Guida (eds.). From the Aegean to the Adriatic: Social Organisations, Modes of Exchange and Interaction in Postpalatial Times (12th–11th BC): 345–414. Rome: Quasar.

Needham, S.
1993 Displacement and exchange in archaeological methodology. In C. Scarre and F. Healy (eds.), *Trade and Exchange in Prehistoric Europe* (Oxbow Monographs): 161–169. Oxford: Oxbow Books.

Needham, S., P. Northover, M. Uckelmann and R. Tabor
2012 South Cadbury: The last of the Bronze Shields. *Archäologisches Korrespondenzblatt* 42(4): 473–492.

O'Brien, S.

2013 Parables of Decline: Popular Fears and the Use of Crises in Aegean Archaeological Interpretation. In E.M. van der Wilt and J. Martínez Jiménez (eds.), *Tough Times: The Archaeology of Crisis and Recovery*: 13–22. Oxford: British Archaeological Reports.

Pacciarelli, M.

2006 Sull'evoluzione dell'armamento in Italia peninsulare e Sicilia nel Bronzo tardo. In Istituto Preistoria E. Protostoria (ed.) *Studi Di Protostoria in Onore Di Renato Peroni*: 246–260. Firenze: All'Insegna del Giglio.

Palailogou, H.

2013 Late Helladic IIIC cremation burials at Chania of Mycenae. In M. Lochner, and F. Ruppenstein (eds.), *Brandbestattungen von Der Mittleren Donau Bis Zur Ägäis Zwischen 1300 Und 750 v. Chr*: 249–279. Wien: Verlag der Österreichischen Akademie der Wissenschaften.

Papadopoulos, T.

1998 *The Late Bronze Age Daggers of the Aegean I: The Greek Mainland*, (Prähistorische Bronzefunde VI.10). Stuttgart: Franz Steiner Verlag.

1999 Warrior graves in Achaean Mycenaean cemeteries. In Lafineur, R. *Polemos*, (Aegaeum 19): 267–277 Liège: Univeritè de Liège.

Papadopoulos, T. and L. Kontorli-Papadopoulou

2000 Four Late Bronze Age Italian imports in Achaea. In P. Åstrom and D. Surenhagen (eds.), *Periplus: Festshrift Fur Hans-Gunter Bucholz Zu Seinem Achtzigsten Geburtstag Am 24 Dezember 1999* (Studies In Mediterranean Archaeology 127): 143–146. Göteborg: Paul Åströms Förlag.

Papazoglou-Manioudaki, L.

1994 A Mycenaean Warrior's tomb at Krini near Patras. *Annual of the British School at Athens* 89: 171–200.

Pilides, D. and M.C. Boileau

2011 Revisiting the Handmade Burnished Ware of Cyprus: new analytical results. In V. Karageorgis and O. Kouka (eds.), *On Cooking Pots, Drinking Cups, Loomweights and Ethnicity in Bronze Age Cyprus and Neighbouring Regions*: 113–128 Nicosia: A.G. Leventis Foundation.

Pulak, C.

1988 The Bronze Age Shipwreck at Ulu Burun, Turkey: 1985 Campaign. *American Journal of Archaeology* 92: 1–37.

Rahmstorf, L.

2008 *Tiryns XVI: Kleinfunde aus Tiryns. Terrakotta, Stein, Bein und Glas/Fayence, vornehmlich der spaten Bronzezeit*. Wiesbaden: Reichert Verlag.

2011 Handmade pots and crumbling loomweights: "Barbarian" elements in the eastern Mediterranean in the last quarter of the 2nd millennium BC. In V. Karageorgis and O. Kouka (eds.), *On Cooking Pots, Drinking Cups, Loomweights And Ethnicity In Bronze Age Cyprus And Neighbouring Regions*: 315–330. Nicosia: A.G. Leventis Foundation.

Rutter, J.

1990 Some Comments on Interpreting the Dark-surfaced Handmade Burnished Pottery of the 13th and 12th Century B.C. Aegean. *Journal of Mediterranean Archaeology* 3: 29–49.

2012 Migrant drinking assemblages in Aegean Bronze Age settings. In J. Maran and P. Stockhammer (eds.), *Materiality and Social Practice: Transformative Capacities of Intercultural Encounters*: 73–88. Oxford: Oxbow Books.

Salzani, L.
1994 Nogara. Rinvenimento di un ripostiglio di bronzi in localitá "Pila del Brancón". *Quaderni di Archeologia del Veneto* 10: 83–94.

Sandars, N.
1963 Later Aegean Bronze Swords. *American Journal of Archaeology* 67: 117–153.
1985 *The Sea Peoples*, 2nd ed. London: Thames and Hudson.

Shalev, S.
2004 Swords and Daggers in Late Bronze Age Canaan (Prähistorische Bronzefunde IV.13). Stuttgart: Franz Steiner Verlag.

Sherratt, S.
2000 Circulation of metals at the end of the Bronze Age in the Eastern Mediterranean. In C. Pare (ed.), *Metals Make the World Go Round*: 82–95. Oxford: Oxbow Books.
2003 The Mediterranean economy: "Globalisation" at the end of the second millennium BC. In W. Dever and S. Gitin (eds.), *Symbiosis, symbolism and the power of the past: Canaan, Ancient Israel and their neighbours from the Late Bronze Age through Roman Palaestina*: 37–62. Winona Lake: Eisenbrauns.
2012 The intercultural transformative capacities or irregularly appropriated goods. In J. Maran and P. Stockhammer (eds.), *Materiality and Social Practice: Transformative Capacities of Intercultural Encounters*: 152–172. Oxford: Oxbow Books.

Snodgrass, A.
1964 *Early Greek Armour and Weapons: From the End of the Bronze Age to 600 B.C.* Edinburgh: Edinburgh University Press.
1971 The first European body-armour. In J. Boardman, M. Browne, T. Powell (eds.), *The European Community in Later Prehistory*: 33–49. London: Routledge, London.

Sørensen, M.L.S.
2013 A Sword for the Chief – a Conversation with Kristian. In S. Sabatini and S. Bergerbrant (eds.), *Counterpoint: Essays in Archaeology and Heritage Studies in Honour of Professor Kristian Kristiansen*: 435–442. Oxford: British Archaeological Reports.

Souyoudzouglou-Haywood, C.
1999 *The Ionian Islands in the Bronze Age and Early Iron Age*. Liverpool: Liverpool University Press.

Stavropoulou Gatsi, M., R. Jung and M. Mehoefer
2012 Tafos "Mykinaiou" polemisti ston Kouvara Aitoloakarnanias. Proti Parousiasi. In A. Kanta and A. Giannikouri (eds.), *Athanasia: The Earthly, the Celestial and the Underworld in the Mediterranean from the Late Bronze and Early Iron Age*: 247–265. Heraklio: Panepistimio Kritis, Eidikos Logariasmos.

Stockhammer, P.W.
2012 Entangled pottery: Phenomena of appropriation in the Late Bronze Age Eastern Mediterranean. In J. Maran and P. Stockhammer (eds.), *Materiality and Social Practice: The Transformative Capacities of Intercultural Encounters*: 89–103. Oxford: Oxbow Books.

Stojić, M.

1996 Le Bassin de la Morava á l'âge de bronze á la période de transition de l'âge de bronze a celui de fer. In N. Tasić, (ed.), *The Yugoslav Danube Basin and the Neighbouring Regions in the 2nd Millennium BC*: 247–256. Belgrade: Arheološki Institut.

Strack, S.

2007 Regional Dynamics and Social Change in the Late Bronze and Early Iron Age: a study of handmade pottery from southern and central Greece. PhD dissertation, University of Edinburgh.

Stubbings, F.

1954 Mycenae 1939–1953: Part VIII. A Winged-Axe Mould. *Annual of the British School at Athens* 47: 297–298.

Tartaron, T.

2004 *Bronze Age Landscape and Society in Southern Epirus, Greece*. Oxford: British Archaeological Reports.

Teržan, B.

2007 Cultural Connections between Caput Adriae and the Aegean in the Late Bronze and Early Iron Age. In I. Galanaki, H. Tomas, Y. Galanakis and R. Laffineur (eds.). *Between the Aegean and Baltic Seas: Prehistory Across Borders* (Aegaeum 27): 157–164. Liège: Univeritè de Liège.

Teržan, B. and S. Karavanić

2013 The Western Balkans in the Bronze Age. In A. Harding and H. Fokkens (eds.), *The Oxford Handbook of the European Bronze Age*: 837–863. Oxford: Oxford University Press.

Tomas, H.

2010 The World Beyond the Northern Margin: The Bronze Aege Aegean and the East Adriatic Coast. In W.A. Parkinson M.L. Galaty (eds.), *Archaic State Interaction: The Eastern Mediterranean in the Bronze Age*: 181–212. Santa Fe: SAR Press.

Trampuž-Orel, N.

1996 Spectrometric Research of the Late Bronze Age Hoard Finds. In B. Teržan (ed.), *Hoards and Individual Metal Finds from the Eneolithic and Bronze Ages in Slovenia, Katalogi in Monografije*: 165–243. Ljubljana: Narodni Muzej.

Turk, P.

1996. The Dating of Late Bronze Age Hoards. In B. Teržan (ed.), *Hoards and Individual Metal Finds from the Eneolithic and Bronze Ages in Slovenia, Katalogi in Monografije*: 89–124. Ljubljana: Narodni Muzej.

Uckelmann, M.

2012 *Die Schilde der Bronzezeit in Nord-, West- und Zentraleuropa* (Prähistorische Bronzefunde III.4). Stuttgart: Franz Steiner Verlag.

Van der Leeuw, S.

2013 Archaeology, networks, information processing, and beyond. In C. Knappett, (ed.), *Network Analysis in Archaeology: New Approaches to Regional Interaction*: 335–348. Oxford: Oxford University Press.

Van Dommelen, P. and M. Rowlands
2012 Material concerns and colonial encounters. In J. Maran and P. Stockhammer (eds.), *Materiality and Social Practice: The Transformative Capacities of Intercultural Encounters*: 20–31. Oxford: Oxbow Books.

Vasić, R.
1999 *Die Fibeln im Zentralbalkan: Vojvodina, Serbien, Kosovo und Mazedonien* (Prahistorische Bronzefunde XIV.12). Stuttgart: Franz Steiner Verlag.

Vermeule, E. and V. Karageorghis
1982 *Mycenaean Pictorial Vase Painting*. London: Harvard University Press.

Vinski-Gasparini, K.
1973 *Kultura polja sa žarama u sjevernoj Hrvatskoj*. Zagreb: Filozofski fakultet.

Wachsmann, S.
2000 To the Sea of the Philistines. In E.D. Oren (ed.), *The Sea Peoples and Their World: A Reassessment* (University Museum Monograph): 103–143. Philadelphia: The University Museum, University of Pennsylvania.
2013 *The Gurob ship-cart model and its Mediterranean context*. Texas: Texas A&M University Press.

Yasur-Landau, A.
2010 *The Philistine and Aegean migration at the end of the late Bronze Age*. Cambridge: Cambridge University Press.

Chapter 14

Distributed Practice and Cultural Identities in the 'Mycenaean' Period

Michael J. Boyd

Concepts of Mycenaean identity

This paper will consider the usefulness of the term 'Mycenaean'. In particular, it addresses how our varied understandings of it may relate to past realities experienced by widely dispersed actors and entities. It will assess if at any time in the past, a concept like our modern notion of 'Mycenaean' was current. Fundamentally, the underlying issue to be explored is whether people, groups, or artefacts identified or identifiable by this or a similar epithet. In relation to the theme of scales and modes of interaction at the heart of this volume, the contribution addresses the relevance of the local scale negotiation of identity through modes of dealing with the dead using a range of case-studies from the Aegean later Bronze Age. This is relevant in approaching questions of wider social frameworks of cultural and ethnic identity in prehistory, including those emerging from our own research traditions.

The term 'Mycenaean' emerged in the earliest days of the discipline, and its proper reconsideration would involve a historiographical excursus (see Burns 2010: 41–72), which is not the purpose of this chapter. But it is important to question what we mean today when we use the term as freely as we sometimes do. In the abstract for the colloquium from which this volume arose, contributors were invited to consider scales and modes of interaction, spatial and temporal gradations of influence, sub-regions or composite entities – in other words to employ a discerning subtlety for which the term and concepts of 'Mycenaean' might seem bluntly unsuited. 'Mycenaean' may be used as shorthand for a chronological period, or for certain styles of pottery or other material culture; but it is also widely employed as a cultural term, in the traditional archaeological sense (Childe 1929; 1933; cf. Jones 1997: 15–26), and even as an ethnic term (Davis and Bennet 1999: 112). More 'neutral' period and geographic designations such as 'Late Bronze Age' or 'third palace period' (Dickinson 1994) are used more rarely because they mask the *intended* (though usually ill-defined) cultural or ethnic sense of 'Mycenaean'.

The subject of this volume is connectivity and interaction, and individual 'Mycenaean' traits or the complete Mycenaean 'package' are certainly evidence of that. Demonstrating connectivity is straightforward but interpretation much less so: connectivity can be demonstrated in many different periods over varying regions, but it is not often used to demonstrate an identity or even ethnicity as persistently and specifically as it has been in the Mycenaean case. Yet the Mycenaean identities seen to arise from the material evidence of the Late Helladic world have not often been explicitly examined. A recent paper (Feuer 2011) takes up this challenge. 'Identity' can refer to different individual and group attributes or characteristics, some more fluid than others (Díaz-Andreu and Lucy 2005); an investigation of the ongoing creation and reproduction of Mycenaean *identities* through the manipulation of symbolic materials in practice could be sensitive to variation in time and place. Yet Feuer argues much more specifically for the appropriateness of 'Mycenaean' as an ethnic term: as a clear modern reflection of a past ethnic reality. The past reality of a Mycenaean ethnic group is for him self-evident, and he asks, for example, 'Could one choose to be Mycenaean', or 'How did the people we today term 'Mycenaean' come into existence?' (Feuer 2011: 507). That a people called the Mycenaeans existed as a point of historical fact is a given. He argues that through 'ethnogenesis' the Mycenaean ethnic identity was created by elite groups in the Early Mycenaean period: he equates Mycenaean ethnicity with the ruling class, a group either already ethnically distinct, or transformed into a separate ethnic group in the process of creating a distinct elite Mycenaean identity marked by features such as tholos tombs, palaces, iconography and writing. This process of 'ethnogenesis' was catalysed by contacts with Crete: "these mainland Proto-Mycenaeans first became Minoanized during Middle Helladic III and Late Helladic I before becoming Mycenaean through the process of ethnogenesis" (Feuer 2011: 529). In many ways this is a forceful reassertion of mainstream positions of the twentieth century (*e.g.* Caskey 1960; *cf* the more nuanced analysis in Davis and Bennet 1999).

The recognition of ethnicity, and indeed of identity more generally, in prehistoric periods is widely regarded as methodologically challenging (Jones 1997; Emberling 1997). The presumption of a common identity for Early Minoan Crete, for example, has recently been challenged: Legarra Herrero notes that "a continuum of possibilities' lies 'between the traditional perception of a homogeneous... culture and... [separate] human populations with completely different traits co-existing..." (2009: 31–32). In many prehistoric examples, most expressions of identity will fall within this 'continuum of possibilities' rather than in the two extremes. Broodbank, in considering a possible Minoan ethnicity, suggests "the chances of identifying ethnic groups and boundaries in prehistory are in fact vanishingly thin" (2004: 52). In the present case, Feuer's argument hinges on three assumptions: first, his assertion that there was a historical Mycenaean ethnicity; second that what he calls 'ethnic markers' – palaces, Linear B, tholos tombs and so on – would have been widely understood in the past as indicating such an identity; and third that the distribution of these markers defines a homogeneous 'ethnic' region in space. One aim of this paper is to examine evidence which might undermine these assumptions. One basic problem with mapping the spread of sets of 'ethnic markers' and drawing boundaries around them is that the maps do nothing to explain the adoption and employment in practice and subsequent development of those traits in specific local or regional circumstances. In a more nuanced analysis Burns notes Hall's assertion that "the association of objects with ethnic categories is neither self-evident nor stable" (Burns 2010: 42; Hall 2002). Broodbank notes that "even if specific elements of material culture did gain emblematic status... the choice of such elements is extremely hard to ascertain even when other information sources suggesting the existence of ethnic groups are available, and effectively impossible if the data consist entirely of patterns of spatial variation in material culture, that might signify a variety of social, economic or other processes" (2004: 53). Mac Sweeney (2009: 106) notes a "current problem where group identities are unthinkingly ascribed to patterns in material culture, and where ethnicity is assumed to lie at their root". A related problem is the assumption of correlation between material culture distribution and common linguistic traits (Davis and Bennet 1999: 113).

Objects and other aspects of context, such as architecture, as material structural conditions, are implicated in practice, which may be both constrained and enabled by them (Barrett 2000). For Feuer, being Mycenaean is the replication of practice: it is to live in a palace or bury in a tholos tomb. The combination of practice and material structural conditions is a basic unit of archaeological study within which it is possible to examine evidence for connectivity and sometimes to question notions of identity. However, the coarse replication of material and architectural forms does not in itself demonstrate conscious replication of practice, and indeed the replication of dominant meanings or ideologies. In particular, as hinted above, we might question how nuanced and diverging identities were created and reproduced in practice (Lucy 2005). Mac Sweeney's approach to the instantiation of group identities seems particularly relevant here: "a form of ideology that must be actively created, negotiated and ascribed to through social practice" (2009: 105). However, with an emphasis on variation in practice, the creation of variable and contextually-specific group identities may offer a useful approach to the study of connectivity in Late Bronze Age.

This paper examines manifestations of one such field of practice in selected areas of the Aegean in order to face this question. This coverage is not meant to be even or exhaustive: instead, the areas are chosen to highlight differing trajectories in the adoption and employment of traits at different local and regional scales, and questioning the possible expressions of identity produced as a result of adherence to, deviation from and recreation of practices and symbolic forms in differing circumstances.

Being and becoming Mycenaean in death?

The field of practice in question is that of mortuary practices. Although mortuary practices are somewhat removed from everyday experience, the mortuary field is the obvious choice as, alongside pottery, it is the only facet of the more common definitions of 'Mycenaean' which is maintained throughout this long period. Other aspects – the palaces, texts, or perhaps aspects of cult and iconography – are only really evidenced in the late Mycenaean period. So not only do mortuary practices have the advantage of longevity, but if there were a period of 'becoming Mycenaean', archaeologically this can only be addressed through mortuary practices and pottery. Mortuary practices have the advantage of letting us begin at the beginning. As a field of practice, it offers opportunities for demonstrative practice in communally expressed action which may draw on non-routine knowledge, materials and symbols and thus may be used to marshal and channel notions of group identity.

The study of mortuary practices in the Aegean has been undergoing a renaissance. For the mainland the work of Voutsaki has emphasised the creation of Mycenaean elite identity through conspicuous funerary consumption (Voutsaki 1995; 1997; 1998; 1999; 2010). However, the glittering attraction of the Mycenae shaft graves sometimes detracts from the breadth of the data. Mycenaean funerary practices can tell us about more than just the concerns of the elite (Papadimitriou 2011), but curiosities more voyeuristic than forensic have led to methodological emphases on elite and 'pristine' contexts, and the often woeful recording of 'disturbed' or 'poor' contexts. As Barrett has said, "we must confront the full diversity of our data... [through] a theoretically competent framework designed to expose the nature of specific practices" (Barrett 1988: 32). Approaches to Mycenaean funerary practice have too often been top-down, with the evidence being aggregated into typological groupings whose presence might indicate certain states of being, roles or social structures (generally with an elite emphasis). The structuring of assemblages in typological rather than contextual nexus can leave the data struggling to surprise us, or tell us anything we didn't already know (Boyd 2014a). A bottom-up approach that centres on the material conditions of human practice would allow us to theorise variation as well as conformity. An emphasis on variability allows us to acknowledge repeated and stereotypical forms and practices as widely and variably understood and developing resources of symbolic representation, rather than as essential components of a reified concept. These forms and practices were inherent in multiple modes of mortuary architecture, material culture and practice, emphasising the range of symbolic resources within which different groups chose to situate themselves. Approached in this manner, we open the way to more nuanced notions of identity through the differential adoption of certain practices across time and space.

Framework of practice

In order to begin it is essential briefly to review developments in mortuary forms and practices in the Peloponnese around the end of the Middle Helladic period and into the Late Helladic – the formative period for Mycenaean identity, if such terms are appropriate. These five developments, which I have analysed in detail elsewhere (Boyd 2016) and so will only briefly review here, occur broadly simultaneously, and it is not clear that any one precipitated any other. Once established, they underpinned much of the mortuary activity for the remainder of the Bronze Age (although their adoption was not accomplished at the same rate in all areas, and cannot be detected in some regions, as discussed below). However, my point here is not simply to produce a more tightly defined version of what death and burial meant in 'the Mycenaean world', nor is it my contention that these developments are in themselves indicative of Mycenaean identity. Instead I am sketching a framework within which to understand human action and especially variation through time and space, and within which it may be possible to address connectivity, interaction and identity.

The five areas of development are: first, new tomb types which changed the possibilities for action during funerals and other interventions; second, the introduction of collective burial; third, the development of a rich variety of secondary treatments of funerary contexts; fourth, significant developments in the use of material culture in funerary contexts; and fifth, the creation of funerary landscapes.

Let us begin with architecture. New tomb types were developed in the Middle Helladic III period (Boyd 2002, 54–64). Their evolving design enabled specific aspects of funerary practice, while constraining others. Prior to this, most Middle Helladic grave types, including shaft graves, shared the characteristic of being more or less elaborate holes in the ground whose scale was prompted by that of the corpse (Boyd 2002: 92). The new types were designed to accommodate the ingress and activities of the mourners, as well as the corpse. The construction of reusable tombs facilitated not only the actions of a group of mourners in the deposition phase of a funeral, but also allowed for and constrained movement and circulation between interior and exterior space over potentially extended periods of time, including beyond the timeframe of a single funeral.

These architectural innovations facilitated practice in two areas. Previously, during a funeral, at the end of the procession stage, the acts at the graveside and the interment itself were conducted in plain view of the mourners. A crowd of mourners may sometimes have restricted viewpoints: some Middle Helladic burials took place on the raised stage of a tumulus in order to counteract this (Boyd 2002: 80). The acts were accessible from multiple angles, and the architecture of simpler graves neither facilitated nor constrained the movements of those involved. The new types of tomb consisted of hidden chambers either built of stone and covered by a prominent mound (tholos tombs), or dug underground (chamber tombs). These chambers were approached by a closable doorway (stomion), and usually this doorway itself was at the end of a narrow passageway (dromos). This created a very directed, very narrow focus, and served to facilitate two groups among the mourners – those few who could fit inside the tomb to observe or direct proceedings, and the larger number remaining outside – though during the proceedings no doubt there would be considerable interchange between these groups (Boyd in press; Papadimitriou 2011).

Beyond the funeral itself, these new tomb types facilitated re-entry, both for future funerals but also for other activities. This relates to the second area of innovation, the introduction of collective burial. Middle Helladic burials had always shown a strong sense of association: not only between burials, often grouped together, but also through focus on certain locales, such as a burial mound, or a disused part of settlement. However, graves were not designed or usually intended for reuse: although instances of reuse exist (Cavanagh and Mee 1998: 31 note 100), many Middle Helladic graves were single inhumations. The new tomb forms created a specific collective space for interment. The innovation of collective interment involved far-reaching changes in the flow of activity in funerary practice, opening up opportunities on several fronts. At the start of the process, the choice was now more often to reopen an existing tomb rather than to dig a new one; this of necessity involved engagement with the material remains of prior activity in the tomb. This may have prompted the development of up to three stages in secondary treatment of material within the tombs (the third area of innovation). These three opportunities, not necessarily evidenced at all times and places, were first, interaction with and rearrangement of material on reopening the tomb prior to the interment; second, the production of a new arrangement of material, including the corpse, at the end of a funeral; and third, the opportunity to return to the tomb at a time other than during a funeral to carry out further activities.

All three of these were opportunities for meaningful engagement with the material remains of the past, not merely to be dismissed as expedient activity involving 'cleaning' or 'sweeping aside'. Without secondary treatment, in many tombs after one or two interments it would become very difficult to move freely without damaging funerary contexts. These tombs would have been quite unsuitable if their purpose were to hold multiple, intact interment contexts. Instead, the tombs facilitated and encouraged practices of interference with material on almost every visit. Interaction with and rearrangement of material became one of the foremost aspects of funerary activity.

A fourth key aspect of mortuary practice was the use of a much wider range of material culture than during preceding periods (Boyd 2014a). Broadly speaking, artefacts were utilised in one of three categories of practice. Some items relate to the laying out or presentation of the corpse: items such as jewellery or dress ornaments may have been fixed as part of the corpse' raiment away from the tomb, at the graveside, or within the chamber. A second group of items – often weaponry – were not fixed to the corpse but nonetheless relate to its presentation. These may often have been introduced as part of the production of the interment context within the tomb during the latter stages of the funeral. The final group of material evidences activities not directly related to the corpse. In many cases drinking and pouring vessels are the primary representatives in this category, both within the tomb and outside its entrance. None of these were new categories of practice, but previously each had been much less common, if not rare; and their co-occurrence is a new feature.

The final aspect of practice is the inhabitation of a new kind of funerary landscape. While isolated tombs are known, most were built in close proximity to each other. Procession is an aspect central to almost any funeral, dictated by the need to move the corpse to the place of burial (Boyd in press). It was certainly an aspect of Middle Helladic practice (Boyd 2002: 39). But the clustering of tholos and chamber tombs facilitated procession through an ancestral landscape, which became an active means to experience, create or rediscover relationships between groups in a landscape full of mnemonic points of reference (Galanakis 2011; for Wright, 2008: 147–148, the inscription of family sub-groups and their place in the community). The act of moving to the grave may sometimes have come to include visits to other tombs where the material remains of past acts might have been redeployed within the present context, allowing for the active participation of different groups, making manifest relations between the mourners. Beyond the funeral itself, ancestral landscapes were still present in many everyday routes of movement. Aside from a few instances where roads have been detected, tombs are by far the commonest evidence we have for landscape routes: in some cases, it would scarcely have been possible to approach a habitation site without negotiating a landscape of tombs.

This is the framework of practice within which any notions of Mycenaean or other identity would have been articulated. The variability in adoption of or reference to aspects of this framework is the space within which we may question broader and narrower questions of identity. What follows is a regional and chronological overview aimed at addressing these questions. We begin with the Peloponnese, often regarded as the Mycenaean heartland, and then move on to selected regions that would normally be regarded as more peripheral.

The Peloponnese

It is well-known by now that the first tholos tombs appeared in Messenia in Middle Helladic III (Cavanagh and Mee 1998: 44; Boyd 2002: 55), and indeed it is still unclear, recent discoveries notwithstanding, that any tholos tombs were built beyond that region's borders before Late Helladic II (for the Corinth tholos, see Kasimi 2013; Servais and Servais-Soyez 1984 for Thorikos; Boyd 2002: 187 and references for Samiko). I have argued elsewhere, following the lead of Korres (Korres 1996; Korres 2011; Boyd 2002: 54–56), that tholos tombs were first invented on a small scale as constructed improvements on pithos burials in tumuli, but quickly underwent a secondary transformation, becoming larger and dominating the funerary monument, with usually only a single tomb within each mound. These rapid architectural changes were driven by the changing funerary practices just outlined, while at the same time the new possibilities presented by architectural developments also drove changes in funerary practices, accelerating the process. Funerary activity within all five of the key areas sketched above can be demonstrated in Messenia at the Middle-Late Bronze Age transition.

It is interesting to compare Messenia with the Argolid at this time, and first with the site of Mycenae in particular. The shaft graves seem so emblematic of twentieth century notions of Mycenaean identity that it is important to be reminded of how anomalous they are. In the field of tomb design, far from adopting the reusable forms appearing elsewhere, the 'Mycenaean Mycenaeans' went down an entirely different route of innovation (Boyd 2015; Papadimitriou 2011). The innovation of the shaft grave was the roof above the burial in the lower part of the shaft; the reason for this innovation may have been to preserve intact and undisturbed the funerary tableau created during the interment process (Boyd 2015). The tombs were not designed for reuse: in early instances where reuse does take place we see a number of responses which make it clear that meaningful engagement with the remains of prior burials was not embraced as part of the ritual framework. Instead, burial contexts were often fairly carefully moved aside, with an intent to keep their material together in a recognisable part of the tomb, and not mix contexts (*e.g.* graves Λ2, I and Ξ: Mylonas 1973). Later in the sequence, shaft graves were made larger so that three or four burials could take place, each having its own space on the floor. So the practices evidenced in the shaft graves differ from the basic framework I have set out above: collective burial was often not intended, except for some of the latest graves; and secondary treatments were entirely different in nature to those attested in the graves of Messenia and elsewhere at this time, or to widespread later practice.

However, innovations in funerary discourse were taking place elsewhere in the Argolid. At Argos, Papadimitriou has shown that all of the burial traits I have outlined were in operation at least by LH I (Papadimitriou 2001a, 2001b). There are two examples of what he calls 'built chamber tombs' – small built tombs with a bipartite or tripartite design not unlike the tholos and chamber tombs. Closer to Mycenae, at Prosymna at least three chamber tombs seem to have been in use in LH I (Blegen 1937; Shelton 1996); there are also suggestions of two further LH I chamber tombs at Schoinohori (Dickinson 1977: 64) and Kokla (Demakopoulou 1993: 59–60).

So, not only were the Mycenae shaft graves anomalous in terms the framework of practice I have sketched, they were also surrounded by sites where the new funerary practices had begun to be adopted. This brings us to a central point about Late Bronze Age burial practices. The activities at the shaft graves clearly speak of an elite, and the case is often further made that burial in tholos tombs as well as some chamber tombs should be taken as evidence of elite activity and particularly elite self-representation. Because of this inferred elite status, activity at these different sites is often treated as interchangeable: although the details of practice may differ, we can still class the activity as 'elite' and hence infer comparable hierarchical organisation at different sites. The disregard for the details of contextualised practice again creates the position where difference is downplayed in favour of a normative synthesis. This is a misreading of the evidence. While the later burials in the Mycenae shaft graves can scarcely be understood as other than elite, elsewhere the evidence is clear: changes in burial practice were not first developed among rarified social groups which were then emulated further down the hierarchy. They were developed and adopted widely, and their use in what we might call elite contexts is a secondary aspect of adoption.

Mycenae itself is an interesting example of this (Boyd 2015; Wright 2008, 147). In LH I burials that embraced the new framework of practice had begun to encroach ever closer to the site: Prosymna, as mentioned, and then the Kalkani hill, close to the existing Mycenae cemetery, but separated from it by the Panayia ridge. One or more chamber tombs were probably built in the Kalkani hill in LH I, although the evidence is ambiguous, and it could be argued, in the case of tomb 518 for example, that the few LH I items found therein could have been introduced during LH II, and thus may not reflect the date of construction accurately (Blegen 1937: 261; Wilkie 1992: 247; Boyd 2002: 87; Boyd 2014b). Nonetheless, whether late in LH I or early in LH II, chamber tombs and then impressive tholos tombs were being built and used in the peripheral regions of Mycenae. This alternative mortuary discourse, effectively alien to the practices evidenced at the shaft graves, brought about the end of that sequence, and impelled those carrying out funerals close to the Mycenae acropolis to adopt the same practices now used around them. To continue to differentiate themselves, they built bigger, finer tombs designed to draw in the largest group of people possible; in scale they misunderstood the point as their huge tombs dominated the landscape and the individual human as she approached and entered. But despite their impressiveness, the tholos tombs of Aegisthus and the Lion represented the capitulation of one group in the face of the irrelevance of the practices they had promoted to wider society, in which new groups found favour in promoting their alternative discourses.

In this case we turn Feuer's (2011) argument of Mycenaean elite ethnogenesis on its head. It was the elite at Mycenae who were late to the party, who had to adopt the 'Mycenaean' practices that others were promoting. If there is a core 'Mycenaean' identity to be found in these practices, at the site of Mycenae it was adopted, not innate, and the groups burying in the shaft graves were the last of the classes or factions at Mycenae to adopt it. In doing so they reimagined the framework through their particular concerns. This late adaptation underlines the diffuse origins of these practices. It is also just one instance of the variable take-up of these practices notable throughout the Peloponnese. The question of the proportion of members of society who might expect chamber or tholos burial has often been debated (Mee and Cavanagh 1984; Dickinson 1983), but it is clear that this proportion varied considerably in time and space. The possibility of burial in a chamber or tholos tomb was open to different numbers of people in different contexts, and this suggests questions of social and corporate group membership – identity – which differed widely (and thus could only very loosely, and not exclusively, have related to ethnicity).

Turning therefore to look at the adoption of these practices elsewhere, it is interesting to contrast the seeming eagerness of some communities to adopt many of the aspects of this package of practice, and to think about the variation in take-up and in implementation. In Messenia, most of the earliest tombs were built in pre-existing Middle Helladic mounds, and hence into an established, and developing, funerary landscape (Boyd 2002: 56). Isolated tombs remained rare throughout; instead groups of two to five were often the norm, with these groups often loosely associated in a wider landscape. By LH II there was a concentration of sites in the Argolid, where besides the tholos tombs at Mycenae and a handful of other sites, chamber tombs began to be used in cemeteries. These early, and small, chamber tomb cemeteries presage their widespread adoption and enlargement in LH III.

Beyond the Argolid and Messenia, adoption is piecemeal. A few individual sites appear elsewhere in the Peloponnese (as well as in Attica and in Boeotia), mostly LH II in date and in many cases again precursors to the explosion of chamber tomb use in LH III (Cavanagh and Mee 1998: fig. 5.3). However, when those LH II outliers were built, they were themselves isolated examples. Such isolated tombs did not in themselves express community burial practices, but rather the idiosyncratic actions of the early-adopters. The well-known tholos tomb at Vapheio (Tsountas 1899), for example, required the import of an architect to create a version of the impressive tombs of the Argolid or Messenia. This tomb stood in isolation, not built into an existing funerary landscape, nor encouraging the creation of one around it. The burial within it also only partly engaged with the framework of practice under discussion: the burial context was preserved in its cist and the remains were neither disinterred nor reused in any activity after the funeral, even though later activity in the tomb did occur (taphonomic processes accounted from the loss of bone material, but the other material was undisturbed). This recalls more the shaft graves than the usual practices of tholos tombs: one may speculate (given the lack of excavation evidence) that similar practices may have occurred in the great tholos tombs of Mycenae, at least initially – the depositional aspects of shaft grave practice may have simply been transferred to the interior of the tombs. The practices at Vapheio suggest, initially at least, the inclinations of a particular group whose control of the action was not ceded to any wider, communal grouping, and where no cemetery of chamber tombs was encouraged, or allowed, to grow around this tomb. Vapheio may well be an example of simple emulation with little significant input from existing local practice.

Many of the more elaborate tholos tombs of LH II may indeed have been encouraged by emulation between corporate or social groups, perhaps 'elite' in nature, even some in Messenia, such as Peristeria 1. However not all of the isolated adoptions of this period fall into this category. The chamber tombs of Epidauros Limira (Dickinson 1977: 63–64; Boyd 2002: 206–208; Gallou 2009), for example, have no obviously 'elite' features. Their adoption in this remote corner of the Peloponnese may be considered in the light of developments in Messenia, the Argolid, and to the south in Kythera and Crete, although local factors have recently also been emphasised (Gallou 2009). It is unknown how many of the tombs date to LH II as those excavated continued in use in LH III, and it is said that 'more than 100' are to be found nearby (Gallou 2009: 88).

However the early adoption in this case is understood, elite emulation is not a likely explanation. In terms of burial practice, as far as can be understood from the limited evidence, the use of these chamber tombs falls within the framework of practice under discussion without significant deviation.

Moving into LH III, the spread of chamber tomb cemeteries is well-documented (Cavanagh and Mee 1998; Dickinson 1983). However a lack of homogeneity is apparent even from a glance at their distribution (Cavanagh and Mee 1998: fig. 6.3): distinct clusters are apparent in Messenia, Elis, Achaea, and in the Argolid; beyond the Peloponnese, they are common in southern Attica, in eastern Boeotia and central Euboea, and farther afield in Kephalonia; elsewhere they are found less commonly in Fthiotida and Phokis, and in the other areas of the Peloponnese numbers are sparse, while elsewhere on the mainland they are rare. Farther afield in the Aegean significant numbers are located on Rhodes and Crete. Geography is obviously part of the explanation for these distribution patterns. But it is also the case that communities of practice grew in some places where elsewhere they simply did not. Regions of long-lived, widespread practice existed beside other areas where Mycenaean burial practices are hardly attested (Cavanagh 2008: 330–331).

In the southwest Peloponnese in LH I-II, as already noted, numerous tombs and cemeteries were in use: these mostly continue into LH III, although fewer new tombs and cemeteries come into use (Cavanagh and Mee 1998: 77–78). In the northwest, in Elis and Achaea, the picture is very different. In LH I-II, apart from the southern part of Elis, most of this large area has very little evidence for any burial practices; in LH III, however, there is an explosion of chamber tomb cemeteries in two distinct clusters, one centred on southern Elis, and the other in Achaea. The choice in LH III of the chamber tomb, dug out of the ground, rather than the built tholos tomb, differentiates these northwestern areas from Messenia: although there are some very early chamber tombs in Messenia at Volimidhia, (and in LH III there are some very significant chamber tomb cemeteries in the east of Messenia at Ellinika), in general the form never became common there, and there are none in the northern part of Messenia. Moreover, the explosion of chamber tomb building in the northwest Peloponnese was taking place at the same time that tomb construction was winding down in Messenia (Cavanagh and Mee 1998: 63–64; Boyd 2002: 213), although mortuary activity did continue in many of those that were already in existence (Zavadil 2013: 239–242). The burial practices of Messenia in LH III had become much less relevant to its neighbours than those of more distant areas such as the Argolid, Attica and Boeotia.

Explanations for the anomalous situation in Messenia have centred on the possibility that emergent palatial elites sought to manipulate manifestations of authority by directly controlling the construction and use of tholos tombs (Bennet 2007). Bennet also notes a general lack of objects of "cultural and intrinsic value" in LH III contexts in Messenian tombs, which he suggests results from palatial control of the funerary sphere, and a move away from conspicuous consumption in view of the lack of competition for authority. It might also be noted that the two tombs he postulates as constructed under palatial authority, tholos III at Englianos, and tholos M1 at Nichoria (if indeed it was built in LH III: Boyd 2014b; Zavadil 2013: 425), are architecturally relatively modest and lack the pretensions of some large early tholoi of Messenia, such as Englianos IV and Peristeria I (see also Cavanagh and Mee 1998: 64). In LH III at Mycenae the great tholos tombs now named after Atreus and Klytemnaestra demonstrate a quite different trajectory for elite funerary practices. But the general paucity even of architecturally modest tomb construction in Messenia in LH III is also a significant contrast with other areas. The great tholoi of Mycenae were accompanied by a swelling funerary landscape composed of at least 27 cemeteries of more than 250 tombs (Shelton 2003). At Englianos only a few chamber tombs were constructed (Murphy 2014), and as noted above great cemeteries of chamber tombs were not widely initiated in LH III elsewhere in Messenia: some of the tombs at Volimidhia might have been constructed in LH III, although the suspicion must be that many were built in the Early Mycenaean period (Boyd 2002: 144–145), and other chamber tombs in Messenia tend to be found individually or in very small groups, with the important exception of the impressive Ellinika cemetery (Zavadil 2013: 274–287). The early chamber tombs at Volimidhia (along with the formally similar examples at Pellana in Laconia) seem symbolically to reference tholos tombs much more explicitly than most later chamber tombs do, and so emphasise once again the possibilities for practice created by such spaces, rather than their mode of construction.

Continuing funerary activity, but with a much reduced emphasis on new tomb construction, may be seen as one possible outcome of long-term funerary activity within the framework of practice set out previously. Given the emphasis on the ancestors (Boyd 2016), the active maintenance of many existing tombs suggests the greater importance of local factors in funerary practice rather than the influence of the LH III palatial hierarchy. The lack of funerary emphasis on Englianos in LH III is a marked point of contrast with the Argolid. In Messenia in LH III burial practices remained a distributed and relatively low-key aspect of wider society and seem not to have been of much concern to the palatial sphere. In the Argolid, on the other hand, both the overall numbers of tombs increased markedly, drawing in ever wider groups to participate in funerary practices, and through the great tombs at Mycenae, as well as the ever-expanding cemeteries there, funerary activity was closely associated with the routine ritual practices of that site, while perhaps drawing in participants from different social groups.

Both of these areas contrast again with the northwest Peloponnese. Here Mycenaean funerary practices begin with the remarkable sites of Portes in Achaea (Kolonas 2009) and Samiko in Elis (Yialouris 1965; Papakonstandinou 1981, 1982, 1983; Boyd 2002: 186–189), both of which are small, complex cemeteries including tumuli (at Portes) or grave enclosures (at Samiko) with subsequent tholos tombs (and, at Portes, other built tombs, and chamber tombs). Samiko is close to the border with Messenia and may well be regarded as within the wider Messenian community of practice (Eder 2011). Portes, however, seems much more isolated. In both these areas, however, until LH III, other evidence for Mycenaean burial practices is almost absent. Nonetheless in LH III chamber tomb burial quickly became a widely-adopted practice that drew in communities and groups. While aspects of social exclusion may have been at work, and not everyone was buried in a chamber tomb, there can be no suggestion that these are purely elite practices. At Kallithea, for example, in Achaea, a cemetery initiated by building a tholos tomb soon became much larger through the construction of numerous chamber tombs. Even if it could be shown that the tholos was purely representative of the elite, which must be questionable, in any case it is clear that a large subset of the community was able through LH III to take part in burial practices here. It is often (though certainly not always) the case that Peloponnesian chamber tomb cemeteries are not the result of socially highly-restricted burial practices, but drew in a much wider segment of their communities (a point originally made by Mee and Cavanagh: 1978).

Thessaly

In Thessaly, the picture is rather different (Voutsaki 1993; Adrimi-Sismani 2007; Papadimitriou 2008). Feuer regards it as a "zone of decreasing integration" (2011: 525). There is no evidence for the development of burial practices within the framework of practice referred to above during the early Mycenaean period. Moreover, there is virtually no Mycenaean pottery – imported or local – in use during this period. Instead, beginning in LH IIB but really taking off in LH IIIA1, we see a wholesale importation of cultural traits: burial practices and pottery at the same time. However, instead of large chamber tomb cemeteries, tholos tombs were constructed with an energy that is unmatched farther south where far fewer tholos tombs were being built by this time. Within a small area around Dimini and Volos, at least four large tholos tombs were built. In these tombs there is a complete shift from prior practice to embrace collective burial, secondary treatment, the use of material culture, and so on. There are also indications of local peculiarities, such as a scarcity of drinking vessels (Voutsaki 1993: 111), indicating less emphasis on drinking or toasting rituals; and ritual burning of bones as part of the secondary treatment after disarticulation has been demonstrated for the recently excavated Kasanaki tholos, and was probably the case in the two Dimini tholoi as well (Adrimi-Sismani 2007; Galanakis forthcoming). Meanwhile at several other sites smaller tholos tombs were constructed and used in small groups throughout LH IIIA and B, and sometimes continuing into LH IIIC. Very few chamber tombs were constructed and used in Thessaly.

In this case, it could be argued that those building and using the large tholoi were acting in conscious imitation of their counterparts farther south: as part of a construction of identity, entailing not only pottery but also burial customs, and at the same time some (but not all) aspects of a palatial system, the latter introduced during LH IIIA and maintained in LH IIIB (Adrimi-Sismani 2007). The relationships between sites and thus between different groups is a matter of discussion, with some favouring the identification of Dimini as a palatial site in the mould of Mycenae or Pylos at the top of a settlement hierarchy (Adrimi-Sismani 2007); others suggest more diffuse relations between sites (Papadimitriou 2008; Pantou 2010; Feuer 2011). In this regard the smaller tholos tombs built in numbers at several sites surrounding the Dimini and Volos area are of great interest. It would be difficult to argue that these were built as an adoption or imitation of 'Mycenaean' practices farther south, as rather few tholos tombs were being built at this time, and even fewer in the very small size relevant here. It seems obvious that these were inspired principally by the larger tholos tombs of the Volos area, most of whose construction dates are early enough in the Thessalian sequence to play that role (Papadimitriou 2008). Yet although we seem therefore to have a handful of 'elite' tombs near Volos and some more modest tombs in the surrounding area, the overall number is very low, and thus compares badly with areas such as the Argolid where much larger numbers of tombs (in the form of chamber tombs, which are very rare in Thessaly) were in use. This suggests that the smaller tholos tombs of Thessaly were nonetheless quite restricted in their demographic. Hence the processes of adoption and use of these burial practices in Thessaly seem quite different to those farther south: whereas elsewhere burial practices were driven by wider communities, with sometimes the elite trailing behind innovation, in Thessaly the opposite may have been the case, with new burial practices trialled in the upper echelons of widely dispersed groups, and perhaps ultimately not penetrating very deeply into everyday use.

Crete

Cretan mortuary practices have been cited in relation to possible Mycenaean presence or control at Knossos, both in general terms in relation to the supposed importation of Mycenaean burial practices, and more particularly in terms of the 'warrior burials' (Popham 1974; Macdonald 1984; neither author takes a definitive view). Laura Preston has challenged this analysis and cast the adoption of new burial practices in LM II at Knossos very much in terms of local elite activity (Preston 1999, 2005, 2007), specifically 'status advertisement', and indeed sees the subsequent adoption of varied burial practices over the rest of the island in LM III also in terms of the actions of local elites, taking their cue from Knossos rather than farther afield (Preston 2004a, 2004b). More can perhaps be said from the point of view of the postulated framework for burial practice: in what sense, if any, were 'Mycenaean' burial practices adopted?

First, the use of bi- and tripartite tombs is certainly evidenced in the Knossos valley in LM II-III, but alongside other types of burial. Moreover, chamber tombs had a long history at Knossos, and one need not invoke mainland precedent to explain their presence (Alberti 2004). The architecturally impressive tombs of LM II Knossos, such as the Kephala tholos and the stone-built Isopata tombs, share some basic features with mainland tholoi. The LH I-LH II transition on the mainland is the time-period of the first adoption of tholos tombs outside Messenia, and as was noted above with the Vapheio tholos, it seems likely that specific architectural expertise was a requirement before architecturally impressive tholoi such as those at Vapheio, Mycenae, Thorikos, Marathon or Kakovatos could be constructed. The Knossos LM II tombs, which probably slightly post-date this group, are architecturally innovative and eschew the stylistic conventions of the mainland. If architectural expertise were imported in this case, perhaps in relation to the corbel-vaulting, it was not employed in creating a copy of a mainland tholos, but rather in creating a hybrid form. In a similar vein, Preston notes that "the inspirations for these tombs are not only distinctly heterogeneous, and diverse in their cultural and contextual origins, but they are combined here in such innovative ways that the overriding impression they convey is of eclectic experimentation with mortuary symbolism" (2000: 125–126). She offers some intriguing insights into specifically local forms of practice that might have been facilitated by these design variations (2007: 300–303).

Second, the tombs at Knossos are indeed collective in form, but where information is available many may have held only one or two inhumations (Preston 1999: 135). While these tombs retain the basic design features that imply reuse, in fact they may not have been reused: even where two burials are found, these may have been carried out simultaneously. As both Alberti (2004) and Preston (2000: 116, 135) have pointed out, this stands in contrast to Middle Minoan practice. We might add that it stands in contrast to mainland practice: while collective burial became the norm on the mainland, the tombs of Knossos, and (slightly later) more widely on Crete (Preston 2000: fig. 9.2) were generally used for rather few burials. Voutsaki noted a similar discrepancy between the tombs of the Argolid and those of the Dodecanese (1993: 133 and figs. 7.2 and 9.3). Whereas in the Peloponnese the inception of Mycenaean burial practices is marked by the intensification of association in burial by the adoption of collective burial, on Crete the practices of LM II-III mark a *reduced* emphasis on the collective aspects of burial.

Third, and in consequence, often the evidence for secondary treatment of the dead is far from clear. Where only one burial is found, there may be little evidence of subsequent activity in the tomb. Excavators have speculated that some of the dead were placed in wooden coffins or on wooden biers as part of interment, and these closed contexts seem often to have been left intact. The use of larnakes – almost totally alien to the mainland – in wider LM IIIA2 Crete has been suggested by Preston as a driving factor in the adoption of new burial practices at this time (2000: 226). The evidence for a lack of concern for the activities of rearrangement, disarticulation and redeposition is a significant departure from mainland practice, and the use of coffins and larnakes in preserving and protecting the individual funerary context suggests that the concern for maintaining an individual presence outweighed in many cases any concern for communal incorporation in an ancestral group.

Fourth, evidence for use of material culture is plentiful, though not unprecedented. Where more than one burial took place in a tomb, it was often clear to the excavators which item was associated with which burial. It is indeed remarkable that in these small spaces, subsequent interments – if they were not all interred simultaneously – could be introduced into such a restricted space without much damage to the existing interment contexts. This, in combination with the occasional emphasis on bronze weaponry which has been much remarked on, contributes further to a sense of the individual's personal image being carefully created and subsequently curated. This, again, is unlike mainland practice, though perhaps the similarities with the shaft graves are telling.

Finally, the growth of cemeteries does mirror to some extent similar events on the mainland. Nonetheless the landscape of the Knossos valley must have been more overburdened by meaning than most other landscapes in Greece by LM II: new tombs and cemeteries were more a re-purposing of resonant zones and pathways than an expansion of the cultural landscape. However, the construction of new tombs and cemeteries can still be seen as a new and meaningful way of occupying the landscape, evocative, however, of the practices of the past (see also Preston 2000: 115) – perhaps in this aspect Cretan burial practices were closest to those of the mainland.

This analysis demonstrates, if such demonstration still be needed, that these were not 'Mycenaean' burials practised by ethnic, embedded Mycenaeans; nor do they demonstrate simple adoption of Mycenaean practices, or indeed identity. Instead they were a pastiche of ideas imported from the mainland in combination with innovation and the memory of past funerary (and other) practice at Knossos. The emphasis on the presentation and segregation of the individual might make sense in terms of the practices of elite groups, but not all the early burials could be termed elite, and this holds true in subsequent periods as well. Instead, we see the creation and differential adoption of new and variable practices which owed only a part of their inspiration to the practices of the mainland.

If LM II-III Cretans were actively and knowledgeably selecting their sources in forging newly appropriate burial practices, the same must surely be true elsewhere. Cretan influence on mainland burial practices has long been noted. Just as on Crete there is nothing to be gained in an analysis that considers how the 'pure' or 'fundamental' Minoan aspects of mortuary practice were subverted by mainland dominance, so on the mainland we should not consider the adoption of Mycenaean burial practices as an internal expression of identity devoid of heterogenous inspiration. Cretan-derived symbolism in the shaft graves has long been noted (*e.g.* Evans 1929), and such symbolism is found more widely in the iconographic aspects of objects such as seals (Younger 2010), usually Cretan imports. Even Mycenaean pottery is a local expression of styles much more widely distributed. The magnificent palatial jars, for example, commonly used in Peloponnesian tholos and chamber tombs of LH IIA, display a mixed Cretan and mainland ancestry, and when no longer produced on the mainland in LH IIB nonetheless continued to be produced and used as palace style jars on Crete in LM II (Dickinson 1972; Mountjoy 1993: 41–44; Kalogeropoulos 2011) – at just the time that other aspects of mainland practice were being adopted into Cretan funerary practice. The use of these jars in mainland burial practices speaks of the active appropriation and manipulation of symbolism within a specific framework of practice, and their subsequent use on Crete demonstrates the reappropriation of this hybrid icon into a different framework of practice, in each case the echoes of distant times and places knowledgeably emphasised.

Summary of regional and chronological variation

Each tomb, throughout its history, presents its own evidence for varying agency drawing on – or sometimes eschewing – the framework of practice sketched at the outset of this section. Drawing together regional and chronological trends, as I do below, identifies some of the more widespread replications or developments in practice, though also gives a false sense of homogeneity. Yet the many examples of variability discussed above do much to dispel any thought of homogeneity. Turning first to the Peloponnese, it is clear that we are in fact dealing with several smaller regions within a broader geographical entity – a point which is hardly novel (*e.g.* Dickinson 1982). In the southwest, broadly speaking Messenia and southern Elis, developing from the Middle Helladic and continuing to the end of the Bronze Age, widely dispersed cemeteries of tholos and (some) chamber tombs hosted collective burials and secondary treatments accomplished with a wide array of material culture. Beginning slightly later in the Argolid, chamber tomb cemeteries and some tholos tombs hosted similar activities, again until the end of the Bronze Age; the evidence in the Corinthia is less abundant. Moving west, in most of Achaea and northern Elis few funerary activities can be detected before LH III; but during LH III large cemeteries of chamber tombs appeared, concentrated in two geographical areas, and exhibiting all the activities mentioned. Finally, in the southeast Peloponnese, broadly Laconia and Arcadia, far fewer examples of tombs and cemeteries exist in both LH I-II and LH III, though they are found widely dispersed and present throughout, beginning in the far southeast at Epidauros Limira, and inland at Vourvoura. This brief overview shows that adoption was piecemeal, with large areas lacking evidence, but with two intensive areas of activity in Messenia and the Argolid in the earlier period, with some quite widespread but isolated evidence elsewhere, and then several additional areas of concentrated activity in LH III. Regional variation between areas with tombs in LH III is not strong: where adopted, all the aspects of practice under discussion are present, though no doubt close examination of tombs and cemeteries would discern differing emphases. These are much more evident in comparing the practices of Thessaly and of central Crete. In Thessaly a few standard-sized tholos tombs, with rather more small tholos tombs, were adopted by restricted groups, and very large cemeteries did not develop. The range of material deposited in tombs was more restricted, suggesting some differences in funerary rituals; ritual burning of bones was perhaps more common here than elsewhere. In the Knossos valley the evidence for reuse of tombs is poor, and the small size of tombs suggests fewer persons inside performing fewer activities. Although disturbed contexts are known, a much greater proportion of undisturbed contexts is seen, sometimes through the use of coffins or larnakes. The emphasis on weaponry here is a strong contrast with Thessaly. Later on, elsewhere in Crete (*e.g.* Chania: Andreadaki-Vlazaki and Protopapadaki 2009), chamber tombs were found with better evidence for reuse and some evidence for secondary treatments (though in this example were a minority type in a larger cemetery of non-mainland types). The conclusion is clear that different groups and communities widely dispersed in time and space developed burial practices which drew to a greater or lesser extent on this framework of practice: from practices which grew within, maintained and replicated themselves and developed within this framework, to others which merely drew upon some aspects of it for inspiration. Moreover, in the southwest and parts of the northeast Peloponnese, the adoption of this framework of practice can be understood as a development with roots in pre-existing practice, whereas elsewhere this seems less to be the case, and effectively new practices were relatively suddenly adopted, sometimes quite widely, and sometimes in much more isolated circumstances.

Conclusions

Mac Sweeney (2009) concludes that group identities need not arise necessarily from ethnicity, nor need they inhere in archaeologically-defined collectives such as sites or regions. She also emphasises the fluidity of group identities. Identities are an evolving project whose material instantiation must always be partial and grounded in momentary concerns (Lucy 2005: 101–108). Two questions arise from the analysis in this paper. First, insofar as notions of identity are projected at all in funerary practices, at what scales might they operate? If fractured reflections of identity are multi-scalar, our analyses must similarly operate in multiple dimensions. Second, and related, the material and symbolic markers mentioned earlier, while no simple reflection of ethnicity, are notably recurrent in the material under consideration. What is invoked in the reproduction – and reimagining – of symbols and practice which do have a wide, though variably understood, recognition?

To address the issue of scales, we should consider the issue of identity at the levels of the individual funeral, the community of the living and the dead as invoked by the tomb and cemetery, regional communities of practice, and the wider 'Mycenaean' world. The projection of individual identity was perhaps most strongly evidenced in preparation for the funeral and the procession to the tomb, when the emphasis of funerary activity was centred on the corpse: its cleaning, dressing, presentation, and public transport (Boyd in press). Aspects such as dress and body modification are largely invisible archaeologically, and might have been used either to promote individual or group identity. The processional and depositional acts incorporating the dead within cemetery and tomb highlight group identity more strongly: wider community networks in the cemetery, and family, or other corporate groups, in the tomb. Variation in practice, such as burial in prominent or isolated tombs rather than cemeteries, and delay in, or eschewing of, subsequent dissolution of the funerary context, vary the balance between communal and individual. Practices perhaps related to social differentiation, involving architectural or material aggrandisement, form another significant variation. The growth in chamber tomb cemeteries in some areas in LH III, the use of tholos tombs in LH I-II Messenia, the sudden appearance of 'Mycenaean' practices in LH III Thessaly, or similarly in LM III Crete, are all regional phenomena indicating strong intra- and inter-site discourse and much weaker inter-regional interaction.

Identities draw variably on individual, local, regional and wider discourse. It is apparent that the specifics of practice are the result of individual choices drawing upon wider frameworks of practice operating at multiple levels. The 'markers', widely reproduced tomb forms, material culture types, or instances of practice, arose out of inter-regional interaction, but are only a sign of weak integration: locally reproduced traditions were much more strongly integrative.

Burial practices did not arise out of and reflect a Mycenaean culture or ethnicity, but rather formed a widely but unevenly adopted and implemented framework of practice. The inception and much of the adoption of these practices did not result from concerns of elite aggrandisement, although there were instances where elites did seek to co-opt and perhaps control the funerary sphere by adopting and adapting aspects of this framework of practice. Burial practices belonged most of the time to a much wider and diverse social groupings, and so to the extent that concepts of identity were projected through these practices, the identities projected were not merely those of the elite. It is also salient to note that in some areas these practices are evidenced far less frequently than others. This differential adoption, implementation and longevity says more about local choices than it does about a reflection of some overarching identity or ethnicity. Nonetheless it also says much about interconnectedness. The echoes of other times and places, distant or near, form a part of the attraction of Mycenaean burial practices, then as now. There can be no doubt that people felt themselves part of traditions of practice, even when operating creatively within those traditions. It is important, in that light, to emphasise again the non-elite aspects of many mortuary acts. For those outside the palaces, many different expressions of identity may have been articulated through funerary practices: local, family, corporate group; and also, by the development and maintenance of widely understood customs, and the use of specific material forms, expressions of identity within wider margins, wider than the borders of any palatial territory. In LH III some areas of practice, such as burials, may stand as alternative discourse to specific elite identities emanating from the palaces.

Where does that leave the Mycenaeans? There can be no doubt that the term, as we use it, is far too generally applied. Late Bronze Age identities were fractured and differentiating, as well as inclusive or widely resonant. Where some aspects of identity seem to us widely reproduced, they are nonetheless evidenced in divergent circumstances. Examination of these circumstances can bring partial understanding of the local chains of consequences which led to their appropriation. But the adaptation or reproduction of these traits does not in itself indicate an adherence to a fixed cultural or political identity, much less an ethnic one. By continuing to use the term 'Mycenaean' as freely as sometimes we do, we run the risk of implying the opposite.

Acknowledgements

I would like to thank the organisers of the Round Table for the invitation to speak, and all of the participants for a lively and useful meeting. This paper has benefitted greatly from the discussions arising from the meeting, and from the suggestions of John Bennet, Borja Legarra Herrero and Barry Molloy.

References

Adrimi-Sismani, V.
2007 Mycenaean northern borders revisited new evidence from Thessaly. In M.L. Galaty and W.A. Parkinson (eds.), *Rethinking Mycenaean Palaces II*: 159–177. Los Angeles: Cotsen Institute.

Alberti, L.
2004 The Late Minoan II-IIIAI warrior graves at Knossos: the burial assemblages. In G. Cadogan, E. Hatzaki and A. Vasilakis (eds.), *Knossos: Palace, City, State*: 127–136. London: British School at Athens.

Andreadaki-Vlazaki, M. and E. Protopapadaki
2009 "Kouklaki" Excavation (73–77 Igoumenou Gabriel Street). In *Khania (Kydonia) a Tour to Sites of Ancient Memory*: 152–165. Khania: Ministry of Culture and Tourism – 25th Ephorate of Prehistoric and Classical Antiquities.

Barrett, J.C.
1988 The Living, the Dead and the Ancestors: Neolithic and Early Bronze Age Mortuary Practices. In J.C. Barrett and I.A. Kinnes (eds.), *The archaeology of context in the Neolithic and Bronze Age: recent trends*: 30–41. Sheffield: Department of Archaeology and Prehistory, University of Sheffield.
2000 A thesis on agency. In M.-A. Dobres and J.E. Robb (eds.), *Agency in Archaeology*: 61–68. Oxford: Routledge.

Bennet, J.
2007 Pylos: The Expansion of a Mycenaean Palatial Center. In M.L. Galaty and W.A. Parkinson (eds.), *Rethinking Mycenaean Palaces II*: 29–39. Los Angeles: Cotsen Institute.

Blegen, C.W.
1937 *Prosymna. The Helladic Settlement Preceding the Argive Heraeum*. Cambridge: University Press.

Boyd, M.J.
2002 *Middle Helladic and Early Mycenaean Mortuary Practices in the Southern and Western Peloponnese*. Oxford: British Archaeological Reports.
2014a Materialities of performance in Mycenaean funerary practices. *World Archaeology* 46(2): 192–205.

2014b The Development of the Bronze Age Funerary Landscape of Nichoria. In D. Nakassis, J. Gulizio and S.A. James (eds.), *KE-RA-ME-JA Studies Presented to Cynthia Shelmerdine*: 191–208. Philadelphia: INSTAP Academic Press.
2015 Explaining the Mortuary Sequence at Mycenae. In A.-L. Schallin and I. Tournavitou (eds.), *Mycenaeans Up to Date: The Archaeology of the NE Peloponnese – Current Concepts and New Directions*: 433–447. Athens: Swedish School.
2016 Becoming Mycenaean? The living, the dead and the ancestors in the transformation of society in the second millennium BC in southern Greece. In C. Renfrew, M.J. Boyd and I. Morley (eds.) *Death shall have no dominion: the archaeology of mortality and immortality – a worldwide perspective*: 200–220. Cambridge: Cambridge University Press.
in press Fields of action in Mycenaean funerary practices. In A. Dakouri-Hild and M.J. Boyd (eds.), *Staging Death: Funerary Performance, Architecture and Landscape in the Aegean*. Berlin: De Gruyter.

Broodbank, C.
2004 Minoanisation. *Proceedings of the Cambridge Philological Society* 50: 46–91.

Burns, B.E.
2010 *Mycenaean Greece, Mediterranean Commerce, and the Formation of Identity*. Cambridge: Cambridge University Press.

Caskey, J.L.
1960 The Early Helladic Period in the Argolid. *Hesperia* 29: 285–303.

Cavanagh, W.G.
2008 Death and the Mycenaeans. In C.W. Shelmerdine (ed.) *The Cambridge Companion to the Aegean Bronze Age*: 327–341. Cambridge: Cambridge University Press.

Cavanagh, W.G. and C.B. Mee
1998 *A private place: death in prehistoric Greece (Studies in Mediterranean Archaeology 125)*. Jonsered: Paul Åströms Förlag.

Childe, V.G.
1929 *The Danube in Prehistory*. Oxford: Clarendon.
1933 Races, peoples and cultures in prehistoric Europe. *History* 18: 193–203.

Davis, J.L. and J. Bennet
1999 Making Mycenaeans: warfare, territorial expansion, and representations of the other in the Pylian kingdom. In R. Laffineur (ed.), *Polemos le contexte guerrier en Égée à l'âge du bronze (Aegaeum 19)*: 105–119. Liège: Université de Liège.

Demakopoulou, K.
1993 Argive Mycenaean Pottery: Evidence from the Necropolis at Kokla. In C. Zerner, P. Zerner and J. Winder (eds.), *Wace and Blegen: Pottery as Evidence for Trade in the Aegean Bronze Age 1939-1989*: 57–75. Amsterdam: J.C. Gieben.

Díaz-Andreu, M. and S. Lucy
2005 Introduction. In M. Díaz-Andreu, S. Lucy, S. Babić and D.N. Edwards (eds.), *The Archaeology of Identity Approaches to gender, age, status, ethnicity and religion*: 1–12. Abingdon: Routledge.

Dickinson, O.T.P.K.

1972 Late Helladic IIA and IIB: Some Evidence from Korakou. *Annual of the British School at Athens* 67: 103–112.

1977 *The origins of Mycenaean civilisation (Studies in Mediterranean Archaeology 49)*. Göteborg: Paul Åströms Förlag.

1982 Parallels and contrasts in the Bronze Age of the Peloponnese. *Oxford Journal of Archaeology* 1(2): 125–138.

1983 Cist graves and chamber tombs. *Annual of the British School at Athens* 78: 55–67.

1994 *The Aegean Bronze Age*. Cambridge: Cambridge University Press.

Eder, B.

2011 Zur historischen Geographie Triphyliens in mykenischer Zeit. In F. Blakolmer, C. Reinholdt, J. Weilhartner and G. Nightingale (eds.) *Österreichische Forschungen zur Ägäischen Bronzezeit 2009*: 105–117. Vienna: Phoibos.

Emberling, G.

1997 Ethnicity in Complex Societies: Archaeological Perspectives. *Journal of Archaeological Research* 5(4): 295–344.

Evans, A.

1929 *The shaft graves and bee-hive tombs of Mycenae and their interrelation*. London: Macmillan.

Feuer, B.

2011 Being Mycenaean: A View from the Periphery. *American Journal of Archaeology* 115: 507–536.

Galanakis, Y.

2011 Mnemonic landscapes and monuments of the past: tumuli, tholos tombs and landscape associations in late Middle Bronze Age and early Late Bronze Age Messenia (Greece). In E. Borgna and S. Müller Celka (eds.) *Ancestral Landscapes. Burial mounds In The Copper And Bronze Ages (Travaux de la Maison de l'Orient 58)*: 219–229. Lyon: Maison de l'Orient et de la Méditerranée – Jean Pouilloux.

Forthcoming Fire, fragmentation, and the body in the Late Bronze Age Aegean. In M. Mina, S. Triantaphyllou and Y. Papadatos (eds.), *Embodied Identities in the Prehistoric Eastern Mediterranean: Convergence of Theory and Practice*. Oxford: Oxbow.

Gallou, C.

2009 Epidaurus Limera: the tale of a Laconian site in Mycenaean times. In W.C. Cavanagh, C. Gallou and M. Georgiadis (eds.), *Sparta and Laconia: from Prehistory to Pre-Modern (British School at Athens Studies 16)*: 85–93. London: British School at Athens.

Hall, J.M.

2002 *Hellenicity: Between Ethnicity and Culture*. Chicago: University of Chicago Press.

Jones, S.

1997 *The Archaeology of Ethnicity Constructing identities in the past and present*. London: Routledge.

Kalogeropoulos, K.

2011 The social and religious significance of palatial jars as grave offerings. In H. Cavanagh, W. Cavanagh and J. Roy (eds.), *Honouring the Dead in the Peloponnese Proceedings of the conference held at Sparta 23-25 April 2009*: 207–235. Nottingham: Centre for Spartan and Peloponnesian Studies. http://www.nottingham.ac.uk/csps/documents/honoringthedead/kalogeropoulos.pdf (accessed 26 February 2013).

Kasimi, P.

2013 Ενας πρώιμος θολωτός μυκηναϊκός τάφος στην Αρχαία Κόρινθο. In K. Kissas and W.-D. Niemeier (eds.), *The Corinthia and the Northeast Peloponnese: Topography and History from Prehistoric Times until the End of Antiquity*: 45–53. München: Hirmer Verlag Gmbh.

Kolonas, L.

2009 *Network of visitable Mycenaean settlements and cemeteries in the Prefecture of Patras*. Athens: Ministry of Culture.

Korres, G.S.

1996 Προϊστορικοί τύμβοι της Μεσσηνίας. *Η Καθημερινή, Επτά Ημέρες* 28/1/96: 22–24.

2011 Middle Helladic tumuli in Messenia. Ethnological conclusions. In E. Borgna and S. Müller Celka (eds.), *Ancestral landscapes. Burial mounds in the copper and Bronze Ages (Travaux de la Maison de l'Orient 58)*: 585–596. Lyon: Maison de l'Orient et de la Méditerranée – Jean Pouilloux.

Legarra Herrero, B.

2009 The Minoan fallacy: cultural diversity and mortuary behaviour on Crete at the beginning of the Bronze Age. *Oxford Journal of Archaeology* 28(1): 29–57.

Lucy, S.

2005 Ethnic and cultural identities. In M. Díaz-Andreu, S. Lucy, S. Babić and D.N. Edwards (eds.), *The Archaeology of Identity Approaches to gender, age, status, ethnicity and religion*: 86–109. Abingdon: Routledge.

Macdonald, C.F.

1984 Part II: Aegean swords and warrior graves: their implications for Knossian military organization. *Annual of the British School at Athens* 79: 56–74.

Mac Sweeney, N.

2009 Beyond Ethnicity: The Overlooked Diversity of Group Identities. *Journal of Mediterranean Archaeology* 22(1): 101–126.

Mee, C.B. and W.G. Cavanagh

1984 Mycenaean tombs as evidence for social and political organisation. *Oxford Journal of Archaeology* 3(3): 45–64.

Mountjoy, P.A.

1993 *Mycenaean Pottery An Introduction*. Oxford: Oxford University Committee for Archaeology.

Murphy, J.

2014 The varying place of the dead in Pylos. In D. Nakassis, J. Gulizio and S.A. James (eds.), *KE-RA-ME-JA Studies Presented to Cynthia Shelmerdine*: 209–221. Philadelphia: INSTAP Academic Press.

Mylonas, G.E.

1973 *Ο ταφικὸς κύκλος Β τῶν Μυκηνῶν (Βιβλιοθήκη τῆς ἐν Ἀθήναις Ἀρχαιολογικῆς Ἑταιρείας 73)*. Athens: Archaeological Society.

Pantou, P.A.

2010 Mycenaean Dimini in Context: Investigating Regional Variability and Socioeconomic Complexities in Late Bronze Age Greece. *American Journal of Archaeology* 114(3): 381–401.

Papadimitriou, N.

2001a *Built Chamber Tombs of Middle and Late Bronze Age Date in Mainland Greece and the Islands*. Oxford: British Archaeological Reports.

2001b T. 164: An Early LH Built Chamber Tomb from Argos. *Annual of the British School at Athens* 96: 41–79.

2008 Both centre and periphery? Thessaly in the Mycenaean period. In A. Tziaphalias (ed.), *Περιφέρεια Θεσσαλίας.1ο Διεθνές Συνεδρίο Ιστορίας και Πολιτισμού της Θεσσαλίας. Πρακτικά Συνεδρίου, 9-11 Νοεμβρίου 2006*: 98–113. Thessaloniki: Peripheria Thessalias.

2011 "Passing away" or "passing through"? Changing funerary attitudes in the Peloponnese at the MBA/LBA transition. In H. Cavanagh, W. Cavanagh and J. Roy (eds.), *Honouring the Dead in the Peloponnese Proceedings of the conference held at Sparta 23-25 April 2009*: 467–491. Nottingham: Centre for Spartan and Peloponnesian Studies. http://www.nottingham.ac.uk/csps/documents/honoringthedead/papadimitriou.pdf (accessed 26 February 2013).

Papakonstandinou, E.

1981 Κάτω Σαμικό. *Archaiologikon Deltion* 36B1: 148–149.

1982 Κάτω Σαμικό. *Archaiologikon Deltion* 37B1: 133–134.

1983 Κάτω Σαμικό. *Archailogikon Deltion* 38B1: 109–110.

Popham, M.R.

1974 Sellopoulo tombs 3 and 4, two Late Minoan graves near Knossos. *Annual of the British School at Athens* 1969: 195–257.

Preston, L.

1999 Mortuary practices and the negotiation of social identities at LM II Knossos. *Annual of the British School at Athens* 94: 131–143.

2000 A mortuary approach to cultural interaction and political dynamics on Late Minoan II-IIIB Crete. PhD dissertation, University of London.

2004a A Mortuary Perspective on Political Changes in Late Minoan II-IIIB Crete. *American Journal of Archaeology* 108: 321–348.

2004b Final Palatial Knossos and Postpalatial Crete: a mortuary perspective on political dynamics. In G. Cadogan, E. Hatzaki and A. Vasilakis (eds.), *Knossos City Palace State (British School at Athens Studies 12)*: 137–145. London: British School at Athens.

2005 The Kephala tholos at Knossos: a study in the reuse of the past. *Annual of the British School at Athens* 100: 61–123.

2007 The Isopata cemetery at Knossos. *Annual of the British School at Athens* 102: 257–314.

Servais, J. and B. Servais-Soyez

1984 La 'tholos' oblongue (tombe IV) et le tumulus (tombe V) sur le Vélatouri. In H.F. Mussche (ed.) *Thorikos VIII 1972/1976: rapport préliminaire sur les 9, 10e, 11e et 12e campagnes de fouilles*: 15–71. Bruxelles: Comité des fouilles belges en Grèce.

Shelton, K.S.
1996 *The Late Helladic Pottery from Prosymna* (SIMA Pocket-Book 138). Jonsered: Paul Åströms Förlag.
2003 The Chamber tombs. In S. Iakovidis and E. French (eds.), *Archaeological Atlas of Mycenae* (Archaeological Society of Athens Library 229): 35. Athens: Archaeological Society.

Tsountas, C.
1899 Ἔρευναι ἐν τῇ Λακωνικῇ καὶ ὁ τάφος τοῦ Βαφειοῦ. *Ephemeris Archaiologiki* 28: 129–172.

Voutsaki, S.
1993 Society and culture in the Mycenaean world: an analysis of mortuary practices in the Argolid, Thessaly and the Dodecanese. PhD dissertation, University of Cambridge.
1995 Social and political processes in the Mycenaean Argolid: the evidence from the mortuary practices. In R. Laffineur and W.-D. Niemeier (eds.), *Politeia society and state in the Aegean Bronze Age Proceedings of the 5th International Aegean Conference (Aegaeum 12)*: 55–66. Liège and Austin: Université de Liège.
1997 The creation of value and prestige in the Aegean Late Bronze Age. *Journal of European Archaeology* 5(2): 34–52.
1998 Mortuary Evidence, Symbolic Meanings and Social Change: A Comparison between Messenia and the Argolid in the Mycenaean Period. In K. Branigan (ed.) *Cemetery and Society in the Aegean Bronze Age (Sheffield Studies in Aegean Archaeology 1)*: 41–58. Sheffield: Academic Press.
1999 Mortuary display, prestige and identity in the shaft grave era. In I. Kilian-Dirlmeier and M. Egg (eds.), *Eliten in der Bronzezeit Ergebnisse zweier Kolloquien in Mainz und Athen (Römisch-Germanisches Zentralmuseum Monographien 43.1)*: 103–118. Mainz: Verlag des Römisch-Germanischen Zentralmuseums in Kommission bei Dr Rudolph Habelt.
2010 Agency and personhood at the onset of the Mycenaean period. *Archaeological Dialogues* 17(1): 65–92.

Wilkie, N.C.
1992 The MME Tholos Tomb. In W.A. McDonald and N.C. Wilkie (eds.), *Excavations at Nichoria in Southwest Greece Vol. II. The Bronze Age Occupation*: 231–344. Minneapolis: University of Minnesota Press.

Wright, J.C.
2008 Chamber tombs, family and state in Mycenaean Greece. In C. Gallou, M. Georgiadis and G.M. Muskett (eds.), *Dioskouroi Studies presented to W.G. Cavanagh and C.B. Mee on the anniversary of their 30-year joint contribution to Aegean Archaeology*: 144–153. Oxford: British Archaeological Reports.

Yialouris, N.
1964 Μυκηναϊκὸς τύμβος Σαμικοῦ. *Archaiologikon Deltion* 20A: 6–40.

Younger, J.G.
2010 Mycenaean Seals and Sealings. In E.H. Cline (ed.), *The Oxford Handbook of the Bronze Age Aegean*: 329–339. Oxford: Oxford University Press.

Zavadil, M.
2013 *Monumenta Studien zu mittel-und späthelladischen Gräbern in Messenien*. Vienna: Verlag der Österreichischen Akademie der Wissenschaften.

Chapter 15

Anatolian-Aegean interactions in the Early Iron Age: Migration, Mobility, and the Movement of People

Naoíse Mac Sweeney

Interaction is predicated on movement. For most of human history, the movement of people was a fundamental and indeed a necessary aspect of interaction and connectivity. However, when discussing interaction and connectivity in the prehistoric Aegean (and indeed in archaeological discussions more generally), the movement of people receives relatively little attention. Instead, within the discipline of modern, theoretically-informed Aegean archaeology we tend to focus far more on the movement of objects, practices, styles, and ideas – the archaeologically visible traces of interaction (many papers in this volume are examples of this general trend). The reasons for this are partly practical, in that archaeologists may reasonably be expected to conduct research on archaeologically visible phenomena. However, another reason for this is disciplinary, and relates to the long and somewhat chequered history of the study of migration in archaeology. The spectre of old-fashioned diffusionist approaches haunts our work, and even those working with new scientific methods such as isotope analysis are cautious in their interpretations and use of language. For disciplinary reasons, many of us do not discuss the movement of people because we feel we *must not*.

In the case of Anatolian-Aegean interactions in the Early Iron Age (c. 1200–800 BCE; hereafter EIA), however, it is impossible to avoid the question of people moving. The reasons for this, like the reasons for the general reluctance to discuss the topic, are twofold. In part, the nature of the evidence frames the terms of the debate. Specifically, the issue of people moving is brought up by later textual sources which seem to make reference to what is known as the 'Ionian Migration': a mass population transfer whereby people from the western Aegean moved to the eastern Aegean during the EIA (see below for textual references). More importantly, however, it is disciplinary history which really determines the parameters of the discourse, and which means that it is impossible to consider Anatolian-Aegean interaction without mentioning migration. For disciplinary reasons, we discuss the movement of people because we feel we *must*.

The same solution can be advanced for both of these problems. The idea of mobility has recently emerged as a means of conceptualising the movement of people which avoids the unsavoury connotations of the term 'migration'. It also enables us to reframe the debate surrounding the Ionian Migration, and to contextualise it within the wider frame of assessing interaction and connectivity.

Migration and mobility

Migration, or the movement of people, is a divisive topic in archaeology. Traditional culture historical approaches used migration as a straightforward explanation for cultural change, postulating that the arrival of new cultural traits could be explained by the arrival of new populations. This approach was criticised strongly in the 1960s and 1970s, in particular as part of the 'New Archaeology' (*e.g.* Binford 1962; 1965; Clark 1966; Renfrew 1973; Hodder 1978). The equation between cultural traits and population groups was overturned, and the concept of archaeological 'cultures' largely abandoned. Instead, cultural change was more often seen in terms of indigenous development and systemic change, paired with active strategies of adoption and adaption. As a result, there was a 'retreat from migrationism' (Adams, Van Gerven and Levy 1978), and migration itself became a *thema non grata* in mainstream Anglophone archaeology for several decades.

From the 1980s on, there has been some criticism of this refusal to engage with the concept of migration, and of what has been labelled as an overly 'immobilist' perspective (Anthony 1990; Chapman and Hamerow 1997: 1). The movement of people, it is argued, is a social phenomenon and a structured process which can indeed be investigated archaeologically. Some scholars have turned to scientific approaches, based on ancient DNA and stable isotopes, to explore the movement of people in the past (*e.g.* Burke and Renfrew 2000; Perkins 2009). Others have tried to construct new theoretical frameworks through which to approach the issue of migration (Härke 1998; Burmeister 2000). Since 1990 there have been periodic prophecies that the pendulum of academic fashion is on the verge of swinging back, and that migration is soon to reappear on the mainstream archaeological agenda (*e.g.* Härke 2004: 456; van Dommelen 2014). However, these mantic utterances have yet to be fulfilled, and the theme of migration remains largely outside the mainstream archaeological agenda.

There are, of course, exceptions to this general rule. In some national traditions, old-school migrationism was never abandoned in the first place, and amongst scholars working in these traditions, migration is still approached within a broadly culture historical framework (such approaches remain common when considering EIA Anatolia, see below for examples). There are also instances where historically-attested migrations are investigated archaeologically, and where the movement of people is not, in itself, a point of dispute (*e.g.* historical migrations to the British Isles in the first millennium CE, see: Sykes 2006; Bowden *et al.* 2008). The central questions for such studies become the nature, mode, and motivation of the movement, rather than the movement *per se.*

Perhaps partly because of these studies, the last decade has seen an explicit shift away from the term 'migration', and a shift towards thinking more fluid and dynamic ways about the movement of people. In archaeology, migration is usually understood as a large-scale phenomenon, taking place in a single direction, and on a permanent basis. Where this definition is not explicitly formulated, it is often tacitly assumed (*e.g.* Antony 1990: 899; Burmeister 2000: 543–546; Yasur-Landau 2010: 13). Some scholars over the decades have sought to nuance this definition, pointing out that in other disciplines such as sociology and anthropology it is widely assumed that there may be a variety of different forms and scales of migration (Greenwood *et al.* 1991; Brettell and Hollifield 2000). Despite this, the most common perception of the term 'migration' within the discipline of archaeology has remained unchanged. Recent decades have seen an increased interest in connectivity and interaction in prehistory (this Round Table is one illustration of this wider trend). This has brought us to something of an impasse. It is clearly nonsense to argue that people in prehistory did not move, and that objects, styles, practices and ideas either spontaneously emerged or were magically transported between locations without human agency. To do so would not only fly in the face of common sense, but would also reduce prehistoric societies to passive recipients – making them the objects, rather than the subjects, of their own histories. It is vital, therefore, that we are able to discuss the movement of people in prehistory. But how can we do this without encountering the problematic associations of the term 'migration'?

Increasingly, rather than the language of migration, archaeologists are beginning to employ other terminology in order to indicate a broader variety of human movement. For example, some scholars have considered the movement of individuals for specific reasons (*e.g.* the movement of craftspeople: Papadopoulos 2009), while others have concentrated on abstractions of people moving (*e.g.* networks and network theory: Knappett 2011; Malkin 2011). One term which is currently growing in popularity is 'mobility' (*e.g.* Hordern and Purcell 2000: Chapter 9; Schlesier and Zellman 2004; Lightfoot 2008; van Dommelen and Knapp 2010; Isayev 2013; van Dommelen 2014 and other papers in the same edition of *World Archaeology*). The concept of 'mobility' encompasses a far greater range of different human activity than allowed for under the current archaeological understanding of migration. Indeed, at one level it can encompass any form of human movement or travel. Mobility can be fleeting or permanent, frequent or rare, over long distances or short ones, involving large groups or solitary individuals, and can be motivated by a wide range of different rationales. The flexibility of the term accounts for much of its appeal – at a basic level, 'mobility' can be used to refer to any movement of people, in any form.

However, I would argue that we should use the term 'mobility' with slightly more precision. In everyday language, the word is associated with more than simply the movement of people. It also relates to the likelihood of people moving – the propensity to travel. How mobile you are is a measure of how likely you are to move, or your personal mobility. I would therefore assert that mobility can be seen as having two crucial aspects – the ability of people to move, and the inclination for people to do so. When addressing the ability of people to move, both enabling and constraining factors must be taken into consideration. These might include physical geography and technological capabilities for travel, as well as social, political, or economic constraints. When considering the inclination of people to travel, again both enabling and constraining factors are important. The pros and cons of mobility must be compared with the pros and cons of staying put. For example, if there were nothing to be gained by travelling to the next village to trade, people would be less inclined to do so than if the rewards were substantial. High levels of personal mobility occur, therefore, when there is both the widespread ability and the potential motivation to undertake travel. Conversely, there are likely to be low levels of mobility in situations where either the ability or the inclination to travel is lacking (Figure 15.1). Of course, mobility may vary in its form and nature. For example, there may be the ability and inclination to travel only relatively short distances or only relatively long ones; or to travel either in groups or individually. Mobility, no less than migration, comes in many different shapes and sizes. It does, however, encompass migration within its broad scope. Migration (at least, in the form that the term is commonly understood in archaeology) is only one type of human movement. Indeed, it is a particularly extreme form of mobility, and one which has perhaps enjoyed more scholarly attention to date than it deserves.

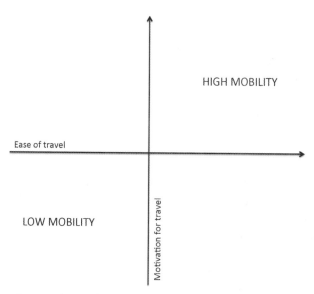

Figure 15.1: Diagram showing the two key factors contributing to situations of high and low mobility

What is there to be gained by an explicit focus on mobility, rather than on migration? By examining the nature of human mobility – or the lack of it – we are investigating a crucial feature shaping interaction. Indeed, it could be argued that a full understanding of interaction would remain incomplete without some consideration of mobility. A focus on mobility helps us to understand, not whether ideas, objects, styles and practices travelled, but rather how and why they did so. Learning about mobility, therefore, crucially contributes to our understanding of the mechanisms and processes of interaction. With this background in mind, I will now turn to mobility and migration in the context of EIA Anatolian-Aegean interactions.

The idea of the 'Ionian Migration'

The scholarship on Anatolian-Aegean interactions during the EIA is dominated by the question of the 'Ionian Migration'. This was said to be a mass population movement from the western Aegean (and primarily from Athens) to coastal Anatolia, resulting in the foundation of the cities which in the historic period would come to be known as the Ionian cities. From north to south, these cities are: Phocaea, Clazomenae, Erythrae, Teos, Lebedus, Colophon, Ephesus, Priene, Myus, Miletus, and the eponymous cities which dominated the islands of Chios and Samos (Figure 15.2). In addition to the original dodecapolis, at some stage in the later Iron Age or archaic period, the city of Smyrna also came to be considered as 'Ionian', joining the official body of the Ionian League (Caspari 1915; Crielaard 2009; Mac Sweeney 2013). Theses cities have often been characterised in an almost cartoonish way in classical scholarship – as predominantly Greek settlements, perched precariously on the edge of a barbarian hinterland (*e.g.* Cook 1975; Emlyn-Jones 1980). According to traditional scholarship therefore, the Ionian Migration was the process by which Greek settlers colonised and Hellenised the Aegean coast of Anatolia. In this context, the term 'colonisation' is used to refer to the deliberate and organised takeover of land by an incoming migrant group, and the subsequent establishment of asymmetrical power relations with the existing inhabitants of that land.

There is, of course, much that is wrong with this traditional picture. Ideas about Iron Age Greek 'colonisation' have been radically rethought in the last two decades, and the old orthodoxy on Greek colonialism has been roundly critiqued (*e.g.* Osborne 1998; Lyons and Papadopoulos 2002; Hurst and Owen 2005; Hodos 2009; van Dommelen 2012). Although there is ongoing discussion about whether current approaches have somewhat thrown the baby out with the bathwater (Zurbach 2012), most scholars now articulate a much more nuanced approach to the phenomenon of Greek colonisation. The specific case of the Ionian Migration, however, is rarely included in discussions of Greek colonisation. With a supposed date in the twelfth and eleventh centuries BCE, it predates the colonisation movements of the historical period (ninth to fifth centuries BCE) by several centuries. In addition (and perhaps partly because of its relatively early date), the evidence available for approaching the question of Greek

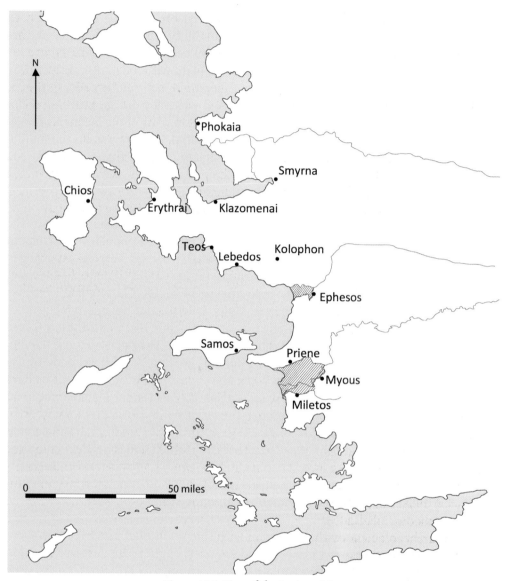

Figure 15.2: Map of the Ionian cities

settlement in Anatolia is generally patchier than that available for considering the later movements. For a number of reasons therefore, much of even the most recent scholarship on the Ionian Migration is still framed in distinctly outdated terms of colonial domination, acculturation, and 'Hellenisation' (*e.g.* Harl 2011; Herda 2013).

It is therefore especially important to reassess the material upon which the traditional myth of the Ionian Migration is based. It is widely known, and yet rarely acknowledged, that the story of the Stephanus Byzantinus Ionian Migration has been pieced together from diverse references in a range of different literary texts.

The earliest attestation of the story is in the writings of the sixth-century author, Hecataeus (although we only have the testimony of Stephanus Byzantinus, an author of compendia from the sixth century CE, of this). Following this, key characters from the story and elements of it are mentioned obliquely in several other Greek and Latin texts (including but not limited to: Herodotus 1.145–7; Pherecydes *FGrHist* 3 F125 and F155; Hellanicus *FGrHist* 4 F48 and F125; Ephorus *FGrHist* 70 F125, F126 and F22; Thucydides 1.2.6; 1.12.4; 2.15.4; 6.82.3 and 7.57.4; Plato, *Euthydemos* 302c; Isocrates, *Panegyricus* 122; Parian Marble A.27; Demon *FGrHist* 327 F22; Polybius 16.12). It is not until the Roman imperial period, however, that we find texts which tell the full story of the Ionian Migration in its entirety. The passage below is from Pausanias, a geographer of the second century CE, and summarises the story succinctly, at least a millennium after the supposed migration is said to have happened, focusing on how and why the migrants set out from Athens:

> Many years later Medon and Neileus, the oldest of the sons of Codrus, quarrelled about the kingship, as Neileus did not agree that Medon should be elevated to rule over him, because Medon was lame in one foot. They referred the matter to the Delphic oracle, and the Pythia gave kingship over the Athenians to Medon. And so Neileus and the rest of the sons of Codrus were sent off to live abroad, taking with them any Athenian who wished to go, and the majority of them on the expedition were Ionians... When they arrived at Asia by ship, each turned their steps to different cities on the coast. (Pausanias 7.2.1–4)

Traditional interpretations of the Ionian Migration story have taken the tales literally, assuming that these later texts contain a kernel (and, indeed, often more than a kernel) of historical truth. It is assumed that we can take the texts at their word, and that there was indeed a mass migration of people in the EIA, that it was primarily from Athens but also incorporated other groups from the western Aegean, and that it resulted in the founding of the Ionian cities. Such traditional approaches have long dominated discussions of the Ionian Migration (*e.g.* Lenschau 1944; Sakellariou 1958; Roebuck 1961; Huxley 1966; Emlyn-Jones 1980; Sourvinou-Inwood 2005; Vanschoonwinkel 2006; Niemeier 2007a; Harl 2011; Herda 2013). Under this approach, archaeological evidence is used as a means of 'proving' the stories told in the texts. The appearance of Protogeometric pottery in Anatolia, for example, is often interpreted as evidence for the arrival of the Ionian migrants. Some scholars, for example, have asserted that "[t]he appearance and distribution of so-called Protogeometric pottery from the late eleventh century BCE onwards is one of the decisive factors for the migration" (Herda 2013: 426), while others claim that the presence of this pottery "shows clearly enough that the western coast of Anatolia was inhabited by Aeolians and Ionians during the 10th century at least" (Akurgal 1962: 369). The archaeological evidence, it is argued, proves the model of a migration.

These traditional approaches have been criticised in recent years for assuming that 'pots equal people', and for taking material culture as a straightforward index of ethnicity (*e.g.* Greaves 2010). It has been argued by some critics that, far from proving the story of the Ionian Migration, the archaeological record in fact disproves the texts. Returning to the example of Protogeometric pottery in Anatolia, it is significant that Protogeometric wares have been found, not just at sites which were said to have been colonised by Ionians, or even just at sites which are widely considered to be 'Greek'. Instead, the distribution of Protogeometric pottery in western Anatolia is relatively dispersed, and includes many sites which are traditionally thought of as indigenous Anatolian sites (*e.g.* Sardis, Teichoussa, Mylasa, Çine-Tepecik, Akpınar: see Figure 15.3). Scholars are also beginning to recognise that

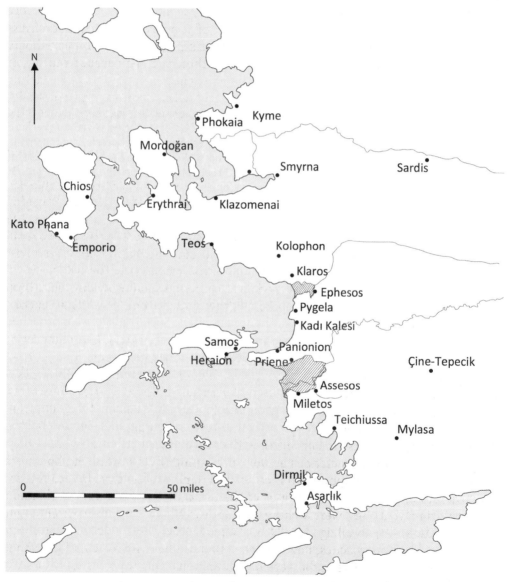

Figure 15.3: Findspots of protogeometric pottery in Ionia

local Anatolian wares continued to be produced alongside Protogeometric pottery, even at sites that later became known as Ionian cities such as Miletus (Kaiser and Zurbach 2015). The appearance of Protogeometric pottery in Anatolia, it might be argued, could just as easily be explained by indigenous appropriation of foreign styles, with imports reaching Anatolia through varied mechanisms of trade and exchange. Indeed, the continued evidence for an indigenous Anatolian presence in the Ionian cities, it could be argued, is inconsistent with the idea of a wholesale migration (Ehrhardt 2006; Herda 2009; Mac Sweeney 2013). It has also been pointed out that Aegean objects, styles, and social practices appeared in Anatolia long before the EIA, and that interaction and the movement of people occurred between these regions long before any putative 'migration' horizon (Hanfmann 1948, 146; Şahoğlu and Sotirakopoulou 2011; see also below). It has therefore been argued that while literary texts might tell one story, "[a]nyone who began their study from the starting point of landscape and archaeology, however, would weave an entirely different tale" (Greaves 2010, xvi). The archaeological evidence, it is argued, disproves the model of a single Ionian Migration.

The question of interconnections between the Aegean and Anatolia during the EIA is often dominated by this debate between those seeking to prove and disprove the Ionian Migration. As mentioned in the introduction to this paper, the disciplinary history is such that any serious treatment of the topic cannot avoid engaging with the concept of 'migration'. Despite coming to very different conclusions, the proponents and detractors of this traditional approach both adopt the same overall methodology and focus on the concept of migration. Both begin with a positivist reading of the texts (i.e., looking for the potential elements of factual 'truth' in the myths), thereby constructing a model of mass migration. Following this, both camps go on to use archaeological evidence either to prove or disprove their model, depending on their stance.

Over the last two decades, however, an altogether different approach to the stories of the Ionian Migration has emerged – one which sidesteps the issue of migration. This approach draws from approaches to foundation myths favoured by literary scholars and ancient historians, who consider these stories as literary constructs, rather than as factually reliable documents (*e.g.* Malkin 1987; Calame 1990, 2003; Hall 1997; Gehrke 2001). Under this approach, the factual accuracy or otherwise of the stories is considerably less important than the social function of the stories – what were the agendas and expectations at work in shaping these stories, and how were the myths used in a strategic and political way? A number of scholars in recent years have, therefore, argued that the stories of the Ionian Migration are more eloquent about the time that they were written in than the time they were written about (*e.g.* Hall 2002, 67–71; Kowalzig 2005, 49–51; Cobet 2007; Crielaard 2009; Mac Sweeney 2013). Under such approaches, however, the texts can tell us almost nothing about EIA interconnections between the Aegean and Anatolia, and can be used exclusively to examine the historical period.

EIA interaction

Is there a possible fourth approach to the question? Can we address the issue of Anatolian-Aegean interconnections in the EIA, without either escaping into the realms of literary invention or falling into the elephant traps of textual positivism? One possible approach that has been advocated by several commentators is to focus exclusively on archaeological evidence from the EIA itself, jettisoning the later texts as irrelevant and anachronistic (*e.g.* Cobet 2007; Greaves 2010). This is indeed a valid approach, but the archaeological evidence currently available is sadly limited, and such an approach allows for only very tentative conclusions to be drawn. EIA levels at western Anatolian sites tend to be very poorly preserved, and were often partly destroyed by construction activity in the later historical periods. In addition, at several sites changes in the levels of groundwater have meant that the EIA remains now lie beneath the water table, making them extremely difficult to excavate. Overall, we can currently only catch small glimpses into the EIA at most sites, and have only rarely found evidence of architecture. Indeed, much of our evidence for EIA activity in western Anatolia is in the form of unstratified or poorly-stratified ceramic deposits. Such deposits are usually identified by the presence of protogeometric pottery, as our understanding of Anatolian EIA ceramics is limited. Research is increasingly being carried out on these local wares, but this remains works in progress. We cannot therefore be confident that we will always recognise EIA deposits even when we do uncover them, especially if these deposits lack protogeometric pottery.

With such severe limitations imposed by the nature of the evidence, it is therefore difficult to arrive at many clear conclusions about Anatolian-Aegean interaction in the EIA. It is evident that there was indeed some interaction. One clear sign of this is the development of Protogeometric styles of pottery around the same time on both the east and west sides of the Aegean Sea. These apparently contemporary developments suggest that similar aesthetic and technological ideas were in circulation around the Aegean basin, with the result that potters in several areas of the Aegean began to decorate ceramics in similar styles. It remains a matter of debate whether the Protogeometric style emerged in one part of the Aegean and 'spread' from there to other areas (as assumed in most traditional discussions of the subject, *e.g.* Desborough 1952; Cook 1962, 23ff; Coldstream 1968, 338; Snodgrass 1971, 66–68; Cook 1975, 785ff), or whether the style emerged more or less simultaneously across the Aegean at the same time (for its independent development in Thessaly and Macedonia, see: Jacob-Felsch 1988; Whitley 1991, 82; Dickinson 2006: 20). In terms of Anatolia and the eastern Aegean, the precision of the dates is such that it is impossible to tell whether Protogeometric pottery appeared here at the same time or later than in the northern and western Aegean. Therefore, although the ceramic evidence may potentially teach us much about patterns of trade, interaction, social dynamics and cultural practices, it cannot furnish us with unequivocal evidence for the unidirectional movement of people from the western to the eastern Aegean.

Beyond Protogeometric ceramics, the archaeological record of EIA western Anatolia is, as mentioned above, somewhat scanty. Nonetheless, several other conclusions can nonetheless still be reached from examining the archaeological material alone. Firstly, it is evident that there was a certain level of settlement continuity. Several of the Ionian cities have yielded remains from the Bronze Age through to the historic period without any noticeable break in occupation (*e.g.* Miletus, Ephesus, Clazomenae, Colophon, Smyrna, Phocaea). The example of Miletus is particularly well known, as the evidence here indicates not only continuous occupation, but also continuous interaction with the Aegean and engagement with Aegean objects, styles, and social practices (indeed, some have interpreted this as evidence for Minoan and Mycenaean 'migration' or 'colonisation' at Miletus: *e.g.* Niemeier 1996, 1997 and 2007b; Niemeier and Niemeier 1997). Although the nature of these settlements seems to have changed over this time, the continued use of these sites as local centres is significant. Continuity is also evident from what we do know of western Anatolian ceramic traditions. Part of the reason why the establishment of a local ceramic chronology has proved so difficult has been the longevity of certain ceramic styles and techniques. Red and buff burnished wares, for example, are found both in Late Bronze Age (hereafter LBA) and EIA contexts, as are the particularly long-lived silver and gold wash wares. Similarly, metal skeuomorphic features, so popular in western Anatolian pottery in the LBA (Mac Sweeney 2011: 109), continue to be popular in the EIA (Kerschner 2006: 370–371).

From even this most cursory and broad-brush look at the archaeological record, we have evidence for both innovation and conservatism; new fashions and long-held traditions; change and continuity. There are indications of interaction, and following from this, some movement of people can be implied. We can be confident in asserting that there was some mobility between the Aegean and Anatolia during the EIA. What type of mobility this may have been, however, remains unclear. Was it a fairly mobile environment, where people moved freely and often, with a high level of individual 'get up and go'? Or was it an environment of relatively low mobility, where people moved only rarely and perhaps in organised groups in a way that we might consider to be 'migration'? The archaeological record remains, to date, inconclusive on this point. However, given that the material remains indicate stability as well as change, continuity as well as innovation, we can assume some level of cultural and likely population continuity in western Anatolia during this time. Whatever the nature and extent of Anatolian-Aegean mobility in the EIA, therefore, we do not seem to be dealing with wholesale population transfer, the emptying of the landscape (or indeed, the filling of an empty landscape), or radical change in social and cultural practices. While it seems clear from the archaeological record that there was indeed some mobility, it seems equally clear that this mobility did not result in a dramatic rupture or sudden transformation.

Ionian mobility, not Ionian Migration

The archaeological record is certainly the most important source of information regarding Anatolian-Aegean connectivity during the EIA. However, I hope to demonstrate here that the later literary sources can usefully contribute to the debate. In order to make sensible use of the sources, we must adopt a rigorous approach to them as items of source material in their own right, considering the contents of each text individually, as well as considering each text in its particular historical and social context. As mentioned above, there is no single text which recounts the entire story of the Ionian Migration before the Roman period. It is possible that such a text did once exist (perhaps as part of Panyassis' *Ionika* or in the writings of Hecataeus) but the surviving fragments and testimonia are such that we cannot be completely sure of this. Some stories were indeed in circulation by the classical period (5th century BCE is our earliest attestation) which mentioned the movement of people from Athens to Ionia. However, these were not the only stories in circulation at the time. For example, earlier texts speak of the city of Colophon being founded by a prophetess from Thebes (*Epigonoi* F4, 8th century BCE), and occupied by settlers from Pylos (Mimnermus F9 *IEG*, 7th century BCE). Other early texts mention colonists coming to individual cities from Crete (*e.g.* Herodorus *FGrHist* 31 F45), Delphi (*e.g.* Theophrastus F631 Rose), Achaea (*e.g.* Timotheus F791 lines 235–236), and even from Phoenicia (*e.g.* Douris of Samos *FGrHist* 76 F74). Some texts also discuss autochthonous or indigenous Anatolian founders (*e.g.* Asius F7 *GEF*; Ion of Chios *FGrHist* 392 F1; Herodorus *FGrHist* 31 F45; Metrodorus F3; Ephorus *FGrHist* 70 F114a). While stories of the 'Ionian Migration' from Athens to Ionia, therefore, did exist in the classical (and perhaps even in the archaic) period, they were far from being the only stories told about the foundation of the Ionian cities.

Table 15.1 presents some texts from the archaic and classical periods (seventh to fourth centuries BCE) which explicitly mention the founding, naming, settlement or occupation of one of the Ionian cities. I have deliberately excluded texts which mention other myths related to the heroes of the Ionian Migration story (*e.g.* Codrus, Neileus, Androclus, *etc.*) but which do not specifically make reference to the foundation of the Ionian cities. I have also excluded texts which talk about the early histories of the cities, unless they make particular mention of the foundation. On this basis, many texts have been excluded from the table which are often cited as 'evidence' in favour the Ionian Migration. The 'evidence' that such texts provide is circumstantial at best, and irrelevant at worst. I have also restricted this table to texts written in the archaic and classical periods only, remaining as chronologically close to the EIA as possible whilst still including enough material to make for a viable discussion. It should be noted that the table does not offer any insights which are statistically meaningful, nor even numerically accurate. I have not attempted to include *every* archaic and classical text which refers to Ionian origins. Nor is this information enough in itself to suggest proportions or quantifiable patterns. Rather, the aim of the table is to illustrate one very basic, and yet absolutely vital, point about the literary material.

Table 15.1: Foundation stories of the Ionian cities in literary texts from the archaic and classical periods (7th-4th centuries BCE)

Reference	Author from	Date (century)	Migration from Athens	Migration from elsewhere	Autochthons or Anatolian migrants
Epigonoi F4 GEF	Teos	7th	■		
Mimnermus F9 IEG	Colophon	7th	■		
Asius F7 GEF	Samos	6th			■
Panyassis Ionika	Halikarnassos	5th	■	■	
Hecataeus FGrHist 1 F141; F228	Miletus	5th	■		■
Timotheus F791, lines 235-6	Miletus	5th	■	■	■
Pherecydes FGrHist 3 F102; F152f; F155	Athens	5th	■	■	
Ion FGrHist 392 F1; F3	Chios	5th	■	■	■
Herodotus 1.145-7	Halikarnassos	5th	■	■	■
Herodorus FGrHist 31 F45	Herakleia	5th			■
Theopompus FGrHist 115 F276; F346	Chios	4th		■	■
Theophrastus F631 Rose	Lesbos	4th			■
Thucydides 1.2.6; 1.12.4; 7.57.4	Athens	4th	■		
Plato, Euthy 302C	Athens	4th	■		
Isocrates, Panegyricus 122	Athens	4th	■		
Ephorus FGrHist 70 F114a; F117; F126; F127	Kyme	4th	■	■	■
Metrodorus F3; F3a	Chios	4th	■		■
Hellanicus FGrHist 4 F48; F101	Lesbos	4th	■		
Douris FGrHist 76 F74	Samos	4th/3rd		■	
Homer, Iliad 2.867-8	Smyrna/ Chios	8th			■

What I hope this table demonstrates is that that the story of the Ionian Migration was not the only or even the dominant myth of Ionian origins. Instead, the picture offered by the literary texts is far more complex and nuanced than is assumed. The cities of Ionia were said to be occupied by a wide range of different people – autochthons and migrants, Greeks and non-Greeks, people from across the western, central and eastern Aegean, and indeed even from elsewhere in the Near East too. The only place which conspicuously does *not* seem to have contributed migrants in these stories is the northern Aegean and continental Europe. This is perhaps interesting, but given the extremely fragmentary nature of the literary record, no firm conclusions can reliably be drawn concerning this. The literary record does not suggest 'an Ionian Migration' in the singular. Rather, it suggests an extremely heterogeneous set of origins for the Ionian cities, and for the people who occupied them. The literary record does not imply migration, but high levels of personal mobility.

The overall picture gained from examining these texts is that people in the EIA Aegean and Anatolia were moving. There were no set routes, destinations, or origins for these movements. Instead, people from almost all parts of the Aegean seem to have been both able and willing to relocate, whether on a temporary or permanent basis. This mobility seems to have included people in Anatolia as well, as the stories tell of people from different parts of Anatolia moving, as well as people from the Ionian cities shifting around to different location within Anatolia (*e.g.* Mimnermus F9 *IEG*; Hecataeus *FGrHist* 1 F141; Herodotus 1.146). There are even suggestions of migration in a westwards direction, with people born in Ionia travelling to the peninsula now known as mainland Greece to found and rule cities there (*e.g.* Herodorus *FGrHist* 31 F45). From a close and detailed reading of the literary sources therefore, we can see that the texts do not suggest any unitary migration horizon, a single moment of migration, or a single direction of migration. Instead, when we read the texts carefully we discover that they suggest instead a period when there were high levels of mobility.

Mobility also fits well with what we know historically about the EIA in the eastern Mediterranean and Near East more generally. It has now been firmly established that the breakdown of several centralised state systems at the end of the Bronze Age did not necessarily entail collapse across the entire social spectrum (Bachhuber and Roberts 2009). Indeed, the idea of the EIA as a 'Dark Age' has now been widely critiqued and largely abandoned, for being both theoretically unsound and inconsistent with the available evidence. However, in comparison to the LBA, the EIA was certainly a time of greater flexibility in political structures. Far from being a sign of 'backwardness', it is now apparent that this flexibility opened up new opportunities for a range of people across the Mediterranean and Near East (*e.g.* for parts of the Levant, see Bell 2009; for Cyprus, see Steele 2004: 208–210; for Anatolia, see Mac Sweeney 2010). Opportunities for independent travel and trade would likely have increased, unencumbered by the impositions of formal laws, taxes, and state military control. With reduced amounts of state control over economic resources, it may also have been possible for a wider range of people to engage in travel (see Sherratt 2000 and 2003 for an increase in tramping trade). It is not my aim here to paint a romantic picture of the EIA as an anarchic (or neoconservative) utopia, where the general population enjoyed relative freedom after the collapse of the exploitative and oppressive system of LBA imperial states. On balance nonetheless, the collapse of states at the end of the Bronze Age and the increased flexibility of political structures in the EIA does seem likely to have given more people the ability to become mobile.

This same situation is also likely to have increased the desirability of mobility. Not only may trade have become more lucrative, but also instability at home, with political uncertainty and perhaps conflict, may also have contributed to some individuals seeking to relocate on a more permanent basis. As well as seeing more people able to move than previously, the EIA is also likely, therefore, to have seen more people who were willing to move. It is perhaps worth noting that at the beginning of the EIA, western Anatolia may indeed have seemed an attractive option for people seeking greater political stability (although of course, not the only option available). At this time, in precisely the area which was later to become known as Ionia, the kingdom of Mira seems to have thrived (Hawkins 1998; 2002). Mira can be considered a 'neo-Hittite' state in the sense that it was once officially a province of the Hittite Empire (although Hittite control over this area was only ever tenuous at best, see Glatz 2009 and Mac Sweeney 2010). It emerged as an independent kingdom as the Hittite empire contracted – opportunistically expanding into the vacuum left by the collapse of Hittite power. Indeed, the ruling dynasty of Mira seems to have been relatively stable, lasting at least three generations (according to the Karabel A inscription, see Hawkins 1998). This argument should not be over-emphasised as it relies on probability and likelihood rather than firm evidence, but such stability may have been attractive at the very start of the EIA.

The idea of high levels of personal mobility also fits well with the evidence of the archaeological record. It would, for example, go some way towards explaining the apparently contemporary development of Protogeometric styles of pottery in different areas of the Aegean. Ceramic and other craft specialists, it has recently been pointed out, are often particularly mobile (Papadopoulos 1996; 2009; Brysbaert 2011). In an environment where individuals were both willing and able to move freely, ideas and technologies could be easily transferred, exchanged, and swapped. This is also consistent with the evidence for continuity in western Anatolia. While people might well have arrived and settled in the region during the EIA, they do not seem to have done so in overwhelming numbers, causing major rupture and sudden cultural and social change. Instead, patterns of mutual exchange and contact are more consistent with a longer-term situation characterised by ongoing high levels of mobility around the Aegean basin as a whole. Although the extremely patchy nature of the archaeological record prevents us from coming to any clear conclusions, at the least it appears to be consistent with a time of high personal mobility. Indeed, high personal mobility could even have contributed to the patchiness of the archaeological record itself. While poor preservation and the priorities of archaeological research are most likely to be the dominant factors in this patchiness, it is also possible that another factor might be the nature of these EIA remains themselves. In a time of high personal mobility, architecture is less likely to be monumental and permanent, and buildings are more likely to be modest and made from less durable materials. Such structures do not survive well in the archaeological record.

The historical and archaeological evidence, therefore, is consistent with the theory that the EIA was a period of high personal mobility around the region of western Anatolia and between different areas of the Aegean. This evidence is far from conclusive, and indeed is both indirect and circumstantial. The amount of evidence available, and the nature of this evidence, is currently too poor to allow for much in the way of certainty. Nonetheless, the evidence is *more* consistent with a theory of high mobility than it is with the two alternative theories of migration and isolation. The testimony of the later literary sources is perhaps the strongest argument in favour of this third theory. These texts, when viewed together as an assemblage, present a relatively cohesive overall picture. People moved around, in different directions, for different reasons, in a chaotic tangle of localised patterns, individual decisions, and random Brownian motion. Such a conclusion encourages us to think in radical new ways about the EIA, and also to reconsider how we approach literary texts (for more on which, see below. It also challenges us to further research. Once we have concluded that this was likely a time of high mobility, many new questions present themselves: What was the nature and extent of this mobility? Were there local and regional patterns? Were there social patterns concerning who was most likely to move, when, and how? While the literary texts have been useful inasmuch as they have helped to establish a model of high mobility in the EIA, they are less helpful in the investigation of these subsequent questions. More, and more detailed, archaeological research is badly needed.

Conclusion

The assertion that the EIA in the Aegean and Anatolia was a time of high mobility is not, in itself, controversial. The idea that this mobility is different and distinct from migration, however, has not yet been much discussed. The concept of mobility is currently being explored in several areas of archaeology, and a consensus is emerging that it is indeed distinct from migration. In this paper, I have argued that the phenomenon of high personal mobility is in fact at the opposite end of the scale from migration. It is during times of relatively low personal mobility that large-scale, unidirectional movements that we would characterise as 'migrations' are more likely to occur. High personal mobility, therefore, is a distinct phenomenon, which occurs in historical contexts where individuals have both the ability and the willingness to engage in travel. Characterising the EIA in this way, therefore, reflects on the nature of EIA society. If we were to portray the phenomenon positively, the EIA emerges as a time of relative independence, where individuals were free to pursue their own entrepreneurial activities without much in the way of external control or imposition, when social structures were flexible, and when cultural boundaries were fluid and permeable. A slightly different choice of language, however, would lead us to portray the EIA as a period of endemic instability, a volatile social and political environment prone to disruption and insecurity. Both characterisations are equally valid, and equally consistent with the evidence available. Indeed, I am not advocating one or the other of these perspectives here – rather, I hope to draw attention to the varying ways that we can potentially choose to portray the same phenomenon.

I have argued in this paper that all our existing evidence – the archaeological, the historical, and the literary – is consistent with the theory of high personal mobility. Despite this, it is evident that the myth of the Ionian Migration still dominates discussions of Anatolia-Aegean interaction during the EIA. The privileged position that the Ionian Migration story is accorded in the academic discourse is often attributed to a bias in favour of the literary sources. Classical archaeologists and historians stand accused of elevating the texts above the archaeology, and of anachronistically imposing a text-led model of Greek migration and colonisation onto the archaeological evidence. I hope I have demonstrated in this paper that a close and rigorous assessment of the literary texts does not result in a migrationist model. Indeed, the literary sources suggest almost exactly the opposite. The problem is not, therefore, with the texts or the literary source material. Once more, the problem lies in the nebulous intricacies of disciplinary history, and in the ways that scholars to date have approached the literary texts.

Existing approaches to the literary material have treated texts as narratives. The contents of each individual text have been analysed, and elements from each of these texts have been brought together to form an overarching grand narrative. For example, it has been argued that Mimnermus' story of migrants coming from Pylos (F9 *IEG*) can be aligned with the classic Ionian Migration story of the sons of Codrus arriving from Athens in the following way: as the family of Codrus were said to have originally hailed from Pylos (*e.g.* Hecataeus *FGrHist* 1 F119; Hellanicus *FGrHist* 4 F125), it was assumed that Mimnermus was 'confused', and mixed up two distinct historical events (the migration of Codrus' father from Pylos to Athens, and the migration of Codrus' sons from Athens to Ionia) in his poem (for this argument, see for example Sakellariou 1958). By such processes, discrepancies between the texts were either ironed out or ignored altogether, and the many contradictory stories contained in the texts have been rationalised into a single, overarching myth. By stitching together the mismatched fragments of diverse literary bodies, scholarship has constructed a Frankenstein's monster of a foundation myth – the myth of the Ionian Migration. And like Frankenstein's monster, the myth of the Ionian Migration has taken on a life of its own, one which has proved dangerous to our understanding of the original source material. Advocates and detractors of the Ionian Migration story have fixated on the same artificial construct, rarely returning to the original texts themselves to assess the accuracy of the original model. In this paper, I have advocated a different approach to the literary material – one which may also be applicable to other comparable contexts. The texts here are not seen as individual narratives, nor as fragments of a larger narrative. Instead, they are seen as elements of a wider corpus. It is from the corpus as a whole that we must draw our characterisation of the EIA, not from any single story or individual text. And where the corpus is partial or fragmentary, we must factor this uncertainty into our conclusions. In an analogy with archaeological practice and the study of material culture, individual texts may usefully be approached as part of an assemblage. Only by studying assemblages of texts, as we would study assemblages of ceramics, tools, or bones, can we get a sense of the big picture.

We are left, perhaps, with the nagging question of where the Ionian cities really did come from, and how they ended up in the historical period identifying themselves as Greek. I have not set out to address this issue in this paper, which has focused instead on disciplinary histories, methodologies, and approaches. To answer this question properly, we would need a far larger paper than is possible here, and a much fuller discussion of the archaeological material. But perhaps, once more, we can fall back on the literary texts to give us a clue. If we read the texts chronologically, beginning with Homer in the eighth century and moving forward in time through those written first in the archaic and then those written in the classical period, we would find an intriguing pattern. Over time, the concern with Greekness gradually increases, as does Ionian self-identification with a conscious sense of Greek identity. To paraphrase the historian John Myres, we seem to be dealing, not with the 'coming of the Greeks' to Anatolia, but rather the '*becoming* of the Greeks' in Anatolia (Myres 1930; Hall 2002, 45–47).

References

Adams, W.Y., D.P. Van Gervan and R.S. Levy
1978 The retreat from migrationism. *Annual Review of Anthropology* 7: 483–532.

Akurgal, E.
1962 The early period and golden age of Ionia. *American Journal of Archaeology* 66: 369–379.

Anthony, D.W.
1990 Migration in archaeology: The baby and the bathwater. *American Anthropologist* 92: 895–914.

Bachhuber, C. and R.G. Roberts (eds.)
2009 *Forces of Transformation: The End of the Bronze Age in the Mediterranean.* Oxford: Oxbow.

Bell, C.
2009 Continuity and Change: The Divergent Destinies of Late Bronze Age Ports in Syria and Lebanon across the LBA/Iron Age Transition. In C. Bachhuber and R. G. Roberts (eds.), *Forces of Transformation: The End of the Bronze Age in the Mediterranean*: 30–38. Oxford: Oxbow.

Binford, L.R.
1962 Archaeology as anthropology. *American Antiquity* 18: 217–225.
1965 Archaeological systems and the study of culture process. *American Antiquity* 31: 203–210.

Bowden, G.K., P. Balaresque, T.E. King, Z. Hansen, A.C. Lee, G. Pergl-Wilson, E. Hurley, S.J. Roberts, P. Waite, J. Jesch, A.L. Jones, M.G. Thomas, S.E. Harding and M.A. Jobling
2008 Excavating past population structures by surname-based sampling: the genetic legacy of the Vikings in northwest England. *Molecular Biology & Evolution* 25: 301–309.

Boyle, K. and C. Renfrew (eds.)
2000 *Archaeogenetics: DNA and the Population Prehistory of Europe.* Cambridge: McDonald Institute for Archaeological Research.

Brysbaert, A. (ed)
2011 *Tracing Prehistoric Social Networks Through Technology.* London: Routledge.

Burmeister, S.
2000 Archaeology and migration. *Current Anthropology* 41: 539–567.

Calame, C.
1990 Narrating the Foundation of a City: The Symbolic Birth of Cyrene. In L. Edmonds (ed.),
    Approaches to Greek Myth: 275–341. London and Baltimore: Johns Hopkins University Press.
2003 *Myth and History in Ancient Greece* [translated by D.W. Berman]. Princeton: Princeton University
    Press.

Caspari, M.C.
1915 The Ionian confederacy. *Journal of Hellenic Studies* 35: 173–188.

Chapman, J. and H. Hamerow (eds.)
1997 *Migrations and Invasions in Archaeological Explanation* (BAR International Series 664). Oxford:
    British Archaeological Reports.

Clark, G.
1966 The invasion hypothesis in British archaeology. *Antiquity* 11: 172–189.

Cobet, J.
2007 Das alte Ionien in der Geschichtsscreibung. In J. Cobet, V. von Graeve, W-D. Neimeier, and
    K. Zimmerman (eds.), *Frühes Ionien. Eine Bestandsaufnahme. Akten des Symposions: 100 Jahre Milet,
    1999*: 724–744. Mainz am Rhein: Phillipp von Zabern.

Coldstream, J.N.
1969 *Greek Geometric Pottery. A survey of ten local styles and their chronology*. London: Methuen and Co.

Cook, J.M.
1962 *The Greeks in Ionia and the East*. London: Thames and Hudson.
1975 Greek settlement in the eastern Aegean and Asia Minor. In I.E.S. Edwards, N.G.L. Hammond
    and E. Sollberger (eds.), *The Cambridge Ancient History, Vol 2, Part 2: History of the Middle East and
    the Aegean Region, c1380–1000 BC*: 773–804. Cambridge: Cambridge University Press.

Crielaard, J-P.
2009 The Ionians in the archaic period: shifting identities in a changing world. In T. Derks and
    N. Roymans (eds.), *Ethnic Constructs in Antiquity: The Role of Power and Tradition*: 37–84. Amsterdam:
    Amsterdam University Press.

Emlyn-Jones, C.J.
1980 *The Ionians and Hellenism: A Study of the Cultural Achievements of the Early Inhabitants of Asia Minor*.
    London: Routledge and Kegan Paul.

Desborough, V.R.d'A.
1952 *Protogeometric Pottery*. Oxford: Clarendon Press.

Dickinson, O.T.P.K.
2006 *The Aegean from Bronze Age to Iron Age: Continuity and Change Between the Twelfth and Eighth
    Centuries BC*. Cambridge: Cambridge University Press.

Gehrke, H.-J.
2001 Myth, history, and collective identity: the uses of the past in ancient Greece and beyond. In N. Luraghi (ed.) *The Historian's Craft in the Age of Herodotus*: 286–313. Oxford: Oxford University Press.

Glatz, C.
2009 Empire as network: spheres of material interaction in Late Bronze Age Anatolia. *Journal of Anthropological Archaeology* 28: 127–141.

Greaves, A.
2010 *The Land of Ionia: Society and Economy in the Archaic Period*. London: Routledge.

Hall, J.
1997 *Ethnic Identity in Greek Antiquity*. Cambridge: Cambridge University Press.
2002 *Hellenicity: Between Ethnicity and Culture*. Chicago and London: University of Chicago Press.

Hanfmann, G.M.A.
1948 Archaeology in Homeric Asia Minor. *American Journal of Archaeology* 52: 135–155.

Härke, H.
1998 Archaeologists and migrations: a problem of attitude? *Current Anthropology* 39: 19–46.
2004 The debate on migration and identity in Europe. *Antiquity* 78: 453–456.

Harl, K.W.
2011 The Greeks in Anatolia: From the Migrations to Alexander the Great. In S.R. Steadmand and G. McMahon (eds.), *The Oxford Handbook to Ancient Anatolia (c.10,000-323 BCE)*: 752–776. Oxford: Oxford University Press.

Hawkins, J.D.
1998 Tarkasnawa King of Mira, "Tarkondemos", Boğazköy sealings and Karabel. *Anatolian Studies* 48: 1–31.
2002 Anatolia: the end of the Hittite Empire and after' in E.A. Braun-Holzinger, H. Mattäus (eds.), *Die nahöstlichen Kulturen und Griechenland an der Wende vom 2. zum 1. Jarhtausend v. Chr.*: 143–151. Mainz: Bibliopolis.

Herda, A.
2013 Greek (and our) views on the Karians. In A. Mouton, I. Rutherford, and I. Yakubovich (eds.), *Luwian Identities: Culture, Language and Religion Between Anatolia and the Aegean*: 421–507. Leiden: Brill.

Hodder, I. (ed.)
1978 *The Spatial Organization of Culture*. Pittsburgh: University of Pittsburgh Press.

Hodos, T.
2009 Colonial Engagements in the Global Mediterranean Iron Age. *Cambridge Archaeological Journal* 19.2: 221–241.

Hordern, P. and N. Purcell
2000 *The Corrupting Sea*. Oxford: Blackwell.

Hurst, H. and S. Owen (eds.)
2005 *Ancient Colonizations. Analogy, similarity and difference*. London: Duckworth.

Huxley, G.L.
1966 *The Early Ionian*. London: Faber and Faber.

Isayev, E.
2013 Mediterranean ancient migrations 2000–2001 BCE. In I. Ness (ed.), *The Encyclopedia of Global Human Migration*. Oxford: Wiley-Blackwell

Jacob-Felsch, M.
1988 Compass-drawn concentric circles in vase painting. A problem of relative chronology at the end of the Bronze Age. In E.B. French and K.A. Wardle (eds.), *Problems in Greek Prehistory*: 198–199. Bristol: Bristol Classical Press.

Kaiser, I. and J. Zurbach
2015 Late Bronze Age Miletos. In C. Maner, N.C. Stampolidis and K. Kopanias (eds.), *Nostoi: Indigenous Culture, Migration and Integration in the Aegean Islands and Western Anatolia during the Late Bronze and Early Iron Age*: 557–580. Istanbul: Koç University Press.

Kerschner, M.
2006 Die Ionische Wanderung im Lichte neuer archäologischer Forschungen in Ephesos. In E. Olshausen and H. Sonnabend (eds.), *'Troianer sind wir gewesen': Migrationen in der anitken Welt. Stuttgart Kolloquium zue Historischen Geographie des Altertums 8, 2002*: 364–382. Stuttgart: Franz Steiner Verlag.

Knappett, C.
2011 *An Archaeology of Interation. Network Perspectives on Material Culture and Society*. Oxford: Oxford University Press.

Kowalzig, B.
2005 Mapping out communitas: performances of theoria in their sacred and political context. In J. Elsner and I. Rutherford (eds.), *Pilgrimage in Graeco-Roman and Early Christian Antiquity: Seeing the Gods*: 41–72. Oxford: Oxford University Press.

Lenschau, T.
1944 Die Gründung Ioniens und der Bund am Panionion. *Klio* 36: 201–237.

Lightfoot, E. (ed.)
2008 *Movement, Mobility, and Migration. Archaeological Review from Cambridge* 23.

Lyons, C.L. and K. Papadopoulos (eds.)
2002 *The Archaeology of Colonialism*. Los Angeles: Getty Institute.

Mac Sweeney, N.
2010 Hittites and Arzawans: A view from western Anatolia. *Anatolian Studies* 60: 7–24.
2011 *Community Identity and Archaeology: Dynamic Communities at Aphrodisias and Beycesultan*. Ann Arbor: University of Michigan Press.
2013 *Foundation Myths and Politics in Ancient Ionia*. Cambridge: Cambridge University Press.

Malkin, I.
1987 *Religion and Colonization in Ancient Greece*. Leiden: Brill.
2011 *A Small Greek World. Networks in the Ancient Mediterranean*. Oxford: Oxford University Press.

Myres, J.L.
1930 *Who Were the Greeks?* Berkeley: University of California Press.

Niemeier, W.-D.
1996 A Linear A Inscription from Miletus (MIL Zb 1). *Kadmos* 35: 87–99.
1997 The Mycenaean Potters' Quarter at Miletus. In R. Laffineur and P.P. Betancourt (eds.), *TEXNH: Craftsmen, Craftswomen and Craftsmanship in the Aegean Bronze Age [Aegaeum 16]*: 347–352. Liège: Université de Liège.
2007a Westkleinasien und Ägais von den Anfängen bis zur Ionischen Wanderung. In J. Cobet, V. von Graeve, W-D. Niemeier, and K. Zimmerman (eds.), *Frühes Ionien. Eine Bestandsaufnahme. Akten des Symposions: 100 Jahre Milet, 1999*: 37–96. Mainz am Rhein: Phillipp von Zabern.
2007b Milet von den Anfängen menschlicher Besiedlung bis zur Ionischen Wanderung. In J. Cobet, V. von Graeve, W-D. Niemeier, and K. Zimmerman (eds.), *Frühes Ionien. Eine Bestandsaufnahme. Akten des Symposions: 100 Jahre Milet, 1999*: 3–20. Mainz am Rhein: Philip von Zabern.

Osborne, R.
1998 Early Greek Colonization? The nature of Greek settlement in the west. In N. Fisher and H. van Wees (eds.), *Archaic Greece: new approaches and new evidence*: 251–270. London: Duckworth.

Papadopoulos, J.K.
1996 Innovations, Imitations and Ceramic Style: Modes of Production and Modes of Dissemination. In R. Laffineur and P.P. Betancourt (eds.), *TEXNH: Craftsmen, Craftswomen and Craftsmanship in the Aegean Bronze Age [Aegaeum 16]*: 449–462. Liège: Université de Liège.
2009 The Relocation of Potters and the Dissemination of Style: Athens, Corinth, Ambrakia, and the Agrinion Group. In J.H. Oakley and O. Palagia (eds.), *Athenian Potters and Painters, II*: 232–240. Oxford: Oxbow.

Perkins, P.
2009 DNA and Etruscan identity. In P. Perkins and J. Swaddling (eds.), *Etruscan by Definition*: 95–111. London: British Museum Press.

Renfrew, C.
1973 *Before Civilization*. London: Metheun.

Roebuck, C.
1961 Tribal Organization in Ionia. *Transactions of the American Philological Society* 92: 495–507.

Şahoğlu, V. and P. Sotirakopoulou (eds.)
2011 *ACROSS: The Cyclades and Western Anatolia during the 3rd Millennium BC*. Istanbul: Sakip Sabançı Müsesi.

Sakellariou, M.B.
1958 *La migration grecque en Ionie*. Athens: Institut Français d'Athènes.

Schlesier, R. and U. Zellman (eds.)
2004 *Mobility and Travel in the Mediterranean from Antiquity to the Middle Ages*. Münster: LIT Verlag.

Sherratt, S.
2000 Circulation of metals and the end of the Bronze Age in the eastern Mediterranean. In C.F.E. Pare (ed.), *Metals make the world go round. The supply and circulation of metals in Bronze Age Europe*: 82–95. Oxford: Oxbow Books.
2003 The Mediterranean economy: 'globalization' at the end of the second millennium B.C.E. In W.G. Dever and S. Gitin (eds.), *Symbiosis, symbolism, and the power of the past. Canaan, ancient Israel, and their neighbors from the Late Bronze Age through Roman Palaestina*: 37–62. Winona Lake: Eisenbrauns.

Snodgrass, A.M.
1971 *The Dark Age of Greece*. Edinburgh: Edinburgh University Press.

Sourvinou-Inwood, C.
2005 *Hylas, the Nymphs, Dionysos and Others: Myth, Ritual, Ethnicity*. Stockholm: Svenska Institut i Athen.

Steele, L.
2004 *Cyprus before History: From the Earliest Settlers to the End of the Bronze Age*. London: Duckworth.

Sykes, B
2006 *Blood of the Isles: Exploring the Genetic Roots of our Tribal History*. London: Corgi Books.

Van Dommelen, P.
2012 Colonialism and migration in the ancient Mediterranean. *Annual Review of Anthropology* 41: 393–409.
2014. Moving On: Archaeological Perspectives on Mobility and Migration. World Archaeology 46(6): 477–483.

Van Dommelen, P. and A.B. Knapp (eds.)
2010 *Material Connections in the Ancient Mediterranean. Mobility, Materiality and Identity*. London: Routledge.

Vanschoonwinkel, J.
2006 Greek migrations to Aegean Anatolia in the Early Dark Age. In G.R. Tsetskhladze (ed.), *Greek Colonisation: An Account of Greek Colonies and Other Settlements Overseas*, vol. 1: 115–142. Leiden: Brill.

Yasur-Landau, A.
2010 *The Philistines and Aegean Migration at the End of the Late Bronze Age*. Cambridge: Cambridge University Press.

Whitley, J.
1991 *Style and Society in Dark Age Greece: The Changing Face of a Pre-Literate Society, 1100–700 BC*. Cambridge: Cambridge University Press.

Zurbach, J.
2012 Mobilités, réseaux, ethnicité. Bilan et perspectives. In L. Capdetrey and J. Zurbach (eds.), *Mobilités grecques. Mouvements, réseaux, contacts en Méditerranée, de l'époque archaïque à l'époque hellénistique (actes de colloque de Naterre, juin 2012). Scripta Antiqua* 46: 261–273. Bordeaux: Ausonius.

Chapter 16

Komai, Colonies and Cities in Epirus and Southern Albania: The Failure of the Polis and the Rise of Urbanism on the Fringes of the Greek World

John K. Papadopoulos

Introduction

One of the primary purposes of this paper is to state the obvious: that much of western and northwestern Greece – the area traditionally referred to as Epirus – together with southern Illyria, remains comparatively little studied, especially in terms of systematic fieldwork, both in the prehistoric and historic periods. In dealing specifically with prehistoric Epirus, Stelios Andreou, Michalis Fotiadis and Kostas Kotsakis have noted that the underdevelopment of research is a chronic condition, adding: "The archaeological imagination has always been resourceful in Epirus. It is time, however, for intensive fieldwork" (Andreou *et al.* 2001: 318). There is a great deal of archaeology to be done here and many dissertations to be written.

My interest in Epirus begins with two Molossian komai – small, ostensibly unwalled villages – that have been systematically investigated, Vitsa Zagoriou and Liatovouni, which provide some idea of the lifeways in this part of the world in the period before full-scale urbanism. Despite their remote locations, these komai were linked to, and interconnected with, a much larger world, including, on the one hand, that of Late Bronze Age (LBA) and Early Iron Age (EIA) Greece and, on the other, the Balkans and central Europe beyond. In addition to the komai there is a whole slew of different types of settlements in southern Illyria and northwest Greece, from full-fledged colonies boasting a metropolis-apoikia relationship, to cities claiming descent from Nostoi (heroes returning from the Trojan War, see below), to fortified 'proto-urban' centres. For the purposes of this paper, my focus is on Epirus and southern Illyria, although many of the processes seen there also hold true for Macedonia (and by extension Thessaly and Thrace, see Archibald 2000), which I will deal with only briefly in terms of comparison. My time frame is the LBA and EIA, down to the end of the Classical period and the beginnings of the Hellenistic era (*c.* 1500–300 BC) (for the synchronization of the absolute chronology of southern Illyria with Greece, see Damiata *et al.* 2007–2008).

In terms of this chronological range, I want to begin at the end in order to focus on a process that took shape in the LBA and EIA, namely a dichotomy between polis and other non-polis states in the EIA and Archaic period which, I would argue, is paralleled by an earlier dichotomy between palatial and non-palatial states in the Late Bronze Age. The aim is to show how two very different systems of political, social and economic organisation not only connected with one another, but how each influenced and determined the other.

Sometime in the 4th or 3rd century BC a way of life that had been there for centuries disappears. For much of their history, at least from the 12th century through to the earlier 4th century BC, the inhabitants of northwest Greece and parts of southern Illyria lived in small unwalled villages, referred to as komai in the Classical Greek sources, which were characteristic of an ἔθνος (ethnos) (see, for example, Thucydides, 1.5; 1.10; 3.94; Herodotus 5.98; Aristotle, *Poetica*, 1448a.36; *Politica* 1261a.28). Nicholas Hammond (2000: 345) has argued that the term ethnos in the Greek sources denotes a tribal state based on kinship (see further Galaty 2002: 109; Hall 2007a: 49–53). In Homer, the term simply refers to "a number of people living together, company, body of men" (see Liddell, Scott and Jones 1940, sv. ethnos; and see further Hall 2007a). This way of life in komai is replaced, sometime in the 4th century BC and evidently rather suddenly, by urbanism at a massive scale. Critical to this development is a political system that stands in stark contrast to the seemingly stable and successful polis.

In spectacular fashion, Philip II in the 4th century BC showed how powerless poleis were in the face of his Macedonian, tribal, clan-based, polis-less state with central authority (for Philip urbanising Macedonia, see below). His son, Alexander III, extended his empire from Greece to the frontiers of India, including all of Egypt. In a similar fashion to Philip II, Pyrrhos of Epirus, in the 3rd century BC, extended his empire from the Peloponnese well into Illyria, before turning his gaze to Sicily and the Italian peninsula. Philip the Macedonian and Pyrrhos the Molossian did much more than build empires; they built cities – *real* cities – ushering in a new form of urbanism (for an overview of Macedonia, see Hammond 1972, 1989; for Epirus, Evangelidis 1947; Dakaris 1951, 1952, 1956, 1971, 1972, 1981, 1982; Hammond 1967; Pliakou 2007, 2011). Just at the time when the Macedonian and Epirote komai were being abandoned in the 4th century BC, large cities, like Pella, were developing exponentially in Macedonia on a very different scale to anything that went before, as were settlements like Antigoneia, together with large-scale building projects, such as the theater at Dodona in Epirus, the former by Philip, the latter by Pyrrhos. This was *synoikismos* at an unprecedented scale (*cf.* Demand 1990). Ironically, it was the tribal, clan-based, polis-less states with central authority that not only ushered in the Hellenistic age, but also paved the way for a new type of urbanism and society, not the relatively long-lived poleis. It is important to begin with what we perhaps know best: colonies and cities.

Colonies and cities in Epirus and southern Illyria

Despite their many differences, Epirus and Illyria are linked by a similar tribal, clan-based system. Hekataios was among the first to name a number of tribes in Epirus. Theopompos (in Strabo 7.7.4f [C323–324]) counted 14 Epirote tribes and, some 300 years later, Strabo records the names of eleven (see Douzougli and Papadopoulos 2010: 2), among which the nucleus of historical Epirus was formed by three tribes far larger than the rest: the Molossians, Chaonians and Thesprotians. The approximate tribal borders, if we can call them that, together with some principal sites discussed in this paper, are presented in Figure 16.1. According to Pseudo-Scymnus, Epirus between 360 and 355 BC was largely organised under the same three tribes (see Hammond 1967: 518), and of these, Dimitrios Evangelidis (1947: 13) noted that the largest and most important was the Molossians (others include the Athamanians, Aithikes, Tymphaioi, Orestai, Paroraioi, Atintanes, Amphilochoi, Kassopaioi). Of all the Epirote tribes, the coastal Thesprotians were the first known to the Greeks and much more open to influences from traders and colonists (Malkin 1998: 138); they are the only Epirote tribe mentioned in Homer (*e.g. Odyssey* 14.315). As for the tribes of southern Illyria, as opposed to Epirus, Strabo (7.7.8 [C326]), in his description of the mountainous country above the Ionian Gulf, specifically names the Bylliones, Taulantioi, Parthinoi, and the Brygoi. The tribal territory of these and other Illyrian tribes extended up the Adriatic coast to the north.

What is especially remarkable about Epirus and southern Illyria is the different types of site that were established there over the course of the EIA and Archaic period, although there was a good deal of fluidity among them. These included true Greek colonies, that is, those sites that could claim a metropolis/apoikia relationship (Graham 1964). There are only three true colonies in this sense in this area: Ambrakia, Apollonia and Epidamnos, all primarily involving Corinthians, sometimes with Kerkyrans and others. Then there were cities, such as Aulon, Orikos, Thronion, claiming descent from the heroes of the Nostoi, the legend of those returning from Troy (for the Nostoi, see Malkin 1998). Together with these there were not only later foundations, such as Antigoneia established by Pyrrhos (for the recent Albanian-Greek project at the site, see Zachos *et al.* 2006), but also indigenous sites that became, by the 4th century BC or later, cities very much organised on a Greek model (*e.g.* Byllis, Nikaia, Amantia, Lissos). It is useful to begin with the implants, as these not only best connect Epirus and Illyria with the Aegean world, but they often leave the largest footprint on the landscape: the true colonies.

The southernmost of the Greek colonies, and the only one in Epirus, was Ambrakia (modern Arta), situated on the navigable Arachthos River some 18 km north of its harbor Ambrakos, on the north shore of the Gulf of Arta (Figure 16.1) (see Hammond 1967; Cabanes 1976; for the topography of Ambrakia and the rescue excavations conducted there, see Karatzeni 1994). A colony of the Corinthians, Ambrakia was founded in the 7th century BC – traditionally sometime between 650 and 625 BC – by

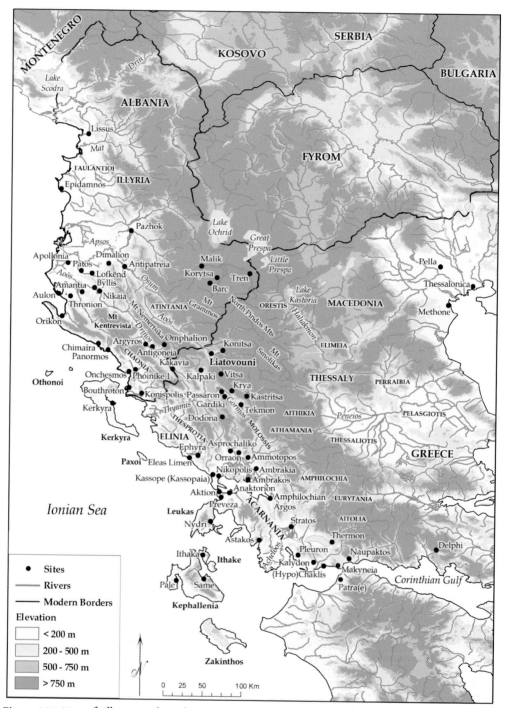

Figure 16.1: Map of Albania and northwest Greece showing principal sites and territory of the ethne mentioned in this paper (UCLA Experiential Technology Center).

Gorgos, the son of the Corinthian tyrant Kypselos, and it quickly became a colonial powerhouse in southern Epirus (for the relations between Ambrakia and Corinth, see Will 1955: 517–527). Although the literary testimonia place the foundation of Ambrakia in the 7th century BC, archaeological evidence, especially in the form of locally produced Thapsos Class ware, suggests a Corinthian interest in the area much earlier, well into the 8th century BC (Papadopoulos 2009).

Farther north, in southern Illyria, Apollonia and Epidamnos were the only colonies in the true Greek sense, that is, formal apoikiai of a sponsoring mother-city or metropolis (see Stocker 2009 on the 'ktisis' of Apollonia). According to Strabo (8.316) and Pseudo-Scymnus (439), Apollonia was a joint foundation of Corinth and Kerkyra; Thucydides (1.26.2) describes it as a Corinthian apoikia (*cf.* Stephanos Byzantinos [sv. "Apollonia"], who only mentions 200 Corinthians under the oikist Gylax), whereas Pausanius (5.22.4) refers to Kerkyra as the sole metropolis (Graham 1964: 130). Of the Greek colonies in southern Illyria, Apollonia was not only one of the largest Greek poleis and Roman centres in the Mediterranean, but is the colony that has been most extensively explored archaeologically (for bibliography, see Dimo *et al.* 2007). Epidamnos (modern Durrës), more or less due west from the modern Albanian capital of Tirana, boasted a Kerkyran and Corinthian pedigree. The Greek colonists were Kerkyrans with some Corinthians and other Dorians (Hammond 1967: 425–426). The colony was at first a mixture of Greeks and Illyrians, specifically Taulantioi, who had called in the Kerkyrans. The Greek founder was Phalios, a Corinthian of Heraclid descent (Hammond 1967: 425; the recent archaeological survey of Epidamnos by Davis *et al.* 2003 is indispensable). Useful overviews of the Greek colonies in southern Illyria have been provided by a number of able commentators (*e.g.* Hammond 1967; Wilkes 1992; Myrto 1998; for a circumscribed account of the relations between Illyrian Albania and the Greeks and Romans, see Hammond 1992).

Other sites on the coast of Epirus and Illyria are only linked with legendary Greek settlers returning from Troy, heroes of the Nostoi (for which see Malkin 1998). Thus Bouthrotos (Buthrotum, Butrint) was founded by Helenos, one of the sons of Priam, who established there a 'little Troy' which was visited by Aeneas (Virgil, *Aeneid* 3.289–355, especially 349 for 'parvam Troiam;' also Stephanos Byzantinos quoting Teuker of Kyzikos, see Hammond 1967: 385, 474); it is worth stressing that there is no tradition of any historical Greek colony at Bouthrotos. Inhabited since prehistoric times, Bouthrotos was located in the tribal territory of the Epirote Chaonians, and was always closely connected to Kerkyra (see, most recently, Hansen *et al.* 2013). Another example was Orikos (Oricum), which was traditionally founded by Lokrians and Euboians, whose ships were driven there by storms on their way home from Troy (Pseudo-Scymnus 442–443; for Orikos see further Bereti *et al.* 2011). Hyperbolic claims by Jean-Paul Descoeudres (in Bereti *et al.* 2011) that Orikos was the first Greek colony on the Adriatic are unfounded. The site of Thronion/Thronium, often identified at Kanina, in the Bay of Vlora, features in legend as an early foundation at the time of the Nostoi, and is also linked with Lokrians and Euboians returning from Troy

(Pausanias 5.22; Hammond 1967: 384–385, 494, 515–516, 523). Another site in the Bay of Vlora, and probably the most important, was ancient Aulon – its name meaning channel, and from which the modern Vlora is derived – which I would equate with the site at Treport (for excavations at Treport, see Bereti 1985, 1992). A little inland, on the Vjosë/Aoös River, was the site of Nymphaion. Since modern times the ancient Nymphaion has been identified with Selenicë, across from Byllis, and is still a modern producer of hydrocarbons, not least a high quality bitumen (for which see Morris 2006, 2014; Cabanes 2007).

Then there was the establishment of a new type of site in the Illyrian hinterland, away from the coastal areas usually inhabited by Greeks, especially during the developed Iron Age, which have come to be known as 'proto-urban' centres (for general overviews, see Lafe 2003; Ceka 2011). These proto-urban centres are different to komai in many important respects, not least that they are fortified. It is not yet fully understood whether sites such as Margëlliç, Gurëzezë, Mashkjezë, Byllis, Klos/Nikaia and Dimal (Kalaja e Krotinës) represent true towns, hilltop refuges, or regional trading and meeting places (for bibliography on these sites, see Papadopoulos *et al.* 2007: 108; 2014: 8–9). Farther south, in the Korçe-Kolonjë region of southeastern Albania, and in the area near Butrint, new settlements were created on naturally defended hilltops in the later Bronze and EIA (Karaiskaj 1976; Bejko *et al.* 2006; Lima 2013). At most, if not all, of these sites evidence for permanent year-round habitation has yet to be furnished, but this is not a phenomenon limited to southern Illyria. At the site of Emporio on the Aegean island of Chios, a dry-stone fortification wall – probably built in the 8th century BC – running around the top of the hill enclosed an area of approximately 2.4 ha and the dearth of habitation finds inside the wall, as well as the area immediately outside, suggests that the fortification was a refuge (Boardman 1967: 4–5; Frederiksen 2011: 137–138, fig. 31).

Also unclear are the processes by which these Illyrian 'proto-urban' sites developed, as well as the relationship of these centres to one another and to the coastal colonies. A particularly vexed problem with all of these sites is the issue of their chronology, and conclusive evidence for the initial stages of their period of use is usually lacking. At Mashkjezë, the earliest cultural layers are dated to the Archaic period on the basis of imported Greek pottery, and a similar date is suggested for Margëlliç, though the latter has furnished some evidence, albeit limited, of use in the Mycenaean period. The exact chronology of Gurëzezë is far from clear, while at Klos-Nikaia there is little that clearly predates the 5th century BC (for the development of occupied hilltops to proto-urban centres, see Korkuti 1982; Ceka 1985a, 1985b; Harding 1992: 22–27). Despite recent research on fortified sites in Chaonia (Butrint, Kalivo and Kepi i Stillos), few have yielded more than mixed deposits of prehistoric ceramics, without absolute dates (Gjipali 2011; Lima 2013). Meanwhile, for the first time, a proto-urban citadel in northern Albania, at the site of Grunas, Shala, has been firmly dated by AMS radiocarbon dates to an initial phase in the EIA (*c.* cal 800 BC), and occupied thereafter through the Early to Middle Iron Ages (Galaty 2007; Galaty *et al.* 2011, 2013).

Looking at the rise of population centres throughout southern Illyria, the development from occupied hilltops to proto-urban sites has been mapped out by several scholars (Korkuti 1982; Ceka 1985a, 1985b; Harding 1992: 22–27). The earliest of three phases is usually dated to the Late Bronze Age and is often named after the type-site of Badher. The second, pre-urban, phase is characterised by the sites at Gajtan and Trajan, while the third, full-fledged proto-urban phase sees numerous fortified hilltop sites all over southern Illyria, generally dated to the 7th–5th centuries BC. It is debatable, however, whether the pre-urban sites such as Gajtan were in any way 'urban' during their earlier phases; evidence for occupation within the walls is scant, and the sites are better characterised as hill-forts rather than towns. Whatever the historical trajectory of proto-urban centres, the important points to bear in mind are, first of all, the continuance of the colonial foundations in the later Classical, Hellenistic and Roman periods, and that, secondly, by the 4th or 3rd century much of southern Illyria lived ostensibly in Greek-looking cities.

At the same time in Epirus we have the beginnings of a new type of urbanism, during which populations appear to have been centralised into new fortified acropoleis. Although few of these fortified hilltops have been systematically investigated, two sites in the Ioannina basin that have seen some archaeological exploration are the prominent hilltops of Kastritsa (Dakaris 1951, 1952; Pliakou 2007: 108–137; Pliakou 2011: 640, figs. 13a-b) and Megalo Gardiki (Figure 16.2; see Dakaris 1956: 46–58, with map, fig. 1; Zachos 1993; see also Hammond 1967: 181–183, 168, map 7; 288, map 13; Pliakou 2007: 60–90; Pliakou 2011: 640, figs. 14a-b, 15). The former has been equated with the ancient Tekmon (Dakaris 1956: 47, map, fig. 1), the latter is usually equated with Passaron, although at least one author prefers to place the ancient Passaron at Kastro Ioannina (Pliakou 2007: 91–107, 143–151; Pliakou 2011: 639–640, figs. 12a–c). Both sites are characterised by impressive enceintes of late Classical or Hellenistic date. Indeed, the bibliography on the chronology and motives behind the establishment of these new administrative centres in Epirus is arguably much greater than the basic facts we possess as to their character (see Dakaris 1971, 1972, 1981, where a 5th century BC date is proposed on the problematic basis of masonry style and the presence/absence of towers; see also Dakaris 1982; Hammond 1967; Hoepfner and Schwandner 1994: 116–119).

In addition to the hilltop settlements in the Ioannina basin, there are what many scholars have termed full-fledged cities, like Kassope in southern Epirus, which are founded at exactly the same time, built on a Hippodamian plan (Figure 16.3; for Kassope, see Dakaris 1971, 1982: 361–373 and, more generally, Hoepfner and Schwandner 1986: 75–140; Antonelli 2005). In terms of size, Hippodamian Kassope is only slightly larger than Megalo Gardiki and smaller than Kastritsa in terms of overall area.

In the centre of all this, in the very heart of Molossis, was the Epirote topos that loomed largest in the Greek imagination: Dodona/Dodone, which was always regarded as one of the Greek oracles (Parke 1967; for Molossian political organisation at Dodone, see Meyer 2012). In addition to listing Dodone as among the Greek oracles, Herodotus

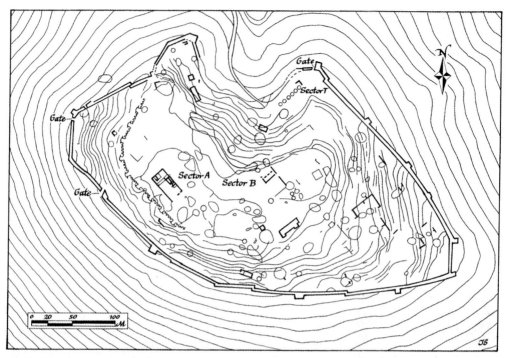

Figure 16.2: Plan of the fortified acropolis of Megalo Gardiki in the Ioannina basin. Simplified drawing by Jack Scott, based on the plan published in Zachos 1993.

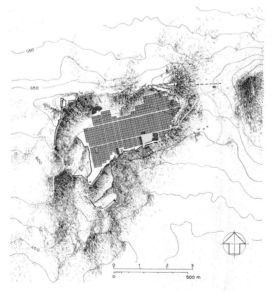

Figure 16.3: Plan of the city of Kassope in southern Epirus in the 4th century BC (after Hoepfner and Schwandner 1986: 82, fig. 62.)

(1.46.3) also describes the envoys of Periander sent to consult the Nekromanteion in Ephyra as another Greek oracle (Herodotus 5.92.7; Hammond 1967: 422; Malkin 1998: 143). Furthermore, Aristotle (*Mete* 352a.33–34) explicitly states that 'ancient Hellas' lay around Dodone and the Acheloös River: "it was there that the Selloi and those who were then called 'Graikoi' and now 'Hellenes' used to live" (the Selloi are Zeus's priests at Dodone, for which see further Hesiod, Fragment 181). This passage dealing with the 'Graikoi' – their name the source of the Latin 'Graeci' and ultimately the 'Greeks' – and 'Hellas' is well discussed by Malkin (1998: 147–148), who notes that two of the three comprehensive names for the 'Greeks' still relevant today – Graikoi, Hellenes and Ionians – were associated with Dodone and Epirus, and it was this which encouraged Hammond (1967: 370) to contend that the real origins of the Greeks were Epirote. The Sanctuary of Zeus at Dodone was well established by the Geometric period, if not earlier, and in the 3rd century BC Pyrrhos built the theatre, which was estimated to hold 13,000–14,000 spectators (Figure 16.4) (Zachos, personal communication).

Figure 16.4: Aerial view of the theatre of Dodone built in the 3rd century BC by Pyrrhos of Epirus (photo courtesy Constantinos Zachos).

By the later 4th and 3rd centuries BC the populations of Epirus and southern Illyria lived primarily in large urban agglomerations: real towns and cities. But what was there before the 4th century BC and before the era of urbanism? There was another type of settlement, one found all over the southern Balkan Peninsula in much of Greece and southern Illyria in the LBA and EIA: komai.

Epirote Komai and their Mediterranean networks

Excavations at Vitsa Zagoriou, published in exemplary fashion by Ioulia Vokotopoulou (1986), together with those in the region of Pogoni excavated by Elias and Ioanna Andreou and those at Liatovouni excavated by Angelika Douzougli, provide a baseline for our knowledge of settlement in Epirus in the period before the Classical (for Liatovouni and for bibliography on the region of Pogoni, see Douzougli and Papadopoulos 2010). These Molossian komai were primarily scattered in the river valleys and lakeside areas of the region. Several, however, including Vitsa Zagoriou, were at higher elevations (1030 m ASL). They were all small, unwalled villages, which could not have maintained more than a few families. The two most extensively explored komai, Vitsa Zagoriou and Liatovouni – we do not know their ancient names – illustrate well the character of these settlements. The κώμη (komē) of Vitsa is barely 60 m in overall length, with a maximum width of not much more than 20 m (Vokotopoulou 1986: plan 1; herein Figure 16.5). The circumscribed area of the settlement was further delineated by the two large cemeteries to the north and south, along with additional tombs on the east side. At Liatovouni, the settlement was located some 220 m north of the cemetery (Douzougli and Papadopoulos 2010: 21, fig. 4). Although the full extent of settlement was not established, the area exposed was approximately 200 square metres, and brought to light a series of walls constructed primarily of unworked pieces of limestone, with no foundation trenches (Figure 16.6). Also uncovered was a more substantial, slightly curvilinear wall, running approximately north-south, with a width of about 0.90–1.10 m, which appears to delimit the extent of the settlement on this side and may have served as a retaining wall (Douzougli and Papadopoulos 2010: 62–66). The total excavated area of the settlement was less than 20 m in length and the overall size of the komē at Liatovouni could not have been much more than that of Vitsa. The hill of Liatovouni, with Profiti Elias at the highest point, some 525 m ASL, is located at what is arguably not only the most strategic position in the valley, right at the confluence of the Aoös and Voidomatis Rivers, but what was and still is the most fertile (Figure 16.7).

The chronological range of both Vitsa and Liatovouni are well established. The finds from the settlement and especially the cemetery at Vitsa date from the 9th century BC to sometime near the end of the third quarter of the 4th century; the latest material from the settlement was found in Oikia Θ (Vokotopoulou 1986, 1994). The settlement and cemetery at Liatovouni covers a longer period

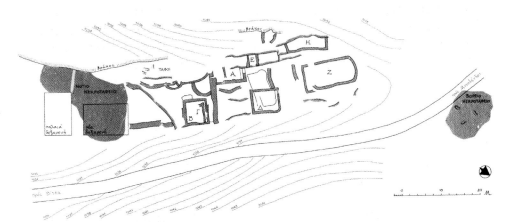

Figure 16.5: Plan of the komē, with adjacent cemeteries, of Vitsa Zagoriou as excavated, showing its total extent (after Vokotopoulou 1986: plan 1).

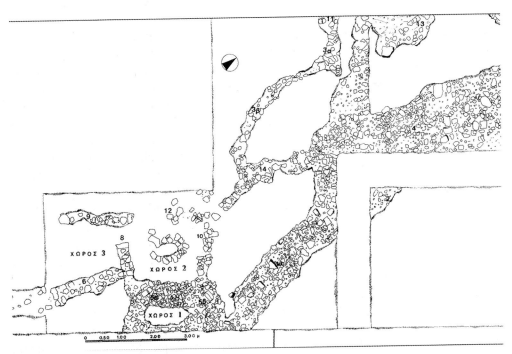

Figure 16.6: Plan of the portion of the komē of Liatovouni actually excavated (after Douzougli and Papadopoulos 2010: 63, fig. 30).

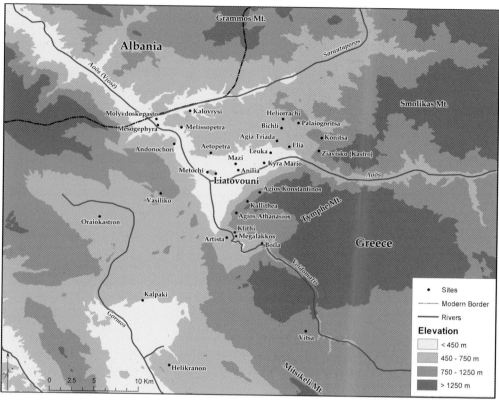

Figure 16.7: The valley of Konitsa in Epirus and its immediate surrounds showing the location of Liatovouni and Vitsa Zagoriou.

of time, beginning as early as the 13th or 12th centuries BC, but it ends at more or less the same time as Vitsa, that is, sometime in the earlier 4th century BC. The earliest burial in the Liatovouni cemetery, Tomb 59 – dubbed the 'hero of Liatovouni' (Douzougli and Papadopoulos 2010: 23–35) – dates to the closing stages of the LBA and it was around this grave that the later tombs of the cemetery were arranged. A few scattered bronze objects, probably deriving from disturbed burials, may be slightly earlier, dating to the Late Helladic IIIB-C Early or Middle period.

Establishing the precise date of the pottery from the Liatovouni settlement must await the full study of the material (which is in the capable hands of Eleni Vasileiou). On the basis of a preliminary survey of the settlement pottery (by Sarah Morris and John Papadopoulos), among the earliest diagnostic pieces are the fragmentary stems of at least ten Mycenaean kylikes (Furumark 1972: Shape 275 and 274), which date to various stages of the Late Helladic IIIC period (Douzougli and Papadopoulos 2010: 65, fig. 32, with *comparanda* in note 267). As for the latest evidence for the occupation of the settlement, it largely comprises late Classical black-gloss pottery, which appears to date as late as the very end of the 5th century BC, and a few fragments may belong to the first quarter or so of the 4th century BC (Douzougli and Papadopoulos 2010: 66).

Vitsa and Liatovouni are not the only known Epirote komai. The Meropi (Nemertsika) mountain range separates the Valley of the Aoös and the Valley of the Gormos. Surface survey and excavations conducted over a number of years in the Valley of the Gormos have brought to light a variety of settlement and cemetery sites from Kephalovryso to Kakolakko, ranging in date from the LBA to the Hellenistic period (for full references, see Douzougli and Papadopoulos 2010: 9, note 66). Just on the Albanian side of the Greek-Albanian border, not far from Kakavia, the site of Tekke Melan – excavated because it was originally thought to be medieval – has yielded important LBA and EIA material (Muçaj and Hobdari 2005). Only a small sondage was excavated (for stratigraphy, see Muçaj and Hobdari 2005: 33, fig. 3), but the material recovered can be dated, on the basis of Aegean *comparanda*, from c. 1350–1200 BC down to about 850–800 BC, dates remarkably close to the beginning of the settlement and cemetery at Liatovouni (for the pottery, see Muçaj and Hobdari 2005: 39–57). The settlement itself is small, resembling a komē, not unlike Vitsa and Liatovouni, but closer in date to the latter. Despite the small scale of the site, and the circumscribed area explored, it represents one of the best preserved insights we have from northern Epirus/southern Illyria of the critical period of transition between the LBA and EIA (for the EIA in Thesprotia, see now Forsén 2009; Tzortzatou and Fatsiou 2009).

Despite their relatively small size and isolated location, the Epirote komai were networked into a larger Mediterranean world, with access to material from all over the Greek world, including various parts of the Aegean, the Italian peninsula, and central Europe beyond. This is not the place to review the full range of the material; of the komai that have been explored, the range of material is perhaps best appreciated from the more recent excavations at Liatovouni (Douzougli and Papadopoulos 2010: 35–62). From the early tombs of the Liatovouni cemetery, dating primarily from the 11th to 8th centuries BC, come a large group of handmade decorated vases generically referred to as 'matt-painted' (Douzougli and Papadopoulos 2010: 44–45, figs. 17–18). Such pottery is found all over Epirus, and also farther north in Albania, as well as western Macedonia, and a related type of pottery is well-known in southern Italy (Douzougli and Papadopoulos 2010: 45). During the later 8th century BC the first imported vessels from southern and western Greece make their appearance, including material from the northwest Peloponnese or else from western Greece or the Ionian islands (*e.g.* the cup Douzougli and Papadopoulos 2010: 47, fig. 19a; for the style, see Papadopoulos 2001). Perhaps the earliest of all the Late Geometric imports at Liatovouni is the fragmentary Thapsos Class oinochoe (inv. 8440), that was probably made at ancient Ambrakia (Douzougli and Papadopoulos 2010: 47, fig. 19b; Papadopoulos 2009).

Corinthian imports include a wide variety of standard shapes (aryballoi, alabastra, oinochoai), both of the Archaic period (Douzougli and Papadopoulos 2010: 50–51, fig. 20), as well as black-gloss vessels of the Classical period. Together with the Thapsos Class pottery, this material provides ample testimony of the movement of people, commodities and ideas between the Molossians and the Corinthian settlers of the Ionian shores. The mountainous interior of Epirus was no barrier to complex connectivity. Corinthian, or Corinthian-inspired, influence is also seen in another category of material from Liatovouni, namely bronze vessels (*e.g.* Douzougli and Papadopoulos 2010: 52, fig. 21). In addition to Corinthian and western Greek pottery, the cemetery at Liatovouni yielded a comparatively large number of Athenian black-figured, red-figured and black-gloss vessels, as well as patterned lekythoi (Douzougli and Papadopoulos 2010: 53–58, figs. 22–26). In addition to the Attic and Corinthian black-gloss pottery, there were a number of plain black vessels, probably from a workshop based in Ambrakia (see Douzougli and Papadopoulos 2010: 59, fig. 27; for the fabric, see Papadopoulos 2009).

In addition to bronze and clay vessels, the Liatovouni cemetery also brought to light a number of miniature core-formed glass vessels, as well as beads of glass and faience (Douzougli and Papadopoulos 2010: 60, fig. 28). Generally considered to have been made on the island of Rhodes, the glass vessels found at Liatovouni almost certainly reached the mountainous interior of Epirus via Ambrakia, together with other commodities, such as bronze vessels and different types of pottery already noted. The cemetery also yielded numerous examples of silver, bronze and iron jewellery, as well as bronze and iron tools and weapons (see Douzougli and Papadopoulos 2010: 26–31, figs. 6–9; 39–43, figs. 14–16). One of the most interesting of the bronze finds was the fragmentary handle of a bronze vessel of unknown form, probably a situla, with close parallels from Tolfa (Coste di Marano) near Rome (Douzougli and Papadopoulos 2010: 61–62, fig. 29).

As for what the Molossians were exchanging for these imported commodities, we may guess at a wide array of animal products (hides, wool, textiles, *etc.*), together with agricultural produce. For a long time, the prevalent view was that the early settlements of Epirus developed an economy largely based on animal husbandry, one in which the agricultural production of cereals, pulses, and legumes must have always been limited in scope and of secondary importance to stock-breeding. This point of view was championed by Hammond (1967: *passim*), Dakaris (1976), and it was also assumed by Vokotopoulou (1986: 340), and others (see references in Douzougli and Papadopoulos 2010: 10). In a number of seminal studies, Paul Halstead and John Cherry, independently from one another, challenged the prevailing view that the mountain environment and pan-Balkan affinities of the material culture of the Pindos indicated transhumant or nomadic pastoralism (see especially Halstead 1987a; 1987b; 1990; also Halstead 1988; 1989; 2000; Cherry 1988). Halstead argued that the archaeological evidence in the Pindos from the late 2nd millennium BC on should be interpreted in terms of sedentary mixed farming, replicating the subsistence strategy that dominated the lowlands of Greece throughout the Neolithic and Bronze Age, adding that a mixed farming economy does not preclude either seasonal use of distant pastures or differences within and between communities in the relative importance of arable and pastoral farming (Halstead 1990: 72). Similarly, Cherry (1988: 9) argued "that specialized pastoralism is an unlikely mode of subsistence in the context of the types of environmental settings and farming systems that existed in early prehistoric Greece and, indeed, is an adaption that has emerged historically only in specific socio-economic and political circumstances" (for further discussion and references, see Douzougli and Papadopoulos 2010: 10–12).

It seems clear that a mixed farming economy prevailed in Epirus through much of the late 2nd and 1st millennia BC. A critical development, as opposed to change, in this subsistence strategy can be traced in Epirus to the years of the 4th century BC, at which time the Epirote komai are abandoned and their cemeteries go out of use. All the archaeological evidence suggests that this was the time of a fundamental reorganisation of an economic, social and political way of life that had been in place for centuries, if not millennia, at which time the previously scattered population was centralised within and around fortified acropoleis or urban centres. Such a reorganisation was not limited to Epirus or southern Illyria, but was part of a broader phenomenon in the Mediterranean, including Italy and the western Mediterranean. The same is true for other parts of Greece as well, not least Macedonia: despite the numerous burials in the EIA cemetery of the tumuli at Vergina, for example, little is known of the contemporary settlement or, indeed, the lifeways of its inhabitants. Precisely the same processes were in place in Macedonia, where small settlements that have defied the archaeological record gave way to cities.

Alexander the Great, in the well-known passage in Arrian (7.9.2), boasted that his father, Philip II, had transformed the Macedonians from stock-breeders to city-dwellers. However controversial this statement may seem, the transformation of Macedonia from a disparate series of villages to mega cities in the 4th century BC is indeed one of the greatest transformations to have occurred in the Greek world. It happened not in the political heart of Greece – the world of the city-states – but on its fringes. By moving their capital from land-locked Aigai to Pella, with its access to the sea, probably in the 5th century BC, Macedonia developed into an outward-looking state not only connected to the Greek world but ready to become a major player on the world stage. This transformation happened within a dynamic area of early Greek colonies and other types of poleis, and an already established kingdom based on a tribal system. Among the Greek cities there were the colonial foundations, especially those in the Chalkidike, but also in Pieria, with the site of Methone near the delta of the Haliakmon and Axios Rivers. For Philip to transform Macedonia from an inward-looking kingdom he had to control these Greek cities or what these cities had access to and what they represented: first Methone in 354 BC, where he famously lost his eye, and slightly later at Olynthos, which he razed to the ground in 348, thereby crushing the Chalkidian League. And at the end of the 4th century, Kassander carried out the *synoikismos* of the Chalkidian cities, establishing on a new scale the city of Poteidaia, appropriately renamed Kassandreia. What Philip achieved in Macedonia, Pyrrhos and others did in Epirus.

The Macedonian coast, like the coast of Epirus and southern Illyria, saw established, polis-like towns and cities, whereas the hinterland was very different. It has been well described by John K. Davies (2000: 258) as "fringe-Greek at best, monarchically governed, with fluid geographical and ethnic boundaries, but no significant urban agglomerations, no clearly developed civic life, and managed by custom rather than law." Yet, it was the latter – whether Epirus, or neighbouring Aitolia and Macedonia, or even the Anatolian hinterland to the east – that became the crucible of political activity that was to determine and define the trajectory of the later Greek, and Anatolian, world. In contrast, the established and evidently stable poleis, which found it so difficult to merge their sovereignties in any way that was both militarily effective and politically acceptable, became irrelevant: a political dead end. Yet one could not exist without the other; the two systems had become irrevocably intertwined, in a sense mutually dependent on one another. This is perhaps best seen in Epirus and southern Illyria, particularly in the coastal zone, where large implanted Greek colonies, heavily fortified, existed side-by-side with small unwalled komai. It remains to trace and attempt to understand the effectiveness of the polis-less, tribal, clan-based ethne, and their political trajectories from prehistory into the historic period.

Poleis vs. Ethne and their Bronze Age ancestry

By the closing stages of the EIA, much if not all of the southern Balkan Peninsula was composed of two very different types of social and political forms of organisation. The first is the distinction that has been drawn between the polis and the ethnos – the latter a looser type of political organisation associated above all with regions such as Achaia, Elis, Aitolia, Akarnania, Thessaly, Macedonia and Epirus in Greece, as well as Illyria, and much of the rest of the Balkan Peninsula beyond (see Hall 2007a; 2007b: 88–92; for Achaia, see Morgan 2000; 2003; for Thessaly, Archibald 2000). As we have seen, various Classical authors regarded unwalled villages (komai) as characteristic of an ethnos. In his description of the Aitolians, for example, Thucydides (3.94.4–5) makes clear reference to unfortified villages (komai). Vitsa Zagorou and Liatovouni were certainly such villages, but at the same time we have proto-urban fortified centres in southern Illyria with little if any evidence for year-round occupation, and there is a similar or related pattern in various parts of the Aegean, as at Emporio, already cited. Archaeologically the situation is far from straightforward precisely because small unwalled villages are not easy to identify in the ground, whereas fortified sites, whatever their nature or date, leave a much more blatant footprint on the landscape. In contrast to many ethne, almost all poleis in the Classical period had walls (Hansen 2006: 73).

Similarly, our literary sources are far from clear-cut, and terms such as 'polis' and 'ethnos' are complex ones that can mean different things in different contexts. As Jonathan Hall (2007a: 50) cautions: the "distinction between polis and ethnos was not... recognised by ancient writers." He further cautions that ethne should not necessarily be regarded as an alternative form of state organisation to the polis (Hall 2007b: 88). Moreover, various ethne in the historic period dwelt in poleis (Hall 2007a, 2007b: 88–91). In discussing the well-known passage in Aristotle (*Politics* 3.5.11), Hall (2007a: 50) notes that Aristotle is differentiating between ethne settled in villages (komai) and ethne, like the Arkadians, settled in poleis. Consequently, Hall goes on to distinguish between consolidated ethne and dispersed ethne. The former are represented by groups such as the Aitolians, Achaians, or Thessalians "who inhabited a contiguous tract of territory in the historic period. Dispersed ethne, on the other hand, are diaspora-type collectivities, whose members were in the historic period scattered throughout different communities – normally poleis – but who conceived of their unity in terms of an original homeland in which their ancestors had cohabited" (Hall 2007b: 90).

Two points are critical here: In much of the literature, something of a linear development is often assumed in the diachronic passage from a tribal (ethnos) to a state (polis) society in early Greece, but there is no clear evidence for such a straightforward linear development. As Hall (2007b: 90) notes: "it is increasingly difficult to maintain that the polis represents an evolutionary development from an earlier, more 'tribal' organization in which ethne were dominant." The second point has to do with the distribution of poleis, and why they emerged in certain parts of the Greek world and not others (the fullest overview, with references, is Hansen 2006). Although a number of scholars have noted that the earliest poleis are usually attested in those regions of Greece that were more strongly influenced by the administrative structures of the Mycenaean palaces (see, for example, Hall 2007b: 91), the argument has never been adequately developed.

However one defines the polis or an ethnos, and despite a good deal of fluidity between the two terms – as in ethne, for example, dwelling in poleis – the two systems are not the same. They represent parallel developments that collided with one another in remarkable ways. Moreover, they are not solely the result of developments in the historic period or in the EIA. The distinction between the polis and the ethnos in the Archaic period, I would argue, has a Bronze Age ancestry in the distinction between the palatial and non-palatial polities. Such a distinction extends beyond tracing the 'borders' of the Mycenaean world. Among the ethne, Achaia and Elis, in the Peloponnese, or what was otherwise the heart of Mycenaean Greece, together with Aitolia, Akarnania, and Macedonia, never boasted a Mycenaean 'palace', and even in Thessaly, the only plausible palatial centre was at Iolkos (equated with the site of Dimini: Adrimi-Sismani 2003; 2004–2005; 2006; 2007, with references to earlier literature; *cf.* Pantou 2010), whereas northern and western Thessaly display a very different material record.

To map the extent of the palatial Mycenaean world is to map the world of the later Greek poleis. Similarly, those areas that in the historic period were inhabited by ethne – whether consolidated or dispersed – never boasted a palatial center. The distinction between poleis/ethne and palatial/non-palatial involved not only a major difference in type of settlement – one barely archaeologically visible, the other characterised by massive Cyclopean fortifications and well defined architectural units such as the megaron – but also in a much more centralised system of administration, typified by the use of Linear B tablets. Here the case of the Peloponnese is particularly telling. The Hither and Further Provinces of Pylos (as they were cast by Ventris and Chadwick 1973: 415–417, *cf.* 119–125, 139–140; but see further Bennet 2007; Small 2007: 52), subsuming most of what came to be known as historic Messenia, had an administrative centre in the Palace of Nestor; the same holds true for the Argolid (see Burns 2010: 163–190), as it now does for Sparta and Lakonia, with the discovery of Linear B tablets at Xirokambi, Agios Vassilios. In contrast, large swathes of the Peloponnese, not least Arkadia, never had a palace, and as already noted, the same appears to be the case for Achaia and Elis (although extensively fortified, Teichos Dymaion does not seem to enclose a palace or other major building, see Dickinson 2006: 25, 41). In the historic period, Arkadia, Achaia and Elis are characterised by ethne, even though the Arkadians dwelt in poleis (Hall 2007b: 88–91; Morgan 2000; 2003). To be sure, there are regions, even in the Peloponnese, that fall between palatial and non-palatial and the classic case may well be the Corinthia, where a palatial centre has never been found. As Daniel Pullen and Thomas Tartaron (2007) have argued, the Corinthia was a political periphery, contested by competing polities centered at Mycenae, or the Argolid more generally, and at Kolonna on Aigina (see further Tartaron 2013: 232–243). The Peloponnese reflects a pattern seen all over the Greek mainland.

The political pattern that emerged in the Late Bronze Age between palatial and non-palatial on the Greek mainland was to continue, albeit much altered, in the EIA, surviving the collapse of the Mycenaean world in an unpredictable and overlooked manner. The distinction between palatial and non-palatial in part mirrors that between the polis and the ethne. This distinction, clearly visible in the Archaic and Classical periods, was to have enormous ramifications in later history.

Back to the end

If we fast-forward to the end of the Classical and the beginning of the Hellenistic era, two things clearly emerge: the first is the failure of the polis. The established and evidently stable polis became irrelevant: a political dead end. City-states like Athens got about as large and as far as a polis could get. The second thing that comes into focus is that, ironically, it was the tribal, clan-based polities with central authority that paved the way for a totally new political, social and economic system to emerge. In contrast to the polis, it was the ethne that effectively merged their political and military trajectories.

As Davies (2000: 258) noted so well, "it was they – whether Epirus, or neighbouring Aitolia and Macedonia, or the Anatolian hinterland to the east – which were the crucible of Greek political activity in the fourth and third centuries BC, rather than the established and stable poleis, which found it so difficult to merge their sovereignties in any way which was at once militarily effective and politically acceptable."

History can now be traced archaeologically: just as Vitsa and Liatovouni and other Epirote komai were being abandoned, the main work of political creativity was being forged in Epirus and in neighbouring tribal areas in the 4th century BC. The establishment of urban agglomerations at sites like Kastritsa, Magalo Gardiki in the Ioannina basin and Kassope in southern Epirus – the latter in the middle of the 4th century, the other two at probably the same time – occurred at the same time as it did in Macedonia. The fall of komai and the development of cities are part and parcel of the same process.

In the Bronze Age, there is a real distinction between the palatial and non-palatial polities, not least in their levels of administrative control. Moreover, threads of continuity can be easily traced, as in the survival in the Early Iron Age and Archaic periods of the term *basileus* from the Mycenaean *pa-si-re-u* (Hall 2007b: 91, 120–121). But what happens in the EIA is that the poleis and ethne – or, more accurately, the political, social and economic processes that underpin them – become irrevocably intertwined, in a sense mutually dependent on one another, which accounts for the fluidity that we see between poleis and ethne in the historic period. In the course of time – sometime in the 4th century BC – it was the tribal clan-based ethne that were to determine and define the trajectory of the Greek world, paving the way for Hellenistic mega-cities, and ultimately Rome.

Acknowledgements

I am grateful to Barry Molloy for the invitation to take part in this Sheffield roundtable and to all my friends in Sheffield for their hospitality and for making my visit so memorable. For reading earlier drafts of this paper and for their many comments, I would like to thank Náoise McSweeney, Barry Molloy and Sarah Morris. I am also grateful to Angelika Douzougli and Konstantinos Zachos for their assistance with all things Epirote.

References

Adrimi-Sismani, V.
2003 Μυκηναϊκή Ιωλκός. *Athens Annals of Archaeology* 32–34: 71–100.
2004–2005 Le palais de Iolkos et sa destruction. *Bulletin de Correspondance Héllenique* 128–129: 1–54.
2006 The palace of Iolkos and its end. In S. Deger-Jalkotzy and I.S. Lemos (eds.), *Ancient Greece from the Mycenaean Palaces to the Age of Homer*: 465–481. Edinburgh: Edinburgh University Press.
2007 Mycenaean northern borders revisited: New evidence from Thessaly. In M.L. Galaty and W.A. Parkinson (eds.), *Rethinking Mycenaean Palaces II*: 159–177. Los Angeles: Cotsen Institute of Archaeology.

Andreou, S., M. Fotiadis and K. Kotsakis
2001 The Neolithic and Bronze Age of northern Greece, with addendum 1996–1999. In T. Cullen (ed.), *Aegean Prehistory: A Review* (*AJA* Supplement 1): 259–327. Boston: Archaeological Institute of America.

Antonelli, L.
2005 Corinto e le ΗΛΕΙΩΝ ΑΠΟΙΚΙΑΙ nell'Epiro meridionale: Nota a ps. Demosthenes VII 32. *Anemos* 3: 89–99.

Archibald, Z.H.
2000 Space, hierarchy, and community in Archaic and Classical Macedonia, Thessaly, and Thrace. In R. Brock and S. Hodkinson (eds.), *Alternatives to Athens: Varieties of Political Organization and Community in Ancient Greece*: 212–233. Oxford: Oxford University Press.

Bejko, L., M.G. Amore and S. Aliu
2006 Korça Basin Archaeological Survey Project: preliminary report for the season of 2005. The Albanian Rescue Archaeology Unit. http://www.gshash.org/index_files/Page1541.htm (2006).

Bennet, J.
2007 Pylos: the expansion of a Mycenaean palatial center. In M.L. Galaty and W.A. Parkinson (eds.), *Rethinking Mycenaean Palaces II* (revised and expanded second edition): 29–39. Los Angeles: Cotsen Institute of Archaeology.

Bereti, V.
1985 Vendbanimi ilir në Treport të Vlorës. *Iliria* 15 (2): 313–320.
1992 Amfora transporti të zbuluara në vendbanimin e Treportit. *Iliria* 22 (1–2): 129–147.

Bereti, V., G. Gonsagra, J.-P. Descoeudres, S. Shruza, and C. Zindel
2011 Orikos: première colonie grecque en Adriatique? La première campagne de fouille Albano-Suisse. In J.-L. Lamboley and M.P. Castiglioni (eds.), *L'Illyrie méridionale et l'Épire dans l'antiquité, V. Actes du Ve Colloque International de Grenoble (8–11 October 2008)*: 419–430. Paris: De Boccard.

Boardman, J.
1967 *Excavations in Chios, 1952–1955: Greek Emporio* (*BSA* Supplement 6). Oxford: Thames and Hudson.

Burns, B.E.
2010 *Mycenaean Greece, Mediterranean Commerce, and the Formation of Identity*. Cambridge: Cambridge University Press.

Cabanes, P.
1976 *L'Épire de la mort de Pyrrhos à la conquête Romaine (272–167 av. J.C.)*. Paris: Belles Lettres.
2007 Les sources littéraires grecques: Le bitume et le Nymphaion. In V. Dimo, F. Lenhardt and F. Quantin (eds.), *Apollonia d'Illyrie: Atlas archéologique et historique* (Mission épigraphique et historique en Albanie, Recherches Archéologiques Franco-Albanaises 1): 42–44. Athens: École françaises d'Athènes.

Ceka, N.
1985a Kultura protogytetate Ilire. *Iliria* 15(1): 111–150
1985b Fortifikimet parahistorike Ilire. *Monumentet* 29: 27–58.

2011 Les fortifications dans les villes d'Illyrie méridionale et d'Épire. In J.-L. Lamboley and M.P. Castiglioni (eds.), *L'Illyrie méridionale et l'Épire dans l'antiquité, V. Actes du Ve Colloque International de Grenoble (8-11 October 2008)*: 649–661. Paris: De Boccard.

Cherry, J.F.
1988 Pastoralism and the role of animals in the pre- and protohistoric economies of the Aegean. In C.R. Whittaker (ed.), *Pastoral Economies in Classical Antiquity, Cambridge Philological Society* (Supplement 14): 6–34. Cambridge: Cambridge Philological Society.

Dakaris, S.
1951 Ανασκαφή εις Καστρίτσαν Ιωαννίνων. *Praktika of the Athens Archaeological Society* 1951: 173–183.
1952 Ανασκαφή εις Καστρίτσαν Ιωαννίνων. *Praktika of the Athens Archaeological Society* 1952: 362–386.
1956 Αρχαιολογικές έρευνες στο λεκανοπέδιο των Ιωαννίνων. In Αφιέρωμα εις την Ήπειρον εις μνήμην Χρίστου Σούλη, 46–80. Athens: Typographeion Myrtidi.
1971 *Cassopaia and the Elean Colonies* (Ancient Greek Cities 4). Athens: Athens Centre of Ekistics.
1972 Θεσπρωτία (Ancient Greek Cities 15). Athens: Athens Centre of Ekistics.
1976 Η κτινοτροφία στην αρχαία Ήπειρο (Lecture, University of Ioannina, November 28, 1976). Ioannina: University of Ioannina.
1981 Η γένεση της πόλις στην αρχαία Ήπειρο. *Δελτίο Κέντρου Ερευνών Ζαγορίου* 1: 7–20.
1982 Von einer kleinen ländlichen Ansiedlung des 8.-4. Jhs. v. Chr. zu einer spätklassischen Stadt in Nordwest-Griechenland. In D. Papenfuss and V.M. Strocka (eds.), *Palast und Hütte: Beiträge zum Bauen und Wohnen im Altertum von Archäologen, Vor- und Frühgeschichtlern*: 357–374. Mainz: Philipp von Zabern.

Damiata, B.N., J.K. Papadopoulos, M.G. Amore, S.P Morris, L. Bejko, J.M. Marston, and J. Southon
2007–2008 Towards an absolute chronology of Albanian archaeology: AMS radiocarbon dates from Apollonia and Lofkënd (Të dhëna mbi kronologjinë absolute të arkeologjisë shqiptare: datime radiokarboni AMS nga Apollonia dhe Lofkëndi)," (in English and Albanian) *Iliria* 33: 135–185.

Davies, J.K.
2000 A wholly non-Aristotelian universe: The Molossians as ethnos, state, and monarchy. In R. Brock and S. Hodkinson (eds.), *Alternatives to Athens: Varieties of Political Organization and Community in Ancient Greece*: 234–258. Oxford: Oxford University Press.

Davis, J., A. Hoti, I. Pojani, S. Stocker, A. Wolpert, P. Acheson and J. Hayes
2003 The Durrës regional archaeological project: Archaeological survey in the territory of Epidamnus/Dyrrachium in Albania. *Hesperia* 72: 41–119.

Demand, N.H.
1990 *Urban Relocation in Archaic and Classical Greece: Flight and Consolidation.* Norman: University of Oklahoma Press.

Dickinson, O.T.P.K.
2006 *The Aegean from Bronze Age to Iron Age: Continuity and Change between the Twelfth and Eighth Centuries BC.* London and New York: Routledge.

Dimo, V., F. Lenhardt and F. Quantin (eds.)
2007 *Apollonia d'Illyrie: Atlas archéologique et historique* (Mission épigraphique et historique en Albanie). Athens: École françaises d'Athènes.

Douzougli, A. and J.K. Papadopoulos
2010 Liatovouni: a Molossian cemetery and settlement in Epirus. *Jahrbuch des Deutschen Archäologischen Instituts* 125: 1–87.

Evangelidis, D.
1947 *Οι Αρχαίοι Κάτοικοι της Ηπείρου*. Athens: Epeirotike Zoe.

Forsén, J.
2009 The "Dark Age" in the Kokytos valley – not so dark after all. In B. Forsén (ed.), *Thesprotia Expedition I: Towards a Regional History* (Papers and Monographs of the Finnish Institute at Athens, Vol. 15): 55–72. Helsinki: Foundation of the Finnish Institute at Athens.

Frederiksen, R.
2011 *Greek City Walls of the Archaic Period, 900–480 BC*. Oxford: Oxford University Press.

Furumark, A.
1972 *Mycenaean Pottery, Vol. 1: Analysis and Classification*. Stockholm and Lund: Swedish Institute in Athens.

Galaty, M.L.
2002 Modeling the formation and evolution of an Illyrian tribal system: ethnographic and archaeological analogs. In W.A. Parkinson (ed.), *The Archaeology of Tribal Societies*: 109–122. Ann Arbor: International Monographs in Prehistory.
2007 "There are prehistoric cities up there": the Bronze and Iron Ages in northern Albania. In I. Galanaki, H. Tomas, Y. Galanakis and R. Laffineur (eds.), *Between the Aegean and Baltics Seas: Prehistory Across Borders. Proceedings of the International Conference Bronze and Early Iron Age Interconnections and Contemporary Developments Between the Aegean and the Regions of the Balkan Peninsula, Central and Northern Europe, University of Zagreb, 11–14 April 2005* (Aegaeum 27): 133–141. Liège: Université de Liège.

Galaty, M.L., O. Lafe, W.E. Lee and Z. Tafilica (eds.)
2013 *Light and Shadow: Isolation and Interaction in the Shala Valley of Northern Albania* (Monumenta Archaeologica 28). Los Angeles: Cotsen Institute of Archaeology.

Galaty, M.L., O. Lafe and Z. Tafilica
2011 Grunas, Shala: a new fortified prehistoric site in the northern Albanian mountains. In J.-L. Lamboley and M.P. Castiglioni (eds.), *L'Illyrie méridionale et l'Épire dans l'antiquité, V. Actes du Ve colloque international de Grenoble (8–11 octobre 2008)*: 13–24. Paris: de Boccard.

Gjipali, I.
2011 Prehistoric settlements in the territory of western Chaonia. In J.-L. Lamboley and M.P. Castiglioni (eds.), *L'Illyrie méridionale et l'Épire dans l'antiquité V. Proceedings of the Ve Colloque International, Grenoble, France, October 8–12, 2008*: 25–40. Paris: De Boccard.

Graham, A.J.
1964 *Colony and Mother City in Ancient Greece*. Manchester: Manchester University Press.

Hall, J.M.
2007a Polis, community and ethnic identity. In H.A. Shapiro (ed.), *The Cambridge Companion to Archaic Greece*: 40–60. Cambridge: Cambridge University Press.
2007b *A History of the Greek World, ca. 1200–479 BCE*. Oxford: Blackwell Publishing.

Halstead, P.

1987a Traditional and ancient rural economy in Mediterranean Europe: Plus ça change? *Journal of Hellenic Studies* 107: 77–87.

1987b Man and other animals in later Greek prehistory. *Annual of the British School at Athens* 82: 71–83.

1988 On redistribution and the Minoan-Mycenaean palatial economies. In E.B. French and K.A. Wardle (eds.), *Problems in Greek Prehistory: Papers Presented at the Centenary Conference of the British School of Archaeology in Athens, Manchester, April 1986*: 519–530. Bristol: Bristol Classical Press.

1989 The economy has a normal surplus: Economic stability and social change among early farming communities of Thessaly, Greece. In P. Halstead and J. O'Shea (eds.), *Bad Year Economics: Cultural Responses to Risk and Uncertainty*: 68–90. Cambridge: Cambridge University Press.

1990 Present to past in the Pindhos: Diversification and specialization in mountain economies. *Rivista di Studi Liguri* 56: 61–80.

2000 Landuse in postglacial Greece: Cultural causes and environmental effects. In P. Halstead and C. Frederick (eds.), *Landscape and Land Use in Postglacial Greece* (Sheffield Studies in Aegean Archaeology 3): 110–128. Sheffield: Sheffield Academic Press.

Hammond, N.G.L.

1967 *Epirus: The Geography, the Ancient Remains, the History, and the Topography of Epirus and Adjacent Areas.* Oxford: Clarendon Press.

1972 *A History of Macedonia.* Oxford: Clarendon Press.

1989 *The Macedonian State: Origins, Institutions and History.* Oxford: Clarendon Press.

1992 The relations of Illyrian Albania with the Greeks and the Romans. In T. Winnifrith (ed.), *Perspectives on Albania*: 29–39. New York: St. Martin's Press.

2000 The *ethne* in Epirus and upper Macedonia. *Annual of the British School at Athens* 95: 345–352.

Hansen, I.L., R. Hodges and S. Leppard

2013 *Butrint 4: The Archaeology and Histories of an Ionian Town.* Oxford and Oakville: Oxbow Books for the Butrint Foundation.

Hansen, M.H.

2006 *Polis: An Introduction to the Ancient Greek City-state.* Oxford: Oxford University Press.

Harding, A.F.

1992 The prehistoric background of Illyrian Albania. In T. Winnifrith (ed.), *Perspectives on Albania*: 14–28. New York: St. Martin's Press.

Hoepfner, W. and E.L. Schwandner

1986 *Haus und Stadt im klassischen Griechenland.* Munich: Deutscher Kunstverlag.

1994 *Wohnen in der klassischen Polis I: Haus und Stadt im klassischen Griechenland.* Munich: Deutscher Kunstverlag.

Karaiskaj, G.

1976 Les fortifications illyriennes du premier âge fu fer dans les environs de Korçë. *Iliria* 4: 197–221.

Karatzeni, V.

1994 Το ιερόν όρος και το επιφανές όρος Κράνεια της Αμβρακίας. In *ΦΗΓΟΣ: Τιμητικός τόμος για τον καθηγητή Σωτήρη Δάκαρη*: 289–299. Ioannina: University of Ioannina.

Korkuti, M.
1982 Die Siedlungen der späten Bronze- und der frühen Eisenzeit in Südwestalbanien. In B. Hänsel (ed.), *Südosteuropa zwischen 1600 und 100 v. Chr.*: 234–253. Berlin: Moreland Editions.

Lafe, O.
2003 *The Earliest Urbanized Settlement in the Hinterland of Apollonia (Albania): 7th–mid 5th century BC*. MA dissertation, University of Cincinnati.

Liddell, H.G., R. Scott and H.S. Jones
1940 *A Greek-English Lexicon*. Oxford: Clarendon Press.

Lima, S.
2013 Butrint and the Pavllas River Valley in the Late Bronze and Early Iron Age. In I.L. Hansen, R. Hodges and S. Leppard, *Butrint 4: The Archaeology and Histories of an Ionian Town*: 31–46. Oxford and Oakville: Oxbow Books for the Butrint Foundation.

Malkin, I.
1998 *The Returns of Odysseus: Colonization and Ethnicity*. Berkeley and Los Angeles: University of California Press.

Meyer, E.A.
2012 Two grants of *politeia* and the Molossians at Dodona. *Zeitscrift für Papyrologie und Epigrafik* 180: 205–216.

Morgan, C.
2000 Politics without the polis: Cities and the Achaean Ethnos, *c.* 800–500 BC. In R. Brock and S. Hodkinson (eds.), *Alternatives to Athens: Varieties of Political Organization and Community in Ancient Greece*: 189–211. Oxford: Oxford University Press.
2003 *Early Greek States Beyond the Polis*. London and New York: Routledge.

Morris, S.P.
2006 *Illyrica pix*: the exploitation of bitumen in ancient Albania. In L. Bejko and R. Hodges (eds.), *New Directions in Albanian Archaeology: Studies Presented to Muzafer Korkuti*: 94–106. Tirana: International Centre for Albanian Archaeology.
2014 Bitumen at Lofkënd: Deposits, sherds, and containers. In J.K. Papadopoulos *et al., The Excavations of the Prehistoric Burial Tumulus at Lofkënd, Albania*, 476–482. Los Angeles: Cotsen Institute of Archaeology.

Muçaj, S. and E. Hobdari
2005 Teqeja e Melanit. *Candavia* 2: 29–92.

Myrto, H.
1998 *Albania Archeologica: Bibliografia Sistematica dei Centri Antichi* I. Bari: Edipuglia.

Pantou, P. A.
2010 Mycenaean Dimini in context: Investigating regional variability and socioeconomic complexities in Late Bronze Age Greece. *American Journal of Archaeology* 114: 381–401.

Papadopoulos, J.K.
2001 Magna Achaea: Akhaian Late Geometric and Archaic pottery in south Italy and Sicily. *Hesperia* 70: 373–460.
2009 The relocation of potters and the dissemination of style: Athens, Corinth, Ambrakia, and the Agrinion group. In J.H. Oakley and O. Palagia (eds.), *Athenian Potters and Painters* II: 232–240. Oxford: Oxbow Books.

Papadopoulos, J.K., L. Bejko and S.P. Morris
2007 Excavations at the prehistoric burial tumulus of Lofkënd in Albania: A preliminary report for the 2004–2005 seasons. *American Journal of Archaeology* 111: 105–147.

Papadopoulos, J. K., S. P. Morris, L. Bejko and L. A. Schepartz
2014 *The Excavations of the Prehistoric Burial Tumulus at Lofkënd, Albania.* Los Angeles: Cotsen Institute of Archaeology.

Parke, H.W.
1967 *The Oracles of Zeus: Dodona, Olympia, Ammon.* Cambridge, MA: Harvard University Press.

Pliakou, G.
2007 Το λεκανοπέδιο των Ιωαννίνων και η ευρύτερη περιοχή της Μολοσσίας στην κεντρική Ήπειρω. Αρχαιολογικά κατάλοιπα, οικιστική οργάνωση και οικονομία. PhD dissertation, University of Thessaloniki.
2011 *Cômai* et ethne: L'organisation spatiale du Bassin d'Ioannina à la lumière du materiel archéologique. In J.-L. Lamboley and M. P. Castiglioni (eds.), *L'Illyrie méridionale et l'Épire dans l'antiquité, V. Actes du Ve Colloque International de Grenoble (8–11 October 2008)*: 631–647. Paris: De Boccard.

Pullen, D.J. and T.F. Tartaron
2007 Where's the palace? The absence of state formation in the Late Bronze Age Corinthia. In M. L. Galaty and W. A. Parkinson (eds.), *Rethinking Mycenaean Palaces II* (revised and expanded second edition): 146–158. Los Angeles: Cotsen Institute of Archaeology

Small, D.B.
2007 Mycenaean polities: states or estates? In M.L. Galaty and W.A. Parkinson (eds.), *Rethinking Mycenaean Palaces II* (revised and expanded second edition): 47–53. Los Angeles: Cotsen Institute of Archaeology.

Stocker, S.R.
2009 Illyrian Apollonia: Toward a New Ktisis and Developmental History of the Colony. PhD dissertation, University of Cincinnati.

Tartaron, T.F.
2013 *Maritime Networks in the Mycenaean World.* Cambridge: Cambridge University Press.

Tzortzatou, A., and L. Fatsiou
2009 New Early Iron Age and Archaic sites in Thesprotia. In B. Forsén (ed.), *Thesprotia Expedition I: Towards a Regional History* (Papers and Monographs of the Finnish Institute at Athens, Vol. 15): 39–53. Helsinki: Foundation of the Finnish Institute at Athens.

Ventris, M., and J. Chadwick
1973 *Documents in Mycenaean Greek*, 2nd ed. Cambridge: Cambridge University Press.

Vokotopoulou, I.
1986 *Βίτσα· Τα νεκροταφεία μίας Μολοσσικής κώμης*. Athens: Greek Ministry of Culture.
1994 Η τελευταία οικία της Μολοσσικής κώμης στη Βίτσα Ζαγορίου. In *ΦΗΓΟΣ: Τιμητικός τόμος για τον καθηγητή Σωτήρη Δάκαρη*: 189–220. Ioannina: University of Ioannina.

Wilkes, J.J.
1992 *The Illyrians*. Oxford: Blackwell.

Will, E.
1955 *Korinthiaka: Recherches sur l'histoire et la civilisaton de Corinthe des origins aux guerres médiques*. Paris: De Boccard.

Zachos, K.L.
1993 Ακρόπολη Μεγάλου Γαρδικίου. *Archaiologikon Deltion* 48, Chronika: 262–267.

Zachos, K. L., D. Çondi, A. Douzougli, G. Pliakou, and V. Karatzeni
2006 The Antigoneia Project: Preliminaty report on the first season. In L. Bejko and R. Hodges (eds.), *New Directions in Albanian Archaeology: Studies Presented to Muzafer Korkuti*, 379–390. Tirana: International Centre for Albanian Archaeology.